Oxford Paperback Reference

New Oxford Rhyming Dictionary

Oxford Paperback Reference

The most authoritative and up-to-date reference books for both students and the general reader.

Many of these titles are also available online at www.oxfordreference.com

New Oxford Rhyming Dictionary

OXFORD

UNIVERSITY PRESS

OXFORD
UNIVERSITY PRESS

Great Clarendon Street, Oxford, OX2 6DP,
United Kingdom

Oxford University Press is a department of the University of Oxford.
It furthers the University's objective of excellence in research, scholarship,
and education by publishing worldwide. Oxford is a registered trade mark of
Oxford University Press in the UK and in certain other countries

First Edition published in 2006 as the *Oxford Dictionary of Rhymes*
First published in paperback 2007
Second Edition published in 2012 as the *New Oxford Rhyming Dictionary*
Second Edition first published in paperback in 2013

Impression: 3

Published in the United States of America by Oxford University Press
198 Madison Avenue, New York, NY 10016, United States of America

British Library Cataloguing in Publication Data
Data available

Library of Congress Control Number: 2013937757

ISBN 978-0-19-967422-0

Printed in Great Britain by
Clays Ltd, St Ives plc

Contents

Preface

The *New Oxford Rhyming Dictionary* is a new work of reference, combining not only a vast range of rhyming words but also practical usage notes and examples in order to meet as far as possible the needs of today's rhyme-makers.

The rhymes of this dictionary are based directly on the pronunciations held in the wider Oxford Dictionaries databases, and are organized primarily on aural rather than orthographic principles. This emphasis on sound is important for at least three reasons. First, organization by sound—and not by the order of the letters of the alphabet—ensures that sounds that are closest together are grouped together. Secondly, the way the rhymes are organized does not depend on spelling: in English, spelling is notoriously irregular in the way letters represent sounds. Finally, the entries in the *New Oxford Rhyming Dictionary* relate to the standard pronunciation of British English and, where two possible pronunciations are correct, the word in question is listed in two different places.

The editorial contributions of Sheila Ferguson to the compilation of this dictionary, and the technical expertise of James McCracken in its inception, are gratefully acknowledged.

Introduction

Rhyme is heard everywhere—because it **works**. In advertising jingles, football chants, birthday-card greetings, tabloid headlines, political slogans, and catchphrases, rhyme makes the sentiments more powerful and more memorable. If you can't beat them, join them; Arrive Alive—Don't Drink and Drive; Dennis the Menace; No More War; hang 'em and flog 'em: in all, words are slammed together, echoed and re-echoed, as one rhyme-word prompts another or confirms the word that prompted it. Listen to any crowd chant or sing, and the punched emphasis on any rhyme shows clearly how important it is to each singer, and to all in keeping time; listen to almost any song on the radio, and its use of rhyme, for better or worse, is a primary factor in what you hear.

This widespread commercial, political, and social use of rhyme is a testimony to its commanding power over our attention and memory; so too, of course, is the artistic use of rhyme by poets and singers, which may in addition to power seek range and subtlety. And as anyone who reads contemporary poetry or listens to contemporary music knows, the idea that rhyme is somehow 'old-fashioned' or has fallen by the wayside is simply nonsense. Many of the best living poets are confirmed rhymers, middle-of-the-road easy-listening ballads and rock anthems rely as much as ever on strong rhymes, and the great innovators of rhyme in recent years have been rappers, from Grandmaster Flash to the Beastie Boys and Eminem: you may like or loathe the songs, but the cleverness and frequent sting of the tumbling rhymes cannot be denied. And unwelcome as the connection might be to some, Eminem, as a heavy and complex rhymer with social purpose, is a descendant of songwriters like Cole Porter, Ira Gershwin, and W. S. Gilbert (of Gilbert & Sullivan), whose comic-operatic songs like "I am the very model of a modern Major-General" were a nineteenth-century equivalent of rap.

Whatever your own concerns with it, rhyme is thus worth attending to for many reasons, and to understand it helpfully some history and analysis are necessary. This introduction is therefore divided into three sections: 'I. Rhyme in history and by type' gives some historical context and explains how rhyme has traditionally been analysed in English; 'II. Rhyme in use and by demonstration' applies those lessons, first tracking one particular type of rhyming-stanza from 1591 to the twentieth century, then ranging over a wide variety of modern poets and singers; and 'III. How to use this book' explains how to find the various kinds of rhyme that exist so you can use them for your own purposes. The technical vocabulary defined in Section I is used without further explanation in Section II, so if you are unfamiliar with such terms as *stressed* and *unstressed rhyme*, or *arch* and *chain rhyme*, it is advisable to read the sections in order. A table listing all the varieties of rhyme appears on pages xvi–xvii and there are inset panels throughout the book which give additional examples and tips.

Rhyme in history and by type

I'm a poet
And I know it.

Rhyme is a basic possibility of language, and must have occurred (if only by chance) in the earliest human speech. It was formalized early in Chinese and Arabic poetry, but in the West the idea of rhyme as a formal characteristic of poetry is relatively recent. No classical Hebrew, Greek, or Latin poets normally used rhyme, depending instead on parallel grammar or metres based on vowel-length, while Anglo-Saxon poets used the repetition of vowels or consonants known as *assonance* and *alliteration*. When rhyme was formally organized in the West as a poetic tool, principally in the twelfth to fourteenth centuries, it was in part its new and striking audibility that enabled it so rapidly to spread across Europe, first as a poetic vogue, and then as an established norm for lyric verse and song.

Rhyme was able to displace alliteration and assonance because both earlier modes depend on the repetition of individual letters that may occur anywhere in a word, and so do not necessarily connect the meanings of the words in which they occur. Charles Churchill's famous tag in *The Prophecy of Famine* (1763) about "apt Alliteration's artful aid" is remembered precisely because it is self-referentially witty, as most alliterative volleys are not. Rhyme, conversely, is based not simply on whole syllables, but on a word's last stressed vowel and all sounds that follow it, so that larger, grammatically significant elements of a word are likely to be involved.

As a formal principle of poetry rhyme thus represented a paradigm shift, one of many during the transition from 'Late Medieval' to 'Renaissance' and 'Early Modern'. Metrically, for example, the new importance of stress signals a shift from classical metres using duration to new metres using accent, and amid such shifts, 'rhyme' and 'rhythm' (both from Greek *rhythmos* and ultimately *rhein*, 'to flow') became distinct. Where alliteration or assonance, however rhythmic, link words only lightly within a line, relying on single sounds without individual meaning, rhyme, by linking multiple syllables (usually) in distinct lines, binds much larger parcels of sense. It is also an intrinsically complex phenomenon, interacting with spelling, poetry's distinctive use of lines, and regional accents, and richly invites variation, while alliteration or assonance can only shift from letter to letter. Rhyme thus helped poets and singers to organize, learn, and present their material, and helped readers or audiences to understand and remember it: a powerful and distinct resource, as Oscar Wilde insisted in calling rhyme "the one chord we have added to the Greek lyre".

His "we" is more dubious. The immediate sources of Western rhyme were Arabic poetry, in which various kinds of rhyme had been used since at least the 8th century CE, and perhaps some Celtic poetry; the primary European distribution system was the Troubadours, Provençal poet-musicians of the twelfth and thirteenth centuries who travelled and corresponded across Europe, the Middle East, North Africa, and Asia Minor. Traces of Late Mediaeval rhyme are as widespread as their contacts, but once rhyme had been adopted (via the 'Sicilian school' at the court of Frederic II Hohenstaufen in Palermo) by the great Italian poets Dante (Dante Alighieri, 1265–1321) and above all Petrarch (Francisco Petrarca, 1304–74), a massive and decisive secondary distribution began, initially in manuscript, then in print also, through the pan-European cultural and educational movement known as Humanism. Though exact dating is contested and uncertain, the 'Gawain-Poet' in the mid-late fourteenth century probably represents the first English sign of Petrarch's influence: *Sir Gawain and the Grene Knyght* itself has a rhyming 'wheel' ending its alliterative stanzas, and the notorious formal complexity of *Pearl* (preserved in the same manuscript) arises precisely from combining rhyme with alliteration. Geoffrey Chaucer (*c.*1344–1400), writing at the same time, was rarely so elaborate, but his *Canterbury Tales* established rhyming couplets as a narrative mode, while *Troylus and Criseyde* did as much for complex stanzas; shorter lyric verse, like the songs to which it is close, was already there. The older traditions of *blank* or unrhymed verse still prospered towards their dramatic flowering in Shakespeare and his fellows, but new traditions of rhymed verse rapidly joined them as normative within both folk and elite poetic cultures.

Notwithstanding some bad-tempered outbursts, like Milton's famous jibe in the 1667 Preface to *Paradise Lost* about "the troublesome and modern bondage of rhyming", rhymed and blank verse co-existed happily until the early twentieth century. Poetic tastes swung this way and that, but no one seriously thought less of Pope or Tennyson for rhyming, nor of Wordsworth or Browning for using blank verse. In the first quarter of the twentieth century, however, some Modernists began to proclaim the supposed death of rhyme and other formal devices. Patently, with Modernism and the birth of *free verse*, a new energy infused and transformed the blank tradition; equally patently, neither rhyme nor other formal devices were wholly absent even from High Modernism (think of T. S. Eliot or e. e. cummings), and both within and around Modernism rhyme flowed unabated, in W. B. Yeats, Robert Frost,

W. H. Auden, Philip Larkin, Robert Lowell, Elizabeth Bishop, Sylvia Plath and a hundred more. The 'New Formalism' announced by critics in the 1980s was certainly a reaction against the formlessness of some (late) Modernist work, but even so, it was not in any serious sense new, and in practice the augmented blank and rhyming traditions continue, now as then, to co-exist to their mutual benefit.

Despite its long prosperity, however, categorizations of rhyme vary in differing national traditions. In French poetry, for example, there are particular concerns with euphony (sweetness of sound) and punning, while in German, alliteration and assonance are designated as types of rhyme. English has a rich vocabulary for rhyme, but names are unstable: in what follows, therefore, alternative names are sometimes provided in parenthesis. Fortunately, however, there is more variation in labelling than understanding, for the basic definition of rhyme as involving two elements (the last stressed vowel + all following letters) creates an obvious structure of **degree**. In *full* (or *perfect*) *rhyme* both elements are correctly matched (as in 'hand/band'), and this can be intensified into *rime riche* (which as a French term always keeps its italics) by extending the rhyming sequences backwards from the last stressed vowels ('right hánd/fright ánd'). The obvious next step is *half-* (or *imperfect*, *near*, *slant*) *rhyme*, with only one element correctly matching, which divides into *vowel rhyme*, with the same last stressed vowel but different following letters ('hand/hang'), and *pararhyme*, with the same letters following different vowels ('hand/bind'). For the mathematically-minded, these four primary variants might be represented as $\{(+1,1), (1,1), (1,0), (0,1)\}$.

A second common analysis is by **type**. If the last stressed vowels are in last syllables ('hánd/bánd', 'cáre/bewáre', 'disgúst/entrúst'), the rhyme is *stressed* (the older term, abandoned as sexist, was *masculine rhyme*). If the last stressed vowels are followed by one or more metrically unstressed syllables ('hánding/stánding', 'Atlántic/gigántic'), the rhyme is *unstressed* (or *feminine*). The use of multiple words to form a rhyme ('poet/know it'), or of rhyming phrases ('on the run/in the sun'), creates *mosaic rhyme*, which if deliberately silly or outrageous ('hypotenuse/lot o' news') is known as *Hudibrastic rhyme*, from Samuel Butler's practice in

Hudibras. There are also three oddities: the logical *auto-* (or *null* or *identical*) *rhyme*, of a word with itself; the illogical *eye-* (or *printers'*) *rhyme*, when words that look as if they rhyme are not so pronounced ('-ough' is notorious: cough, bough, rough, dough); and the playful variety of *spelling rhymes*, using humorous distortion or abbreviations (compare '& Co./although' with '& Co./dump any'). To these can be added *wrenched rhyme*, when 'normal' pronunciation is overridden to create a rhyme by distorting one last vowel into conformity with the other ('hand/brigánd'); and two further types of distorted rhyme, *embedded rhyme*, of one word with a medial part of another ('band/handfast'), especially popular in song when the rhyme can be sounded in delivery, and which can be displayed on the page as *broken rhyme*, when the word containing the medial rhyming syllable is split between lines. In his last collection, *A Scattering of Salts* (1995), the underrated American poet James Merrill (1926–95) combined both in 'Snow Jobs', a wicked take on twentieth-century political integrity: "Like blizzards on a screen the scan-/dals thickened at a fearful rate / Followed by laughter from a can / and hot air from the candidate."

Expanding slightly, a third common analysis is by the **position** of rhyming words within lines. *Terminal rhyme*, between words ending lines, is predominant, but *medial rhyme* (at least one non-terminal word) remains common in song lyrics, libretti, and comic poetry—think of Gilbert & Sullivan, Tom Lehrer, or Eliot's *Old Possum's Book of Practical Cats*. There is one strict form of *medial rhyme*, *leonine rhyme*, when the word in the middle of the line (technically, preceding the caesura) rhymes with the end-word of the same line (as in "And louder rose the ragged crows" or "And blessed with bread the waters red", both from Charles Causley's 'Christ at the Cheesewring'). *Initial rhyme*, with at least one word beginning a line, is rarer, but as *autorhyme* can be created by repeated lines and formulae (as in the Psalms) or refrains that vary only slightly (as in many ballads).

Expanding again, the final common analysis is of **relation**, the pattern in which rhymes are combined (or *rhyme scheme*). Using the quatrain as an example, and the standard notation of rhyme schemes (in which successive letters, *a b c* ..., represent rhyming lines), if all lines rhyme, it is *monorhyme* (*aaaa*); if two lines rhyme and two are blank, it is *single rhyme* (*aabc*, *abac*, *abca*, *abbc*, *abcb*, *abcc*); if successive pairs of lines rhyme, it is *couplet rhyme* (*aabb*); if alternating lines rhyme, it is *cross-rhyme* (*abab*); and if the rhymes have mirror symmetry, it is *arch-* (or *chiasmic*) *rhyme* (*abba*). Once a pattern is sufficiently established to generate expectations of rhyme, rhymes may be *accelerated* by shortening the line (as in lines 3–4 of limericks) or by bringing a line forward (as *ababcdd*, where the second *d* is earlier than expected); or equally be *delayed*, by lengthening the line (as at the end of Spenserian stanzas) or by putting a line back (as *ababcdced*, where the second *d* is later than expected). And if a rhyme-sound is carried over from one stanza to another—as in the *terza rima* made famous by Dante, rhyming *aba bcb cdc* and so on—it is *chain rhyme*.

Finally, critics also talk of *semantic rhyme*, between words with related meanings (as 'glass/vitreous' or 'cake/bake'), and *thematic rhyme*, between words that are linked in a given work ('free/ slavery' or 'redeem/dream', for example, in a poem about Emancipation). There is also, therefore, *counter-semantic rhyme*, between words with opposed meanings, as 'make/break', 'raise/ raze', or, famously, 'death/breath'. In theory these are all desirable qualities in a rhyme, but in practice are intimately dependent on diction, the verbal range and register of a poem: if a semantic or thematic rhyme fits, all well and good, but if diction is forced, to admit for the sake of a rhyme a word that stands out as one the speaker of the poem would not use, even a perfectly semantic rhyme will not turn any profit.

These four kinds of analysis, by degree, type, position, and relation, enable accurate discussion, and offer writers a way forward in composition and revision. They are not complete— the effects and uses of rhyme exceed all handy analysis, especially where accents and non-standard spelling are involved, and it can *always* surprise—but there are nevertheless connections between particular poetic effects and particular combinations of rhyme, awareness of which can guide writers to control, as much as readers to understand, what is going on.

The varieties of rhyme

Degree

rime riche	full rhyme + preceding elements	right hand / fright and
full rhyme	last stressed vowel + following elements	hand / band
vowel rhyme (half-rhyme)	last stressed vowel only	hand / hang
pararhyme (half-rhyme)	following elements only	hand / bind

Type

stressed rhyme (masculine)	last stressed vowel in last syllable	hand / band
unstressed rhyme (feminine)	last stressed vowel not in last syllable	handing / standing
mosaic rhyme	involving multiple words	tanned hands / bandstand
Hudibrastic rhyme	deliberately silly mosaic rhyme	handstand / grand, planned
autorhyme (identical or null rhyme)	repetition	hypotenuse / lot o'news
eye rhyme	in spelling only, not pronunciation	cough / bough
spelling rhyme	with distorted orthography	Charles II / beckoned
wrenched rhyme	last vowel mis-stressed	hand / brigánd
embedded rhyme	with a medial syllable in a word	handout / band
broken rhyme	displays embedded rhyme	band / hand-/out...

Position

terminal rhyme (end rhyme)	between words ending lines
medial rhyme (internal rhyme)	at least one rhyme-word is not terminal
leonine rhyme	between the mid- and end-words of the same line
initial rhyme	between words beginning lines

Relation

monorhyme	*aaaa*	hand / band / sand / land
single rhyme	*aabc*	hand / band / foot / arm
	abac	hand / foot / band / arm
	abca	hand / foot / arm / band
	abbc	hand / foot / put / arm
	abcb	hand / foot / arm / put
	abcc	hand / foot / arm / harm
couplet rhyme	*aabb*	hand / band / foot / put
cross-rhyme	*abab*	hand / foot / band / put
arch-rhyme	*abba*	hand / foot / put / band
delayed, accelerated	relative to any established pattern	
chain rhyme	chaining successive stanzas together with a shared rhyme	
semantic	between words with related meanings	alive / survive
counter-semantic	between words with opposed meanings	save / grave
thematic	between meanings thematic to a given work	

Rhyme in use and by demonstration

I'm a poet
And I know it:
Thus I show it
And sometimes blow it.

The broadest rules of thumb are that:

(1) the consonance of full rhyme tends to confirm sense, while the dissonance of half-rhyme tends to question or ironize sense;

(2) stressed rhyme tends to affirmation, and unstressed rhyme to comedy;

(3) medial rhymes tend to call for accelerated delivery;

(4) cross-rhyme marches while arch-rhyme curvets, monorhyme hammers, couplets epigrammatize, and so on.

As with all such rough rules there are infinite exceptions, and one can always work against the grain—but to try, for example, to write a grave or joyous anthem using unstressed pararhymes ('handing/ binding', 'finger/clanger') is a needlessly uphill task: real anthems prefer stressed full rhyme, in couplets (such as 'high/die/sneer/ here' in 'The Red Flag') or even triplets ('glare/air/there', 'victorious/glorious/over us'). This last, from the British national anthem, 'God Save the Queen', is a warning as well as an example: the unstressed 'victorious/glorious' and mosaic pararhyme '/over us' are in practice neither as comedic nor as dissonant as one might in theory expect; deliberately overstated lyrics and a clever melody (falling on 'victorious' and 'glorious' but rising with 'over us') enable the anthem to carry its risky rhymes, usually without difficulty. More private poems are unlikely to command such resources, and risk will be correspondingly higher.

An interesting lesson in the powers of rhyme is offered by *ottava rima*, an eight-line Italian stanza rhyming *abababcc*. Now strongly associated in English with the wicked comedy of Lord Byron's *Beppo* and *Don Juan*, *ottava rima* started in Italian as a straightforward narrative stanza, and its earliest major appearances in English are translations, beginning in 1591 with Sir John Harington's of *Orlando Furioso* by Ludovico Ariosto (1474–1533). Harington was Elizabeth I's godson, and having translated one canto about an orgy to circulate among the ladies of the Queen's Bedchamber, he was set to translating the other 45 as a punishment; one that he took in good part:

> Of Dames, of Knights, of armes, of loves delight,
>   Of curtesies, of high attempts I speake,
> Then when the Moores transported all their might
>   On Affrick seas the force of France to breake,
> Incited by the youthfull heate and spite
>   Of *Agramant* their king that vowd to wreake
> The death of king *Trayano* (lately slayne)
> Upon the Romane Emperour *Charlemaine*.

> I will no less *Orlandos* acts declare
>   (A tale in prose ne verse yet song or sayd)
> Who fell bestraught with love, a hap most rare
>   To one that erst was counted wise and stayd.
> If my sweet Saint that causeth my like care
>   My slender muse afford some gracious ayd,
> I make no doubt but I shall have the skill
> As much as I have promist to fulfil.
>
> Vouchsafe (O Prince of most renowmed race,
>   The ornament and hope of this our time)
> T'accept this gift presented to your grace
>   By me your servant, rudely here in rime,
> And though I paper pay and inke in place
>   Of deeper debt, yet take it for no cryme:
> It may suffise a poore and humble debter
> To say and if he could it should be better.

(Book I, stanzas 1–3)

Ottava rima breaks down into a cross-rhymed sestet + terminal couplet (6+2, *ababab-cc*), and works well as a beast of narrative burden because the tick-tock sestet can carry action while the couplet offers space for a summary comment or moral reflection. In English, however, the need for two triple rhymes tests skill, and Harington's first *b*-rhyme, 'speake/breake/wreake', signals that pararhyme will be allowed. It also begins with witty self-deprecation, "I speake"—Virgil's famous formula opening his *Aeneid* was "*Arma virumque cano*", meaning 'Arms and the man *I sing*'—and the rhyming reminders of "speake" underscore that humility. Similarly, allowing his second *c*-rhyme, 'skill/fulfil', as mildly wrenched, Harington sticks to stressed rhyme (even in 'lately slayne/*Charlemaine*') until the third *c*-rhyme, 'debter/better'—a fine example of the link between unstressed rhyme and (ironic) comedy. The third stanza aptly served Harington's private needs (his book is fulsomely dedicated to Elizabeth), and the rhyming sequences in the sestet, 'race/place/grace' and 'time/rime/cryme', skilfully insinuate a personal apology to his godmother into the fabric of his penance.

Little is known about Edward Fayrfax other than that in 1600 he published a translation of Torquato Tasso's *Il Goffredo* (later retitled *Gerusalemme Liberata*) as *Godfrey of Bulloigne or The Recoverie of Ierusalem*. Tasso (1544–95), fearful of the Inquisition, produced a sombre Christian epic about the Crusaders' conquest of Jerusalem in 1099, lacking Ariosto's lively fantasy but also in *ottava rima*; Fayrfax followed suit:

> The sacred armies and the godly knight
>> That the great sepulchre of Christ did free
> I sing; much wrought his valour and foresight,
>> And in that glorious war much suffer'd he:
> In vain 'gainst him did hell oppose her might,
>> In vain the Turks and Morians armed be;
> His soldiers wild, to brawls and mutines prest,
> Reduced he to peace; so heaven him blest.
>
> O heavenly muse, that not with fading bays
>> Deckest thy brow by th' Heliconian spring,
> But sittest, crown'd with stars' immortal rays,
>> In heaven, where legions of bright angels sing,
> Inspire life in my wit, my thoughts upraise,
>> My verse ennoble, and forgive the thing,
> If fictions light I mix with truth divine,
> And fill these lines with others' praise than thine.
>
> Thither thou know'st the world is best inclined
>> Where luring Parnass most his sweet imparts,
> And truth convey'd in verse of gentle kind,
>> To read perhaps will move the dullest hearts;
> So we, if children young diseas'd we find,
>> Anoint with sweets the vessel's foremost parts,
> To make them taste the potions sharp we give;
> They drink deceived; and so deceiv'd they live.
>
> (Book I, stanzas 1–3)

As that last line attests, Fayrfax was capable of power and delicacy, and he was a more faithful translator than Harington, but it isn't only Tasso's epic subject and often gloomy tone that weigh him down. Metrically Fayrfax is too often flat-footed ("Reduced he to peace; so heaven him blest"); syntactically he tends as unhappily to echo Spenser ("Anoint with sweets the vessel's foremost parts") as to anticipate Milton ("Where luring Parnass most his sweet imparts"); but his rhymes do not help. In the first *a*-rhyme the wrenching of 'foresíght' to match 'knight/.../might' is earlier and more awkward than Harington's 'skill/fulfil', and the first *c*-rhyme, 'prest/blest', is, if then allowable, unfortunate. But most tellingly, there is no unstressed or half-rhyme in these stanzas, and readers must wait until stanza 17 for the first variation from stressed full rhyme ('asunder/wonder') and stanza 30 for the second ('given/uneven'). Such constant and heavy chiming may work well in an anthem or in shorter stanzas demanding only double rhymes, but in an epic with triple rhymes it soon begins to thump and annoy.

Listened to one-by-one, Fayrfax wasn't doing anything particularly wrong in his lines or his rhymes. A verse-translator's lot is never easy, and there are anxieties and a grimness in Tasso's work that Fayrfax perhaps catches in what may seem like stumbles and relentlessness. The slalom of each sestet and halt of each couplet are constantly demanding, and freedom of movement always burdened by fidelity of translation. Yet with the best will in the world, Fayrfax (some shining moments excepted) is duller to read than Harington, and failure in variety, especially of rhyme, is a primary reason. Though complex, this phenomenon is familiar to everyone who has written in rhyme: each line seems fine in itself, each achieved rhyme acceptable; but as lines accumulate the whole seems more and more a botch-job, a series of local solutions without larger purpose.

Primo Levi pinned part of the problem in 'Rhyming on the Counterattack', when he observed that the rhyming poet:

is committed to ending a verse not with the word dictated by discursive logic but with another, strange word, which must be drawn from the few that end 'in the right way'. And so he is compelled to deviate, to leave the path that is easier because it is predictable; now, reading what is predictable bores us and so does not inform us. The restriction of rhyme obliges the poet to resort to the unpredictable: compels him to invent, to 'find'; and to enrich his lexicon with unusual terms; to bend his syntax; in short, innovate.

(*The Mirror Maker: Stories and Essays* (trans. Raymond Rosenthal, 1989; London: Minerva, 1990), p.113)

Just so: but such innovation cannot, especially in a long poem, be allowed to accumulate higgledy-piggledy, and the "restriction of rhyme" is not a restriction to stressed full rhyme. One need not go as far as Vladimir Nabokov, who in creating chess-problems liked "form to bulge and burst like a sponge bag containing a small furious devil", to recognize that variation of rhyme is necessary in any extended use of a stanza-form; and to discipline such variant rhymes over thousands of lines demands a coherent attitude—an overarching capacity to govern expedience and guide virtuosity.

Enter Byron. He knew Harington's and Fayrfax's translations as well as their originals, and having taken the form for a brisk spin in the 99 stanzas of *Beppo* (1818), promptly embarked on the 2,000+ stanzas of *Don Juan* (1818–24), left unfinished at his premature death:

> I want a hero: an uncommon want,
>> When every year and month sends forth a new one,
> Till, after cloying the gazettes with cant,
>> The age discovers he is not the true one;
> Of such as these I should not care to vaunt,
>> I'll therefore take our ancient friend Don Juan,
> We all have seen him in the pantomime
> Sent to the devil, somewhat ere his time.
>
> Vernon, the butcher Cumberland, Wolfe, Hawke,
>> Prince Ferdinand, Granby, Burgoyne, Keppel, Howe,
> Evil and good, have had their tithe of talk,
>> And fill'd their sign-posts then, like Wellesley now;
> Each in their turn like Banquo's monarchs stalk,
>> Followers of fame, 'nine farrow' of that sow:
> France, too, had Buonaparté and Dumourier
> Recorded in the Moniteur and Courier.
>
> Barnave, Brissot, Condorcet, Mirabeau,
>> Petion, Clootz, Danton, Marat, La Fayette,
> Were French, and famous people, as we know;
>> And there were others, scarce forgotten yet,
> Joubert, Hoche, Marceau, Lannes, Dessaix, Moreau,
>> With many of the military set,
> Exceedingly remarkable at times,
> But not at all adapted to my rhymes.

(Canto I, stanzas 1–3)

It is Byron's personality that is so compelling, but from the outset rhyme is foregrounded as a principal pleasure. The first *a*-rhyme, 'want/cant/vaunt', sharply establishes semantic pararhyme, while an outrageous unstressed mosaic *b*-rhyme, 'new one/true one', comically imposes English pronunciation on '/Juan'. In the second stanza 'Howe/now/sow' is disrespectfully close to 'How now, brown cow?', while the notably unstressed 'Dumóur-i-er/ Cóur-i-er', if better pronounced than 'Juan', undermines the dignity of being mentioned in Parisian dispatches. The third stanza opens (like the second, but this time using French names) with a clever catalogue, improbably establishing the *a*-rhyme as 'Mirabeau' and *b*-rhyme as 'La Fayette', awakening readers' anticipation. Both are stressed, and after the experience of

'Dumourier/Courier' apparently demand French rhymes—but Byron promptly supplies English ones, 'as we know' and 'forgotten yet', making such interlingual rhyming sound easy, which it isn't. By way of comparison, William Aytoun's 'To Britain' (in *The Oxford Book of Sonnets*) wobbles perilously when its rhyme for 'Waterloo' is '*sauve qui peut*', and James Lasdun's 'Powder Compact' has to labour to earn its last rhyme of '*memento mori*' and 'reliquary'.

Critically, and like Harington ("this gift presented to your grace / By me your servant, rudely here in rime") but unlike Fayrfax, who was more worried about irreverence, Byron then addresses the issue of rhyming directly. Without Harington's need for personal apology, he has no call to be self-deprecating, and his downbeat return in the third couplet to plain speech and stressed monosyllabic rhyme (times/rhymes) declares a personal presence that will be mediated largely through manipulations of rhyme. Every stanza thereafter has some new rhyming delight to offer, but always contained within the tonal mesh Byron generates by patterning voices, and supported by his narrative presence and wit. It is a mode many have attempted, but in which few have succeeded in Byron's measure; Auden perhaps came closest, in his long *Letter to Lord Byron* (1936), but abandoned *ottava rima* for the more English rhyme royal (a heptet rhyming *ababbcc*). Yet if *ottava rima* has not since Byron found an English-language poet able to handle it at its traditional narrative length, it has not, thanks to William Butler Yeats (1865–1939), fallen into disuse.

Much of what Yeats achieved with form is remarkable, but nothing more so than his late adoption of *ottava rima* as a lyric stanza, most famously in 'Sailing to Byzantium', most devastatingly in 'The Circus Animals' Desertion'. Part of his skill lies in his handling of *end-stopping*, the reinforcement of line-breaks with punctuation—marks, and *enjambent*, the wrapping of syntax from one line to the next, helping to blur and digest the necessary triple rhymes; but even in the earlier and easier 'Sailing to Byzantium' there is also a discord generated by pararhyme:

> THAT is no country for old men. The young
> In one another's arms, birds in the trees
> —Those dying generations—at their song,
> The salmon-falls, the mackerel-crowded seas,

> Fish, flesh, or fowl, commend all summer long
> Whatever is begotten, born, and dies.
> Caught in that sensual music all neglect
> Monuments of unageing intellect.

The awkward additional near-pararhyme of 'men' and 'young' across a disruptive full stop anticipates the *a*-pararhyme, 'young/song', and any comfort in the fullness of the first *b*-rhyme, 'trees/seas', and second *a*-rhyme, 'song/long', is lost in the second *b*-rhyme, '/dies' (again medially augmented, with 'is'), and the wrenching of 'intelléct' into conformity with 'neglect'.

In 'Among School Children' the discord grows worse:

> I WALK through the long schoolroom questioning;
> A kind old nun in a white hood replies;
> The children learn to cipher and to sing,
> To study reading-books and histories,
> To cut and sew, be neat in everything
> In the best modern way—the children's eyes
> In momentary wonder stare upon
> A sixty-year-old smiling public man.

There is a problem with stressing '-ing' endings as rhymes (as Shakespeare showed in sonnet 87, 'Farewell thou art too deare for my possessing'), and the extra stress on 'quéstioníng' is not helped by its rhyme: in any poetic opening 'sing' summons Virgil and the epic tradition, but here its subject is 'The children', not the Yeatsian 'I' who 'walks' and is briefly stared at, and smiles in practised habit or with nerves. Wrenching recurs with 'everything', while pararhyme sounds immediately in 'replies/histories', and again, despairingly, in 'upon/man'.

Such discord could be traced in other late poems in *ottava rima*; its terminus is 'The Circus Animals' Desertion':

> I sought a theme and sought for it in vain,
> I sought it daily for six weeks or so.
> Maybe at last, being but a broken man,
> I must be satisfied with my heart, although
> Winter and summer till old age began
> My circus animals were all on show,
> Those stilted boys, that burnished chariot,
> Lion and woman and the Lord knows what.

The wrenched or pararhyming couplet has a Byronic gravity-in-levity, so that mock-seriousness and serious mockery are hard to tell apart, but it sounds rather hollow after the initial autorhyme of 'I sought' (picked up in 'at last'), the discordant *a*-pararhymes 'vain/man/began' (interacting with 'daily', 'broken', and 'animals'), and the qualifying or negative *b*-rhymes 'or so/although/on show'. So potent are these systematic dissonances that they become, in Eliot's phrase, the 'objective correlative' or physical embodiment of Yeats's dissatisfaction with himself: fuller rhymes and greater harmony would not correct a fault, but undo the whole.

Few of us can hope to redesign the coachwork of a major stanza in this way, but the general lesson holds good for all rhymers. Rhyme in any concentration demands sharp attention from the writer (and subsequently all readers); which does not mean slavish adherence to one sort of rhyme, but rather a plan within which variations can be marshalled. Harington, Byron, and Yeats share a professional poetic understanding of rhyme as in counterpoint to itself and to other prescribed elements of a form, an understanding that Fayrfax did not really have: and in 'free verse' (which means only a lack of **pre**scription, not any **pro**scription) the stakes will usually be higher, for rhyme will be operating in relative isolation. Hence (in part) Auden's wry observation that in free verse an 'infallible ear' is always required: a single bad rhyme, awkwardly wrenched or introducing a false note in diction or syntax, can bring ruin, yet a great poet can all but bend our ears to his or her will.

T. S. Eliot (1888–1965) went as far as anyone in the 'Dante' section of *The Dry Salvages*, the third of his *Four Quartets* (1942), abandoning rhyme itself but substituting a pattern of alternating stressed and unstressed endings ('re-enáctment/sháme/awáreness', 'hárm/vírtue/stáins' etc.) that manage with the faintest vowel rhymes and some help from layout to be heard as equivalent to full rhyme in Dantean *terza rima*—a lesson well learned by the Canadian poet-performer Leonard Cohen (b.1934), whose persistently 'mournful' sound owes much to unstressed endings (some rhyming, some blank). Almost as radical as Eliot though in a different manner, a recent sonnet called 'In Iowa' by the Irish Nobel Laureate Seamus Heaney (b.1937), has the quatrain rhyme-sequences 'Mennonites/afternoon/windscreen/

flits', 'gap/snow/seat/brow', and 'gears/wilderness/darkness/
tatters', plus the couplet 'hiss/waters'. This 4-4-4-2 structure
suggests a Shakespearean sonnet (rather than the Petrarchan 4-4-
3-3), which should properly have the rhyme scheme *abab cdcd
efef gg*, comprising three cross-rhymed quatrains and a couplet; in
Heaney's version, the third quatrain is arch-rhymed (*effe*) rather
than cross-rhymed, but otherwise, allowing for the persistent
pararhyme, the pairings of '-noon/-screen', '-ites/flits', 'snow/
brow', and 'hiss/waters' seem to be in the right places. The
supposed *c*-rhyme, 'gap/seat', however, is not a rhyme at all—
neither vowels nor following sounds match—and yet the pairing
seems in this company to strain towards being one. There is in the
poem no syntactical connection between "the open gap/of a field"
and the "iron seat" of a "mowing machine", but as expectation of
(para)rhyme tries to bind the words together I find myself
imagining the kinds of gaps iron seats often have, how
uncomfortable they are, and the elevated view the seats of farm-
machines offer over rolling farmland; even, ranging more widely
with the ideas of 'gap' and 'seat', that for Heaney, as intensely Irish
as he is cosmopolitan, to be 'In Iowa' is to be strikingly out of place.
In almost anyone else's work, 'gap/seat' would simply be a duff
moment, a failure of form or at best a shrug of defeat; in Heaney's
it is the free stroke of a master.

As in Yeats, and persistently in the First World War poems of
Wilfred Owen, half-rhyming serves Heaney by generating but also
containing anxieties and questionings; it is equally possible to go
the other way, and build intensities of full rhyme. Perhaps the
most notorious of all post-1945 lyrics, the terrifying 'Daddy' by
Sylvia Plath (1932–63), returns again and again, always unevenly,
to the same crooning rhyme-sound, 'do/shoe/blue/you/achoo/
gobbledygoo', while only occasionally and with tremendous power
delivering the rhyme that demands that sound, 'Jew'. Many other
aspects of 'Daddy' are irregular—the rhythm can sound jaunty,
which for some adds insult to injury, and the diction is sometimes
wilfully childish—but it is the hammering rhymes that most
people remember.

Such an extreme strategy is necessarily a one-off, but insistence of
rhyme can be very profitably harnessed. The lyrics of The
Waterboys' great lament 'Old England', from *This is the Sea* (1985),

for example, written by Mike Scott (b.1958) builds through triple and quadruple rhymes to a climactic description of a place "where criminals are televised politicians fraternize/journalists are dignified and everyone is civilised/and children stare with Heroin eyes". The complex beat and wrenched delivery more acceptable in song allows each of the medial and terminal rhymes, 'televised-fraternize/dignified-civilised', to sound clearly, building through their variations (-ised, -ize, -ied) an arch that apparently ends with 'civilised' as the full rhyme for 'televised'; only to be trumped, after the blow of the blank 'stare' where another medial rhyme might be expected, by the delayed, now hideously unexpected "Heroin eyes" and its horrible closeness to "fraternize". As the phrase is repeated it begins to sound like 'heroinise', and so to suggest (in a corporate-style word) a strategy of heroin-induced anaesthesia as a means of dulling exclusion and poverty, yet remains "Heroin eyes", a glassy pin-pointedness that is vile to see in anyone, and in massed children a peculiarly terrible thing. Rap lyrics and slam poetry also tend to try this route, often with real success, but can easily fall into the trap parodied by Blondie in 'Rapture', where a "man from Mars" who knows about "stars" hungrily eats up "cars", "bars", and "guitars" only because they rhyme.

Relatedly, one might think of Bob Dylan (Robert Zimmerman, b.1941), often accused of 'just trying to make it rhyme', but to many, a rhymer of astonishing skill. Helped in performance by the ambiguity between long lines with regular medial rhymes and enjambed short rhyming lines, one of his tricks is the use of prepositions as rhyme-words, as in 'Like a Rolling Stone': "Ain't it hard when you discover that / He really wasn't where it's at". The preceding "diplomat / Who carried on his shoulder a Siamese cat" is embarrassing for Dylan's defenders, but the rhymes on 'that' and 'at' carry in performance (if not on the page) a vengeful and insistent sneer made all the more powerful by the simple, functional words. Like most live performers Dylan also knows the value of stretching his vowels, and in the same song his recurrent rhymes for 'feel', as each stanza ends with an elongated 'meal' or 'steal', offset the far curter rhymes on the prepositions.

If a rhyming rock-and-roll villain is sought, the better candidate is Jim Morrison (James Douglas Morrison, 1943–71) of The Doors, who immortally declared both in the song 'Riders on the Storm' and the poem 'The Hitchhiker' that 'There's a killer on the road', but ruined things by adding—very much with rhyme but wholly without reason—that 'His brain is squirming like a toad'. It isn't that one cannot accept a squirming toad, nor that toads aren't killers, nor even that some connection between the look of a killer's brain and a toad squirming is beyond imagination, but that the rhyme is lazy, an obvious and weak choice when several far more interesting possibilities were readily available ('goad', 'mode', 'load'), never mind a raft of pararhymes beginning with 'mad' and 'bad', and vowel rhymes beginning with 'roam' and 'lone'. In a looping and self-consciously eerie (or portentous) song like 'Riders on the Storm', the clang of 'road/toad' cannot be easily borne without clear and apparent justification, and the results are notorious even among Morrison's most ardent defenders as a poet.

Rhyme of course has humbler and more homely uses than poetry and song, in proverbs, slogans, jingles, and birthday cards, but even when literary quality is in no way necessary, the rules of thumb remain useful. The notorious tweeness of printed birthday-card rhymes has much to do with tin-eared metre, but their stale sentimentality is equally to do with tired and rehashed rhymes, devoid of any effort to refurbish their meaning. Compare 'love/dove', 'love/above', 'dear/near' and the rest of their ilk with 'love/prove', 'love/give', and 'dear/far': yes, the dissonances could spiral out of control to undo a loving or celebratory tone, but they could equally introduce sufficient spine to lift the verse from limp servility to convention. The celebrated awfulness as a poet of William McGonagall (1830–1902) also has as much to do with his clumsy strivings after full rhyme as his obsession with commemorating transport disasters at interminable length. And I suspect that the condescension often shown to the plaintive or jolly (and once hugely popular) poems of Pam Ayres (b.1947), collected in such volumes as *Thoughts of a Late-Night Knitter* and *Some of Me Poetry* (both 1978), similarly has as much to do with her forced rhymes as her everyday subjects and calculated self-presentation as an amateur.

Finally, the issues that regional or national accents pose for rhyme are also best treated as resources, not problems. Occasional use of regional accent to create a rhyme in a poem that is otherwise

accentless on the page is unwise; even intended comedy readily
slides into snideness or jeering, and neither readers nor audiences
tend to be forgiving. Systematic use of one's own regional accent,
however, once derided by the establishment, is back with a
vengeance, and may be indicated by spelling, as in 'giver/nivver'
(for 'never'), or left to a reader's discretion. Tony Harrison, born to
working-class parents in Leeds in 1937, famously pointed out in
'Them and [Uz]' (freely available is a wonderful reading by
Harrison at the British Council website) that to Wordsworth, born
in Cumberland, 'matter/water' was a full rhyme—but poetry "you
see / 's been dubbed by [ʌs] into RP". '[Uz]' and '[ʌs]' represent the
northern- and southern-English pronunciations of the pronoun
'us'—'[Uz]' rhymes with southern 'buzz' or 'booze', and '[ʌs]' with
'bus'—while 'RP' is Received Pronunciation, the supposedly
accentless but in fact specifically southern sound that is 'normal'
or 'proper', the 'Queen's' or 'BBC' English, in terms of which
northerners (among others) are deemed to speak with an 'inferior'
accent. Harrison's trenchant claim is that much great poetry has
been rendered 'southern' on the page when its creators would in
life have spoken with a northern (or whatever) accent, and even so
small a thing as the short northern 'a' (making 'past' like 'pasta', not
'parsed') can have tremendous effects. His English teacher at
Leeds Grammar School, to which he won a scholarship, once
stopped him from reading Keats's 'Ode to a Nightingale' aloud
because his accent 'barbarised' our "glorious heritage". Instead
Harrison "played the drunken porter in *Macbeth*", and he has
described his career as a "long, slow-burning revenge" on that
teacher, poetically bringing home to the English the bigoted class
and regional snobberies that divide them as a nation. Beyond
domestic politics, in 'A Cold Coming', published in the news pages
of *The Independent* during the First Gulf War in 1991, Harrison
persistently rhymed 'Iraq' with a short 'a'— 'Iraq/back', or '/sack',
or '/black', but never '/park' or '/dark'—and the snap of the short
vowels is integral to a poem of bitter questions.

Similar issues recur fiercely in post-colonial poetry. The St Lucian
Nobel Laureate Derek Walcott (b.1930), for example, late in
'Nearing Forty' (from *The Gulf*, 1969) rhymes 'clerk' with 'work',
forcing readers to choose between the received southern-English
pronunciation, 'clark', a pararhyme ('clark/work'), and a common

but non-standard and *déclassé* pronunciation, 'clurk', a full rhyme ('clurk/work') that semantic harmony (clerks working) and the peaceful resolution of Walcott's poem seem to want. Or again, the Jamaican poet Edward Baugh (b.1937), responding in 'Nigger Sweat' (from *A Tale from the Rainforest*, 1988) to a notice in the Visa Section of the U. S. Embassy in Kingston requiring applicants to 'Kindly keep [documents] dry', pointedly rhymes the affirmatory patois pronoun 'weself' with 'life', fighting with semantic pararhyme against the humiliation of a place seemingly designed to "bruk-spirit" in those who must wait there.

The most general lessons, then, are variety and control. Those committed to verse may wish to experiment systematically with given stanzas using full and half-, or monosyllabic and mosaic, or stressed and unstressed rhyme; much may be learned in doing so. Those desiring rhymes only for light or occasional verse may equally profit by considering carefully the kind of rhyme they want, as well as their desired content. And for the comically or satirically minded, rhyme is a calculation that should never be ignored.

How to use this book

I'm a poet
And I know it:
As proud as William of Orange
I rhyme my way ... ~~cringe range binge~~ zorange

The *New Oxford Rhyming Dictionary* offers a toolkit to writers of all kinds. It will allow you to look up rhymes for specific words; browse sets of rhymes for inspiration; use the tips in the notes to create extra sets of rhymes; and learn from the poetry panels how other writers past and present have used rhyme.

The first half of the book is set out in 35 sections, each representing the sound of a word ending. The sounds (or phonic elements) are indicated using the most common spelling in English, starting with the vowel sounds, such as '-ay', '-ee', '-ow', '-oo', and moving on to consonant sounds, such as '-b', '-g', '-k', '-sh', and '-z'. There are 13 sections of words ending in vowel sounds, and 22 sections of words ending in consonant sounds. The sections are divided in approximately alphabetical order by sound, so that in the '-b' section you will find the following subsections: '-ab', '-arb', '-eb', '-airb', '-abe', '-eeb', '-ib', '-ibe', '-ob', etc. The consistent sequencing of subsections in this manner will enable you to source vowel rhymes across sections. Once you are familiar with the book, all this will allow you to browse the text, as well as to use the index to guide you. Browsing is a good way to make exciting and unexpected rhyming connections.

To find rhymes for a specific word, simply go to the index (which has over 45,000 words to choose from, including proper names); there you will find a number which directs you to a corresponding section in the main text (e.g. 1.1 or 12.55). At that numbered section, you will find a list of all the words which rhyme with your chosen word. A subsection which begins with a bullet point and the first word in bold indicates a list of words which are full or perfect rhymes for each other. Other subsections will offer near or half-rhymes for your chosen word. In practice, the further away in the text you get from your chosen word, the less 'perfectly' the words will rhyme with it.

For example, if you look up the word 'candy' in the index, it will direct you to section 4.12 where you will find several subsections. The one which begins with the word '**Andy**' is the section you want for full rhymes. There you will find 'brandy', 'dandy', and 'Gandhi' among others. In the neighbouring sections, you will find 'hardy', 'lardy', 'daddy', and 'laddie', all of which are pararhymes for 'candy'.

The notes within sections will help you to create whole new sets of rhymes, and will enable you to link different rhyming sets in the book. For instance you can make additional rhymes for words such as 'shallow' (and the other words in that section), by adding '-ness' to make 'shallowness', 'sallowness', and 'fallowness'. Also, by adding '-(r)ed' to words like 'blur' and 'deter', you can create a new set of rhyming words: 'absurd', 'overheard', and so on. The in-text notes will thus help you to make new and unexpected rhymes.

In some cases, derived words (words with suffixes such as '-ness', '-ly', '-ed' and so on) are not listed explicitly, but the notes will indicate when extra rhyming lists can be created by adding these to an existing list of words.

The poetry panels contain useful information on types of rhymes and give examples from many different styles of writing, from sonnets and songs, to nursery rhymes and limericks. Their purpose is both to illustrate technical aspects of rhyme and to inspire you to explore the possibilities for yourself. Searching for rhymes has never been more fun or enlightening. Good luck and good rhyming!

JOHN LENNARD
May 2005

List of sections

Section 1: -ar

1.1

- **aargh**, Accra, afar, ah, aha, aide-mémoire, ajar, Alcazar, are, Armagh, armoire, Artois, au revoir, baa, bah, bar, barre, bazaar, beaux-arts, Bekaa, bête noire, Bihar, bizarre, blah, Bogotá, Bonnard, bra, cafard, café noir, Calabar, car, Carr, Castlebar, catarrh, Changsha, char, charr, cigar, comme ci comme ça, commissar, coup d'état, de haut en bas, devoir, Dhofar, Directoire, Du Bois, Dumas, Dunbar, éclat, embarras de choix, escritoire, fah, famille noire, far, feu de joie, film noir, foie gras, Fra, galah, gar, guar, guitar, ha, hah, ha-ha, Halacha, hurrah, hussar, huzza, insofar, Invar, jar, je ne sais quoi, ka, kala-azar, Kandahar, Khimar, Khorramshahr, knar, Krasnodar, Kwa, la-di-da, lah, Lehár, Loire, ma, mama, mamma, mar, Mardi Gras, ménage à trois, mirepoix, moire, nam pla, Navarre, noir, objet d'art, pa, pah, Panama, papa, par, Pará, Paraná, pas, pâté de foie gras, peau-de-soie, pietà, Pinot Noir, pooh-bah, poult-de-soie, pya, rah, registrar, Saar, Salazar, Sana'a, sang-froid, scar, schwa, Seychellois, shah, Shangri-La, shikar, ska, sol-fa, spa, spar, star, Starr, Stranraer, ta, tahr, tar, tartare, tata, tra-la, tsar, Twa, Villa, voilà, waratah, yah

1.2

- penniä • caviar

1.3

- boyar

1.4

- Akbar • handlebar • sandbar • kasbah
- baba • rebar • heelbar • Finbar
- millibar • coolibah • minibar
- Zanzibar • sidebar • crossbar
- **crowbar**, towbar
- rollbar • Nicobar • isobar • durbar

1.5

- cha-cha

1.6

- Dada • radar • zamindar • Pindar
- chowkidar • havildar • Godard
- doodah
- **purdah**, sirdar

1.7

- Afar • Sofar

This poem, written in *couplets*, uses simple rhymes on single syllable words and on words with a final stressed syllable (these are called *stressed* or *masculine rhymes*):

This is the midnight—let no star
Delude us—dawn is very far
This is the tempest long foretold—
Slow to make head but sure to hold

(Rudyard Kipling, 'The Storm Cone')

1.8

- gaga • Elgar
- **Degas**, Hagar
- budgerigar • nougat • Bulgar

1.9

- **ha-ha**, Praha
- brouhaha • Mudéjar • pakeha • Doha
- hoo-ha • Omaha

1.10

- Sharjah • nightjar

1.11

- **Dakar**, fracas
- tramcar • Shankar
- **Farquhar**, kaka, markka, taka
- railcar • cablecar • streetcar • Indycar
- Hamilcar • tricar • sidecar • stockcar
- boxcar • chukar • Issachar • motorcar
- advocaat

1.12

- verglas • Alar • Mylar • foulard
- hoopla

1.13

- Dagmar • Kalmar • grandma • Tamar
- **Valdemar**, Waldemar
- Weimar • Bislama • grandmama
- Kostroma • Fermat

1.14

- dinar • webinar • seminar • sonar
- Fragonard

1.15

- grandpa • feldspar • oompah
- fluorspar • grandpapa

1.16

- Marat • rah-rah • bajra • baccarat
- Aymara • Seurat

1.17

- ahimsa • paisa • pulsar

1.18

- entrechat

1.19

- Qatar • Telstar • sitar • Ishtar • co-star
- lodestar • sunstar • megastar
- superstar • avatar • earthstar

1.20

- Cathar

1.21

- Avar • Alvar
- **bolivar**, Bolívar
- cultivar • shalwar • samovar

1.22

- Valois • chamois
- **fatwa**, patois
- wah-wah • Hardwar • memoir
- Renoir • peignoir • pissoir
- Chippewa
- **François**, Françoise
- renvoi • Vaudois • boudoir
- pourboire • bourgeois • abattoir
- fille de joie • Delacroix • repertoire
- conservatoire • reservoir

1.23

• Magyar • Chechnya • Iyyar

1.24

• **César**, quasar

Section 2: **-air**

2.1

• **affair**, affaire, air, Altair, Althusser, Anvers, Apollinaire, Astaire, aware, Ayer, Ayr, bare, bear, bêche-de-mer, beware, billionaire, Blair, blare, Bonaire, cafetière, care, chair, chargé d'affaires, chemin de fer, Cher, Clair, Claire, Clare, commissionaire, compare, concessionaire, cordon sanitaire, couvert, Daguerre, dare, debonair, declare, derrière, despair, doctrinaire, éclair, e'er, elsewhere, ensnare, ere, extraordinaire, Eyre, fair, fare, fayre, Finisterre, flair, flare, Folies-Bergère, forbear, forswear, foursquare, glair, glare, hair, hare, heir, Herr, impair, jardinière, Khmer, Kildare, La Bruyère, lair, laissez-faire, legionnaire, luminaire, mal de mer, mare, mayor, meunière, mid-air, millionaire, misère, Mon-Khmer, multimillionaire, ne'er, Niger, nom de guerre, outstare, outwear, pair, pare, parterre, pear, père, pied-à-terre, Pierre, plein-air, prayer, questionnaire, rare, ready-to-wear, rivière, Rosslare, Santander, savoir faire, scare, secretaire, share, snare, solitaire, Soufrière, spare, square, stair, stare, surface-to-air, swear, Tailleferre, tare, tear, their, there, they're, vin ordinaire, Voltaire, ware, wear, Weston-super-Mare, where, yeah

2.2

• Molière • première • son et lumière • Robespierre

2.3

• threadbare • Colbert • Rambert
• **forbear**, forebear
• Flaubert • bugbear • Camembert

2.4

• armchair • deckchair • wheelchair
• pushchair

2.5

• fanfare • carfare • welfare • airfare
• **Mayfair**, Playfair
• fieldfare • warfare • funfair
• thoroughfare

Rime riche (or identical rhyme) includes rhymes created with homophones (words which sound the same but have different meanings and spellings):

''All things thy fancy hath desired of me
Thou hast received. I have prepared for thee
Within my house a spacious chamber, where
Are delicate things to handle and to wear [...]

(Edna St Vincent Millay, 'The Suicide')

2.6

- camelhair •maidenhair •longhair
- horsehair •shorthair
- mohair

2.7

- haircare •skincare •Medicare
- childcare •aftercare

2.8

- Sinclair •Baudelaire

2.9

- nightmare •commère

2.10

- **ampere**, milliampere
- compère

2.11

- confrère

2.12

- corsair

2.13

- timeshare
- ploughshare (*US* plowshare)

2.14

- hectare

2.15

- adware •flatware •hardware
- glassware •shapewear •neckwear
- **headsquare**
- headwear •setsquare •delftware
- menswear •shareware •tableware
- rainwear •freeware •beachwear
- T-square •creamware •sleepware
- swimwear •tinware •knitwear
- giftware •kitchenware •womenswear
- anywhere •everywhere •activewear
- nightwear •software •sportswear
- loungewear •nowhere •stoneware
- cookware •footwear •somewhere
- ovenware •ironware •underwear
- leisurewear •Delaware •Tupperware
- outerwear •otherwhere •silverware
- workwear •earthenware

> Try rhyming one word with a set of two: nightwear, might wear; nowhere, go there.

2.16

- Gruyère

Section 3: **-ay**

3.1

- **affray**, agley, aka, allay, Angers, A-OK, appellation contrôlée, array, assay, astray, au fait, auto-da-fé, away, aweigh, aye, bay, belay, betray, bey, Bombay, Bordet, boulevardier, bouquet, brae, bray, café au lait, Carné, cassoulet, Cathay, chassé, chevet, chez, chiné, clay, convey, Cray, crème brûlée, crudités, cuvée, cy-pres, day, decay, deejay, dégagé, distinguée, downplay, dray, Dufay, Dushanbe, eh, embay, engagé, essay, everyday, faraway, fay, fey, flay, fray, Frey, fromage frais, gainsay, gay, Gaye, Genet, giclee, gilet, glissé, gray, grey, halfway, hay, heigh, hey, hooray, Hubei, Hué, hurray, inveigh, jay, jeunesse dorée, José, Kay, Kaye, Klee, Kray, Lae, lay, lei, Littré, Lough Neagh, lwei, Mae, maguey, Malay, Mallarmé, Mandalay, Marseilles, may, midday, midway, misplay, Monterrey, Na-Dene, nay, né, née, neigh, Ney, noway, obey, O'Dea, okay, olé, outlay, outplay, outstay, outweigh, oyez, part-way, pay, Pei, per se, pince-nez, play, portray, pray, prey, purvey, qua, Quai d'Orsay, Rae, rangé, ray, re, reflet, relevé, roman-à-clef, Santa Fé, say, sei, Shar Pei, shay, slay, sleigh, sley, spae, spay, Spey, splay, spray, stay, straightaway, straightway, strathspey, stray, Sui, survey, sway, Taipei, Tay, they, today, tokay, Torbay, Tournai, trait, tray, trey, two-way, ukiyo-e, underlay, way, waylay, Wei, weigh, wey, Whangarei, whey, yea

3.2

- **déshabillé**, plié

3.3

- **Chevalier**, Duvalier
- tablier
- **atelier**, Tortelier
- Rainier •croupier •Le Verrier •Kyrie
- Du Maurier •couturier •Cartier
- métier
- **Poitier**, Poitiers
- bustier •Olivier •Cuvier •Lavoisier
- Le Corbusier

3.4

- foyer

3.5

- **Niue**, roué

3.6

- habitué

3.7

- abbé •thebe •sickbay •yohimbe
- flambé •sorbet •rosebay

3.8

- Elche •seviche
- **Croce**, mezza voce
- Duce

3.9

- **Allende**, duende
- Wednesday
- **heyday**, mayday, payday
- bidet • weekday • Halliday • holiday
- Friday • Hobday • washday
- Corday
- **magna cum laude**, summa cum laude
- **Daudet**, démodé
- noonday • Tuesday
- **Domesday**, doomsday
- Yaoundé • someday
- **Monday**, sundae, Sunday
- Muscadet • workaday • faraday
- Saturday • yesterday • workday
- birthday • Thursday

> Try rhyming one word with a set of two: bidet, key day; sundae, one day.   **i**

3.10

- café • cybercafé • parfait • coryphée
- buffet

3.11

- distingué • reggae • Sergei • Tenzing Norgay • nosegay

3.12

- Piaget • negligee • protégé • Roget
- Fabergé

3.13

- popinjay

3.14

- parquet
- **appliqué**, piqué
- **Biscay**, risqué
- communiqué • tourniquet • sobriquet
- manqué

- **cloqué**, croquet
- Malplaquet

3.15

- **ballet**, Calais, chalet, Hallé, palais, pis aller
- matchplay • parlay
- **cor anglais**, franglais
- **melee**, pappardelle, Pelé
- endplay • Nestlé • airplay
- **belay**, relay
- replay • screenplay • Millais • inlay
- misplay • cantabile • roundelay
- teleplay • pipeclay • byplay • volet
- bobsleigh • cosplay • foreplay
- swordplay • horseplay • outlay
- paso doble • stroke play • soufflé
- bouclé • gunplay • cabriolet
- Rabelais • underlay • Beaujolais
- Charolais • interplay • overlay
- wordplay

> Create extra rhymes by adding *-ing* or *-ed* to words like belay and replay.   **i**

3.16

- gamay
- **lamé**, Niamey
- Aimée • animé • consommé • Lomé
- **résumé**, resume
- gourmet • entremets

3.17

- Manet • carnet
- **nota bene**, René
- Binet • estaminet
- **gratiné**, matinée
- **cloisonné**, donnée, Dubonnet, Monet
- Mornay • panettone • Chardonnay
- Hogmanay

3.18

- frappé • jaspé
- **épée**, Pepe

- Príncipe
- **coupé**, Nupe, toupée
- agape • canapé

3.19

- Le Carré • Sierra Madre • ashtray
- **mare**, soirée
- padre • Castlereagh • beret • sempre
- X-ray • affairé • hairspray • respray
- Tigray • stingray • in-tray • émigré
- vertebrae
- **foray**, moray
- **chambray**, chambré, hombre, ombré
- André • osprey • entrée
- **con amore**, Doré, Fauré
- sucre • outré • Vouvray
- **bourrée**, Blu-ray
- sunray
- **Desirée**, Dies Irae
- **curé**, purée
- cabaret

3.20

- **déclassé**, glacé, laissez-passer
- passé
- **fiancé**, fiancée
- essay • naysay
- **lycée**, plissé
- pensée
- **repoussé**, retroussé
- hearsay

3.21

- **attaché**, cachet, papier-mâché, sachet, sashay
- Beaumarchais • recherché • cliché
- crochet • touché • ricochet • Pinochet

3.22

- **latte**, maté, pâté, pattée, satay
- concertante • backstay • commedia dell'arte, écarté, Jubilate
- **fouetté**, jeté, mantellette
- Deo volente • mainstay • décolleté

- cinéma-vérité • diamanté • bobstay
- homestay
- **forte**, panforte, prêt-à-porter
- forestay • sauté • velouté

3.23

- Pathé

3.24

- pavé • névé • corvée • duvet
- champlevé • survey

3.25

- Kabwe • hatchway • trackway
- tramway • gangway • Yahweh
- archway • parkway • pathway
- headway • segue • expressway
- **airway**, fairway, stairway
- railway • gateway
- **freeway**, keyway, leeway, seaway
- speedway • breezeway • Midway
- ridgeway
- **shipway**, slipway
- Kitwe • alleyway • Hemingway
- anyway • carriageway • entryway
- steerageway • taxiway • passageway
- **byway**, highway, skyway
- **guideway**, tideway
- bridleway • Steinway • driveway
- Otway
- **doorway**, Norway
- Broadway • walkway
- **Galway**, hallway
- causeway • roadway • throughway
- sluiceway • footway • subway
- someway • runway • clearway
- areaway • entranceway • flyaway
- **stowaway**, throwaway
- hideaway • foldaway
- **breakaway**, takeaway
- galloway • rollaway
- **colourway** (*US* colorway), mulloway
- Greenaway • Stornoway • runaway
- caraway • tearaway • castaway
- getaway • straightaway • waterway

- motorway - cutaway - Hathaway
- giveaway - companionway - sternway

3.26

- **soigné**, soignée

3.27

- blasé
- **Bizet**, Champs-Élysées, frisée
- **exposé**, rosé

Section 4: -ee

4.1

absentee, açaí, addressee, adoptee, agree, allottee, amputee, appellee, appointee, appraisee, après-ski, assignee, asylee, attendee, bailee, bain-marie, Bangui, bargee, bawbee, be, Bea, bee, bootee, bouquet garni, bourgeoisie, Brie, BSc, buckshee, Capri, cc, chimpanzee, cohabitee, conferee, consignee, consultee, Cree, debauchee, decree, dedicatee, Dee, degree, deportee, dernier cri, detainee, devisee, devotee, divorcee, draftee, dree, Dundee, dungaree, eau-de-vie, emcee, employee, endorsee, en famille, ennui, enrollee, escapee, esprit, evacuee, examinee, expellee, fee, fiddle-de-dee, flea, flee, fleur-de-lis, foresee, franchisee, free, fusee (*US* fuzee), Gardaí, garnishee, gee, ghee, glee, goatee, grandee, Grand Prix, grantee, Guarani, guarantee, he HMRC, indictee, inductee, internee, interviewee, invitee, jamboree, Jaycee, jeu d'esprit, key, knee, Lea, lee, legatee, Leigh, lessee, Ley, licensee, loanee, lychee, manatee, Manichee, maquis, Marie, marquee, me, Midi, mortgagee, MSc, nominee, obligee, Otomi, parolee, Parsee, parti pris, patentee, Pawnee, payee, pea, pee, permittee, plc, plea, pledgee, pollee, presentee, promisee, quay, ratatouille, referee, refugee, releasee, repartee, retiree, returnee, rupee, scot-free, scree, sea, secondee, see, settee, Shanxi, Shawnee, shchi, she, shea, si, sirree, ski, spree, standee, suttee, tant pis, tea, tee, tee-hee, Tennessee, testee, the, thee, three, thuggee, Tiree, Torquay, trainee, Tralee, transferee, tree, Trincomalee, trustee, tutee, twee, Twi, undersea, vestee, vis-à-vis, wagon-lit, Waikiki, warrantee, we, wee, whee, whoopee, ye, yippee, Zuider Zee

4.2

Agnus Dei, clayey, Pompeii

4.3

• Danaë • filariae • torii • differentiae • prima facie • facetiae • reliquiae

4.4

Hawaii, skyey

A combination of *unstressed* (or *feminine*) rhyme, *autorhyme*, and *medial rhyme* gives this passage a lilting and soft cadence:

Time for you and time for me,
And time yet for a hundred indecisions,
And for a hundred visions and revisions,
Before the taking of a toast and tea.

(T. S. Eliot, 'The Love Song of J. Alfred Prufrock')

> Two successive lines that rhyme are called a *rhyming couplet*; this example
> from a well-known Shakespeare sonnet is also a *heroic couplet* (written in
> iambic pentameter which means five stressed syllables: ti-TUM ti-TUM ti-TUM
> ti-TUM ti-TUM):
>
> So long as men can breathe or eyes can see,
> So long lives this, and this gives life to thee.
>
> (William Shakespeare, Sonnet XVIII 'Shall I Compare thee to a Summer's Day?')

4.5

• strawy

4.6

• Towy

4.7

• **blowy**, doughy, joey, showy, snowy, toey, towy, Zoë
• shadowy •meadowy •echoey
• **sallowy**, tallowy
• yellowy
• **billowy**, pillowy, willowy
• arrowy •furrowy •tomatoey

4.8

• **bluey**, chewy, chop suey, cooee, Dewey, dewy, Drambuie, feng shui, gluey, gooey, hooey, Hughie, Louie, Louis, phooey, rouille, screwy, Wanganui
• mildewy •sinewy

4.9

• Anouilh

4.10

• **abbey**, cabby, crabby, flabby, gabby, grabby, Rabbie, scabby, shabby, tabby, yabby
• namby-pamby

• **Abu Dhabi**, Babi, Darby, derby, kohlrabi, Mugabe, Punjabi, Wahhabi
• **Entebbe**, plebby
• cobwebby
• **Achebe**, baby, maybe
• Naseby •crybaby •bushbaby
• **freebie**, Hebe, phoebe
• Libby •Digby
• **astilbe**, Philby, trilby
• Dimbleby •nimby •Whitby
• **frisbee**, Thisbe
• Grimsby •renminbi •honeybee
• oribi
• **Bobbie**, bobby, Gobbi, hobby, knobby, lobby, snobby, swabbie
• Dolby •zombie •Crosby
• **corbie**, warby
• Albee •Formby •Port Moresby
• **adobe**, dhobi, dobe, Nairobi, obi, Robey
• Toynbee
• **booby**, jube, newbie, Newby, ruby
• would-be
• **chubby**, clubby, cubby, grubby, hubby, nubby, scrubby, shrubby, stubby, tubby

> Create extra rhymes by
> changing words like chubby to
> chubbiness, or to chubbier and
> chubbiest.

• rugby •bumblebee •brumby •busby
• Niobe •Jacobi •Lockerbie •Allenby
• Willoughby •wallaby •wannabe
• Araby •tsessebi •herby

4.11

• **Apache**, catchy, patchy, scratchy, snatchy

- **hibachi**, Karachi, Liberace, starchy, vivace
- **sketchy**, stretchy, tetchy
- squelchy •Strachey
- **caliche**, Campeche, peachy, preachy, screechy
- **bitchy**, itchy, kitschy, pitchy, Richie, titchy, twitchy
- Medici •semplice
- **blotchy**, bocce, notchy, splotchy
- **grouchy**, pouchy, slouchy
- **sotto voce**, viva voce
- **Bertolucci**, smoochy, Vespucci
- **archduchy**, duchy, touchy
- churchy

4.12

- **baddy**, caddie, caddy, daddy, faddy, kabaddi, laddie, paddy
- **alcalde**, Chaldee, Fittipaldi, Vivaldi
- **Andy**, bandy, brandy, candy, dandy, Gandhi, glissandi, handy, jim-dandy, Kandy, Mandy, modus operandi, Nandi, randy, Río Grande, sandhi, sandy, sforzandi, shandy
- **cadi**, cardy, Guardi, Hardie, hardy, jihadi, lardy, Mahdi, mardy, Saadi, samadhi, tardy, Yardie
- foolhardy •autostrade
- **already**, Eddie, eddy, Freddie, heady, neddy, oven-ready, ready, reddy, steady, teddy, thready
- **bendy**, effendi, Gassendi, modus vivendi, trendy, Wendy

- **Monteverdi**, Verdi
- **Adie**, Brady, lady, milady, Sadie, shady
- landlady •charlady •saleslady
- **beady**, greedy, needy, reedy, seedy, speedy, tweedy, weedy

> Create extra rhymes by changing words like needy to neediness, or to needier and neediest. ⓘ

- wieldy
- **biddy**, diddy, giddy, kiddie, middy, midi
- higgledy-piggledy
- **Cindy**, Hindi, indie, Indy, Lindy, Rawalpindi, shindy, Sindhi, Sindy, windy
- perfidy •raggedy •tragedy •remedy
- **comedy**, tragicomedy
- Kennedy •Cassidy •accidie •subsidy
- **bona fide**, Heidi, mala fide, tidy, vide

4.13

- **body**, embody, Irrawaddy, Kirkcaldy, noddy, Passamaquoddy, shoddy, Soddy, squaddie, toddy, wadi
- **secondi**, spondee, tondi
- anybody •everybody •busybody
- dogsbody •homebody
- **bawdy**, gaudy, Geordie, Lordy

Rhyming on proper names is often used for humour, and to add topicality—Cole Porter managed to squeeze in more than most in his song 'You're the Top':

You're a melody from a symphony by Strauss,
You're a Bendel bonnet, a Shakespeare sonnet, you're Mickey Mouse.
You're the Nile, you're the Tower of Pisa,
You're the smile on the Mona Lisa,
I'm a worthless check, a total wreck, a flop,
But if, baby, I'm the bottom, you're the top! ...

You're the top, you're Mahatma Gandhi,
You're the top, you're Napoleon Brandy ...

(Cole Porter, 'You're the Top')

- **baldy**, Garibaldi, Grimaldi
- Maundy
- **cloudy**, dowdy, Gaudí, howdy, rowdy, Saudi
- **Jodie**, roadie, toady, tody
- **Goldie**, mouldy (*US* moldy), oldie
- **broody**, foodie, Judy, moody, Rudi, Trudy, Yehudi
- **goody**, hoodie, woody
- **Burundi**, Kirundi, Mappa Mundi
- Rushdie
- **bloody**, buddy, cruddy, cuddy, muddy, nuddy, ruddy, study
- **barramundi**, bassi profundi, Lundy, undy
- fuddy-duddy • understudy
- Lombardy • nobody • somebody
- organdie (*US* organdy) • burgundy
- Arcady
- **chickadee**, Picardy
- malady • melody • Lollardy
- psalmody • Normandy • threnody
- hymnody • jeopardy • chiropody
- parody • rhapsody • prosody
- bastardy • custody
- **birdie**, curdy, hurdy-gurdy, nerdy, sturdy, vinho verde, wordy
- olde worlde

4.14

- **daffy**, taffy
- Amalfi
- **Cavafy**, Gaddafi
- Effie
- **beefy**, Fifi, leafy
- **cliffy**, iffy, jiffy, Liffey, niffy, sniffy, spiffy, squiffy, stiffy, whiffy
- salsify
- **coffee**, toffee
- wharfie
- **Sophie**, strophe, trophy
- **Dufy**, goofy, Sufi
- **fluffy**, huffy, puffy, roughie, roughy, scruffy, snuffy, stuffy, toughie

> Create extra rhymes by changing words like fluffy to fluffiness.   [i]

- comfy • atrophy
- **anastrophe**, catastrophe
- **calligraphy**, epigraphy, tachygraphy
- **dystrophy**, epistrophe
- **autobiography**, bibliography, biography, cardiography, cartography, chirography, choreography, chromatography, cinematography, cosmography, cryptography, demography, discography, filmography, geography, hagiography, historiography, hydrography, iconography, lexicography, lithography, oceanography, orthography, palaeography (*US* paleography), photography, pornography, radiography, reprography, stenography, topography, typography
- apostrophe
- **gymnosophy**, philosophy, theosophy
- **furphy**, murphy, scurfy, surfy, turfy

4.15

- **Aggie**, baggy, craggy, draggy, jaggy, Maggie, quaggy, saggy, scraggy, shaggy, slaggy, snaggy
- Hwange
- **dreggy**, eggy, leggy, Peggy
- dengue • plaguy
- **Carnegie**, Malpighi
- **ciggy**, piggy, spriggy
- **boggy**, cloggy, doggy, foggy, froggy, groggy, moggie, smoggy, soggy

> Create extra rhymes for words like moggie by adding -*gy* to smog etc. (see section 18.8).   [i]

- demagogy
- **corgi**, porgy
- **bogey**, bogie, dogie, fogey, hoagie, stogy, yogi
- **boogie**, boogie-woogie, sastrugi
- **buggy**, druggy, fuggy, muggy, puggy
- **lungi**, sarangi
- Lalage • lurgy

4.16

- **Rajshahi**, spahi, surahi
- tarakihi •towhee •takahe

4.17

- haji •algae •Angie
- **argy-bargy**, Panaji
- **edgy**, sedgy, solfeggi, veggie, wedgie
- **cagey**, stagy
- **mangy**, rangy
- **Fiji**, gee-gee, squeegee
- **Murrumbidgee**, ridgy, squidgy
- **dingy**, fringy, mingy, stingy, whingy
- cabbagy •prodigy •effigy •villagey
- porridgy •strategy •cottagey
- **dodgy**, podgy, splodgy, stodgy
- pedagogy
- **Georgie**, orgy
- ogee •Fuji
- **bhaji**, budgie, pudgy, sludgy, smudgy
- bulgy
- **bungee**, grungy, gungy, scungy, spongy
- **allergy**, analogy, genealogy, hypallage, metallurgy, mineralogy, tetralogy
- elegy
- **antilogy**, trilogy
- aetiology (*US* etiology), amphibology
- **andrology**, anthology, anthropology, apology, archaeology (*US* archeology), astrology, biology, campanology, cardiology, chronology, climatology, cosmology, craniology, criminology, dermatology, ecology, embryology, entomology, epidemiology, etymology, geology, gynaecology (*US* gynecology), haematology (*US* hematology), hagiology, horology, hydrology, iconology, ideology, immunology, iridology, kidology, meteorology, methodology, musicology, mythology, necrology, neurology, numerology, oncology, ontology, ophthalmology, ornithology, parasitology, pathology, pharmacology, phraseology, phrenology, physiology, psychology, radiology, reflexology, scatology, Scientology, seismology, semiology, sociology, symbology, tautology, technology, terminology, theology, topology, toxicology, urology, zoology •eulogy •energy •synergy
- •apogee •liturgy •lethargy
- **burgee**, clergy
- zymurgy •dramaturgy

4.18

- **ackee**, Bacchae, baccy, cracky, Jackie, lackey, tacky, wacky
- latchkey •talcy
- **cranky**, Frankie, hanky, hanky-panky, lanky, manky, swanky, wanky, Yankee
- **Askey**, Pulaski
- Polanski •Blavatsky •Stanislavsky
- ticky-tacky
- **Iraqi**, Kawasaki, khaki, larky, malarkey, menarche, Nagasaki, narky, parky, raki, saké, saki, sarky, souvlaki, sparky, sukiyaki, teriyaki
- passkey
- **matriarchy**, patriarchy
- diarchy •oligarchy •synarchy
- hierarchy
- **Becky**, kaiseki, recce, techie
- Elkie •Palenque
- **Esky**, pesky
- **Dostoevsky**, Paderewski
- **achy**, Blakey, flaky, quaky, shaky, snaky, wakey-wakey
- headachy
- **beaky**, cheeky, cliquey, cock-a-leekie, creaky, freaky, Geikie, Kon-Tiki, Leakey, leaky, peaky, reeky, sleeky, sneaky, squeaky, streaky, Thessaloníki, tiki, tzatziki

> Create extra rhymes by changing words like cheeky to cheekiness. 🛈

4.19

- **brickie**, Dickie, hickey, icky, mickey, Nicky, picky, quickie, rickey, Rikki, sickie, sticky, tricky, Vicky
- **milky**, silky, Wilkie
- **Chinky**, dinky, Helsinki, inky, Kinki, kinky, minke, pinkie, pinky, slinky, stinky, stotinki
- **frisky**, risky, whisky
- **Dzerzhinsky**, Kandinsky, kolinsky, Nijinsky, Stravinsky
- doohickey • smart-alecky • garlicky
- colicky • gimmicky • panicky • finicky
- plasticky
- **crikey**, Nike, psyche, spiky
- **choccy**, cocky, flocky, gnocchi, hockey, jockey, oche, pocky, rocky, schlocky, stocky
- **conchae**, donkey, honky, shonky, wonky
- Brodsky
- **Malinowski**, Minkowski, Stokowski, Tchaikovsky
- Chomsky • Trotsky • droshky
- jabberwocky
- **balky**, chalky, corky, gawky, Gorky, Milwaukee, pawky, porky, talkie, walkie-talkie
- Sikorsky • Mussorgsky

4.20

- **chokey**, croaky, folkie, folky, hokey, hokey-cokey, hoki, jokey, karaoke, Loki, okey-dokey, Okie, pokey, poky, smoky, trochee
- **adzuki**, bouzouki, fluky, kabuki, kooky, pukey, saluki, spooky, Sukie, Suzuki, verrucae
- **bookie**, cookie, hookey, hooky, nooky, rookie
- netsuke
- **clucky**, ducky, happy-go-lucky, Kentucky, lucky, mucky, plucky, yucky
- **bulky**, sulky
- **chunky**, clunky, flunkey, funky, hunky, junkie, junky, monkey, punky, spunky

- **dusky**, husky, musky
- synecdoche • Malachy • hillocky
- bullocky
- **Andromache**, logomachy, theomachy
- hummocky • anarchy • monarchy
- Cherokee • tussocky
- **herky-jerky**, jerky, mirky, murky, perky, quirky, smirky, turkey
- turnkey • Albuquerque

4.21

- **Ali**, alley, Allie, Ally, bally, dally, dilly-dally, farfalle, galley, Halley, mallee, Mexicali, pally, Raleigh, rally, reveille, sally, tally, valley
- Chablis • brambly
- **badly**, Bradley, Hadlee, madly, sadly
- scraggly
- **dangly**, gangly
- crackly • Shankly • Bramley
- **Manley**, manly, Osmanli, Stanley
- slatternly
- **Langley**, tangly
- amply • Ashley
- **Attlee**, fatly, patly
- aptly • shilly-shally
- **Bali**, barley, Cali, Carly, Charlie, Dali, Diwali, finale, gnarly, Gurkhali, Kali, Kigali, Mali, Marley, marly, Pali, parley, snarly, Somali, Svengali, tamale
- **Barclay**, Berkeley, clerkly, sparkly
- Darnley • ghastly • Hartley • Barnsley
- blackguardly

4.22

- **belly**, Botticelli, casus belli, Corelli, Delhi, deli, Ellie, Grappelli, jelly, Kelly, lamellae, Machiavelli, Mahaweli, nelly, Schiaparelli, Shelley, shelly, smelly, tagliatelle, telly, Torricelli, vermicelli, welly, Zeffirelli
- trebly
- **assembly**, trembly
- **deadly**, Hedley, medley, redly
- friendly • freckly

- **cleanly**, eco-friendly, user-friendly
- heavenly •fleshly •wetly •directly
- Bentley •deathly
- **Lesley**, Leslie, Presley, Wesley
- yellow-belly •underbelly
- **bailey**, bailie, capercaillie, Cayley, ceilidh, daily, Daley, Daly, Disraeli, Eilidh, feyly, gaily, Haley, Hayley, Israeli, Rayleigh, scaly, shaly, ukulele
- ably •ungainly •maidenly •shapely
- stately •saintly •paisley •Ainsley
- comradely

4.23

- **campanile**, dele, eely, Ely, fusilli, Gigli, Ismaili, Keeley, Keneally, KwaNdebele, Lely, Matabele, mealie, mealy, Ndebele, sapele, Sindebele, steely, Swahili, wheelie
- **biweekly**, weakly, weekly
- seemly
- **cleanly**, queenly
- **beastly**, Priestley, priestly
- Keighley •measly

4.24

- **Billie**, billy, Chile, chilli (*US* chili), chilly, Dili, dilly, filly, frilly, ghillie, gillie, Gilly, hilly, Lillee, lily, Lyly, papillae, Philly, Piccadilly, piccalilli, silly, skilly, stilly, Tilly, willy, willy-nilly

> Create extra rhymes by changing words like chilly to chilliness. ℹ

- **Ridley**, tiddly
- **Brindley**, spindly
- sniffly
- **giggly**, niggly
- **jingly**, shingly, Zwingli
- **prickly**, sickly
- **crinkly**, tinkly, twinkly, wrinkly
- dimly
- **Finlay**, inly, McKinlay
- musicianly
- **kingly**, tingly

- Shipley •pimply
- **bristly**, gristly
- princely •fitly
- **drizzly**, grisly, grizzly, Sisley
- Kingsley •Cybele •hillbilly •jubilee
- rockabilly •bodily
- **bibliophily**, cartophily, toxophily
- Galilee •family •stepfamily
- subfamily
- **Emily**, Semele
- **facsimile**, simile
- homily •contumely
- **cicely**, Sicily
- icily •volatile •Maithili •weevily

4.25

- **drily**, kylie, Riley, shyly, slyly, smiley, Smily, wily, wryly

> Create extra rhymes for words like drily by adding -*ly* to high etc. (see section 6.1). ℹ

- idly •kindly •wifely •likely •timely
- Christly
- **knightly**, nightly, sightly, sprightly
- lively •fortnightly •housewifely
- **Barbirolli**, brolly, collie, dolly, folly, golly, holly, jolly, lolly, Mollie, molly, nollie, Ollie, polly, poly, trolley, volley, wally
- knobbly
- **Bodley**, godly, oddly
- wanly •Copley •fait accompli
- costly
- **hotly**, motley
- softly-softly
- **Bengali**, Cawley, crawly, creepy-crawly, Macaulay, Morley, Nepali, poorly, rawly, scrawly, squally
- lordly
- **courtly**, portly
- **jowly**, Pauli
- **aïoli**, coaly, coley, Foley, goalie, guacamole, holey, Holi, holy, lowly, moly, pinole, ravioli, roly-poly, Rowley, shoaly, soli
- nobly •Oakley •homely
- **lonely**, only

- ghostly •Moseley
- **coyly**, doily, oily

4.26

- **boule**, coolie, coulée, duly, Friuli, goolie, Hooley, Julie, mooli, newly, puli, schoolie, stoolie, Thule, truly, unruly
- **googly**, Hooghly
- muesli •absolutely •torulae
- **ampullae**, bullae, bully, fully, Lully, pulley, Woolley, woolly
- goodly •patchouli •nebuly
- vox populi •formulae •uvulae
- **dully**, gulley, gully, sully
- nubbly
- **crumbly**, grumbly
- **cuddly**, Dudley
- **plug-ugly**, ugly
- jungly
- **comely**, rumly
- slovenly •cousinly •crumply
- Huxley •Uttley
- **bimonthly**, monthly
- lovely

4.27

- **biyearly**, really, yearly
- Beardsley •lawyerly •immediately
- hourly •cowardly •surely •marbly
- pebbly
- neighbourly (*US* neighborly)
- **dribbly**, scribbly
- Kimberley
- **bobbly**, wobbly
- Stromboli
- **bubbly**, lubberly, rubbly, stubbly
- husbandly •hyperbole
- **creaturely**, teacherly
- Wycherley •elderly
- **fiddly**, twiddly
- orderly •puddly
- **Offaly**, waffly
- snuffly
- **straggly**, waggly
- spangly •laggardly •beggarly

- **jiggly**, squiggly, wiggly, wriggly
- niggardly •sluggardly •leisurely
- gingerly •soldierly •curmudgeonly
- rascally •treacly •tickly •broccoli
- knuckly •melancholy •sailorly
- scholarly •gentlemanly •seamanly
- anomaly •yeomanly •womanly
- mannerly •panoply •Connolly
- **Gallipoli**, ripply, tripoli
- dimply
- **monopoly**, oligopoly
- rumply •purply •matronly
- squirrelly •scoundrelly •Thessaly
- thistly •tinselly •muscly
- **Natalie**, philately, rattly
- dastardly
- **headmasterly**, masterly
- schoolmasterly •westerly •painterly
- easterly •Italy •winterly
- **sisterly**, systole
- writerly •doctorly •quarterly
- fatherly •grandfatherly •weatherly
- northerly
- **brotherly**, motherly, southerly, unbrotherly •grandmotherly
- gravelly• Beverley• weaselly• frizzly
- wizardly• miserly •Rosalie

4.28

- **Burghley**, Burley, burly, curly, early, girlie, hurley, hurly-burly, pearly, Shirley, surly, swirly, twirly
- worldly •Berkeley •termly •earthly

4.29

- **chamois**, clammy, gammy, Grammy, hammy, jammy, mammae, mammee, mammy, Miami, ramie, rammy, Sammy, shammy, whammy
- **acme**, drachmae
- Lakshmi
- **army**, balmy, barmy, gourami, macramé, origami, palmy, pastrami, salami, smarmy, swami, tsunami, Yanomami
- **Clemmie**, Emmy, jemmy, lemme, semi

- elmy
- **Amy**, cockamamie, flamy, gamy, Jamie, Mamie, samey
- **beamy**, creamy, dreamy, gleamy, Mimi, preemie, seamy, steamy

> Try rhyming one word with a set of two: steamy, see me. ℹ

- **gimme**, shimmy, Timmy
- pygmy •filmy
- **arch-enemy**, enemy
- synonymy •Jeremy •sashimi
- **blimey**, gorblimey, grimy, limey, slimy, stymie, thymy
- **commie**, mommy, pommie, pommy, tommy
- **dormy**, stormy
- **foamy**, homey, loamy, Naomi, Salome
- polychromy

4.30

- **fumy**, gloomy, plumy, rheumy, roomie, roomy, spumy
- excuse-me •mushroomy •perfumy
- **Brummie**, chummy, crumby, crummy, dummy, gummy, lumme, mummy, plummy, rummy, scrummy, scummy, slummy, tummy, yummy
- academy •sodomy •blasphemy
- infamy
- **bigamy**, polygamy, trigamy
- **endogamy**, exogamy, heterogamy, homogamy, misogamy, monogamy
- hypergamy •alchemy •Ptolemy
- anomie •antinomy
- **agronomy**, astronomy, autonomy, bonhomie, Deuteronomy, economy, gastronomy, heteronomy, metonymy, physiognomy, taxonomy
- thingummy •Laramie •sesame
- blossomy
- **anatomy**, atomy
- **hysterectomy**, mastectomy, tonsillectomy, vasectomy
- epitome
- **dichotomy**, lobotomy, tracheotomy, trichotomy
- colostomy •bosomy

- **squirmy**, thermae, wormy
- taxidermy

4.31

- **Annie**, ca'canny, canny, cranny, Danny, fanny, granny, nanny, tranny

> Create extra rhymes by changing words like cranny to crannies. ℹ

- **Ariadne**, Evadne
- daphne
- **Agni**, Cagney
- **acne**, Arachne, hackney
- hootenanny
- **Afghani**, ani, Armani, Azerbaijani, Barney, biriani, blarney, Carney, frangipani, Fulani, Galvani, Giovanni, Hindustani, Killarney, maharani, Mbabane, Modigliani, Omani, Pakistani, Rafsanjani, Rajasthani, rani, sarnie
- McCartney
- **antennae**, any, Benny, blenny, Dene, fenny, jenny, Kenny, Kilkenny, Lenny, many, penne, penny, Rennie
- catchpenny •pinchpenny
- pyrotechny
- **Bahraini**, brainy, Chaney, Eugénie, grainy, Janey, Khomeini, rainy, veiny, waney, zany
- **halfpenny**, shove-halfpenny, twopenny-halfpenny
- **Athene**, bambini, beanie, Bellini, Bernini, bikini, Boccherini, Borromini, capellini, catenae, Cellini, Cherubini, Cyrene, Fellini, fettuccine, genie, greeny, grissini, Heaney, Houdini, Jeanie, linguine, martini, Mazzini, mankini, meanie, Mussolini, Mycenae, Paganini, Panini, porcini, Puccini, queenie, rapini, Rossellini, Rossini, Santoríni, Selene, sheeny, spaghettini, Sweeney, teeny, teeny-weeny, tortellini, Toscanini, Trini, tweeny, wahine, weeny, zucchini
- monokini

4.32

- **blini**, cine, Finney, finny, Ginny, guinea, hinny, mini, Minnie, ninny, pinny, Pliny, shinny, skinny, spinney, tinny, whinny
- **kidney**, Sidney, Sydney
- chimney
- **jitney**, Whitney
- Disney
- **aborigine**, polygeny, polygyny
- **androgyny**, homogeny, misogyny, progeny
- Gemini
- **niminy-piminy**, Rimini
- **dominie**, hominy, Melpomene
- ignominy • Panini • larceny • telecine
- satiny • destiny • mountainy
- **mutiny**, scrutiny
- **briny**, Heine, liny, piny, shiny, spiny, tiny, whiny
- sunshiny
- **Bonnie**, bonny, Connie, johnny, Lonnie, Ronnie, Suwannee
- Rodney
- **Cockney**, Procne
- Romney • Novotný • Grozny
- **brawny**, corny, horny, lawny, mulligatawny, scrawny, tawny, thorny
- Orkney • Courtney
- **brownie**, browny, downy, townie

4.33

- **abalone**, Albinoni, Annigoni, Antonioni, baloney, Bodoni, boloney, bony, calzone, cannelloni, canzone, cicerone, coney, conversazione, coronae, crony, Gaborone, Giorgione, macaroni, Manzoni, Marconi, mascarpone, minestrone, Moroni, Mulroney, padrone, panettoni, pepperoni, phoney, polony, pony, rigatoni, Shoshone, Sloaney, stony, Toni, tony, zabaglione
- **cartoony**, lacunae, loony, Moonie, moony, Nguni, puny, Rooney, spoony, uni

- Sunni
- **bunny**, dunny, funny, gunny, honey, money, runny, sonny, sunny, tunny
- twopenny • chutney • beermoney

4.34

- **Léonie**, peony
- Tierney
- **Briony**, bryony, Hermione
- tourney • ebony • Albany
- chalcedony • Alderney
- **Persephone**, Stephanie, telephony
- **antiphony**, epiphany, polyphony, tiffany
- symphony
- **cacophony**, homophony, theophany, Zoffany
- euphony • agony • garganey
- Antigone
- **cosmogony**, mahogany, theogony
- balcony • Gascony • Tuscany
- calumny
- **felony**, Melanie, miscellany
- villainy • colony
- **Chamonix**, salmony, scammony, Tammany
- harmony
- **anemone**, Emeny, hegemony, lemony, Yemeni
- **alimony**, palimony
- agrimony • acrimony
- **matrimony**, patrimony
- ceremony • parsimony • antimony
- sanctimony • testimony • simony
- Romany • Germany • threepenny
- timpani • sixpenny • tuppenny
- **accompany**, company
- barony • saffrony • tyranny
- synchrony • irony • saxony • cushiony
- Anthony • betony
- **Brittany**, dittany, litany
- **botany**, cottony, monotony
- **gluttony**, muttony
- Bethany • oniony • raisiny
- **attorney**, Burney, Czerny, Ernie, ferny, gurney, journey, Verny

4.35

- **hangi**, slangy, tangy, twangy
- **clingy**, dinghy, springy, stingy, stringy, swingy, thingy, zingy
- puddingy
- **Missolonghi**, pongy

4.36

- **crappie**, crappy, flappy, gappy, happi, happy, nappy, pappy, sappy, scrappy, slap-happy, snappy, strappy, tapis, yappy, zappy

> Create extra rhymes by changing words like happy to happiness. [i]

- **campy**, scampi, vampy
- **harpy**, okapi, serape, sharpie
- raspy
- **Giuseppe**, peppy, preppy
- kelpie
- **kempy**, tempi
- Gillespie
- **crêpey**, kepi, scrapie
- **creepy**, sleepy, tepee, weepy
- **chippy**, clippie, dippy, drippy, grippy, hippy, Lippi, lippy, Mississippi, nippy, slippy, snippy, tippy, trippy, whippy, Xanthippe, zippy
- chickpea
- **crimpy**, gimpy, skimpy, wimpy
- **crispy**, wispy
- turnipy • recipe • praecipe • gossipy
- **pipy**, stripy
- **choppy**, copy, floppy, jalopy, moppy, poppy, sloppy, soppy, stroppy
- **Pompey**, swampy
- **waspie**, waspy
- photocopy • cowpea
- **dopey**, Hopi, Opie, ropy, soapy, topi

4.37

- **croupy**, droopy, goopy, groupie,

loopy, pupae, roupy, snoopy, soupy, Tupi
- whoopee
- **duppy**, guppy, puppy, yuppie
- **gulpy**, pulpy
- **bumpy**, clumpy, dumpy, frumpy, grumpy, humpy, jumpy, lumpy, plumpy, rumpy-pumpy, scrumpy, stumpy

> Create a different rhyming set by changing words like bumpy to bumpiness. [i]

- hiccupy • chirrupy • calliope
- pericope • syncope
- **colonoscopy**, horoscopy, microscopy, stereoscopy
- Penelope • canopy • satrapy
- **lycanthropy**, misanthropy, philanthropy
- **aromatherapy**, chemotherapy, hypnotherapy, physiotherapy, psychotherapy, radiotherapy, therapy
- entropy • syrupy (*US* sirupy) • chirpy

4.38

- **Barry**, Carrie, carry, Cary, Clarrie, Gary, glengarry, harry, intermarry, lari, Larry, marry, miscarry, parry,
- tarry • angry • chapelry cavalry
- lamprey • Crabtree
- **gantry**, pantry
- Langtry • polyandry
- **askari**, Bari, Cagliari, calamari, Campari, charivari, curare, Ferrari, Harare, Kalahari, Mari, Mata Hari, Qatari, Rastafari, safari, sari, Scutari, shikari, sparry, starry, Stradivari, tamari, terramare, Vasari, Zanzibari
- compadre • chantry
- **beriberi**, berry, BlackBerry, bury, Ceri, cherry, Derry, ferry, Gerry, jerry, Kerry, merry, perry, Pondicherry, sherry, terry, very, wherry, wolfberry
- débris • Hendry • Geoffrey • belfry
- **devilry**, revelry
- **Henri**, henry

- peltry
- **entry**, gentry, sentry
- pedantry
- **peasantry**, pheasantry, pleasantry
- vestry • every • elderberry
- checkerberry • whortleberry
- chokecherry • daredevilry
- Londonderry • knobkerrie

4.39

- **airy**, Azeri, canary, carabinieri, Carey, Cary, chary, clary, contrary, dairy, Dari, faerie, fairy, glairy, glary, Guarneri, hairy, lairy, Mary, miserere, nary, Nyerere, prairie, Salieri, scary, Tipperary, vary, wary
- carefree • masonry • blazonry
- Aintree • pastry • masturbatory
- freemasonry • stonemasonry • Petrie

4.40

- hara-kiri • ribaldry • chivalry • Tishri
- figtree • wintry • poetry • casuistry
- Babbittry • banditry • pedigree
- punditry • verdigris • sophistry
- porphyry • gadgetry • registry
- Valkyrie
- **marquetry**, parquetry
- basketry • trinketry • daiquiri
- **coquetry**, rocketry
- circuitry • varletry • filigree
- palmistry
- **biochemistry**, chemistry, photochemistry
- **gimmickry**, mimicry
- **asymmetry**, symmetry
- **craniometry**, geometry, micrometry, optometry, psychometry, pyrometry, sociometry, trigonometry
- tenebrae • ministry • cabinetry
- tapestry • carpentry • papistry
- piripiri • puppetry
- **agroforestry**, floristry, forestry
- ancestry • corsetry • artistry
- dentistry • Nyree • rivalry • pinetree

4.41

- **Florrie**, Laurie, lorry, Macquarie, quarry, sorry, whare
- Rhodri • Godfrey • hostelry
- Coventry • quixotry
- **cacciatore**, Corey, dory, Florey, flory, furore, glory, gory, hoary, hunky-dory, lory, Maury, monsignori, Montessori, multistorey, Pori, Rory, satori, saury, storey, story, Tory, vainglory
- Aubrey • aumbry
- **Audrey**, bawdry, tawdry
- laundry
- **gallimaufry**, orphrey
- palfrey • paltry • outlawry • centaury
- clerestory (*US* clearstory)
- understorey
- **cowrie**, kauri, Lowry, Maori
- Cowdrey • foundry • Rowntree
- ochry (*US* ochery) • poultry
- coxcombry • matsuri • Kirkcudbright
- shoetree
- **Hurri**, potpourri
- kukri • century • penury • estuary
- residuary • augury • mercury

4.42

- **curry**, dhurrie, flurry, hurry, Murray, scurry, slurry, surrey, worry

> Create extra rhymes by [i]
> adding -*ing* to words like curry.

- penumbrae • sundry
- **comfrey**, Humphrey
- hungry • Cymru • sultry
- **country**, upcountry
- Guthrie • backcountry

4.43

- **beery**, bleary, cheery, dearie, dreary, Dun Laoghaire, eerie, eyrie (*US* aerie), Kashmiri, leery, peri, praemunire, query, smeary, teary, theory, weary
- Deirdre • incendiary • intermediary

- subsidiary
- **auxiliary**, ciliary, domiciliary
- apiary •topiary •farriery •furriery
- justiciary
- **bestiary**, vestiary
- breviary •aviary •hosiery
- **diary**, enquiry, expiry, fiery, friary, inquiry, miry, priory, spiry, wiry
- **podiatry**, psychiatry
- **dowry**, floury, flowery, loury, showery, towery
- brewery •jewellery (US jewelry)
- **curie**, de jure, fioriture, fury, houri, Jewry, jury, Manipuri, Missouri, moory, Newry, tandoori, Urey
- statuary •actuary •sanctuary
- obituary •sumptuary •voluptuary
- January •electuary •ossuary
- mortuary
- **Bradbury**, Cadbury
- **blackberry**, hackberry
- cranberry •waxberry
- **Barbary**, barberry
- Shaftesbury •raspberry
- **bayberry**, blaeberry
- Avebury •Aylesbury •Sainsbury
- **bilberry**, tilbury
- bribery
- **corroboree**, jobbery, robbery, slobbery, snobbery
- dogberry •Roddenberry •Fosbury
- strawberry •Salisbury
- **crowberry**, snowberry
- chokeberry
- **Rosebery**, Shrewsbury
- **blueberry**, dewberry
- Dewsbury •Bloomsbury •gooseberry
- **blubbery**, rubbery, shrubbery
- Sudbury •mulberry •huckleberry
- Bunbury •husbandry •loganberry
- Canterbury •Glastonbury
- **Burberry**, turbary
- hatchery •archery
- **lechery**, treachery
- **stitchery**, witchery
- debauchery •butchery •camaraderie
- **cindery**, tindery
- industry •dromedary •lapidary
- spidery •bindery •doddery
- quandary •powdery •boundary

- bouldery •embroidery
- **prudery**, rudery
- do-goodery •shuddery •thundery
- prebendary •legendary •secondary
- amphorae •wafery
- **midwifery**, periphery
- infantry •housewifery •spoofery
- puffery •sulphury (US sulfury)
- Calgary
- **beggary**, Gregory
- vagary
- **piggery**, priggery, whiggery
- brigandry •bigotry •allegory
- vinegary •category •subcategory
- **hoggery**, toggery
- pettifoggery •demagoguery
- roguery •sugary
- **buggery**, skulduggery, snuggery, thuggery
- Hungary •humbuggery
- ironmongery •lingerie •treasury
- usury •menagerie •pageantry
- Marjorie •kedgeree •gingery
- imagery •orangery •savagery
- forgery •soldiery •drudgery
- **perjury**, surgery
- microsurgery
- **hackery**, quackery, Thackeray, Zachary
- mountebankery •knick-knackery
- gimcrackery •peccary •grotesquerie
- **bakery**, fakery, jacquerie
- **chickaree**, chicory, hickory, Terpsichore, trickery
- whiskery •apothecary
- **crockery**, mockery, rockery
- falconry •jiggery-pokery
- **cookery**, crookery, rookery
- brusquerie
- **puckery**, succory
- cuckoldry
- **calorie**, gallery, Malory, salary, Valerie
- saddlery •balladry •gallantry
- kilocalorie •diablerie •chandlery
- harlotry •celery •pedlary
- exemplary
- **helotry**, zealotry
- **nailery**, raillery
- Tuileries

- **ancillary**, artillery, capillary, codicillary, distillery, fibrillary, fritillary, Hilary, maxillary, pillory
- mamillary •tutelary •corollary
- **bardolatry**, hagiolatry, iconolatry, idolatry
- **cajolery**, drollery
- **foolery**, tomfoolery
- **constabulary**, vocabulary
- scapulary •capitulary •formulary
- scullery •jugglery •cutlery
- chancellery •epistolary •burglary
- mammary •fragmentary
- passementerie •flimflammery
- **armory**, armoury, gendarmerie
- almonry
- **emery**, memory
- creamery •shimmery •primary
- rosemary •yeomanry
- **parfumerie**, perfumery
- **flummery**, Montgomery, mummery, summary, summery
- gossamery •customary •infirmary
- **cannery**, granary, tannery
- canonry
- **antennary**, bimillenary, millenary, venery
- tenantry •chicanery
- **beanery**, bicentenary, catenary, centenary, deanery, greenery, machinery, plenary, scenery, senary, septenary
- **disciplinary**, interdisciplinary
- hymnary •missionary
- **ordinary**, subordinary
- valetudinary •imaginary •millinery
- culinary •seminary •preliminary
- luminary •urinary •veterinary
- mercenary •sanguinary
- **binary**, finery, pinery, quinary, vinery, winery
- Connery •Conakry •ornery •joinery
- **buffoonery**, poltroonery, sublunary, superlunary
- **gunnery**, nunnery
- consuetudinary •visionary
- exclusionary •legionary •pulmonary
- coronary •reactionary •expansionary
- **concessionary**, confessionary,

discretionary
- **confectionery**, insurrectionary, lectionary
- **deflationary**, inflationary, probationary, stationary, stationery
- **expeditionary**, petitionary, prohibitionary, traditionary, transitionary •contractionary
- dictionary •cautionary
- **ablutionary**, counter-revolutionary, devolutionary, elocutionary, evolutionary, revolutionary, substitutionary
- functionary
- **diversionary**, reversionary
- **fernery**, quaternary, ternary
- peppery •extempore •weaponry
- **apery**, drapery, japery, napery, papery, vapoury (US vapory)
- **frippery**, slippery
- **coppery**, foppery
- popery •dupery •trumpery
- February •heraldry •knight-errantry
- arbitrary •registrary •library
- contrary •horary •supernumerary
- itinerary •honorary •funerary
- **contemporary**, extemporary, temporary
- literary •brasserie •chancery
- **accessory**, intercessory, pessary, possessory, tesserae
- **dispensary**, incensory, ostensory, sensory, suspensory
- tracery
- **pâtisserie**, rotisserie
- emissary •dimissory
- **commissary**, promissory
- janissary •necessary •derisory
- glossary •responsory •sorcery
- grocery •greengrocery
- **delusory**, illusory
- compulsory •vavasory •adversary
- **anniversary**, bursary, cursory, mercery, nursery
- haberdashery
- **evidentiary**, penitentiary, plenipotentiary, residentiary
- **beneficiary**, fishery, judiciary
- noshery •gaucherie •fiduciary

• luxury •tertiary
• **battery**, cattery, chattery, flattery, tattery
• **factory**, manufactory, olfactory, phylactery, refractory, satisfactory
• **artery**, martyry, Tartary
• **mastery**, plastery
• **directory**, ex-directory, interjectory, rectory, refectory, trajectory
• peremptory
• **alimentary**, complementary, complimentary, documentary, elementary, parliamentary, rudimentary, sedimentary, supplementary, testamentary
• investigatory
• **adulatory**, aleatory, approbatory, celebratory, clarificatory, classificatory, commendatory, congratulatory, consecratory, denigratory, elevatory, gyratory, incantatory, incubatory, intimidatory, modificatory, participatory, placatory, pulsatory, purificatory, reificatory, revelatory, rotatory
• natatory •elucidatory •castigatory
• mitigatory •justificatory
• imprecatory •equivocatory
• flagellatory •execratory •innovatory
• **eatery**, excretory
• **glittery**, jittery, skittery, twittery
• **benedictory**, contradictory, maledictory, valedictory, victory
• **printery**, splintery
• **consistory**, history, mystery
• presbytery
• **inhibitory**, prohibitory
• hereditary •auditory •budgetary
• **military**, paramilitary
• solitary •cemetery •limitary
• vomitory •dormitory •fumitory
• **interplanetary**, planetary, sanitary
• primogenitary •dignitary
• **admonitory**, monitory
• unitary •monetary •territory
• secretary •undersecretary
• plebiscitary •repository •baptistery
• transitory
• **depositary**, depository, expository,

suppository
• niterie
• **Godwottery**, lottery, pottery, tottery
• bottomry •watery •psaltery
• **coterie**, notary, protonotary, rotary, votary
• upholstery
• **bijouterie**, charcuterie, circumlocutory
• persecutory •statutory •salutary
• executory
• **contributory**, retributory, tributary
• interlocutory
• **buttery**, fluttery
• introductory •adultery •effrontery
• perfunctory •blustery •mediatory
• retaliatory •conciliatory •expiatory
• **denunciatory**, renunciatory
• **appreciatory**, depreciatory
• **initiatory**, propitiatory
• **dietary**, proprietary
• extenuatory
• **mandatary**, mandatory
• predatory •sedentary •laudatory
• prefatory •offertory •negatory
• obligatory
• **derogatory**, interrogatory, supererogatory
• nugatory
• **expurgatory**, objurgatory, purgatory
• precatory
• **explicatory**, indicatory, vindicatory
• **confiscatory**, piscatory
• dedicatory •judicatory
• qualificatory •pacificatory
• supplicatory
• **communicatory**, excommunicatory
• masticatory •prognosticatory
• invocatory •obfuscatory
• revocatory •charlatanry
• **depilatory**, dilatory, oscillatory
• assimilatory •consolatory
• voluntary •emasculatory
• ejaculatory
• **ambulatory**, circumambulatory, perambulatory
• regulatory
• **articulatory**, gesticulatory
• manipulatory •copulatory

- expostulatory •circulatory
- **amatory**, declamatory, defamatory, exclamatory, inflammatory, proclamatory
- crematory •segmentary
- lachrymatory
- **commentary**, promontory
- **informatory**, reformatory
- momentary
- **affirmatory**, confirmatory
- explanatory •damnatory
- condemnatory
- **cosignatory**, signatory
- combinatory
- **discriminatory**, eliminatory, incriminatory, recriminatory
- comminatory •exterminatory
- hallucinatory •procrastinatory
- monastery •repertory
- emancipatory •anticipatory
- **exculpatory**, inculpatory
- **declaratory**, preparatory
- respiratory •perspiratory
- vibratory
- **migratory**, transmigratory
- **exploratory**, laboratory, oratory
- inauguratory •adjuratory
- corroboratory •reverberatory
- refrigeratory •compensatory
- desultory •dysentery
- **exhortatory**, hortatory
- salutatory •gustatory •lavatory
- inventory
- **conservatory**, observatory
- improvisatory
- **accusatory**, excusatory
- lathery
- **feathery**, heathery, leathery
- **dithery**, slithery
- carvery
- **reverie**, severy
- **Avery**, bravery, knavery, quavery, Savery, savory, savoury, slavery, wavery
- thievery
- **livery**, quivery, shivery
- silvery
- **ivory**, salivary
- ovary
- **discovery**, recovery

- servery •equerry •reliquary
- antiquary •cassowary •stipendiary
- colliery •pecuniary •chinoiserie
- misery •wizardry •citizenry
- **advisory**, provisory, revisory, supervisory
- **causerie**, rosary

- **blurry**, firry, furry

- **bassi**, Brassey, brassie, chassis, gassy, Haile Selassie, lassie, Malagasy, Manasseh, massé, massy, sassy, Tallahassee
- **Cotopaxi**, maxi, taxi, waxy
- Anglesey
- **antsy**, Clancy, fancy, Nancy
- **paparazzi**, patsy
- Yangtze •necromancy •cartomancy
- geomancy •bibliomancy
- chiromancy •ataraxy
- **Adivasi**, brassy, classy, dalasi, Darcy, farcy, Farsi, glassy, grassy
- chancy •ardency •Nazi
- **Bessie**, Crécy, dressy, Jessie, messy, Nessie, tressy
- **prexy**, sexy
- **Chelsea**, Elsie
- Dempsey •Montmorency
- discrepancy •incessancy
- **Betsy**, tsetse
- epilepsy •narcolepsy •nympholepsy
- apoplexy •catalepsy
- **Basie**, Casey, Gracie, lacy, O'Casey, pace, pacy, precis, racy, spacey, Stacey, Sulawesi, Tracy
- cadency •complacency
- **blatancy**, patency
- **Assisi**, fleecy, greasy, Tbilisi
- decency

- **Chrissie**, Cissy, kissy, missy, prissy, sissy

- **dixie**, pixie, tricksy, Trixie
- **chintzy**, De Quincey, wincey
- **efficiency**, proficiency, sufficiency
- **Gypsy**, tipsy
- **ditzy**, glitzy, itsy-bitsy, Mitzi, ritzy, Uffizi
- Eurydice
- **odyssey**, theodicy
- sub judice •prophecy •anglice
- chaplaincy •policy •baronetcy
- governessy •Pharisee •actressy
- **clerisy**, heresy
- secrecy •statice •captaincy
- courtesy
- **dicey**, icy, pricey, spicy, vice

> Try rhyming one word with a set of two: dicey, high sea.   ⓘ

- stridency •sightsee
- **bossy**, Flossie, flossy, glossy, mossy, posse
- **boxy**, doxy, epoxy, foxy, moxie, poxy, proxy
- bonxie
- **poncey**, sonsy
- **dropsy**, popsy
- biopsy •heterodoxy •orthodoxy
- autopsy

4.47

- **gorsy**, horsey, saucy
- normalcy •schmaltzy
- **discordancy**, mordancy
- Orczy •mousy •bouncy •viscountcy
- paramountcy •folksy •potency
- **Debussy**, goosey, juicy, Lucy, Senussi, Watusi
- **lucency**, translucency
- **cutesy**, rootsy
- pussy
- **booksy**, look-see
- **Abruzzi**, footsie, tootsie, Tutsi
- Sadducee
- **fussy**, hussy, mussy
- fubsy •Dulcie •gutsy •bankruptcy

4.48

- radiancy
- **immediacy**, intermediacy

- expediency •idiocy •saliency
- resiliency •leniency
- **incipiency**, recipiency
- recreancy •pruriency •deviancy
- subserviency •transiency •pliancy
- **buoyancy**, flamboyancy
- **fluency**, truancy
- constituency •abbacy •embassy
- celibacy •absorbency
- **incumbency**, recumbency
- **ascendancy**, intendancy, interdependency, pendency, resplendency, superintendency, tendency, transcendency
- candidacy
- **presidency**, residency
- despondency •redundancy •infancy
- sycophancy •argosy •legacy
- profligacy •surrogacy
- extravagancy •plangency •agency
- regency
- **astringency**, contingency, stringency
- intransigency •exigency •cogency
- pungency
- **convergency**, emergency, insurgency, urgency
- vacancy •piquancy •fricassee
- mendicancy •efficacy •prolificacy
- insignificancy •delicacy •intricacy
- advocacy •fallacy •galaxy
- **jealousy**, prelacy
- repellency •valency •Wallasey
- articulacy •corpulency •inviolacy
- excellency •equivalency •pharmacy
- supremacy •clemency •Christmassy
- **illegitimacy**, legitimacy
- intimacy •ultimacy •primacy
- dormancy •diplomacy •contumacy
- stagnancy
- **lieutenancy**, subtenancy, tenancy
- pregnancy
- **benignancy**, malignancy
- effeminacy •prominency
- obstinacy •pertinency •lunacy
- immanency
- **impermanency**, permanency
- rampancy •papacy •flippancy
- occupancy
- **archiepiscopacy**, episcopacy
- transparency •leprosy •inerrancy
- **flagrancy**, fragrancy, vagrancy

- conspiracy •idiosyncrasy
- minstrelsy •magistracy •piracy
- vibrancy
- **adhocracy**, aristocracy, autocracy, bureaucracy, democracy, gerontocracy, gynaecocracy (*US* gynecocracy), hierocracy, hypocrisy, meritocracy, mobocracy, monocracy, plutocracy, technocracy, theocracy
- accuracy •obduracy •currency
- **curacy**, pleurisy
- confederacy •numeracy
- degeneracy •itinerancy •inveteracy
- **illiteracy**, literacy
- innocency •trenchancy •deficiency
- **fantasy**, phantasy
- intestacy •ecstasy •expectancy
- latency •chieftaincy •intermittency
- **consistency**, insistency, persistency
- instancy •militancy •impenitency
- precipitancy •competency
- hesitancy •apostasy •constancy
- accountancy •adjutancy
- **consultancy**, exultancy
- impotency •discourtesy
- inadvertency •privacy
- **irrelevancy**, relevancy
- solvency •frequency •delinquency
- adequacy •poignancy

4.49

- **arsy-versy**, Circe, mercy, Percy, pursy
- colonelcy •verdancy •conversancy
- **conservancy**, fervency
- curtsy •controversy

4.50

- **ashy**, flashy, Lubumbashi, mashie, plashy, splashy, trashy
- Gramsci
- **banshee**, Comanche
- **marshy**, Ustashe
- **branchy**, Ranchi
- **Bangladeshi**, fleshy
- Frenchy •chichi
- **dishy**, fishy, maharishi, squishy, swishy, Vichy

> Create extra rhymes by changing words like dishy to dishiness. [i]

- rubbishy
- **sloshy**, squashy, washy
- bolshie •conchie •wishy-washy
- **paunchy**, raunchy
- sushi •munshi
- **bushy**, cushy, pushy
- **brushy**, gushy, mushy, plushy, rushy, slushy
- **bunchy**, crunchy, punchy

4.51

- **batty**, bratty, catty, chatty, Cincinnati, Dolcelatte, fatty, flattie, Hattie, natty, patty, ratty, Satie, Scarlatti, scatty, Tati, tattie, tatty

> Create extra rhymes by changing words like batty to battiness. [i]

- faculty
- **Alicante**, andante, ante, anti, Ashanti, Bramante, Chianti, Dante, dilettante, Fante, Ferranti, infante, scanty, shanty (*US* chanty), spumante, vigilante, Zante
- **Asti**, pasty
- pederasty
- **Amati**, arty, Astarte, castrati, chapatti, clarty, coati, ex parte, Frascati, glitterati, Gujarati, hearty, illuminati, karate, Kiribati, lathi, literati, Marathi, obbligati (*US* obligati), party, tarty
- **crafty**, draughty (*US* drafty)
- auntie •nasty •contrasty
- **amaretti**, amoretti, Betti, Betty, confetti, cornetti, Donizetti, Getty, Giacometti, Hettie, jetty, machete, Marinetti, Nettie, petit, petty, Rossetti, Serengeti, spaghetti, sweaty, vaporetti, yeti
- **hefty**, lefty
- **felty**, sheltie
- penalty •specialty •empty
- **al dente**, aplenty, cognoscenti,

divertimenti, lisente, plenty, portamenti, sente, twenty, twenty-twenty, venti
- seventy - peasanty
- **chesty**, testy, zesty
- Ghiberti

4.52

- **Albacete**, eighty, Haiti, Katy, Kuwaiti, Leyte, matey, pratie, slaty, weighty
- safety - frailty
- **dainty**, painty
- **hasty**, pastie, pasty, tasty
- suzerainty
- **Beatty**, entreaty, graffiti, meaty, Nefertiti, peaty, sleety, sweetie, Tahiti, titi, treaty
- **beastie**, yeasty

4.53

- **banditti**, bitty, chitty, city, committee, ditty, gritty, intercity, kitty, megacity, nitty-gritty, Pitti, pity, pretty, shitty, slitty, smriti, spitty, titty, vittae, witty

> Create extra rhymes by changing words like bitty to bittiness. [i]

- **fifty**, fifty-fifty, nifty, shifty, swiftie, thrifty
- **guilty**, kiltie, silty
- **flinty**, linty, minty, shinty
- **ballistae**, Christie, Corpus Christi, misty, twisty, wristy
- sixty
- **deity**, gaiety (US gayety), laity, simultaneity, spontaneity
- **contemporaneity**, corporeity, femineity, heterogeneity, homogeneity
- **anxiety**, contrariety, dubiety, impiety, impropriety, inebriety, notoriety, piety, satiety, sobriety, ubiety, variety
- moiety
- **acuity**, ambiguity, annuity,

assiduity, congruity, contiguity, continuity, exiguity, fatuity, fortuity, gratuity, ingenuity, perpetuity, perspicuity, promiscuity, suety, superfluity, tenuity, vacuity
- rabbity
- **improbity**, probity
- acerbity - witchetty - crotchety
- heredity
- **acidity**, acridity, aridity, avidity, cupidity, flaccidity, fluidity, frigidity, humidity, hybridity, insipidity, intrepidity, limpidity, liquidity, lividity, lucidity, morbidity, placidity, putridity, quiddity, rabidity, rancidity, rapidity, rigidity, solidity, stolidity, stupidity, tepidity, timidity, torpidity, torridity, turgidity, validity, vapidity
- **commodity**, oddity
- **immodesty**, modesty
- **crudity**, nudity
- **fecundity**, jocundity, moribundity, profundity, rotundity, rubicundity
- absurdity - difficulty - gadgety
- majesty - fidgety - rackety
- **pernickety**, rickety
- biscuity
- **banality**, duality, fatality, finality, ideality, legality, locality, modality, morality, natality, orality, reality, regality, rurality, tonality, totality, venality, vitality, vocality
- fidelity
- **ability**, agility, civility, debility, docility, edibility, facility, fertility, flexility, fragility, futility, gentility, hostility, humility, imbecility, infantility, juvenility, liability, mobility, nihility, nobility, nubility, puerility, senility, servility, stability, sterility, tactility, tranquillity (US tranquility), usability, utility, versatility, viability, virility, volatility
- ringlety
- **equality**, frivolity, jollity, polity, quality

- **credulity**, garrulity, sedulity
- nullity
- **amity**, calamity
- extremity • enmity
- **anonymity**, dimity, equanimity, magnanimity, proximity, pseudonymity, pusillanimity, unanimity
- comity
- **conformity**, deformity, enormity, multiformity, uniformity
- subcommittee • pepperminty
- infirmity
- **Christianity**, humanity, inanity, profanity, sanity, urbanity, vanity
- amnesty
- **lenity**, obscenity, serenity
- **indemnity**, solemnity
- mundanity • amenity
- **affinity**, asininity, clandestinity, divinity, femininity, infinity, masculinity, salinity, trinity, vicinity, virginity
- **benignity**, dignity, malignity
- honesty
- **community**, immunity, importunity, impunity, opportunity, unity

> ⓘ Create extra rhymes by changing words like community to communities.

- **confraternity**, eternity, fraternity, maternity, modernity, paternity, taciturnity
- **serendipity**, snippety
- uppity
- **angularity**, barbarity, bipolarity, charity, circularity, clarity, complementarity, familiarity, granularity, hilarity, insularity, irregularity, jocularity, linearity, parity, particularity, peculiarity, polarity, popularity, regularity, secularity, similarity, singularity, solidarity, subsidiarity, unitarity, vernacularity, vulgarity
- alacrity • sacristy
- **ambidexterity**, asperity, austerity, celerity, dexterity, ferrety, posterity, prosperity, severity, sincerity,

temerity, verity
- celebrity • integrity • rarity
- **authority**, inferiority, juniority, majority, minority, priority, seniority, sonority, sorority, superiority
- mediocrity • sovereignty • salubrity
- entirety
- **biosecurity**, cybersecurity, futurity, immaturity, impurity, maturity, obscurity, purity, security, surety • touristy
- **audacity**, capacity, fugacity, loquacity, mendacity, opacity, perspicacity, pertinacity, pugnacity, rapacity, sagacity, sequacity, tenacity, veracity, vivacity, voracity
- laxity
- **sparsity**, varsity
- necessity
- **complexity**, perplexity
- **density**, immensity, propensity, tensity
- scarcity • obesity
- **felicity**, toxicity
- **fixity**, prolixity
- **benedicite**, nicety
- **anfractuosity**, animosity, atrocity, bellicosity, curiosity, fabulosity, ferocity, generosity, grandiosity, impecuniosity, impetuosity, jocosity, luminosity, monstrosity, nebulosity, pomposity, ponderosity, porosity, preciosity, precocity, reciprocity, religiosity, scrupulosity, sinuosity, sumptuosity, velocity, verbosity, virtuosity, viscosity
- paucity • falsity • caducity • russety
- **adversity**, biodiversity, diversity, perversity, university
- **sacrosanctity**, sanctity
- chastity
- **entity**, identity
- quantity • certainty
- **cavity**, concavity, depravity, gravity
- travesty • suavity
- **brevity**, levity, longevity
- velvety • naivety
- **activity**, nativity
- equity

- **antiquity**, iniquity, obliquity, ubiquity
- propinquity

4.54

- **almighty**, Aphrodite, Blighty, flighty, mighty, nightie, whitey
- ninety •feisty
- **dotty**, grotty, hottie, knotty, Lanzarote, Lottie, Pavarotti, potty, Scottie, snotty, spotty, totty, yachtie, zloty

> Create extra rhymes by changing words like dotty to dottiness. [i]

- **lofty**, softie
- Solti •novelty
- **Brontë**, démenti, Monte, Monty, Visconti
- frosty
- **forty**, haughty, naughty, pianoforte, rorty, shorty, sortie, sporty, UB40, warty
- **balti**, faulty, salty
- **flaunty**, jaunty
- **doughty**, outie, pouty, snouty
- **bounty**, county, Mountie
- frowsty •viscounty
- **Capote**, coatee, coyote, dhoti, floaty, goaty, oaty, peyote, roti, throaty
- jolty
- **postie**, toastie, toasty
- hoity-toity •pointy
- **agouti**, beauty, booty, cootie, cutie, Djibouti, duty, fluty, fruity, rooty, snooty, tutti-frutti

4.55

- **footy**, putti, sooty, tutti
- shufti •casualty •deputy
- **butty**, cutty, gutty, nutty, puttee, putty, rutty, smutty
- **mufti**, tufty
- bhakti •subtlety •humpty-dumpty
- **Bunty**, runty
- **bustee**, busty, crusty, dusty, fusty, gusty, lusty, musty, rusty, trusty

- fealty •realty
- **propriety**, society
- **loyalty**, royalty
- cruelty
- **Krishnamurti**, Trimurti
- liberty •puberty
- **faggoty**, maggoty
- Hecate •chocolatey •Cromarty
- commonalty •personalty •property
- carroty •guaranty •mayoralty
- warranty •admiralty •severalty
- poverty
- **Alberti**, Bertie, dirty, flirty, shirty, thirty
- uncertainty
- **Kirstie**, thirsty
- bloodthirsty

4.56

- Cathy
- **Iolanthe**, Xanthe
- McCarthy •breathy
- **healthy**, stealthy, wealthy
- lengthy
- **heathy**, Lethe
- pithy •filthy
- **bothy**, frothy, mothy, wrathy
- toothy
- **polymathy**, timothy
- apathy •telepathy •empathy
- antipathy •sympathy
- **encephalopathy**, homeopathy, osteopathy
- Dorothy •earthy

4.57

- **prithee**, smithy, withy
- swarthy
- **mouthy**, Southey
- smoothie •worthy •airworthy
- blameworthy •praiseworthy
- seaworthy •Galsworthy
- roadworthy •noteworthy
- newsworthy •trustworthy

4.58

- **navvy**, savvy
- **ave**, Garvey, Harvey, larvae, Mojave

- **bevvy**, bevy, Chevy, heavy, levee, Levi, levy, top-heavy
- envy
- **cavy**, Davy, Devi, gravy, navy, slavey, venae cavae, wavy
- **bivvy**, chivvy, civvy, divvy, Livy, privy, skivvy, spivvy
- Sylvie • ivy • grovy
- **groovy**, movie
- **covey**, lovey, lovey-dovey, luvvy
- anchovy • Muscovy • Pahlavi
- **curvy**, Nervi, nervy, scurvy, topsy-turvy

4.59

- Myfanwy • Malawi • Zimbabwe
- Anhui • Dewi
- **kiwi**, peewee, weewee
- **Conwy**, Goronwy
- **soliloquy**, ventriloquy
- colloquy • obloquy

4.60

- Mascagni • Daubigny • bouilli

4.61

- **jazzy**, snazzy
- palsy-walsy • Ramsay
- **pansy**, tansy
- **Anasazi**, Ashkenazi, Ashkenazy, Benghazi, Ghazi, kamikaze, khazi, Stasi, Swazi
- prezzie
- **frenzy**, Mackenzie

- **Bel Paese**, Buthelezi, crazy, daisy, Farnese, glazy, hazy, lazy, Maisie, mazy, oops-a-daisy, Piranesi, upsy-daisy, Veronese
- stir-crazy

> Create extra rhymes by changing words like crazy to craziness.   **i**

- **breezy**, cheesy, easy, easy-peasy, Kesey, Parcheesi, queasy, sleazy, wheezy, Zambezi
- teensy • speakeasy
- **busy**, dizzy, fizzy, frizzy, Izzy, Lizzie, tizzy
- **flimsy**, whimsy
- **Kinsey**, Lindsay, Lynsey
- poesy
- **Aussie**, cossie, mossie
- Swansea • gauzy • causey
- **ballsy**, palsy
- **blowsy**, Dalhousie, drowsy, frowzy, housey-housey, lousy
- cosy (*US* cozy), dozy, Josie, mafiosi, mosey, nosy, posey, posy, prosy, Rosie, rosy
- **Boise**, noisy

4.62

- **bluesy**, boozy, choosy, doozy, floozie, jacuzzi, medusae, newsy, oozy, Pusey, snoozy, Susie, Uzi, woozy
- woodsy • Wolsey • jalousie
- **fuzzy**, muzzy, scuzzy
- sudsy • clumsy • klutzy
- **durzi**, furzy, jersey, kersey, Mersey
- Guernsey

Section 5: -i

5.1

- canaille

5.2

- millefeuille

5.3

- fauteuil

Section 6: **-iy**

6.1

- **ally**, Altai, apply, assai, awry, ay, aye, Baha'i, belie, bi, Bligh, buy, by, bye, bye-bye, chi, Chiangmai, Ciskei, comply, cry, Cy, Dai, defy, deny, Di, die, do-or-die, dry, Dubai, dye, espy, eye, fie, fly, forbye, fry, Frye, goodbye (US goodby), guy, hereby, hi, hie, high, I, imply, I-spy, July, kai, lie, lye, Mackay, misapply, my, nearby, nigh, Nye, outfly, passer-by, phi, pi, pie, ply, pry, psi, Qinghai, rai, rely, rocaille, rye, scry, serai, shanghai, shy, sigh, sky, Skye, sky-high, sly, spin-dry, spry, spy, sty, Sukhotai, supply, Tai, Thai, thereby, thigh, thy, tie, Transkei, try, tumble-dry, underlie, Versailles, Vi, vie, whereby, why, wry, Wye, xi, Xingtai, Yantai

6.2

- uraei

6.3

- leylandii • radii • bindi-eye • nuclei

- genii • Sinai • denarii • caducei
- minutiae • sestertii

6.4

- aye-aye

6.5

- rabbi • standby • lay-by • nimbi • alibi
- rhombi • go-by • incubi • succubi
- syllabi • lullaby • hushaby

6.6

- **deadeye**, red-eye
- Sendai • solidi
- **nidi**, tie-dye
- eisteddfodau • Bondi • fundi

6.7

- Delphi
- **deify**, reify
- **preachify**, speechify
- edify • ladyfy
- **acidify**, humidify, rigidify, solidify
- **commodify**, modify
- codify • amplify • jellify • exemplify
- vilify • simplify

Cross-rhyme is a rhyme pattern with alternating end rhymes (in the pattern *abab*):

Drink and dance and laugh and lie,
    Love, the reeling midnight through,
For tomorrow we shall die!
    (But, alas, we never do.)

(Dorothy Parker, 'The Flaw in Paganism')

- **mollify**, qualify
- nullify •uglify •ramify
- **humify**, tumefy
- mummify •magnify •damnify
- **dignify**, signify
- personify •unify •typify •stupefy
- yuppify
- **clarify**, scarify
- **terrify**, verify
- petrify •electrify •gentrify •rarefy
- vitrify •horrify •transmogrify
- glorify •putrefy •purify
- **classify**, pacify
- calcify •Nazify •specify •intensify
- ossify •detoxify •falsify •crucify
- **dulcify**, emulsify
- **diversify**, versify
- **beatify**, gratify, ratify, stratify
- sanctify •satisfy
- **objectify**, rectify
- **identify**, misidentify
- testify •prettify •mystify •quantify
- **fortify**, mortify
- notify •beautify •fructify •stultify
- justify •certify •liquefy
- **hi-fi**, sci-fi

> Create extra rhymes by changing word endings from *-fy* to *-fying*, *-fies*, or *-fied*. ⓘ

6.8

- Haggai •Belgae •gilgai •fungi
- sarcophagi •mamaguy •assegai

6.9

- magi

6.10

- pink-eye •Mordecai •sockeye
- **croci**, foci
- buckeye •Diadochi •Malachi

6.11

- **ally**, phalli

- Adlai •gadfly •blackfly •damselfly
- sandfly •barfly •mayfly
- **Eli**, Ely
- greenfly •bacilli •multiply •styli
- whitefly •wall eye •horsefly
- housefly
- **alveoli**, E. coli, gladioli
- blowfly •lapis lazuli •reguli •stimuli
- flocculi •ranunculi •firefly
- discoboli •astragali •dragonfly
- alkali •Lorelei •Naphtali •butterfly
- hoverfly

6.12

- rami •calami

6.13

- decani •Iceni •Gemini •Anno Domini •termini •acini
- **personae**, tostone
- Brunei •alumni •goldeneye

6.14

- magpie •Philippi •sweetie-pie
- occupy

6.15

- panfry •certiorari •spray-dry •papyri
- **a fortiori**, a posteriori, a priori, memento mori, sori, thesauri, tori
- outcry •blow-dry •samurai
- caravanserai •stir-fry

6.16

- Masai •narcissi •prophesy •nisi
- colossi •flocci •bonsai •loci •fuci
- thyrsi

6.17

- gun-shy •work-shy

6.18

- cacti • necktie
- **aqua vitae**, curriculum vitae
- pigsty • hogtie • crosstie • shut-eye
- conducti • tongue-tie

6.19

- lecythi • mythi

6.20

- Levi

6.21

- lapsus linguae • Paraguay • Uruguay

6.22

- banzai • tiger's-eye • bird's-eye

Section 7: -or

7.1

- **abhor**, adore, afore, anymore, ashore, awe, bandore, Bangalore, before, boar, Boer, bore, caw, chore, claw, cocksure, comprador, cor, core, corps, craw, Delors, deplore, door, draw, drawer, evermore, explore, flaw, floor, for, forbore, fore, foresaw, forevermore, forswore, four, fourscore, furthermore, Gábor, galore, gnaw, gore, grantor, guarantor, guffaw, hard-core, Haugh, haw, hoar, ignore, implore, Indore, interwar, jaw, Johor, Lahore, law, lessor, lor, lore, macaw, man-o'-war, maw, mirador, mor, more, mortgagor, Mysore, nevermore, nor, oar, obligor, offshore, onshore, open-jaw, or, ore, outdoor, outwore, paw, poor, pore, pour, rapport, raw, roar, saw, scaur, score, senhor, señor, shaw, ship-to-shore, shop-floor, shore, signor, Singapore, snore, soar, softcore, sore, spore, squaw, store, straw, swore, Tagore, tau, taw, thaw, Thor, threescore, tor, tore, torr, trapdoor, tug-of-war, two-by-four, underfloor, underscore, war, warrantor, Waugh, whore, withdraw, wore, yaw, yore, your

7.2

- Dior

7.3

- Melchior • Gwalior • excelsior

7.4

- hellebore • usquebaugh • Tombaugh

7.5

- jackdaw • battledore
- **landau**, Landor
- chador • vendor • humidor • lobster thermidor • cuspidor • corridor
- stevedore • Isidore • condor
- stormdoor • Sodor • Theodore
- toreador • troubadour • picador
- commodore • parador • Labrador
- matador • conquistador • Salvador
- Ecuador

The use of *rime riche* (or *identical rhyme*) underlines the fear in the voice of the narrator and makes it appear that he is trying to convince himself that nothing untoward is happening by chanting a comforting refrain:

Once upon a midnight dreary, while I pondered weak and weary,
Over many a quaint and curious volume of forgotten lore,
While I nodded, nearly napping, suddenly there came a tapping,
As of some one gently rapping, rapping at my chamber door.
'Tis some visitor,' I muttered, 'tapping at my chamber door -
Only this, and nothing more.'

(Edgar Allan Poe, 'The Raven')

> *Rhyme schemes* are referred to by letters indicating the rhyming words for each line, so the rhyme scheme *abab* (known as *cross-rhyme*) is one in which the first and third, and second and fourth lines rhyme:
>
> I don't go to parties. Well, what are they for,
> If you don't need to find a new lover?
> You drink and you listen and drink a bit more
> And you take the next day to recover.
>
> (Wendy Cope, 'Being Boring')

7.6

• **therefore**, wherefore
• Roquefort • semaphore • ctenophore
• pinafore

7.7

• Igor • rigor • gewgaw

7.8

• hee-haw

7.9

• lockjaw

7.10

• Angkor • hardcore • décor • Agincourt
• manticore • ichor • encore
• kwashiorkor • underscore

7.11

• Danelaw • in-law • son-in-law
• sister-in-law • by-law • outlaw
• folklore • coleslaw • subfloor

7.12

• Blackmore • Sedgemoor • claymore

• **Seymour**, Timor
• Brynmor • Barrymore • Baltimore
• Broadmoor • Growmore • sophomore
• sagamore • blackamoor • sycamore
• Tullamore

7.13

• mackinaw • Elsinore

7.14

• millepore
• **forepaw**, pawpaw
• downpour • southpaw

7.15

• jackstraw • bedstraw • uproar
• wire-draw

7.16

• Nassau • hacksaw • heartsore
• bedsore • Ensor • fretsaw • chainsaw
• **Esau**, seesaw
• jigsaw
• **ripsaw**, whipsaw
• eyesore • Warsaw • bowsaw
• footsore • Luxor • plesiosaur
• stegosaur • Arkansas • Chickasaw
• dinosaur • brontosaur

7.17

• Bradshaw • seashore

- **kickshaw**, rickshaw
- scrimshaw •trishaw •dogshore
- **alongshore**, longshore
- foreshore

7.18

- cantor •lector •caveat emptor
- **centaur**, mentor, stentor
- Wichita •Choctaw •coldstore •Utah
- drugstore •megastore •Minotaur
- superstore

7.19

- Hathor

7.20

- Ifor •Gwynfor •herbivore •carnivore
- omnivore •insectivore

7.21

- bezoar

Section 8: **-ow**

8.1

- **allow**, avow, Bilbao, Bissau, bough, bow, bow-wow, brow, cacao, chow, ciao, cow, dhow, Dow, endow, Foochow, Frau, Hangzhou, Hough, how, Howe, kowtow, Lao, Liao, Macao, Macau, miaow, Mindanao, mow, now, ow, Palau, plough (*US* plow), pow, prow, row, scow, Slough, sough, sow, Tao, thou, vow, wow, Yangshao

8.2

- luau

8.3

- Moldau

Stressed (or *masculine*) *rhymes* can be created with single and multi-syllable words where the stress is on the last syllable. In 'When We Two Parted', Byron alternates double and single syllable words, and *stressed* and *unstressed* rhymes:

The dew of the morning
　Sunk chill on my brow—
It felt like the warning
　Of what I feel now.
Thy vows are all broken,
　And light is thy fame:
I hear thy name spoken,
　And share in its shame.

(Lord Byron, 'When We Two Parted')

8.4

- hoosegow • Oberammergau

8.5

- anyhow
- **know-how**, nohow
- somehow

8.6

- **Dachau**, Kraków

8.7

- Breslau
- snowplough (*US* snowplow)
- Tokelau

8.8

- Mau Mau

8.9

- Donau • Lucknow

8.10

- middlebrow
- **eyebrow**, highbrow
- Hausfrau • lowbrow • Jungfrau

8.11

- Nassau • Dessau

8.12

- **bow-wow**, powwow

Section 9: **-oh**

9.1

- **aglow**, ago, alow, although, apropos, art nouveau, Bamako, Bardot, beau, Beaujolais Nouveau, below, bestow, blow, bo, Boileau, bons mots, Bordeaux, Bow, bravo, bro, cachepot, cheerio, Coe, crow, Defoe, de trop, doe, doh, dos-à-dos, do-si-do, dough, dzo, Flo, floe, flow, foe, foreknow, foreshow, forgo, Foucault, froe, glow, go, good-oh, go-slow, grow, gung-ho, Heathrow, heave-ho, heigh-ho, hello, ho, hoe, ho-ho, jo, Joe, kayo, know, lo, low, maillot, malapropos, Marceau, mho, Miró, mo, Mohs, Monroe, mot, mow, Munro, no, Noh, no-show, oh, oho, outgo, outgrow, owe, Perrault, pho, po, Poe, pro, quid pro quo, reshow, righto, roe, Rouault, row, Rowe, sew, shew, show, sloe, slow, snow, so, soh, sow, status quo, stow, Stowe, strow, tally-ho, though, throw, tic-tac-toe, to-and-fro, toe, touch-and-go, tow, trow, undergo, undersow, voe, whacko, whoa, wo, woe, Xuzhou, yo, yo-ho-ho, Zhengzhou, Zhou

> The combination of *terminal* (or *end*) *rhymes* and *medial* (or *internal*) *rhymes* helps give this Nursery Rhyme its typical bounce:
>
> Mary, Mary, quite contrary,
> How does your garden grow?
> With silver bells and cockleshells,
> And pretty maids all in a row.

9.2

- **Bulawayo**, Galileo, Mayo, Montevideo

9.3

- **brio**, Clio, Krio, Leo, Milhaud, Rio, Theo, trio

9.4

- Cleo •Carpaccio •Boccaccio
- capriccio •braggadocio •Palladio
- cardio •radio •video •audio •rodeo
- studio
- **Caravaggio**, DiMaggio
- adagio
- **arpeggio**, Correggio
- Sergio •radicchio •Tokyo •intaglio
- seraglio
- **billy-o**, punctilio
- **folio**, imbroglio, olio, polio, portfolio
- cameo •Romeo
- **Borneo**, Tornio
- Antonio •Scipio •Scorpio
- **barrio**, Mario
- **impresario**, Lothario, Polisario, Rosario, scenario
- stereo •embryo
- **Blériot**, Ontario
- vireo •Florio
- **oratorio**, Oreo
- curio •Ajaccio •Lazio •nuncio
- pistachio
- **fellatio**, Horatio, ratio
- **ab initio**, ex officio
- patio •Subbuteo •physio

9.5

• **bio**, Cetshwayo, Io, ngaio, Ohio

9.6

• **arroyo**, boyo

9.7

• **duo**, Luo

9.8

• in vacuo • moto perpetuo • continuo

9.9

• **jabot**, sabot
• **ambo**, flambeau, mambo, Rambo, Rimbaud, Tambo
• **Gabo**, Garbo, lavabo
• elbow • Strabo • rainbow
• **gazebo**, grebo, placebo
• Igbo • bilbo
• **akimbo**, bimbo, limbo
• Maracaibo • yobbo
• **combo**, Negombo
• longbow • crossbow • oxbow
• **hobo**, lobo, oboe
• **Colombo**, dumbo, gumbo, jumbo, mumbo-jumbo, umbo
• Malabo • Mirabeau • turbo

9.10

• **gazpacho**, macho
• nacho • pasticcio • honcho • gaucho
• Ayacucho

9.11

• **foreshadow**, shadow
• Faldo
• **accelerando**, bandeau, Brando, glissando, Orlando
• eyeshadow

• **aficionado**, amontillado, avocado, Bardo, Barnardo, bastinado, bravado, Colorado, desperado, Dorado, eldorado, incommunicado, Leonardo, Mikado, muscovado, Prado, renegado, Ricardo, stifado
• commando
• **eddo**, Edo, meadow, semifreddo
• **crescendo**, diminuendo, innuendo, kendo
• **carbonado**, dado, Feydeau, gambado, Oviedo, Toledo, tornado
• **aikido**, bushido, credo, Guido, Ido, libido, lido, speedo, teredo, torpedo, tuxedo
• widow • dildo • window
• **Dido**, Fido, Hokkaido
• **condo**, rondeau, rondo, secondo, tondo
• Waldo
• **dodo**, Komodo, Quasimodo
• **escudo**, judo, ludo, pseudo, testudo, Trudeau
• weirdo • sourdough • fricandeau
• tournedos • Murdo

9.12

• Sappho • nympho • info • boffo
• Castel Gandolfo
• **buffo**, Truffaut

9.13

• Hidalgo
• **charango**, Durango, fandango, mango, Okavango, quango, Sango, tango
• Glasgow
• **Argo**, argot, cargo, Chicago, embargo, escargot, farrago, largo, Margot, Otago, Santiago, virago
• Lego • Marengo
• **Diego**, galago, Jago, lumbago, sago, Tierra del Fuego, Tobago, Winnebago
• **amigo**, ego, Vigo
• **bingo**, dingo, Domingo, flamingo, gringo, jingo, lingo
• Bendigo • indigo • archipelago

- vertigo • Sligo
- **doggo**, logo
- **bongo**, Congo, drongo, Kongo, pongo
- **a-gogo**, go-go, pogo, Togo
- Hugo
- **fungo**, mungo
- **ergo**, Virgo

9.14

- Tajo
- **boho**, coho, Moho, Soho
- Idaho • Arapaho • Navajo

9.15

- banjo • Gorgio
- **dojo**, mojo, Tojo

9.16

- **tacho**, taco, tobacco, wacko
- **blanco**, Franco
- **churrasco**, fiasco, Tabasco
- **Arco**, Gran Chaco, mako
- **art deco**, dekko, echo, Eco, El Greco, gecko, secco
- **flamenco**, Lysenko, Yevtushenko
- **alfresco**, fresco, Ionesco
- **Draco**, shako
- **Biko**, Gromyko, pekoe, picot, Puerto Rico, Tampico
- **sicko**, thicko, tricot, Vico
- **ginkgo**, pinko, stinko
- **cisco**, disco, Disko, Morisco, pisco, San Francisco
- zydeco • magnifico • calico • Jellicoe
- haricot • Jericho • Mexico • galactico
- kleftico • simpatico • politico • portico
- **psycho**, Tycho
- **Morocco**, Rocco, sirocco, socko
- bronco
- **Moscow**, roscoe
- Rothko
- **coco**, cocoa, loco, moko, Orinoco, poco, rococo
- osso buco • Acapulco
- **Cuzco**, Lambrusco

- **bucko**, stucco
- **bunco**, junco, unco
- guanaco • Monaco • turaco • Turco

9.17

- **aloe**, callow, fallow, hallow, mallow, marshmallow, sallow, shallow, tallow

> Create extra rhymes by adding -*ness* to words like callow. [i]

- **Pablo**, tableau
- cashflow • Anglo • matelot
- **Carlo**, Harlow, Marlowe
- **Bargello**, bellow, bordello, cello, Donatello, fellow, jello, martello, mellow, morello, niello, Novello, Pirandello, Portobello, Punchinello, Uccello, violoncello, yellow
- pueblo • bedfellow • playfellow
- Oddfellow • Longfellow
- schoolfellow • Robin Goodfellow
- airflow • halo • Day-Glo
- **filo**, kilo
- **armadillo**, billow, cigarillo, Murillo, Negrillo, peccadillo, pillow, tamarillo, Utrillo, willow
- inflow • Wicklow • furbelow • Angelo
- pomelo • uniflow
- **kyloe**, lilo, milo, silo
- **Apollo**, follow, hollow, Rollo, swallow, wallow
- Oslo • São Paulo • outflow
- **bolo**, criollo, polo, solo, tombolo
- rouleau • regulo • modulo • mudflow
- diabolo • bibelot • pedalo • underflow
- buffalo
- **brigalow**, gigolo
- bungalow
- **Michelangelo**, tangelo
- piccolo • tremolo • alpenglow • tupelo
- contraflow • afterglow • overflow
- furlough • workflow

9.18

- **ammo**, Gamow
- Rameau • Malmö
- **demo**, memo

- Elmo •Palermo
- **emo**, primo, supremo
- limo
- **gizmo**, gran turismo, machismo, verismo
- Eskimo •Geronimo
- **duodecimo**, octodecimo, sextodecimo
- **altissimo**, fortissimo, generalissimo, pianissimo
- proximo •centimo •ultimo •Cosmo
- Pontormo
- **chromo**, duomo, Homo, majordomo, momo, Nkomo, promo, slo-mo
- **Profumo**, sumo
- Alamo •dynamo •paramo

9.19

- **Mano**, piano
- **Americano**, Arno, boliviano, Bolzano, Carnot, chicano, guano, Kano, Ilano, Locarno, Lugano, Marciano, Marrano, meccano, oregano, Pisano, poblano, Romano, siciliano, soprano, Sukarno
- **Renault**, steno, tenno
- techno •Fresno •Pernod
- **ripieno**, volcano
- **albino**, bambino, babycino, beano, Borodino, Borsalino, cappuccino, casino, chino, Comino, concertino, Filipino, fino, Gino, keno, Ladino, Latino, Leno, maraschino, merino, Monte Cassino, Navarino, neutrino, Pacino, palomino, pecorino, Reno, San Marino, Sansovino, Torino, Trevino, Valentino, vino, Zeno
- **minnow**, winnow
- Llandudno •Gobineau •domino
- Martineau
- **lino**, rhino, wino
- tonneau •Grodno
- **Livorno**, porno
- Mezzogiorno
- **cui bono?**, kimono, Mono, no-no, phono
- **Bruno**, Gounod, Juneau, Juno, Uno
- Huguenot •pompano
- **Brno**, inferno, journo, Salerno, Sterno

9.20

- capo •Gestapo
- **Aleppo**, depot
- **downtempo**, tempo, uptempo
- Expo
- **cheapo**, Ipoh, peep-bo, repo
- hippo
- **hypo**, typo
- **oppo**, topo, troppo
- compo •Limpopo

9.21

- **arrow**, barrow, farrow, harrow, Jarrow, marrow, narrow, sparrow, taro, tarot, Varro, yarrow

> Create extra rhymes by adding -s to words like arrow. ⓘ

- gabbro •Avogadro •Afro •aggro
- macro •cilantro •Castro
- wheelbarrow
- **Faro**, Kilimanjaro, Pissarro, Pizarro, Tupamaro
- Pedro •allegro •hedgerow •velcro
- escrow
- **metro**, retro
- electro •Jethro
- **bolero**, caballero, dinero, Faeroe, pharaoh, ranchero, sombrero, torero
- scarecrow •Ebro
- **Montenegro**, Negro
- repro •in vitro •Pyrrho •synchro
- windrow •impro •intro •bistro
- Babygro •McEnroe
- **biro**, Cairo, giro, gyro, tyro
- fibro •micro •maestro
- **borrow**, Corot, morrow, sorrow, tomorrow
- cockcrow •cointreau
- **Moro**, Sapporo, Thoreau
- Mindoro •Yamoussoukro
- Woodrow
- **burro**, burrow, furrow
- upthrow
- **De Niro**, hero, Nero, Pierrot, Pinero, Rio de Janeiro, sub-zero, zero
- **bureau**, chiaroscuro, Douro, enduro, euro, Ishiguro, Oruro, Truro

- Politburo •guacharo •Diderot
- vigoro •Prospero •Cicero •in utero
- Devereux •Jivaro •overthrow

9.22

- **basso**, El Paso, Picasso, Sargasso, Tasso
- **fatso**, paparazzo, terrazzo
- Brasso
- **espresso**, gesso
- **intermezzo**, mezzo
- scherzo
- **peso**, say-so
- **calypso**, dipso
- schizo •Mato Grosso •torso •also
- **amoroso**, capriccioso, oloroso, so-so
- **Caruso**, Robinson Crusoe, Rousseau, trousseau
- so-and-so
- **Curaçao**, curassow
- **Thurso**, verso

9.23

- basho •Sancho •chat show
- peep show •sideshow •poncho
- roadshow •dumbshow

9.24

- **bateau**, chateau, gateau, gelato, mulatto, plateau
- **de facto**, ipso facto
- alto
- **canto**, Esperanto, manteau, panto, portmanteau
- **antipasto**, impasto -
- **agitato**, Ambato, castrato, esparto, inamorato, legato, moderato, obbligato (*US* obligato), ostinato, pizzicato, rubato, staccato, tomato, vibrato, Waikato
- contralto
- **allegretto**, amaretto, amoretto, Canaletto, cornetto, falsetto, ghetto, larghetto, libretto, Loreto, Orvieto,

ristretto, Soweto, stiletto, Tintoretto, vaporetto, zucchetto
- **perfecto**, recto
- **cento**, cinquecento, divertimento, lento, memento, pimiento, portamento, Risorgimento, Sacramento, Sorrento, Trento
- **manifesto**, pesto, presto
- concerto
- **Cato**, Plato, potato
- **Benito**, bonito, burrito, coquito, graffito, Hirohito, incognito, Ito, magneto, Miskito, mosquito, Quito, Tito, veto
- ditto •in flagrante delicto •mistletoe
- **pinto**, Shinto
- tiptoe
- **Callisto**, fritto misto
- cogito •Felixstowe •Sillitoe

9.25

- **blotto**, Giotto, grotto, lotto, motto, Otto, risotto, Watteau
- Cocteau
- **molto**, Sholto
- **pronto**, Toronto
- Ariosto
- **auto**, Oporto, Porto, quarto
- **in toto**, koto, Kumamoto, Kyoto, photo, Sesotho, Yamamoto
- **Bhutto**, butoh, Maputo, Pluto, prosciutto, ritenuto, sostenuto, tenuto
- Cousteau •putto •gusto •Pashto
- undertow •Erato

9.26

- litho
- **Clotho**, Otho

9.27

- salvo
- **arvo**, bravo, centavo, multum in parvo, octavo
- Sarajevo
- **in vivo**, relievo

- **ab ovo**, de novo, Denovo, Porto Novo, Provo
- Kosovo • servo

9.28

- bagnio
- **dal segno**, jalapeño
- **cursillo**, piquillo, Trujillo
- caudillo • El Niño • yo-yo

9.29

- garbanzo • Chimborazo
- Lorenzo • whizzo
- **proviso**, Valparaiso
- **Alfonso**, Alonzo, gonzo
- **arioso**, bozo, Gozo, mafioso, virtuoso
- **muso**, ouzo

Section 10: **-oy**

10.1

- **ahoy**, alloy, Amoy, annoy, boy, buoy, cloy, coy, destroy, employ, enjoy, Hanoi, hoi polloi, hoy, Illinois, joy, koi, oi, ploy, poi, Roy, savoy, soy, tatsoi, toy, trompe l'œil, troy

10.2

- **naoi**, pronaoi

10.3

- sandboy •bellboy •rentboy •playboy
- pageboy •lifebuoy •tomboy
- **ballboy**, tallboy
- cowboy •houseboy
- **doughboy**, hautboy, lowboy
- homeboy •toyboy •schoolboy
- bootboy •newsboy •busboy
- choirboy •paperboy •attaboy

10.4

- hobbledehoy

10.5

- killjoy

10.6

- decoy •didicoi •Khoikhoi

10.7

- alloy •saveloy

10.8

- dromoi

10.9

- tannoy

10.10

- charpoy
- **sepoy**, teapoy
- topoi

10.11

- Elroy •Leroy
- **Gilroy**, Kilroy
- Fitzroy •viceroy •Norroy •corduroy
- Fauntleroy

10.12

- Tolstoy

10.13

- **envoi**, envoy
- convoy

10.14

- Iroquois

10.15

- Yayoi

10.16

- borzoi

Section 11: **-oo**

11.1

- **accrue**, adieu, ado, anew, Anjou, aperçu, askew, ballyhoo, bamboo, bedew, bestrew, billet-doux, blew, blue, boo, boohoo, brew, buckaroo, canoe, chew, clew, clou, clue, cock-a-doodle-doo, cockatoo, construe, coo, Corfu, coup, crew, Crewe, cru, cue, déjà vu, derring-do, dew, didgeridoo, do, drew, due, endue, ensue, eschew, feu, few, flew, flu, flue, foreknew, glue, gnu, goo, grew, halloo, hereto, hew, Hindu, hitherto, how-do-you-do, hue, Hugh, hullabaloo, imbrue, imbue, jackaroo, Jew, kangaroo, Karroo, Kathmandu, kazoo, Kiangsu, knew, Kru, K2, kung fu, Lahu, Lanzhou, Lao-tzu, lasso, lieu, loo, Lou, Manchu, mangetout, mew, misconstrue, miscue, moo, moue, mu, nardoo, new, non-U, nu, ooh, outdo, outflew, outgrew, peekaboo, Peru, pew, plew, Poitou, pooh, pooh-pooh, potoroo, pursue, queue, revue, roo, roux, rue, screw, Selous, set-to, shampoo, shih-tzu, shoe, shoo, shrew, Sioux, skean dhu, skew, skidoo, slew, smew, snafu, sou, spew, sprue, stew, strew, subdue, sue, switcheroo, taboo, tattoo, thereto, thew, threw, thro, through, thru, tickety-boo, Timbuktu, tiramisu, to, to-do, too, toodle-oo, true, true-blue, tu-whit tu-whoo, two, vendue, view, vindaloo, virtu, wahoo, wallaroo, Waterloo, well-to-do, whereto, whew, who, withdrew, woo, Wu, yew, you, zoo

11.2

- leu

11.3

- bayou

11.4

- babu •Malibu •caribou •booboo
- **marabou**, marabout

11.5

- statue •Machu Picchu •virtue

11.6

- **sadhu**, Tamil Nadu

Medial (or *internal*) *rhyme* is used here to emphasize and summarize the main idea of the first stanza of this poem; this is also a good example of rhyming used in free verse:

Your clear eye is the one absolutely beautiful thing.
I want to fill it with colour and ducks,
The zoo of the new ...

(Sylvia Plath, 'Child')

- hairdo •Pompidou •fondue
- **hoodoo**, kudu, voodoo
- Urdu •amadou •Xanadu

11.7

- samfu •tofu •Khufu

11.8

- ragout
- **fugu**, Ouagadougou
- Telugu •burgoo

11.9

- bijou

11.10

- **Oahu**, yahoo
- yoo-hoo

11.11

- juju •carcajou •kinkajou

11.12

- **Baku**, raku
- haiku •Shikoku •cuckoo

11.13

- Yalu •igloo •Oulu
- **Honolulu**, KwaZulu, lulu, Zulu
- Pagalu •Angelou •ormolu
- superglue •curlew

11.14

- **Camus**, Jammu
- rimu •muumuu •tinamou

11.15

- Manu •Vishnu •Ainu •ingénue
- parvenu

11.16

- tapu •quipu •coypu •hoopoe

11.17

- Andrew
- **Maseru**, Nehru
- aircrew •écru •breakthrough
- Hebrew •see-through •corkscrew
- walk-through
- **Nakuru**, Nauru
- froufrou •guru •woodscrew
- thumbscrew •run-through •Timaru

11.18

- shiatsu •keiretsu •ju-jitsu
- Clarenceux

11.19

- **cachou**, cashew
- sandshoe •fichu
- **issue**, Mogadishu, tissue
- Honshu •horseshoe •snowshoe
- Kyushu •gumshoe •overshoe

11.20

- **Bantu**, stand-to
- **Manawatu**, Vanuatu
- passe-partout •gentoo •lean-to
- pistou
- **into**, thereinto
- manitou •onto •Motu
- **Basotho**, Hutu, Lesotho, Mobutu, Sotho, tutu
- **hereunto**, thereunto, unto
- surtout

11.21

• rendezvous

11.22

• Askew
• **undervalue**, value
• Matthew •countervalue •argue
• début •nephew •Pegu •ecu •rescue
• Verdelho
• **menu**, venue
• ague •Jehu •emu •preview •Jesu
• mildew •miscue

• **continue**, sinew
• in situ •barbecue •curlicue
• honeydew •clerihew •retinue
• avenue •residue •impromptu •shoyu
• Autocue •Kikuyu •Bartholomew
• interview •Montague •overview
• curfew •purlieu •purview

> Try rhyming one word with a
> set of two: menu, when you;
> preview, sea view.
> [i]

11.23

• kudzu

Section 12: -ə ('-uh')

12.1

- **huh**, ugh, uh-huh

12.2

- **abaya**, betrayer, conveyor, Eritrea, flayer, Freya, gainsayer, layer, Malaya, Marbella, Maya, Mayer, Nouméa, obeyer, payer, player, portrayer, prayer, preyer, purveyor, slayer, sprayer, stayer, strayer, surveyor, waylayer, weigher
- tracklayer ● bricklayer ● minelayer
- record-player ● taxpayer ● ratepayer
- naysayer ● soothsayer ● crocheter

12.3

- **Achaea**, aliyah, Almería, Apia, Bahía, Caesarea, Cassiopeia, Chaldea, Cytherea, Euboea, foreseer, freer, galleria, gynaecea, Iphigenia, Kampuchea, kea, keyer, Latakia, Leah, Lucia, Nicaea, Nicosia, onomatopoeia, Oriya, osteria, Pangaea, Pantelleria, pharmacopoeia, pizzeria, ria, rupiah, sangría, seer, sharia, Shia, skier, spiraea (*US* spirea), Tanzania, taqueria, Tarpeia, Thea, trachea, trattoria, urea
- sightseer

12.4

- **adhere**, Agadir, Anglosphere, appear, arrear, auctioneer, austere, balladeer, bandolier, Bashkir, beer, besmear, bier, blear, bombardier, brigadier, buccaneer, cameleer, career, cashier, cavalier, chandelier, charioteer, cheer, chevalier, chiffonier, clavier, clear, Coetzee, cohere, commandeer, conventioneer, Cordelier, corsetière, Crimea, dear, deer, diarrhoea (*US* diarrhea), domineer, Dorothea, drear, ear, electioneer, emir, endear, engineer, fear, fleer, Freer, fusilier, gadgeteer, Galatea, gazetteer, gear, gondolier, gonorrhoea (*US* gonorrhea), Greer, grenadier, hand-rear, hear, here, Hosea, idea, interfere, Izmir, jeer, Judaea, Kashmir, Keir, kir, Korea, Lear, leer, Maria, marketeer, Medea, Meir, Melilla, mere, Mia, Mir, mishear, mountaineer, muleteer, musketeer, mutineer, near, orienteer, pamphleteer, panacea, paneer, peer, persevere, pier, Pierre, pioneer, pistoleer, privateer, profiteer, puppeteer, queer, racketeer, ratafia, rear, revere, rhea, rocketeer, Sapir, scrutineer, sear, seer, sere, severe, Shamir, shear, sheer, sincere, smear, sneer, sonneteer, souvenir, spear, sphere, steer, stere, summiteer, Tangier, tear, tier, Trier, Tyr, veer, veneer, Vere, Vermeer, vizier, volunteer, Wear, weir, we're, year, Zaïre

12.5

- **Gambia**, Zambia
- **Arabia**, labia, Swabia
- **Libya**, Namibia, tibia
- euphorbia
- **agoraphobia**, claustrophobia, homophobia, hydrophobia, phobia, technophobia, xenophobia, Zenobia
- Nubia ● rootbeer ● cumbia
- **Colombia**, Columbia
- **exurbia**, Serbia, suburbia

In this well-known poem Robert Frost uses an interesting *rhyme pattern* called *chain rhyme*, in which the rhyme-sound is echoed from stanza to stanza, with the third line signalling the main rhyme of the following stanza ('here' with 'queer/near/year'):

Whose woods these are I think I know.
His house is in the village, though;
He will not see me stopping here
To watch his woods fill up with snow.

My little horse must think it queer
To stop without a farmhouse near
Between the woods and frozen lake
The darkest evening of the year.

(Robert Frost 'Stopping by Woods on a Snowy Evening')

- Wiltshire • Flintshire
- **gaillardia**, Nadia, tachycardia
- steadier • compendia
- **Acadia**, Arcadia, nadir, stadia
- reindeer
- **acedia**, encyclopedia, media, multimedia
- **Lydia**, Numidia
- India • belvedere • Claudia
- **Cambodia**, odea, plasmodia, podia, roe-deer
- **Mafia**, raffia, tafia
- Philadelphia • hemisphere
- planisphere • Montgolfier • Sofia
- ecosphere • biosphere • atmosphere
- thermosphere • ionosphere
- stratosphere • headgear • switchgear
- logia • nemesia • menhir

12.6

- **myalgia**, nostalgia
- sporangia
- **florilegia**, quadriplegia
- Phrygia • Thuringia • loggia • Borgia
- **apologia**, eulogia
- Perugia
- **Czechoslovakia**, Slovakia
- Saskia
- **clarkia**, souvlakia
- rudbeckia
- **fakir**, Wallachia
- Ischia
- **Antalya**, espalier, pallia, rallier

- shilly-shallyer • Somalia
- **hotelier**, Montpellier, sommelier, St Helier
- **Australia**, azalea, bacchanalia, Castalia, dahlia, echolalia, genitalia, inter alia, Lupercalia, Mahalia, marginalia, paraphernalia, regalia, Saturnalia, Thalia, Westphalia
- **Amelia**, camellia, Celia, Cordelia, Cornelia, Delia, Elia, epithelia, Karelia, Montpelier, Ophelia, psychedelia
- **bougainvillea**, Brasília, cilia, conciliar, familiar, haemophilia (*US* hemophilia), Hillier, juvenilia, memorabilia, necrophilia, paedophilia (*US* pedophilia), sedilia
- chanticleer
- **collier**, volleyer
- cochlea • haulier
- **Anatolia**, magnolia, melancholia, Mongolia
- **Apulia**, dulia, Julia, peculiar
- **nuclear**, sub-nuclear, thermonuclear
- buddleia

12.7

- Grasmere • cashmere
- **Emyr**, premier
- **macadamia**, Mesopotamia
- **academia**, anaemia (*US* anemia), Bohemia, Euphemia, hypoglycaemia, leukaemia (*US* leukemia),

septicaemia (*US* septicemia), uraemia
- **bulimia**, Ymir
- arrhythmia • Vladimir • encomia
- **costumier**, parfumier
- Windermere
- **Hermia**, hyperthermia, hypothermia

12.8

- **Campania**, Catania, pannier
- apnoea
- **Oceania**, Tanya, Titania
- **biennia**, denier, quadrennia, quinquennia, septennia, triennia
- **Albania**, balletomania, bibliomania, crania, dipsomania, egomania, erotomania, kleptomania, Lithuania, Lusitania, mania, Mauritania, megalomania, miscellanea, monomania, nymphomania, Pennsylvania, Pomerania, pyromania, Rainier, Romania, Ruritania, Tasmania, Transylvania, Urania
- **Armenia**, bergenia, gardenia, neurasthenia, ostopenia, proscenia, sarcopenia, schizophrenia, senior, Slovenia
- **Abyssinia**, Bithynia, curvilinear, Gdynia, gloxinia, interlinear, Lavinia, linear, rectilinear, Sardinia, triclinia, Virginia, zinnia
- insignia • Sonia • insomnia • Bosnia
- **California**, cornea
- **Amazonia**, ammonia, Antonia, Babylonia, begonia, bonier, Catalonia, catatonia, Cephalonia, Estonia, Ionia, Laconia, Livonia, Macedonia, mahonia, Patagonia, pneumonia, pogonia, Rondônia, sinfonia, Snowdonia, valonia, zirconia
- **junior**, petunia
- **hernia**, journeyer

12.9

- Dampier
- **Napier**, rapier, tapir
- Shakespeare • sepia • Olympia

- copier • compeer • photocopier
- **cornucopia**, dystopia, Ethiopia, myopia, subtopia, Utopia

12.10

- **barrier**, carrier, farrier, harrier, tarrier
- **Calabria**, Cantabria
- Andrea • Kshatriya • Bactria
- **Amu Darya**, aria, Zaria
- Alexandria
- **Ferrier**, terrier
- destrier
- **aquaria**, area, armamentaria, Bavaria, Bulgaria, caldaria, cineraria, columbaria, filaria, frigidaria, Gran Canaria, herbaria, honoraria, malaria, pulmonaria, rosaria, sacraria, Samaria, solaria, tepidaria, terraria
- **atria**, gematria
- **Assyria**, Illyria, Styria, Syria
- **Laurier**, warrior
- **hypochondria**, mitochondria
- Austria
- **auditoria**, ciboria, conservatoria, crematoria, emporia, euphoria, Gloria, moratoria, phantasmagoria, Pretoria, sanatoria, scriptoria, sudatoria, victoria, Vitoria, vomitoria
- Maurya
- **courier**, Fourier
- **currier**, furrier, spurrier, worrier
- **Cumbria**, Northumbria, Umbria
- **Algeria**, anterior, bacteria, Bashkiria, cafeteria, criteria, cryptomeria, diphtheria, exterior, hysteria, Iberia, inferior, interior, Liberia, listeria, Nigeria, posterior, Siberia, superior, ulterior, wisteria
- **Etruria**, Liguria, Manchuria, Surya

12.11

- **cassia**, glacier
- **apraxia**, dyspraxia
- banksia • eclampsia
- **estancia**, fancier, financier, Landseer

- **intarsia**, mahseer, Marcia, tarsier
- **bartsia**, bilharzia
- **anorexia**, dyslexia
- intelligentsia ●dyspepsia
- **Dacia**, fascia
- **Felicia**, Galicia, indicia, Lycia, Mysia
- **asphyxia**, elixir, ixia
- dossier ●nausea
- **Andalusia**, Lucia
- overseer ●Mercia ●Hampshire
- Berkshire ●Caernarvonshire
- Cheshire ●differentia ●Breconshire
- Devonshire ●Ayrshire
- **Galatia**, Hypatia, solatia
- **alopecia**, godetia, Helvetia
- **Alicia**, Leticia
- Derbyshire ●Berwickshire
- Cambridgeshire ●Warwickshire
- Argyllshire ●quassia ●Shropshire
- Yorkshire ●Staffordshire
- Hertfordshire ●Bedfordshire
- Herefordshire ●Oxfordshire
- Forfarshire ●Lancashire
- Lincolnshire ●Monmouthshire
- Buckinghamshire ●Nottinghamshire
- Northamptonshire ●Leicestershire
- Wigtownshire ●Worcestershire

12.12

- astrantia ●Bastia
- **Dei gratia**, hamartia
- poinsettia
- **in absentia**, Parmentier
- Izvestia
- **meteor**, wheatear
- Whittier ●cottier ●Ostia
- **consortia**, courtier
- protea ●Yakutia ●frontier ●Althea
- Anthea ●Parthia
- **Pythia**, stichomythia
- **Carinthia**, Cynthia
- forsythia ●Scythia ●clothier ●salvia
- Latvia ●Yugoslavia ●envier
- **Flavia**, Moldavia, Moravia, Octavia, paviour (*US* pavior), Scandinavia, Xavier
- **Bolivia**, Livia, Olivia, trivia
- Sylvia ●Guinevere ●Elzevir
- **Monrovia**, Segovia
- Retrovir ●effluvia ●colloquia

- Goodyear ●yesteryear ●brassiere
- Abkhazia
- **Anastasia**, aphasia, brazier, dysphasia, dysplasia, euthanasia, fantasia, Frazier, glazier, grazier, gymnasia, Malaysia
- **amnesia**, anaesthesia (*US* anesthesia), analgesia, freesia, Indonesia, Silesia, synaesthesia
- **artemisia**, Kirghizia, Tunisia
- **ambrosia**, crozier, hosier, osier, symposia

12.13

- **acquire**, admire, afire, applier, aspire, attire, ayah, backfire, barbwire, bemire, briar, buyer, byre, choir, conspire, crier, cryer, defier, denier, desire, dire, drier, dryer, dyer, enquire, entire, esquire, expire, fire, flyer, friar, fryer, Gaia, gyre, hellfire, hire, hiya, ire, Isaiah, jambalaya, Jeremiah, Josiah, Kintyre, latria, liar, lyre, Maia, Maya, Mayer, messiah, mire, misfire, Nehemiah, Obadiah, papaya, pariah, peripeteia, perspire, playa, Praia, prior, pyre, quire, replier, scryer, shire, shyer, sire, skyer, Sophia, spire, squire, supplier, Surabaya, suspire, tier, tire, transpire, trier, tumble-dryer, tyre, Uriah, via, wire, Zechariah, Zedekiah, Zephaniah

> Create extra rhymes by changing words like acquire to acquiring. ⓘ

- homebuyer

12.14

- sapphire ●backfire ●campfire
- shellfire ●ceasefire ●misfire ●spitfire
- speechifier
- **humidifier**, solidifier
- modifier ●codifier ●amplifier
- vilifier
- **mollifier**, qualifier
- nullifier ●magnifier ●indemnifier

- signifier •personifier •unifier
- typifier •stupefier
- **clarifier**, scarifier
- **terrifier**, verifier
- gentrifier •glorifier •purifier
- **classifier**, pacifier
- specifier •intensifier •crucifier
- emulsifier •versifier
- **gratifier**, ratifier
- sanctifier •identifier •testifier
- prettifier •quantifier •fortifier
- beautifier •stultifier •justifier
- liquefier •wildfire •watchfire
- bonfire •crossfire •bushfire •gunfire
- surefire •lammergeier •multiplier
- outlier •Niemeyer •quagmire
- vampire •empire •occupier •umpire
- hairdryer •prophesier •satire
- Blantyre •saltire •haywire •tripwire
- retrochoir •underwire

12.15

- **drawer**, tawer

12.16

- **bower**, cower, devour, dower,
  embower, empower, endower, flour,
  flower, gaur, Glendower, glower,
  hour, lour, lower, our, plougher
  (*US* plower), power, scour, shower,
  sour, Stour, sweet-and-sour, tower
- Beckenbauer •Eisenhower
- Schopenhauer •safflower
- passion flower •bellflower
- mayflower •cauliflower •wallflower
- **cornflour**, cornflower
- sunflower •elderflower •man-hour
- Adenauer •manpower •brainpower
- willpower •horsepower •firepower
- water power •rush hour
- watchtower

12.17

- **anoa**, Balboa, blower, boa, foregoer,
  goer, grower, hoer, jerboa, knower,
  Krakatoa, Lebowa, lower, moa,

mower, Mururoa, Noah, o'er, proa,
protozoa, rower, Samoa, sewer,
Shenandoah, shower, sower,
spermatozoa, Stour, thrower, tower
- shadower •widower •racegoer
- **theatregoer** (*US* theatergoer)
- churchgoer •echoer
- **follower**, swallower
- snowblower •lawnmower •genoa
- winnower •harrower •winegrower
- borrower •burrower •vetoer

12.18

- **annoyer**, Boyer, destroyer,
  employer, enjoyer, Goya, hoya,
  lawyer, Nagoya, paranoia, sequoia,
  soya

12.19

- **Amur**, brewer, chewer, Dewar, doer,
  ewer, hewer, Kahlua, lassoer, Nuer,
  pursuer, renewer, screwer, sewer,
  skewer, skua, spewer, strewer, suer,
  tattooer, viewer, who're, wooer
- evil-doer •wrongdoer •issuer
- snowshoer •rescuer •interviewer

12.20

- **abjure**, adjure, allure, amour,
  assure, Bahawalpur, boor,
  Borobudur, Cavour, coiffure,
  conjure, couture, cure, dastur,
  de nos jours, doublure, dour,
  embouchure, endure, ensure, enure,
  gravure, immature, immure, impure,
  inure, Jaipur, Koh-i-noor, Kultur,
  liqueur, lure, manure, mature, moor,
  Moore, Muir, mure, Nagpur, Namur,
  obscure, parkour, photogravure, plat
  du jour, Pompadour, procure, pure,
  rotogravure, Ruhr, Saussure, secure,
  simon-pure, spoor, Stour, sure, tour,
  Tours, velour, Yom Kippur, you're

> Create extra rhymes by
> adding -*ing* or -(*e*)*d* to words like
> abjure.

- tambour •prefecture •caricature
- armature
- **tamandua**, tandoor
- Dartmoor •Exmoor •Hawksmoor
- paramour •Papua •Jabalpur
- Manipur •Jodhpur •Kuala Lumpur
- Kolhapur •Karlsruhe •Joshua
- cynosure •Fraktur •détour •contour
- Padua
- **jaguar**, Managua, Nicaragua
- vacua •valuer •Langmuir •mantua
- arguer •residua
- **continua**, continuer
- pedicure •manicure •sinecure
- epicure •conure
- **bordure**, ordure
- Saumur •nunciature •overture
- couverture •coverture
- purpure

12.21

- **abba**, blabber, dabber, grabber, jabber, stabber, yabber
- **Alba**, Galba
- **amber**, camber, caramba, clamber, Cochabamba, gamba, mamba, Maramba, samba, timbre
- **Annaba**, arbor, arbour, barber, Barbour, harbour (US harbor), indaba, Kaaba, Lualaba, Pearl Harbor, Saba, Sabah, Shaba
- **sambar**, sambhar
- **rebbe**, Weber
- Elba
- **Bemba**, December, ember, member, November, Pemba, September
- **belabour** (US belabor), caber, labour (US labor), neighbour (US neighbor), sabre (US saber), tabor
- chamber •bedchamber
- antechamber
- **amoeba** (US ameba), Bathsheba, Bourguiba, Geber, Sheba, zariba
- **cribber**, dibber, fibber, gibber, jibba, jibber, libber, ribber
- Wilbur
- **limber**, marimba, timber
- winebibber
- **calibre** (US caliber), Excalibur
- **briber**, fibre (US fiber), scriber, subscriber, Tiber, transcriber
- **clobber**, cobber, jobber, mobber,

robber, slobber
- **ombre**, sombre (US somber)
- **carnauba**, catawba, dauber, Micawber
- **jojoba**, Manitoba, October, sober
- **Aruba**, Cuba, Nuba, scuba, tuba, tuber
- Drouzhba •Toowoomba •Yoruba
- Hecuba

12.22

- **blubber**, clubber, grubber, lubber, rubber, scrubber, snubber
- **Columba**, cumber, encumber, Humber, lumbar, lumber, number, outnumber, rumba, slumber, umber
- cucumber •landlubber
- Addis Ababa •Córdoba
- Aqaba •djellaba •mastaba
- **Berber**, disturber, Djerba, Thurber

12.23

- **catcher**, dacha, focaccia, garnacha, patcher, scratcher, snatcher, stature, thatcher
- **facture**, fracture, manufacture
- **capture**, enrapture, rapture
- flycatcher •oystercatcher
- **archer**, departure, kwacha, marcher, starcher, viscacha
- pasture
- **etcher**, fetcher, fletcher, lecher, sketcher, stretcher
- **conjecture**, lecture
- sepulture
- **denture**, misadventure, peradventure
- **divesture**, gesture, vesture
- texture •architecture •nature
- magistrature
- **bleacher**, creature, feature, headteacher, Katowice, Nietzsche, preacher, screecher, teacher
- schoolteacher
- **ditcher**, hitcher, pitcher, stitcher, twitcher
- Chibcha
- **picture**, stricture
- filcher •simcha

- **cincture**, tincture
- scripture
- **admixture**, commixture, fixture, intermixture, mixture
- expenditure •forfeiture
- discomfiture •garniture
- **primogeniture**, progeniture
- miniature •furniture •temperature
- portraiture •literature
- **divestiture**, vestiture

12.24

- **botcher**, gotcha, top-notcher, watcher, wotcha
- **imposture**, posture
- firewatcher •birdwatcher
- **debaucher**, scorcher, torture
- **Boucher**, voucher
- **cloture**, encroacher, poacher, reproacher
- jointure •moisture
- **cachucha**, future, moocher, smoocher, suture
- butcher
- **kuccha**, scutcher, toucher
- structure
- **culture**, vulture
- **conjuncture**, juncture, puncture
- rupture •sculpture •viniculture
- agriculture •sericulture
- arboriculture •pisciculture
- horticulture •silviculture
- subculture •counterculture
- aquaculture •acupuncture
- substructure •infrastructure
- candidature •ligature •judicature
- implicature
- **entablature**, tablature
- prelature •nomenclature •filature
- legislature •musculature
- premature •biosignature •signature
- aperture • curvature
- **lurcher**, nurture, percher, searcher

12.25

- **adder**, bladder, khaddar, ladder, madder
- **Esmeralda**, Valda

- scaffolder •lambda
- **Amanda**, Aranda, Baganda, Banda, brander, candour (*US* candor), coriander, dander, expander, gander, germander, goosander, jacaranda, Leander, Luanda, Lysander, meander, memoranda, Menander, Miranda, oleander, panda, pander, pasanda, philander, propaganda, Rwanda, sander, Skanda, stander, Uganda, understander, Vanda, veranda, withstander, zander
- backhander •Laplander •stepladder
- inlander •outlander •Netherlander
- overlander •gerrymander
- pomander
- **calamander**, salamander
- bystander
- **ardour** (*US* ardor), armada, Bader, cadre, carder, cicada, Dalriada, enchilada, Garda, gelada, Granada, Haggadah, Hamada, intifada, lambada, larder, Masada, Nevada, panada, piña colada, pousada, promenader, retarder, Scheherazade, Theravada, Torquemada, tostada
- **Alexander**, commander, demander, Lahnda, slander
- Pravda •autostrada

12.26

- **bedder**, cheddar, Edda, Enzedder, header, Kedah, shedder, shredder, spreader, tedder, threader, treader, Vedda
- **elder**, Griselda, welder, Zelda
- **addenda**, agenda, amender, ascender, attender, bender, blender, Brenda, contender, corrigenda, descender, engender, extender, fazenda, fender, gender, Glenda, Gwenda, hacienda, Länder, lender, mender, offender, pudenda, recommender, referenda, render, sender, slender, spender, splendour (*US* splendor), surrender, suspender, tender, Venda, weekender, Wenda
- parascender •bartender
- homesteader •newsvendor
- spot-welder

- **abrader**, Ada, blockader, crusader, dissuader, evader, fader, grader, Grenada, invader, masquerader, Nader, parader, persuader, raider, Rigveda, Seder, serenader, trader, upgrader, Veda, wader
- **attainder**, remainder
- rollerblader
- **Aïda**, bleeder, Breda, breeder, cedar, conceder, corrida, Derrida, Elfreda, e-reader, Etheldreda, feeder, follow-my-leader, interceder, interpleader, kneader, leader, Leda, Lieder, misleader, pleader, reader, seceder, seeder, speeder, stampeder, succeeder, weeder
- **fielder**, midfielder, wielder, yielder
- outfielder •bandleader •ringleader
- cheerleader •copyreader
- mind-reader •sight-reader
- stockbreeder •proofreader
- newsreader

12.27

- **bidder**, consider, Jiddah, kidder, whydah
- **bewilder**, builder, guilder, Hilda, Matilda, St Kilda, Tilda, tilde
- **Belinda**, Cabinda, cinder, Clarinda, Dorinda, hinder, Kinder, Linda, Lucinda, Melinda, tinder
- Drogheda •shipbuilder •bodybuilder
- coachbuilder •boatbuilder •Candida
- spina bifida
- **calendar**, calender
- Phillida •cylinder •Phasmida
- Andromeda •Mérida •Florida
- Cressida •lavender •provender
- **chider**, cider, divider, eider, glider, Guider, Haida, hider, Ida, insider, Oneida, outsider, provider, rider, Ryder, Saida, slider, spider, strider, stridor
- Wilder
- **binder**, blinder, finder, grinder, kinda, minder, ringbinder, winder
- Fassbinder •spellbinder •highbinder
- bookbinder •pathfinder
- rangefinder •viewfinder •backslider

- paraglider •childminder •outrider
- joyrider •roughrider •ringsider
- Tynesider •sidewinder

12.28

- **dodder**, fodder, plodder, prodder
- **Isolde**, solder
- **absconder**, anaconda, Fonda, Golconda, Honda, nonda, ponder, responder, squander, Wanda, wander, yonder
- hot-rodder
- **awarder**, boarder, border, defrauder, hoarder, Korda, marauder, order, recorder, sordor, warder
- **alder**, Balder, Calder
- **launder**, maunder
- sailboarder •skateboarder
- keyboarder •snowboarder
- camcorder •video recorder
- **chowder**, Gouda, howdah, Lauda, powder
- **bounder**, compounder, expounder, flounder, founder, grounder, impounder, pounder, propounder, rounder, sounder
- gunpowder
- **Clodagh**, coda, coder, exploder, loader, Oder, odour (*US* odor), pagoda, Rhoda, Sargodha, Schroder, soda, vocoder
- **beholder**, boulder, folder, holder, moulder (*US* molder), polder, scolder, shoulder, smoulder (*US* smolder), upholder, withholder

> Try rhyming one word with a [i]
> set of two: shoulder, told her;
> smoulder, hold her.

- cardholder •shareholder
- stakeholder
- **freeholder**, keyholder
- leaseholder •copyholder
- policyholder •stockholder
- **smallholder**, stallholder
- householder •freeloader
- **avoider**, embroider
- joinder •Schadenfreude

12.29

- **Barbuda**, barracuda, Bermuda, brooder, Buxtehude, colluder, deluder, excluder, intruder, Judah, Luda, Neruda, obtruder, Tudor
- mouthbrooder
- **Buddha**, do-gooder
- **Kaunda**, Munda
- **judder**, rudder, shudder, udder
- numdah
- **asunder**, blunder, chunder, hereunder, plunder, rotunda, sunder, thereunder, thunder, under, up-and-under, wonder
- husbander • seconder • Shetlander
- mainlander • Greenlander
- Queenslander • midlander
- Little Englander
- **Highlander**, islander
- Icelander • Hollander • lowlander
- Newfoundlander • woodlander
- colander • Canada • Kannada
- ambassador • forwarder
- **birder**, Gerda, girder, herder, murder

12.30

- **chaffer**, gaffer, Jaffa, kafir, Staffa
- **alfalfa**, alpha, Balfour, Wadi Halfa
- **camphor**, chamfer
- Luftwaffe
- **laugher**, staffer
- **heifer**, zephyr
- **chafer**, trefa, wafer
- cockchafer
- **feoffor**, reefer
- **differ**, sniffer
- pilfer • titfer • umbellifer • Jennifer
- conifer • apocrypha • thurifer
- **crucifer**, Lucifer
- Potiphar • aquifer
- **cipher**, encipher, fifer, Haifa, knifer, lifer

> Try rhyming one word with a [i]
> set of two: lifer, knife her.

- **coffer**, cougher, Offa, offer, proffer, quaffer, scoffer

- golfer • phosphor • Forfar • Altdorfer
- **chauffeur**, gofer, goffer, gopher, loafer, Nuku'alofa, Ophir, shofar, sofa
- Fraunhofer
- **hoofer**, loofah, opera buffa, roofer, spoofer, tufa, woofer
- waterproofer
- **bluffer**, buffer, duffer, puffer, snuffer, suffer

> Create extra rhymes for [i]
> words like bluffer by adding -er
> to gruff etc. (see section 17.15).

- **sulphur** (*US* sulfur) • telegrapher
- **calligrapher**, serigrapher
- **autobiographer**, bibliographer, biographer, cartographer, choreographer, cinematographer, crystallographer, geographer, Hagiographa, hagiographer, iconographer, lexicographer, lithographer, oceanographer, palaeographer (*US* paleographer), photographer, pornographer, radiographer, stenographer, topographer, typographer
- **philosopher**, theosopher
- metaphor • Christopher • surfer
- Bonhoeffer • windsurfer

12.31

- **blagger**, bragger, dagger, flagger, Jagger, lagger, nagger, quagga, saggar, shagger, stagger, swagger
- **alga**, realgar, Trafalgar
- **anger**, clangour (*US* clangor), Katanga, languor, manga, panga, sangar, tanga, Tauranga, Zamboanga
- sandbagger • carpetbagger • Erlanger
- **Aga**, Braga, dagga, dargah, laager, lager, naga, Onondaga, raga, saga
- **beggar**, eggar, Gregor, mega, Megger
- Edgar • Helga • Heidegger
- bootlegger
- **Jaeger**, maigre, Meleager, Noriega, Ortega, rutabaga, Sagar
- **Antigua**, beleaguer, bodega, eager,

intriguer, leaguer, meagre (*US* meager), reneger, Riga, Seeger, Vega
- **chigger**, configure, digger, figure, Frigga, jigger, ligger, rigger, rigor, rigour, snigger, swigger, transfigure, trigger, vigour (*US* vigor)
- **churinga**, finger, linger, malinger
- gravedigger •ladyfinger •forefinger
- omega •vinegar •Honegger
- outrigger •Minnesinger
- **Auriga**, Eiger, liger, saiga, taiga, tiger

12.32

- **dogger**, flogger, Hoggar, hogger, jogger, logger, slogger, Wagga Wagga
- **brolga**, Olga, Volga
- **conga**, conger, donga, Rarotonga
- pettifogger •footslogger
- **cataloguer** (*US* cataloger)
- **auger**, augur
- **ogre**, Saratoga, toga, yoga
- **beluga**, cougar, Kaluga, Kruger, Luger
- **sugar**, Zeebrugge
- **bugger**, hugger, lugger, mugger, plugger, rugger, slugger, Srinagar, tugger
- **mulga**, vulgar
- **hunger**, sangha, Younger
- scandalmonger •scaremonger
- fishmonger
- **warmonger**, whoremonger
- ironmonger •hugger-mugger
- costermonger •Málaga
- **Berger**, burger, burgher
- hamburger •beefburger
- cheeseburger •Limburger
- Vegeburger •Erzgebirge
- Luxembourger

12.33

- azure
- **leisure**, made-to-measure, measure, pleasure, treasure
- countermeasure

- **Australasia**, embrasure
- seizure
- **closure**, composure, enclosure, exposure, foreclosure
- Hoosier

12.34

- Brahe •Fatiha •aloha

12.35

- **badger**, cadger
- **Alger**, neuralgia
- **ganja**, grandeur, phalanger
- **charger**, enlarger, maharaja, raja
- slàinte •turbocharger
- **dredger**, edger, hedger, ledger, pledger, St Leger

> ⓘ Create extra rhymes for words like dredger by adding -er to hedge etc. (see section 20.3).

- **avenger**, revenger
- **gauger**, golden-ager, major, old-stager, pager, rampager, sergeant major, stager, wager
- **arranger**, changer, danger, endanger, exchanger, Grainger, hydrangea, manger, ranger, stranger
- moneychanger •teenager
- bushranger
- **besieger**, paraplegia, procedure
- abridger
- **cringer**, ginger, impinger, infringer, injure, ninja, whinger, winger
- dowager •voyager •harbinger
- bondager •wharfinger •packager
- Scaliger
- **challenger**, Salinger
- **pillager**, villager
- armiger •scrimmager
- **rummager**, scrummager
- manager •derringer •forager
- porringer •encourager
- **Massinger**, passenger
- presager •messenger •Kissinger
- **integer**, vintager
- cottager •frontager •ravager
- salvager •scavenger

- **Elijah**, Niger, obliger
- **codger**, dodger, lodger, roger, todger
- **forger**, Georgia, gorger
- gouger
- **lounger**, scrounger
- sunlounger • soldier
- **Abuja**, puja

12.36

- **bludger**, grudger, nudger, trudger
- indulger
- **blunger**, conjure, expunger, plunger, sponger
- **astrologer**, mythologer
- tanager • onager • massager • potager
- **merger**, perjure, purger, scourger, urger, verdure, verger

12.37

- **alpaca**, attacker, backer, clacker, claqueur, cracker, Dhaka, hacker, Hakka, knacker, lacquer, maraca, paca, packer, sifaka, slacker, smacker, stacker, tacker, tracker, whacker, yakka
- Kafka
- **anchor**, banker, Bianca, canker, Casablanca, Costa Blanca, flanker, franker, hanker, lingua franca, Lubyanka, rancour (*US* rancor), ranker, Salamanca, spanker, Sri Lanka, tanka, tanker, up-anchor, wanker

> Try rhyming one word with a set of two: hanker, thank her. ⓘ

- **Alaska**, lascar, Madagascar, Nebraska
- Kamchatka • linebacker • outbacker
- **hijacker**, skyjacker
- Schumacher • backpacker
- safecracker • wisecracker
- nutcracker • firecracker • ransacker
- scrimshanker • bushwhacker
- **barker**, haka, Kabaka, Lusaka, marker, moussaka, nosy parker, Oaxaca, Osaka, parka, Shaka, Zarqa

- **asker**, masker
- backmarker • biomarker • waymarker
- **Becker**, checker, Cheka, chequer, Dekker, exchequer, Flecker, mecca, Neckar, Necker, pecker, Quebecker, Rebecca, Rijeka, trekker, weka, wrecker
- **sepulchre** (*US* sepulcher) • Cuenca
- **burlesquer**, Francesca, Wesker
- woodpecker

12.38

- **acre**, baker, breaker, Chandrasekhar, faker, forsaker, Jamaica, Laker, maker, nacre, partaker, Quaker, raker, saker, shaker, staker, taker, undertaker, waker
- bellyacher • matchmaker • bedmaker
- dressmaker
- **haymaker**, playmaker
- sailmaker • rainmaker
- **lacemaker**, pacemaker
- peacemaker • dealmaker • hitmaker
- filmmaker • kingmaker
- printmaker • holidaymaker
- cabinetmaker • moneymaker
- merrymaker • watchmaker
- clockmaker • lawmaker • homemaker
- bookmaker • troublemaker
- boilermaker • heartbreaker
- safebreaker • Windbreaker
- tie-breaker • strikebreaker
- icebreaker • jawbreaker
- housebreaker • muckraker
- boneshaker • caretaker • piss-taker
- stavesacre • wiseacre
- **beaker**, Costa Rica, Dominica, eureka, Frederica, Griqua, jobseeker, leaker, loudspeaker, seeker, shrieker, sika, sneaker, speaker, squeaker, streaker, Tanganyika, theca, tikka, Topeka, wreaker

12.39

- **bicker**, clicker, dicker, flicker, kicker, liquor, nicker, picker, pricker, shicker, slicker, snicker, sticker, ticker, tricker, vicar, whicker, Wicca, wicker

- **bilker**, milker, Rilke
- **blinker**, clinker, drinker, finca, freethinker, Glinka, Inca, inker, jinker, shrinker, sinker, Soyinka, stinker, stotinka, thinker, tinker, Treblinka, winker
- **frisker**, whisker
- **kibitka**, Sitka
- Cyrenaica •Bandaranaike
- perestroika •Baedeker •melodica
- Boudicca •trafficker •angelica
- replica
- **basilica**, silica
- **frolicker**, maiolica, majolica
- bootlicker •res publica •mimicker
- Anneka •arnica •Seneca •Lineker
- picnicker
- **electronica**, harmonica, Honecker, japonica, Monica, moniker, Salonica, santonica, veronica
- Guernica •Africa •paprika
- **America**, erica
- headshrinker •Armorica •brassica
- Jessica •lip-syncer •fossicker
- Corsica
- **Attica**, hepatica, sciatica, viatica
- Antarctica •billsticker
- **erotica**, exotica
- swastika

12.40

- **balalaika**, biker, duiker, Formica, hiker, mica, pica, pika, piker, striker
- **blocker**, chocker, docker, Fokker, interlocker, knocker, locker, mocha, mocker, ocker, quokka, rocker, saltimbocca, shocker, soccer, stocker
- vodka •polka
- **concha**, conker, conquer, Dzongkha, plonker, stonker
- Oscar •Kotka •Knickerbocker
- footlocker
- **caulker** (US calker), corker, hawker, Lorca, Majorca, Minorca, orca, porker, squawker, stalker, talker, walker, yorker
- deerstalker •jaywalker •sleepwalker
- streetwalker •hillwalker
- shopwalker
- **Asoka**, broker, carioca, choker, coca,

croaker, evoker, invoker, joker, mediocre, ochre (US ocher), poker, provoker, revoker, Rioja, smoker, soaker, soca, Stoker, tapioca
- judoka •shipbroker •stockbroker
- pawnbroker •troika

12.41

- **bazooka**, euchre, farruca, lucre, palooka, pooka, rebuker, snooker, Stuka, verruca
- babushka
- **booker**, cooker, hookah, hooker, looker, Sukkur
- Junker •onlooker •yarmulke
- Hanukkah •manuka
- **chukka** (US chukker), ducker, felucca, fucker, mucker, plucker, pucker, pukka, shucker, succour (US succor), sucker, trucker, tucker, yucca
- **skulker**, sulker
- **bunker**, hunker, lunker, punkah, spelunker
- **busker**, tusker
- latke •motherfucker •bloodsucker
- seersucker •abaca •stomacher
- **Linacre**, spinnaker
- massacre
- **Jataka**, Karnataka
- Tripitaka •Ithaca
- **burka**, circa, Gurkha, jerker, lurker, mazurka, shirker, smirker, worker
- tearjerker •autoworker •craftworker
- metalworker •networker
- caseworker •fieldworker
- teleworker •shopworker •outworker
- homeworker •stoneworker
- woodworker

12.42

- **Allah**, calla, Caracalla, Haller, inshallah, pallor, Valhalla, valour (US valor), Whyalla
- **gabbler**, tabla
- **ambler**, gambler, rambler, scrambler
- **Adler**, saddler

- handler
- **angler**, dangler, strangler, wrangler
- tackler •trampler •antler •dazzler
- **Carla**, challah, Douala, gala, Guatemala, Gujranwala, impala, kabbala, Kampala, koala, La Scala, Lingala, Mahler, Marsala, masala, nyala, parlour (*US* parlor), Sinhala, snarler, tala, tambala, Uppsala
- garbler •chandler •sparkler
- sampler
- **a cappella**, Arabella, Bella, bestseller, Capella, cellar, Cinderella, citronella, Clarabella, corella, Daniela, Della, dispeller, dweller, Ella, expeller, favela, fella, fellah, feller, Fenella, Floella, foreteller, Heller, impeller, interstellar, Keller, Louella, Mandela, mortadella, mozzarella, Nigella, novella, paella, panatella, patella, predella, propeller, queller, quinella, repeller, rosella, rubella, salmonella, Santiago de Compostela, seller, smeller, speller, Stella, stellar, tarantella, teller, umbrella, Viyella
- Puebla
- **assembler**, dissembler, trembler
- **medlar**, pedlar
- ländler
- **fin de siècle**, Hekla
- Kepler
- **exempla**, exemplar, Templar
- **tesla**, wrestler
- embezzler •Rockefeller
- knee-trembler •saltcellar
- bookseller •storyteller

12.43

- **Adela**, bailer, bailor, baler, Benguela, bewailer, derailleur, hailer, inhaler, jailer, loudhailer, mailer, nailer, railer, retailer, sailer, sailor, scaler, Scheele, shillelagh, tailor, Taylor, trailer, Venezuela, vuvuzela, wailer, whaler
- fabler •Daimler •blackmailer
- abseiler •wassailer •boardsailor
- wholesaler
- **appealer**, candela, Coahuila,

concealer, dealer, feeler, healer, Keeler, kneeler, Leila, peeler, Philomela, reeler, revealer, Schiele, sealer, sheila, Shelagh, spieler, squealer, stealer, tequila, velar, Vila, wheeler, wheeler-dealer
- enfant terrible
- **Anguilla**, Aquila, Attila, Camilla, cedilla, chiller, chinchilla, driller, Drusilla, fibrillar, filler, flotilla, fulfiller, Godzilla, gorilla, griller, guerrilla, killer, Manila, manilla, mantilla, miller, pillar, Priscilla, sapodilla, sarsaparilla, Schiller, scilla, scintilla, spiller, swiller, thriller, tiller, vanilla, vexilla, villa, Willa, willer, zorilla

> Try rhyming one word with a set of two: chiller, kill her.

- kiblah •fiddler
- **kindler**, swindler
- sniffler •sigla •stickler
- **sprinkler**, twinkler, winkler
- **Himmler**, Simla
- crippler
- **Hitler**, Littler, Mitla
- grizzler •Polyfilla •drosophila
- downhiller •Angela •painkiller
- weedkiller •ladykiller •Pamela
- **similar**, verisimilar
- propyla •caterpillar •canceller
- **councillor** (*US* councilor), counsellor (*US* counselor)

12.44

- **beguiler**, compiler, Delilah, filer, Isla, miler, reviler, smiler, styler, tiler, Tyler
- idler
- **stifler**, trifler
- recycler •Kreisler •profiler
- stockpiler •freestyler •Rottweiler
- **ayatollah**, choler, collar, corolla, dollar, dolour (*US* dolor), Hezbollah, holler, scholar, squalor, wallah, Waller, white-collar
- **cobbler**, gobbler
- **Doppler**, poplar
- ostler

- **brawler**, caller, crawler, drawler, faller, forestaller, hauler, installer, mauler, Paula, stonewaller, trawler
- warbler •dawdler •footballer
- reed-warbler
- **fowler**, growler, howler, prowler, scowler
- **Angola**, barbola, bipolar, bowler, bronchiolar, canola, carambola, circumpolar, coaler, Coca-Cola, cola, comptroller, consoler, controller, Ebola, eidola, extoller, Finola, Gorgonzola, granola, Hispaniola, kola, Lola, lunisolar, mandola, molar, multipolar, Ndola, patroller, payola, pianola, polar, roller, Savonarola, scagliola, scroller, sola, solar, stroller, tombola, Tortola, troller, Vignola, viola, Zola
- ogler
- **teetotaller** (*US* teetotaler)
- potholer •steamroller •logroller
- roadroller
- **boiler**, broiler, Euler, oiler, spoiler, toiler
- potboiler

12.45

- **chermoula**, cooler, hula, moolah, Petula, ruler, Shula, Tallulah, Tula
- bugler •pre-schooler

12.46

- **ampulla**, bulla, fuller, Müller, pula, puller
- titular •Weissmuller •wirepuller
- **incunabula**, tabular
- preambular •glandular •coagula
- **angular**, quadrangular, rectangular, triangular
- **Dracula**, facula, oracular, spectacular, vernacular
- **cardiovascular**, vascular
- **annular**, granular
- scapula •capsular •spatula
- tarantula •nebula •scheduler
- calendula
- **irregular**, regular

- **Benbecula**, molecular, secular, specular
- cellular •fibula •Caligula •singular
- **auricular**, curricula, curricular, diverticula, funicular, lenticular, navicular, particular, perpendicular, testicular, vehicular, vermicular
- primula
- **insular**, peninsula
- **fistula**, Vistula
- globular
- **modular**, nodular
- **binocular**, jocular, ocular
- oscular
- **copula**, popular
- consular •formula •tubular •uvula
- jugular
- **avuncular**, carbuncular
- **crepuscular**, majuscular, minuscular, muscular
- pustular
- **circular**, semicircular, tubercular
- Ursula

12.47

- **colour** (*US* color), cruller, culler, medulla, mullah, Muller, nullah, sculler, Sulla
- **doubler**, troubler
- **bumbler**, grumbler, stumbler, tumbler
- bundler •muffler •juggler •bungler
- suckler •coupler
- **hustler**, rustler
- **butler**, cutler
- puzzler •swashbuckler •technicolor
- **multicolour** (*US* multicolor)
- **watercolour** (*US* watercolor)

12.48

- **areola**, rubeola
- Viola
- **dueller** (*US* dueler), jeweller (*US* jeweler)
- **babbler**, dabbler, parabola
- **labeller** (*US* labeler)
- **dribbler**, nibbler, quibbler, scribbler
- **libeller** (*US* libeler)
- **hobbler**, nobbler, squabbler, wobbler

- bubbler
- **fumbler**, mumbler, rumbler
- **burbler**, hyperbola
- bachelor
- **paddler**, straddler
- mandala •panhandler •meddler
- ladler •wheedler
- **diddler**, piddler, riddler, tiddler, twiddler
- **coddler**, modeller (US modeler), toddler, twaddler, waddler
- **fondler**, gondola
- **yodeller** (US yodeler)
- doodler
- **muddler**, puddler
- hurdler •waffler
- **shuffler**, snuffler
- **haggler**, straggler
- **mangler**, wangler
- finagler
- **giggler**, wiggler, wriggler
- **smuggler**, struggler
- pergola •heckler
- **Agricola**, Nicola, pickler, tickler, tricolour (US tricolor)
- chronicler
- **snorkeller** (US snorkeler)
- chuckler
- **enameller** (US enameler)
- **signaller** (US signaler)
- **tunneller** (US tunneler)
- grappler •stapler
- **stippler**, tippler
- Coppola
- **gospeller** (US gospeler)
- cupola
- **caroller** (US caroler)
- Kerala
- **quarreller** (US quarreler)
- chancellor
- **penciller** (US penciler)
- whistler
- **battler**, prattler, rattler, tattler
- dismantler •startler
- **fettler**, settler, settlor
- **belittler**, victualler (US victualer)
- **hospitaller** (US hospitaler)
- **bottler**, throttler
- **hosteller** (US hosteler)
- **caviller** (US caviler), traveller (US traveler)
- **marveller** (US marveler)

- **leveller** (US leveler), reveller (US reveler)
- **driveller** (US driveler), sniveller (US sniveler)
- **groveller** (US groveler)
- **shoveler**, shoveller
- chiseller (US chiseler), sizzler
- **bamboozler**, methuselah
- guzzler

12.49

- **curler**, pearler, purler, twirler, whirler
- curdler •burglar •Koestler

12.50

- **Alabama**, clamour (US clamor), crammer, gamma, glamour (US glamor), gnamma, grammar, hammer, jammer, lamber, mamma, rammer, shammer, slammer, stammer, yammer
- Padma •magma •drachma
- **Alma**, halma, Palma
- Cranmer •asthma •mahatma
- **miasma**, plasma
- jackhammer •sledgehammer
- yellowhammer •windjammer
- flimflammer •programmer
- **amah**, armour (US armor), Atacama, Brahma, Bramah, charmer, cyclorama, dharma, diorama, disarmer, drama, embalmer, farmer, Kama, karma, lama, llama, Matsuyama, panorama, Parma, pranayama, Rama, Samar, Surinamer, Vasco da Gama, Yama, Yokohama
- snake-charmer •docudrama
- melodrama
- **contemner**, dilemma, Emma, emmer, Jemma, lemma, maremma, stemma, tremor
- **Elmer**, Selma, Thelma, Velma
- Mesmer
- **claimer**, crema, defamer, framer, proclaimer, Shema, tamer

12.51

- **beamer**, blasphemer, Colima, creamer, dreamer, emphysema, femur, Iwo Jima, Kagoshima, lemur, Lima, oedema (*US* edema), ottava rima, Pima, reamer, redeemer, schema, schemer, screamer, seamer, Selima, steamer, streamer, terza rima, Tsushima
- daydreamer
- **dimmer**, glimmer, limber, limner, shimmer, simmer, skimmer, slimmer, strimmer, swimmer, trimmer, zimmer
- **enigma**, sigma, stigma
- **Wilma**, Wilmer
- charisma •Gordimer •polymer
- ulema •anima •enema
- **cinema**, minima
- maxima •Bessemer •eczema
- dulcimer •Hiroshima
- **Fatima**, Latimer
- optima •Mortimer •anathema
- **climber**, Jemima, mimer, old-timer, part-timer, primer, rhymer, timer
- Oppenheimer •two-timer
- **bomber**, comma, momma, prommer
- dogma •dolma

12.52

- **dormer**, former, korma, Norma, performer, pro-forma, stormer, transformer, trauma, warmer
- sixth-former •barnstormer
- **aroma**, carcinoma, chroma, coma, comber, diploma, glaucoma, Homer, lymphoma, melanoma, misnomer, Oklahoma, Omagh, roamer, Roma, romer, sarcoma, soma
- beachcomber
- **bloomer**, boomer, consumer, Duma, humour (*US* humor), Nkrumah, perfumer, puma, roomer, rumour (*US* rumor), satsuma, stumer, Sumer, tumour (*US* tumor)
- zeugma •fulmar
- **bummer**, comer, drummer, hummer, midsummer, mummer, plumber, rummer, strummer, summa, summer
- latecomer •newcomer •agama
- welcomer
- **astronomer**, monomer
- ashrama •isomer •gossamer
- customer
- **affirmer**, Burma, derma, Irma, murmur, squirmer, terra firma, wormer

12.53

- **Alana**, Anna, bandanna, banner, Branagh, canna, canner, Diana, fanner, Fermanagh, Guyana, Hannah, Havana, hosanna, Indiana, Joanna, lanner, Louisiana, manna, manner, manor, Montana, nana, planner, Pollyanna, Rosanna, savannah, scanner, spanner, Susanna, tanner
- Abner •Jaffna •Patna •caravanner
- **Africana**, Afrikaner, Americana, ana, banana, Botswana, bwana, cabana, caragana, Christiana, Dana, darner, Edwardiana, garner, Georgiana, Ghana, Gloriana, Guiana, gymkhana, Haryana, iguana, Lana, lantana, liana, Lipizzaner, Ljubljana, Mahayana, mana, mañana, marijuana, nirvana, Oriana, pacarana, piranha, prana, Purana, Rosh Hashana, Santayana, Setswana, sultana, Tatiana, Tijuana, Tirana, tramontana, Tswana, varna, Victoriana, zenana
- Gardner •partner
- **antenna**, Avicenna, duenna, henna, Jenna, Jenner, Morwenna, Ravenna, senna, Siena, sienna, tenner, tenor, Vienna
- Edna •interregna •Etna •Pevsner

12.54

- **abstainer**, arcana, campaigner, Cana, caner, cantilena, complainer, container, detainer, drainer, entertainer, explainer, Gaenor,

gainer, Gaynor, grainer, Jena, Lena, maintainer, Marlene, N'Djamena, obtainer, ordainer, planar, planer, profaner, Rayner, retainer, scena, seiner, Sinn Feiner, strainer, sustainer, trainer, uniplanar
• straightener
• **Adelina**, Angelina, arena, Argentina, ballerina, Ballymena, Bettina, Bukovina, Burkina, cantina, Cartagena, casuarina, catena, Christina, cleaner, concertina, congener, contravener, convener, Cortina, demeanour (US demeanor), deus ex machina, duodena, Edwina, Ena, farina, Filipina, galena, Georgina, Gina, gleaner, hyena, Ina, intervener, kachina, kina, Magdalena, marina, Martina, Medina, Messalina, Messina, misdemeanour (US misdemeanor), Nina, novena, ocarina, Palestrina, Pasadena, Philomena, piscina, retsina, Rowena, Sabrina, scarlatina, screener, Selina, semolina, Seraphina, Serena, Sheena, signorina, sonatina, subpoena, Taormina, tsarina, verbena, vina, weaner, wiener, Wilhelmina, Zena
• sweetener •pipecleaner

12.55

• **beginner**, Berliner, Corinna, dinner, grinner, inner, Jinnah, sinner, skinner, spinner, thinner, winner
• echidna
• **Krishna**, Mishnah, Ramakrishna
• vintner •prisoner •Pilsner
• Kitchener •Modena •bargainer
• imaginer
• **Elinor**, Helena
• milliner
• **examiner**, stamina
• **epiphenomena**, phenomena, prolegomena
• **alumina**, noumena, numina
• determiner

• **mariner**, submariner
• foreigner •larcener •Porsena
• patina •retina •Pristina
• Herzegovina •breadwinner
• prizewinner
• **angina**, assigner, china, consignor, decliner, definer, Dinah, diner, diviner, forty-niner, hardliner, incliner, Indo-China, liner, maligner, Medina, miner, minor, mynah, recliner, refiner, Regina, Salina, Shekinah, shiner, signer, South Carolina, Steiner, twiner, vagina, whiner
• headliner •jetliner •airliner
• mainliner •eyeliner •moonshiner
• Landsteiner •Niersteiner
• Liechtensteiner

12.56

• **belladonna**, Connor, donna, goner, gonna, honour (US honor), Maradona, Mashona, O'Connor, Shona, wanna
• **corner**, fauna, forewarner, Lorna, Morna, mourner, sauna, scorner, suborner, warner
• softener •Faulkner
• **downer**, uptowner
• sundowner
• **Arizona**, Barcelona, boner, condoner, corona, Cremona, Desdemona, donor, Fiona, groaner, Iona, Jonah, kroner, Leona, loaner, loner, moaner, Mona, owner, Pamplona, persona, postponer, Ramona, stoner, toner, Valona, Verona, Winona
• landowner •homeowner •shipowner
• **coiner**, joiner, purloiner
• **crooner**, harpooner, lacuna, lacunar, lampooner, Luna, lunar, mizuna, Oona, oppugner, Poona, pruner, puna, schooner, spooner, Tristan da Cunha, tuna, tuner, Una, vicuña, yokozuna
• honeymooner •Sunna •Brookner
• koruna

12.57

- **Corunna**, front-runner, gunner, oner, punner, runner, scunner, stunner
- columnar •guv'nor •forerunner
- roadrunner •gunrunner

12.58

- Catriona •ironer •questioner
- **gardener**, hardener, pardoner
- deadener •widener •Londoner
- stiffener •toughener •wagoner
- tobogganer •provisioner •sojourner
- jacana •darkener •reckoner
- weakener
- **sickener**, thickener
- falconer •Eleanor
- **almoner**, Brahmana
- commoner •summoner •dampener
- sharpener •tympana •opener
- coroner •fastener •chastener
- **christener**, listener
- loosener •fashioner •confectioner
- **pensioner**, tensioner
- **probationer**, stationer, vacationer
- **commissioner**, conditioner, exhibitioner, missioner, munitioner, parishioner, partitioner, petitioner, positioner, practitioner, requisitioner
- extortioner •executioner •flattener
- **Smetana**, threatener
- westerner •easterner
- **enlightener**, frightener, whitener
- **lengthener**, strengthener
- marathoner •northerner
- southerner •Taverner •scrivener
- enlivener •governor •Ramayana
- reasoner •poisoner

12.59

- **Annapurna**, burner, discerner, earner, learner, Myrna, Smyrna, spurner, taverna, turner, Verner, Werner, yearner
- woodturner

12.60

- **banger**, clanger, ganger, hangar, hanger, haranguer, Sanger, Stavanger
- headbanger •doppelgänger
- straphanger •cliffhanger
- paperhanger
- **bringer**, clinger, flinger, humdinger, pinger, ringer, singer, slinger, springer, stinger, stringer, swinger, winger, wringer, zinger
- Schrödinger •mud-slinger
- gunslinger •bell-ringer •klipspringer
- Helsingor
- **prolonger**, tonga, wronger
- ponga

12.61

- **clapper**, crapper, dapper, flapper, grappa, kappa, knapper, mapper, nappa, napper, rapper, sapper, scrapper, snapper, strapper, tapper, trapper, wrapper, yapper, Zappa
- **catalpa**, scalper
- **camper**, damper, hamper, pamper, scamper, stamper, Tampa, tamper, tramper
- **Caspar**, jasper
- handicapper •kidnapper
- whippersnapper
- **carper**, harper, scarper, sharper
- **clasper**, gasper, grasper, rasper
- **leper**, pepper, salt-and-pepper
- **helper**, yelper
- temper
- **Vespa**, vesper
- Culpeper •sidestepper
- **caper**, draper, escaper, gaper, paper, raper, scraper, shaper, taper, vapour (*US* vapor)
- sandpaper •endpaper •flypaper
- wallpaper •notepaper •newspaper
- skyscraper
- **Arequipa**, beeper, bleeper, creeper, Dnieper, keeper, leaper, peeper, reaper, sleeper, sweeper, weeper
- gamekeeper •gatekeeper
- **greenkeeper** (*US* greenskeeper)

- peacekeeper •innkeeper
- wicketkeeper •timekeeper
- shopkeeper
- **Scorekeeper**, storekeeper
- housekeeper •goalkeeper
- zookeeper •bookkeeper •treecreeper
- minesweeper

12.62

- **Agrippa**, chipper, clipper, dipper,
  equipper, flipper, gripper, hipper,
  kipper, nipper, Pippa, ripper,
  shipper, sipper, skipper, slipper,
  stripper, tipper, tripper, whipper,
  zipper
- **crimper**, shrimper, simper,
  whimper, Whymper
- **crisper**, whisper
- mudskipper •caliper •Philippa
- juniper •gossiper
- **worshipper** (*US* worshiper)
- **griper**, piper, sniper, swiper, viper,
  wiper
- bagpiper •sandpiper
- **bopper**, chopper, copper, cropper,
  Dopper, dropper, hopper, improper,
  Joppa, poppa, popper, proper,
  shopper, stopper, swapper, topper,
  whopper
- stomper •prosper •bebopper
- teenybopper •grasshopper
- clodhopper •sharecropper
- name-dropper •eavesdropper
- window-shopper •doorstopper
- show-stopper
- **gawper**, pauper, torpor, warper

12.63

- **coper**, doper, eloper, Europa,
  groper, hoper, L-dopa, moper,
  no-hoper, opah, toper
- interloper
- **blooper**, cooper, Cowper, duper,
  grouper, Hooper, looper, pea-souper,
  pupa, scooper, snooper, stupa, stupor,
  super, trooper, trouper, whooper
- pooper-scooper •party-pooper
- paratrooper •mea culpa •chutzpah

- **crupper**, cuppa, scupper, supper,
  upper
- **gulper**, kalpa, pulper
- **bumper**, dumper, gazumper,
  jumper, lumper, stumper, thumper
- showjumper •diaper •galloper
- developer
- **scalloper**, walloper
- **chirper**, sherpa, usurper

12.64

- **jarrah**, para, Tara
- **abracadabra**, Aldabra
- Alhambra •Vanbrugh
- **Cassandra**, Sandra
- **Aphra**, Biafra
- **Niagara**, pellagra, Viagra
- **bhangra**, Ingres
- Capra •Cleopatra
- **mantra**, tantra, yantra
- Basra
- **Asmara**, Bukhara, carbonara,
  Carrara, cascara, Connemara,
  Damara, Ferrara, Gemara,
  Guadalajara, Guevara, Honiara, Lara,
  marinara, mascara, Nara, Sahara,
  Samara, samsara, samskara, shikara,
  Tamara, tiara, Varah, Zara
- **candelabra**, macabre, sabra
- Alexandra •Agra •fiacre
- **Chartres**, Montmartre, Sartre,
  Sinatra, Sumatra
- Shastra •Maharashtra •Le Havre
- gurdwara
- **Berra**, error, Ferrer, sierra, terror
- zebra •ephedra •Porto Alegre
- **belles-lettres**, Petra, raison d'être,
  tetra
- **Electra**, plectra, spectra
- Clytemnestra •extra
- **chèvre**, Sèvres
- Ezra

12.65

- **airer**, bearer, carer, Clara, darer,
  declarer, Demerara, Éire, habanera,
  Halmahera, parer, Perak, primavera,
  repairer, Rivera, Riviera, Sarah,

scarer, sharer, snarer, sparer,
squarer, starer, swearer, tearer,
wearer
- cause célèbre •torch-bearer
- swordbearer •pallbearer •wayfarer
- seafarer •capoeira •Phaedra
- **sacra**, simulacra
- **Libra**, vers libre
- ex cathedra
- **chypre**, Ypres
- **palaestra** (*US* palestra) •urethra
- joie de vivre
- **mirror**, sirrah
- Coimbra •Middlesbrough •Indra
- Sintra
- **aspidistra**, sistra
- algebra •orchestra •vertebra
- **Beira**, Fujairah, Hegira, Lyra, Myra,
naira, palmyra, spirogyra
- Hydra •Lycra
- **begorra**, Gomorrah, horror
- double entendre •genre •amour
propre •Le Nôtre •contra
- **Cosa Nostra**, rostra

12.66

- **abhorrer**, adorer, Andorra, angora,
aura, aurora, bora, Bora-Bora, borer,
Camorra, Cora, corer, Dora,
Eleonora, Eudora, explorer, fedora,
flora, fora, ignorer, Isadora, Kia-Ora,
Laura, Leonora, Maura, menorah,
Nora, pakora, Pandora, pourer,
roarer, scorer, senhora, señora,
signora, snorer, soarer, Sonora, sora,
storer, Theodora, Torah, Tuscarora,
Vlorë
- goalscorer •cobra •okra •Oprah
- Socotra •Moira •Sudra
- chaulmoogra •supra
- **Brahmaputra**, sutra
- Zarathustra •Louvre •fulcra
- Tripura
- **borough**, burgh, Burra, curragh,
demurrer, thorough
- Rubbra
- **penumbra**, umbra
- tundra •chakra •ultra •kookaburra

12.67

- **Altamira**, chimera, clearer, Elvira,
era, hearer, Hera, hetaera,
interferer, lempira, lira, lire,
Madeira, Megaera, monstera,
rangatira, rearer, scorzonera, sera,
shearer, smearer, sneerer, steerer,
Thera, Utsire, Vera

> ℹ️ Create extra rhymes for
> words like clearer by adding -*er*
> to dear and near etc. (see
> section 12.4).

- **acquirer**, admirer, enquirer, firer,
hirer, inquirer, requirer, wirer
- **devourer**, flowerer, scourer
- **Angostura**, Bonaventura, bravura,
Bujumbura, caesura, camera obscura,
coloratura, curer, Dürer, durra,
Estremadura, figura, fioritura,
Führer, insurer, Jura, juror, Madura,
nomenklatura, procurer, sura, surah,
tamboura, tempura, tourer
- **labourer** (*US* laborer) •Canberra
- Attenborough
- **Barbara**, Scarborough
- Marlborough •Farnborough
- Deborah •rememberer
- Gainsborough •Edinburgh
- Aldeburgh •blubberer
- Loughborough
- **lumberer**, slumberer
- Peterborough
- **Berbera**, gerbera
- manufacturer •capturer •lecturer
- posturer •torturer •nurturer
- philanderer •gerrymanderer
- slanderer
- **renderer**, tenderer
- dodderer
- **squanderer**, wanderer
- borderer •launderer •flounderer
- embroiderer •Kundera
- **blunderer**, plunderer, thunderer,
wonderer
- murderer •amphora •pilferer
- offerer •sufferer
- **staggerer**, swaggerer

- sniggerer
- **lingerer**, malingerer
- treasurer • usurer • injurer • conjuror
- perjurer • lacquerer
- **Ankara**, hankerer
- **bickerer**, dickerer
- tinkerer • conqueror • heuchera
- cellarer • cholera
- **camera**, stammerer
- **armourer** (*US* armorer)
- **ephemera**, remora
- kumara • woomera • murmurer
- Tanagra • genera • gunnera
- **Tampere**, tamperer
- Diaspora
- **emperor**, Klemperer, tempera, temperer
- **caperer**, paperer
- whimperer • whisperer • opera
- corpora • tessera • viscera • sorcerer
- **adventurer**, venturer
- **batterer**, chatterer, flatterer, natterer, scatterer, shatterer
- banterer
- **barterer**, charterer
- plasterer • shelterer • pesterer
- et cetera • caterer
- **titterer**, twitterer
- **potterer**, totterer
- fosterer
- **slaughterer**, waterer
- **falterer**, palterer
- saunterer • poulterer
- **bolsterer**, upholsterer
- loiterer • roisterer • fruiterer
- **flutterer**, mutterer, splutterer, stutterer, utterer
- adulterer • musterer • plethora
- gatherer • ditherer • furtherer
- **favourer** (*US* favorer), waverer
- **deliverer**, shiverer
- hoverer
- **manoeuvrer** (*US* maneuverer)
- **discoverer**, recoverer

12.68

- **deferrer**, demurrer, referrer, stirrer, transferor, transferrer
- chef-d'œuvre, oeuvre

12.69

- **amasser**, gasser, macassar, Makassar, Mombasa, Nasser
- **relaxer**, waxer
- salsa
- **cancer**, romancer
- piazza • necromancer • madrasa
- **Kinshasa**, Lhasa, passer, Tarrasa, Vaasa
- **advancer**, answer, chancer, dancer, enhancer, lancer, prancer
- tazza
- **addresser**, aggressor, assessor, compressor, confessor, contessa, depressor, digresser, dresser, guesser, intercessor, lesser, Odessa, oppressor, possessor, professor, represser, successor, transgressor, Vanessa
- **Alexa**, flexor, vexer
- **Elsa**, Kielce
- **censer**, censor, dispenser, fencer, Mensa, sensor, Spenser
- seltzer
- **Faenza**, Henze
- indexer • hairdresser • predecessor
- **microprocessor**, processor
- **acer**, bracer, chaser, debaser, embracer, facer, macer, mesa, pacer, placer, racer, spacer, tracer
- Ailsa • steeplechaser
- **greaser**, Lisa, Nerissa, piecer, Raisa, releaser
- pizza

12.70

- **Alissa**, Clarissa, kisser, Larissa, Marisa, Melissa, Orissa, reminiscer
- **fixer**, mixer, sixer
- **convincer**, mincer, pincer, rinser, wincer
- **Amritsar**, Maritsa, spritzer
- howitzer • kibitzer • purchaser
- artificer • officer • surfacer • Pulitzer
- Wurlitzer • promiser • harnesser
- menacer
- **practiser** (*US* practicer)
- **de-icer**, dicer, enticer, gricer, paise,

pricer, ricer, slicer, splicer
- Schweitzer
- **Barbarossa**, dosser, embosser, fossa, glosser, josser, Ossa, Saragossa, tosser
- boxer •sponsor •matzo •bobbysoxer
- **Chaucer**, courser, endorser (*US* indorser), enforcer, forcer, reinforcer, saucer, Xhosa
- **balsa**, waltzer
- **dowser**, grouser, Hausa, mouser, Scouser
- **announcer**, bouncer, denouncer, pouncer, pronouncer, renouncer, trouncer
- schnauzer

12.71

- **anorexia nervosa**, bulimia nervosa, curiosa, Formosa, grocer, samosa, Via Dolorosa
- **coaxer**, hoaxer
- greengrocer
- **rejoicer**, voicer
- **Abu Musa**, Appaloosa, babirusa, inducer, introducer, juicer, producer, reducer, rusa, seducer, sprucer, traducer
- **discusser**, fusser, trusser
- **propulsor**, Tulsa, ulcer
- oncer •conveyancer •piercer
- influencer •Odense •balancer
- silencer •grimacer •trespasser
- harasser •remembrancer
- **licenser**, licensor
- traverser •canvasser •sequencer
- **bursar**, converser, curser, cursor, disburser, mercer, purser, rehearser, reverser, vice versa

12.72

- **Asher**, clasher, Falasha, flasher, lasher, masher, Natasha, pasha, rasher, Sasha, slasher, smasher, thrasher
- haberdasher •gatecrasher •Marsha
- rancher
- **flesher**, fresher, pressure, thresher

- welsher
- **adventure**, bencher, censure, dementia, front-bencher, trencher, venture, wencher
- backbencher •acupressure
- **acacia**, Asia, Croatia, Dalmatia, ex gratia, geisha
- **Lucretia**, magnesia, Rhodesia, Venetia
- **Fischer**, fisher, fissure, justiciar, Laetitia, militia, Patricia, Phoenicia, Tricia
- **clincher**, flincher, lyncher, wincher
- Frobisher •furbisher •brandisher
- Yiddisher •kingfisher •establisher
- embellisher
- **abolisher**, demolisher, polisher
- publisher •skirmisher •replenisher
- finisher •punisher
- **burnisher**, furnisher
- perisher
- **flourisher**, nourisher
- Britisher •ravisher •languisher
- vanquisher •well-wisher
- extinguisher •Elisha

12.73

- **josher**, washer
- moksha •tonsure •dishwasher
- whitewasher •Portia •launcher
- **brochure**, kosher, Scotia
- fuchsia •pusher •penpusher
- **blusher**, crusher, flusher, gusher, Prussia, rusher, Russia, usher
- **cruncher**, luncher, puncher
- cowpuncher •Udmurtia
- **inertia**, Persia

12.74

- **attar**, batter, bespatter, chatter, clatter, flatter, hatter, Kenyatta, latter, matamata, matter, natter, patter, platter, ratter, regatta, satyr, scatter, shatter, smatter, spatter, splatter, yatter
- **abstractor**, actor, attractor, compactor, contractor, enactor,

exactor, extractor, factor, infractor, protractor, redactor, refractor, tractor, transactor

• **Atlanta**, banter, canter, infanta, levanter, manta, ranter, Santa, tam-o'-shanter
• **adaptor**, captor, chapter, raptor
• **Antofagasta**, aster, Astor, canasta, Jocasta, oleaster, pasta, piastre (*US* piaster), pilaster, poetaster, Rasta, Zoroaster
• **dragster**, gagster
• Baxter •prankster •hamster
• **gangsta**, gangster
• malefactor •benefactor
• pitter-patter •subcontractor
• chiropractor • oviraptor

12.75

• **barter**, Bata, cantata, carter, cassata, charter, chipolata, ciabatta, darter, desiderata, errata, garter, imprimatur, Inkatha, Jakarta, Magna Carta, Maratha, martyr, Odonata, passata, persona non grata, rata, Renata, Río de la Plata, serenata, sonata, Sparta, starter, strata, taramasalata, tartar, Tatar, Zapata
• **after**, drafter, grafter, hereafter, laughter, rafter, thereafter, whereafter
• **chanter**, enchanter, granter, planter, supplanter, transplanter, Vedanta
• **blaster**, caster, castor, faster, grandmaster, headmaster, master, pastor, plaster
• alabaster •telecaster •forecaster
• broadcaster •sportscaster
• newscaster •sandblaster
• bandmaster •taskmaster
• pastmaster •paymaster •ringmaster
• quizmaster •spymaster
• housemaster •Scoutmaster
• toastmaster •schoolmaster
• harbourmaster (*US* harbormaster)
• quartermaster •substrata
• sought-after

12.76

• **abetter**, begetter, better, bettor, biretta, bruschetta, carburettor (*US* carburetor), debtor, feta, fetter, forgetter, getter, go-getter, Greta, Henrietta, letter, Loretta, mantelletta, operetta, petter, Quetta, setter, sinfonietta, sweater, upsetter, Valletta, vendetta, whetter
• **bisector**, collector, connector, convector, corrector, defector, deflector, detector, director, ejector, elector, erector, hector, injector, inspector, nectar, objector, perfecter, projector, prospector, protector, rector, reflector, rejector, respecter, sector, selector, Spector, spectre (*US* specter), vector
• **belter**, delta, helter-skelter, melter, pelta, Shelta, shelter, swelter, welter
• **pre-emptor**, tempter
• **assenter**, cementer, centre (*US* center), concentre (*US* concenter), dissenter, enter, eventer, fermenter (*US* fermentor), fomenter, frequenter, inventor, lamenter, magenta, placenta, polenta, precentor, presenter, preventer, renter, repenter, tenter, tormentor
• **inceptor**, preceptor, receptor, sceptre (*US* scepter)
• **arrester**, Avesta, Chester, contester, ester, Esther, fester, fiesta, Hester, investor, jester, Leicester, Lester, molester, Nestor, pester, polyester, protester, quester, semester, sequester, siesta, sou'wester, suggester, tester, trimester, vesta, zester
• Webster •dexter •Leinster
• Dorchester •Poindexter •newsletter
• genuflector •implementer
• experimenter •trendsetter
• **epicentre** (*US* epicenter)
• typesetter •jobcentre •photosetter
• Cirencester •interceptor •Sylvester

12.77

- **cater**, crater, creator, curator, data, debater, delator, dumbwaiter, equator, fascinator, freighter, frustrater, gaiter, grater, gyrator, hater, later, legator, mater, negator, pater, peseta, plater, rotator, skater, slater, stater, tater, traitor, ultimata, understater, upstater, waiter

> ℹ️ Create extra rhymes for words like crater by adding *-er* to collate etc. (see section 30.7).

- painter
- **taster**, waster
- gamester •aviator •tailgater
- hesitater •shirtwaister
- **Akita**, Anita, arboreta, beater, beta, Bhagavadgita, cheater, cheetah, Demeter, Dieter, dolce vita, eater, eta, Evita, excreta, fetor, granita, greeter, heater, Juanita, litre (*US* liter), Lolita, maltreater, margarita, meter, metre, Peta, peter, praetor (*US* pretor), repeater, Rita, saltpetre (*US* saltpeter), secretor, Senhorita, señorita, Sita, skeeter, teeter, terra incognita, theta, treater, tweeter, ureter, veleta, zeta
- **Batista**, Dniester, Easter, feaster, keister, leister, quaestor
- speedster
- **deemster**, teamster
- scenester •browbeater •windcheater
- beefeater
- **millilitre** (*US* milliliter)
- **decilitre** (*US* deciliter)
- **centilitre** (*US* centiliter)
- **kilolitre** (*US* kiloliter)
- ammeter •Machmeter
- **millimetre** (*US* millimeter)
- **decimetre** (*US* decimeter)
- altimeter
- **centimetre** (*US* centimeter)
- **nanometre** (*US* nanometer)
- **micrometer**, micrometre
- **decametre** (*US* dekameter)
- **kilometre** (*US* kilometer) •autopista
- anteater

12.78

- **bitter**, committer, critter, embitter, emitter, fitter, flitter, fritter, glitter, gritter, hitter, jitter, knitter, litter, permitter, pitta, quitter, remitter, sitter, skitter, slitter, spitter, splitter, submitter, titter, transmitter, twitter, witter
- **drifter**, grifter, lifter, shifter, sifter, snifter, uplifter
- **constrictor**, contradictor, depicter, dicta, evictor, inflicter, predictor, victor
- **filter**, kilter, philtre (*US* philter), quilter, tilter
- **Jacinta**, midwinter, Minter, Pinta, Pinter, printer, splinter, sprinter, tinter, winter
- sphincter
- **assister**, ballista, bistre (*US* bister), blister, enlister, glister, lister, mister, resistor, Sandinista, sister, transistor, tryster, twister, vista
- trickster
- **minster**, spinster
- **hipster**, quipster, tipster
- cohabiter •arbiter •presbyter
- **exhibitor**, inhibitor, prohibiter
- Manchester •Chichester •Silchester
- Rochester •Colchester
- **creditor**, editor, subeditor
- auditor •Perdita •taffeta •shopfitter
- forfeiter •outfitter •counterfeiter
- register •marketer
- **cricketer**, picketer
- Alistair •weightlifter •filleter
- fillister •shoplifter
- **diameter**, heptameter, hexameter, parameter, pentameter, tetrameter
- Axminster •Westminster
- **limiter**, perimeter, scimitar, velocimeter
- **accelerometer**, anemometer, barometer, gasometer, geometer, manometer, micrometer, milometer, olfactometer, optometer, pedometer, photometer, pyrometer, speedometer, swingometer, tachometer, thermometer

- Kidderminster • janitor
- **banister**, canister
- **primogenitor**, progenitor, senator
- **administer**, maladminister, minister, sinister
- monitor • per capita • carpenter
- spanakopita • Jupiter • trumpeter
- character • barrister • ferreter
- teleprinter
- **chorister**, forester
- **interpreter**, misinterpreter
- capacitor • ancestor • Exeter
- stepsister
- **elicitor**, solicitor
- babysitter • house-sitter • bullshitter
- competitor • catheter • harvester
- riveter • banqueter • non sequitur
- loquitur
- **inquisitor**, visitor
- **compositor**, expositor

12.79

- **all-nighter**, biter, blighter, fighter, igniter, inciter, indicter, inviter, lighter, mitre (*US* miter), overnighter, reciter, righter, sighter, smiter, writer

> ℹ Create extra rhymes for words like writer by adding -er to bright and tight etc. (see section 30.26).

- shyster • rhymester • backbiter
- expediter • prizefighter • dogfighter
- bullfighter • gunfighter • lamplighter
- highlighter • downlighter
- moonlighter • uplighter • firelighter
- screenwriter • scriptwriter
- copywriter • signwriter • typewriter
- songwriter • ghostwriter
- underwriter
- **blotter**, cotta, cottar, dotter, gotta, hotter, jotter, knotter, otter, pelota, plotter, potter, ricotta, rotter, spotter, squatter, terracotta, totter, trotter
- crofter
- **concocter**, doctor, proctor

- Volta • prompter • wanter
- **adopter**, dioptre
- **Costa**, coster, defroster, foster, Gloucester, impostor, paternoster, roster
- **lobster**, mobster
- oxter • monster • songster
- witchdoctor • helicopter
- teleprompter • globetrotter

12.80

- **aorta**, daughter, exhorter, exporter, extorter, Horta, importer, mortar, porter, quarter, slaughter, snorter, sorter, sporter, supporter, three-quarter, torte, transporter, underwater, water
- **altar**, alter, assaulter, defaulter, falter, Gibraltar, halter, Malta, palter, psalter, salter, vaulter, Walter
- **flaunter**, haunter, saunter, taunter, vaunter
- **exhauster**, Forster
- fraudster • granddaughter
- stepdaughter • manslaughter
- ripsnorter • pole-vaulter • backwater
- headquarter • freshwater
- breakwater • rainwater • seawater
- dishwater • flatwater • tidewater
- Whitewater • saltwater • rosewater
- shearwater • firewater
- **doubter**, grouter, outer, pouter, scouter, shouter, spouter, touter
- **counter**, encounter, mounter
- **jouster**, ouster
- revcounter
- **bloater**, boater, Botha, Dakota, doter, emoter, floater, gloater, iota, Kota, Minnesota, motor, promoter, quota, rota, rotor, scoter, voter
- **bolter**, coulter (*US* colter), Volta
- **boaster**, coaster, poster, roaster, toaster
- roadster • oldster
- **bolster**, holster, pollster, soulster, upholster
- billposter

12.81

- **exploiter**, goitre (*US* goiter), loiter, reconnoitre (*US* reconnoiter), Reuter
- **anointer**, appointer, jointer, pointer
- **cloister**, hoister, oyster, roister
- **accoutre** (*US* accouter), commuter, computer, disputer, hooter, looter, neuter, pewter, polluter, recruiter, refuter, rooter, saluter, scooter, shooter, souter, suitor, tooter, transmuter, tutor, uprooter
- **booster**, rooster
- doomster •freebooter •sharpshooter
- peashooter •six-shooter
- troubleshooter •prosecutor
- persecutor •prostitutor
- telecommuter
- **footer**, putter
- Gupta •Worcester •Münster
- pussyfooter •executor
- **contributor**, distributor
- **collocutor**, interlocutor
- **abutter**, aflutter, butter, Calcutta, clutter, constructor, cutter, declutter, flutter, gutter, mutter, nutter, scutter, shutter, splutter, sputter, strutter, stutter, utter
- **abductor**, conductor, destructor, instructor, obstructor
- insulter
- **Arunta**, Bunter, chunter, Grantha, grunter, Gunter, hunter, junta, punter, shunter
- **corrupter**, disrupter, interrupter
- sculptor
- **adjuster**, Augusta, bluster, buster, cluster, Custer, duster, fluster, lustre (*US* luster), muster, thruster, truster
- huckster •Ulster •dumpster
- **funster**, Munster, punster
- **funkster**, youngster
- gangbuster •filibuster •blockbuster
- semiconductor •headhunter
- woodcutter
- **lacklustre** (*US* lackluster)

12.82

- **theatre** (*US* theater)
- realtor

- **amphitheatre** (*US* amphitheater)
- **proprietor**, rioter
- breakfaster •comforter •Lancaster
- Doncaster
- **Alasdair**, baluster
- **bardolater**, idolater
- **amateur**, shamateur
- schemata •stigmata •automata
- traumata •covenanter
- Mahabharata •orator •warranter
- **Alberta**, asserter, Bizerta, converter, deserter, Goethe, inserter, kurta, perverter, reverter, subverter
- frankfurter

12.83

- Cather •naphtha
- **anther**, panther, Samantha
- **Arthur**, MacArthur, Martha
- **ether**, Ibiza
- Tabitha •Hiawatha •author •Gotha
- Luther •Gunther •Agatha •Golgotha
- **Bertha**, Jugurtha

12.84

- **blather**, foregather, gather, slather
- **farther**, father, lather, rather
- grandfather •stepfather •godfather
- forefather
- **altogether**, feather, heather, leather, nether, tether, together, weather, wether, whether

> Create extra rhymes by
> adding -*ing* to words like feather.　　i

- bather •sunbather
- **bequeather**, breather
- **dither**, hither, slither, swither, thither, whither, wither, zither
- **either**, neither
- **bother**, pother
- Rhondda •mouther •loather
- **smoother**, soother
- **another**, brother, mother, other, smother, t'other
- grandmother •stepmother
- godmother •housemother
- stepbrother •further

12.85

- **cadaver**, slaver
- **halva**, salver, salvor
- **balaclava**, Bratislava, carver, cassava, Costa Brava, guava, Java, kava, larva, lava, palaver
- woodcarver
- **clever**, endeavour (*US* endeavor), ever, forever, however, howsoever, never, never-never, sever, Trevor, whatever, whatsoever, whenever, whensoever, wheresoever, wherever, whichever, whichsoever, whoever, whomever, whomsoever, whosoever
- **delver**, elver
- Denver
- **Ava**, caver, craver, deva, engraver, enslaver, favour (*US* favor), flavour (*US* flavor), graver, haver, laver, paver, quaver, raver, saver, savour (*US* savor), shaver, vena cava, waiver, waver
- lifesaver •semiquaver
- **achiever**, beaver, believer, cleaver, deceiver, diva, Eva, fever, Geneva, griever, heaver, leaver, lever, Neva, perceiver, receiver, reiver, reliever, retriever, Shiva, underachiever, viva, weaver, weever
- cantilever

12.86

- **aquiver**, downriver, forgiver, giver, quiver, river, shiver, sliver, upriver
- silver •mitzvah •lawgiver •Oliver
- **miniver**, Nineveh
- quicksilver
- **conniver**, contriver, diver, driver, fiver, Godiva, Ivor, jiver, Liver, reviver, saliva, skiver, striver, survivor, viva
- skydiver •slave-driver •piledriver
- screwdriver
- **bovver**, hover
- Moskva
- **revolver**, solver
- windhover
- **Canova**, Casanova, clover, Dover, drover, Grsbover, Jehovah, left-over,

Markova, Moldova, moreover, Navrátilová, nova, ova, over, Pavlova, rover, trover, up-and-over
- layover •flyover •handover
- changeover
- **makeover**, takeover
- walkover •spillover •pullover
- Hanover •turnover •hangover
- wingover •sleepover •slipover
- **popover**, stopover
- Passover •crossover •once-over
- pushover •leftover

12.87

- **disapprover**, hoover, improver, louvre (*US* louver), manoeuvre (*US* maneuver), mover, outmanoeuvre (*US* outmaneuver), reprover, Suva, Tuva, Vancouver
- **cover**, Glover, hardcover, lover, plover, undercover
- vulva •triumvir •slipcover •Cordova
- baklava •helluva •Ulanova •Genova
- Vaishnava •Ostrava •Vltava
- **fervour** (*US* fervor), Minerva, Nerva, observer, server, swerver
- time-server

12.88

- Aconcagua
- **aqua**, sub-aqua
- **Chihuahua**, Kurosawa, Massawa, Okinawa, Tokugawa
- Qwaqwa •Quechua
- **Chichewa**, rewarewa
- Ojibwa •Interlingua •siliqua •Iowa
- Medawar •Te Kanawa •Ottawa

12.89

- Antakya
- **Britannia**, lasagne
- Katya •Vanya
- **Kenya**, Mantegna, Sardegna, tenure
- failure •Montagna
- **behaviour** (*US* behavior), misbehaviour (*US* misbehavior),

saviour (*US* savior)
- **seguidilla**, tortilla
- Monsignor
- **Melanesia**, Micronesia, Polynesia
- Tigrinya •De Falla •Vaisya
- Lockyer •Bologna •sawyer •bowyer
- **alleluia**, hallelujah
- La Coruña
- **bunya**, gunyah

12.90

- **Balthazar**, Belshazzar, jazzer
- **bonanza**, Braganza, Constanza, extravaganza, kwanza, organza, Panzer, stanza
- **parser**, plaza, tabula rasa
- Shevardnadze •dopiaza
- Nebuchadnezzar •Demelza
- **cadenza**, cleanser, credenza, influenza, Penza
- **appraiser**, blazer, eraser, Fraser, gazer, glazer, grazer, laser, mazer, praiser, razor, salmanazar, taser, Weser
- stargazer •trailblazer •hellraiser
- **appeaser**, Caesar, easer, Ebenezer, El Giza, freezer, geezer, geyser, Louisa, Pisa, seizer, squeezer, teaser, Teresa, Theresa, visa, wheezer
- crowd-pleaser •stripteaser
- **fizzer**, quizzer, scissor
- Windsor

12.91

- **adviser**, chastiser, coryza, despiser, deviser, divisor, Dreiser, Eliza, incisor, Kaiser, Liza, miser, Mount Isa, provisor, reviser, riser, sizer, visor
- aggrandizer •subsidizer
- merchandiser •standardizer
- methodizer •philosophizer
- mythologizer •catechizer

- **immobilizer**, mobilizer
- utilizer •idealizer •verbalizer
- idolizer •evangelizer
- **nationalizer**, rationalizer
- monopolizer •moralizer •neutralizer
- liberalizer •generalizer •catalyser
- tantalizer •totalizer •Breathalyzer
- civilizer •minimizer •maximizer
- victimizer •systemizer •itemizer
- economizer •compromiser
- atomizer •mechanizer
- homogenizer •scrutinizer
- immunizer •lionizer •modernizer
- organizer •recognizer •colonizer
- womanizer •sermonizer •patronizer
- synchronizer •westernizer
- theorizer •plagiarizer •tenderizer
- deodorizer •popularizer •memorizer
- mesmerizer •summarizer
- temporizer •terrorizer •enterpriser
- pulverizer •criticizer •exerciser
- franchiser •proselytizer •sanitizer
- sensitizer •privatizer •systematizer
- advertiser •sympathizer •improviser
- rozzer •bonzer
- **causer**, hawser

12.92

- **bowser**, browser, carouser, dowser, espouser, Mauser, rouser, trouser, wowser
- rabble-rouser
- **composer**, discloser, dozer, exposer, Mendoza, mimosa, opposer, ponderosa, poser, proposer, proser, Rosa, Somoza, Spinoza
- bulldozer •Tannhäuser
- **abuser**, accuser, boozer, bruiser, chooser, cruiser, diffuser, infuser, lollapalooza, loser, Marcuse, medusa, mezuzah, misuser, peruser, refuser, snoozer, Sousa, user, yakuza
- battlecruiser •buzzer

Section 13: **-er**

- à deux, agent provocateur, astir, auteur, aver, bestir, blur, bon viveur, burr, Chandigarh, coiffeur, concur, confer, connoisseur, cordon-bleu, cri de cœur, cur, danseur, Darfur, defer, demur, de rigueur, deter, entrepreneur, er, err, farceur, faute de mieux, fir, flâneur, Fleur, force majeure, fur, hauteur, her, infer, inter, jongleur, Kerr, littérateur, longueur, masseur, Monseigneur, monsieur, Montesquieu, Montreux, murre, myrrh, occur, pas de deux, Pasteur, per, pisteur, poseur, pot-au-feu, prefer, prie-dieu, pudeur, purr, raconteur, rapporteur, refer, répétiteur, restaurateur, saboteur, sabreur, seigneur, Sher, shirr, sir, skirr, slur, souteneur, spur, stir, tant mieux, transfer, Ur, vieux jeu, voyageur, voyeur, were, whirr

13.2

- transfer

13.3

- langur

13.4

- larkspur •hotspur

13.5

- milieu •Richelieu

Section 14: -b

14.1

- **blab**, cab, confab, crab, Crabbe, dab, drab, fab, flab, gab, grab, jab, kebab, lab, nab, scab, slab, smash-and-grab, stab, tab

> ℹ Create extra rhymes by adding -(b)y to words like fab.

- Moab • baobab • rehab • pedicab
- minicab • taxicab • Skylab

14.2

- **barb**, carb, garb, hijab, nawab, Punjab, sahib
- rhubarb • mihrab

14.3

- **Aurangzeb**, bleb, celeb, deb, ebb, pleb, reb, web, Webb
- Caleb • Deneb • Zagreb • cobweb

14.4

- **fines herbes**, Malherbe

14.5

- **Abe**, babe
- astrolabe

14.6

- **Antibes**, Beeb, Delibes, dweeb, glebe, grebe, Maghrib, plebe

14.7

- **bib**, crib, dib, fib, glib, jib, lib, nib, rib, sib, snib, squib
- memsahib • Carib • sparerib
- Sennacherib

14.8

- **ascribe**, bribe, gybe, imbibe, jibe, proscribe, scribe, subscribe, transcribe, tribe, vibe
- diatribe • circumscribe

14.9

- **blob**, bob, cob, dob, fob, glob, gob, hob, job, knob, lob, mob, nob, rob, slob, snob, sob, squab, stob, swab, throb, yob

> ℹ Create extra rhymes by changing words like bob to bobbing.

- nabob • skibob • thingamabob
- corncob • hobnob • doorknob
- heartthrob

14.10

- **absorb**, bedaub, daub, orb, sorb

14.11

- **daube**, enrobe, globe, Job, lobe, probe, robe, strobe
- Anglophobe • technophobe
- homophobe • xenophobe • earlobe
- bathrobe • microbe • wardrobe

14.12

- **boob**, cube, droob, j'adoube, jube, lube, rube, tube
- jujube • Danube

14.13

- **blub**, bub, chub, Chubb, club, cub, drub, dub, flub, grub, hub, nub, pub, rub, scrub, shrub, slub, snub, stub, sub, tub
- Beelzebub • hubbub • syllabub
- wolfcub • nightclub • bathtub
- twintub • washtub

14.14

- Jacob
- **Arab**, carob, scarab, Shatt al-Arab
- cherub

14.15

- **acerb**, blurb, curb, disturb, herb, kerb, perturb, Serb, superb, verb
- suburb • potherb • willowherb
- exurb • adverb • proverb

14.16

- alb • Elbe • stilb • bulb • flashbulb

Section 15: -ch

15.1

- **attach**, batch, catch, crosshatch, detach, hatch, latch, match, mismatch, natch, outmatch, patch, scratch, snatch, thatch
- Lukács • eyepatch • crosspatch
- sasquatch

15.2

- **arch**, larch, march, parch, starch
- frogmarch • cornstarch

15.3

- **etch**, fetch, ketch, kvetch, lech, outstretch, retch, sketch, stretch, vetch, wretch
- backstretch

15.4

- **mph**, pH, Rh

15.5

- **beach**, beech, beseech, bleach, breach, breech, each, impeach, leach, leech, outreach, peach, pleach, preach, reach, screech, speech, teach

> Create extra rhymes by adding *-ing* to words like beseech. ⓘ

- horseleech

15.6

- **bewitch**, bitch, ditch, enrich, fitch, flitch, glitch, hitch, itch, kitsch, Mitch, pitch, quitch, rich, snitch, stitch, switch, titch, twitch, which, witch

> Create extra rhymes by adding *-ed* to words like bewitch. ⓘ

- Redditch • Greenwich • eldritch
- ostrich • backstitch • hemstitch
- topstitch • Shostakovich • tsarevich
- Sandwich
- **dipswitch**, Ipswich

In the opening stanzas of this nonsense poem, Lewis Carroll invents words to rhyme with each other. It is one way to ensure you get a perfect rhyme!

'Twas brillig, and the slithy toves
    Did gyre and gimble in the wabe:
All mimsy were the borogoves,
    And the mome raths outgrabe.

''Beware the Jabberwock, my son!
    The jaws that bite, the claws that catch!
Beware the Jubjub bird, and shun
    The frumious Bandersnatch!''

(Lewis Carroll, 'Jabberwocky')

15.7

- **blotch**, botch, crotch, notch, outwatch, scotch, splotch, swatch, topnotch, watch
- hopscotch •butterscotch
- hotchpotch •wristwatch •skywatch
- fobwatch •dogwatch •stopwatch

15.8

- **debauch**, nautch, porch, scorch, torch
- blowtorch

15.9

- **avouch**, couch, crouch, debouch, grouch, ouch, pouch, slouch, vouch

15.10

- **approach**, broach, brooch, coach, encroach, loach, poach, reproach, roach
- stagecoach •slowcoach •cockroach

15.11

- **hooch**, mooch, pooch, smooch

15.12

- **butch**, putsch

15.13

- **clutch**, crutch, Dutch, hutch, inasmuch, insomuch, much, mutch, scutch, such, thrutch, touch
- nonesuch

15.14

- **besmirch**, birch, church, lurch, perch, search, smirch
- Christchurch •pikeperch
- wordsearch

15.15

- **belch**, squelch
- **filch**, zilch
- gulch

Section 16: **-d**

16.1

- **ad**, add, Allahabad, bad, Baghdad, bedad, begad, cad, Chad, clad, dad, egad, fad, forbade, gad, glad, grad, had, jihad, lad, mad, pad, plaid, rad, Riyadh, sad, scad, shad, Strad, tad, trad
- chiliad • oread
- **dryad**, dyad, naiad, triad
- Sinbad • Ahmadabad • Jalalabad
- Faisalabad • Islamabad • Hyderabad
- grandad • Soledad • Trinidad
- doodad • Galahad • Akkad • ecad
- **cycad**, nicad
- ironclad • nomad • maenad
- **monad**, trichomonad
- gonad • scratch pad • sketch pad
- keypad • helipad • launch pad
- notepad • footpad • touch pad • farad
- tetrad • Stalingrad • Leningrad
- Conrad • Titograd • undergrad
- Volgograd • Petrograd • hexad
- Mossad • Upanishad • pentad
- heptad • octad

16.2

- **Assad**, aubade, avant-garde, backyard, ballade, bard, Bernard, bombard, canard, card, charade, chard, couvade, croustade, Cunard, facade, glissade, guard, hard, ill-starred, interlard, lard, Montagnard, nard, pard, petard, pomade, promenade, regard, retard, rodomontade, roulade, saccade, Sade, salade, sard, shard, unmarred, unscarred, yard

> Create extra rhymes for [i] words like bard by adding -(r)ed to words like mar and star etc. (see section 1.1)

- Bayard • galliard • Savoyard
- Svalbard
- **bombarde**, Lombard
- Goddard • blackguard • vanguard
- Asgard • safeguard • Midgard
- bodyguard • lifeguard • Bogarde
- coastguard • mudguard • rearguard
- fireguard • Kierkegaard • diehard
- blowhard
- **Jacquard**, placard
- flashcard • railcard • racecard • Picard
- scorecard • showcard • phonecard
- **Ballard**, mallard
- Willard • Abelard • bollard • Barnard
- **Maynard**, reynard
- communard • Oudenarde • Stoppard
- Gerard • Everard • brassard
- **Hansard**, mansard
- Trenchard • Ostade • leotard
- boulevard • scrapyard • farmyard
- barnyard • graveyard • brickyard
- shipyard
- **dockyard**, stockyard
- foreyard • courtyard • boatyard
- woodyard • junkyard • churchyard

16.3

- **abed**, ahead, bed, behead, Birkenhead, bled, bread, bred, coed, cred, crossbred, dead, dread, Ed, embed, Enzed, fed, fled, Fred, gainsaid, head, infrared, ked, lead, led, Med, misled, misread, Ned, outspread, premed, pure-bred, read, red, redd, said, samoyed, shed, shred, sked, sled, sped, Spithead, spread, stead, ted, thread, tread, underbred, underfed, wed
- trackbed • flatbed • deathbed
- airbed • daybed • seabed

- **reed bed**, seedbed
- sickbed •childbed •hotbed •roadbed
- footbed •sunbed •sofa bed
- waterbed •feather bed •breastfed
- dripfed •spoonfed •Szeged
- blackhead
- **cathead**, fathead, Flathead
- masthead
- **bedhead**, deadhead, redhead
- egghead
- **airhead**, stairhead
- railhead •maidenhead •Gateshead
- beachhead •greenhead •meathead
- bighead •bridgehead
- **dickhead**, thickhead
- **pinhead**, skinhead
- pithead •Holyhead •sleepyhead
- fountainhead •whitehead •godhead
- blockhead
- **drophead**, hophead, mophead
- hothead •hogshead
- **sorehead**, warhead
- Roundhead •bonehead •arrowhead
- bullhead •wooden-head •sub-head
- bulkhead
- **chucklehead**, knucklehead
- drumhead •muttonhead •spearhead
- go-ahead •dunderhead •figurehead
- loggerhead •hammerhead
- letterhead •bobsled •cirriped •biped
- moped •quadruped

16.4

- flatbread •bedspread •teabread
- sweetbread •retread •crispbread
- wingspread •widespread •cornbread
- shortbread •sowbread •proofread
- pure-bred •gingerbread
- thoroughbred •aforesaid •Holinshed
- cowshed •woodshed •woolshed
- bloodshed •watershed •Stansted
- farmstead •bedstead •Hemel

Hempstead •roadstead •homestead
- newly-wed

16.5

- **Baird**, hearing-impaired, laird, shit-scared, undeclared, underprepared, unimpaired, unpaired, unprepared, unshared

> Create extra rhymes for words like laird by adding -d to care etc. (see section 2.1). ℹ

16.6

- **abrade**, afraid, aid, aide, ambuscade, arcade, balustrade, barricade, Belgrade, blade, blockade, braid, brigade, brocade, cannonade, carronade, cascade, cavalcade, cockade, colonnade, crusade, dissuade, downgrade, enfilade, esplanade, evade, fade, fusillade, glade, grade, grenade, grillade, handmade, harlequinade, homemade, invade, jade, lade, laid, lemonade, limeade, made, maid, man-made, marinade, masquerade, newlaid, orangeade, paid, palisade, parade, pasquinade, persuade, pervade, raid, serenade, shade, Sinéad, spade, staid, stockade, stock-in-trade, suede, tailor-made, they'd, tirade, trade, Ubaid, underpaid, undismayed, unplayed, unsprayed, unswayed, upbraid, upgrade, wade

> Create extra rhymes for words like abrade by adding -ed to array etc. (see section 3.1). ℹ

Unstressed (or *feminine*) *rhymes* have at least one unstressed syllable following the final stress of the rhyme-word:

Christians have burned each other, quite persuaded
That all the Apostles would have done as they did.

(Lord Byron, 'Don Juan')

- nightshade • renegade • decade
- Medicaid • motorcade • switchblade
- Adelaide • accolade • rollerblade
- marmalade • razor blade • handmaid
- barmaid • Teasmade • milkmaid
- dairymaid • bridesmaid • housemaid
- chambermaid
- parlourmaid (US parlormaid)
- mermaid • nursemaid • escapade
- ram raid • centigrade • multigrade
- comrade • retrograde • lampshade
- eyeshade • sunshade

16.7

- **accede**, bead, Bede, bleed, breed, cede, concede, creed, deed, Eid, exceed, feed, Gide, God speed, greed, he'd, heed, impede, interbreed, intercede, Jamshid, knead, lead, mead, Mede, meed, misdeed, mislead, misread, need, plead, proceed, read, rede, reed, Reid, retrocede, screed, secede, seed, she'd, speed, stampede, steed, succeed, supersede, Swede, tweed, weak-kneed, we'd, weed

> ⓘ Create extra rhymes for words like accede by adding -d to agree etc. (see section 4.1).

- breastfeed • greenfeed • dripfeed
- chickenfeed • spoonfeed • nosebleed
- Nibelungenlied • invalid • Ganymede
- Runnymede • airspeed • millipede
- velocipede • centipede • Siegfried
- filigreed • copyread • crossbreed
- proofread • flaxseed • hayseed
- rapeseed • linseed • pumpkinseed
- aniseed • oilseed • birdseed • ragweed
- knapweed • seaweed • chickweed
- stinkweed • blanket weed • bindweed
- pondweed • duckweed • tumbleweed
- fireweed • waterweed • silverweed

16.8

- **amid**, backslid, bid, did, forbid, grid, hid, id, kid, Kidd, lid, Madrid, mid, outbid, outdid, quid, rid, skid, slid,

squid, underbid, yid
- scarabaeid • Aeneid • nereid
- spermatozoid
- **Clwyd**, Druid, fluid
- noctuid • rabid • carabid • ibid
- morbid • turbid • wretched

16.9

- **plaided**, unpadded
- **backhanded**, candid, candied, heavy-handed, high-handed, offhanded, red-handed, short-handed, unbranded, underhanded
- **retarded**, unregarded
- **bareheaded**, boneheaded, fatheaded, hard-headed, hot-headed, light-headed, pig-headed, pinheaded, thickheaded, unleaded, unwedded, wooden-headed, wrong-headed
- **intended**, splendid, unamended, unapprehended, unattended, unblended, undefended, untended
- **gadid**, unaided, unpersuaded, unshaded
- **reeded**, unheeded, unimpeded, unneeded, unseeded
- unshielded • katydid
- **lopsided**, misguided, one-sided, undecided, undivided, unguided, unprovided
- **broadminded**, like-minded, simple-minded, single-minded, small-minded, tough-minded
- disembodied
- **sordid**, unrecorded, unrewarded
- **unclouded**, uncrowded
- **unbounded**, unfounded, ungrounded
- **outmoded**, spring-loaded, unexploded
- unwounded
- **unhooded**, wooded
- **cold-blooded**, hot-blooded, red-blooded, unstudied, warm-blooded
- **underfunded**, unfunded
- unheralded • aphid • triffid
- **jagged**, ragged

- **cross-legged**, legged
- dogged • rugged

16.10

- carangid • alleged • aged
- **frigid**, rigid
- turgid • naked • wicked • whizz-kid
- orchid • crooked
- **pallid**, valid
- gelid • skidlid • eyelid
- **solid**, squalid, stolid
- Euclid • unsullied • annelid
- chrysalid • Ozalid • desmid • timid
- Fatimid
- **humid**, tumid
- pyramid • MacDiarmid • crannied
- arachnid • Enid • hominid • honied
- **Leonid**, Oceanid
- salmonid • Achaemenid
- unaccompanied • Sassanid • learned
- winged
- **rapid**, sapid, vapid
- **intrepid**, tepid
- **insipid**, lipid
- limpid • poppied • torpid
- **Cupid**, stupid
- canopied

16.11

- **arid**, married
- Alfred • Manfred • acrid • Astrid
- **serried**, unburied, viverrid
- varied • sacred • hatred • mirid
- Mildred • kindred • Wilfred • Ingrid
- Winifred • hybrid
- **florid**, forehead, horrid, torrid
- storied • Mordred • putrid
- **hurried**, unworried
- unwearied • lurid • ascarid
- unsalaried • liveried
- **Abbasid**, acid, antacid, flaccid, Hasid, placid
- alcid
- **rancid**, unfancied
- **deuced**, lucid, pellucid, Seleucid
- cussed • cursed

16.12

- **caryatid**, cravatted, dratted, fatted, matted
- **distracted**, protracted
- unadapted • unformatted • Hampstead
- **downhearted**, good-hearted, hard-hearted, heavy-hearted, kind-hearted, light-hearted, lion-hearted, overparted, tender-hearted, uncharted, warm-hearted, wholehearted
- unplanted
- **fetid**, indebted, minareted, rosetted
- **aspected**, disaffected, disconnected, invected, unaffected, uncollected, unconnected, uncorrected, undetected, undirected, unelected, unexpected, uninflected, unprotected, unselected, unsuspected
- unmelted
- **discontented**, malcontented, unaccented, undented, under-represented, unfermented, unfrequented, unlamented, unrepresented, unscented
- **indigested**, predigested, Quested, uncontested, undigested, unmolested, unrequested, untested
- unprecedented • undocumented
- unornamented
- **belated**, elated, mismated, outdated, overinflated, striated, unabated, undated, unrated, unrelated, unstated, X-rated
- **sainted**, unacquainted, unpainted, untainted
- untasted • unmediated
- **ciliated**, unaffiliated
- fimbriated
- **historiated**, storiated
- unappropriated • glaciated
- unsubstantiated • undifferentiated
- unappreciated
- **uninitiated**, unvitiated
- unassociated • unalleviated
- unpunctuated • unsegregated
- uninvestigated • unmitigated
- unexpurgated • dedicated
- uncomplicated • elasticated

- undomesticated • unsophisticated
- **overeducated**, self-educated, undereducated, uneducated
- unreciprocated • unassimilated
- pixilated • castellated • unventilated
- unregulated • uninsulated
- unallocated • unarticulated
- unaspirated • unmodulated
- **underpopulated**, unpopulated
- unformulated • mentholated
- unconsummated • uncoordinated
- unhyphenated • uncontaminated
- unilluminated • opinionated
- unanticipated • uncelebrated
- unconsecrated • unsaturated
- unliberated • uncorroborated
- undecorated • unillustrated
- unseparated • unincorporated
- unadulterated • uncompensated
- unpremeditated
- **self-motivated**, unmotivated
- uncultivated • antiquated
- **conceited**, uncompleted, undefeated, unheated, untreated
- **half-witted**, nitwitted, quick-witted, uncommitted, unfitted
- ungifted
- **self-inflicted**, unconstricted, unencrypted, unpredicted, unrestricted
- stilted
- **unprinted**, unstinted
- unscripted
- **limp-wristed**, tight-fisted, unassisted, unlisted, unresisted
- uninhabited • uninhibited
- **unaccredited**, uncredited, unedited
- ringletted • limited • uncarpeted
- unmerited • untouristed
- **self-interested**, uninterested
- multifaceted • unsolicited • unvisited
- **benighted**, clearsighted, shortsighted, uninvited, unlighted, unrequited, unsighted
- foresighted
- **besotted**, carotid, unspotted
- unprompted • unwanted • unadopted
- **undistorted**, unescorted, unreported, unsorted, unsupported
- unsalted • undaunted • undoubted
- **unaccounted**, uncounted, unmounted

- sugarcoated • wonted
- unexploited
- **self-appointed**, unpointed
- **undiluted**, undisputed, unpolluted, unsuited, voluted
- convoluted • unexecuted
- **barefooted**, club-footed, light-footed, splay-footed, sure-footed, wrong-footed
- worsted
- **unattributed**, undistributed
- **uninstructed**, unobstructed, unreconstructed
- **uncorrupted**, uninterrupted
- maladjusted • multitalented
- untalented
- uncovenanted • propertied
- unwarranted • unpatented
- **concerted**, uncontroverted, unconverted
- extroverted • introverted

16.13

- avid • unenvied • David
- **livid**, vivid
- ivied • Ovid • bovid
- **beloved**, Dyfed
- **fervid**, perfervid
- languid • equid
- **illiquid**, liquid
- frenzied • palsied

16.14

- **abide**, applied, aside, astride, backslide, beside, bestride, betide, bide, bride, chide, Clyde, cockeyed, coincide, collide, confide, cried, decide, divide, dried, elide, five-a-side, glide, guide, hide, hollow-eyed, I'd, implied, lied, misguide, nationwide, nide, offside, onside, outride, outside, pan-fried, pied, pie-eyed, pitch-side, popeyed, pride, provide, ride, Said, shied, side, slide, sloe-eyed, snide, square-eyed, starry-eyed, statewide, Strathclyde, stride, subdivide, subside, tide, tried, undyed, wall-eyed, wide, worldwide

> Create extra rhymes for
> words like abide by changing
> comply etc. to complied (see
> section 6.1). ⓘ

- carbide •unmodified
- **overqualified**, unqualified
- **dignified**, signified
- unverified •countrified
- unpurified •unclassified
- unspecified •sissified
- unsanctified
- **self-satisfied**, unsatisfied
- unidentified •unquantified
- unfortified •unjustified •uncertified
- formaldehyde •oxhide •rawhide
- cowhide •allied •landslide •bolide
- paraglide •polyamide •bromide
- thalidomide •selenide •cyanide
- unoccupied

16.15

- hayride •chloride •joyride •telluride
- sun-dried •fluoride •saccharide

16.16

- **backside**, trackside
- bedside •airside
- **Tayside**, wayside
- lakeside •stateside •graveside
- **quayside**, seaside, Teesside
- beachside •hillside •ringside
- suicide •herbicide •regicide
- fungicide •filicide •Barmecide
- homicide
- **germicide**, spermicide
- tyrannicide •parricide
- **fratricide**, matricide, patricide
- uxoricide •countryside •infanticide
- insecticide •pesticide •parasiticide
- mountainside •Merseyside
- Tyneside
- **dioxide**, dockside, hydroxide, monoxide, oxide, peroxide
- alongside
- **diopside**, topside
- broadside •downside •roadside
- poolside •upside •nearside

- fireside •Humberside •underside
- genocide •waterside •riverside
- silverside •overside
- kerbside (*US* curbside) •Burnside

16.17

- peptide •eventide •Whitsuntide
- springtide •riptide •Shrovetide
- Yuletide •noontide •nucleotide

16.18

- **bod**, clod, cod, god, hod, mod, nod, od, odd, plod, pod, prod, quad, quod, rod, scrod, shod, sod, squad, tod, Todd, trod, wad
- demigod •amphipod •unipod
- **ipod**, tripod
- isopod •myriapod •decapod
- cephalopod •monopod •macropod
- gastropod •arthropod •sauropod
- ramrod •Nimrod •hotrod •pushrod
- goldenrod •Novgorod •slipshod
- roughshod •eisteddfod •tightwad

16.19

- **aboard**, abroad, accord, afford, applaud, award, bawd, board, broad, chord, Claude, cord, ford, fraud, gaud, Gawd, hoard, horde, laud, lord, maraud, milord, sward, sword, toward, unawed, unexplored, unrestored, ward

> Create extra rhymes for
> words like applaud by adding -ed
> to soar and thaw etc. (see
> section 7.1). ⓘ

- fjord

16.20

- scratchboard
- **backboard**, blackboard
- gangboard •clapboard •dashboard
- **cardboard**, hardboard
- draughtboard •bargeboard

- dartboard
- **breadboard**, headboard
- pegboard (*US* Peg-board)
- chessboard •fretboard
- **sailboard**, tailboard
- drainboard
- **baseboard**, pasteboard
- skateboard
- **freeboard**, keyboard, seaboard
- cheeseboard •switchboard
- billboard
- **springboard**, stringboard
- **chipboard**, clipboard, shipboard
- running board •storyboard
- noticeboard •diving board
- sandwich board •sideboard
- signboard •whiteboard •washboard
- **floorboard**, scoreboard, strawboard
- chalkboard •soundboard •outboard
- snowboard
- mouldboard (*US* moldboard)
- **buckboard**, duckboard
- shuffleboard •shovelboard
- fibreboard (*US* fiberboard)
- smorgasbord
- chequerboard (*US* checkerboard)
- clapperboard •scraperboard
- plasterboard
- centreboard (*US* centerboard)
- mortar board •weatherboard
- motherboard •surfboard

16.21

- record •telerecord •needlecord
- **ripcord**, whipcord
- discord •tape-record •misericord
- harpsichord •clavichord
- **concord**, Concorde
- drawcord •monochord •pentachord
- landlord •warlord •slumlord
- overlord •broadsword
- greensward

16.22

- **aloud**, becloud, cloud, crowd,
  enshroud, loud, Macleod, proud,
  shroud, Stroud, unavowed,
  unbowed, unendowed, unploughed
  (*US* unplowed)

- thundercloud

> Create extra rhymes for
> words like cloud by adding -*ed* to
> allow etc. (see section 8.1). [i]

16.23

- **abode**, bestrode, bode, code,
  commode, corrode, download,
  encode, erode, explode, forebode,
  goad, implode, load, lode,
  middle-of-the-road, mode, node, ode,
  offload, outrode, road, rode, sarod,
  Spode, strode, toad, upload, woad

> Create extra rhymes for
> words like abode by adding -*ed*
> to bestow etc. (see section 9.1). [i]

- geode
- **diode**, triode
- barcode •zip code •unhallowed
- carload •cartload •payload
- trainload •caseload •freeload
- peakload •shipload •coachload
- boatload •truckload •wagonload
- workload •anode •internode
- epode •antipode •electrode
- railroad
- **byroad**, highroad
- rhapsode •episode •cestode
- webisode
- **nematode**, trematode
- cathode

16.24

- **avoid**, Boyd, Coed, droid, Floyd,
  Freud, Lloyd, overjoyed,
  self-employed, unalloyed,
  underemployed, unemployed, void

> Create extra rhymes for
> words like avoid by adding -*ed* to
> alloy etc. (see section 10.1). [i]

- geoid •amoeboid (*US* ameboid)
- globoid •cuboid •gadoid •typhoid
- fungoid •discoid •tabloid •colloid
- celluloid •mongoloid •alkaloid
- coralloid •crystalloid •prismoid
- arachnoid •sphenoid •hominoid

- **crinoid**, echinoid
- solenoid ▪humanoid ▪paranoid
- hypoid ▪anthropoid ▪gabbroid
- android ▪steroid ▪thyroid ▪hydroid
- spheroid ▪meteoroid ▪Murgatroyd
- Polaroid
- haemorrhoid (*US* hemorrhoid)
- asteroid ▪schizoid ▪factoid ▪mastoid
- deltoid ▪planetoid ▪ovoid ▪trapezoid
- rhizoid

16.25

- **allude**, brood, collude, conclude, crude, delude, dude, elude, étude, exclude, extrude, exude, feud, food, illude, include, intrude, Jude, lewd, mood, nude, obtrude, occlude, Oudh, preclude, protrude, prude, pseud, pultrude, rood, rude, seclude, shrewd, snood, transude, unglued, unsubdued, who'd, you'd
- habitude

> Create extra rhymes for words like allude by adding -(e)d to chew etc. (see section 11.1). ⓘ

- magnitude ▪seafood ▪wholefood
- Quaalude ▪postlude ▪interlude
- Ermintrude ▪Gertrude ▪unvalued
- prelude ▪quietude ▪hebetude
- longitude ▪amplitude
- **similitude**, verisimilitude
- solitude ▪plenitude ▪finitude
- decrepitude ▪turpitude ▪pulchritude
- **crassitude**, lassitude
- **solicitude**, vicissitude
- **attitude**, beatitude, gratitude, latitude, platitude
- exactitude ▪sanctitude ▪aptitude
- rectitude ▪ineptitude ▪promptitude
- fortitude ▪multitude ▪certitude
- servitude ▪consuetude

16.26

- **could**, good, hood, Likud, misunderstood, pud, should, stood, understood, withstood, wood, would

- Gielgud ▪manhood ▪maidenhood
- nationhood ▪statehood ▪sainthood
- priesthood ▪kinghood ▪babyhood
- likelihood ▪livelihood ▪puppyhood
- childhood ▪wifehood ▪knighthood
- falsehood ▪widowhood ▪boyhood
- cousinhood ▪adulthood
- neighbourhood (*US* neighborhood)
- husbandhood ▪bachelorhood
- toddlerhood ▪womanhood
- parenthood ▪sisterhood
- spinsterhood ▪fatherhood
- **brotherhood**, motherhood
- girlhood ▪Talmud ▪Malamud
- matchwood ▪Dagwood ▪Blackwood
- sandalwood ▪sapwood ▪basswood
- Atwood
- **Harewood**, Larwood
- hardwood ▪lancewood ▪heartwood
- redwood ▪Wedgwood ▪Elmwood
- bentwood ▪Hailwood ▪lacewood
- beechwood ▪greenwood ▪Eastwood
- cheesewood ▪driftwood ▪stinkwood
- Littlewood ▪giltwood ▪Hollywood
- satinwood ▪plywood ▪wildwood
- pinewood ▪whitewood ▪softwood
- **dogwood**, logwood
- cottonwood ▪coachwood ▪rosewood
- fruitwood ▪Goodwood ▪brushwood
- firewood ▪ironwood ▪underwood
- Isherwood ▪wormwood

16.27

- **blood**, bud, crud, cud, dud, flood, Judd, mud, rudd, scud, spud, stud, sudd, thud
- redbud ▪lifeblood
- stick-in-the-mud

16.28

- multi-layered
- **beard**, weird
- greybeard (*US* graybeard)
- bluebeard ▪Iliad ▪Olympiad ▪myriad
- period
- **hamadryad**, jeremiad, semi-retired, underwired, undesired, unexpired, uninspired

One of the most popular types of poem in English is the *limerick*, a five-line humorous poem with the rhyme scheme *aabba*, which uses a three-beat metre (made up of two unstressed and one stressed beats, ti-ti-TUM, called *anapaestic*):

There was an Old Man with a beard,
Who said, 'It is just as I feared!
Two Owls and a Hen,
Four Larks and a Wren,
Have all built their nests in my beard!'

(Edward Lear, 'There was an Old Man with a beard')

- **coward**, Howard, underpowered, unpowered
- froward
- **leeward**, steward
- **gourd**, Lourdes, self-assured, uncured, uninsured, unobscured, unsecured
- **scabbard**, tabard
- halberd • starboard
- unremembered • tribade • cupboard
- **unencumbered**, unnumbered
- **good-natured**, ill-natured
- Richard • pilchard • pochard • orchard
- unstructured • uncultured
- **standard**, sub-standard
- unconsidered • unhindered
- unordered • Stafford • Bradford
- **Sandford**, Sanford, Stanford
- **Hartford**, Hertford
- **Bedford**, Redford
- Telford • Wexford • Chelmsford
- Clifford • Pickford • Guildford
- Linford • Mitford • Hereford
- Longford • Oxford • Watford
- Crawford • Salford • Rutherford
- **haggard**, laggard
- niggard • unsugared • sluggard
- unmeasured • uninjured • tankard
- becard • bewhiskered • unconquered
- drunkard

16.29

- **ballad**, salad

- **collard**, Lollard, pollard
- bicoloured (*US* bicolored), dullard, multicoloured (*US* multicolored), particoloured (*US* particolored), self-coloured (*US* self-colored), uncoloured (*US* uncolored), varicoloured (*US* varicolored), versicoloured (*US* versicolored)
- **enamored**, Muhammad
- ill-humoured (*US* ill-humored)
- **Seanad**, unmannered
- Leonard • synod • unhonoured
- **Bernard**, gurnard
- unhampered
- **leopard**, shepherd
- untempered
- **Angharad**, Harrod
- Herod • hundred • unanswered
- uncensored • unsponsored
- Blanchard • dastard • unchartered
- bastard • unlettered • unsheltered
- self-centred (*US* self-centered) • it'd
- unfiltered • unregistered • unwatered
- unaltered • dotard • untutored
- **uncluttered**, unuttered
- **bustard**, custard, mustard
- method • unbothered • Harvard
- unflavoured (*US* unflavored)
- **lily-livered**, undelivered
- undiscovered

16.30

- landward • backward
- **Edward**, headward
- hellward • heavenward • leftward
- **northwestward**, southwestward, westward
- wayward
- **leeward**, seaward
- **eastward**, northeastward, southeastward
- windward • inward • cityward
- skyward • sideward • rightward
- onward
- **forward**, henceforward, shoreward, straightforward, thenceforward
- awkward • northward
- **downward**, townward

- outward • southward • poleward
- homeward • oceanward • Woodward
- sunward • upward • frontward
- rearward • afterward • earthward
- halyard
- **lanyard**, Spaniard
- untenured • steelyard • vineyard
- poniard
- **haphazard**, hazard, mazzard
- **blizzard**, gizzard, izard, lizard, vizard, wizard
- buzzard

16.31

- **absurd**, bird, Byrd, curd, engird, gird, Heard, herd, Kurd, misheard, nerd, overheard, reheard, third, turd, undergird, undeterred, unheard, unstirred, word

> Create extra rhymes for [i]
> words like absurd by adding -(e)d
> to blur etc. (see section 13.1).

- blackbird • yardbird • cage bird
- jailbird • seabird • ladybird
- dickybird • mockingbird • whirlybird
- hummingbird • nightbird • songbird
- shorebird • bluebird • lovebird
- lyrebird • bowerbird • thunderbird
- waterbird • weaverbird • Sigurd
- swineherd • cowherd • goatherd
- potsherd • catchword • password
- headword • swear word • keyword
- byword • watchword • crossword

> **This poem shows how effective**
> *delayed rhyme* **can be. The rhyme**
> **scheme is** *abbcac*, **and the very**
> **delayed** *a*-**rhyme**
> **('blurred/absurd') stands out:**
>
> Side by side, their faces blurred,
> The earl and countess lie in stone,
> Their proper habits vaguely shown
> As jointed armour, stiffened pleat,
> And that faint hint of the absurd—
> The little dogs under their feet.
>
> (Philip Larkin, 'An Arundel Tomb')

- foreword • loanword • buzzword
- afterword

16.32

- undersubscribed • self-absorbed
- **undisturbed**, unperturbed

16.33

- jagged • gatelegged
- **bewigged**, ship-rigged, square-rigged
- outrigged • waterlogged

16.34

- **uncharged**, undischarged
- **gilt-edged**, unfledged, unhedged
- **aged**, unassuaged, unengaged, unwaged
- unabridged
- **privileged**, underprivileged
- unacknowledged • undamaged
- unmanaged • unchanged • untinged
- unchallenged

16.35

- Schwarzwald • Buchenwald
- **beheld**, eld, geld, held, meld, self-propelled, upheld, weld, withheld
- Ziegfeld • unparalleled • spot-weld
- unscaled
- **afield**, field, midfield, misfield, shield, unaneled, unconcealed, unhealed, unpeeled, unrevealed, unsealed, wield, yield

> Create extra rhymes for [i]
> afield by adding -ed to conceal
> etc. (see section 23.7).

- backfield • battlefield • Mansfield
- Garfield • Sheffield • Lee-Enfield
- airfield • Wakefield • Masefield
- Greenfield • Lichfield • brickfield
- Springfield • Smithfield • minefield

- cornfield • brownfield • outfield
- snowfield
- **coalfield**, goldfield, Sutton Coldfield
- oilfield • Bloomfield • Nuffield
- upfield • Huddersfield • Sellafield
- chesterfield • windshield
- gumshield
- **build**, deskilled, gild, guild, self-willed, sild, unfilled, unfulfilled, unskilled, untilled, upbuild

> [i] Create extra rhymes for words like build by adding -ed to words like grill etc. (see Section 23.8).

- Brunhild • Roskilde

16.36

- **child**, Childe, mild, self-styled, undefiled, wild, Wilde
- grandchild • stepchild • brainchild
- godchild • Rothschild • schoolchild
- love child • unreconciled
- **bald**, scald, so-called, uncalled, unwalled
- Archibald • piebald • skewbald
- Theobald • Cumbernauld

16.37

- **behold**, bold, cold, enfold, fold, foretold, gold, hold, mould (US mold), old, outsold, scold, self-controlled, sold, told, uncontrolled, undersold, unpolled, uphold, withhold, wold

> [i] Create extra rhymes for words like behold by adding -(e)d to bowl and console etc. (see section 23.17).

- scaffold • tenfold
- **elevenfold**, sevenfold
- twelvefold
- **eightfold**, gatefold
- threefold • sheepfold • billfold
- pinfold • sixfold • manifold
- manyfold • twentyfold
- **blindfold**, ninefold

- fivefold • fourfold • thousandfold
- twofold • hundredfold
- centrefold (US centerfold)
- millionfold • mangold • marigold
- handhold • stranglehold • threshold
- freehold • leasehold • copyhold
- stronghold • shorthold • household
- toehold • foothold • commonhold
- cuckold • Leopold • Courtauld
- Cotswold
- **unoiled**, unsoiled, unspoiled
- shopsoiled
- **Gould**, unschooled
- unscheduled • thick-skulled

16.38

- Roald • unlabelled (US unlabeled)
- ribald • untroubled • unruffled
- newfangled • unwrinkled
- bespectacled
- untrammelled (US untrammeled)
- Arnold • Reginald
- **Donald**, Macdonald, Ronald
- unexampled • unprincipled
- uncrumpled • Harold
- **Fitzgerald**, Gerald, herald
- emerald • embattled • unmetalled
- untitled • disgruntled
- untravelled (US untraveled)
- unrivalled (US unrivaled) • Tynwald
- Ostwald • Oswald • sozzled • world
- dreamworld • underworld
- afterworld • netherworld

16.39

- **unarmed**, unharmed
- **ashamed**, self-proclaimed, unclaimed, unframed, unnamed, unreclaimed, untamed
- **undreamed**, unredeemed
- **undimmed**, unskimmed, untrimmed
- **unclimbed**, unprimed, unrhymed
- **malformed**, unformed, uninformed, unreformed, untransformed
- uncombed • unconsumed
- unplumbed • unaccustomed
- unfathomed • unconfirmed

This poem by Tennyson begins in a powerful and striking way with a mixture of alliteration in the first line and *stressed* (or *masculine*) *rhyme*:

He clasps the crag with crooked hands;
Close to the sun in lonely lands,
Ring'd with the azure world, he stands.

(Alfred Lord Tennyson, 'The Eagle')

16.40

- **and**, band, bland, brand, expand, firsthand, gland, grand, hand, land, manned, misunderstand, offhand, rand, righthand, Samarkand, sand, stand, strand, thirdhand, underhand, undermanned, understand, unplanned, untanned, withstand

> Create extra rhymes for words like and by adding -(n)ed to ban etc. (see section 25.1). ℹ️

- graduand ∘hatband ∘armband
- **headband**, headstand
- neckband ∘sweatband
- waistband ∘waveband ∘wristband
- broadband ∘showband ∘noseband
- saraband ∘backhand ∘chargehand
- farmhand ∘deckhand ∘stagehand
- freehand ∘millhand ∘behindhand
- longhand
- **beforehand**, forehand
- shorthand ∘gangland ∘Lapland
- flatland ∘no-man's-land ∘Saarland
- farmland ∘grassland ∘marshland
- fenland ∘wetland ∘Sudetenland
- wasteland ∘dreamland ∘peatland
- Matabeleland ∘Ngamiland
- fairyland ∘Dixieland ∘Swaziland
- Thailand ∘Rhineland ∘swampland
- washland ∘homeland ∘Heligoland
- Basutoland
- **clubland**, scrubland
- timberland ∘borderland
- wonderland ∘Nagaland ∘Helgoland
- **Bechuanaland**, Gondwanaland
- Mashonaland ∘Damaraland
- Nyasaland ∘platteland ∘hinterland
- fatherland ∘motherland

- Namaqualand ∘Öland ∘allemande
- confirmand ∘ordinand ∘Ferdinand
- Talleyrand ∘firebrand ∘Krugerrand
- honorand ∘Witwatersrand
- greensand ∘quicksand ∘analysand
- Streisand ∘ampersand
- **bandstand**, grandstand, handstand
- hatstand ∘kickstand ∘inkstand
- washstand ∘hallstand ∘news-stand

16.41

- **command**, demand, remand
- reprimand ∘countermand
- **amend**, append, apprehend, ascend, attend, befriend, bend, blend, blende, commend, comprehend, condescend, contend, defriend, depend, emend, end, expend, extend, fend, forfend, friend, impend, interdepend, lend, mend, misapprehend, misspend, offend, on-trend, Oostende, Ostend, perpend, portend, rend, reprehend, scrag-end, send, spend, subtend, suspend, tail end, tend, transcend, trend, underspend, unfriend, upend, vend, weekend, wend
- U-bend ∘dividend ∘bookend
- ill-omened ∘bin-end ∘stipend
- penfriend ∘boyfriend ∘girlfriend
- godsend ∘parascend ∘repetend
- **ingrained**, self-contained, self-restrained, self-sustained, unascertained, unconstrained, undertrained, undrained, unexplained, unfeigned, unrestrained, unstained, unstrained, unsustained, untrained
- crackbrained ∘harebrained

- featherbrained •tearstained
- **fiend**, unscreened, unweaned

- dewpond •Trebizond
- **unadorned**, unmourned, unwarned

16.42

- **downwind**, Lind, prescind, rescind, Sind, upwind, wind

> Create extra rhymes for words like downwind by changing grin etc. to grinned (see section 25.13). ⓘ

- Wedekind •wunderkind •Rosalind
- unexamined •undetermined
- tamarind •uncurtained •headwind
- tradewind •tailwind •crosswind
- woodwind •whirlwind
- **affined**, behind, bind, blind, find, grind, hind, humankind, interwind, kind, mankind, mind, nonaligned, resigned, rind, unaligned, unassigned, unconfined, undefined, undersigned, undesigned, unlined, unrefined, unsigned, wynd

> Create extra rhymes for words like affined by adding -(e)d to assign etc. (see section 25.21). ⓘ

- spellbind •womankind •snowblind
- sunblind •colourblind •purblind
- mastermind
- **abscond**, beau monde, beyond, blonde, bond, correspond, demi-monde, despond, fond, frond, Gironde, haut monde, pond, respond, ronde, second, wand
- Eurobond •vagabond •millpond

16.43

- **abound**, aground, around, astound, bound, compound, confound, dumbfound, expound, found, ground, hound, impound, interwound, mound, pound, profound, propound, redound, round, sound, stoneground, surround, theatre-in-the-round (*US* theater-in-the-round), underground, wound

> Create extra rhymes for words like abound by adding -ed to clown etc. (see section 25.29). ⓘ

- spellbound •westbound •casebound
- eastbound •windbound •hidebound
- fogbound •stormbound
- northbound •housebound
- outbound •southbound •snowbound
- weatherbound •earthbound
- hellhound •greyhound •foxhound
- newshound •wolfhound
- bloodhound •background
- battleground •campground
- fairground •playground
- whip-round •foreground
- showground •merry-go-round
- runaround •turnaround •ultrasound
- **pre-owned**, unowned
- unchaperoned •poind •untuned
- Lund

An unusual rhyming device is to rhyme a word with itself: this is called *autorhyme* (or *identical* or *null rhyme*), and can have a slowing or deadening effect:

We paused before a House that seemed
A Swelling of the Ground—
The Roof was scarcely visible—
The Cornice—in the Ground—

(Emily Dickinson, 'Because I could not stop for Death')

16.44

- **bund**, fund, Lund, rotund
- moribund •cummerbund
- Rosamund •orotund

16.45

- **unironed**, viand
- prebend
- **beribboned**, riband
- husband •house husband
- unquestioned •escutcheoned
- **brigand**, ligand
- legend
- **fecund**, second, split-second
- millisecond •nanosecond
- microsecond •rubicund •jocund
- Langland •garland •parkland
- **Cartland**, heartland
- headland •Shetland •Lakeland
- mainland
- **eland**, Leland, Wieland, Zealand, Zeeland
- Greenland •heathland •Cleveland
- Friesland •Queensland •midland
- England •Finland •Maryland
- **dryland**, highland, island
- Iceland •Holland •dockland
- Scotland
- **foreland**, Westmorland
- **Auckland**, Falkland
- Portland •Northland
- **lowland**, Poland, Roland
- Oakland •Copland •Newfoundland
- woodland •Buckland •upland
- **Jutland**, Rutland
- Ireland •moorland
- **Cumberland**, Northumberland
- Sunderland •Switzerland
- Sutherland •Hammond
- **almond**, Armand
- **Edmund**, Redmond
- **Desmond**, Esmond
- Raymond •Grimond •Richmond
- Sigmund •Sigismund •Osmond
- Dortmund •unsummoned
- diamond •gourmand
- unopened
- **errand**, gerund
- reverend •Bertrand •dachshund

- unchastened
- **old-fashioned**, unimpassioned
- unsanctioned
- **aforementioned**, undermentioned, unmentioned
- unconditioned •unsweetened
- unenlightened •unleavened
- self-governed •unseasoned
- wizened •thousand

16.46

- **learned**, unearned, unreturned, unturned, upturned

16.47

- winged •smooth-tongued

16.48

- unscathed
- **loudmouthed**, mealy-mouthed

16.49

- **unpaved**, unsaved, unshaved
- **broadleaved**, unrelieved
- uncontrived
- **unapproved**, unimproved, unmoved
- **ungloved**, unloved
- **undeserved**, unobserved
- **undissolved**, uninvolved, unresolved, unsolved

16.50

- **unfazed**, unglazed
- unappeased
- **undersized**, undisguised, unrevised, unsized, unsurprised
- unanalysed (*US* unanalyzed)
- unspecialized •pearlized •satinized
- unmodernized •unpressurized
- unpublicized •uncommercialized
- uncircumcised • unadvertised
- unsupervised

- **self-imposed**, undisclosed, unenclosed, unexposed, unopposed, unposed

- toffee-nosed • undiagnosed
- **unamused**, unbruised, underused, used

Section 17: **-f**

17.1

- **caff**, carafe, faff, gaff, gaffe, naff, Najaf, piaffe, Taff
- Piaf • chiffchaff • decaf • pilaf • Olaf
- paraph • riffraff • Asaph

17.2

- **barf**, behalf, calf, chaff, coif, giraffe, Graf, graph, half, laugh, scarf, scrum half, staff, strafe, wing half
- headscarf • mooncalf • bar graph
- telegraph • polygraph • epigraph
- serigraph • cardiograph • radiograph
- spectrograph • micrograph
- lithograph • heliograph
- choreograph • tachograph
- stylograph • holograph • seismograph
- **chronograph**, monograph
- phonograph • paragraph
- cinematograph • pictograph
- autograph • photograph • flagstaff
- jackstaff • distaff • tipstaff • epitaph
- pikestaff • cenotaph

17.3

- **chef**, clef, deaf, def, eff, Geoff, Jeff, Kiev, ref, teff, tone-deaf
- Nureyev • Prokofiev • Ipatieff
- Kislev • Diaghilev • Turgenev

17.4

- **chafe**, Rafe, safe, vouchsafe, waif

17.5

- **aperitif**, beef, belief, brief, chief, enfeoff, fief, grief, interleaf, leaf, Leif, lief, Mazar-e-Sharif, misbelief, motif, naif, O'Keeffe, reef, seif, Sharif, sheaf, shereef, sportif, Tenerife, thief
- tea leaf • fig leaf • bas-relief • flyleaf
- drop-leaf • broadleaf • cloverleaf
- massif • leitmotif

17.6

- **biff**, cliff, glyph, if, kif, miff, niff, quiff, riff, skew-whiff, skiff, sniff, spliff, stiff, tiff, whiff
- mischief • handkerchief
- neckerchief • kerchief • Cardiff
- Radcliffe
- **bailiff**, calif, caliph
- Wyclif • Northcliffe • anaglyph
- hieroglyph • tariff
- **serif**, sheriff
- midriff • hippogriff • mastiff • caitiff
- plaintiff • pontiff • Joseph

17.7

- **fife**, Fyfe, knife, life, pro-life, rife, still-life, strife, wife
- shelf-life • midlife • wildlife
- nightlife • lowlife • afterlife
- jackknife • penknife • paperknife
- spaewife • alewife • midwife
- fishwife • housewife • goodwife

17.8

- **boff**, cough, doff, far-off, off, quaff, roll-on roll-off, scoff, telling-off, toff, trough
- **lay-off**, payoff, playoff
- show-off • Khrushchev • Gorbachev

- stand-off • Meyerhof • Cracow
- Schwarzkopf • Chekhov • Cherenkov
- take-off • kick-off • Kalashnikov
- Baryshnikov • Rimsky-Korsakov
- Kirchhoff • Karloff • Wolof • spin-off
- Rachmaninov • Ustinov • Godunov
- Stroganoff • Romanov • rip-off
- eavestrough • Sakharov • cut-off
- Molotov

17.9

- **corf**, dwarf, morph, orfe, Orff, swarf, wharf, Whorf
- Ludendorff • Düsseldorf • biomorph
- pseudomorph

17.10

- langlauf

17.11

- **loaf**, oaf
- Lagerlöf • sugarloaf

17.12

- **coif**, Cruyff

17.13

- **aloof**, behoof, goof, hoof, pouffe, proof, roof, shadoof, spoof, Tartuffe, underproof, woof
- flameproof • rainproof • greaseproof
- heatproof • windproof • bulletproof
- childproof • shockproof • mothproof
- stormproof • soundproof • foolproof
- sunroof • ovenproof • rustproof
- fireproof • showerproof
- shatterproof • waterproof
- weatherproof

17.14

- **pouffe**, woof

17.15

- **bluff**, buff, chough, chuff, cuff, duff, enough, fluff, gruff, guff, huff, luff, muff, puff, rough, ruff, scruff, scuff, slough, snuff, stuff, Tough, tuff
- handcuff • earmuff • powder puff
- dandruff • woodruff • feedstuff
- greenstuff • foodstuff

17.16

- seraph

17.17

- **scurf**, serf, soixante-neuf, surf, turf
- windsurf • Astroturf

17.18

- Ralph
- **elf**, herself, himself, itself, myself, oneself, ourself, self, shelf, themself, thyself, yourself
- mantelshelf • bookshelf • sylph
- **golf**, Rolf, Wolf
- Randolph • Rudolph
- **Wolfe**, Woolf
- aardwolf • werewolf • Beowulf
- **engulf**, gulf
- Ranulf

17.19

- Kulturkampf
- **lymph**, nymph
- Arc de Triomphe • oomph
- **bumf**, galumph, harrumph, humph
- triumph

Section 18: -g

18.1

- **bag**, blag, brag, Bragg, crag, dag, drag, fag, flag, gag, hag, jag, lag, mag, nag, quag, rag, sag, scrag, shag, slag, snag, sprag, stag, swag, tag, wag, zag

> Create extra rhymes by changing words like brag to bragging. ⓘ

- ragbag • saddlebag
- **handbag**, sandbag
- gasbag • manbag • ratbag • air bag
- mailbag
- **fleabag**, tea bag
- beanbag • windbag • kitbag • dillybag
- carpet bag • washbag • growbag
- nosebag
- **bumbag**, scumbag
- punchbag • Stalag • jetlag • greylag
- gulag • dishrag • bullyrag • Morag
- ragtag • hashtag • dog tag • Sontag
- wigwag • chinwag
- scallywag (*US* scallawag) • zigzag

18.2

- **Camargue**, Den Haag, Prague
- Reichstag • Bundestag

18.3

- **beg**, cleg, egg, Eigg, Greg, keg, leg, Meg, peg, skeg, teg, yegg
- filibeg • blackleg • peg-leg • dogleg
- foreleg • Oleg • bootleg • nutmeg
- Winnipeg • clothes peg • thalweg

18.4

- **Craig**, Hague, Haig, plague, taig, vague

18.5

- **fatigue**, Grieg, intrigue, league, renege
- colleague
- **Blitzkrieg**, Sitzkrieg

18.6

- **big**, brig, dig, fig, frig, gig, grig, jig, lig, pig, prig, rig, snig, sprig, swig, tig, trig, twig, Whig, wig
- Liebig • shindig • whirligig
- thingamajig • Pfennig • Gehrig
- thimblerig • Meurig • oilrig • Leipzig
- Schleswig • bigwig • periwig
- Ludwig • earwig • Danzig
- Zagazig

18.7

- Braunschweig

18.8

- **agog**, befog, blog, bog, clog, cog, dog, flog, fog, frog, grog, hog, Hogg, hotdog, jog, log, nog, prog, slog, smog, snog, sprog, tautog, tog, trog, wog
- hangdog • lapdog • seadog • sheepdog
- watchdog • bulldog • gundog • firedog
- underdog • pettifog • pedagogue
- demagogue • synagogue • sandhog
- hedgehog • warthog • groundhog
- roadhog • backlog • Kellogg • weblog
- eclogue
- epilogue (*US* epilog)
- prologue (*US* prolog) • footslog
- ideologue
- dialogue (*US* dialog) • duologue
- Decalogue

- **analog**, analogue (*US* analog)
- monologue •apologue
- catalogue (*US* catalog) •travelogue
- eggnog •leapfrog •bullfrog
- Taganrog
- **golliwog**, polliwog
- phizog •Herzog

18.9

- **Borg**, morgue
- Aalborg •Swedenborg •Helsingborg
- cyborg •Cherbourg

18.10

- **brogue**, disembogue, drogue, pirog, pirogue, prorogue, rogue, vogue

18.11

- fugue

18.12

- **bug**, chug, Doug, drug, dug, fug, glug, hug, jug, lug, mug, plug, pug, rug, shrug, slug, smug, snug, thug, trug, tug

> Create extra rhymes by changing words like bug to bugging. [i]

- bedbug •ladybug •doodlebug
- humbug •firebug •thunderbug
- **jitterbug**, litterbug
- shutterbug •Rawlplug •earplug
- fireplug •hearthrug

18.13

- **Berg**, burg, erg, exergue
- Hamburg •Battenberg •Strasberg
- Habsburg •Salzburg •Strasbourg
- Pressburg •Spielberg •Tilburg
- **Lindbergh**, Strindberg
- Wittenberg •Vicksburg •Pittsburgh
- Ginsberg •Johannesburg
- Königsberg •Gettysburg •Freiburg
- Heidelberg •Heisenberg •iceberg
- **Bromberg**, homburg, Romberg
- Gothenburg •Warburg •Jo'burg
- Gutenberg •Duisburg •Magdeburg
- Brandenburg •Hindenburg
- Mecklenburg •Wallenberg
- Orenburg •Nuremberg
- Luxembourg •St Petersburg
- Williamsburg •Schoenberg
- Würzburg •Esbjerg

Section 19: **-zh**

19.1

- **décolletage**, découpage, Lesage, maquillage, paysage, plage, potage, vernissage
- triage •persiflage •fuselage •collage
- ménage •badinage
- counter-espionage •mirage
- entourage •corsage •repêchage
- frottage
- **montage**, photomontage
- cabotage

19.2

- Courrèges

19.3

- **auberge**, barège
- concierge

19.4

- **beige**, cortège, Liège, manège

19.5

- **Limoges**, loge, Vosges

19.6

- **Bruges**, rouge

19.7

- mélange

Section 20: **-ge**

20.1

- **badge**, cadge, hajj, Madge

20.2

- **barge**, charge, enlarge, large, marge, raj, reportage, sarge, sparge, Swaraj, taj, undercharge

> Create extra rhymes by changing words like barge to barging. ⓘ

- turbocharge •countercharge
- cover charge •surcharge
- camouflage •espionage
- **barrage**, garage
- massage •dressage •sabotage

20.3

- **allege**, dredge, edge, fledge, hedge, kedge, ledge, pledge, reg, sedge, sledge, veg, wedge
- straight edge

20.4

- **age**, assuage, backstage, cage, downstage, engage, enrage, gage, gauge, mage, multistage, offstage, onstage, Osage, page, Paige, rage, rampage, sage, stage, swage, under-age, upstage, wage
- greengage •ribcage •birdcage
- teenage •saxifrage •outrage
- space-age

20.5

- **besiege**, liege, prestige, siege

20.6

- **abridge**, bridge, fridge, frig, midge, ridge
- quayage •verbiage •foliage •lineage
- ferriage
- **stowage**, towage
- **buoyage**, voyage
- sewage
- **Babbage**, cabbage
- garbage •cribbage
- **Burbage**, herbage
- adage •bandage •yardage •headage
- appendage •windage •bondage
- vagabondage •cordage •poundage
- wordage •staffage •roughage
- baggage •mortgage •luggage
- **package**, trackage
- tankage •wreckage •breakage
- leakage
- **linkage**, shrinkage, sinkage
- **blockage**, dockage, lockage
- boscage •corkage •soakage
- truckage •tallage •assemblage
- railage
- **grillage**, pillage, spillage, stillage, tillage, village
- pupillage (US pupilage) •sacrilege
- ensilage •mucilage •cartilage
- sortilege •tutelage •curtilage
- privilege
- **mileage**, silage
- **acknowledge**, college, foreknowledge, knowledge
- **haulage**, stallage
- spoilage •Coolidge

20.7

- damage
- **image**, scrimmage
- pilgrimage

- **homage**, West Bromwich
- plumage
- **rummage**, scrummage
- **manage**, mismanage, pannage, stage-manage
- carnage
- **cranage**, drainage
- spinach •concubinage •libertinage
- linage •nonage •coinage
- **dunnage**, tonnage
- orphanage •baronage •patronage
- parsonage •personage •Stevenage
- cozenage •scrappage •seepage
- slippage •equipage •stoppage
- warpage • groupage

20.8

- **carriage**, disparage, Harwich, intermarriage, marriage, miscarriage
- undercarriage
- **cartridge**, partridge
- Selfridge •Cambridge •Bainbridge
- Knightsbridge •umpirage
- **borage**, forage, Norwich, porridge
- Oxbridge •storage •self-storage
- drawbridge •Trowbridge •tollbridge
- footbridge
- **courage**, demurrage, encourage
- umbrage •suffrage
- **peerage**, steerage
- sewerage •moorage
- harbourage (*US* harborage)
- pasturage •pilferage •anchorage
- acreage •vicarage •brokerage
- cellarage •Coleridge
- haemorrhage (*US* hemorrhage)
- amperage •factorage •hectarage
- **litreage** (*US* literage), metreage (*US* meterage) •fosterage
- **porterage**, quarterage
- tutorage •average
- **beverage**, Beveridge
- leverage •overage •coverage

20.9

- passage
- **message**, presage
- sausage •dosage
- **misusage**, usage

- cartage
- **advantage**, vantage
- curettage •percentage •vestige
- freightage •wastage
- **mintage**, vintage
- hermitage •baronetage •heritage
- **cottage**, pottage, wattage
- hostage
- **portage**, shortage
- outage •dotage •voltage •postage
- anecdotage •footage •frontage
- pilotage •parentage •Carthage
- **ravage**, savage
- salvage •selvedge •pavage •cleavage
- lovage •language •sandwich
- **envisage**, visage

20.10

- oblige

20.11

- **bodge**, dodge, Hodge, lodge, splodge, stodge, wodge
- horologe •hodgepodge

20.12

- **engorge**, forge, George, gorge

20.13

- gouge

20.14

- doge

20.15

- **huge**, kludge, luge, scrooge, smoodge, stooge
- refuge •centrifuge
- subterfuge

20.16

- **adjudge**, begrudge, bludge, budge,

drudge, fudge, grudge, judge, misjudge, nudge, pudge, sludge, smudge, trudge

> Create extra rhymes by changing words like adjudge to adjudging. ℹ

20.17

- **converge**, dirge, diverge, emerge, merge, purge, scourge, serge, splurge, spurge, submerge, surge, urge, verge
- demiurge •upsurge •dramaturge
- thaumaturge

20.18

- bilge
- **bulge**, divulge, indulge, promulge

20.19

- **Falange**, flange
- **avenge**, henge, revenge, Stonehenge
- **arrange**, change, counterchange, estrange, exchange, grange, interchange, Lagrange, mange, part-exchange, range, short-change, strange
- **binge**, cringe, fringe, hinge, impinge, singe, springe, swinge, syringe, tinge, twinge, whinge

> Create extra rhymes by changing words like binge to bingeing. ℹ

- challenge •orange •scavenge
- lozenge •blancmange
- **lounge**, scrounge
- **blunge**, expunge, grunge, gunge, lunge, plunge, scunge, sponge

> **'Orange' is a word which famously has no full rhyme. Here the poet uses a device called** *eye rhyme* **(words that look the same when printed but which sound different) to play on this rhyming fact:**
>
> Most Saturday afternoons
> At the local Hippodrome
> Saw the Pathe-News rooster,
> Then the recurring dream
>
> Of a lonesome drifter
> Through uninterrupted range.
> Will Hunter, so gifted
> He could peel an orange
>
> In a single fluent gesture,
> Was the leader of our gang.
>
> (Paul Muldoon, 'The Weepies')

Section 21: -k

21.1

- **aback**, alack, attack, back, black, brack, clack, claque, crack, Dirac, drack, flack, flak, hack, jack, Kazakh, knack, lack, lakh, mac, mach, Nagorno-Karabakh, pack, pitchblack, plaque, quack, rack, sac, sack, shack, shellac, slack, smack, snack, stack, tach, tack, thwack, track, vac, wack, whack, wrack, yak, Zack
- cardiac • zodiac
- **haemophiliac** (*US* hemophiliac), necrophiliac, sacroiliac
- umiak
- **bibliomaniac**, dipsomaniac, egomaniac, kleptomaniac, maniac, megalomaniac, monomaniac, nymphomaniac, pyromaniac
- insomniac • celeriac • Syriac
- hypochondriac • Mauriac • theriac
- amnesiac
- **aphrodisiac**, Dionysiac
- **Dayak**, kayak
- Kerouac • bivouac

21.2

- hatchback • saddleback • camelback
- **flashback**, splashback
- fatback • hardback • halfback
- fastback • redback • shellback
- **setback**, wetback
- bareback
- **payback**, playback
- **tailback**, whaleback
- zwieback • feedback • greenback
- sweepback • leaseback • switchback
- kickback • stickleback
- **slingback**, wingback
- piggyback
- **dieback**, tieback
- **fightback**, right-back

- softback
- **clawback**, drawback
- talkback
- **callback**, fallback
- horseback • outback
- **blowback**, throwback
- rollback • yellowback • crookback
- fullback • touchback • comeback
- humpback • hunchback • cutback
- fireback • pickaback • huckaback
- Blumenbach • diamondback
- cornerback • paperback • quarterback
- razorback

21.3

- blackjack • applejack • flapjack
- steeplejack • cheapjack • skipjack
- **hijack**, skyjack
- bootjack • lumberjack • crackerjack
- ack-ack • click-clack • eyeblack
- kulak • shoeblack • bootblack
- yashmak • Tarmac • Cormac
- Potomac • sumac
- **Karnak**, Nanak, Pontianak
- knick-knack • almanac • Pasternak
- backpack • woolpack • mudpack
- power pack • Mubarak • backtrack
- **amtrac**, Amtrak
- half-track • serac • racetrack
- rickrack • gimcrack • tribrach
- wisecrack • sidetrack • soundtrack
- bladderwrack • sandarac • Skagerrak
- Bergerac • Bacharach • bric-à-brac
- tamarack • anorak

21.4

- ransack • knapsack • Barsac • Cossack
- Husák • woolsack • rucksack
- cul-de-sac • haversack • hard tack

- haystack •tic-tac •chimney stack
- smokestack •Blu-Tack •thumbtack
- counter-attack •Medevac
- **Czechoslovak**, Slovak
- Sarawak •bushwhack •Arawak
- cognac •Armagnac •Balzac •Anzac
- Prozac •Muzak

21.5

- **arc**, ark, Bach, bark, barque, Braque, Clark, clerk, dark, embark, hark, impark, Iraq, Ladakh, Lamarck, lark, macaque, marc, mark, marque, narc, nark, Newark, park, quark, sark, shark, snark, spark, stark, Vlach
- **matriarch**, patriarch
- tanbark •ringbark •stringy-bark
- Offenbach •ironbark •oligarch
- salesclerk •titlark •skylark
- meadowlark •woodlark •mudlark
- landmark •checkmark •Denmark
- benchmark •waymark •trademark
- seamark •Bismarck •telemark
- tidemark •Kitemark •pockmark
- Ostmark •hallmark •Goldmark
- Deutschmark •bookmark •footmark
- earmark •watermark •birthmark
- anarch •car park •skatepark
- ballpark
- **Petrarch**, tetrarch
- **hierarch**, squirearch
- exarch •Pesach •loan shark
- Plutarch •aardvark

21.6

- **beck**, bedeck, check, cheque, Chiang Kai-shek, crosscheck, Czech, deck, dreck, exec, fleck, heck, hitech, keck, lek, neck, peck, Québec, rec, reck, sec, sneck, spec, speck, spot-check, tec, tech, Toulouse-Lautrec, trek, wreck

> Create extra rhymes by **i**
> adding -ing to words like check.

- Hayek •Baalbek •pinchbeck
- Steinbeck •Warbeck
- **Brubeck**, Lübeck

- Uzbek •Beiderbecke •hacek
- soundcheck •Dubcek •foredeck
- sundeck •afterdeck •quarterdeck
- **Dalek**, Palekh
- fartlek •Chichimec •Olmec •redneck
- breakneck •V-neck •bottleneck
- swan-neck •roughneck •rubberneck
- halterneck •leatherneck •turtleneck
- henpeck •kopek •shipwreck •Hasek
- Aztec •Mixtec •Toltec •infotech
- discothèque •Zapotec

21.7

- **ache**, awake, bake, betake, Blake, brake, break, cake, crake, drake, fake, flake, forsake, hake, Jake, lake, make, mistake, opaque, partake, quake, rake, sake, shake, sheikh, slake, snake, splake, stake, steak, strake, take, undertake, wake, wideawake
- bellyache •clambake •headache
- backache •pancake •teacake
- seedcake •beefcake •cheesecake
- fishcake •johnnycake •tipsy cake
- rock cake •shortcake •oatcake
- oilcake •fruitcake •cupcake
- pat-a-cake •cornflake •snowflake
- rattlesnake •handbrake •mandrake
- heartbreak •airbrake •daybreak
- jailbreak •canebrake •windbreak
- tiebreak •corncrake •outbreak
- footbrake •muckrake •earache
- firebreak •namesake •keepsake
- handshake •milkshake •heartache
- beefsteak •sweepstake •stocktake
- out-take •uptake •grubstake
- wapentake •toothache •seaquake
- kittiwake •moonquake •earthquake

21.8

- **antique**, batik, beak, bespeak, bezique, bleak, boutique, cacique, caïque, cheek, chic, clique, creak, creek, critique, Dominique, eke, freak, geek, Greek, hide-and-seek, keek, Lalique, leak, leek, Martinique, meek, midweek, Mozambique, Mustique, mystique, oblique, opéra comique, ortanique, peak, Peake, peek, physique, pique, pratique, reek, seek, shriek, Sikh, sleek, sneak, speak, Speke, squeak, streak, teak, technique, tongue-in-cheek, tweak, unique, veronique, weak, week, wreak

> **i** Create extra rhymes by adding -ly to words like bleak.

- stickybeak • grosbeak • houseleek
- forepeak • technospeak • textspeak
- newspeak • doublespeak • hairstreak
- tugrik • fenugreek • Realpolitik
- Ostpolitik • pipsqueak • workweek

21.9

- **artic**, brick, chick, click, crick, dick, flick, hand-pick, hic, hick, kick, lick, mick, miskick, nick, pic, pick, prick, quick, rick, shtick, sic, sick, slick, snick, spic, stick, thick, tic, tick, trick, Vic, wick
- **alcaic**, algebraic, Aramaic, archaic, choleraic, Cyrenaic, deltaic, formulaic, Hebraic, Judaic, Mishnaic, Mithraic, mosaic, Pharisaic, prosaic, Ptolemaic, Romaic, spondaic, stanzaic, trochaic
- **logorrhoeic** (US logorrheic), mythopoeic, onomatopoeic
- **echoic**, heroic, Mesozoic, Palaeozoic (US Paleozoic), Stoic
- Bewick
- **disyllabic**, monosyllabic, polysyllabic, syllabic
- **choriambic**, dithyrambic, iambic
- alembic
- amoebic (US amebic)
- **aerobic**, agoraphobic, claustrophobic, homophobic, hydrophobic, phobic, technophobic, xenophobic
- **cherubic**, cubic, pubic
- **Arabic**, Mozarabic
- acerbic • apparatchik • dabchick
- peachick

21.10

- **Chadic**, Cycladic, Helladic, maenadic, nomadic, sporadic, triadic
- heraldic • Icelandic • asdic
- **bardic**, Haggadic, Lombardic, Sephardic
- **medic**, paramedic, Samoyedic
- Wendic • Vedic
- **comedic**, cyclopedic, encyclopedic, medick, orthopaedic (US orthopedic)
- **acidic**, Druidic, hasidic
- dik-dik
- **Indic**, syndic
- **aperiodic**, episodic, geodic, melodic, methodic, monodic, parodic, periodic, prosodic, psalmodic, rhapsodic, Roddick, spasmodic, threnodic
- Nordic
- **ludic**, pudic
- Talmudic
- **autobiographic**, autographic, bibliographic, biographic, calligraphic, cartographic, choreographic, cinematographic, cryptographic, demographic, geographic, graphic, hagiographic, historiographic, holographic, hydrographic, iconographic, lithographic, monographic, orthographic, palaeographic (US paleographic), photographic, pictographic, pornographic, reprographic, Sapphic, seraphic, stenographic, telegraphic, traffic, typographic, xerographic

> **i** Create extra rhymes by adding -al to words like autobiographic.

- **Efik**, malefic
- **Delphic**, Guelphic
- **anaglyphic**, beatific, calorific, colorific, hieroglyphic, honorific, horrific, Indo-Pacific, pacific, prolific, scientific, soporific, specific, terrific, transpacific, triglyphic
- **catastrophic**, dystrophic,

philosophic, strophic, theosophic, trophic
- **anamorphic**, biomorphic, metamorphic, Orphic, polymorphic, zoomorphic
- **Kufic**, Sufic
- demagogic • yogic

21.11

- **bathypelagic**, magic, tragic
- **neuralgic**, nostalgic
- **lethargic**, Tajik
- Belgic
- **paraplegic**, quadriplegic, strategic
- **dialogic**, ethnologic, hydrologic, isagogic, logic, monologic, mythologic, pathologic, pedagogic, teleologic
- georgic • muzhik
- **allergic**, dramaturgic
- **anarchic**, heptarchic, hierarchic, monarchic, oligarchic
- psychic • sidekick • dropkick
- synecdochic • Turkic
- **Alec**, cephalic, encephalic, Gallic, intervallic, italic, medallic, mesocephalic, metallic, phallic, Salic, tantalic, Uralic, Vandalic
- catlick • garlic
- **angelic**, archangelic, evangelic, melic, melick, philatelic, psychedelic, relic
- Ehrlich • Gaelic
- **acrylic**, bibliophilic, Cyrillic, dactylic, exilic, idyllic, imbecilic, necrophilic
- niblick • skinflick
- **acyclic**, cyclic, polycyclic
- **alcoholic**, anabolic, apostolic, bucolic, carbolic, chocoholic, colic, diabolic, embolic, frolic, hydraulic, hyperbolic, melancholic, metabolic, parabolic, rollick, shambolic, shopaholic, symbolic, vitriolic, workaholic
- saltlick • cowlick • souslik • gemütlich
- public • Catholic

21.12

- **aerodynamic**, balsamic, ceramic, cryptogamic, cycloramic, dynamic, hydrodynamic, Islamic, panoramic, psychodynamic, thermodynamic
- **Kalmyk**, ophthalmic
- **chasmic**, cytoplasmic, ectoplasmic, miasmic, orgasmic, phantasmic
- **karmic**, psalmic
- **academic**, alchemic, endemic, epidemic, pandemic, polemic, totemic
- **anaemic** (*US* anemic), epistemic, systemic
- **bulimic**, gimmick, metronymic, mimic, pantomimic, patronymic
- filmic
- **eurhythmic**, logarithmic, rhythmic
- cataclysmic • seismic
- **agronomic**, astronomic, atomic, comic, economic, ergonomic, gastronomic, metronomic, palindromic, physiognomic, subatomic, taxonomic, tragicomic
- **cosmic**, macrocosmic, microcosmic
- **gnomic**, monochromic, ohmic, photochromic
- humic
- **hypodermic**, taxidermic, thermic

21.13

- **aldermanic**, botanic, Brahmanic, Britannic, epiphanic, galvanic, Germanic, Hispanic, interoceanic, Koranic, manganic, manic, mechanic, messianic, oceanic, organic, panic, Puranic, Romanic, satanic, shamanic, talismanic, titanic, transoceanic, tympanic, volcanic
- **anthropogenic**, arsenic, autogenic, callisthenic (*US* calisthenic), carcinogenic, cariogenic, cryogenic, erotogenic, eugenic, fennec, hallucinogenic, Hellenic, hypo-allergenic, photogenic,

pyrogenic, radiogenic, schizophrenic, telegenic
- **polytechnic**, pyrotechnic, technic
- Chetnik
- **ethnic**, multi-ethnic
- Selznick
- **hygienic**, scenic
- peacenik • beatnik
- **actinic**, clinic, cynic, Finnic, Jacobinic, rabbinic
- **picnic**, pyknic
- hymnic • Iznik • Dominic
- **anachronic**, animatronic, bionic, Brythonic, bubonic, Byronic, canonic, carbonic, catatonic, chalcedonic, chronic, colonic, conic, cyclonic, daemonic, demonic, diatonic, draconic, electronic, embryonic, euphonic, harmonic, hegemonic, histrionic, homophonic, hypersonic, iconic, ionic, ironic, isotonic, laconic, macaronic, Masonic, Miltonic, mnemonic, monotonic, moronic, Napoleonic, philharmonic, phonic, Platonic, Plutonic, polyphonic, quadraphonic, sardonic, saxophonic, siphonic, Slavonic, sonic, stereophonic, subsonic, subtonic, symphonic, tectonic, Teutonic, thermionic, tonic, transonic, ultrasonic
- Dubrovnik
- **Munich**, Punic, runic, tunic
- refusenik • nudnik • kibbutznik
- sputnik • Metternich

21.14

- priapic • aspic • epic
- **philippic**, prototypic, stereotypic
- Olympic • nitpick
- **ectopic**, gyroscopic, heliotropic, horoscopic, isotopic, isotropic, kaleidoscopic, macroscopic, microscopic, misanthropic, myopic, philanthropic, phototropic, telescopic, topic, tropic
- Ethiopic • biopic
- **Inupik**, Yupik
- toothpick

21.15

- **Amharic**, barbaric, Garrick, Pindaric, samsaric
- fabric • cambric • Aelfric • chivalric
- **geriatric**, paediatric (US pediatric), Patrick, psychiatric, theatric
- tantric
- **epigastric**, gastric
- **alphanumeric**, atmospheric, chimeric, cleric, climacteric, congeneric, Derek, derrick, Eric, esoteric, exoteric, ferric, generic, hemispheric, Herrick, Homeric, hysteric, mesmeric, numeric, skerrick, spheric, stratospheric

> i Create extra rhymes by adding -al to words like atmospheric.

- red-brick • Cedric
- **calendric**, Kendrick
- **anthropometric**, asymmetric, diametric, geometric, isometric, kilometric, metric, obstetric, psychometric, pyrometric, sociometric
- **electric**, hydroelectric, photoelectric
- **androcentric**, centric, concentric, eccentric, egocentric, ethnocentric, Eurocentric, geocentric, phallocentric, theocentric
- airbrick • hayrick • Friedrich
- Dietrich
- **empiric**, lyric, panegyric, Pyrrhic, satiric, satyric, vampiric
- pinprick • citric • oneiric • hydric
- nitric
- **aleatoric**, allegoric, anaphoric, camphoric, categoric, choric, Doric, euphoric, historic, metaphoric, meteoric, phantasmagoric, phosphoric, pyrophoric, semaphoric, sophomoric, theophoric, Warwick, Yorick
- con trick
- **auric**, boric, folkloric
- **Kubrick**, rubric
- Ugric • Cymric • xeric • firebrick

- **Rurik**, sulphuric (*US* sulfuric), telluric, Zürich
- Frederick • Roderick • undertrick
- agaric • Alaric • choleric • limerick
- turmeric
- **archbishopric**, bishopric
- rhetoric • maverick • overtrick
- Masaryk

21.16

- **boracic**, classic, Jurassic, neoclassic, potassic, thoracic, Triassic
- ataraxic • carsick • heartsick
- geodesic
- **anorexic**, dyslexic
- airsick • basic • seasick
- **extrinsic**, intrinsic
- **fossick**, virtuosic
- toxic • homesick • lovesick

21.17

- **achromatic**, acrobatic, Adriatic, aerobatic, anagrammatic, aquatic, aristocratic, aromatic, Asiatic, asthmatic, athematic, attic, autocratic, automatic, axiomatic, bureaucratic, charismatic, chromatic, cinematic, climatic, dalmatic, democratic, diagrammatic, diaphragmatic, diplomatic, dogmatic, dramatic, ecstatic, emblematic, emphatic, enigmatic, epigrammatic, erratic, fanatic, hepatic, hieratic, hydrostatic, hypostatic, idiomatic, idiosyncratic, isochromatic, lymphatic, melodramatic, meritocratic, miasmatic, monochromatic, monocratic, monogrammatic, numismatic, operatic, panchromatic, pancreatic, paradigmatic, phlegmatic, photostatic, piratic, plutocratic, pneumatic, polychromatic, pragmatic, prelatic, prismatic, problematic, programmatic, psychosomatic, quadratic, rheumatic, schematic, schismatic, sciatic, semi-automatic, Socratic, somatic, static, stigmatic, sub-aquatic, sylvatic, symptomatic, systematic, technocratic, thematic, theocratic, thermostatic, traumatic
- **anaphylactic**, ataractic, autodidactic, chiropractic, climactic, didactic, galactic, lactic, prophylactic, syntactic, tactic
- asphaltic
- **antic**, Atlantic, corybantic, frantic, geomantic, gigantic, mantic, necromantic, pedantic, romantic, semantic, sycophantic, transatlantic
- synaptic
- **bombastic**, drastic, dynastic, ecclesiastic, elastic, encomiastic, enthusiastic, fantastic, gymnastic, iconoclastic, mastic, monastic, neoplastic, orgastic, orgiastic, pederastic, periphrastic, plastic, pleonastic, sarcastic, scholastic, scholiastic, spastic
- matchstick • candlestick • panstick
- slapstick • cathartic
- **Antarctic**, arctic, subantarctic, subarctic
- Vedantic • yardstick
- **aesthetic** (*US* esthetic), alphabetic, anaesthetic (*US* anesthetic), antithetic, apathetic, apologetic, arithmetic, ascetic, athletic, balletic, bathetic, cosmetic, cybernetic, diabetic, dietetic, diuretic, electromagnetic, emetic, energetic, exegetic, frenetic, genetic, Helvetic, hermetic, homiletic, kinetic, magnetic, metic, mimetic, parenthetic, pathetic, peripatetic, phonetic, photosynthetic, poetic, prophetic, prothetic, psychokinetic, splenetic, sympathetic, syncretic, syndetic, synthetic, telekinetic, theoretic, zetetic
- **apoplectic**, catalectic, dialectic, eclectic, hectic
- Celtic
- **authentic**, crescentic
- **aseptic**, dyspeptic, epileptic, nympholeptic, peptic, proleptic, sceptic (*US* skeptic), septic
- **domestic**, majestic

• cretic
• **analytic**, anchoritic, anthracitic,
  arthritic, bauxitic, calcitic, catalytic,
  critic, cryptanalytic, Cushitic,
  dendritic, diacritic, dioritic,
  dolomitic, enclitic, eremitic,
  hermitic, lignitic, mephitic,
  paralytic, parasitic, psychoanalytic,
  pyritic, Sanskritic, saprophytic,
  Semitic, sybaritic, syenitic,
  syphilitic, troglodytic
• **apocalyptic**, cryptic, diptych,
  elliptic, glyptic, styptic, triptych
• **aoristic**, artistic, autistic, cystic,
  deistic, distich, egoistic, fistic,
  holistic, juristic, logistic, monistic,
  mystic, puristic, sadistic, Taoistic,
  theistic, truistic, veristic
• fiddlestick
• **dipstick**, lipstick
• **impolitic**, politic
• polyptych •hemistich •heretic
• nightstick
• **abiotic**, amniotic, antibiotic,
  autoerotic, chaotic, demotic,
  despotic, erotic, exotic, homoerotic,
  hypnotic, idiotic, macrobiotic,
  meiotic, narcotic, neurotic, osmotic,
  patriotic, prebiotic, psychotic, quixotic,
  robotic, sclerotic, semiotic,
  symbiotic, zygotic, zymotic
• **Coptic**, optic, panoptic, synoptic
• **acrostic**, agnostic, diagnostic,
  gnostic, prognostic
• knobstick •chopstick •aeronautic
• **Baltic**, basaltic, cobaltic
• caustic •swordstick •photic •joystick
• **psychotherapeutic**, therapeutic
• acoustic •broomstick •cultic
• **fustic**, rustic
• drumstick •gearstick •lunatic

21.18

• **homeopathic**, polymathic,
  psychopathic, telepathic
• ethic
• **Eolithic**, megalithic, Mesolithic,
  monolithic, mythic, neolithic,
  Palaeolithic (US Paleolithic)

• **Gothic**, Visigothic
• Sothic •anacoluthic
• **Narvik**, Slavic
• pelvic •civic •Bolshevik •Ludovic
• Keflavik •Menshevik •Reykjavik
• Chadwick •candlewick •Gatwick
• Sedgwick •Prestwick •bailiwick
• Warwick •Brunswick •Lerwick
• Herdwick •Ashkenazic •Keswick
• forensic
• **aphasic**, phasic
• **amnesic**, analgesic, mesic
• metaphysic •music

21.19

• **alike**, bike, dyke, haik, hike, kike,
  like, mic, mike, mislike, pike, psych,
  psyche, shrike, spike, strike, trike,
  tyke, Van Dyck, vandyke

> Create extra rhymes by
> changing words like bike to
> biking. ⓘ

• pushbike •motorbike •Klondike
• Thorndike •Updike •hitchhike
• crablike •lamblike
• **fanlike**, manlike, panlike
• trap-like •catlike •starlike •calf-like
• **glass-like**, grass-like
• branch-like •plant-like •thread-like
• gem-like •deathlike •waiflike
• vein-like •wraithlike •fiendlike
• leaf-like •dreamlike •queen-like
• sheeplike •witchlike •sylphlike
• piglike
• **springlike**, string-like, wing-like
• lip-like •princelike •ladylike
• businesslike •lifelike •childlike
• **Christlike**, vice-like
• knob-like
• **godlike**, rod-like
• doglike •rock-like •swanlike
• foxlike •warlike •lord-like
• horselike •globe-like
• **dome-like**, homelike
• ghostlike •rose-like •toylike
• root-like •tooth-like •hood-like
• wolf-like •hook-like

> Try rhyming one word with a set of two: hooklike, look like. ⓘ

- wool-like • suchlike • sponge-like
- **nunlike**, sunlike
- dovelike • lion-like • flower-like
- soundalike • lookalike
- statesmanlike • seamanlike
- sportsmanlike • womanlike
- workmanlike • fatherlike • worm-like
- handspike • garpike • marlinspike
- turnpike

21.20

- **ad hoc**, amok, Bangkok, baroque, belle époque, bloc, block, bock, brock, chock, chock-a-block, clock, cock, crock, doc, dock, floc, flock, frock, hock, hough, interlock, jock, knock, langue d'oc, lock, Locke, Médoc, mock, nock, o'clock, pock, post hoc, roc, rock, schlock, shock, smock, sock, Spock, stock, wok, yapok
- manioc • Antioch • sjambok
- gemsbok • rhebok • steenbok
- springbok • grysbok • Lombok
- Zadok • Languedoc
- **burdock**, Murdoch
- hollyhock • forehock • spatchcock
- blackcock • Hancock • petcock
- haycock • gamecock
- **Leacock**, peacock, seacock
- Hickok • Hitchcock • poppycock
- stopcock • gorcock
- **Alcock**, ballcock
- monocoque • woodcock • shuttlecock
- moorcock • weathercock

21.21

- matchlock • padlock • armlock
- Belloc
- **deadlock**, headlock, wedlock
- hemlock • fetlock • airlock
- breeze block • gridlock • ziplock
- flintlock • Shylock
- **forelock**, oarlock, warlock
- roadblock • woodblock • sunblock

- gunlock • lovelock • firelock
- hammerlock • fetterlock • interlock
- Enoch • kapok • epoch • shamrock
- bedrock • pibroch • Sheetrock
- Ragnarök • bedsock • windsock
- shell shock • aftershock • fatstock
- Bartók
- **deadstock**, headstock
- penstock • tailstock • feedstock
- tick-tock • laughing stock • livestock
- **nostoc**, Rostock, Vladivostok, Vostok
- rootstock • Woodstock • bloodstock
- gunstock

21.22

- **auk**, baulk, Bork, caulk (*US* calk), chalk, cork, dork, Dundalk, Falk, fork, gawk, hawk, Hawke, nork, orc, outwalk, pork, squawk, stalk, stork, talk, torc, torque, walk, york
- pitchfork • nighthawk • goshawk
- mohawk • sparrowhawk • tomahawk
- back talk • peptalk • beanstalk
- sweet-talk • crosstalk • small talk
- smooth-talk • catwalk • jaywalk
- cakewalk • space walk
- **sheep walk**, sleepwalk
- skywalk • sidewalk • crosswalk
- boardwalk • rope-walk

21.23

- gowk

21.24

- **awoke**, bespoke, bloke, broke, choke, cloak, Coke, convoke, croak, evoke, folk, invoke, joke, Koch, moke, oak, okey-doke, poke, provoke, revoke, roque, smoke, soak, soke, spoke, stoke, stony-broke (*US* stone-broke), stroke, toke, toque, woke, yoke, yolk
- Holyoake • artichoke • gentlefolk
- menfolk • kinsfolk • womenfolk
- townsfolk • fisherfolk • holmoak

• woodsmoke •cowpoke •slowpoke
• backstroke •breaststroke •keystroke
• heatstroke •sidestroke •downstroke
• sunstroke •upstroke •masterstroke
• counterstroke •equivoque

21.25

• **hoick**, oik

21.26

• guestbook

21.27

• **archduke**, chibouk, duke, Farouk, fluke, gook, kook, Luke, nuke, peruke, puke, rebuke, Seljuk, snook, souk, spook, spruik, stook, tuque, zouk
• gobbledegook •sail-fluke
• Marmaduke •Pentateuch

21.28

• **betook**, book, brook, Brooke, Chinook, chook, Coke, cook, Cooke, crook, forsook, Gluck, hook, look, mistook, nook, partook, rook, schnook, schtuck, Shilluk, shook, Tobruk, took, undercook, undertook
• handbook
• **chapbook**, scrapbook
• cash book •passbook •sketchbook
• chequebook •netbook •textbook
• **daybook**, playbook
• casebook •phrase book •dybbuk
• pocketbook •copybook •storybook
• guidebook •logbook •songbook
• scorebook •hornbook •sourcebook
• schoolbook •notebook
• **cookbook**, lookbook
• yearbook •picture book
• wordbook •workbook
• caoutchouc •Windhoek •billhook
• fishhook •skyhook •buttonhook
• tenterhook •wet look •outlook

• Inuk •inglenook •Sihanouk
• Pembroke •Innsbruck •donnybrook
• Uruk •Osnabrück •Beaverbrook
• nainsook

21.29

• **buck**, Canuck, chuck, cluck, cruck, duck, fuck, luck, muck, pluck, puck, ruck, schmuck, shuck, struck, stuck, suck, truck, tuck, upchuck, yuck
• blackbuck •reedbuck •sawbuck
• roebuck •bushbuck •megabuck
• woodchuck •shelduck •Habakkuk
• stagestruck •awestruck •moonstruck
• dumbstruck •thunderstruck

21.30

• elegiac •Newark •Lubbock
• **Caradoc**, haddock, paddock, shaddock
• Marduk •piddock •Norfolk •Suffolk
• charlock
• **hillock**, pillock
• lilac
• **ballock**, pollack, pollock, rowlock
• bullock •hammock
• **hummock**, slummock, stomach
• **bannock**, Zanuck
• Kilmarnock •Greenock •monarch
• eunuch
• **arrack**, barrack, Baruch, carrack
• **cassock**, hassock
• tussock •Taoiseach •mattock
• **buttock**, futtock
• havoc •bulwark •wazzock •Isaac

21.31

• **berk**, berserk, Burke, cirque, dirk, Dunkirk, erk, irk, jerk, kirk, lurk, mirk, murk, outwork, perk, quirk, shirk, smirk, stirk, Turk, work
• Selkirk •Falkirk •Atatürk
• patchwork •handwork •waxwork
• **artwork**, part-work
• craftwork •headwork •legwork
• metalwork •guesswork
• **fretwork**, network

- breastwork •daywork •spadework

> Try rhyming one word with a set of two: spadework, made work. ℹ️

- framework •brainwork
- **casework**, lacework
- paintwork •beadwork •fieldwork
- needlework •teamwork •piecework
- brickwork •handiwork •bodywork
- basketwork •donkeywork •telework
- clockwork •knotwork •formwork
- coursework •falsework
- groundwork •housework
- coachwork •roadwork •homework
- stonework •woodwork •bookwork
- footwork •brushwork •firework
- ironwork •underwork •wickerwork
- paperwork •openwork •camerawork
- **masterwork**, plasterwork
- earthwork

21.32

- **calque**, talc
- catafalque
- **elk**, whelk
- **bilk**, ilk, milk, silk
- Liebfraumilch •buttermilk •volk
- **bulk**, hulk, skulk, sulk

21.33

- **ankh**, bank, blank, clank, crank, dank, drank, embank, flank, franc, frank, hank, lank, outflank, outrank, Planck, plank, point-blank, prank, rank, sank, shank, shrank, spank, stank, swank, tank, thank, wank, yank

> Create extra rhymes by adding -ing to words like bank. ℹ️

- sandbank •piggy bank •mountebank
- fog bank •mudbank •Bundesbank
- databank •riverbank •Burbank
- gangplank •Poulenc •redshank

- greenshank •sheepshank
- scrimshank •Cruikshank
- think tank •Franck •Eysenck
- **bethink**, blink, brink, chink, cinque, clink, dink, drink, fink, Frink, gink, ink, interlink, jink, kink, link, mink, pink, plink, prink, rink, shrink, sink, skink, slink, stink, sync, think, wink, zinc
- rinky-dink •Humperdinck •iceblink
- cufflink •bobolink •Maeterlinck
- lip-sync •countersink •doublethink
- kiddiewink
- tiddlywink (US tiddledywink)
- hoodwink

21.34

- **bonk**, clonk, conk, cronk, honk, Leblanc, pétanque, plonk, tronc, zonk
- honky-tonk •oink •Munch
- **bunk**, chunk, clunk, drunk, dunk, flunk, funk, gunk, hunk, junk, Monck, monk, plunk, punk, shrunk, skunk, slunk, spunk, stunk, sunk, thunk, trunk
- chipmunk •quidnunc •cyberpunk
- punch-drunk •countersunk

21.35

- **Basque**, Monégasque
- **ask**, bask, cask, flask, Krasnoyarsk, mask, masque, task
- facemask
- **arabesque**, burlesque, Dantesque, desk, grotesque, humoresque, Junoesque, Kafkaesque, Moresque, picaresque, picturesque, plateresque, Pythonesque, Romanesque, sculpturesque, statuesque
- **bisque**, brisk, disc, disk, fisc, frisk, risk, whisk
- laserdisc •obelisk •basilisk
- odalisque •tamarisk •asterisk
- **mosque**, Tosk
- kiosk •Nynorsk •brusque

- **busk**, dusk, husk, musk, rusk, tusk
- subfusc • Novosibirsk
- mollusc (*US* mollusk) • damask
- Vitebsk
- **Aleksandrovsk**, Sverdlovsk
- Khabarovsk • Komsomolsk

- **Omsk**, Tomsk
- **Gdansk**, Murmansk, Saransk
- Smolensk
- **Chelyabinsk**, Minsk
- **Donetsk**, Novokuznetsk
- **Irkutsk**, Yakutsk

Section 22: -kh

22.1

- Sassenach

22.2

- quaich

22.3

- Reich

22.4

- **Bloch**, Clough, loch, lough, och
- torgoch

22.5

- Tough

22.6

- Harlech • cromlech • coronach
- Rhydderch

Section 23: -l

23.1

- **Al**, bacchanal, cabal, canal, Chagall, Chantal, chaparral, gal, grand mal, Guadalcanál, Hal, La Salle, mall, Natal, pal, pall-mall, petit mal, sal, shall, Val
- Iqbal •Parsifal •mescal •decal
- caracal •Amytal •Nembutal
- Pentothal

23.2

- **Amal**, Arles, banal, Barisal, Basle, Bhopal, Carl, chorale, corral, dhal, entente cordiale, Escorial, farl, femme fatale, Funchal, gayal, gnarl, halal, Karl, kraal, locale, marl, morale, musicale, Pascal, pastorale, procès-verbal, Provençal, rationale, real, rial, riyal, snarl, Taal, Taj Mahal, timbale, toile, Vaal, Vidal, Waal
- Stendhal •Heyerdahl •housecarl
- cantal •hartal •Wiesenthal
- Lilienthal •neanderthal •Emmental
- Hofmannsthal •Wuppertal
- Transvaal •Roncesvalles •Kursaal

23.3

- **Adele**, Aix-la-Chapelle, aquarelle, artel, au naturel, bagatelle, béchamel, befell, bell, belle, boatel, Brunel, Cadell, carousel, cartel, cell, Chanel, chanterelle, clientele, Clonmel, compel, Cornell, crime passionnel, dell, demoiselle, dispel, dwell, el, ell, Estelle, excel, expel, farewell, fell, Fidel, fontanelle, foretell, Gabrielle, gazelle, gel, Giselle, hell, hotel, impel, knell, lapel, mademoiselle, maître d'hôtel, Manuel, marcel, matériel, mesdemoiselles, Michel, Michelle, Miguel, misspell, morel, moschatel, Moselle, motel, muscatel, nacelle, Nell, Nobel, Noel, organelle, outsell, Parnell, pell-mell, personnel, propel, quell, quenelle, rappel, Raquel, Ravel, rebel, repel, Rochelle, Sahel, sardelle, sell, shell, show-and-tell, smell, Snell, spell, spinel, swell, tell, undersell, vielle, villanelle, well, yell

> [i] Create extra rhymes by changing words like compel to compelling.

- Buñuel •Pachelbel •handbell
- barbell •harebell •decibel •doorbell
- cowbell •bluebell •Annabel
- mirabelle •Christabel •Jezebel
- **Isabel**, Isobel
- nutshell •infidel •asphodel
- zinfandel •Grenfell •Hillel •parallel
- Cozumel •caramel •Fresnel
- pimpernel •pipistrelle •Tricel
- filoselle

23.4

- clamshell •eggshell •seashell
- cockleshell •bombshell
- tortoiseshell •razorshell •Oftel
- caravel •Maxwell •Cherwell
- stairwell •Bakewell •speedwell
- inkwell •Sitwell •wishing well
- bridewell •Sizewell •Rockwell
- Cromwell •Bothwell
- **Boswell**, Roswell
- Orwell •Caldwell •groundswell
- ne'er-do-well

23.5

- **ail**, ale, assail, avail, bail, bale, bewail, brail, Braille, chain mail, countervail, curtail, dale, downscale, drail, dwale, entail, exhale, fail, faille, flail, frail, Gael, Gail, gale, Grail, grisaille, hail, hale, impale, jail, kale, mail, male, webmail, nail, nonpareil, outsail, pail, pale, quail, rail, sail, sale, sangrail, scale, shale, snail, stale, swale, tail, tale, they'll, trail, upscale, vail, vale, veil, surveil, wail, wale, whale, Yale

> Create extra rhymes by adding -s or -(e)d to words like ail. ℹ

- Passchendaele • Airedale
- Wensleydale • Clydesdale
- Chippendale • Coverdale • Abigail
- galingale • martingale • nightingale
- farthingale • Windscale • timescale
- blackmail • airmail
- **email**, female
- Ishmael • voicemail • vermeil

23.6

- hangnail • treenail • hobnail
- doornail • toenail • thumbnail
- fingernail
- **handrail**, landrail
- cantrail • guard rail • Israel • contrail
- monorail • abseil • headsail • resale
- skysail • wassail • topsail • foresail
- wholesale • lugsail • wagtail
- tattletale • fantail • bangtail
- rat's-tail • telltale
- **detail**, retail
- pigtail • bristletail • pintail
- **ringtail**, springtail
- fishtail • ponytail • hightail • bobtail
- **cocktail**, mocktail
- cottontail

- **foxtail**, oxtail
- horsetail • folktale • swallowtail
- dovetail • shirt tail • travail

23.7

- **allele**, anele, anneal, appeal, Bastille, Beale, Castile, chenille, cochineal, cockatiel, conceal, congeal, creel, deal, eel, Emile, feel, freewheel, genteel, Guayaquil, heal, heel, he'll, keel, Kiel, kneel, leal, Lille, Lucille, manchineel, meal, misdeal, Neil, O'Neill, ordeal, peal, peel, reel, schlemiel, seal, seel, she'll, spiel, squeal, steal, steel, Steele, teal, underseal, veal, weal, we'll, wheel, zeal
- airmobile • Dormobile • snowmobile
- Popemobile • bookmobile
- automobile • mouthfeel • piecemeal
- **sweetmeal**, wheatmeal
- fishmeal • inchmeal • cornmeal
- wholemeal • bonemeal • oatmeal
- kriegspiel • bonspiel • Glockenspiel
- newsreel • imbecile • Jugendstil
- cartwheel • treadwheel • millwheel
- pinwheel • flywheel • gearwheel
- waterwheel

23.8

- **bill**, Brazil, brill, Camille, chill, cookchill, dill, distil (US distill), downhill, drill, Edgehill, Estoril, fill, freewill, frill, fulfil (US fulfill), Gill, goodwill, grill, grille, hill, ill, instil, kill, krill, mil, mill, nil, Phil, pill,

> The juxtaposition of simple *stressed* (or *masculine*) *rhymes* ('chill/will') with more complex *unstressed* (or *feminine*) *rhymes* ('vision/indecision') underpins the statement of death's inevitability in this passage:
>
> And so it stays just on the edge of vision,
> A small unfocused blur, a standing chill
> That slows each impulse down to indecision.
> Most things may never happen; this one will
>
> (Philip Larkin, 'Aubade')

quadrille, quill, rill, Seville, shill,
shrill, sill, skill, spadille, spill, squill,
still, stock-still, swill, thill, thrill, till,
trill, twill, until, uphill, will
• hwyl • bank bill • handbill • waxbill
• **playbill**, waybill
• cranesbill • sibyl • crossbill • sawbill
• hornbill • storksbill • shoebill
• spoonbill • duckbill • razorbill
• gerbil • wind chill • Churchill • idyll
• daffodil • autofill • back-fill • landfill
• monofil • fibrefill (*US* fiberfill)
• chlorophyll • bluegill

23.9

• anthill • Edgehill • sidehill • molehill
• foothill • dunghill
• **sigil**, strigil, vigil
• strongyle • Virgil • Gaitskell • orchil
• roadkill • Danakil • overkill
• **amyl**, Tamil
• treadmill • windmill • gristmill
• sawmill • watermill • vinyl • mini-pill
• overspill • Caryl
• **mandrel**, mandrill
• Avril
• **beryl**, Cheryl, chrysoberyl, imperil,
  Merrill, peril, Sheryl
• tendril • April • Cyril • fibril • nombril
• nostril • Bovril • tumbril • escadrille
• espadrille • gracile • Cecil • utensil
• codicil • windowsill
• **dactyl**, pterodactyl
• pastille • standstill
• **dentil**, lentil, ventil
• quintile • pistil • postil • tormentil
• ethyl

23.10

• **anvil**, Granville
• Jacksonville • Nashville
• **Greville**, Neville
• Melville • Grenville • weevil
• Merthyr Tydfil • Louisville
• Mandeville • Stanleyville • Knoxville
• Orville • Townsville • Léopoldville
• Huntsville • Elisabethville
• vaudeville • Bougainville

• Brazzaville • chervil • tranquil
• Anwyl • pigswill • jonquil
• whippoorwill • frazil • fusil

23.11

• **aisle**, Argyle, awhile, beguile, bile,
  Carlisle, Carlyle, compile, De Stijl,
  ensile, file, guile, I'll, interfile, isle,
  Kabyle, kyle, lisle, Lyle, Mikhail,
  mile, Nile, pile, rank-and-file, resile,
  rile, Ryle, Sieg Heil, smile, spile,
  stile, style, tile, vile, Weil, while,
  wile, worthwhile
• **labile**, stabile
• **immobile**, mobile
• nubile • aedile • crocodile • cinephile
• profile • audiophile • bibliophile
• Francophile • Anglophile
• technophile • necrophile
• Russophile
• paedophile (*US* pedophile)
• **agile**, fragile
• chamomile
• **penile**, senile
• juvenile • stockpile • isopropyl
• woodpile • sterile • febrile • virile
• puerile • facile • decile • flexile
• **extensile**, prehensile, tensile
• **fissile**, missile
• domicile • docile • reconcile

23.12

• tactile • pantile
• **erectile**, insectile, projectile
• **gentile**, percentile
• reptile
• **sextile**, textile
• hairstyle • freestyle • fictile • epistyle
• peristyle • acetyl • lifestyle • hostile
• homestyle
• **butyl**, futile, rutile, utile
• ductile • fluviatile • infantile
• decastyle • mercantile • cyclostyle
• volatile • hypostyle • tetrastyle
• hexastyle • versatile • fertile
• turnstile • servile • meanwhile
• erstwhile • exile

23.13

- **boll**, Chabrol, Coll, doll, Guignol, haute école, loll, moll, pol, poll, skol, sol, troll, vol
- obol •aldol •Panadol •Algol •argol
- Gogol •googol •alcohol •glycol
- protocol •paracetamol
- **ethanol**, methanol, bioethanol
- Sebastopol •Interpol •folderol
- cholesterol •Lysol •Limassol
- parasol •aerosol •girasol •entresol
- atoll
- **Dettol**, metol
- sorbitol •capitol •Athol •menthol
- benzol

23.14

- **all**, appal (*US* appall), awl, Bacall, ball, bawl, befall, Bengal, brawl, call, caul, crawl, Donegal, drawl, drywall, enthral (*US* enthrall), fall, forestall, gall, Galle, Gaul, hall, haul, maul, miaul, miscall, Montreal, Naipaul, Nepal, orle, pall, Paul, pawl, Saul, schorl, scrawl, seawall, Senegal, shawl, small, sprawl, squall, stall, stonewall, tall, thrall, trawl, wall, waul, wherewithal, withal, yawl
- carryall •blackball •handball
- patball •hardball •netball •baseball
- paintball •speedball •heelball
- meatball •stickball •pinball •spitball
- racquetball •basketball •volleyball
- **eyeball**, highball
- oddball •softball •mothball
- korfball •cornball
- **lowball**, no-ball, snowball
- goalball
- **cueball**, screwball
- goofball •stoolball •football
- puffball •punchball •fireball
- rollerball •cannonball •butterball
- catchall •bradawl •holdall
- Goodall

23.15

- landfall •pratfall •deadfall

- rainfall •windfall •pitfall •icefall
- nightfall •rockfall •shortfall
- downfall •outfall •snowfall •dewfall
- footfall •waterfall •overfall
- keelhaul •guildhall •Whitehall
- shorthaul •overhaul •catcall •recall
- Rockall •rollcall •photocall •overcall
- Bokmål •pub crawl •overall
- coverall •Walsall •tattersall
- headstall •bookstall •fingerstall
- **therewithal**, wherewithal
- paywall •gadwall •whitewall
- Cornwall •firewall •caterwaul
- Kirkwall

23.16

- **afoul**, befoul, cowl, foul, fowl, growl, howl, jowl, owl, prowl, Rabaul, scowl, yowl
- gamefowl •peafowl •wildfowl
- moorfowl •waterfowl

23.17

- **barcarole**, bole, bowl, cajole, coal, Cole, condole, console, control, dhole, dole, droll, enrol (*US* enroll), extol, foal, goal, hole, Joel, knoll, kohl, mol, mole, Nicole, parol, parole, patrol, pole, poll, prole, rôle, roll, scroll, Seoul, shoal, skoal, sole, soul, stole, stroll, thole, Tirol, toad-in-the-hole, toll, troll, vole, whole
- Creole
- **carriole**, dariole
- cabriole •capriole
- **aureole**, gloriole, oriole
- wassail-bowl •fishbowl •dustbowl
- punchbowl •rocambole •farandole
- girandole •manhole •rathole
- armhole •arsehole •hellhole
- **keyhole**, kneehole
- peephole

> Try rhyming one word with a set of two: peephole, keep whole. [i]

- sinkhole •pinhole •cubbyhole
- hidey-hole •pigeonhole

- **eyehole**, spyhole
- foxhole
- **knothole**, pothole
- **borehole**, Warhol
- porthole •soundhole •blowhole
- stokehole •bolthole •loophole
- **lughole**, plughole
- chuckhole •buttonhole •bunghole
- earhole •waterhole •wormhole
- charcoal •caracole •Seminole
- pinole

23.18

- tadpole •flagpole •bargepole
- redpoll •maypole •beanpole
- ridgepole •Walpole •bibliopole
- Monopole •quadrupole •Metropole
- bankroll •bedroll •payroll
- banderole •rigmarole •fumarole
- casserole •profiterole •rissole
- insole •camisole •console •oversoul
- turnsole •citole •pistole

23.19

- **boil**, Boyle, broil, coil, Dáil, Doyle, embroil, Fianna Fáil, foil, Hoyle, moil, noil, oil, roil, Royle, soil, spoil, toil, voile
- parboil •trefoil •jetfoil •airfoil
- cinquefoil •milfoil •tinfoil
- multifoil •aerofoil •hydrofoil
- counterfoil •gargoyle •turmoil
- charbroil •topsoil •subsoil

23.20

- **Banjul**, befool, Boole, boule, boules, boulle, cagoule, cool, drool, fool, ghoul, Joule, mewl, misrule, mule, O'Toole, pool, Poole, pul, pule, Raoul, rule, school, shul, sool, spool, Stamboul, stool, Thule, tomfool, tool, tulle, you'll, yule
- mutule •kilojoule •playschool
- intercool •Blackpool
- ampoule (US ampule) •cesspool
- Hartlepool •Liverpool
- whirlpool

- **ferrule**, ferule
- curule •homeschool
- cucking-stool •faldstool
- toadstool •footstool •animalcule
- granule •capsule •ridicule •molecule
- minuscule •fascicule •graticule
- vestibule •reticule •globule
- **module**, nodule
- floccule •noctule •opuscule
- pustule •majuscule •virgule

23.21

- **bull**, full, Istanbul, pull, push-pull, wool
- Kabul •bagful
- **manful**, panful
- **capful**, lapful
- hatful •carful •armful •artful
- wilful (US willful) •sinful •fitful
- eyeful •boxful •potful
- **awful**, lawful
- woeful •joyful •rueful •useful
- tubful
- **jugful**, mugful
- cupful •earful •ring pull •lambswool
- schedule •residual

23.22

- **annul**, cull, dull, gull, hull, lull, mull, null, scull, skull, Solihull, trull, Tull
- seagull •multihull •monohull
- numbskull •Elul

23.23

- **Baal**, betrayal, defrayal, portrayal
- Raphael
- **empyreal**, genial, hymeneal, peritoneal

23.24

- beau idéal, ideal, real, surreal
- labial •microbial •connubial
- **adverbial**, proverbial
- prandial •radial •medial •mondial
- **cordial**, exordial, primordial

- **custodial**, plasmodial
- preludial • collegial • vestigial
- monarchial • Ezekiel • bronchial
- parochial • pallial • Belial
- **familial**, filial
- proemial • binomial • Nathaniel
- **bicentennial**, biennial, centennial, decennial, millennial, perennial, Tenniel, triennial
- cranial
- **congenial**, genial, menial, venial
- **finial**, lineal, matrilineal, patrilineal
- corneal
- **baronial**, ceremonial, colonial, matrimonial, monial, neocolonial, postcolonial, patrimonial, testimonial
- participial • marsupial
- **burial**, Meriel
- terrestrial
- **actuarial**, adversarial, aerial, areal, bursarial, commissarial, filarial, malarial, notarial, secretarial, vicarial
- Gabriel
- **atrial**, patrial
- vitriol
- **accessorial**, accusatorial, advertorial, ambassadorial, arboreal, armorial, auditorial, authorial, boreal, censorial, combinatorial, consistorial, conspiratorial, corporeal, curatorial, dictatorial, directorial, editorial, equatorial, executorial, gladiatorial, gubernatorial, immemorial, imperatorial, janitorial, lavatorial, manorial, marmoreal, memorial, monitorial, natatorial, oratorial, oriel, pictorial, piscatorial, prefectorial, professorial, proprietorial, rectorial, reportorial, sartorial, scriptorial, sectorial, senatorial, territorial, tonsorial, tutorial, uxorial, vectorial, visitorial
- Umbriel • industrial
- **arterial**, bacterial, cereal, criterial, ethereal, ferial, funereal, immaterial, imperial, magisterial, managerial, material, ministerial, presbyterial, serial, sidereal, venereal, biomaterial

- **mercurial**, Muriel, seigneurial, tenurial, Uriel
- entrepreneurial
- **axial**, biaxial, coaxial, triaxial
- uncial • lacteal
- **bestial**, celestial
- gluteal
- **convivial**, trivial
- **jovial**, synovial
- **alluvial**, diluvial, fluvial, pluvial
- **colloquial**, ventriloquial
- gymnasial • ecclesial • ambrosial

23.25

- **denial**, dial, espial, Lyall, mistrial, myall, Niall, phial, trial, vial, viol
- sundial
- **knawel**, withdrawal
- **avowal**, Baden-Powell, bowel, disembowel, dowel, Howell, Powell, rowel, towel, trowel, vowel
- semivowel
- **bestowal**, koel, Lowell, Noel
- **loyal**, royal, viceroyal
- **accrual**, construal, crewel, cruel, dual, duel, fuel, gruel, jewel, newel, renewal, reviewal
- eschewal
- artefactual (*US* artifactual), contractual, factual, tactual
- perpetual
- **aspectual**, effectual, intellectual
- **conceptual**, perceptual
- **contextual**, textual
- **habitual**, ritual
- conflictual • instinctual • spiritual
- mutual • punctual • virtual • casual
- **audio-visual**, televisual, visual
- usual • gradual • individual
- menstrual • actual
- **asexual**, bisexual, heterosexual, homosexual, psychosexual, sexual, transsexual, unisexual
- **accentual**, conventual, eventual
- Samuel
- **annual**, biannual, Emanuel, Emmanuel, manual
- Lemuel
- **consensual**, sensual
- continual

23.26

- **babble**, bedabble, dabble, drabble, gabble, grabble, rabble, scrabble
- **amble**, bramble, Campbell, gamble, gambol, ramble, scramble, shamble
- psychobabble • technobabble
- **barbel**, garble, marble
- **pebble**, rebel, treble
- **assemble**, dissemble, Kemble, resemble, tremble
- **Abel**, able, Babel, cable, enable, fable, gable, label, Mabel, sable, stable, table
- **enfeeble**, feeble, Keble
- **dibble**, dribble, fribble, Gribble, kibble, nibble, quibble, scribble
- **Abu Simbel**, cymbal, gimbal, nimble, symbol, thimble, timbal
- mandible
- **credible**, edible
- **descendible**, extendible, vendible
- audible
- **frangible**, tangible
- **illegible**, legible
- **eligible**, intelligible
- negligible • dirigible • corrigible
- submergible • fallible • indelible
- gullible
- **cannibal**, Hannibal
- discernible • terrible • horrible
- thurible
- **irascible**, passible
- expansible • collapsible • impassible
- **accessible**, compressible, impressible, inexpressible, irrepressible, repressible
- flexible
- **apprehensible**, comprehensible, defensible, distensible, extensible, ostensible, reprehensible, sensible
- indexible
- **admissible**, dismissible, immiscible, impermissible, irremissible, miscible, omissible, permissible, remissible, transmissible
- **convincible**, vincible
- **compossible**, impossible, possible
- **irresponsible**, responsible
- forcible
- **adducible**, crucible, deducible,

inducible, irreducible, producible, reducible, seducible
- **coercible**, irreversible, reversible, submersible
- **biocompatible**, compatible
- contractible • partible
- **indefectible**, perfectible
- contemptible
- **imperceptible**, perceptible, susceptible
- **comestible**, digestible, suggestible
- **irresistible**, resistible
- exhaustible
- **conductible**, deductible, destructible, tax-deductible
- **corruptible**, interruptible
- combustible
- **controvertible**, convertible, invertible
- discerptible • persuasible • feasible
- **divisible**, risible, visible
- **implausible**, plausible
- fusible
- **Bible**, intertribal, libel, scribal, tribal
- **bobble**, Chernobyl, cobble, gobble, hobble, knobble, nobble, squabble, wobble
- ensemble
- **bauble**, corbel, warble
- **coble**, ennoble, Froebel, global, Grenoble, ignoble, noble
- foible • rouble • Hasdrubal • chasuble
- **soluble**, voluble
- **bubble**, double, Hubble, nubble, rubble, stubble, trouble
- **bumble**, crumble, fumble, grumble, humble, jumble, mumble, rough-and-tumble, rumble, scumble, stumble, tumble, umbel

> Create extra rhymes by changing words like bumble to bumbling. [i]

- **payable**, sayable
- **seeable**, skiable
- amiable
- **dyeable**, flyable, friable, liable, pliable, triable, viable
- towable
- **doable**, suable, wooable
- affable • effable • exigible • cascabel
- takable • likable • salable • tenable

- tunable • capable • dupable
- **arable**, parable
- **curable**, durable
- taxable
- **fixable**, mixable
- actable • collectible
- **datable**, hatable, relatable
- eatable
- **notable**, potable
- mutable • savable • livable • movable
- lovable • equable • sizable
- usable
- **burble**, herbal, verbal

23.27

- satchel • Rachel • Mitchell

23.28

- **addle**, paddle, saddle, skedaddle, staddle, straddle
- **candle**, Coromandel, dandle, Handel, handle, mishandle, Randall, sandal, scandal, vandal
- **manhandle**, panhandle
- packsaddle • side-saddle
- **backpedal**, heddle, medal, meddle, pedal, peddle, treadle
- **Grendel**, Kendall, Lendl, Mendel, Rendell, sendal, Wendell
- **cradle**, ladle
- **beadle**, bipedal, credal, needle, wheedle
- **diddle**, fiddle, griddle, kiddle, Liddell, middle, piddle, riddle, twiddle
- **brindle**, dwindle, kindle, spindle, swindle, Tyndale
- **paradiddle**, taradiddle
- pyramidal • apsidal
- **bridal**, bridle, fratricidal, genocidal, germicidal, homicidal, idle, idol, infanticidal, insecticidal, intertidal, matricidal, parricidal, patricidal, pesticidal, regicidal, sidle, suicidal, tidal, tyrannicidal, uxoricidal
- **coddle**, doddle, model, noddle, swaddle, toddle, twaddle, waddle
- **fondle**, rondel
- mollycoddle

- **caudal**, chordal, dawdle
- **poundal**, roundel
- **Gödel**, modal, yodel
- crinoidal
- **boodle**, caboodle, canoodle, doodle, feudal, noodle, poodle, strudel, udal
- **befuddle**, cuddle, fuddle, huddle, muddle, puddle, ruddle
- **bundle**, trundle
- prebendal • synodal
- **antipodal**, tripodal
- citadel
- **curdle**, engirdle, girdle, hurdle, nurdle
- dirndl

23.29

- **baffle**, raffle, snaffle
- falafel
- **piffle**, riffle, skiffle, sniffle, whiffle
- nymphal • apocryphal
- **Eiffel**, rifle, stifle, trifle
- **coffle**, offal, waffle
- **duffel**, kerfuffle, muffle, ruffle, scuffle, shuffle, snuffle, truffle
- triumphal

23.30

- **draggle**, gaggle, haggle, raggle-taggle, straggle, waggle
- algal
- **angle**, bangle, bespangle, dangle, entangle, fandangle, jangle, mangel, mangle, spangle, strangle, tangle, wangle, wide-angle, wrangle
- triangle • quadrangle • rectangle
- pentangle • right angle • gargle
- **bagel**, finagle, Hegel, inveigle, Schlegel
- **beagle**, eagle, illegal, legal, paralegal, regal, spread eagle, viceregal
- porbeagle
- **giggle**, higgle, jiggle, niggle, sniggle, squiggle, wiggle, wriggle

> Create extra rhymes by changing words like giggle to giggling. ⓘ

- **commingle**, cringle, dingle, Fingal, intermingle, jingle, mingle, shingle, single, swingle, tingle
- prodigal •madrigal •warrigal
- surcingle •Christingle
- **boggle**, goggle, joggle, synagogal, toggle, woggle
- **diphthongal**, Mongol, pongal
- hornswoggle
- **bogle**, mogul, ogle
- Bruegel
- **bugle**, frugal, fugal, google
- **Dougal**, Mughal
- Portugal •conjugal
- **juggle**, smuggle, snuggle, struggle
- **bungle**, fungal, jungle
- McGonagall •astragal
- **burghal**, burgle, Fergal, gurgle

23.31

- Tintagel •evangel •angel •archangel
- brinjal •Nigel •cudgel

23.32

- **cackle**, crackle, grackle, hackle, jackal, mackle, shackle, tackle
- **ankle**, rankle
- **Gaskell**, mascle, paschal
- tabernacle •ramshackle
- **débâcle**, diarchal, matriarchal, monarchal, patriarchal, sparkle
- rascal
- **deckle**, freckle, heckle, Jekyll, shekel, speckle
- faecal (US fecal), treacle
- **chicle**, fickle, mickle, nickel, pickle, prickle, sickle, strickle, tickle, trickle
- **besprinkle**, crinkle, sprinkle, tinkle, twinkle, winkle, wrinkle
- fiscal
- **laical**, Pharisaical
- vehicle •stoical •cubicle •radical
- **medical**, paramedical
- **Druidical**, juridical, veridical
- syndical
- **methodical**, periodical, rhapsodical, synodical
- Talmudical •graphical •pontifical

- **magical**, tragical
- strategical
- **alogical**, illogical, logical
- **dramaturgical**, liturgical, metallurgical, surgical
- **anarchical**, hierarchical, monarchical, oligarchical
- psychical
- **angelical**, evangelical, helical
- umbilical •biblical •encyclical
- **diabolical**, follicle, hyperbolical, symbolical
- **dynamical**, hydrodynamical
- **academical**, agrochemical, alchemical, biochemical, chemical, petrochemical, photochemical, polemical
- inimical •rhythmical •seismical
- **agronomical**, anatomical, astronomical, comical, economical, gastronomical, physiognomical
- **botanical**, Brahmanical, mechanical, puritanical, sanicle, tyrannical
- ecumenical
- **geotechnical**, pyrotechnical, technical
- **clinical**, cynical, dominical, finical, Jacobinical, pinnacle, rabbinical
- **canonical**, chronicle, conical, ironical
- tunicle •pumpernickel •vernicle
- apical •epical
- **atypical**, prototypical, stereotypical, typical
- **misanthropical**, semi-tropical, subtropical, topical, tropical
- theatrical
- **chimerical**, clerical, hemispherical, hysterical, numerical, spherical
- calendrical
- **asymmetrical**, diametrical, geometrical, metrical, symmetrical, trimetrical
- electrical •ventricle
- **empirical**, lyrical, miracle, panegyrical, satirical
- cylindrical
- **ahistorical**, allegorical, categorical, historical, metaphorical, oratorical, phantasmagorical, rhetorical
- auricle •rubrical •curricle

- **classical**, fascicle, neoclassical
- farcical • vesicle
- **indexical**, lexical
- **commonsensical**, nonsensical
- **bicycle**, icicle, tricycle
- upcycle • paradoxical • Popsicle
- versicle
- **anagrammatical**, apostatical, emblematical, enigmatical, fanatical, grammatical, mathematical, piratical, prelatical, problematical, sabbatical
- **impractical**, practical, syntactical, tactical
- canticle
- **ecclesiastical**, fantastical
- **article**, particle, nanoparticle
- **alphabetical**, arithmetical, heretical, hypothetical, metathetical, metical, parenthetical, poetical, prophetical, reticle, synthetical, theoretical
- dialectical
- **conventicle**, identical
- sceptical (*US* skeptical) • testicle
- **analytical**, apolitical, critical, cryptanalytical, diacritical, eremitical, geopolitical, hypercritical, hypocritical, political, socio-political, subcritical
- **deistical**, egoistical, logistical, mystical, papistical
- **optical**, synoptical
- **aeronautical**, nautical, vortical
- **cuticle**, pharmaceutical, therapeutical
- vertical • ethical • mythical • clavicle
- periwinkle • lackadaisical

- **metaphysical**, physical, quizzical
- whimsical • musical
- **Carmichael**, cervical, cycle, Michael
- unicycle • monocycle • motorcycle
- **cockle**, grockle
- corncockle • snorkel
- **bifocal**, focal, local, univocal, varifocal, vocal, yokel
- **archducal**, coucal, ducal, pentateuchal
- **buckle**, chuckle, knuckle, muckle, ruckle, suckle, truckle
- **peduncle**, uncle
- parbuckle • carbuncle • turnbuckle
- pinochle • furuncle • honeysuckle
- **demoniacal**, maniacal, megalomaniacal, paradisiacal, zodiacal
- manacle • barnacle • cenacle
- binnacle • monocle • epochal
- reciprocal
- **coracle**, oracle
- spectacle
- **pentacle**, tentacle
- receptacle • obstacle
- equivocal
- **circle**, encircle
- semicircle

23.33

- sewellel
- **camel**, enamel, entrammel, mammal, trammel
- **miasmal**, phantasmal
- Carmel
- **abysmal**, baptismal, catechismal, dismal, paroxysmal

More unusual— and trickier— rhymes often include *unstressed* (or *feminine*) *rhymes* involving words with multiple syllables. Lord Byron used many of these, typically for comic effect:

And there are dresses splendid, but fantastical,
Masks of all times and nations, Turks and Jews,
And harlequins and clowns, with feats gymnastical,
Greeks, Romans, Yankee-doodles, and Hindoos;
All kinds of dress, except the ecclesiastical,
All people, as their fancies hit, may choose

(Lord Byron, *'Beppo'*)

- animal •minimal •lachrymal
- maximal
- **decimal**, infinitesimal
- septimal •optimal •primal •Rommel
- **abnormal**, conformal, formal, normal, paranormal, subnormal
- chromosomal •Kümmel
- **Brummell**, pommel, pummel
- **epidermal**, geothermal, isothermal, pachydermal, taxidermal, thermal

23.34

- **annal**, channel, flannel, impanel, multichannel, panel
- cracknel
- **grapnel**, shrapnel
- carnal
- **antennal**, crenel, fennel, kennel
- regnal
- **anal**, decanal
- **adrenal**, officinal, penal, renal, venal
- **signal**, spignel
- hymnal •cardinal •libidinal •ordinal
- **attitudinal**, latitudinal, longitudinal
- altitudinal
- **imaginal**, paginal
- **marginal**, submarginal
- aboriginal •virginal •disciplinal
- seminal
- **criminal**, liminal, subliminal
- **abdominal**, nominal, phenomenal, pronominal
- noumenal
- **germinal**, terminal
- **vaticinal**, vicinal
- sentinel •intestinal •Juvenal
- **doctrinal**, final, semi-final, spinal, urinal, vaginal
- quarterfinal
- **cantonal**, O'Connell
- cornel •nounal
- **atonal**, Donal, hormonal, Monel, patronal, polytonal, tonal, zonal
- motional
- **lagoonal**, monsoonal, tribunal
- communal
- **Chunnel**, funnel, gunnel, gunwale, runnel, tunnel

- autumnal •meridional
- **embryonal**, Lionel
- **diagonal**, heptagonal, hexagonal, octagonal, tetragonal
- trigonal •orthogonal •occasional
- **divisional**, provisional, visional
- **delusional**, fusional, illusional
- regional •original •coronal •arsenal
- medicinal
- **impersonal**, interpersonal, personal, transpersonal
- **irrational**, national, passional, rational
- **factional**, fractional, redactional, transactional
- **confessional**, congressional, expressional, impressional, obsessional, processional, professional, progressional, recessional, secessional, sessional, successional
- **connectional**, correctional, directional, interjectional, intersectional, sectional, unidirectional
- **ascensional**, attentional, conventional, declensional, intentional, tensional, three-dimensional, two-dimensional
- **conceptional**, exceptional, perceptional
- **durational**, locational, oblational, relational, vocational
- rotational
- **additional**, positional, tuitional, volitional
- **fictional**, jurisdictional
- inscriptional •optional •proportional
- **devotional**, emotional, notional, promotional
- **constitutional**, evolutional, institutional, substitutional
- **constructional**, fluxional, instructional
- **conjunctional**, cross-functional, dysfunctional, functional, multifunctional
- versional •seasonal
- **colonel**, diurnal, eternal, external, fraternal, infernal, internal, journal, kernel, maternal, nocturnal, paternal, supernal, vernal

23.35

- **apple**, chapel, chappal, Chappell, dapple, grapple, scrapple
- scalpel
- **ample**, trample
- pineapple
- **carpal**, carpel
- **example**, sample
- sepal
- **stemple**, temple
- **maple**, papal, staple
- **peepul**, people, steeple
- tradespeople •sportspeople
- townspeople •workpeople
- **cripple**, fipple, nipple, ripple, stipple, tipple, triple
- **dimple**, pimple, simple, wimple
- Oedipal •maniple •manciple
- municipal
- **principal**, principle
- participle •multiple
- **archetypal**, disciple, typal
- prototypal
- **hopple**, popple, stopple, topple
- gospel
- **Constantinople**, copal, nopal, opal, Opel
- **duple**, pupal, pupil, scruple
- quadruple •septuple •sextuple
- quintuple •octuple
- **couple**, supple
- **crumple**, rumple, scrumple
- syncopal •episcopal •purple

23.36

- **apparel**, barrel, carol, Carole, carrel, Carroll, Darrell, Darryl, Farrell
- gambrel •spandrel
- **astral**, plastral
- cracker-barrel
- **Errol**, feral
- **petrel**, petrol
- spectral
- **central**, epicentral, ventral
- **ancestral**, kestrel, orchestral
- dextral •Sacheverell •mayoral
- sacral •wastrel •cerebral
- **anhedral**, cathedral, dihedral,

tetrahedral
- hypaethral (*US* hypethral), urethral
- **squirrel**, Tyrol, Wirral
- **timbrel**, whimbrel
- minstrel •arbitral •sinistral •integral
- triumviral
- **spiral**, viral
- **amoral**, Balmoral, coral, immoral, laurel, moral, quarrel, sorel, sorrel
- **cockerel**, Cockerell
- dotterel •rostral
- **aboral**, aural, choral, floral, goral, oral
- **austral**, claustral
- scoundrel •cloistral •carbon-neutral
- neutral •figural •augural
- **demurral**, Durrell
- mongrel •sepulchral •lustral
- spheral •retiral
- **crural**, jural, mural, neural, plural, rural
- **illiberal**, liberal
- natural •federal •peripheral
- doggerel •mackerel •pickerel
- **bicameral**, unicameral
- admiral
- **ephemeral**, femoral
- **humeral**, numeral
- general •mineral •funeral
- **spatio-temporal**, temporal
- corporal •tesseral •visceral
- **bilateral**, collateral, equilateral, lateral, multilateral, quadrilateral, trilateral, unilateral
- pastoral
- **electoral**, pectoral, prefectoral, protectoral
- **clitoral**, literal, littoral, presbyteral
- **dipteral**, peripteral
- doctoral •several •behavioural
- **conferral**, deferral, referral, transferral

23.37

- **hassle**, Kassel, passel, tassel, vassal
- **axel**, axle
- **cancel**, hansel, Hänsel, Mansell
- transaxle
- **castle**, metatarsal, parcel, tarsal
- chancel •sandcastle •Newcastle

- **Bessel**, nestle, pestle, redressal, trestle, vessel, wrestle
- Edsel •Texel
- **intercensal**, pencil, stencil
- pretzel •staysail •mainsail •Wiesel
- **abyssal**, bristle, epistle, gristle, missal, scissel, thistle, whistle
- pixel •plimsoll
- **tinsel**, windsail
- **schnitzel**, spritsail
- Birtwistle
- **paradisal**, sisal, trysail
- **apostle**, colossal, dossal, fossil, glossal, jostle, throstle
- **consul**, proconsul, tonsil
- **dorsal**, morsel
- **council**, counsel, groundsel
- Mosul •fo'c's'le, forecastle
- **bustle**, hustle, muscle, mussel, Russell, rustle, tussle
- gunsel •corpuscle
- **disbursal**, dispersal, Purcell, rehearsal, reversal, succursal, tercel, transversal, traversal, universal
- Herzl

23.38

- **circumstantial**, financial, substantial
- **court-martial**, impartial, marshal, martial, partial
- **especial**, special
- **cadential**, confidential, consequential, credential, deferential, differential, essential, evidential, existential, experiential, exponential, influential, intelligential, irreverential, jurisprudential, penitential, pestilential, potential, preferential, presidential, providential, prudential, quintessential, referential, residential, reverential, sapiential, sciential, sentential, sequential, tangential, torrential
- **abbatial**, craniofacial, facial, fascial, glacial, interracial, multiracial, palatial, primatial, racial, spatial
- **artificial**, beneficial, initial, interstitial, judicial, official,

sacrificial, solstitial, superficial
- provincial •seneschal •equinoctial
- **asocial**, precocial, psychosocial, social
- **crucial**, fiducial
- bushel
- **antenuptial**, nuptial
- **commercial**, controversial, Herschel, inertial, infomercial

23.39

- **battle**, cattle, chattel, embattle, prattle, rattle, Seattle, tattle
- fractal
- **cantle**, covenantal, mantel, mantle, Prandtl
- pastel •Fremantle •tittle-tattle
- **startle**, stratal
- Nahuatl
- **fettle**, kettle, metal, mettle, nettle, petal, Popocatépetl, settle
- **dialectal**, rectal
- **dental**, gentle, mental, Oriental, parental, rental
- transeptal
- **festal**, vestal
- gunmetal
- **antenatal**, fatal, hiatal, natal, neonatal, ratel
- **beetle**, betel, chital, decretal, fetal
- blackbeetle
- **acquittal**, belittle, brittle, committal, embrittle, it'll, kittle, little, remittal, skittle, spittle, tittle, victual, whittle
- **edictal**, rictal
- **lintel**, pintle, quintal
- **Bristol**, Chrystal, crystal, pistol
- varietal •coital •phenobarbital
- orbital •pedestal •sagittal •vegetal
- digital •skeletal •Doolittle
- **congenital**, genital, primogenital, urogenital
- capital •lickspittle •hospital •marital
- **entitle**, mistitle, recital, requital, title, vital
- subtitle •surtitle
- **axolotl**, bottle, dottle, glottal, mottle, pottle, throttle, wattle
- **fontal**, horizontal

- **hostel**, intercostal, Pentecostal
- greenbottle •bluebottle •Aristotle
- **chortle**, immortal, mortal, portal
- Borstal
- **anecdotal**, sacerdotal, teetotal, total
- **coastal**, postal
- subtotal
- **brutal**, footle, pootle, refutal, rootle, tootle
- **buttle**, cuttle, rebuttal, scuttle, shuttle, subtle, surrebuttal
- **buntal**, contrapuntal, frontal
- crustal •societal •pivotal
- **hurtle**, kirtle, myrtle, turtle

23.40

- Ethel •lethal •brothel •betrothal
- **Cavell**, cavil, gavel, gravel, ravel, travel
- **Havel**, larval, marvel, Marvell, rondavel
- **bedevil**, bevel, devil, dishevel, kevel, level, revel, split-level
- daredevil •she-devil •eye level
- **naval**, navel
- **coeval**, evil, Khedival, medieval, primeval, retrieval, shrieval, upheaval
- **civil**, drivel, shrivel, snivel, swivel
- carnival •Percival •perspectival
- festival •aestival (*US* estival)
- **adjectival**, arrival, deprival, genitival, imperatival, infinitival, outrival, relatival, revival, rival, substantival, survival
- archival
- **grovel**, hovel, novel
- oval
- **approval**, removal
- **Lovell**, shovel
- interval •serval •narwhal

- **coequal**, equal, prequel, sequel
- **bilingual**, lingual, monolingual, multilingual
- rorqual •Hywel
- **Daniel**, spaniel

23.41

- **basil**, bedazzle, dazzle, frazzle, razzle
- damsel •razzle-dazzle •Basel
- **bezel**, embezzle
- Denzil
- **appraisal**, hazel, nasal, phrasal
- wych hazel
- **diesel**, easel, teasel, weasel
- **chisel**, drizzle, fizzle, frizzle, grizzle, mizzle, pizzle, sizzle, swizzle, twizzle
- **reprisal**, revisal
- **nozzle**, shemozzle
- **acausal**, causal, clausal, menopausal, monocausal
- **arousal**, carousal, espousal, spousal, tousle
- **disposal**, proposal, counterproposal
- **accusal**, bamboozle, foozle, ouzel, perusal, refusal
- **guzzle**, muzzle, nuzzle, puzzle
- mangel-wurzel

23.42

- **birl**, burl, churl, curl, earl, Erle, furl, girl, herl, hurl, knurl, merle, pas seul, pearl, purl, Searle, skirl, squirl, swirl, twirl, whirl, whorl
- salesgirl
- **ballgirl**, call girl
- cowgirl •showgirl •schoolgirl
- choirgirl •weathergirl •Husserl

Section 24: -m

24.1

- **am**, Amsterdam, Assam, Bram, cam, cham, cheongsam, clam, cram, dam, damn, drachm, dram, exam, femme, flam, gam, glam, gram, ham, jam, jamb, lam, lamb, mam, mesdames, Omar Khayyám, Pam, pram, pro-am, ram, Sam, scam, scram, sham, Siam, slam, Spam, swam, tam, tram, Vietnam, wham, yam
- in memoriam • ad nauseam
- **iamb**, Priam
- grandam • Edam • goddam
- quondam • Potsdam • cofferdam
- Rotterdam • Oxfam • Birmingham
- Abraham • logjam • CAD-CAM
- minicam • Nicam
- **Eelam**, Elam
- flimflam • oriflamme • Suriname
- ad personam • diazepam • tangram
- ashram • pangram • telegram
- milligram • epigram • centigram
- dithyramb
- **program**, programme

- cardiogram • radiogram • echogram
- mammogram
- aerogramme (*US* aerogram)
- microgram • dirham
- electrocardiogram • ideogram
- heliogram • diaphragm • diagram
- parallelogram • kilogram • hologram
- encephalogram • anagram
- monogram • sonogram • kissogram
- pentagram • cryptogram • photogram
- tam-tam • wigwam
- whim-wham

24.2

- **alarm**, arm, Bairam, balm, barm, becalm, calm, charm, embalm, farm, forearm, Guam, harm, imam, ma'am, malm, Montcalm, Notre-Dame, palm, psalm, qualm, salaam, smarm

> Create extra rhymes by adding -*ed* to words like alarm.

- yardarm • sidearm • gendarme
- wind farm • Islam • schoolmarm

It is well known that rap depends on rhyming for its structure and power; this example includes *medial (internal) rhyme*, *stressed (masculine) rhyme*, *unstressed (feminine) rhyme*, and *half-rhyme*:

Don't u call this a regular jam
I'm gonna rock this land
I'm gonna take this itty bitty world by storm
And I'm just gettin warm

[...]

Listen to my gear shift
I'm blastin, outlastin
Kinda like Shaft, so u could say I'm shaftin
Old English filled my mind
And I came up with a funky rhyme

(LL Cool J, 'Mama said knock you out')

- tonearm • napalm • firearm
- underarm • short-arm

24.3

- **ahem**, Belém, Clem, condemn, contemn, crème de la crème, em, gem, hem, Jem, LibDem, phlegm, pro tem, rem, Shem, stem, them
- **carpe diem**, per diem
- proem • idem • modem • diadem
- mayhem • Bethlehem • ad hominem
- ad valorem • brainstem
- apophthegm (*US* apothegm)

24.4

- **acclaim**, aflame, aim, became, blame, came, claim, dame, exclaim, fame, flame, frame, game, lame, maim, misname, name, proclaim, same, shame, tame
- endgame • counterclaim • nickname
- byname • filename • forename
- surname • airframe • mainframe
- Ephraim • doorframe • subframe
- underframe • aspartame

24.5

- **abeam**, agleam, beam, blaspheme, bream, cream, deem, deme, downstream, dream, esteem, extreme, gleam, hakim, kilim, meme, midstream, Nîmes, ream, régime, scheme, scream, seam, seem, steam, stream, supreme, team, teem, theme, upstream

> Create extra rhymes by adding -*ing* to words like beam. [i]

- cross-beam • hornbeam • moonbeam
- sunbeam • academe • morpheme
- phoneme • jet stream • airstream
- daydream • mainstream • Brylcreem
- millstream • slipstream
- bloodstream • monotreme
- buttercream • raceme • septime
- centime

24.6

- **bedim**, brim, crim, dim, glim, grim, Grimm, gym, him, hymn, Jim, Kim, limb, limn, nim, prim, quim, rim, scrim, shim, Sim, skim, slim, swim, Tim, trim, vim, whim

> Create extra rhymes by changing words like bedim to bedims or bedimmed. [i]

- poem • goyim • cherubim • Hasidim
- **seraphim**, teraphim
- Elohim • Sikkim • Joachim • prelim
- forelimb • Muslim • Blenheim
- paynim • minim • pseudonym
- homonym • anonym • synonym
- eponym • acronym • antonym
- metonym • Antrim • megrim
- Leitrim • pilgrim • Purim • interim
- passim • maxim • kibbutzim
- Midrashim • literatim
- **seriatim**, verbatim
- victim

> Try rhyming one word with a set of two: victim, picked him. [i]

- system • ecosystem • subsystem
- item • Ashkenazim

24.7

- **begrime**, Chaim, chime, climb, clime, crime, dime, grime, half-time, I'm, lime, mime, mistime, part-time, prime, rhyme, rime, slime, sublime, sub-prime, thyme, time
- paradigm • Mannheim • Waldheim
- Sondheim • Trondheim
- Guggenheim • Anaheim • Durkheim
- quicklime • brooklime • birdlime
- pantomime • ragtime • pastime
- bedtime • airtime
- **daytime**, playtime
- teatime • mealtime • dreamtime
- meantime • peacetime • springtime
- anytime • maritime • flexitime
- lifetime • nighttime • wartime
- downtime • noontime • sometime
- one-time • lunchtime • summertime
- wintertime • enzyme

24.8

- **aplomb**, bomb, bombe, CD-ROM, dom, from, glom, mom, pom, prom, Rom, shalom, Somme, therefrom, Thom, tom, wherefrom
- stink bomb • firebomb • sitcom
- Telecom • non-com • intercom
- coulomb • pompom • tomtom

24.9

- **conform**, corm, dorm, form, forme, haulm, lukewarm, Maugham, misinform, norm, outperform, perform, shawm, storm, swarm, transform, underperform, warm

> Create extra rhymes by adding -ing to words like conform. [i]

- landform • platform • multi-platform
- cubiform
- **fungiform**, spongiform
- aliform • bacilliform
- **cuneiform**, uniform
- variform • vitriform • cruciform
- unciform • retiform • multiform
- oviform • triform • microform
- chloroform • cairngorm • sandstorm
- barnstorm
- **brainstorm**, rainstorm
- windstorm • snowstorm • firestorm
- thunderstorm

24.10

- Lebensraum

24.11

- **brome**, chrome, comb, Crome, dome, foam, gnome, holm, Holme, hom, home, Jerome, loam, Nome, ohm, om, roam, Rome, tome
- Guillaume • Jedrome • Beerbohm
- radome • astrodome • Styrofoam
- megohm • Stockholm • Bornholm
- motorhome • backcomb • honeycomb
- **cockscomb**, coxcomb

- toothcomb • genome • gastronome
- metronome • syndrome • palindrome
- polychrome • Nichrome
- monochrome • velodrome
- hippodrome • aerodrome
- cyclostome • rhizome

24.12

- **abloom**, assume, backroom, bloom, Blum, boom, broom, brume, combe, consume, doom, entomb, exhume, flume, foredoom, fume, gloom, groom, Hume, illume, inhume, Khartoum, khoum, loom, neume, perfume, plume, presume, resume, rheum, room, spume, subsume, tomb, vroom, whom, womb, zoom
- catacomb • heirloom • broadloom
- taproom • guardroom • staffroom
- darkroom • classroom
- bathroom
- **bedroom**, headroom
- legroom • restroom
- **dayroom**, playroom
- saleroom • stateroom • salesroom
- tearoom • green room • sickroom
- anteroom • bridegroom • stockroom
- strongroom • box room • washroom
- storeroom • boardroom • ballroom
- courtroom • houseroom • showroom
- cloakroom • elbow room
- **poolroom**, schoolroom
- newsroom
- **gunroom**, sunroom
- mushroom • common room
- workroom • hecatomb • vacuum
- legume • volume • costume
- Leverhulme

24.13

- **Qum**, stum
- Aksum

24.14

- **become**, benumb, Brum, bum, chum, come, crumb, cum, drum,

dumb, glum, gum, ho-hum, hum,
Kara Kum, lum, mum, numb, plum,
plumb, Rhum, rhumb, rum, scrum,
scum, slum, some, strum, stum,
succumb, sum, swum, thrum, thumb,
tum, yum-yum
• natatorium

> Create extra rhymes by adding -*ly* to words like come and crumb. ⓘ

• stumblebum • dumdum • bubblegum
• philtrum • outcome • sugarplum
• lanthanum • kettledrum
• breadcrumb • humdrum • eardrum

24.15

• um
• **Graeme**, graham
• **athenaeum**, atheneum, coliseum,
Liam, lyceum, mausoleum, museum,
peritoneum, propylaeum, Te Deum
• Rijksmuseum

24.16

• columbium
• **erbium**, terbium, ytterbium
• scandium • compendium
• **palladium**, radium, stadium,
vanadium
• **medium**, tedium
• **cryptosporidium**, cymbidium,
idiom, iridium, rubidium
• indium
• **exordium**, Gordium, rutherfordium
• **odeum**, odium, plasmodium,
podium, sodium
• **allium**, gallium, pallium, thallium,
valium
• **berkelium**, epithelium, helium,
nobelium, Sealyham
• **beryllium**, cilium, psyllium, trillium
• **linoleum**, petroleum
• thulium • cadmium
• **epithalamium**, prothalamium
• **freemium**, gelsemium, premium
• **chromium**, encomium
• holmium • fermium

• **biennium**, millennium
• **cranium**, geranium, germanium,
Herculaneum, titanium, uranium
• **helenium**, proscenium, rhenium,
ruthenium, selenium
• **actinium**, aluminium,
condominium, delphinium
• **ammonium**, euphonium,
harmonium, pandemonium,
pelargonium, plutonium, polonium,
zirconium
• neptunium
• **europium**, opium
• **aquarium**, armamentarium, barium,
caldarium, cinerarium,
columbarium, dolphinarium,
frigidarium, herbarium, honorarium,
planetarium, rosarium, sanitarium,
solarium, sudarium, tepidarium,
terrarium, vivarium
• atrium
• **delirium**, Miriam
• **equilibrium**, Librium
• yttrium
• **auditorium**, ciborium,
conservatorium, crematorium,
emporium, moratorium, sanatorium,
scriptorium, sudatorium, vomitorium
• opprobrium
• **cerium**, imperium, magisterium
• **curium**, tellurium
• potassium • axiom • calcium
• francium • lawrencium • copernicium
• americium
• **Latium**, solatium
• **lutetium**, technetium
• Byzantium • strontium • consortium
• protium • promethium • lithium
• **alluvium**, effluvium
• requiem • colloquium • gymnasium
• **caesium** (*US* cesium), magnesium,
trapezium
• Elysium • symposium

24.17

• **jeroboam**, Noam, Siloam
• brougham
• **residuum**, triduum
• continuum • Brabham • album
• sachem • Beecham • Mitchum

- **Adam**, macadam, madam, Madame
- **avizandum**, fandom, memorandum, nil desperandum, random, tandem
- tarmacadam
- **shahdom**, stardom, tsardom
- **beldam**, seldom
- **addendum**, corrigendum, referendum
- heirdom •sheikhdom •Gaeldom
- thanedom •saintdom
- **Edom**, freedom, Needham
- **chiefdom**, fiefdom
- queendom •heathendom
- crippledom •officialdom •Wyndham
- Christendom •kingdom •princedom
- wisdom •fogeydom •yuppiedom
- **rodham**, Sodom
- condom
- **boredom**, whoredom
- thraldom •Oldham •popedom
- dukedom
- **Carborundum**, corundum
- poppadom •pauperdom •martyrdom
- reductio ad absurdum •serfdom
- earldom

24.18

- amalgam •Targum •begum
- Brigham •lingam •ogham •sorghum
- Nahum •Belgium •dodgem
- Brummagem •stratagem •Rackham
- Malcolm •Ascham •Beckham
- welcome •vade mecum •stickum
- dinkum •modicum •hypericum
- capsicum •viaticum •practicum
- Occam
- **hokum**, locum, oakum
- bunkum
- **alum**, Calum, mallam, vallum
- Pablum
- **Haarlem**, Harlem, Malayalam, slalom
- **antebellum**, cerebellum, elm, helm, overwhelm, pelham, realm, underwhelm, vellum
- emblem •bedlam •peplum
- exemplum •wychelm •Kenelm
- Salem •velum
- **aspergillum**, chillum, film, vexillum

- Whitlam •clingfilm •telefilm
- microfilm
- **asylum**, hilum, phylum, whilom
- **column**, olm, solemn
- problem •golem •hoodlum • Ulm
- **incunabulum**, pabulum
- coagulum •pendulum •speculum
- curriculum •cimbalom •paspalum
- Absalom •Jerusalem •tantalum

24.19

- minimum •maximum •optimum
- **chrysanthemum**, helianthemum
- cardamom •Pergamum •sesamum
- per annum •magnum •damnum
- **Arnhem**, Barnum
- **envenom**, venom
- interregnum •Cheltenham •arcanum
- **duodenum**, plenum
- platinum •antirrhinum •Bonham
- summum bonum •Puttnam
- ladanum •molybdenum •laudanum
- **origanum**, polygonum
- organum •tympanum
- **laburnum**, sternum
- gingham •Gillingham •Birmingham
- Cunningham •Walsingham
- Nottingham •wampum •carom
- Abram •panjandrum •tantrum
- angstrom •alarum •candelabrum
- **plectrum**, spectrum
- **arum**, harem, harum-scarum, Sarum
- **sacrum**, simulacrum
- maelstrom •cerebrum •pyrethrum
- Ingram
- **sistrum**, Tristram
- Hiram
- **grogram**, pogrom
- **nostrum**, rostrum
- **cockalorum**, decorum, forum, jorum, Karakoram, Karakorum, Mizoram, pons asinorum, quorum
- wolfram •fulcrum •Durham
- conundrum •buckram •lustrum
- **serum**, theorem
- labarum •marjoram •pittosporum
- Rotherham •Bertram

24.20

- **hansom**, ransom, Ransome, transom
- Wrexham • sensum • Epsom • jetsam
- lissom • winsome • gypsum • alyssum
- **blossom**, opossum, possum
- flotsam • awesome • balsam • Folsom
- noisome • twosome

> Try rhyming one word with a set of two: twosome, lose some. ℹ

- fulsome • buxom • Hilversum
- irksome • Gresham • meerschaum
- petersham • nasturtium
- **atom**, Euratom
- factum
- **bantam**, phantom
- sanctum
- **desideratum**, erratum, post-partum, stratum
- substratum • rectum • momentum
- septum
- **datum**, petrolatum, pomatum, Tatum, ultimatum
- arboretum • dictum • symptom
- ad infinitum
- **bottom**, rock-bottom
- quantum
- **autumn**, postmortem
- **factotum**, Gotham, scrotum, teetotum, totem
- sputum
- **accustom**, custom
- diatom • anthem • Bentham • Botham
- fathom • rhythm • biorhythm
- algorithm • logarithm • sempervivum
- ovum • William

24.21

- **chasm**, spasm
- enthusiasm • orgasm • sarcasm
- ectoplasm • cytoplasm • iconoclasm
- cataplasm • pleonasm • phantasm
- besom • dirigisme
- **abysm**, arrivisme, chrism, chrisom, ism, prism, schism
- **Shiism**, theism
- **Maoism**, Taoism
- egoism • truism • Babism • cubism
- sadism • nudism • Sufism • ageism
- holism • cataclysm • monism • papism
- verism • aneurysm • purism • Nazism
- sexism • racism • paroxysm • autism
- macrocosm • microcosm • bosom

24.22

- **affirm**, berm, confirm, firm, germ, herm, midterm, perm, sperm, squirm, term, therm, worm
- pachyderm • echinoderm
- wheatgerm • endosperm
- gymnosperm • isogeotherm
- ragworm • flatworm • threadworm
- tapeworm
- **eelworm**, mealworm
- silkworm • ringworm • inchworm
- blindworm • lobworm • roundworm
- slow-worm • screw worm
- woodworm
- **bookworm**, hookworm
- bloodworm • lugworm • lungworm
- earthworm

Section 25: -n

25.1

- **Aberfan**, Adrianne, an, Anne,
artisan, astrakhan, ban, began,
Belmopan, bipartisan, bran, can,
Cannes, Cézanne, Cheyenne, clan,
courtesan, cran, dan, Dayan, Diane,
divan, élan, Elan, fan, flan, foreran,
Fran, Friedan, Gell-Mann, gran, Han,
Hunan, Ivan, Jan, Japan, Jinan,
Joanne, Kazan, Klan, Kordofan,
Lacan, Lausanne, Leanne, Limousin,
Louvain, man, Mann, Marianne,
Milan, Moran, nan, Oran, outran,
outspan, Pan, panne, parmesan,
partisan, pavane, pecan, Pétain, plan,
Pusan, ran, rataplan, rattan,
Rosanne, Sagan, Saipan, saran, scan,
scran, sedan, span, spick-and-span,
Spokane, Suzanne, Tainan, tan, than,
tisane, trepan, van, vin, Wuhan,
Xian, Yerevan, Yunnan, Zhongshan
- koan • kanban • Seremban
- **Cardin**, Teilhard de Chardin
- Rodin • Ramadan • dauphin
- turbofan • Afghan • Gauguin
- Callaghan

25.2

- cancan
- **ashcan**, trash can
- billycan • jerrycan • oilcan
- Leninakan • gamelan • Ameslan
- Acrilan • Catalan • adman
- **bagman**, ragman, swagman
- **packman**, Pac-man
- sandman • gasman • taxman • Batman
- jazzman • yardman • legman
- chessman • repairman • mailman
- apeman • spaceman • caveman
- he-man • freedman • linkman
- middleman • Winckelmann
- wingman • hitman • handyman
- bogeyman • everyman • iceman
- conman • strongman
- **lawman**, strawman
- snowman • patrolman • oilman
- schoolman • newsman
- **frontman**, stuntman
- wireman • anchorman • Telemann
- newspaperman • Superman
- motorman
- weatherman • merman • Poznan

25.3

- sampan • tarpan
- **bedpan**, deadpan
- skidpan • inspan • wingspan
- marzipan
- **frypan**, taipan
- lifespan • Chopin • saltpan • outspan
- dustpan • tragopan • Perrin
- trimaran • catamaran • Poussin
- Anshan • gratin • kaftan • suntan
- Chambertin • orang-utan • minivan
- Ativan • caravan • banyan

25.4

- **Abadan**, Abidjan, adhan, Amman,
Antoine, Arne, Aswan, Avon,
Azerbaijan, Baltistan, Baluchistan,
Bantustan, barn, Bhutan, Dagestan,
darn, dewan, Farne, guan, Hahn,
Hanuman, Hindustan, Huascarán,
Iban, Iran, Isfahan, Juan,
Kazakhstan, khan, Koran, Kurdistan,
Kurgan, Kyrgyzstan, macédoine,
Mahon, maidan, Marne, Michoacán,
Oman, Pakistan, pan, Pathan,
Qumran, Rajasthan, Shan, Siân,
Sichuan, skarn, soutane, Sudan,

Tai'an, t'ai chi ch'uan, Taiwan, Tajikistan, Taklimakan, tarn, Tatarstan, Tehran, Tenochtitlán, Turkestan, Turkmenistan, tzigane, Uzbekistan, Vientiane, yarn, Yinchuan, yuan, Yucatán
- Autobahn • Lindisfarne
- Bildungsroman • Nisan • Khoisan
- Afghanistan • bhagwan • Karajan

25.5

- **Adrienne**, again, amen, Ardennes, Behn, Ben, Benn, Bren, cayenne, Cévennes, Dairen, den, en, fen, gen, glen, Glenn, Guyenne, Gwen, hen, julienne, Karen, ken, Len, Loren, men, Nene, Ogaden, paren, pen, Penn, Phnom Penh, Rennes, Shenzhen, Sun Yat-sen, ten, then, Tlemcen, when, wren, yen, zazen, Zen
- paraben • Chechen • Nurofen
- peahen • moorhen • Origen
- allergen • admen
- **bagmen**, ragmen, swagmen
- packmen • gasmen • taxmen
- jazzmen • ramen • yardmen • legmen
- chessmen • repairmen • flamen
- mailmen • cavemen • he-men
- freedmen • milkmen • linkmen
- middlemen • wingmen • hitmen
- handymen • bogeymen • hymen
- icemen • conmen • strongmen
- **lawmen**, strawmen
- **cognomen**, nomen, praenomen, snowmen
- patrolmen • oilmen • Shumen
- newsmen
- **frontmen**, stuntmen
- **firemen**, wiremen
- anchormen • newspapermen
- motormen
- weathermen • mermen • playpen
- pigpen • fountain pen • bullpen
- samisen • Leuven • Ceinwen
- somewhen

25.6

- **Auvergne**, bairn, cairn

25.7

- **abstain**, appertain, arcane, arraign, ascertain, attain, Bahrain, bane, blain, brain, Braine, Cain, Caine, campaign, cane, cinquain, chain, champagne, champaign, Champlain, Charmaine, chicane, chow mein, cocaine, Coleraine, Coltrane, complain, constrain, contain, crane, Dane, deign, demesne, demi-mondaine, detain, disdain, domain, domaine, drain, Duane, Dwane, Elaine, entertain, entrain, explain, fain, fane, feign, gain, Germaine, germane, grain, humane, Hussein, inane, Jain, Jane, Jermaine, Kane, La Fontaine, lain, lane, legerdemain, Lorraine, main, Maine, maintain, mane, mise en scène, Montaigne, moraine, mundane, obtain, ordain, pain, Paine, pane, pertain, plain, plane, Port-of-Spain, profane, rain, Raine, refrain, reign, rein, retain, romaine, sane, Seine, Shane, Sinn Fein, skein, slain, Spain, Spillane, sprain, stain, strain, sustain, swain, terrain, thane, train, twain, Ujjain, Ukraine, underlain, urbane, vain, vane, vein, Verlaine, vicereine, wain, wane, Wayne
- watch chain • mondaine • Haldane
- ultramundane • Cellophane
- novocaine • sugar cane
- marocain

25.8

- **airplane**, terreplein
- **sailplane**, tailplane
- mainplane
- **seaplane**, ski-plane
- chilblain
- **biplane**, triplane
- warplane • towplane • Tamerlane
- monoplane • aeroplane • gyroplane
- hydroplane • châtelaine • aquaplane
- balletomane • Moulmein
- Charlemagne • frangipane • propane
- windowpane • counterpane
- membrane • checkrein • lamebrain

- migraine •ingrain •quatrain
- grosgrain •wholegrain •scatterbrain
- suzerain •birdbrain •sixain
- elastane •Beltane •Aquitaine
- octane
- **Fonteyn**, montane
- Holstein •Bloemfontein •butane
- bloodstain •chevrotain
- **ethane**, methane
- polyurethane •Alfvén •paravane
- weathervane •vervain •Gawain

25.9

- **Aberdeen**, Amin, aquamarine,
  baleen, bean, been, beguine, Benin,
  between, canteen, careen, Claudine,
  clean, contravene, convene, cuisine,
  dean, Dene, e'en, eighteen, fascine,
  fedayeen, fifteen, figurine, foreseen,
  fourteen, Francine, gean, gene,
  glean, gombeen, green, Greene,
  Halloween, intervene, Janine, Jean,
  Jeannine, Jolene, Kean, keen, Keene,
  Ladin, langoustine, latrine, lean,
  limousine, machine, Maclean,
  magazine, Malines, margarine,
  marine, Mascarene, Massine,
  Maxine, mean, Medellín, mesne,
  mien, Moline, moreen, mujahedin,
  Nadine, nankeen, Nazarene, Nene,
  nineteen, nougatine, obscene,
  palanquin, peen, poteen, preen,
  quean, queen, Rabin, Racine, ramin,
  ravine, routine, Sabine, saltine,
  sardine, sarin, sateen, scene, screen,
  seen, serene, seventeen, shagreen,
  shebeen, sheen, sixteen, spleen,
  spring-clean, squireen, Steen,
  submarine, supervene, tambourine,
  tangerine, teen, terrine, thirteen,
  transmarine, treen, tureen,
  Tyrrhene, ultramarine, umpteen,
  velveteen, wean, ween, Wheen,
  yean

> Try rhyming one word with a   i
> set of two or more: foreseen, one
> more scene.

- soybean •buckbean

25.10

- gradine •sanidine
- **codeine**, Roedean
- undine •iodine
- **Aberdeen**, gaberdine
- almandine •grenadine •Geraldine
- caffeine •Delphine •Josephine
- morphine •carrageen •aubergine
- indigene •hygiene •phosgene
- Eugene •Tolkien •Kathleen
- **Arlene**, Charlene, Darlene, Marlene,
  praline
- **Hellene**, philhellene
- **Aileen**, Raelene, scalene
- spring-clean •crimplene •Abilene
- Ghibelline •Cymbeline •terylene
- vaseline •acetylene •Mytilene
- Eileen •colleen •Pauline
- mousseline •Hölderlin •nepheline
- Evangeline
- **Jacqueline**, Sakhalin
- Emmeline •tourmaline •trampoline
- gasoline •naphthalene •Rosaleen
- rosaline

25.11

- gamine •bromine •thiamine
- dopamine •amphetamine •histamine
- quinine •strychnine •mezzanine
- spalpeen •Philippine •lycopene
- gangrene •terrene •silkscreen
- windscreen •citrine •Dexedrine
- putting green •Benzedrine
- pseudoephedrine
- **Irene**, polystyrene
- widescreen •sight screen
- **chlorine**, chorine, Doreen, Maureen,
  Noreen, taurine
- smokescreen •rood screen
- sunscreen •fluorine •helleborine
- Gadarene •Hippocrene
- **glycerine** (US glycerin),
  nitroglycerine (US nitroglycerin)
- nectarine •wintergreen •Methedrine
- evergreen •wolverine •vaccine
- glassine •Essene •Rexine •piscine
- epicene •glycine •pyroxene

- **Palaeocene** (*US* Paleocene)
- Pliocene •Miocene •Holocene
- damascene •kerosene •Plasticine
- Pleistocene

25.12

- diamantine •dentine •Benedictine
- **Christine**, pristine, Sistine
- Springsteen •tontine •protein
- Justine •libertine •mangosteen
- brigantine •Augustine •nicotine
- galantine •guillotine •carotene
- quarantine •astatine •travertine
- brilliantine •ethene •polythene
- hypersthene •olivine •Slovene
- go-between •fanzine
- **benzene**, benzine
- bombazine •organzine

25.13

- **agin**, akin, begin, Berlin, bin, Boleyn, Bryn, chin, chin-chin, Corinne, din, fin, Finn, Flynn, gaijin, gin, Glyn, grin, Gwyn, herein, Ho Chi Minh, in, inn, Jin, jinn, kin, Kweilin, linn, Lynn, mandolin, mandoline, Min, no-win, pin, Pinyin, quin, shin, sin, skin, spin, therein, thin, Tientsin, tin, Tonkin, Turin, twin, underpin, Vietminh, violin, wherein, whin, whipper-in, win, within, Wynne, yin
- weigh-in •lutein •lie-in •Samhain
- **Bowen**, Cohen, Owen, throw-in
- **heroin**, heroine
- benzoin
- **bruin**, ruin, shoo-in
- Bedouin •Islwyn
- **genuine**, Menuhin
- **cabin**, Scriabin
- Portakabin •sin bin •swingbin
- **bobbin**, dobbin, robin
- **haemoglobin** (*US* hemoglobin)
- Reuben •dubbin •dustbin •Jacobin
- **kitchen**, lichen
- Cochin •urchin

25.14

- Aladdin •stand-in
- **Dunedin**, lead-in
- **Blondin**, Girondin
- Odin
- **paladin**, Saladin
- Borodin •Baffin •elfin
- **biffin**, griffin, tiffin
- **boffin**, coffin
- dolphin •endorphin •bowfin
- yellowfin
- **muffin**, puffin
- ragamuffin •paraffin •perfin
- bargain •Begin •Kosygin
- **hoggin**, noggin
- imagine •margin •engine
- **pidgin**, pigeon, smidgen, wigeon
- stool pigeon •wood pigeon •origin
- Pugin •virgin

25.15

- grimalkin •lambkin •napkin •gaskin
- lambskin •catkin
- **Larkin**, parkin
- calfskin •sharkskin •welkin
- Potemkin •Jenkin •redskin
- bearskin •snakeskin •Deakin
- sealskin •sheepskin •chicken
- limpkin •pipkin
- **griskin**, siskin
- pigskin •spillikin •ramekin
- **manikin**, mannequin, pannikin
- minikin •larrikin •Zworykin
- wineskin •bodkin •Hodgkin
- Donkin
- **Algonquin**, Tonkin
- Hopkin
- **Kropotkin**, Watkin
- walk-in •foreskin •doeskin
- moleskin •goatskin •oilskin
- coonskin •wolfskin •Pushkin
- **bumpkin**, pumpkin
- **buskin**, Ruskin
- buckskin •deerskin •baldachin
- manakin

- **firkin**, gherkin, jerkin, merkin, Perkin

25.16

- **Alun**, Malin, Tallinn
- Jacklin •franklin
- **chaplain**, Chaplin
- ratline
- **Carlin**, call-in, marlin, marline, Stalin
- **Helen**, Llewelyn
- Mechlin
- **Emlyn**, gremlin, Kremlin
- Galen •capelin •kylin •Evelyn
- **Enniskillen**, penicillin, villein
- Hamelin •Marilyn •discipline
- **Colin**, Dolin
- **goblin**, hobgoblin
- Loughlin
- **Joplin**, poplin
- compline •tarpaulin
- **Magdalen**, maudlin
- **bowline**, pangolin
- Ventolin •moulin •Lublin •Brooklyn
- masculine •insulin •globulin
- mullein •Dublin •dunlin •muslin
- kaolin •chamberlain •Michelin
- madeleine •Mary Magdalene
- Gwendolen •francolin •mescaline
- formalin •lanolin
- **adrenalin**, noradrenalin
- crinoline •zeppelin •cipolin
- Carolyn •Jocelyn •porcelain •Ritalin
- Ottoline
- **javelin**, ravelin
- Rosalyn
- **merlin**, purlin
- Dunfermline •purslane

25.17

- **examine**, famine, gamin
- admin •jasmine •Yasmin •Brahmin
- women •specimen •madwomen
- clanswomen •charwomen
- craftswomen •draughtswomen
- gentlewomen •Welshwomen
- Frenchwomen
- **airwomen**, chairwomen
- laywomen •stateswomen

- saleswomen •policewomen
- kinswomen •Englishwomen
- businesswomen •Irishwomen
- congresswomen •countrywomen
- jurywomen •servicewomen
- tribeswomen
- **Scotswomen**, yachtswomen
- forewomen •horsewomen
- sportswomen •oarswomen
- councilwomen •townswomen
- noblewomen •spokeswomen
- frontierswomen •alderwomen
- anchorwomen •washerwomen
- Ulsterwomen •churchwomen
- **catechumen**, illumine, lumen
- bitumen
- **albumen**, albumin
- Duralumin •cumin •Benjamin
- theremin •vitamin
- **determine**, ermine, vermin

25.18

- tannin
- **antivenin**, Lenin
- Kalinin •linen •bedlinen
- underlinen •feminine
- **Cronin**, phone-in, ronin, serotonin
- Bakunin •run-in •melanin •santonin
- crankpin •backspin •hatpin
- tenpin •hairpin •tailspin •wheelspin
- **Crippen**, pippin
- stickpin •kingpin •Crispin •linchpin
- tiepin •topspin •clothespin
- **lupin**, lupine
- pushpin •terrapin •Turpin •Karin
- Keirin •chagrin •aspirin •Catrin
- Kathryn •Gagarin
- **Erin**, Perrin, serin
- Sanhedrin •epinephrine •dextrin
- brethren •Montenegrin •pyrethrin
- peregrine
- **Corin**, florin, foreign
- doctrine •sovereign •Aldrin
- Paludrine •murrain
- **Kirin**, stearin
- Lohengrin
- **burin**, urine
- tambourin •mandarin •warfarin
- **saccharin**, saccharine

- tamarin •Catherine
- **navarin**, savarin
- culverin •Mazarin

25.19

- assassin •Yeltsin •sasine
- Solzhenitsyn •rebbetzin
- **biomedicine**, medicine
- ceresin
- **ricin**, Terramycin
- **tocsin**, toxin
- Wisconsin •oxytocin •niacin
- moccasin •characin •Capuchin
- **Latin**, satin
- plantain •captain
- **marten**, martin
- cretin
- **pecten**, pectin
- Quentin
- **clandestine**, destine, intestine
- sit-in •quintain •bulletin •chitin
- **Austen**, Mostyn
- **fountain**, mountain
- **gluten**, highfalutin, Rasputin
- **Dustin**, Justin
- biotin •legatine •gelatin •keratin
- **certain**, Curtin
- Kirsten •Gethin •lecithin •Bleddyn
- **Gavin**, ravin, ravine, savin, spavin
- **Alvin**, Calvin
- Marvin
- **Bevin**, Kevin, levin, Previn, replevin
- **kelvin**, Melvin
- riboflavin •covin •Mervyn

25.20

- Gladwin
- **anguine**, sanguine
- Alcuin •Darwin •Tarquin
- **Cledwyn**, Edwin
- penguin
- **Delwyn**, Selwyn
- sequin •Chindwin •Dilwyn
- harlequin
- **Blodwen**, Godwin
- Olwen •Baldwin •Alwyn •Goldwyn
- Goodwin •Irwin •Gershwin

- **muezzin**, resin
- seisin •rosin

25.21

- **align**, assign, benign, brine, chine, cline, combine, condign, confine, consign, dine, divine, dyne, enshrine, entwine, fine, frontline, hardline, interline, intertwine, kine, Klein, line, Main, malign, mine, moline, nine, on-line, opine, outshine, pine, Rhein, Rhine, shine, shrine, sign, sine, spine, spline, stein, Strine, swine, syne, thine, tine, trine, twine, Tyne, underline, undermine, vine, whine, wine
- Sabine •carbine •Holbein •woodbine
- concubine •columbine •turbine
- sardine •Aldine •muscadine
- celandine •anodyne •androgyne

25.22

- catchline •dragline •tramline
- landline •strapline •chatline
- carline
- **breadline**, deadline, headline, redline
- neckline •hemline •helpline
- **airline**, hairline
- saline •mainline
- **baseline**, bassline, waistline
- dateline
- **beeline**, feline, treeline
- streamline •slimline •sibylline
- Adeline •bodyline •storyline
- Catiline •aquiline
- **byline**, skyline
- **guideline**, sideline, tideline
- lifeline •pipeline •sight line •hotline
- **jawline**, Pauline, shoreline
- outline
- **snowline**, towline
- coastline •clothesline •microcline
- Fräulein •Ursuline •touchline
- bloodline •plumb line •punchline
- buntline •timberline •borderline
- underline •alkaline •opaline
- Caroline •coralline •crystalline

- waterline • landmine • carmine
- goldmine

> Try rhyming one word with a set of two: goldmine, sold mine. [i]

- calamine • melamine

25.23

- canine • asinine • leonine • saturnine
- Antonine • pavonine • rapine
- **alpine**, cisalpine
- pitchpine • orpine
- **lupine**, supine
- porcupine • vulpine • salamandrine
- alexandrine • sapphirine • taurine
- endocrine • aventurine • vulturine
- colubrine • lacustrine • estuarine
- viperine • passerine • catarrhine
- **intrauterine**, uterine
- adulterine • riverine • ensign
- **internecine**, V-sign
- piscine • porcine • cosine • thylacine
- countersign
- **hircine**, ursine
- shoeshine • moonshine • sunshine
- earthshine
- **adamantine**, Byzantine, elephantine
- Tridentine • Levantine • Bechstein
- Epstein • amethystine • Rubinstein
- Frankenstein • Palestine • Philistine
- turpentine • Einstein • Eisenstein
- **cispontine**, transpontine
- serotine • infantine • Wittgenstein
- Argentine • Palatine
- **Ballantyne**, valentine
- eglantine • Hammerstein
- clementine • vespertine • serpentine
- Florentine
- **Lichtenstein**, Liechtenstein
- Constantine • nemertine • Bernstein
- **hyacinthine**, labyrinthine
- Jugurthine • grapevine • bovine
- Glühwein • cervine • equine

25.24

- **aide-de-camp**, aides-de-camp, anon,

Asunción, au courant, begone, Bonn, bon vivant, Caen, Canton, Carcassonne, Ceylon, chaconne, chateaubriand, ci-devant, Colón, colon, Concepción, con (*US* conn), cretonne, don, Duchamp, Evonne, foregone, fromage blanc, Gabon, Garonne, gone, guenon, hereupon, Inchon, Jean, john, Jon, Le Mans, León, Luzon, Mont Blanc, Narbonne, odds-on, on, outgone, outshone, Perón, phon, piñon, Pinot Blanc, plafond, Ramón, Saigon, Saint-Saëns, Sand, Schwann, scone, shone, side-on, sine qua non, Sorbonne, spot-on, swan, thereon, thereupon, ton, Toulon, undergone, upon, Villon, wan, whereon, whereupon, won, wonton, yon, Yvonne

- **crayon**, rayon

> Try rhyming one word with a set of two: rayon, lay on. [i]

- **Leon**, Lyons, neon, prion
- Ceredigion • Mabinogion • nucleon
- Amiens • dupion • parathion
- Laocoon
- **gluon**, Rouen
- bon-bon • Audubon

25.25

- radon • Chalcedon • Proudhon
- Mogadon • pteranodon • iguanodon
- mastodon • chiffon • Ctesiphon
- bouffant • balafon • Xenophon
- Bellerophon
- **argon**, Sargon
- Dagon • woebegone • bygone
- **doggone**, logon
- dodecagon • Dijon • demijohn • ancon
- archon • racon • Comecon • emoticon
- stereopticon • icon • walk-on • neocon
- Yukon • zircon • salon • Fablon
- decathlon • Teflon • Dralon • Simplon
- Babylon • papillon • propylon
- epsilon • nylon • Orlon
- **eidolon**, roll-on, Solon
- mouflon • Ascalon • Ashqelon

- echelon • Avalon
- **gnomon**, Jomon

25.26

- **Agamemnon**, Memnon
- **ninon**, xenon
- noumenon • Trianon • xoanon
- organon • Simenon • Maintenon
- **crampon**, kampong, tampon
- Nippon • coupon
- **Akron**, Dacron, macron
- electron • natron • Hebron • positron
- Heilbronn • micron
- **boron**, moron, oxymoron
- neutron • interferon
- **fleuron**, Huron, neuron
- Oberon • mellotron • aileron
- cyclotron • Percheron • Mitterrand
- vigneron • croissant • Maupassant
- garçon • Cartier-Bresson • exon
- frisson • Oxon • chanson • Tucson
- soupçon • Aubusson • Besançon
- penchant • torchon • cabochon
- **Anton**, canton, Danton
- lepton
- **piton**, Teton
- krypton • feuilleton • magneton
- chiton
- **photon**, proton
- **croûton**, futon
- eschaton • peloton • contretemps
- telethon
- **talkathon**, walkathon
- Avon • tableau vivant • vol-au-vent

25.27

- par avion • Messiaen
- **chignon**, filet mignon
- Avignon • Sauvignon • Semillon
- Roussillon • sabayon
- **demi-pension**, pension
- **bouillon**, court-bouillon
- K-meson • soi-disant • blouson

25.28

- **adorn**, born, borne, bourn, Braun, brawn, corn, dawn, drawn, faun, fawn, forborne, forewarn, forlorn, freeborn, horn, lawn, lorn, morn, mourn, newborn, Norn, outworn, pawn, porn, prawn, Quorn, sawn, scorn, Sean, shorn, spawn, suborn, sworn, thorn, thrawn, torn, Vaughan, warn, withdrawn, worn, yawn

> Create extra rhymes by adding -ing to words like dawn and fawn. |i|

- airborne • Ayckbourn • seaborne
- Eastbourne • stillborn • highborn
- Osborne • winterbourne
- waterborne • firstborn • Apeldoorn
- althorn • hartshorn • leghorn
- greenhorn • bighorn • inkhorn
- tinhorn • windborne • foghorn
- longhorn • shorthorn
- shoehorn • Flügelhorn
- bullhorn • alpenhorn • Matterhorn
- acorn • seedcorn • sweetcorn
- barleycorn • unicorn • Capricorn
- leprechaun • tricorne • einkorn
- popcorn • Runcorn • peppercorn
- lovelorn • frogspawn • wire-drawn
- wartorn • blackthorn • hawthorn
- careworn • time-worn • shopworn
- toilworn

25.29

- **brown**, Browne, clown, crown, down, downtown, drown, frown, gown, low-down, noun, renown, run-down, town, upside-down, uptown
- crackdown • clampdown • Ashdown
- markdown • letdown • meltdown
- **breakdown**, shakedown, takedown
- kick-down • thistledown • sit-down
- climbdown • countdown
- Southdown
- **godown**, hoedown, showdown, slowdown
- put-down • touchdown • tumbledown
- comedown
- **rundown**, sundown
- shutdown • eiderdown
- ballgown • nightgown

When a rhyme is formed using words within a line rather than at the end of lines, it is called a *medial* (or *internal*) *rhyme*. The particular kind shown here is known as a *leonine rhyme*, a type of *medial rhyme* in which the rhymes occur between the mid- and end-words of the same line; it can, as in this poem by Blake, have a dramatic linking effect:

And Priests in black gowns were walking their rounds,
And binding with briars my joys and desires.

(William Blake, 'The Garden of Love')

- pronoun •Jamestown •Freetown
- midtown •Bridgetown •Kingstown
- shanty town •Georgetown
- ecotown •Motown
- hometown •toytown •Newtown
- Charlottetown •Chinatown

25.30

- **alone**, atone, Beaune, bemoan, blown, bone, Capone, clone, Cohn, Cologne, condone, cone, co-own, crone, drone, enthrone, flown, foreknown, foreshown, groan, grown, half-tone, home-grown, hone, Joan, known, leone, loan, lone, mephedrone, moan, Mon, mown, ochone, outflown, outgrown, own, phone, pone, prone, Rhône, roan, rone, sewn, shown, Simone, Sloane, Soane, sone, sown, stone, strown, throne, thrown, tone, trombone, Tyrone, unbeknown, undersown, windblown, zone

> Create extra rhymes for words like alone by adding -n to words like blow and sew (see section 9.1).

- Dione •backbone •hambone
- breastbone •aitchbone
- **tail bone**, whalebone
- cheekbone •shin bone •hip bone
- wishbone •splint bone •herringbone
- thigh bone •jawbone •marrowbone
- knuckle bone •collarbone
- methadone •headphone •cellphone
- heckelphone •payphone •Freefone
- **radio-telephone**, telephone
- videophone •francophone

- megaphone •speakerphone
- allophone •Anglophone •xylophone
- gramophone •homophone
- vibraphone •microphone
- saxophone •answerphone
- dictaphone
- **sarrusophone**, sousaphone
- silicone •pine cone •snow cone
- flyblown •cyclone •violone
- hormone •pheromone •Oenone
- chaperone •progesterone
- testosterone

25.31

- **flagstone**, ragstone
- **Blackstone**, jackstone
- sandstone •capstone •hearthstone
- headstone •gemstone •whetstone
- hailstone •gravestone
- **freestone**, keystone
- greenstone •Wheatstone
- Tinseltown •ringtone •pitchstone
- millstone •whinstone •siltstone
- holystone •semitone
- stepping stone •coping stone
- baritone •acetone •dulcitone
- tritone •drystone •milestone
- limestone
- **grindstone**, rhinestone
- cobblestone •gallstone •brownstone
- lodestone •soapstone •duotone
- microtone •bluestone •tombstone
- moonstone •touchstone
- **bloodstone**, mudstone
- sunstone •ironstone •undertone
- monotone •cornerstone
- Silverstone •overtone
- **kerbstone** (*US* curbstone)
- turnstone

- birthstone • flavone • endzone
- cortisone • ozone

25.32

- **adjoin**, Boulogne, coign, coin, conjoin, Des Moines, Dordogne, enjoin, groin, groyne, join, loin, purloin, quoin, subjoin
- Burgoyne • Gascogne • tenderloin
- sirloin • talapoin

25.33

- **afternoon**, attune, autoimmune, baboon, balloon, bassoon, bestrewn, boon, Boone, bridoon, buffoon, Cameroon, Cancún, cardoon, cartoon, Changchun, cocoon, commune, croon, doubloon, dragoon, dune, festoon, galloon, goon, harpoon, hoon, immune, importune, impugn, Irgun, jejune, June, Kowloon, lagoon, lampoon, loon, macaroon, maroon, monsoon, moon, Muldoon, noon, oppugn, picayune, platoon, poltroon, pontoon, poon, prune, puccoon, raccoon, Rangoon, ratoon, rigadoon, rune, saloon, Saskatoon, Sassoon, Scone, soon, spittoon, spoon, swoon, Troon, tune, tycoon, typhoon, Walloon
- **fortune**, misfortune
- vodun • veldskoen • honeymoon
- forenoon • tablespoon • teaspoon
- soupspoon • dessertspoon • Neptune
- tribune • triune • opportune

25.34

- Gudrun

25.35

- **begun**, bun, done, Donne, dun, fine-spun, forerun, fun, gun, Gunn, hon, Hun, none, nun, one, one-to-one, outdone, outgun, outrun, plus-one, pun, run, shun, son, spun, stun, sun, ton, tonne, tun, underdone, Verdun, won

> ℹ Create extra rhymes by changing words like gun to gunning.

- honeybun • handgun • flashgun
- air gun • sixgun • popgun • shotgun
- **blowgun**, shogun
- speargun • scattergun • homespun
- endrun • sheep run • grandson
- stepson • godson • kiloton • megaton
- anyone • everyone • someone

> ℹ Try rhyming one word with a set of two: someone, become one.

25.36

- **Eritrean**, Ghanaian, Himalayan, Malayan, Tigrayan
- **Actaeon**, Aegean, aeon (*US* eon), Augean, Behan, Cadmean, Caribbean, Carolean, Chaldean, Cyclopean, empyrean, epicurean,

---

The use of past participles in an *aaaa...* pattern at the end of each line in this sonnet lends it an odd relentlessness. This is an example of *wrenched monorhyme*:

WILD, wild the storm, and the sea high running,
Steady the roar of the gale, with incessant undertone muttering,
Shouts of demoniac laughter fitfully piercing and pealing,
Waves, air, midnight, their savagest trinity lashing,

(Walt Whitman, 'Patroling Barnegat')

These four lines from John Donne's poem 'The Sun Rising' use a *rhyming pattern* (or rhyme scheme) known as *arch-rhyme* (*abba*):

> BUSY old fool, unruly Sun,
> Why dost thou thus,
> Through windows, and through curtains, call on us?
> Must to thy motions lovers' seasons run?

(John Donne, 'The Sun Rising')

European, Fijian, Galilean, Hasmonean, Hebridean, Herculean, Ian, Jacobean, Kampuchean, Laodicean, lien, Linnaean (*US* Linnean), Maccabean, Mandaean (*US* Mandean), Medicean, monogenean, Nabataean (*US* Nabatean), Orphean, paean, paeon, pean, peon, Periclean, piscean, plebeian, Pyrenean, Pythagorean, Sabaean, Sadducean, Sisyphean, skean, Tanzanian, Tennesseean, Terpsichorean, theodicean, Tyrolean

25.37

- **antipodean**, Crimean, Judaean, Korean
- Albion
- **Gambian**, Zambian
- lesbian
- **Arabian**, Bessarabian, Fabian, gabion, Sabian, Swabian
- **amphibian**, Libyan, Namibian
- Sorbian
- **Danubian**, Nubian
- Colombian •Serbian •Nietzschean
- **Chadian**, Trinidadian
- **Andean**, Kandyan
- guardian
- **Acadian**, Akkadian, Arcadian, Barbadian, Canadian, circadian, Grenadian, Hadean, Orcadian, Palladian, radian, steradian
- **Archimedean**, comedian, epicedian, median, tragedian
- **ascidian**, Derridean, Dravidian, enchiridion, Euclidean, Floridian, Gideon, Lydian, meridian, Numidian,

obsidian, Pisidian, quotidian, viridian
- **Amerindian**, Indian
- **accordion**, Edwardian
- **Cambodian**, collodion, custodian, melodeon, nickelodeon, Odeon
- Freudian •Bermudian •Burundian
- Burgundian
- **Falstaffian**, Halafian
- **Christadelphian**, Delphian, Philadelphian
- nymphean •ruffian •Brobdingnagian
- Carolingian •Swedenborgian
- **logion**, Muskogean
- Jungian
- **magian**, Pelagian
- collegian
- **callipygian**, Cantabrigian, Phrygian, Stygian
- Merovingian •philologian •Fujian
- Czechoslovakian •Pickwickian
- Algonquian •Chomskian
- Kentuckian
- **battalion**, galleon, medallion, rapscallion, scallion
- **Anglian**, ganglion
- Heraklion
- **Dalian**, Malian, Somalian
- **Chellean**, Machiavellian, Orwellian, Sabellian, Trevelyan, triskelion
- Wesleyan
- **alien**, Australian, bacchanalian, Castalian, Deucalion, episcopalian, Hegelian, madrigalian, mammalian, Pygmalion, Salian, saturnalian, sesquipedalian, tatterdemalion, Thessalian, Westphalian
- **anthelion**, Aristotelian, Aurelian, carnelian, chameleon, Karelian, Mendelian, Mephistophelian, Pelion, Sahelian

- **Abbevillian**, Azilian, Brazilian, caecilian, Castilian, Chilean, Churchillian, civilian, cotillion, crocodilian, epyllion, Gillian, Lilian, Maximilian, Pamphylian, pavilion, postilion, Quintilian, reptilian, Sicilian, Tamilian, vaudevillian, vermilion, Virgilian
- **Aeolian**, Anatolian, Eolian, Jolyon, Mongolian, napoleon, simoleon
- **Acheulian**, Boolean, cerulean, Friulian, Julian, Julien
- bullion
- **mullion**, scullion, Tertullian
- Liverpudlian
- **Bahamian**, Bamian, Damian, Mesopotamian, Samian
- **anthemion**, Bohemian
- **Endymion**, prosimian, Simeon, simian
- isthmian •antinomian
- **Permian**, vermian
- Oceanian
- **Albanian**, Azanian, Iranian, Jordanian, Lithuanian, Mauritanian, Mediterranean, Panamanian, Pennsylvanian, Pomeranian, Romanian, Ruritanian, Sassanian, subterranean, Tasmanian, Transylvanian, Tripolitanian, Turanian, Ukrainian, Vulcanian
- **Armenian**, Athenian, Fenian, Magdalenian, Mycenaean (*US* Mycenean), Slovenian, Tyrrhenian
- **Argentinian**, Arminian, Augustinian, Carthaginian, Darwinian, dominion, Guinean, Justinian, Ninian, Palestinian, Sardinian, Virginian
- **epilimnion**, hypolimnion
- Bosnian
- **Bornean**, Californian, Capricornian
- **Aberdonian**, Amazonian, Apollonian, Babylonian, Baconian, Bostonian, Caledonian, Catalonian, Chalcedonian, Ciceronian, Devonian, draconian, Estonian, Etonian, gorgonian, Ionian, Johnsonian, Laconian, Macedonian, Miltonian, Newtonian, Oregonian, Oxonian,

Patagonian, Plutonian, Tennysonian, Tobagonian, Washingtonian
- **Cameroonian**, communion, Mancunian, Neptunian, Réunion, union
- **Hibernian**, Saturnian
- **Campion**, champion, Grampian, rampion, tampion
- thespian •Mississippian •Olympian
- Paralympian •Crispian
- **Scorpian**, scorpion
- **cornucopian**, dystopian, Ethiopian, Salopian, subtopian, Utopian
- Guadeloupian
- **Carian**, carrion, clarion, Marian
- **Calabrian**, Cantabrian
- Cambrian •Bactrian
- **Lancastrian**, Zoroastrian
- Alexandrian •Maharashtrian
- **equestrian**, pedestrian
- **agrarian**, antiquarian, apiarian, Aquarian, Arian, Aryan, authoritarian, barbarian, Bavarian, Bulgarian, Caesarean (*US* Cesarean), centenarian, communitarian, contrarian, Darien, disciplinarian, egalitarian, equalitarian, establishmentarian, fruitarian, Gibraltarian, grammarian, Hanoverian, humanitarian, Hungarian, latitudinarian, libertarian, librarian, majoritarian, millenarian, necessarian, necessitarian, nonagenarian, octogenarian, ovarian, Parian, parliamentarian, planarian, predestinarian, prelapsarian, proletarian, quadragenarian, quinquagenarian, quodlibetarian, Rastafarian, riparian, rosarian, Rotarian, sabbatarian, Sagittarian, sanitarian, Sauveterrian, sectarian, seminarian, septuagenarian, sexagenarian, topiarian, totalitarian, Trinitarian, ubiquitarian, Unitarian, utilitarian, valetudinarian, vegetarian, veterinarian, vulgarian
- **Adrian**, Hadrian
- **Assyrian**, Illyrian, Syrian, Tyrian
- morion •Austrian

- **Dorian**, Ecuadorean, historian, Hyperborean, Nestorian, oratorian, praetorian (*US* pretorian), salutatorian, Salvadorean, Singaporean, stentorian, Taurean, valedictorian, Victorian
- Ugrian • Zarathustrian
- **Cumbrian**, Northumbrian, Umbrian
- **Algerian**, Cancerian, Chaucerian, Cimmerian, criterion, Hesperian, Hitlerian, Hyperion, Iberian, Liberian, Nigerian, Presbyterian, Shakespearean, Siberian, Spenserian, Sumerian, valerian, Wagnerian, Zairean
- **Arthurian**, Ben-Gurion, centurion, durian, holothurian, Khachaturian, Ligurian, Missourian, Silurian, tellurian
- **Circassian**, Parnassian
- halcyon • Capsian • Hessian
- **Albigensian**, Waldensian
- Dacian • Keatsian
- **Cilician**, Galician, Lycian, Mysian, Odyssean
- Leibnizian • Piscean • Ossian
- Gaussian • Joycean • Andalusian
- Mercian • Appalachian • Decian
- **Ordovician**, Priscian
- Lucian
- **himation**, Montserratian
- **Atlantean**, Dantean, Kantian
- **bastion**, Erastian, Sebastian
- Mozartian • Brechtian • Thyestean
- Fortean • Faustian • protean
- Djiboutian
- **fustian**, Procrustean
- **Gilbertian**, Goethean, nemertean
- pantheon
- **Hogarthian**, Parthian
- **Lethean**, Promethean
- Pythian • Corinthian • Scythian
- **Lothian**, Midlothian
- Latvian • Yugoslavian
- **avian**, Batavian, Flavian, Moldavian, Moravian, Octavian, Scandinavian, Shavian
- **Bolivian**, Maldivian, oblivion, Vivian
- **Chekhovian**, Harrovian, Jovian, Pavlovian

- **alluvion**, antediluvian, diluvian, Peruvian
- Servian • Malawian • Zimbabwean
- Abkhazian • Dickensian
- **Caucasian**, Malaysian, Rabelaisian
- Keynesian
- **Belizean**, Cartesian, Indonesian, Milesian, Salesian, Silesian
- **Elysian**, Frisian, Parisian, Tunisian
- Holmesian
- **Carthusian**, Malthusian, Venusian

25.38

- **Brian**, cyan, Gaian, Geminian, Hawaiian, ion, iron, Ixion, lion, Lyon, Mayan, Narayan, O'Brien, Orion, Paraguayan, prion, Ryan, scion, Uruguayan, Zion
- andiron
- **gridiron**, midiron
- dandelion • anion • Bruneian
- **cation**, flatiron
- **gowan**, Palawan, rowen
- **anthozoan**, bryozoan, Goan, hydrozoan, Minoan, protozoan, protozoon, rowan, Samoan, spermatozoon
- Ohioan • Chicagoan • Virgoan
- Idahoan
- **doyen**, Illinoisan, Iroquoian
- **Ewan**, Labuan, McEwan, McLuhan, Siouan
- Saskatchewan • Papuan • Paduan
- Nicaraguan • gargantuan
- **carbon**, chlorofluorocarbon, graben, hydrocarbon, Laban, radiocarbon
- ebon • Melbourne • Theban
- **gibbon**, ribbon
- **Brisbane**, Lisbon
- Tyburn
- **auburn**, Bourbon
- Alban • Manitoban • Cuban
- stubborn
- **Durban**, exurban, suburban, turban, urban

25.39

- **congestion**, digestion, ingestion,

question, suggestion
• richen •Chibchan
• **Christian**, unchristian
• exhaustion
• **escutcheon**, scutcheon
• combustion •birchen

25.40

• **Abaddon**, gladden, gladdon, Ibadan, madden, sadden
• **abandon**, Brandon, Rwandan, Ugandan
• **Baden**, Baden-Baden, Coloradan, garden, harden, lardon, Nevadan, pardon
• Wiesbaden •bear garden
• tea garden
• **Armageddon**, deaden, leaden, redden
• **Eldon**, Sheldon
• **Brendan**, tendon
• Dresden
• **Aden**, Aidan, Haydn, laden, maiden
• handmaiden
• **cedarn**, cotyledon, dicotyledon, Eden, monocotyledon, Sweden
• wealden
• **bestridden**, forbidden, hidden, midden, outridden, ridden, stridden, unbidden
• Wimbledon
• **linden**, Lindon, Swindon
• Wisden •Mohammedan •Myrmidon
• harridan •hagridden •Sheridan
• bedridden •Macedon •Huntingdon
• **Dryden**, guidon, Leiden, Poseidon, Sidon, widen
• **Culloden**, hodden, modern, sodden, trodden
• Cobden •downtrodden
• **Auden**, broaden, cordon, Gordon, Hordern, Jordan, warden
• churchwarden •louden •bounden
• **loden**, Snowdon
• **beholden**, embolden, golden, olden
• hoyden •Bermudan •wooden
• Mukden •gulden •sudden
• **Blunden**, London
• Riordan •bourdon •bombardon

• celadon •Clarendon
• **burden**, guerdon

25.41

• deafen
• **griffon**, stiffen
• antiphon
• **hyphen**, siphon
• **often**, soften
• orphan •ibuprofen
• **roughen**, toughen
• colophon
• **dragon**, flagon, lagan, pendragon, wagon
• snapdragon •bandwagon •jargon
• Megan
• **Copenhagen**, pagan, Reagan
• Nijmegen
• **Antiguan**, Egan, freegan, Keegan, Regan, vegan
• Wigan •cardigan •Milligan •polygon
• hooligan •mulligan •ptarmigan
• Branigan •Oregon •Michigan
• Rattigan
• **tigon**, trigon
• toboggan
• **Glamorgan**, gorgon, Morgan, morgen, organ
• **Brogan**, hogan, Logan, slogan
• Cadogan •decagon
• **Aragon**, paragon, tarragon
• hexagon •pentagon •heptagon
• octagon •Bergen •Spitsbergen

25.42

• **abrasion**, Australasian, equation, Eurasian, evasion, invasion, occasion, persuasion, pervasion, suasion, Vespasian
• **adhesion**, cohesion, Friesian, lesion
• **circumcision**, collision, concision, decision, derision, division, elision, envision, excision, imprecision, incision, misprision, precisian, precision, provision, scission, vision
• subdivision •television •Eurovision

- LaserVision
- **corrosion**, eclosion, erosion, explosion, implosion
- **allusion**, collusion, conclusion, confusion, contusion, delusion, diffusion, effusion, exclusion, extrusion, fusion, illusion, inclusion, interfusion, intrusion, obtrusion, occlusion, preclusion, profusion, prolusion, protrusion, reclusion, seclusion, suffusion, transfusion
- Monaghan •Belgian
- **Bajan**, Cajun, contagion, Trajan
- **Glaswegian**, legion, Norwegian, region
- **irreligion**, religion
- Injun •Harijan •oxygen •antigen
- sojourn •donjon •Georgian
- **theologian**, Trojan
- Rügen
- **bludgeon**, curmudgeon, dudgeon, gudgeon, trudgen
- dungeon •glycogen •halogen
- collagen •Imogen •carcinogen
- hallucinogen •androgen
- **oestrogen** (US estrogen)
- hydrogen •nitrogen
- **burgeon**, sturgeon, surgeon

25.43

- **blacken**, bracken, slacken
- Sri Lankan
- **Alaskan**, Gascon, Madagascan, Nebraskan
- **Aachen**, darken, hearken, kraken, Marcan, Petrarchan
- Interlaken
- **beckon**, Deccan, pekan, reckon
- Mencken
- **awaken**, bacon, betaken, forsaken, Jamaican, mistaken, partaken, shaken, taken, waken
- godforsaken
- **archdeacon**, beacon, Costa Rican, deacon, Dominican, Mohican, Mozambican, Puerto Rican, weaken
- **quicken**, sicken, stricken, thicken, Wiccan
- silken
- **Incan**, Lincoln

- **brisken**, Franciscan
- barbican •Rubicon •Gallican
- Anglican
- **Helicon**, pelican
- **basilican**, Millikan, silicon
- publican •pantechnicon •Copernican
- African •American •hurricane
- **lexicon**, Mexican
- Corsican •Vatican •liken
- **Brocken**, Moroccan
- **falcon**, Lorcan, Majorcan, Minorcan
- **Balcon**, Balkan
- gyrfalcon
- **awoken**, bespoken, betoken, broken, foretoken, oaken, outspoken, plain-spoken, ryokan, spoken, token, woken
- heartbroken
- **Lucan**, toucan, lebkuchen
- Saarbrücken •Buchan •Vulcan
- **drunken**, Duncan, shrunken, sunken
- **Etruscan**, molluscan (US molluskan), Tuscan
- Ardnamurchan •lochan

25.44

- **Alan**, gallon, talon
- raglan
- **biathlon**, heptathlon, pentathlon, tetrathlon, triathlon
- **Guatemalan**, Marlon
- **Ellen**, felon, Magellan, Mellon, melon
- Veblen •Declan •watermelon
- Venezuelan •Elan
- **Anguillan**, Dillon, Dylan, kiln, Macmillan, Milne, villain
- limekiln •abutilon
- **pylon**, upsilon
- **Hohenzollern**, pollan, pollen, Stollen
- Lachlan
- **befallen**, fallen
- chapfallen •crestfallen
- **Angolan**, colon, Nolan, semicolon, stolen, swollen
- kulan
- **woollen** (US woolen)

- **challan**, sullen
- myrobalan
- gonfalon • castellan
- **ortolan**, portolan
- **Köln**, merlon

25.45

- **Alabaman**, Amman, Ammon, Drammen, gammon, Mammon, salmon
- **Bradman**, Caedmon, madman, madmen
- **flagman**, flagmen
- **trackman**, trackmen
- **hangman**, hangmen
- **chapman**, chapmen
- **cragsman**, cragsmen
- **cracksman**, cracksmen, Flaxman
- **batsman**, batsmen
- **batman**, batmen
- Tasman
- **clansman**, clansmen, Klansman, Klansmen, landsman, landsmen
- backgammon
- **barman**, barmen, Brahman, Carman, Carmen, shaman, Sharman, Tutankhamen
- **craftsman**, craftsmen, draftsman, draftsmen, draughtsman, draughtsmen, raftsman, raftsmen
- **marksman**, marksmen
- atman
- **guardsman**, guardsmen
- **leman**, Lemmon, lemon, Yemen
- **headman**, headmen, Stedman
- Beckmann
- **bellman**, bellmen, Hellman
- **gentleman**, gentlemen
- **penman**, penmen
- Helpmann
- **pressman**, pressmen
- **freshman**, freshmen
- **Welshman**, Welshmen
- **Frenchman**, Frenchmen, henchman, henchmen
- desman
- **headsman**, headsmen
- **helmsman**, helmsmen
- **lensman**, lensmen
- **airman**, airmen, chairman, chairmen
- **Bremen**, caiman, Damon, Eamon, layman, laymen, stamen

- **railman**, railmen
- **brakesman**, brakesmen
- **statesman**, statesmen
- **tradesman**, tradesmen
- **salesman**, salesmen
- **gamesman**, gamesmen
- **plainsman**, plainsmen
- **railwayman**, railwaymen
- **highwayman**, highwaymen
- **cacodemon**, daemon, demon, Freeman, freemen, Philemon, Riemann, Schliemann, seaman, seamen, semen
- Friedman
- **liegeman**, liegemen
- **Eastman**, policeman, policemen
- **beadsman**, beadsmen, seedsman, seedsmen
- **fieldsman**, fieldsmen
- **wheelsman**, wheelsmen
- **persimmon**, Rimmon
- **pitchman**, pitchmen
- Bridgman • milkman • Hillman
- **signalman**, signalmen
- Lippmann
- **pitman**, pitmen, Whitman
- **guildsman**, guildsmen
- **kinsman**, kinsmen
- Betjeman • regimen
- **clergyman**, clergymen
- **tallyman**, tallymen
- talisman
- **Englishman**, Englishmen
- **businessman**, businessmen
- **cameraman**, cameramen
- **Cornishman**, Cornishmen
- **journeyman**, journeymen
- **cavalryman**, cavalrymen
- **ferryman**, ferrymen
- **vestryman**, vestrymen
- **dairyman**, dairymen
- **Irishman**, Irishmen
- **quarryman**, quarrymen
- **Orangeman**, Orangemen
- **congressman**, congressmen
- **countryman**, countrymen
- **infantryman**, infantrymen
- **nurseryman**, nurserymen
- **liveryman**, liverymen
- **midshipman**, midshipmen
- **harvestman**, harvestmen
- **serviceman**, servicemen

- **Hyman**, Simon
- Eichmann
- **rifleman**, riflemen
- **Feynman**, lineman, linemen
- Weismann • Wiseman
- **tribesman**, tribesmen
- **linesman**, linesmen
- **exciseman**, excisemen
- **common**, Roscommon
- **watchman**, watchmen
- **Godman**, hodman, hodmen
- Hoffman
- **frogman**, frogmen
- **stockman**, stockmen
- **dolman**, dolmen
- **Scotsman**, Scotsmen, yachtsman, yachtsmen
- Boltzmann • Cotman
- **bondsman**, bondsmen
- **Bormann**, doorman, doormen, foreman, foremen, Mormon, Norman, storeman, storemen
- Kauffmann • Walkman
- **horseman**, horsemen, Norseman, Norsemen
- **sportsman**, sportsmen
- **oarsman**, oarsmen, outdoorsman, outdoorsmen
- swordsman
- **longshoreman**, longshoremen
- **bowmen**, cowman, cowmen, ploughman (*US* plowman), ploughmen (*US* plowmen)
- **councilman**, councilmen
- Hauptmann • Housman
- **groundsman**, groundsmen, roundsman, roundsmen, townsman, townsmen
- **warehouseman**, warehousemen
- **Bowman**, Oklahoman, Oman, omen, Roman, showman, showmen, yeoman, yeomen
- **coachman**, coachmen
- **Coleman**, Goldman
- **nobleman**, noblemen
- **postman**, postmen
- **spokesman**, spokesmen
- **boatman**, boatmen
- **lifeboatman**, lifeboatmen
- dragoman
- **crewman**, crewmen, energumen,

human, ichneumon, Newman, numen, Schumann, subhuman, Trueman
- woman
- **woodman**, woodmen
- **bookman**, bookmen
- Pullman
- **Bushman**, Bushmen
- **footman**, footmen
- **woodsman**, woodsmen
- **ombudsman**, ombudsmen
- clanswoman
- **backwoodsman**, backwoodsmen
- charwoman
- **craftswoman**, draughtswoman
- gentlewoman • Welshwoman
- Frenchwoman
- **airwoman**, chairwoman
- laywoman • stateswoman
- saleswoman • policewoman
- kinswoman • Englishwoman
- businesswoman • Irishwoman
- congresswoman • countrywoman
- jurywoman • servicewoman
- tribeswoman
- **Scotswoman**, yachtswoman
- forewoman • horsewoman
- sportswoman • oarswoman
- townswoman • spokeswoman
- Dutchwoman • frontierswoman
- alderwoman • anchorwoman
- washerwoman • Ulsterwoman
- churchwoman • acumen • summon
- **Dutchman**, Dutchmen
- **gunman**, gunmen
- **busman**, busmen, dustman, dustmen
- **huntsman**, huntsmen
- Newcomen • Layamon
- **privateersman**, privateersmen, steersman, steersmen
- **frontiersman**, frontiersmen
- fireman • Dobermann • lumbermen
- abdomen • Omdurman
- **alderman**, aldermen
- Turkoman
- **cellarman**, cellarmen, telamon
- cyclamen
- **Highlandman**, Highlandmen
- Solomon • trawlerman • cinnamon
- **Chinaman**, Chinamen

> The tension between *full rhymes*
> and *half-rhymes* offers scope to
> play with language and
> pronunciation. In 'It Ain't
> Necessarily So', achieving a *full
> rhyme* depends on distorting the
> pronunciation of the second
> word, called a *wrenched rhyme*:
>
> Oh Jonah, he lived in de whale
> Fo' he made his home in
> Dat fish's abdomen
> Oh Jonah, he lived in de whale
>
> (George and Ira Gershwin, 'It Ain't
> Necessarily So')

- **trencherman**, trenchermen
- **fisherman**, fishermen, militiaman, militiamen
- **washerman**, washermen
- ottoman
- **waterman**, watermen
- **Ulsterman**, Ulstermen
- **Burman**, firman, German, Herman, sermon, Sherman
- **churchman**, churchmen
- **turfman**, turfmen
- Bergman
- **kirkman**, kirkmen, workman, workmen
- Perelman
- **herdsman**, herdsmen

25.46

- **Buchanan**, cannon, canon, colcannon, Louisianan, Montanan, Rhiannon, Shannon
- Botswanan
- **Lennon**, pennon, tenon
- Canaan
- **Burkinan**, Henan
- finnan
- **phenomenon**, prolegomenon
- Parthenon
- **Arizonan**, Conan, Ronan
- Lebanon •Algernon •Vernon
- Groningen •Vlissingen
- **Tongan**, wrong'un

- cap'n, happen
- **dampen**, lampern
- aspen
- **parpen**, sharpen, tarpon
- weapon •hempen
- **capon**, misshapen
- **cheapen**, deepen, steepen
- tympan •ripen •saucepan •open
- lumpen

25.47

- **Aran**, Arran, baron, barren, Darren, Karen, Sharon, yarran
- **Biafran**, saffron
- plastron •Saharan •Sumatran
- **heron**, perron
- rhododendron •chevron
- **Aaron**, Charon, Dáil Eireann
- apron
- **matron**, patron
- Libran
- **decahedron**, dodecahedron, octahedron, polyhedron, tetrahedron
- children •citron •grandchildren
- stepchildren •godchildren
- schoolchildren
- **Byron**, Chiron, environ, Myron, siren
- **sporran**, warren
- squadron •Cochran
- **Andorran**, Doran, Lauren, loran
- cauldron
- **Kieran**, Madeiran, schlieren
- **Honduran**, Van Buren
- Aldebaran •Auberon •Acheron
- **Cameron**, Decameron
- **cateran**, Lateran
- veteran
- **dipteran**, hemipteran
- lepidopteran •Lutheran

25.48

- Masson
- **flaxen**, Jackson, klaxon, Sachsen, Saxon, waxen
- Samson
- **Branson**, Jansen, Manson, Nansen

- **arson**, Carson, fasten, parson, sarsen
- **Bresson**, delicatessen, Essen, lessen, lesson
- Texan
- **Belsen**, keelson, Nelson
- Mendelssohn • Empson
- **Benson**, ensign
- Stetson
- **basin**, caisson, chasten, diapason, hasten, Jason, mason
- Bateson • handbasin • washbasin
- Freemason • stonemason • Nielsen
- Stevenson
- **christen**, glisten, listen
- **Gibson**, Ibsen
- **Blixen**, Nixon, vixen
- **Nilsson**, Stillson, Wilson
- Nicholson • Simpson • Whitsun
- Robinson • Acheson
- **Addison**, Madison
- Edison

> Try rhyming one word with a   i
> set of two or more: Edison, fed his
> son.

- Atkinson • Dickinson • Alison
- **Tennyson**, venison
- unison
- **caparison**, comparison, garrison, Harrison
- Ericsson • Morrison
- **archdiocesan**, diocesan
- jettison • Davisson
- **bison**, Meissen, Tyson
- Michelson • Robson
- **coxswain**, oxen
- **Mommsen**, Thompson
- **Johnson**, Jonson, sponson, Swanson
- Watson
- **coarsen**, hoarsen, Orson
- **boatswain**, bosun
- Robeson • Jolson • moisten • loosen
- Wolfson • Cookson • Hudson
- Bunsen • tutsan
- **Grierson**, Pearson
- Culbertson • Richardson • Anderson
- Jefferson • Ferguson • Rowlandson
- Amundsen • Emerson • Jespersen
- Saracen • Peterson • Williamson
- **person**, worsen
- Bergson • chairperson • layperson

- salesperson • sportsperson
- spokesperson

25.49

- **ashen**, fashion, passion, ration
- **abstraction**, action, attraction, benefaction, compaction, contraction, counteraction, diffraction, enaction, exaction, extraction, faction, fraction, interaction, liquefaction, malefaction, petrifaction, proaction, protraction, putrefaction, redaction, retroaction, satisfaction, stupefaction, subtraction, traction, transaction, tumefaction, vitrifaction
- **expansion**, mansion, scansion, stanchion
- sanction
- **caption**, contraption
- **harshen**, Martian
- **cession**, discretion, freshen, session
- **abjection**, affection, circumspection, collection, complexion, confection, connection, convection, correction, defection, deflection, dejection, detection, direction, ejection, election, erection, genuflection, imperfection, infection, inflection, injection, inspection, insurrection, interconnection, interjection, intersection, introspection, lection, misdirection, objection, perfection, predilection, projection, protection, refection, reflection, rejection, resurrection, retrospection, section, selection, subjection, transection, vivisection
- **exemption**, pre-emption, redemption
- **abstention**, apprehension, ascension, attention, circumvention, comprehension, condescension, contention, contravention, convention, declension, detention, dimension, dissension, extension, gentian, hypertension, hypotension,

intention, intervention, invention,
mention, misapprehension,
obtention, pension, prehension,
prevention, recension, retention,
subvention, supervention,
suspension, tension
- **conception**, contraception,
deception, exception, inception,
interception, misconception,
perception, reception
- Übermenschen •subsection
- **ablation**, aeration, agnation,
Alsatian, Amerasian, Asian, aviation,
cetacean, citation, conation,
creation, Croatian,
counterdemonstration,
counterproliferation, crustacean,
curation, Dalmatian, delation,
dilation, donation, duration, elation,
fixation, Galatian, geolocation,
glocalization, gyration, Haitian,
halation, Horatian, ideation, illation,
lavation, legation, libation, location,
lunation, mutation, natation, nation,
negation, notation, nutation,
oblation, oration, ovation, potation,
relation, rogation, rotation,
Sarmatian, sedation, Serbo-Croatian,
station, staycation, taxation, Thracian,
vacation, vexation, vocation, zonation
- **accretion**, Capetian, completion,
concretion, deletion, depletion,
Diocletian, excretion, Grecian,
Helvetian, repletion, Rhodesian,
secretion, suppletion, Tahitian,
venetian
- **academician**, addition, aesthetician
(*US* esthetician), ambition, audition,
beautician, clinician, coition,
cosmetician, diagnostician,
dialectician, dietitian, Domitian,
edition, electrician, emission,
fission, fruition, Hermitian, ignition,
linguistician, logician, magician,
mathematician, Mauritian,
mechanician, metaphysician,
mission, monition, mortician,
munition, musician, obstetrician,
omission, optician, paediatrician
(*US* pediatrician), patrician, petition,
Phoenician, physician, politician,
position, rhetorician, sedition,
statistician, suspicion, tactician,

technician, theoretician, Titian,
tuition, volition
- **addiction**, affliction, benediction,
constriction, conviction, crucifixion,
depiction, dereliction, diction,
eviction, fiction, friction, infliction,
interdiction, jurisdiction,
malediction, restriction, transfixion,
valediction
- **distinction**, extinction, intinction
- **ascription**, circumscription,
conscription, decryption,
description, Egyptian, encryption,
inscription, misdescription,
prescription, subscription,
superscription, transcription
- proscription
- **concoction**, decoction
- **adoption**, option
- **abortion**, apportion, caution,
contortion, distortion, extortion,
portion, proportion, retortion,
torsion
- auction
- **absorption**, sorption
- **commotion**, devotion, emotion,
groschen, Laotian, locomotion,
lotion, motion, notion, Nova Scotian,
ocean, potion, promotion
- **ablution**, absolution, allocution,
attribution, circumlocution,
circumvolution, Confucian,
constitution, contribution,
convolution, counter-revolution,
destitution, dilution, diminution,
distribution, electrocution,
elocution, evolution, execution,
institution, interlocution,
irresolution, Lilliputian, locution,
perlocution, persecution, pollution,
prosecution, prostitution,
restitution, retribution, Rosicrucian,
solution, substitution, volution
- cushion •resumption •München
- pincushion
- **Belorussian**, Prussian,
Russian
- **abduction**, conduction,
construction, deduction, destruction,
eduction, effluxion, induction,
instruction, introduction,
misconstruction, obstruction,
production, reduction, ruction,

seduction, suction, underproduction
- **avulsion**, compulsion, convulsion, emulsion, expulsion, impulsion, propulsion, repulsion, revulsion
- **assumption**, consumption, gumption, overconsumption, presumption
- **luncheon**, scuncheon, truncheon
- **compunction**, conjunction, dysfunction, expunction, function, junction, malfunction, multifunction, unction
- **abruption**, corruption, disruption, eruption, interruption
- T-junction •liposuction
- **animadversion**, aspersion, assertion, aversion, bioconversion, Cistercian, coercion, conversion, desertion, disconcertion, dispersion, diversion, emersion, excursion, exertion, extroversion, immersion, incursion, insertion, interspersion, introversion, Persian, perversion, submersion, subversion, tertian, version
- excerption

25.50

- **baton**, batten, fatten, flatten, harmattan, Manhattan, Mountbatten, paten, patten, pattern, platen, Saturn, slattern

> Create extra rhymes by adding -ing to words like batten. 🛈

- Shackleton •Appleton
- **Hampton**, Northampton, Rockhampton, Southampton, Wolverhampton

- **Canton**, lantern, Scranton
- **Langton**, plankton
- Clapton
- **Aston**, pastern
- Gladstone
- **Caxton**, Paxton
- capstan •Ashton •phytoplankton
- **Akhenaten**, Akhetaten, Aten, Barton, carton, Dumbarton, hearten, Parton, smarten, spartan, tartan
- Grafton
- **Carlton**, Charlton
- Charleston •kindergarten
- Aldermaston
- **Breton**, jetton, Sowetan, threaten, Tibetan
- lectern
- **Elton**, melton, Skelton
- **Denton**, Fenton, Kenton, Lenten, Trenton
- Repton
- **Avestan**, Midwestern, northwestern, Preston, southwestern, western
- sexton
- **Clayton**, Deighton, Leighton, Paton, phaeton, Satan, straighten, straiten
- Paignton •Maidstone
- **beaten**, Beaton, Beeton, Cretan, Keaton, neaten, Nuneaton, overeaten, sweeten, uneaten, wheaten
- chieftain
- **eastern**, northeastern, southeastern
- browbeaten •weatherbeaten
- **bitten**, bittern, Britain, Briton, Britten, handwritten, hardbitten, kitten, Lytton, mitten, smitten, underwritten, witan, written
- Clifton

This poem by Robert Burns uses dialect to create vibrant rhymes:

O wad some Power the giftie gie us
To see oursels as ithers see us!
It wad frae monie a blunder free us
An' foolish notion:
What airs in dress an' gait wad lea'e us,
An' ev'n devotion!

(Robert Burns, 'To a Louse')

In this poem by Stevie Smith, the use of *pararhymes* throughout (the words Singleton/Edmonton appear to be *stressed* but in fact, both words have initial stress, SIN and ED, making them *pararhymes*) creates an unconvincing feel which undermines the meaning of the words:

Come, wed me, Lady Singleton,
And we will have a baby soon
And we will live in Edmonton
Where all the friendly people run.

(Stevie Smith, 'Lady "Rogue" Singleton')

- **Milton**, Shilton, Stilton, Wilton
- Middleton •singleton •simpleton
- **Clinton**, Linton, Minton, Quinton, Winton
- **cistern**, Liston, piston, Wystan
- brimstone •Winston •Kingston
- Addington •Eddington
- Workington
- **Arlington**, Darlington
- skeleton
- **Ellington**, wellington
- exoskeleton
- **cosmopolitan**, megalopolitan, metropolitan, Neapolitan
- Burlington •Hamilton •badminton
- lamington •Germiston •Penistone
- Bonington •Orpington •Samaritan
- **Carrington**, Harrington
- sacristan •Festschriften
- Sherrington •typewritten

- Warrington •puritan •Fredericton
- Lexington •Occitan •Washington
- Whittington •Huntington
- Galveston •Livingstone
- Kensington
- **Blyton**, brighten, Brighton, Crichton, enlighten, frighten, heighten, lighten, righten, tighten, titan, triton, whiten

> Create extra rhymes by adding *-ing* to words like brighten.

- **begotten**, cotton, forgotten, ill-gotten, misbegotten, rotten
- **Compton**, Crompton
- wanton •Longton
- **Boston**, postern
- **boughten**, chorten, foreshorten, Laughton, Morton, Naughton, Orton, quartan, quartern, shorten, tauten, torten, Wharton
- **Alton**, Dalton, Galton, saltern, Walton
- Taunton •Allston •Launceston
- **croton**, Dakotan, Minnesotan, oaten, verboten
- **Bolton**, Doulton, molten
- Folkestone •Royston
- **Luton**, newton, rambutan, Teuton
- Houston •Fulton
- **button**, glutton, Hutton, mutton
- sultan
- **doubleton**, subaltern
- fronton •Augustan •Dunstan
- tungsten •quieten •Pinkerton
- charlatan •Wollaston •Palmerston
- Edmonton •automaton •Sheraton

The *unstressed rhymes* in this song partly depend on accent and knowledge of local pronunciation which underlines the strong link between the authors and their subject (the Beastie Boys and their city).

Brooklyn, Bronx, Queens and Staten
From the Battery to the top of Manhattan
Asian, Middle-Eastern and Latin
Black, White, New York you make it happen

(Beastie Boys, 'An Open Letter to NYC')

- Geraldton • Chatterton • Betterton
- Chesterton • Athelstan
- **burton**, curtain, uncertain
- Hurston

25.51

- Melanchthon
- **lengthen**, strengthen
- Nathan
- **Elizabethan**, Ethan
- Phaethon • python • leviathan
- Jonathan • marathon • earthen
- Carmarthen • leathern • heathen
- northern • southern • burthen
- **Avon**, Cavan, cavern, raven, tavern
- **Caernarfon**, Dungarvan, Javan
- Wilhelmshaven • Tórshavn
- **Bevan**, Devon, eleven, Evan, heaven, leaven, Pleven, seven, Severn
- Hesvan
- **craven**, graven, haven, maven, shaven, Stratford-upon-Avon
- **even**, Sivan, Steven
- **driven**, forgiven, given, misgiven, Niven, riven, shriven, thriven
- **silvern**, sylvan
- Godgiven • Sullivan
- **enliven**, Ivan, liven
- **cloven**, interwoven, woven
- Beethoven • Eindhoven • proven
- **coven**, govern, misgovern, oven, sloven
- cordovan • Donovan • Quechuan
- Bronwen • Iowan

25.52

- **Italian**, stallion
- **cañon**, canyon, companion
- **hellion**, rebellion
- Kenyan

- **Melanesian**, Micronesian, Polynesian
- **billion**, jillion, million, bajillion, modillion, multibillion, multimillion, pillion, septillion, sextillion, squillion, trillion, zillion
- **minion**, opinion, pinion
- carillon • slumgullion
- **bunion**, Bunyan, grunion, onion, Runyon
- roentgen • damson • Kansan • Tarzan
- **blazon**, brazen, emblazon, liaison, raisin
- Spätlesen
- **reason**, season, treason
- **arisen**, grison, imprison, mizzen, prison, risen, uprisen
- Pilsen • crimson • malison
- **benison**, denizen
- orison • citizen
- **bedizen**, greisen, horizon, kaizen
- Stockhausen
- **chosen**, frozen
- Lederhosen • poison • Susan
- **cousin**, cozen, dozen
- Amazon

25.53

- **adjourn**, astern, Berne, burn, churn, concern, discern, earn, fern, fohn, kern, learn, Lucerne, quern, Sauternes, spurn, stern, Sterne, tern, terne, Traherne, turn, urn, Verne, yearn

> Create extra rhymes by [i]
> adding -ed to words like adjourn.

- Bayern • Blackburn • heartburn
- Hepburn • Raeburn • Swinburne
- **Gisborne**, Lisburn
- sideburn • sunburn • Bannockburn
- lady-fern • Vättern • extern
- **cittern**, gittern
- Comintern • taciturn
- **nocturn**, nocturne
- U-turn • upturn

Section 26: -ng

26.1

- **bang**, Battambang, bhang, clang, Da Nang, dang, fang, gang, hang, harangue, kiang, Kuomintang, Kweiyang, Laing, Luang Prabang, meringue, Nanchang, Pahang, pang, parang, Penang, prang, Pyongyang, rang, sang, satang, Shang, shebang, Shenyang, slambang, slang, spang, sprang, Sturm und Drang, tang, thang, trepang, twang, vang, whang, Xizang, yang, Zaozhuang

> Create extra rhymes by adding *-ing* to words like bang. ⓘ

- **Xinjiang**, Zhanjiang, Zhenjiang
- Palembang •whiz-bang •charabanc
- pressgang •chaingang •Wolfgang
- strap-hang •ylang-ylang •boomslang
- Semarang •boomerang •linsang
- Sittang •mustang

26.2

- **Kaifeng**, Yancheng
- ginseng

26.3

- **Beijing**, bing, bring, Chungking, cling, ding, dingaling, fling, I Ching, king, Kunming, ling, Ming, Nanjing, Peking, ping, ring, sing, Singh, sling, spring, sting, string, swing, Synge, thing, ting, wing, wring, Xining, zing
- **saying**, slaying
- bricklaying •minelaying
- **being**, far-seeing, unseeing
- sightseeing •well-being
- blackberrying
- **dairying**, unvarying
- unwearying
- **self-pitying**, unpitying
- **belying**, dying, lying, self-denying, tying, vying
- unedifying •unsatisfying •outlying
- drawing •underdrawing
- **easygoing**, flowing, going, knowing, mowing, outgoing, showing, sowing, thoroughgoing, toing and froing
- seagoing •ongoing •foregoing
- theatregoing •churchgoing
- following •borrowing •annoying
- **bluing**, doing, misdoing
- evil-doing •wrongdoing

26.4

- stabbing •ribbing •winebibbing
- zorbing •probing •tubing •rubbing
- hatching •backscratching •etching
- **preaching**, teaching
- schoolteaching •firewatching
- birdwatching •heartsearching

26.5

- scaffolding
- **freestanding**, hardstanding, landing, misunderstanding, notwithstanding, outstanding, standing, stranding, understanding, upstanding
- **Harding**, self-regarding
- undemanding
- **heading**, Reading, steading, wedding
- gelding
- **ending**, impending, microlending, uncomprehending, unoffending, unpretending

- sub-heading •heartrending
- goaltending
- **arcading**, grading, lading, shading, unfading, upbraiding
- **exceeding**, leading, misleading, pleading, reeding, self-feeding, sheading, unheeding
- **Fielding**, yielding
- inbreeding •stockbreeding
- **forbidding**, Ridding
- building •wingding •shipbuilding
- bodybuilding •outbuilding
- **confiding**, hiding, riding, siding
- wilding
- **binding**, finding
- paragliding •wadding
- corresponding •hot-rodding
- **according**, hoarding, recording, unrewarding, waterboarding
- sailboarding •snowboarding
- telerecording •videorecording
- Dowding
- **grounding**, sounding, surrounding
- **foreboding**, loading
- **Golding**, holding, moulding (*US* molding), scolding
- landholding •shareholding
- smallholding •roadholding
- wounding
- **peasepudding**, pudding
- underfunding •wording

26.6

- **strafing**, understaffing
- debriefing •spiffing •offing
- morphing •roofing •stuffing
- **geotagging**, lagging, unflagging
- legging
- **digging**, rigging, wigging
- Vereeniging
- **dogging**, frogging, microblogging, nogging
- mugging •turbocharging •edging
- **aging**, engaging, staging
- unchanging •unchallenging
- managing •discouraging •cottaging
- obliging •lodging •ungrudging
- urging

26.7

- **backing**, blacking, packing, sacking, tracking, whacking
- **landbanking**, ranking, spanking
- nerve-racking
- **marking**, sarking
- **making**, taking, undertaking
- matchmaking •dressmaking
- haymaking
- **lacemaking**, pacemaking
- peacemaking •filmmaking
- printmaking •cabinetmaking
- moneymaking •merrymaking
- winemaking •home-making
- shoemaking •toolmaking
- bookmaking •troublemaking
- backbreaking •heartbreaking
- strikebreaking •housebreaking
- breathtaking •painstaking
- piss-taking •stocktaking
- **self-seeking**, unspeaking
- **licking**, ticking
- **freethinking**, shrinking, sinking, unblinking, unthinking, unwinking
- Mafeking •finicking •politicking
- **liking**, Viking
- **self-cocking**, self-mocking, shocking, stocking
- stonking •bluestocking •Hawking
- sleepwalking •streetwalking
- hillwalking •firewalking
- **soaking**, Woking
- pawnbroking •thought-provoking
- **booking**, Brooking
- onlooking •scrapbooking
- **spelunking**, trunking
- motherfucking •bloodsucking
- bollocking
- **hardworking**, working
- erl-king •tear-jerking •metalworking
- outworking

26.8

- **brambling**, rambling
- hatchling •brandling
- **gangling**, wrangling
- crackling •sapling
- **fatling**, Gatling
- **mantling**, scantling
- **darling**, sparling, starling
- sampling •starveling
- **dwelling**, misspelling,

self-propelling, spelling, swelling, telling, upwelling
• trembling • vetchling • fledgling
• kettling
• **nestling**, wrestling
• storytelling
• **failing**, grayling, mailing, paling, railing, sailing, tailing, unavailing, veiling, wailing
• changeling • boardsailing
• parasailing
• **appealing**, ceiling, Darjeeling, dealing, feeling, Keeling, peeling, revealing, self-sealing, shieling, wheeler-dealing, wheeling
• **reedling**, seedling
• weakling • Riesling
• **deskilling**, filling, grilling, killing, Pilling, quilling, Schilling, self-fulfilling, shilling, Trilling, unfulfilling, willing
• sibling • kindling • piffling
• **inkling**, sprinkling, tinkling
• **Kipling**, stripling
• princeling • witling
• **brisling**, quisling
• painkilling
• **filing**, piling, reviling, tiling, unsmiling
• motorcycling • hairstyling • rockling
• gosling
• **calling**, Pauling
• lordling • porkling
• **cowling**, fowling
• **foundling**, groundling
• **ruling**, schooling
• intercooling • wirepulling
• grumbling
• **buckling**, duckling, Suckling
• youngling • coupling • dumpling
• puzzling • swashbuckling
• **shearling**, yearling
• hireling
• **towelling** (*US* toweling)
• **gruelling** (*US* grueling)
• **babbling**, dabbling
• marbling • scribbling
• **mumbling**, rumbling
• sanderling • middling • doodling
• underling • rifling • shuffling
• strangling • fingerling

• **enamelling** (*US* enameling)
• rustling • rattling
• **bitterling**, chitterling
• titling
• **sterling**, Stirling
• **nurseling**, nursling
• earthling

26.9

• **charming**, disarming, pharming
• **Fleming**, lemming
• **Deeming**, scheming, steaming
• trimming • timing • heartwarming
• house-warming
• **coaming**, gloaming, homing, Wyoming
• assuming
• **becoming**, coming, forthcoming, mumming, up-and-coming
• oncoming • shortcoming
• homecoming • upcoming
• mind-numbing
• **Canning**, Manning, undermanning
• **Denning**, kenning
• **caning**, entertaining, self-sustaining, uncomplaining
• **greening**, leaning, meaning, overweening, screening, spring-cleaning
• sweetening • evening
• **beginning**, inning, thinning, twinning, underpinning, winning
• prizewinning
• **lining**, signing, Twining, vining
• lightning
• **aborning**, awning, dawning, morning, mourning, spawning, warning
• **Browning**, Downing, drowning
• landowning • tuning • cunning
• gunrunning • unquestioning
• widening • stiffening • reckoning
• thickening • happening • sharpening
• opening • fastening • christening
• unthreatening
• **lightening**, unenlightening
• self-governing
• **reasoning**, seasoning
• poisoning

- **discerning**, Herning, turning, yearning
- woodturning

26.10

- hanging • headbanging
- straphanging • cliffhanging
- mud-slinging • gunslinging
- bell-ringing • upbringing • longing
- tonguing
- **tapping**, wrapping
- **camping**, glamping
- kneecapping • backslapping
- **kidnapping** (US kidnaping)
- helping
- **scraping**, shaping
- **safekeeping**, sweeping, unsleeping
- gamekeeping • station-keeping
- greenkeeping • peacekeeping
- wicketkeeping • timekeeping
- shopkeeping • housekeeping
- goalkeeping • bookkeeping
- minesweeping
- **chipping**, clipping, dripping, snipping, whipping
- **dropping**, sopping, stopping, topping
- clodhopping • show-stopping
- wife-swapping
- **coping**, roping
- grouping • showjumping

26.11

- handspring • hamstring • herring
- headspring • wellspring
- **airing**, ballbearing, bearing, Behring, Bering, caring, daring, fairing, file-sharing, hardwearing, pairing, paring, raring, sparing, Waring, wearing
- talebearing • childbearing
- wayfaring • seafaring • cheeseparing
- time-sharing • mainspring • keyring
- gee-string • watch spring • offspring
- **boring**, flooring, Goring, riproaring, roaring, scoring, shoring
- drawstring • goalscoring
- outpouring • bowstring • shoestring
- bullring

- **auctioneering**, clearing, coasteering, earring, electioneering, engineering, gearing, geoengineering, orienteering, privateering, shearing

> Create extra rhymes for
> words like auctioneering by
> adding -ing to appear etc. (see
> section 12.4). ⓘ

- God-fearing • puppeteering
- **firing**, retiring, uninspiring, untiring, wiring
- **during**, mooring, reassuring, Turing
- posturing • restructuring
- meandering • rendering
- **pondering**, wandering
- ordering • maundering
- **plundering**, thundering, wondering
- offering • suffering • fingering
- scaremongering • hankering
- **flickering**, Pickering
- tinkering • hammering • glimmering
- unmurmuring • tampering
- whimpering • whispering
- **smattering**, unflattering
- earthshattering • schoolmastering
- Kettering • self-catering • wittering
- **quartering**, watering
- faltering • roistering • muttering
- gathering • woolgathering
- blithering
- **flavouring** (US flavoring), unwavering
- quivering
- **manoeuvring** (US maneuvering)
- covering • wallcovering
- **Goering**, stirring, unerring

26.12

- waxing
- **passing**, surpassing
- **Lancing**, Lansing
- **blessing**, distressing, dressing, Lessing, pressing, unprepossessing
- hairdressing
- **bracing**, casing, facing, lacing, placing, self-effacing, spacing, tracing

> Try rhyming one word with a
> set of two: bracing, may sing. ⓘ

- steeplechasing • interfacing
- unceasing • Gissing • unconvincing
- unpromising
- **enticing**, icing
- self-sacrificing • crossing
- kick-boxing
- **rejoicing**, voicing
- conveyancing • embarrassing
- videoconferencing
- **dashing**, flashing, lashing, thrashing
- square-bashing • tongue-lashing
- **lynching**, unflinching
- garnishing • furnishing • ravishing
- Cushing
- **Flushing**, gushing, unblushing
- inrushing • onrushing

26.13

- matting • exacting
- **Banting**, ranting
- parting
- **enchanting**, planting
- **everlasting**, fasting, lasting
- narrowcasting
- **letting**, setting, wetting
- **self-respecting**, self-selecting, unreflecting, unsuspecting
- tempting
- **unconsenting**, unrelenting
- excepting
- **arresting**, unprotesting, unresting, westing
- bloodletting • trendsetting
- pace-setting • typesetting
- photosetting
- **grating**, plating, rating, slating, uprating, weighting
- painting
- **pasting**, tasting
- undeviating • self-perpetuating
- unaccommodating • self-deprecating
- suffocating • self-regulating
- undiscriminating • underpainting
- unhesitating
- **beating**, fleeting, greeting, Keating, meeting, self-defeating, sweeting
- easting
- **fitting**, sitting, unbefitting, unremitting, witting

- **printing**, unstinting
- **listing**, twisting, unresisting
- shopfitting • marketing
- telemarketing • pickpocketing
- weightlifting • side-splitting
- carpeting • trumpeting
- uninteresting • visiting
- **backlighting**, lighting, self-righting, sighting, unexciting, uninviting, whiting, writing
- infighting • prizefighting
- dogfighting • bullfighting
- handwriting • screenwriting
- scriptwriting • copywriting
- skywriting • signwriting
- typewriting • songwriting • knotting
- prompting
- **costing**, frosting
- **self-supporting**, unsporting
- **malting**, salting
- ripsnorting • outing
- **accounting**, mounting
- coating
- **Boulting**, revolting
- **posting**, roasting
- billposting • disappointing
- **non-polluting**, shooting, suiting, Tooting
- sharpshooting • footing
- off-putting
- **cutting**, Nutting
- bunting
- **disgusting**, self-adjusting, trusting
- blockbusting • linocutting
- woodcutting • disquieting
- **disconcerting**, shirting, skirting

26.14

- pennyfarthing • plaything
- silversmithing • anything
- everything • northing • nothing
- something • rebirthing • farthing
- scathing • sheathing
- **tithing**, writhing
- southing • clothing • underclothing
- Worthing • carving • woodcarving
- delving
- **craving**, engraving, paving, raving, saving, shaving
- **self-deceiving**, unbelieving, weaving

- **living**, misgiving, thanksgiving, unforgiving
- skydiving •piledriving •coving
- **approving**, reproving, unmoving
- unloving
- **Irving**, serving, unswerving
- time-serving •lapwing •waxwing
- batwing •redwing •lacewing
- beeswing •forewing •downswing
- outswing •viewing •upswing
- underwing •phrasing •stargazing
- trailblazing •hellraising •unpleasing
- **rising**, surprising
- self-aggrandizing •uncompromising
- unpatronizing •uprising
- enterprising •appetizing
- **Dowsing**, housing
- unimposing
- **amusing**, confusing, musing

26.15

- **along**, belong, bong, chaise longue, dong, Geelong, gong, Guangdong, Haiphong, Heilong, Hong Kong, Jong, King Kong, long, mah-jong, Mao Zedong, Mekong, nong, pong, prolong, prong, sarong, Shillong, song, souchong, strong, thong, throng, tong, Vietcong, wrong

> Create extra rhymes by adding -*ing* to words like belong. [i]

- billabong •dingdong •Wollongong
- Chittagong •headlong •livelong
- sidelong •lifelong •oblong •oolong
- singalong •furlong •pingpong
- Armstrong •headstrong •part song
- plainsong •evensong •singsong
- swansong •birdsong •biltong
- diphthong

26.16

- boing

26.17

- **Jung**, Kung, Taichung
- Bandung •Nibelung •Hornung

26.18

- **among**, bung, clung, dung, flung, hung, lung, outflung, rung, shantung, slung, sprung, strung, stung, sung, swung, tongue, underslung, wrung, young
- aqualung •hamstrung •ox tongue

26.19

- vingt-et-un

Section 27: **-p**

27.1

- **bap**, cap, chap, clap, crap, dap, entrap, enwrap, flap, frap, gap, giftwrap, hap, Jap, knap, lap, Lapp, map, nap, nappe, pap, rap, sap, schappe, scrap, slap, snap, strap, tap, trap, wrap, yap, zap
  - stopgap • mayhap • mishap • madcap
  - blackcap • redcap • kneecap
  - handicap
- **nightcap**, whitecap
- **snowcap**, toecap
  - foolscap • hubcap • skullcap
  - dunce cap • handclap • dewlap
  - mudflap • thunderclap • burlap
  - bitmap • catnap • kidnap • Saranwrap
  - mantrap • claptrap • deathtrap
  - chinstrap • jockstrap • mousetrap
  - bootstrap • suntrap • firetrap
  - heeltap

27.2

- **Arp**, carp, harp, scarp, sharp, tarp
  - cardsharp

27.3

- **cep**, Dieppe, hep, misstep, outstep, pep, prep, rep, schlepp, skep, step, steppe, strep
  - quickstep • sidestep • doorstep
  - goosestep • footstep • one-step

27.4

- **agape**, ape, cape, chape, crape, crêpe, drape, escape, gape, grape, jape, misshape, nape, rape, scrape, shape, tape
  - landscape • seascape • cityscape
  - skyscape • townscape • snowscape
  - roofscape • moonscape • broomrape
  - shipshape • videotape • sellotape
  - ticker tape

27.5

- **asleep**, beep, bleep, cheap, cheep, creep, deep, heap, Jeep, keep, leap, neap, neep, peep, reap, seep, sheep, skin-deep, sleep, steep, Streep, sweep, veep, weep

> Create extra rhymes by   ⓘ
> adding -ing to words like beep.

- slagheap • scrapheap • antheap
- housekeep • upkeep • chimney sweep

A *pararhyme* (one kind of *half-rhyme*) is one in which the final consonant of the stressed syllable matches but the stressed vowel does not, as in cape/keep. Wilfred Owen made frequent use of it:

It seemed that out of the battle I escaped
Down some profound dull tunnel, long since scooped
Through granites which Titanic wars had groined.
Yet also there encumbered sleepers groaned ...

(Wilfred Owen, 'Strange Meeting')

27.6

- **blip**, chip, clip, dip, drip, equip, flip, grip, gyp, harelip, hip, kip, lip, nip, outstrip, pip, quip, rip, scrip, ship, sip, skip, slip, snip, strip, tip, toodle-pip, trip, whip, yip, zip
- biochip • microchip • woodchip
- sheepdip • skinny-dip • rosehip
- landslip • payslip
- **fillip**, Philip
- gymslip • side-slip • polyp • oxlip
- cowslip • pillowslip
- **julep**, tulip
- Cudlipp • paperclip • catnip • parsnip
- turnip • handgrip • cantrip • hairgrip
- airstrip • filmstrip • kirby grip
- weatherstrip • gossip • airship
- midship • kinship • godship • warship
- gunship • worship • wingtip
- fingertip • horsewhip • bullwhip
- bunyip

27.7

- **gripe**, hype, mistype, pipe, ripe, sipe, skype, slype, snipe, stripe, swipe, tripe, type, wipe

> Create extra rhymes by changing words like grip to gripping. ⓘ

- guttersnipe • bagpipe • standpipe
- tailpipe • drainpipe • pitchpipe
- windpipe • hornpipe • blowpipe
- stovepipe • hosepipe • soilpipe
- pinstripe • archetype • logotype
- phenotype • linotype • Monotype
- electrotype • daguerreotype
- subtype • stereotype
- collotype
- **genotype**, stenotype
- prototype • sideswipe

27.8

- **atop**, bop, chop, clop, cop, crop, dop, drop, Dunlop, estop, flop, fop, glop, hop, intercrop, knop, kop, lop, mop, op, plop, pop, prop, screw-top, shop, slop, sop, stop, strop, swap, tiptop, top, underprop, whop, wop
- co-op • bebop • sweatshop • carhop
- hedgehog • bellhop • hiphop • flipflop
- clip-clop • bellyflop • megaflop
- gigaflop • teraflop • rollmop • coin-op
- lollipop • backdrop • airdrop
- sharecrop • namedrop • raindrop
- eavesdrop • Ribbentrop • Winthrop
- agitprop • outcrop • snowdrop
- stonecrop • turboprop • dewdrop
- gumdrop • teardrop • malaprop
- Aesop • sweetsop • milksop
- pawnshop • window-shop • toyshop
- **bookshop**, cookshop
- barbershop • workshop • ragtop
- blacktop • tanktop • laptop • backstop
- flat-top • hardtop • palmtop • desktop
- tabletop • maintop • treetop • hilltop
- whistle-stop • ripstop • longstop
- foretop • doorstop • shortstop
- clifftop • screwtop • rooftop
- worktop

27.9

- **dorp**, gawp, scaup, scorp, Thorpe, warp, whaup, yawp
- Klerksdorp • Scunthorpe

27.10

- **aslope**, cope, dope, elope, grope, hope, interlope, lope, mope, nope, ope, pope, rope, scope, slope, soap, taupe, tope, trope
- myope • telescope • periscope
- stereoscope • bioscope • stroboscope
- kaleidoscope • CinemaScope
- gyroscope • microscope • horoscope
- stethoscope • antelope • envelope
- zoetrope • skipping-rope • tightrope
- towrope • heliotrope • lycanthrope
- philanthrope • thaumatrope
- misanthrope
- **isotope**, radioisotope

27.11

- **bloop**, cock-a-hoop, coop, croup, droop, drupe, dupe, goop, group,

Guadeloupe, hoop, loop, poop, recoup, roup, scoop, sloop, snoop, soup, stoep, stoop, stoup, stupe, swoop, troop, troupe, whoop

> Create extra rhymes by adding *-ing* to words like droop. [i]

- hula-hoop •cantaloupe •nincompoop
- playgroup •subgroup •peer group

27.12

- Krupp

27.13

- **cup**, grown-up, pup, scup, straight-up, stuck-up, summing-up, sup, totting-up, tup, two-up, up, washing-up
- pick-me-up •fry-up •wind-up
- round-up •hold-up •catch-up
- backup •markup •check-up
- **break-up**, make-up, shake-up, take-up

> Try rhyming one word with a set of two: makeup, wake up. [i]

- teacup
- **hiccup**, pickup, stick-up
- link-up
- **cock-up**, lock-up
- walk-up
- **hook-up**, lookup
- buttercup •snarl-up •pile-up
- pull-up •warm-up •clean-up •pin-up
- line-up •grown-up
- **run-up**, sun-up, ton-up
- turn-up •hang-up •slap-up •zip-up
- top-up •chirrup •press-up •piss-up
- toss-up
- **nosh-up**, wash-up
- punch-up •start-up
- **let-up**, set-up
- meetup •sit-up •cut-up •rave-up

27.14

- ketchup
- **callop**, escallop, escalope, gallop,

galop, Salop, shallop
- **develop**, envelop
- **collop**, dollop, gollop, lollop, scallop, scollop, trollop, Trollope, wallop
- codswallop •Stanhope •larrup
- satrap •caltrop
- **stirrup**, syrup (*US* sirup)
- Europe
- **archbishop**, bishop
- tittup

27.15

- **burp**, chirp, Earp, slurp, twerp, usurp
- Antwerp

27.16

- **alp**, scalp
- **help**, kelp, whelp, yelp
- **gulp**, pulp

27.17

- **amp**, camp, champ, clamp, cramp, damp, encamp, gamp, lamp, ramp, samp, scamp, stamp, tamp, tramp, vamp
- firedamp •headlamp •wheel clamp
- sidelamp •spotlamp •blowlamp
- sunlamp
- **hemp**, kemp, temp
- **blimp**, chimp, crimp, gimp, imp, limp, pimp, primp, scrimp, shrimp, simp, skimp, wimp
- **chomp**, clomp, comp, pomp, romp, stomp, swamp, tromp, whomp, yomp
- **bump**, chump, clump, crump, dump, flump, frump, gazump, grump, hump, jump, lump, outjump, plump, pump, rump, scrump, slump, stump, sump, thump, trump, tump, ump, whump

> Create extra rhymes by adding *-ing* to words like bump. [i]

- ski-jump •showjump •handpump
- mugwump

27.18

• asp

• **clasp**, gasp, grasp, hasp, rasp
• **crisp**, lisp, will-o'-the-wisp, wisp
• wasp • woodwasp • cusp

Section 28: -s

28.1

- **alas**, Alsace, amass, ass, Bass, chasse, crass, crevasse, en masse, gas, Hamas, lass, mass, morass, sass, tarantass, tass, wrasse
- Díaz • Phidias • palliasse
- **materfamilias**, paterfamilias
- Asturias • Aphrodisias • Trias
- Donbas • Vargas • Ofgas • biogas
- teargas • jackass • Hellas • Ulfilas
- Stanislas • Candlemas • landmass
- Martinmas • biomass • Childermas
- Esdras • Mithras • hippocras
- sassafras • demitasse • gravitas

28.2

- **arse**, baas, brass, carse, class, coup de grâce, farce, glass, grass, Grasse, impasse, Kars, kick-ass, kvass, Laplace, Maas, Madras, outclass, pass, sparse, stained glass, surpass, upper class, volte-face
- badass • lardass • sandglass
- **eyeglass**, spyglass
- wine glass • tooth glass • subclass
- hourglass
- fibreglass (*US* fiberglass) • underclass
- masterclass • weather glass • bypass
- underpass • wheatgrass • ryegrass
- knotgrass • sawgrass • bluegrass
- goosegrass • smart-arse

28.3

- **acquiesce**, address, assess, Bess, bless, bouillabaisse, caress, cess, chess, coalesce, compress, confess, convalesce, cress, deliquesce, digress, dress, duchesse, duress, effervesce, effloresce, evanesce, excess, express, fess, finesse, fluoresce, guess, Hesse, impress, incandesce, intumesce, jess, largesse, less, manageress, mess, ness, noblesse, obsess, oppress, outguess, phosphoresce, politesse, possess, press, priestess, princess, process, profess, progress, prophetess, regress, retrogress, stress, success, suppress, tendresse, top-dress, transgress, tress, tristesse, underdress, vicomtesse, yes
- Jewess • shepherdess • Borges
- battledress • Mudéjares • headdress
- protectress • egress • ingress
- minidress • nightdress • congress
- sundress • procuress • murderess
- letterpress • watercress • shirtdress
- access

28.4

- scarce

28.5

- **abase**, ace, apace, backspace, base, bass, brace, case, chase, dace, efface, embrace, encase, enchase, enlace, face, grace, interlace, interspace, in-your-face, lace, mace, misplace, outface, outpace, pace, place, plaice, race, space, Thrace, trace, upper case
- airbase • freebase • wheelbase
- database • steeplechase • paperchase
- paleface • typeface • whiteface
- boldface • coalface • interface
- staircase • briefcase • slipcase
- packing case • doorcase • showcase

- notecase •pillowcase •suitcase
- bookcase •nutcase •marketplace
- anyplace •everyplace •showplace
- shoelace •bootlace •someplace
- Lovelace •fireplace •commonplace
- workplace •birthplace
- tenace •mixed-race
- airspace •aerospace •hyperspace
- carapace •workspace •ratrace
- millrace •Fuentes •rosace

28.6

- **anis**, apiece, Berenice, caprice, cassis, cease, coulisse, crease, Dumfries, fils, fleece, geese, grease, Greece, kris, lease, Lucrece, MacNeice, Matisse, McAleese, Nice, niece, obese, peace, pelisse, piece, police, Rees, Rhys, set piece, sublease, surcease, two-piece, underlease
- mantelpiece •headpiece •hairpiece
- tailpiece •Greenpeace
- chimney piece •frontispiece
- timepiece •codpiece •crosspiece
- mouthpiece •showpiece •earpiece
- masterpiece
- centrepiece (*US* centerpiece)
- altarpiece •workpiece •ambergris
- calabrese

28.7

- **abyss**, amiss, bis, bliss, Chris, Diss, hiss, kiss, Majlis, miss, piss, reminisce, sis, Swiss, this, vis
- dais
- **Powys**, prowess
- **loess**, Lois
- **Lewes**, lewis
- abbess •ibis
- **Anubis**, pubis
- cannabis •arabis •duchess
- purchase
- **caddis**, Gladys
- Candice
- **Sardis**, Tardis
- vendace •Charybdis
- **bodice**, goddess
- demigoddess •Aldiss •jaundice
- de profundis •prejudice •hendiadys
- cowardice •stewardess •preface
- Memphis •aphis •edifice •benefice
- orifice •artifice •office
- **surface**, surface-to-surface
- undersurface •haggis •aegis
- burgess
- **clerkess**, Theodorákis
- Colchis

28.8

- **Alice**, chalice, challis, malice, palace, Tallis

Monorhyme describes a poem or part of a poem in which all the lines have the same *end rhyme*; the rhyme pattern is *aaaa* (or as part of a larger stanza, it could also be *bbbb* or *cccc* etc.). Shakespeare sometimes makes use of it as in this section from *The Merchant of Venice*:

ARAGON: The fire seven times tried this;
Seven times tried that judgement is
That did never choose amiss.
Some there be that shadows kiss;
There be fools alive, iwis,
Silvered o'er; and so was this.
Take what wife you will to bed,
I will ever be your head.
So be gone; you are sped.

(William Shakespeare, *The Merchant of Venice*, 2.9.62-71)

- aurora australis
- **Ellis**, trellis
- necklace
- **aurora borealis**, Baylis, digitalis, Fidelis, rayless
- ageless • aimless • keyless
- **amaryllis**, cilice, Dilys, fillis, Phyllis
- ribless • lidless • rimless
- **kinless**, sinless, winless
- lipless • witless • contactless
- annus mirabilis • annus horribilis
- syphilis
- **eyeless**, skyless, tieless
- **polis**, solace, Wallace
- joyless
- **Dulles**, portcullis
- accomplice
- **Annapolis**, Indianapolis, Minneapolis
- Persepolis
- **acropolis**, cosmopolis, Heliopolis, megalopolis, metropolis, necropolis
- chrysalis • surplice • amice • premise
- airmiss • Amis • in extremis • Artemis
- promise
- **pomace**, pumice
- Salamis
- **dermis**, epidermis, kermis

28.9

- **anise**, Janice
- Daphnis • Agnes
- **harness**, Kiwanis
- **Dennis**, Ennis, Glenys, menace, tennis, Venice
- **feyness**, gayness, greyness (*US* grayness)
- **finis**, penis
- **Glynis**, Innes, pinnace
- Widnes • bigness • lychnis • illness
- dimness • hipness
- **fitness**, witness
- Erinys • iciness
- **dryness**, flyness, shyness, slyness, wryness
- cornice
- **Adonis**, Clones, Issigonis
- coyness
- **Eunice**, Tunis
- **Bernice**, furnace

- Thespis • precipice • coppice • hospice
- auspice • Serapis

28.10

- **arris**, Clarice, Harries, Harris, Paris
- mattress • actress • benefactress
- Polaris • enchantress
- **derris**, Nerys, terrace
- Emrys • empress
- **directress**, Electress
- temptress • sempstress
- **Apollinaris**, heiress
- waitress • seamstress • ex libris
- **headmistress**, mistress
- housemistress • toastmistress
- schoolmistress • ancestress
- dentifrice
- **iris**, Osiris
- **tigress**, Tigris
- cypress
- **Boris**, doch-an-dorris, Doris, Horace, Maurice, Norris, orris
- **cantoris**, Dolores, loris
- laundress • fortress • jointress
- hubris • buttress
- **conductress**, instructress, seductress
- huntress • peeress • Beatrice
- arbitress • berberis • anchoress
- ephemeris • ambassadress
- adventuress • clitoris • authoress
- avarice

28.11

- **glacis**, Onassis
- abscess
- **anaphylaxis**, axis, praxis, taxis
- Chalcis • Jancis • synapsis
- catharsis
- **Frances**, Francis
- thesis • Alexis • amanuensis
- **prolepsis**, sepsis, syllepsis
- **basis**, oasis, stasis
- **amniocentesis**, anamnesis, ascesis, catechesis, diesis, exegesis, mimesis, prosthesis, psychokinesis, telekinesis
- **ellipsis**, paralipsis
- Lachesis

- **analysis**, catalysis, dialysis, paralysis, psychoanalysis
- electrolysis •nemesis
- **genesis**, parthenogenesis, pathogenesis
- diaeresis (*US* dieresis) •metathesis
- parenthesis
- **photosynthesis**, synthesis
- **hypothesis**, prothesis
- **crisis**, Isis
- proboscis •synopsis
- **apotheosis**, chlorosis, cirrhosis, diagnosis, halitosis, hypnosis, kenosis, meiosis, metempsychosis, misdiagnosis, mononucleosis, myxomatosis, necrosis, neurosis, osmosis, osteoporosis, prognosis, psittacosis, psychosis, sclerosis, symbiosis, thrombosis, toxoplasmosis, trichinosis, tuberculosis
- **archdiocese**, diocese, elephantiasis, psoriasis
- anabasis •apodosis
- **emphasis**, underemphasis
- **anamorphosis**, metamorphosis
- periphrasis •entasis •protasis
- **hypostasis**, iconostasis

28.12

- **Attis**, gratis, lattice
- **malpractice**, practice, practise
- **Atlantis**, mantis
- pastis
- **Lettice**, lettuce, Thetis
- **apprentice**, compos mentis, in loco parentis, prentice
- **Alcestis**, testis
- poetess •armistice
- **appendicitis**, arthritis, bronchitis, cellulitis, colitis, conjunctivitis, cystitis, dermatitis, encephalitis, gastroenteritis, gingivitis, hepatitis, laryngitis, lymphangitis, meningitis, nephritis, neuritis, osteoarthritis, pericarditis, peritonitis, pharyngitis, sinusitis, tonsillitis
- **epiglottis**, glottis
- solstice

- **mortise**, rigor mortis
- countess •viscountess
- **myosotis**, notice, Otis
- poultice •justice •giantess •clematis
- Curtis •interstice •Tethys
- Glenrothes •Travis
- **Jarvis**, parvis
- **clevis**, crevice, Nevis
- **Elvis**, pelvis
- **Avis**, Davies, mavis
- Leavis •Divis •novice •Clovis
- **Jervis**, service
- **marquess**, marquis

28.13

- **advice**, bice, Brice, choc ice, concise, dice, entice, gneiss, ice, imprecise, lice, mice, nice, precise, price, rice, sice, slice, speiss, spice, splice, suffice, syce, thrice, top-slice, trice, twice, underprice, vice, Zeiss
- merchandise •paradise •sacrifice
- packice •woodlice •fieldmice
- titmice •dormice •allspice
- cockatrice •edelweiss

28.14

- **across**, boss, Bros, cos, cross, crosse, doss, dross, emboss, en brosse, floss, fosse, gloss, Goss, joss, Kos, lacrosse, loss, moss, MS-DOS, Ross, toss
- Laos
- **Áyios Nikólaos**, chaos
- Eos •Helios
- **Chios**, Khíos
- Lesbos •straw boss •Phobos •rooibos
- extrados •kudos •reredos •intrados
- Calvados •Argos •Lagos •logos
- Marcos •telos
- **Delos**, Melos
- Byblos •candyfloss
- **tholos**, Vólos
- bugloss •omphalos •Pátmos
- **Amos**, Deimos, Sámos
- Demos •peatmoss •cosmos •Los Alamos •Lemnos •Hypnos •Minos
- Mykonos •tripos •topos •Atropos
- **Ballesteros**, pharos, Saros
- Imbros •criss-cross •rallycross •Eros

- albatross •monopteros •Dos Passos
- Náxos •Hyksos •Knossos •Santos
- benthos
- **bathos**, pathos
- ethos •Kórinthos

28.15

- **coarse**, corse, course, divorce, endorse (*US* indorse), enforce, force, gorse, hoarse, horse, morse, Norse, perforce, reinforce, sauce, source, torse
- Wilberforce •workforce •packhorse
- carthorse •racehorse •sea horse
- hobby horse •Whitehorse
- **sawhorse**, warhorse
- clothes horse •shire horse
- workhorse •racecourse •concourse
- intercourse •watercourse
- outsource

28.16

- **douse**, dowse, Gauss, grouse, house, Klaus, louse, Manaus, mouse, nous, Rouse, souse, spouse, Strauss
- Windaus •madhouse •cathouse
- Gasthaus •guardhouse •farmhouse
- glasshouse •bathhouse •almshouse
- penthouse •guesthouse •warehouse
- playhouse
- **bakehouse**, steakhouse
- **alehouse**, jailhouse
- **gatehouse**, statehouse
- treehouse •wheelhouse •greenhouse
- clearing house •meeting house
- counting house •ice house
- **lighthouse**, White House
- doghouse •dollhouse
- **chophouse**, flophouse
- dosshouse
- **hothouse**, pothouse
- **poorhouse**, storehouse, whorehouse
- courthouse •malthouse •Bauhaus
- town house •outhouse •coach house
- roadhouse •smokehouse •boathouse
- oast house •schoolhouse

- Wodehouse •cookhouse •clubhouse
- nuthouse •beerhouse •powerhouse
- summerhouse •barrelhouse
- **porterhouse**, slaughterhouse, Waterhouse
- workhouse •lobscouse •woodlouse
- field mouse •titmouse •dormouse

28.17

- **adiós**, chausses, Close, Davos, dose, engross, gross, Grosz, jocose, morose, Rhos, verbose
- grandiose •religiose •otiose
- globose •viscose •bellicose •varicose
- vorticose •cellulose •lachrymose
- lactose •comatose •siliquose

28.18

- **bourgeois**, Boyce, choice, Joyce, pro-choice, rejoice, Royce, voice

28.19

- **abstruse**, abuse, adduce, Ballets Russes, Belarus, Bruce, burnous, caboose, charlotte russe, conduce, deduce, deuce, diffuse, douce, educe, excuse, goose, induce, introduce, juice, Larousse, loose, luce, misuse, moose, mousse, noose, obtuse, Palouse, papoose, produce, profuse, puce, recluse, reduce, Rousse, seduce, sluice, Sousse, spruce, traduce, truce, use, vamoose, Zeus
- cayuse •calaboose •mongoose
- Aarhus •verjuice •couscous
- footloose •ventouse •refuse
- Odysseus •Idomeneus •hypotenuse
- Syracuse

28.20

- **puss**, schuss, wuss
- Anschluss •sourpuss

28.21

• **bus**, buss, concuss, cuss, fuss, Gus, huss, muss, plus, pus, Russ, sus, suss, thus, truss, us

> Create extra rhymes by i adding -ing to words like fuss.

• trolleybus • minibus • blunderbuss

28.22

• **Andreas**, Antaeus, Laius, Menelaus
• **Aeneas**, Apuleius, Judas Maccabaeus, Linnaeus, Piraeus, uraeus

28.23

• **Bierce**, fierce, Pearce, Peirce, pierce, tierce
• **Fabius**, scabious
• Eusebius
• **amphibious**, Polybius
• dubious • Thaddeus • compendious
• radius • tedious
• **fastidious**, hideous, insidious, invidious, perfidious

> Create extra rhymes by i adding -ly to words like fastidious.

• Claudius
• **commodious**, melodious, odious
• studious • Cepheus
• **Morpheus**, Orpheus

> *Unstressed* (or *feminine*) *rhymes* are rhymes with a stressed syllable followed by one or more unstressed syllables; here the rhyme is spread over two words at the end of each line:
>
> ''No,'' said Lizzie, ''no, no, no;
> Their offers should not charm us,
> Their evil gifts would harm us.''
>
> (Christina Rossetti, 'Goblin Market')

• Pelagius • callipygous • Vitellius
• **alias**, Sibelius, Vesalius
• **Aurelius**, Berzelius, contumelious, Cornelius, Delius
• **bilious**, punctilious, supercilious
• coleus • Julius • nucleus • Equuleus
• abstemious
• **Ennius**, Nennius
• **contemporaneous**, cutaneous, extemporaneous, extraneous, instantaneous, miscellaneous, Pausanias, porcellaneous, simultaneous, spontaneous, subcutaneous
• **genius**, heterogeneous, homogeneous, ingenious
• **consanguineous**, ignominious, Phineas, sanguineous
• **igneous**, ligneous
• Vilnius
• **acrimonious**, antimonious, ceremonious, erroneous, euphonious, felonious, harmonious, parsimonious, Petronius, sanctimonious, Suetonius
• Apollonius • impecunious
• calumnious • Asclepius • impious
• Scorpius
• **copious**, Gropius, Procopius
• Marius • pancreas • retiarius
• **Aquarius**, calcareous, Darius, denarius, gregarious, hilarious, multifarious, nefarious, omnifarious, precarious, Sagittarius, senarius, Stradivarius, temerarious, various, vicarious
• Atreus
• **delirious**, Sirius
• vitreous
• **censorious**, glorious, laborious, meritorious, notorious, uproarious, uxorious, vainglorious, victorious
• opprobrious
• **lugubrious**, salubrious
• **illustrious**, industrious
• **cinereous**, deleterious, imperious, mysterious, Nereus, serious, Tiberius
• **curious**, furious, injurious, luxurious, penurious, perjurious,

spurious, sulphureous
(US sulfureous), usurious
- **Cassius**, gaseous
- Alcaeus • Celsius
- **Theseus**, Tiresias
- **osseous**, Roscius
- nauseous
- **caduceus**, Lucius
- Perseus • Statius • Propertius
- Deo gratias • plenteous • piteous
- bounteous
- **Grotius**, Photius, Proteus
- **beauteous**, duteous
- **courteous**, sestertius
- **Boethius**, Prometheus
- envious • Octavius
- **devious**, previous
- **lascivious**, niveous, oblivious
- obvious
- **Vesuvius**, Vitruvius
- **impervious**, pervious
- aqueous • subaqueous • obsequious
- Dionysius

28.24

- **Ananias**, bias, Darius, dryas, Elias,
  eyas, Gaius, hamadryas, Lias,
  Mathias, pious, Tobias
- joyous • Shavuoth • tempestuous
- spirituous • tortuous • sumptuous
- voluptuous • virtuous • mellifluous
- superfluous • congruous • vacuous
- fatuous • anfractuous • arduous
- **ingenuous**, strenuous, tenuous
- flexuous • sensuous • impetuous
- contemptuous • incestuous
- **assiduous**, deciduous
- **ambiguous**, contiguous, exiguous
- **inconspicuous**, perspicuous
- promiscuous
- **continuous**, sinuous
- nocuous • fructuous • tumultuous
- unctuous
- **Abbas**, shabbos
- **choriambus**, iambus
- Arbus
- **Phoebus**, rebus
- gibbous
- **cumulonimbus**, nimbus

- omnibus • ceteris paribus • Erebus
- rhombus • incubus • succubus
- bulbous • Columbus • syllabus
- colobus • Barnabas • righteous
- rumbustious

28.25

- **horrendous**, stupendous,
  tremendous
- Barbados • Indus • solidus • Lepidus
- **Midas**, nidus
- Aldous • Judas • Enceladus • exodus
- hazardous • Dreyfus • Josephus
- Sisyphus • typhus • Dollfuss
- **amorphous**, anthropomorphous,
  polymorphous
- **rufous**, Rufus
- Angus • Argus
- **Las Vegas**, magus, Tagus
- negus
- **anilingus**, cunnilingus, dingus,
  Mingus
- bogus
- **fungous**, fungus, humongous
- **anthropophagous**, oesophagus (US
  esophagus), sarcophagus
- analogous
- **homologous**, tautologous
- Areopagus • craniopagus • asparagus
- **Burgas**, Fergus, Lycurgus
- Carajás • frabjous
- **advantageous**, contagious,
  courageous, outrageous, rampageous
- egregious
- **irreligious**, litigious, prestigious,
  prodigious, religious, sacrilegious
- umbrageous • gorgeous

28.26

- **Bacchus**, Caracas, Gracchus
- Damascus
- **Aristarchus**, carcass, Hipparchus,
  Marcus
- **discus**, hibiscus, meniscus, viscous
- umbilicus • Copernicus
- Ecclesiasticus • Leviticus • floccus

- **caucus**, Dorcas, glaucous, raucous
- **Archilochus**, Cocos, crocus, focus, hocus, hocus-pocus, locus
- autofocus
- **fucus**, Lucas, mucous, mucus, Ophiuchus, soukous
- ruckus •fuscous •abacus
- diplodocus •Telemachus
- Callimachus •Caratacus •Spartacus
- circus

28.27

- **Callas**, callous, callus, Dallas, Pallas, phallus
- Nablus •manless
- **hapless**, mapless
- **atlas**, fatless, hatless
- **braless**, parlous
- armless •artless
- **jealous**, zealous
- endless •legless •sexless •airless
- talus •bacillus •windlass •Nicklaus
- obelus •strobilus
- **acidophilus**, Theophilus
- angelus •Aeschylus •perilous
- scurrilous •Wenceslas •nautilus
- **Silas**, stylus
- jobless
- **godless**, rodless
- Patroclus •topless •coxless
- **lawless**, oarless
- **Aeolus**, alveolus, bolas, bolus, gladiolus, holus-bolus, solus, toeless
- Troilus •Douglas •useless •Tibullus
- garrulous •querulous •fabulous
- miraculous •calculus •famulus
- crapulous •patulous •nebulous
- **credulous**, sedulous
- pendulous •regulus
- **emulous**, tremulous
- bibulous •acidulous
- **meticulous**, ridiculous
- **mimulus**, stimulus
- scrofulous •flocculus •Romulus
- **populace**, populous
- convolvulus
- **altocumulus**, cirrocumulus, cumulus, stratocumulus, tumulus
- scrupulous

- **furunculous**, homunculus, ranunculus
- Catullus •troublous
- **gunless**, sunless
- **cutlass**, gutless
- earless •Heliogabalus
- libellous (*US* libelous) •discobolus
- scandalous •Daedalus •astragalus
- Nicholas •anomalous •Sardanapalus
- tantalus
- marvellous (*US* marvelous)
- frivolous •furless •surplus

28.28

- Lammas •Cadmus •Las Palmas
- **chiasmus**, Erasmus
- Nostradamus
- **famous**, ignoramus, Seamus, shamus
- **Polyphemus**, Remus
- grimace •Michaelmas
- **Christmas**, isthmus
- litmus
- **animus**, equanimous, magnanimous, pusillanimous, unanimous
- **anonymous**, eponymous, Hieronymus, pseudonymous, synonymous
- Septimus
- **Mimas**, primus, thymus, timeous
- Thomas
- **enormous**, ginormous
- **brumous**, hummus, humous, humus, spumous, strumous
- blasphemous
- **bigamous**, polygamous, trigamous
- **endogamous**, monogamous
- **calamus**, hypothalamus, thalamus
- venomous
- **autonomous**, bonhomous, heteronomous
- Pyramus
- **dichotomous**, hippopotamus, trichotomous
- Thermos

28.29

- pandanus

- **badness**, madness, sadness
- Magnus • aptness
- **fatness**, patness
- redness • wetness
- **anus**, Coriolanus, heinous, Janus, Punta Arenas, Silvanus
- **genus**, intravenous, Maecenas, Malvinas, Salinas, venous, Venus
- Cygnus • proteinous • ruinous
- libidinous
- **multitudinous**, platitudinous, pulchritudinous, vicissitudinous
- **cartilaginous**, farraginous, oleaginous
- **fuliginous**, indigenous, oxygenous, polygynous, rubiginous, vertiginous
- **androgynous**, autogenous, endogenous, erogenous, exogenous, homogenous, hydrogenous, misogynous
- ferruginous • ominous
- **bituminous**, leguminous, luminous, numinous, voluminous
- **conterminous**, coterminous, terminus, verminous
- larcenous • gelatinous • cretinous
- mountainous
- **glutinous**, mutinous
- resinous
- **Aquinas**, Delphinus, echinus, Linus, Longinus, minus, Plotinus, sinus, vinous
- oddness • wanness • hotness
- **Faunus**, rawness
- Kaunas
- **bonus**, Cronus, Jonas, lowness, onus, Tithonus

> Try rhyming one word with a set of two: onus, phone us. ⓘ

- oldness
- **newness**, twoness
- fulness
- **alumnus**, rumness
- oneness • Oceanus • Eridanus
- diaphanous • polyphonous
- **cacophonous**, homophonous
- porcellanous • villainous
- membranous • tyrannous
- synchronous • Uranus • tetanus
- monotonous • gluttonous

- **cavernous**, ravenous
- treasonous • poisonous • Avernus

28.30

- **Chiapas**, tapas
- **campus**, grampus, hippocampus, pampas
- **metacarpus**, streptocarpus
- trespass • Priapus • Lepus
- **Aristippus**, Lysippus
- Olympus • Oedipus • platypus
- pompous
- **corpus**, porpoise
- **Canopus**, opus
- **lupus**, upas
- **compass**, encompass, rumpus
- octopus
- **multipurpose**, purpose

28.31

- **Arras**, embarrass, harass
- **gynandrous**, polyandrous
- Pancras • charas • Tatras • disastrous
- ferrous • leprous • ambidextrous
- **Carreras**, mayoress
- scabrous
- **cirrus**, Pyrrhus
- chivalrous
- **citrous**, citrus
- ludicrous • tenebrous
- **Cyrus**, Epirus, papyrus, virus
- fibrous • hydrous • Cyprus
- retrovirus • monstrous
- **brachiosaurus**, brontosaurus, canorous, chorus, Epidaurus, giganotosaurus, Horus, megalosaurus, pelorus, porous, sorus, stegosaurus, Taurus, thesaurus, torus, tyrannosaurus
- walrus
- ochrous (*US* ocherous)
- cumbrous • wondrous • lustrous
- **Algeciras**, Severus
- desirous
- **Arcturus**, Epicurus, Honduras
- barbarous • tuberous • slumberous
- Cerberus • rapturous
- **lecherous**, treacherous
- torturous • vulturous • Pandarus
- slanderous • ponderous

- **malodorous**, odorous
- thunderous • murderous
- **carboniferous**, coniferous, cruciferous, melliferous, odoriferous, pestiferous, somniferous, splendiferous, umbelliferous, vociferous
- **phosphorous**, phosphorus
- sulphurous (US sulfurous)
- **Anaxagoras**, Pythagoras
- **clangorous**, languorous
- **rigorous**, vigorous
- dangerous • verdurous
- **cankerous**, cantankerous, rancorous
- decorous • Icarus • valorous
- dolorous • idolatrous
- **amorous**, clamorous, glamorous
- timorous
- **humerus**, humorous, numerous
- murmurous • generous • sonorous
- onerous • obstreperous • Hesperus
- vaporous • viviparous • viperous
- **Bosporus**, prosperous
- stuporous • cancerous
- **Monoceros**, rhinoceros
- sorcerous • adventurous • Tartarus
- nectarous • dexterous • traitorous
- preposterous • slaughterous
- **boisterous**, roisterous
- uterus • adulterous • stertorous
- cadaverous • feverous
- **carnivorous**, herbivorous, insectivorous, omnivorous
- Lazarus

28.32

- **Crassus**, Halicarnassus, Lassus
- tarsus
- **nexus**, plexus, Texas
- Paracelsus
- **census**, consensus
- Croesus • narcissus • Ephesus
- Dionysus • colossus • Pegasus
- Caucasus • petasus
- **excursus**, thyrsus, versus

28.33

- **factious**, fractious

- anxious • captious
- **precious**, semi-precious
- infectious
- **conscientious**, contentious, licentious, pretentious, sententious, tendentious
- **Athanasius**, audacious, bodacious, cactaceous, capacious, carbonaceous, contumacious, Cretaceous, curvaceous, disputatious, edacious, efficacious, fallacious, farinaceous, flirtatious, foliaceous, fugacious, gracious, hellacious, herbaceous, Ignatius, loquacious, mendacious, mordacious, ostentatious, perspicacious, pertinacious, pugnacious, rapacious, sagacious, salacious, saponaceous, sebaceous, sequacious, setaceous, spacious, tenacious, veracious, vexatious, vivacious, voracious
- **facetious**, Lucretius, specious
- **adventitious**, Aloysius, ambitious, auspicious, avaricious, capricious, conspicuous, delicious, expeditious, factitious, fictitious, flagitious, judicious, lubricious, malicious, Mauritius, meretricious, nutritious, officious, pernicious, propitious, repetitious, seditious, siliceous, superstitious, supposititious, surreptitious, suspicious, vicious

> ⓘ Create extra rhymes by adding -ly to words like ambitious.

- **noxious**, obnoxious
- **conscious**, subconscious, unselfconscious
- **cautious**, tortious
- **atrocious**, ferocious, precocious
- Confucius • luscious
- **bumptious**, scrumptious
- **compunctious**, rambunctious

28.34

- cactus • saltus • Diophantus • Sanctus
- **Rastus**, Theophrastus
- **altostratus**, cirrostratus

nimbostratus, stratus
- **conspectus**, prospectus
- **momentous**, portentous
- **asbestos**, Festus
- **apparatus**, Donatus, hiatus, status
- **acetous**, boletus, Cetus, Epictetus, fetus, Miletus, quietus
- Hephaestus
- **Benedictus**, ictus, rictus
- Quintus ●linctus ●eucalyptus ●cistus
- coitus
- **circuitous**, fortuitous, gratuitous
- Hippolytus ●calamitous ●tinnitus
- Iapetus ●crepitus
- **precipitous**, serendipitous
- impetus ●emeritus ●spiritous
- **Democritus**, Theocritus
- Tacitus ●necessitous
- **complicitous**, duplicitous, felicitous, solicitous
- covetous
- **iniquitous**, ubiquitous
- **detritus**, Heraclitus, Polyclitus, Titus, Vitus
- **Pocahontas**, Pontus
- **Plautus**, tortoise
- cobaltous
- **Duns Scotus**, lotus
- hostess
- **arbutus**, Brutus
- Eustace ●conductus ●cultus
- coitus interruptus ●Augustus
- riotous ●Herodotus ●Oireachtas

28.35

- Malthus
- **acanthus**, agapanthus, clianthus, dianthus, helianthus, polyanthus
- Hyacinthus ●Aegisthus ●traverse
- **canvas**, canvass
- Selvas ●grievous ●mischievous
- redivivus ●fulvous ●nervous
- **Peleus**, rebellious
- Kansas ●Jesus

28.36

- **amerce**, asperse, averse, biodiverse, burse, coerce, converse, curse, diverse, Erse, hearse, immerse, intersperse,

nurse, perse, perverse, purse, reimburse, submerse, terce, terse, transverse, verse, worse
- commerce ●metaverse ●wet nurse
- sesterce ● adverse ●universe
- obverse

28.37

- handkerchiefs ●fisticuffs

28.38

- **axe** (*US* ax), Backs, Bax, fax, flax, lax, max, pax, Sachs, sax, saxe, tax, wax

> Create extra rhymes for axe by adding -*s* to attack etc. (see section 21.1). [i]

- co-ax ●addax ●Fairfax ●Ceefax
- Halifax ●Telefax ●Filofax ●banjax
- Ajax
- pickaxe (*US* pickax) ●gravlax
- gravadlax ●poleaxe ●toadflax
- parallax
- battleaxe (*US* battleax)
- minimax ●climax ●Betamax ●anthrax
- hyrax
- **borax**, storax, thorax
- syntax ●surtax ●beeswax ●earwax
- **Berks**, Lourenço Marques, Marks, Marx, Parks, Sparks
- **annex**, convex, ex, flex, hex, perplex, Rex, sex, specs, Tex, Tex-Mex, vex
- ibex ●index ●codex ●tubifex
- spinifex ●pontifex ●Telex ●triplex
- simplex ●multiplex
- **ilex**, silex
- complex ●duplex ●circumflex ●Amex
- annexe ●Kleenex ●apex ●Tipp-Ex
- haruspex ●perspex ●Pyrex
- **Durex**, Lurex, murex
- Middlesex ●unisex ●Semtex ●latex
- **cortex**, Gore-tex, vortex
- vertex ●Jacques
- **breeks**, idée fixe, maxixe, Weeks

28.39

- **admix**, affix, commix, fix, Hicks,

intermix, MI6, mix, nix, Nyx, pix, Pnyx, prix fixe, pyx, Ricks, six, Styx, transfix, Wicks

> Create extra rhymes for affix by adding -s to brick etc. (see section 21.9). ℹ️

- Aquarobics • radix • appendix
- crucifix • suffix • Alex • calyx
- **Felix**, helix
- kylix • Horlicks • prolix • spondulicks
- hydromechanics • phoenix
- **Ebonics**, onyx
- mechatronics • sardonyx
- Paralympics • semi-tropics
- subtropics • Hendrix
- **dominatrix**, matrix
- administratrix • oryx • tortrix
- executrix • Beatrix • cicatrix
- **Essex**, Wessex
- kinesics • coccyx • Sussex
- **informatics**, mathematics
- Dianetics • geopolitics • bioethics
- cervix • astrophysics • yikes

28.40

- **box**, cox, detox, fox, Foxe, Knox, lox, outfox, ox, phlox, pox, Stocks

> Create extra rhymes for cox by adding -s to block etc. (see section 21.20). ℹ️

- matchbox
- **bandbox**, sandbox
- hatbox • haybox • mailbox • brainbox
- paintbox • squeezebox • pillbox
- icebox • strongbox • horsebox
- saltbox • soundbox • soapbox
- shadow-box • shoebox • jukebox
- toolbox • snuffbox • gearbox • firebox
- tinderbox • thunderbox • pillar box
- pepperbox • chatterbox • letter box
- workbox • paradox • heterodox
- orthodox • dementia praecox
- Wilcox • backblocks • dreadlocks
- Goldilocks • Magnox • equinox
- chickenpox • smallpox • cowpox
- aurochs • xerox
- volvox
- **Faux**, Fawkes

- **Boaks**, coax, hoax, Oaks, stokes
- yoicks
- **Fuchs**, gadzooks, Jukes
- **Brooks**, Crookes

28.41

- **crux**, dux, flux, lux, luxe, tux
- afflux • efflux • Benelux • conflux
- **bollocks**, Pollux
- **flummox**, lummox
- Lennox • barracks • Trossachs
- **circs**, Merckx, Perks
- gasworks • steelworks • printworks
- waterworks • calx
- **Franks**, Hanks, Manx, Shanks
- Fairbanks • phalanx • Gollancz
- spindleshanks
- **jinks**, jinx, lynx, methinks, minx, sphinx

> Create extra rhymes for jinx by adding -s to blink etc. (see section 21.33). ℹ️

- **larynx**, pharynx
- **Bronx**, Tonks, yonks
- Monks • quincunx

28.42

- Hals • rinkhals • valse • else • grilse
- **false**, waltz
- **convulse**, dulse, pulse
- impulse

28.43

- glimpse

28.44

- **askance**, bromance, expanse, finance, Hans, Hanse, manse, nance, Penzance, Romance
- underpants • happenstance
- microfinance
- **advance**, Afrikaans, à outrance, chance, dance, enhance, entrance, faience, France, glance, lance,

mischance, outdance, perchance, prance, Provence, stance, trance
- nuance • tap-dance • square dance
- freelance • convenance
- **cense**, commence, common sense, condense, dense, dispense, expense, fence, hence, Hortense, immense, offence (*US* offense), pence, prepense, pretence (*US* pretense), sense, spence, suspense, tense, thence, whence
- ring-fence • recompense
- frankincense
- **chintz**, convince, evince, Linz, mince, Port-au-Prince, prince, quince, rinse, since, Vince, wince
- province
- **bonce**, ensconce, nonce, ponce, response, sconce
- séance • pièce de résistance
- **announce**, bounce, denounce, flounce, fluid ounce, jounce, mispronounce, ounce, pounce, pronounce, renounce, trounce
- **dunce**, once

[28.45]

- **abeyance**, conveyance, purveyance
- creance • ambience
- **irradiance**, radiance
- **expedience**, obedience
- audience
- **dalliance**, mésalliance
- salience
- **consilience**, resilience
- emollience • ebullience
- **convenience**, lenience, provenience
- **impercipience**, incipience, percipience
- variance • experience
- **luxuriance**, prurience
- nescience • omniscience
- insouciance • deviance
- subservience • transience
- **alliance**, appliance, compliance, defiance, misalliance, neuroscience, reliance, science
- allowance

- **annoyance**, clairvoyance, flamboyance
- **fluence**, pursuance
- perpetuance • affluence • effluence
- mellifluence • confluence
- congruence • issuance • continuance
- disturbance
- **attendance**, dependence, interdependence, overdependence, resplendence, superintendence, tendance, transcendence
- cadence
- **antecedence**, credence, impedance
- riddance • diffidence • confidence
- accidence • precedence • dissidence
- **coincidence**, incidence
- evidence
- **improvidence**, providence
- residence
- **abidance**, guidance, misguidance, subsidence
- **correspondence**, despondence
- **accordance**, concordance, discordance
- **avoidance**, voidance
- **imprudence**, jurisprudence, prudence
- impudence • abundance • elegance
- arrogance • extravagance
- allegiance • indigence
- **counter-intelligence**, intelligence
- negligence • diligence • intransigence
- exigence
- **divulgence**, effulgence, indulgence, refulgence
- **convergence**, divergence, emergence, insurgence, resurgence, submergence
- significance
- **balance**, counterbalance, imbalance, outbalance, valance
- parlance • repellence • semblance
- **bivalence**, covalence, surveillance, valence
- sibilance • jubilance • vigilance
- pestilence • silence • condolence
- virulence • ambulance • crapulence
- flatulence • feculence • petulance
- opulence • fraudulence • corpulence
- **succulence**, truculence
- turbulence • violence • redolence

- indolence • somnolence • excellence
- insolence • nonchalance
- **benevolence**, malevolence
- **ambivalence**, equivalence
- Clemence • vehemence
- **conformance**, outperformance, performance
- adamance • penance • ordinance
- eminence • imminence
- **dominance**, prominence
- abstinence • maintenance
- continence • countenance
- sustenance
- **appurtenance**, impertinence, pertinence
- provenance • ordnance • repugnance
- ordonnance • immanence
- **impermanence**, permanence
- assonance • dissonance • consonance
- governance • resonance • threepence
- halfpence • sixpence
- **comeuppance**, tuppence, twopence
- **clarence**, transparence
- **aberrance**, deterrence, inherence, Terence
- remembrance • entrance
- **Behrens**, forbearance
- fragrance • hindrance • recalcitrance
- **abhorrence**, Florence, Lawrence, Lorentz
- monstrance
- **concurrence**, co-occurrence, occurrence, recurrence
- encumbrance
- **adherence**, appearance, clearance, coherence, interference, perseverance
- **assurance**, durance, endurance, insurance
- **exuberance**, protuberance
- preponderance • transference
- **deference**, preference, reference
- difference • inference • conference
- sufferance • circumference
- belligerence • tolerance • ignorance
- temperance • utterance • furtherance
- **irreverence**, reverence, severance
- deliverance • renascence • absence
- **acquiescence**, adolescence, arborescence, coalescence, convalescence, deliquescence,

effervescence, essence, evanescence, excrescence, florescence, fluorescence, incandescence, iridescence, juvenescence, luminescence, obsolescence, opalescence, phosphorescence, pubescence, putrescence, quiescence, quintessence, tumescence
- **obeisance**, Renaissance
- puissance
- **impuissance**, reminiscence
- **beneficence**, maleficence
- **magnificence**, munificence
- reconnaissance • concupiscence
- reticence
- **delicense**, licence, license
- nonsense
- **nuisance**, translucence
- innocence • conversance • sentience
- **impatience**, patience
- conscience
- **repentance**, sentence
- acceptance • acquaintance
- **acquittance**, admittance, intermittence, pittance, quittance, remittance
- **assistance**, coexistence, consistence, distance, existence, insistence, outdistance, persistence, resistance, subsistence
- instance • exorbitance
- concomitance
- **impenitence**, penitence
- appetence
- **competence**, omnicompetence
- inheritance • capacitance • hesitance
- Constance • importance • potence
- **conductance**, inductance, reluctance
- substance • circumstance
- omnipotence • impotence
- inadvertence • grievance
- **irrelevance**, relevance
- **connivance**, contrivance
- observance • sequence • consequence
- subsequence • eloquence
- **grandiloquence**, magniloquence
- brilliance • poignance
- **omnipresence**, pleasance, presence
- complaisance • malfeasance

- **incognizance**, recognizance
- usance • recusance

28.46

- **apse**, collapse, craps, elapse, lapse, perhaps, schnapps

> Create extra rhymes for apse ⓘ
> by adding -s to tap etc. (see
> section 27.1).

- prolapse • synapse • Lesseps
- quadriceps
- **biceps**, triceps
- forceps
- **traipse**, trapes
- jackanapes • Pepys
- **Chips**, eclipse, ellipse, thrips
- Phillips • apocalypse
- **amidships**, midships
- **cripes**, Stars and Stripes
- copse • Cheops • Pelops • Cyclops
- triceratops • corpse • Stopes
- **oops**, whoops
- turps • mumps • goosebumps

28.47

- **congrats**, stats
- ersatz • Graz
- **godets**, Metz, pantalettes
  (US pantalets)
- Odets
- **Bates**, Fates, Gates, Trucial States, United States, Yeats

- annates
- **eats**, Keats
- foresheets
- **Biarritz**, blitz, Fritz, glitz, it's, its, Ritz, spitz, spritz, St Kitts
- blewits • Colditz • rickets • giblets
- Austerlitz • Chemnitz • Leibniz
- Massachusetts • slivovitz
- Clausewitz • Auschwitz • Horowitz
- Golan Heights • house lights
- footlights
- **Scots**, Watts
- **Cinque Ports**, orts, quartz
- undershorts
- **thereabouts**, whereabouts
- **Coats**, John o'Groats, Oates
- Hakenkreuz
- **cahoots**, Schütz
- slyboots
- **kibbutz**, Lutz, Perutz, putz
- **futz**, klutz, Smuts
- Roberts • polyunsaturates
- **deserts**, Hertz
- megahertz • kilohertz • outskirts
- Weltschmerz
- draughts (US drafts)
- Helmholtz • schmaltz
- Schulz
- **Hants**, Northants, pants
- sweatpants • smarty-pants
- shin splints • Mainz • Y-fronts
- arrondissements • Barents

28.48

- maths • meths • cloths

Section 29: -sh

29.1

- **abash**, ash, Ashe, bash, brash, cache, calash, cash, clash, crash, dash, encash, flash, gash, gnash, hash, lash, mash, Nash, panache, pash, plash, rash, sash, slash, smash, soutache, splash, stash, thrash, trash

> Create extra rhymes by adding -*ing* to words like cash. ℹ

- earbash • kurbash • calabash
- slapdash • pebbledash • balderdash
- spatterdash • car crash • backlash
- backslash • whiplash • eyelash
- goulash • newsflash • thunderflash
- mishmash • gatecrash • Midrash
- potash • succotash

29.2

- **démarche**, gouache, harsh, marsh, moustache (*US* mustache)
- Saltmarsh

29.3

- **afresh**, Andhra Pradesh, Bangladesh, crème fraîche, enmesh, flesh, fresh, intermesh, Kesh, Madhya Pradesh, Marrakesh, mesh, nesh, thresh, Uttar Pradesh
- parfleche • horseflesh • gooseflesh
- micromesh • Gilgamesh
- synchromesh

29.4

- **crèche**, flèche, kesh

29.5

- **babiche**, Dalglish, fiche, Laois, leash, niche, nouveau riche, pastiche, quiche, Rajneesh, schottische
- microfiche • corniche • hashish
- baksheesh

29.6

- **bish**, dish, fish, Frisch, Gish, knish, pish, squish, swish, wish

> Create extra rhymes by adding -*ing* to words like fish. ℹ

- **clayish**, greyish (*US* grayish)
- puppyish • babyish
- **dandyish**, sandyish
- toadyish • fogeyish • monkeyish
- sissyish • Gypsyish • prettyish
- heavyish • dryish
- **lowish**, slowish
- sallowish • yellowish • narrowish
- boyish • tomboyish
- **bluish**, Jewish, newish, shrewish
- Pollyannaish • prima donna-ish
- nebbish
- **slobbish**, snobbish, yobbish
- rubbish • furbish
- **baddish**, caddish, faddish, kaddish, laddish, radish, saddish
- **blandish**, brandish, outlandish, Standish
- Cavendish • Netherlandish
- horseradish • hardish • reddish
- Wendish • old-maidish • Swedish
- fiendish • Yiddish • widish
- **childish**, mildish, wildish
- **cloddish**, oddish

- baldish •roundish
- **modish**, toadish
- **coldish**, oldish
- prudish •goodish •Kurdish

29.7

- raffish •damselfish
- **catfish**, flatfish
- **garfish**, starfish
- redfish
- **elfish**, selfish, shellfish
- devilfish
- **crayfish**, waifish
- stiffish •kingfish •jellyfish
- killifish •filefish •pipefish
- white fish
- **offish**, standoffish
- codfish •dogfish •rockfish •crawfish
- swordfish
- **blowfish**, oafish
- goldfish

> Try rhyming one word with a set of two: goldfish, cold fish.   ⓘ

- **bonefish**, stonefish
- wolfish
- **huffish**, roughish, toughish
- mudfish •monkfish •cuttlefish
- lungfish •lumpfish •spearfish
- angelfish •parrotfish •silverfish
- **haggish**, waggish
- vaguish
- **biggish**, piggish, priggish, whiggish
- **doggish**, hoggish
- **roguish**, voguish
- **puggish**, sluggish, thuggish
- largish

29.8

- **blackish**, brackish, quackish
- **Frankish**, prankish
- **clerkish**, darkish, sparkish
- peckish •rakish
- **cliquish**, freakish, weakish
- **sickish**, thickish
- pinkish
- **hawkish**, mawkish
- folkish •bookish •textbookish

- puckish
- **monkish**, punkish
- **quirkish**, Turkish
- **establish**, stablish
- Spanglish
- **embellish**, hellish, relish
- **palish**, Salish
- English •stylish
- **abolish**, demolish, spit-and-polish
- **Gaulish**, smallish, tallish
- owlish •Polish
- **coolish**, foolish, ghoulish, mulish
- bullish •dullish •publish
- accomplish •ticklish •purplish
- devilish
- **churlish**, girlish
- famish •Amish •schoolmarmish
- **blemish**, Flemish
- Hamish •squeamish •dimmish
- warmish •gnomish •Carchemish
- skirmish

29.9

- **banish**, clannish, mannish, Spanish, tannish, vanish
- **garnish**, tarnish, varnish
- **replenish**, Rhenish
- Danish
- **cleanish**, greenish
- **diminish**, finish, Finnish, thinnish
- swinish
- **admonish**, astonish, donnish
- Cornish
- **brownish**, clownish, townish
- **buffoonish**, cartoonish, soonish
- **Hunnish**, nunnish, punish
- maidenish •hoydenish •paganish
- womanish •vixenish •kittenish
- heathenish
- **burnish**, furnish
- **longish**, strongish
- youngish
- **Lappish**, snappish
- **dampish**, scampish, trampish, vampish
- sharpish •apish
- **cheapish**, sheepish, steepish
- **blimpish**, impish, wimpish
- foppish •waspish •uppish

- **frumpish**, grumpish, lumpish, plumpish
- parish
- **cherish**, perish
- **bearish**, fairish, garish, squarish
- nightmarish • Irish
- **moreish**, whorish
- **flourish**, nourish
- **nearish**, queerish
- sourish
- **boorish**, Moorish
- gibberish • Micawberish • vulturish
- spiderish • vigorish • vinegarish
- tigerish • ogreish • Quakerish
- **lickerish**, liquorice (*US* licorice)
- ochreish (*US* ocherish)
- vapourish (*US* vaporish) • viperish
- spinsterish • Pooterish • amateurish
- feverish • liverish • impoverish
- minxish • niceish • coarsish • closish

29.10

- **cattish**, fattish, flattish
- smartish
- **coquettish**, fetish, pettish, wettish
- leftish • Kentish
- **latish**, straightish
- sweetish
- **British**, skittish, twittish
- Pictish
- **brightish**, lightish, rightish, slightish, whitish
- **hottish**, Scottish, sottish
- softish • shortish • saltish
- **loutish**, stoutish
- goatish
- **coltish**, doltish
- **brutish**, Jutish
- sluttish • smoothish
- **lavish**, ravish
- elvish
- **knavish**, slavish
- **peevish**, thievish
- spivvish • dervish
- **anguish**, languish
- vanquish
- **distinguish**, extinguish
- relinquish

29.11

- **awash**, Boche, Bosch, bosh, brioche, cloche, cohosh, cosh, dosh, Foch, galosh, gosh, josh, mosh, nosh, posh, quash, slosh, splosh, squash, swash, tosh, wash
- kibosh
- **mackintosh**, McIntosh
- backwash • car wash • brainwash
- wish-wash
- **eyewash**, Siwash
- limewash • whitewash • hogwash
- mouthwash • musquash

29.12

- Porsche

29.13

- **gauche**, guilloche

29.14

- **barouche**, cartouche, douche, farouche, louche, ruche, sloosh, swoosh, tarboosh
- scaramouch

29.15

- **bush**, Hindu Kush, kurus, mush, push, whoosh, woosh
- shadbush • ambush • redbush
- spicebush • saltbush • kiddush
- cush-cush • bell push

29.16

- **ablush**, blush, brush, crush, flush, gush, hush, hush-hush, lush, mush, plush, rush, shush, slush, thrush, tush

> Create extra rhymes by adding *-ing* to words like blush. ⓘ

• **airbrush**, hairbrush
• sagebrush • paintbrush • onrush
• song thrush • outrush • toothbrush
• woodrush • bulrush • uprush

29.17

• kirsch

29.18

• Smersh

29.19

• welsh • milch • Walsh • mulch

29.20

• Romansh

• **blanch**, Blanche, branch, ranch, tranche
• avalanche
• **backbench**, bench, blench, clench, Dench, drench, entrench, French, frontbench, quench, stench, tench, trench, wench, wrench
• crossbench • workbench
• **cinch**, clinch, finch, flinch, inch, lynch, Minch, pinch, squinch, winch
• chaffinch • greenfinch • hawfinch
• goldfinch • bullfinch
• **carte blanche**, conch
• **graunch**, haunch, launch, paunch, raunch, staunch
• **brunch**, bunch, crunch, hunch, lunch, munch, punch, scrunch

> Create extra rhymes by adding -ing to words like bunch. ⓘ

• honeybunch • keypunch

Section 30: -t

30.1

- **at**, bat, brat, cat, chat, cravat, drat, expat, fat, flat, frat, gat, gnat, hat, hereat, high-hat, howzat, lat, mat, matt, matte, Montserrat, Nat, outsat, pat, pit-a-pat, plait, plat, prat, Rabat, rat, rat-tat, Sadat, sat, scat, Sebat, shabbat, shat, skat, slat, spat, splat, sprat, stat, Surat, tat, that, thereat, tit-for-tat, vat, whereat

> Create extra rhymes by changing words like bat to batting. ℹ

- fiat • floreat • exeat • caveat
- **Croat**, Serbo-Croat
- Nanga Parbat • brickbat • dingbat
- **combat**, wombat
- fruitbat • numbat • acrobat • backchat
- whinchat • chitchat • samizdat
- concordat • Arafat • Jehoshaphat
- butterfat • Kattegat • trans-fat
- hard hat • sun hat • fat cat • hellcat
- requiescat • scaredy-cat • Magnificat
- copycat • pussycat • wildcat • bobcat
- tomcat • Sno-Cat • polecat • muscat
- meerkat • mudflat • cervelat
- **doormat**, format
- diplomat • laundromat • Zermatt
- Donat • cowpat

30.2

- Eurocrat • ziggurat • muskrat
- theocrat • jurat • Ballarat • democrat
- technocrat • bureaucrat • aristocrat
- autocrat • plutocrat • babysat
- Comsat • Randstad • Darmstadt
- diktat • habitat • Eisenstadt
- Kronstadt • cryostat • aerostat
- aegrotat • rheostat • haemostat
- thermostat • photostat

30.3

- **apart**, apparat, art, baht, Bart, Barthes, cart, carte, chart, clart, dart, Eilat, fart, ghat, Gujarat, Gujrat, hart, Harte, heart, heart-to-heart, impart, Jat, kart, kyat, Maat, Mansart, mart, outsmart, part, quarte, salat, savate, Scart, smart, start, tart, zakat

> Create extra rhymes by adding -ed or -ing to words like chart. ℹ

- Hobart • wallchart • flow chart
- Bogart • Stuttgart • Earhart
- greenheart • sweetheart • Leichhardt
- Reinhardt • Bernhardt • handcart
- Descartes • dogcart • go-kart
- pushcart • dustcart • rampart
- forepart • underpart • Bonaparte
- counterpart • Bundesrat • Robsart
- Mozart • Hallstatt • kick-start
- push-start • upstart

30.4

- **abet**, aiguillette, anisette, Annette, Antoinette, arête, Arlette, ate, baguette, banquette, barbette, barrette, basinet, bassinet, beget, Bernadette, beset, bet, Bette, blanquette, Brett, briquette, brochette, brunette (*US* brunet), Burnett, cadet, caravanette, cassette, castanet, charette, cigarette (*US* cigaret), clarinet, Claudette, Colette, coquette, corvette, couchette, courgette, croquette, curette, curvet,

Debrett, debt, dinette, diskette, duet, epaulette (*US* epaulet), flageolet, flannelette, forget, fret, galette, gazette, Georgette, get, godet, grisette, heavyset, Jeanette, jet, kitchenette, La Fayette, landaulet, launderette, layette, lazaret, leatherette, let, Lett, lorgnette, luncheonette, lunette, Lynette, maisonette, majorette, maquette, Marie-Antoinette, marionette, Marquette, marquisette, martinet, met, minaret, minuet, moquette, motet, musette, Nanette, net, noisette, nonet, novelette, nymphet, octet, Odette, on-set, oubliette, Paulette, pet, Phuket, picquet, pillaret, pincette, pipette, piquet, pirouette, planchette, pochette, quartet, quickset, quintet, regret, ret, Rhett, roomette, rosette, roulette, satinette, septet, serviette, sestet, set, sett, sextet, silhouette, soubrette, spinet, spinneret, statuette, stet, stockinet, sublet, suffragette, Suzette, sweat, thickset, threat, Tibet, toilette, tret, underlet, upset, usherette, vedette, vet, vignette, vinaigrette, wagonette, wet, whet, winceyette, yet, Yvette

- quodlibet - alphabet
- **ramjet**, scramjet
- propjet - turbojet - etiquette - outlet
- triolet - calumet - cermet

30.5

- dragnet - Fastnet - telnet - hairnet
- keepnet - driftnet - fishnet - jaconet
- alkanet - Intranet - Ethernet
- aigrette - asset - handset - headset
- **hic jacet**, placet
- **preset**, teaset
- filmset
- **inset**, twinset
- videlicet - scilicet - mindset - typeset
- offset - onset - outset - photoset
- moonset - subset - sunset - upset
- Somerset - Exocet - avocet
- trebuchet - epithet - Tevet
- marmoset

30.6

- **famille verte**, terre-verte

30.7

- **abate**, ablate, aerate, ait, await, backdate, bait, bate, berate, castrate, collate, conflate, crate, create, cremate, date, deflate, dictate, dilate, distraite, donate, downstate, eight, elate, equate, estate, fate, fellate, fête, fixate, freight, frustrate, gait, gate, gestate, gradate, grate, great, gyrate, hate, hydrate, inflate, innate, interrelate, interstate, irate, Kate, Kuwait, lactate, late, locate, lustrate, mandate, mate, migrate, misdate, misstate, mistranslate, mutate, narrate, negate, notate, orate, ornate, Pate, placate, plate, prate, prorate, prostrate, pulsate, pupate, quadrate, rate, rotate, sate, sedate, serrate, short weight, skate, slate, spate, spectate, spruit, stagnate, state, straight, strait, Tate, tête-à-tête, Thwaite, translate, translocate, transmigrate, truncate, underrate, understate, underweight, update, uprate, upstate, up-to-date, vacate, vibrate, wait, weight

30.8

- labiate
- **irradiate**, radiate
- mediate - ideate - repudiate
- **palliate**, retaliate
- **affiliate**, ciliate, conciliate, humiliate
- **exfoliate**, foliate
- nucleate - permeate - delineate
- calumniate - expiate
- **expatriate**, repatriate
- recreate - inebriate
- **aureate**, excoriate
- procreate
- **appropriate**, expropriate, impropriate, misappropriate

- **infuriate**, luxuriate
- asphyxiate •nauseate

> Try rhyming one word with a ⓘ
> set of two or more: nauseate,
> because we ate.

- **annunciate**, enunciate
- **instantiate**, substantiate,
  transubstantiate
- **differentiate**, potentiate
- **expatiate**, ingratiate, satiate
- **appreciate**, depreciate
- **initiate**, officiate, propitiate, vitiate
- **associate**, dissociate, negotiate
- excruciate •aviate
- **abbreviate**, alleviate, deviate
- obviate •exuviate •inchoate
- actuate •perpetuate •effectuate
- habituate •fluctuate •punctuate
- graduate •individuate •menstruate
- **accentuate**, eventuate
- evacuate
- **evaluate**, valuate
- superannuate •infatuate
- **attenuate**, extenuate
- insinuate •situate

30.9

- jailbait •rebate •whitebait •probate
- stereobate •approbate •incubate
- stylobate •exacerbate •masturbate
- mandate •candidate •validate
- consolidate •intimidate •dilapidate
- cuspidate •fluoridate •elucidate
- antedate •liquidate •chordate
- update •inundate •fecundate
- accommodate •caliphate •phosphate
- Margate •Irangate •tailgate
- lychgate •Lydgate
- **delegate**, relegate
- Billingsgate •obligate •fumigate
- abnegate •aggregate •segregate
- irrigate •congregate •castigate
- investigate •reinvestigate
- **litigate**, mitigate
- instigate
- **circumnavigate**, navigate
- promulgate •elongate •toll gate
- Newgate •sluice gate •conjugate

- subjugate •floodgate •vulgate
- objurgate •expurgate •propagate
- arrogate •abrogate
- **derogate**, interrogate
- corrugate •subrogate •watergate

30.10

- defalcate •demarcate •cheapskate
- eradicate •abdicate
- **dedicate**, medicate, predicate
- **indicate**, syndicate, vindicate
- adjudicate •defecate
- **certificate**, pontificate
- confiscate •replicate •explicate
- spifflicate •triplicate •implicate
- complicate •overcomplicate
- **duplicate**, quadruplicate,
  quintuplicate
- supplicate •fornicate
- **communicate**, excommunicate,
  intercommunicate, tunicate
- **divaricate**, prevaricate
- fabricate •deprecate •metricate
- extricate
- **lubricate**, rubricate
- desiccate •intoxicate •masticate
- authenticate •domesticate
- sophisticate •prognosticate
- rusticate •hypothecate •manducate
- educate •obfuscate •inculcate
- bifurcate •suffocate •allocate
- dislocate •reciprocate •coruscate
- altercate •advocate •equivocate
- furcate

30.11

- circumvallate •bedplate •template
- breastplate •nameplate •faceplate
- chelate •fishplate •sibilate •jubilate
- flagellate •legislate •invigilate
- **assimilate**, dissimilate
- **depilate**, epilate
- fibrillate
- **correlate**, intercorrelate
- vacillate •tessellate •oscillate
- cantillate
- **hyperventilate**, ventilate
- titillate •scintillate •constellate

- mutilate •oblate •hotplate
- electroplate •bookplate •footplate
- congratulate
- **confabulate**, tabulate
- **ambulate**, circumambulate, perambulate
- adulate •coagulate
- **strangulate**, triangulate
- ejaculate
- **calculate**, miscalculate
- emasculate •granulate •encapsulate
- regulate •speculate •emulate
- infibulate •acidulate
- **articulate**, gesticulate, matriculate
- **simulate**, stimulate
- **manipulate**, stipulate
- insulate •capitulate
- discombobulate •modulate
- **flocculate**, inoculate
- osculate
- **copulate**, populate
- **expostulate**, postulate
- ovulate •formulate •ululate
- **accumulate**, cumulate
- undulate •pustulate •circulate
- lanceolate
- **annihilate**, violate
- number plate •fingerplate •escalate
- percolate •immolate
- crenellate (*US* crenelate)
- extrapolate •copperplate
- **interpellate**, interpolate
- desolate •insufflate •isolate
- apostolate •contemplate

30.12

- bedmate •flatmate •classmate
- checkmate •helpmate •messmate
- playmate •stalemate •stablemate
- teammate •inmate •shipmate
- acclimate •sublimate •animate
- decimate •approximate
- **estimate**, guesstimate, underestimate
- intimate •primate •housemate
- soulmate •schoolmate •room-mate
- consummate •amalgamate
- diplomate •automate •glutamate
- workmate

30.13

- **agnate**, magnate
- **incarnate**, khanate
- impregnate
- **coordinate**, subordinate
- decaffeinate •paginate •originate
- oxygenate
- **cachinnate**, machinate
- pollinate
- **contaminate**, laminate
- **disseminate**, ingeminate, inseminate
- **discriminate**, eliminate, incriminate, recriminate
- **abominate**, dominate, nominate
- **illuminate**, ruminate
- fulminate •culminate
- **exterminate**, germinate, terminate, verminate
- marinate •peregrinate •indoctrinate
- chlorinate •urinate
- **assassinate**, deracinate, fascinate
- vaccinate •hallucinate •Latinate
- procrastinate •predestinate
- agglutinate •rejuvenate •resinate
- designate •redesignate •cognate
- neonate •lunate •alienate
- carbonate •hibernate •odonate
- hyphenate •emanate
- **impersonate**, personate
- fractionate •detonate •intonate
- consternate •alternate •Italianate
- resonate

30.14

- palpate •emancipate
- **anticipate**, dissipate, participate
- constipate •cuspate •exculpate
- inculpate •syncopate •extirpate

30.15

- serrate •concentrate •airfreight
- ingrate •filtrate •arbitrate
- exfiltrate •magistrate •orchestrate
- calibrate •recalibrate •celebrate
- emigrate •immigrate
- denigrate •penetrate

• defenestrate •administrate •aspirate
• perpetrate •decerebrate •desecrate
• execrate •consecrate •integrate
• **carbohydrate**, hydrate
• nitrate •quadrate •prostrate
• **borate**, quorate
• portrait •polyunsaturate
• acculturate •depurate •indurate
• triturate •inaugurate •suppurate
• substrate •adumbrate
• **ameliorate**, meliorate
• deteriorate
• **collaborate**, elaborate
• liberate •corroborate •reverberate
• saturate
• **confederate**, federate
• desiderate •moderate
• preponderate
• **proliferate**, vociferate
• perforate •invigorate •exaggerate
• refrigerate •decorate
• **accelerate**, decelerate
• exhilarate •illustrate •tolerate
• commemorate
• **demonstrate**, remonstrate
• **agglomerate**, conglomerate
• enumerate
• **generate**, venerate
• **incinerate**, itinerate
• exonerate •remunerate •evaporate
• exasperate •separate
• **cooperate**, operate
• incorporate
• **recuperate**, vituperate
• perorate
• **lacerate**, macerate
• incarcerate •eviscerate •expectorate
• **alliterate**, iterate, obliterate,
  transliterate
• adulterate •asseverate •sequestrate
• commiserate •birth rate •sensate
• condensate •decussate •compensate
• tergiversate

30.16

• **lactate**, tractate
• apartheid •peltate •edentate
• testate •dictate •meditate •agitate
• vegetate •interdigitate

• **cogitate**, excogitate
• **ingurgitate**, regurgitate
• **facilitate**, habilitate, militate
• debilitate •imitate •decapitate
• palpitate •crepitate •precipitate
• irritate
• **acetate**, capacitate, triacetate
• necessitate •felicitate •resuscitate
• gravitate •levitate •hesitate
• **apostate**, prostate
• pernoctate •potentate •annotate
• amputate •permutate •orientate
• auscultate •commentate •superstate
• devastate •salivate •elevate
• activate •captivate •titivate
• motivate •cultivate •ovate •excavate
• **enervate**, renovate
• innovate •aggravate •rotavate

30.17

• catchweight •middleweight
• pennyweight •heavyweight
• flyweight •lightweight •paperweight
• hundredweight •bantamweight
• welterweight •counterweight
• featherweight •birthweight
• solmizate

30.18

• **accrete** autocomplete, beat
  beet, bittersweet, bleat, cheat, cleat,
  clubfeet, compete, compleat, complete,
  conceit, Crete, deceit, delete, deplete,
  discreet, discrete, eat, effete, élite,
  entreat, escheat, estreat, excrete, feat,
  feet, fleet, gîte, greet, heat, leat, leet,
  Magritte, maltreat, marguerite, meat,
  meet, meet-and-greet, mesquite, mete,
  mistreat, neat, outcompete, peat,
  Pete, petite, pleat, receipt, replete,
  sangeet, seat, secrete, sheet, skeet,
  sleet, splay-feet, street, suite, sweet,
  teat, treat, tweet, wheat

> Create extra rhymes by   ⓘ
> adding -ing to words like bleat.

• backbeat •heartbeat •deadbeat
• breakbeat •offbeat •browbeat

- downbeat • drumbeat • upbeat
- sugar beet • Blackfeet • flatfeet
- forefeet • exegete • polychaete
- lorikeet • parakeet
- **athlete**, biathlete, decathlete, heptathlete, pentathlete, triathlete
- kick-pleat • paraclete • obsolete
- gamete • crabmeat • sweetmeat
- mincemeat • forcemeat • backstreet
- concrete • window seat

30.19

- spreadsheet • mainsheet • flysheet
- time sheet • broadsheet
- groundsheet • flowsheet • news-sheet
- dust sheet • worksheet
- aesthete (*US* esthete) • wholewheat
- meadowsweet • buckwheat
- bittersweet

30.20

- **acquit**, admit, backlit, bedsit, befit, bit, Brit, Britt, chit, commit, demit, dit, emit, fit, flit, frit, git, grit, hit, intermit, it, kit, knit, legit, lickety-split, lit, manumit, mishit, mitt, nit, omit, outsit, outwit, permit, pit, Pitt, pretermit, quit, remit, retrofit, shit, sit, skit, slit, snit, spit, split, sprit, squit, submit, tit, transmit, twit, whit, wit, writ, zit
- **albeit**, howbeit
- poet
- **bluet**, cruet, intuit, suet, Yuit
- Inuit • floruit • Jesuit
- **Babbitt**, cohabit, habit, rabbet, rabbit
- **ambit**, gambit
- jackrabbit • barbet • Nesbit • rarebit
- **adhibit**, exhibit, gibbet, inhibit, prohibit
- titbit (*US* tidbit) • flibbertigibbet
- **Cobbett**, gobbet, hobbit, obit, probit
- orbit • Tobit
- **cubit**, two-bit
- **hatchet**, latchet, ratchet
- Pritchett
- **crotchet**, rochet

30.21

- adit
- **bandit**, pandit
- **accredit**, credit, edit, subedit
- Chindit • conduit
- **audit**, plaudit
- pundit • refit • misfit • benefit
- **profit**, prophet, soffit
- forfeit • outfit • Tophet • photofit
- **buffet**, tuffet
- comfit • counterfeit • surfeit • agate
- **margate**, target
- frigate • Tlingit • hogget
- **drugget**, nugget
- Brigitte • gadget • eejit
- **Bridget**, digit, fidget, midget, widget
- budget
- **Blackett**, bracket, jacket, packet, placket, racket
- blanket • gasket • bedjacket
- straitjacket • lifejacket • leatherjacket
- **downmarket**, market, upmarket
- **basket**, casket
- breadbasket • Euromarket
- Newmarket • hypermarket
- **Becket**, Beckett
- **cricket**, midwicket, picket, picquet, piquet, pricket, snicket, thicket, ticket, wicket

> Try rhyming one word with a set of two: ticket, stick it.

- trinket
- **biscuit**, brisket, frisket
- identikit
- **brocket**, crocket, Crockett, docket, locket, pocket, rocket, socket, sprocket

> Try rhyming one word with a set of two: socket, shock it.

- airpocket • pickpocket • skyrocket
- drookit • toolkit
- **bucket**, Nantucket, tucket
- **Blunkett**, junket
- musket • rust bucket
- **circuit**, short-circuit

30.22

- **mallet**, palette, pallet, valet
- tablet •pamphlet •aglet •anklet
- candlelit •hamlet
- **Caplet**, chaplet
- lamplit •flatlet •mantlet
- **haslet**, Hazlitt
- **scarlet**, Scarlett, starlet, starlit, varlet
- armlet •lancelet •branchlet
- **martlet**, tartlet
- plantlet •pellet •reglet •necklet
- playlet •lakelet •bracelet
- **platelet**, statelet
- wavelet •leaflet •eaglet •streamlet
- **billet**, filet, fillet, millet, skillet, willet
- **driblet**, triblet
- piglet •singlet •gimlet •inlet
- **kinglet**, ringlet, springlet, winglet
- **ripplet**, triplet
- wristlet
- **eyelet**, islet, stylet, twilit
- pikelet
- **collet**, Smollett, wallet
- goblet •rodlet
- omelette (US omelet) •droplet
- torchlit
- **corselet**, corselette
- gauntlet (US gantlet) •owlet
- townlet •toadlet •notelet •toilet
- moonlit •sextuplet •fruitlet
- **bullet**, pullet
- **booklet**, brooklet, hooklet
- quadruplet •annulet •septuplet
- rivulet •quintuplet
- **gullet**, mullet
- doublet •floodlit
- **runlet**, sunlit
- couplet •cutlet •frontlet •violet
- coverlet •circlet •verselet

30.23

- **dammit**, Hammett, Mamet
- **emmet**, semmit
- **helmet**, pelmet
- remit •limit •kismet •climate
- **comet**, grommet, vomit

- Goldschmidt
- **plummet**, summit
- Hindemith
- **hermit**, Kermit, permit
- **gannet**, granite, Janet, planet
- magnet •Hamnett •pomegranate
- **Barnet**, garnet
- **Bennett**, genet, jennet, rennet, senate, sennet, sennit, tenet
- **innit**, linnet, minute, sinnet
- **cygnet**, signet
- cabinet •definite •Plantagenet
- **bonnet**, sonnet
- **cornet**, hornet
- unit
- **punnet**, whodunnit (US whodunit)
- bayonet •dragonet •falconet
- baronet •coronet
- **alternate**, burnet
- sandpit •carpet •armpit •decrepit
- cesspit •bear pit •fleapit
- **pipit**, sippet, skippet, snippet, tippet, Tippett, whippet
- limpet •incipit •limepit
- **moppet**, poppet
- cockpit •cuckoo-spit •pulpit •puppet
- **crumpet**, strumpet, trumpet
- parapet •turnspit

30.24

- caret •Sanskrit •Prakrit
- **ferret**, inherit, merit
- egret •secret
- **dispirit**, skirret, spirit
- floret •pomfret •bowsprit
- barbiturate
- **turret**, worrit
- culprit •floweret •Margaret
- cellaret (US cellarette)
- **banneret**, lanneret
- hypocrite •preterite (US preterit)
- **Everett**, leveret
- favourite (US favorite)
- **interpret**, misinterpret
- **basset**, facet, tacet, tacit
- **Narragansett**, transit
- lancet
- **cresset**, Knesset
- exit •resit

- **complicit**, elicit, explicit, illicit, implicit, licit, solicit
- Tilsit •plebiscite •babysit •deficit
- **cosset**, posset
- Quonset •whatsit
- **corset**, Dorset, faucet
- **gusset**, russet
- dulcet
- **tercet**, verset
- ashet •planchet •bullshit •Bastet
- tomtit •bluetit

30.25

- davit •brevet •velvet •affidavit
- **civet**, privet, rivet, trivet
- private •covet •aquavit •banquet
- halfwit •peewit •dimwit •nitwit
- **exquisite**, visit
- requisite •perquisite
- **closet**, posit
- apposite •opposite
- composite

30.26

- **affright**, alight, alright, aright, bedright, bight, bite, blight, bright, byte, cite, dight, Dwight, excite, fight, flight, fright, goodnight, height, ignite, impolite, indict, indite, invite, kite, knight, light, lite, might, mite, night, nite, outfight,

> The use of *stressed* (or *masculine*) *rhyme* followed by *wrenched rhyme* (where the last vowel is mis-stressed—eye/symmetry) can have a dramatic deadening effect if one chooses not to force the word to rhyme: here, it practically halts the flow which the stanza has built up:
>
> Tyger Tyger, burning bright,
> In the forests of the night;
> What immortal hand or eye,
> Could frame thy fearful symmetry?
>
> (William Blake, 'The Tyger')

outright, plight, polite, quite, right, rite, shite, sight, site, skintight, skite, sleight, slight, smite, Snow-white, spite, sprite, tight, tonight, trite, twite, underwrite, unite, uptight, white, wight, wright, write
- Shiite •Trotskyite •McCarthyite
- Vishnuite •Sivaite •albite
- snakebite •frostbite •soundbite
- kilobyte •columbite •love bite
- Moabite •megabyte •gigabyte
- Jacobite •Rechabite •jadeite
- lyddite •expedite •cordite •erudite
- Luddite •recondite •troglodyte
- hermaphrodite •extradite

30.27

- graphite •prizefight •dogfight
- cockfight •neophyte •saprophyte
- bullfight •gunfight •firefight
- gesundheit •Fahrenheit •malachite
- blatherskite

30.28

- halite •candlelight •fanlight
- lamplight •gaslight •flashlight
- starlight •headlight •penlight
- daylight •tail light
- **Peelite**, pelite
- street light •phyllite •analyte
- rubellite •Carmelite •proselyte
- Monothelite
- **highlight**, skylight, stylite, twilight
- sidelight •limelight •night light
- spotlight •torchlight •lowlight
- cryolite •microlight •moonlight

> Try rhyming one word with a set of two: moonlight, soon light. 🛈

- cellulite •floodlight •sunlight
- rushlight •Pre-Raphaelite •firelight
- acolyte •Bakelite •Armalite
- Ishmaelite •phonolite •cosmopolite
- electrolyte •Israelite •corallite
- heteroclite •chrysolite •socialite
- satellite •tantalite •overflight
- **pearlite**, perlite
- searchlight

30.29

- **Hamite**, samite
- marmite •Semite •Vegemite
- eremite •Hashemite •Fatimite
- chromite •Edomite •sodomite
- stalagmite •Elamite •dolomite
- Adullamite •dynamite •catamite
- Benthamite
- **termite**, thermite
- Samnite •sennight •midnight
- lignite •selenite •gelignite
- kaolinite •Leninite
- **finite**, transfinite
- watchnight •fortnight •Sunnite
- **exurbanite**, suburbanite, urbanite
- manganite •ammonite •Mennonite
- Canaanite •Maronite •bentonite
- Irvingite •respite •alexandrite
- Arkwright •cartwright •nephrite
- playwright •wainwright
- wheelwright •millwright
- shipwright •copyright •Nazirite
- pyrite •eyebright •nitrite •contrite
- chlorite •forthright •downright
- Fulbright •upright •meteorite
- diorite •fluorite
- Labourite (*US* Laborite) •sybarite
- Thatcherite •phosphorite •azurite
- anchorite •Hitlerite •dolerite
- Amorite •Minorite •laterite
- Hutterite •birthright

30.30

- calcite •campsite

> Try rhyming one word with a set of two: campsite, damp site. ⓘ

- website •dacite •insight
- Monophysite •magnesite •eyesight
- hindsight •bombsight •foresight
- bauxite •quartzite •leucocyte
- Hussite •gunsight •phagocyte
- marcasite •parasite •anthracite
- haemocyte •microsite •oversight
- worksite
- **bipartite**, multipartite, partite, quadripartite, sexpartite, tripartite
- transvestite •airtight •Hittite
- magnetite •appetite •stalactite

- watertight •Levite •Muscovite
- Hepplewhite •bobwhite

30.31

- **allot**, begot, Bernadotte, blot, bot, capot, clot, cocotte, cot, culotte, dot, forgot, garrotte (*US* garrote), gavotte, got, grot, hot, jot, knot, lot, Mayotte, motte, not, Ott, outshot, plot, pot, rot, sans-culotte, Scot, Scott, shallot, shot, slot, snot, sot, spot, squat, stot, swat, swot, tot, trot, twat, undershot, Wat, Watt, what, wot, yacht

> Create extra rhymes by adding -(*t*)*ing* to words like blot. ⓘ

- robot •hotshot •peridot •microdot
- Wyandot •polka dot •fylfot •mascot
- Caldecott •carrycot •apricot
- boycott •dovecote •sandlot •melilot
- polyglot •Camelot •ocelot
- monoglot •sub-plot •Lancelot
- cachalot •counterplot •Wilmot
- guillemot •motmot •bergamot

30.32

- cannot •slip knot •forget-me-not
- touch-me-not •topknot •whatnot
- **crackpot**, jackpot
- blackspot •dashpot •sexpot •despot
- fleshpot •teapot •stinkpot •tinpot
- **gallipot**, talipot
- chimney pot •nightspot •stockpot
- tosspot •hotspot •hotpot •stewpot
- fusspot •sunspot •flowerpot
- pepperpot •lobster pot
- tommyrot
- **dogtrot**, jogtrot
- foxtrot
- **slapshot**, snapshot
- mailshot •grapeshot •slingshot
- eyeshot •potshot •bloodshot
- mugshot •buckshot •troubleshot
- gunshot •upshot •earshot
- Aldershot •Hottentot •aliquot
- diddly-squat •Ofwat •loquat
- kumquat •somewhat •megawatt
- kilowatt •paraquat •terawatt

30.33

• **abort**, apport, assort, athwart, aught, besought, bethought, bort, bought, brought, caught, cavort, comport, consort, contort, Cort, court, distraught, escort, exhort, export, extort, fort, fought, fraught, import, methought, misreport, mort, naught, nought, Oort, ought, outfought, port, Porte, purport, quart, rort, short, snort, sort, sought, sport, support, swart, taught, taut, thought, thwart, tort, transport, wart, wrought

> Create extra rhymes by ⓘ
> adding -ing to words like contort.

• cohort • backcourt • Port Harcourt
• forecourt • onslaught • dreadnought
• Connacht • aeronaut • Argonaut
• juggernaut • cosmonaut • astronaut
• aquanaut • davenport • carport
• passport • airport
• **Freeport**, seaport
• Shreveport
• **heliport**, teleport
• Stockport • outport • Coalport
• spoilsport
• **Newport**, viewport
• hoverport
• **forethought**, malice aforethought
• afterthought • worrywart

30.34

• **about**, bout, clout, devout, doubt, down-and-out, drought, flout, gout, grout, knout, Kraut, lout, mahout, misdoubt, nowt, out, out-and-out, owt, pout, Prout, right about, rout, scout, shout, snout, spout, sprout, stout, thereabout, thereout, throughout, timeout, tout, trout, way-out, without
• **layout**, payout
• buyout • blowout • layabout
• gadabout • roundabout • knockabout
• walkabout • runabout • turnabout
• hereabout • roustabout

• **handout**, standout
• readout • hideout • dugout • blackout
• checkout
• **breakout**, stakeout, takeout
• strikeout
• **knockout**, lockout
• walkout
• **cookout**, lookout
• workout • sell-out • fallout • pull-out
• umlaut • litter lout • spin-out
• **burnout**, turnout
• hangout • wipeout
• **copout**, dropout
• waterspout • beansprout • clearout
• sauerkraut • washout • printout
• white-out • shoot-out
• **cut-out**, shut-out

30.35

• **afloat**, bloat, boat, capote, coat, connote, cote, dote, emote, float, gloat, goat, groat, misquote, moat, mote, note, oat, outvote, promote, quote, rote, shoat, smote, stoat, Succoth, table d'hôte, Terre Haute, throat, tote, vote, wrote

> Create extra rhymes by ⓘ
> changing words like float and
> note to floating and noting.

• flatboat
• **mailboat**, sailboat, whaleboat
• speedboat • keelboat
• **dreamboat**, steamboat
• lifeboat • iceboat • longboat
• sauceboat • houseboat
• **rowboat**, showboat
• U-boat • tugboat • gunboat
• powerboat • motorboat • riverboat
• workboat • Haggadoth • anecdote
• scapegoat • redingote • nanny goat
• zygote • redcoat • tailcoat • raincoat
• waistcoat • greatcoat • petticoat
• topcoat • housecoat • undercoat
• entrecôte • surcoat • turncoat
• matelote • banknote • headnote
• endnote • keynote • woodnote
• footnote • compote • whitethroat

- shofroth •bluethroat •cut-throat
- creosote •mitzvoth •mezuzoth

30.36

- **adroit**, dacoit, Detroit, doit, droit, exploit, maladroit, quoit
- introit •Bayreuth

30.37

- **acute**, argute, astute, beaut, Beirut, boot, bruit, brut, brute, Bute, butte, Canute, cheroot, chute, commute, compute, confute, coot, cute, depute, dilute, dispute, flute, fruit, galoot, hoot, impute, jute, loot, lute, minute, moot, mute, newt, outshoot, permute, pollute, pursuit, recruit, refute, repute, root, route, salute, Salyut, scoot, shoot, Shute, sloot, snoot, subacute, suit, telecommute, Tonton Macoute, toot, transmute, undershoot, uproot, Ute, volute
- Paiute •jackboot •freeboot •top boot
- snow boot •gumboot •marabout
- statute •bandicoot •Hakluyt
- archlute •absolute •dissolute
- **irresolute**, resolute
- jackfruit •passion fruit •breadfruit
- grapefruit •snakeroot •beetroot
- arrowroot •autoroute

30.38

- tracksuit •catsuit •pantsuit
- Hatshepsut
- **sweatsuit**, wetsuit
- playsuit •spacesuit •swimsuit
- bodysuit •drysuit •lawsuit
- jumpsuit •offshoot •troubleshoot
- parachute •Aleut
- **attribute**, contribute, tribute
- execute •prosecute •persecute
- destitute •institute •prostitute
- constitute •substitute •malamute
- electrocute •hirsute

> Try rhyming one word with a set of two: hirsute, fur suit. ⓘ

30.39

- **afoot**, clubfoot, foot, hotfoot, kaput, put, soot, splay-foot, underfoot, wrong-foot, Yakut
- Blackfoot •flatfoot •barefoot
- pussyfoot •forefoot •crowfoot
- coltsfoot •goosefoot •tenderfoot
- per caput •Rajput •output
- throughput •Inuktitut

30.40

- **abut**, but, butt, cut, glut, gut, hut, intercut, jut, Mut, mutt, nut, phut, putt, rut, scut, shortcut, shut, slut, smut, strut, tut, undercut

> Create extra rhymes by changing words like cut to cutting. ⓘ

- sackbut •scuttlebutt •catgut
- midgut •Vonnegut •rotgut •haircut
- offcut •cross-cut •linocut •crew cut
- woodcut •uppercut •chestnut
- hazelnut •beechnut •peanut
- wing nut •cobnut •locknut •walnut
- groundnut •doughnut (US donut)
- coconut •butternut

30.41

- peart
- **immediate**, intermediate
- idiot
- **collegiate**, intercollegiate
- orgeat •Eliot •affiliate
- **foliate**, trifoliate
- **aculeate**, Juliet
- Uniate •opiate
- **chariot**, Harriet, Judas Iscariot, lariat, Marryat
- **compatriot**, expatriate, patriot
- **heriot**, Herriot
- **commissariat**, lumpenproletariat, proletariat, salariat, secretariat, vicariate
- inebriate •Cypriot
- **baccalaureate**, laureate, professoriate

- appropriate • licentiate • satiate
- **initiate**, novitiate, patriciate
- associate • cruciate • Cheviot • soviet
- roseate
- **Byatt**, diet, quiet, riot, ryot, Wyatt
- inchoate
- **Ewart**, Stewart
- Verwoerd
- **graduate**, undergraduate
- attenuate • situate
- **abbot**, Cabot
- Albert • lambert • Egbert • Delbert
- **filbert**, Gilbert
- halibut • celibate • Robert • Osbert
- Norbert
- **Hubert**, Schubert
- Humbert • Cuthbert
- **burbot**, Herbert, sherbet, turbot
- Frankfort • effort • comfort

30.42

- **braggart**, faggot (US fagot), maggot
- legate
- **bigot**, gigot, Piggott, spigot
- ingot • profligate • aggregate • yogurt
- conjugate • abrogate • surrogate
- **ergot**, virgate
- Bagehot • patriarchate • wainscot
- Sickert • predicate • syndicate
- **certificate**, pontificate
- Calicut • delicate • silicate • triplicate
- **duplicate**, quadruplicate
- intricate • Connecticut • Alcott
- ducat • advocate
- **ballot**, palate
- **charlotte**, harlot
- **appellate**, Helot, prelate, zealot
- flagellate • distillate
- **Pilate**, pilot
- copilot • gyropilot • autopilot
- triangulate
- **ejaculate**, immaculate
- amulet • spatulate
- **articulate**, denticulate
- **consulate**, proconsulate
- postulate • ungulate
- **inviolate**, ultraviolet
- chocolate • cardinalate • desolate
- isolate • disconsolate • Merlot

30.43

- gamut
- **imamate**, marmot
- animate
- **approximate**, proximate
- **estimate**, guesstimate,
  underestimate
- **illegitimate**, legitimate
- intimate
- **penultimate**, ultimate
- primate • foumart • consummate
- Dermot
- **discarnate**, incarnate
- impregnate • rabbinate
- **coordinate**, inordinate,
  subordinate, superordinate
- infinite • laminate • effeminate
- discriminate • innominate
- determinate • Palatinate • pectinate
- obstinate • agglutinate • designate
- tribunate • importunate • Arbuthnot
- bicarbonate • umbonate • fortunate
- pulmonate
- **compassionate**, passionate
- affectionate
- **extortionate**, proportionate
- sultanate • companionate
- principate • Rupert • episcopate
- **carat**, carrot, claret, garret, karat,
  parrot
- emirate • aspirate • vertebrate
- levirate
- **duumvirate**, triumvirate
- pirate • quadrat • accurate • indurate
- obdurate
- **Meerut**, vizierate
- priorate • curate • elaborate
- deliberate • confederate
- **considerate**, desiderate
- **immoderate**, moderate
- ephorate
- **imperforate**, perforate
- **agglomerate**, conglomerate
- numerate
- **degenerate**, regenerate
- separate • temperate • desperate
- disparate • corporate • professorate
- commensurate • pastorate
- inveterate
- **directorate**, electorate,

inspectorate, protectorate, rectorate
- **illiterate**, literate, presbyterate
- doctorate • Don Quixote • marquisate
- concert • cushat • precipitate

30.44

- Evert • sievert
- **divot**, pivot
- **covert**, lovat
- culvert • adequate • stalwart • desert

30.45

- **advert**, alert, animadvert, assert, avert, Bert, blurt, Burt, cert, chert, concert, controvert, convert, curt, desert, dessert, dirt, divert, exert, flirt, girt, hurt, inert, insert, introvert, Kurt, malapert, overt, pert, pervert, quirt, shirt, skirt, spirt, spurt, squirt, Sturt, subvert, vert, wort, yurt
- Engelbert • Colbert • sweatshirt
- nightshirt • pay dirt • Frankfurt
- miniskirt • underskirt • expert
- Blackshirt • redshirt • T-shirt
- Brownshirt • undershirt • extrovert
- ragwort • milkwort • pillwort
- nipplewort • lungwort • bladderwort
- liverwort

30.46

- **semi-detached**, unattached, unhatched, unmatched
- **farfetched**, outstretched
- unwatched • untouched

30.47

- Taft
- **abaft**, aft, craft, daft, draft, draught, engraft, graft, haft, kraft, raft, shaft, understaffed, unstaffed, waft

Create extra rhymes for [i]
words like abaft by adding -ed to
laugh etc. (see section 17.2).

- backdraft • handcraft • aircraft
- stagecraft • spacecraft • statecraft
- needlecraft • priestcraft • witchcraft
- kingcraft • handicraft • woodcraft
- Wollstonecraft • bushcraft
- watercraft • hovercraft • crankshaft
- camshaft • layshaft • driveshaft
- turboshaft • countershaft
- **bereft**, cleft, deft, eft, heft, klepht, left, reft, theft, weft
- **adrift**, drift, gift, grift, lift, rift, shift, shrift, sift, squiffed, swift, thrift, uplift
- **airlift**, chairlift, stairlift
- facelift • skilift • shoplift • Festschrift
- spendthrift • spindrift • snowdrift
- makeshift • downshift • upshift
- **aloft**, croft, loft, oft, soft, toft

Create extra rhymes for [i]
words like aloft by adding -ed to
cough etc. (see section 17.8).

- hayloft • Ashcroft • Cockcroft
- undercroft • Lowestoft
- **tuft**, unstuffed
- Delft

30.48

- **abreact**, abstract, act, attract, bract, compact, contract, counteract, diffract, enact, exact, extract, fact, humpbacked, hunchbacked, impact, interact, matter-of-fact, pact, protract, redact, refract, retroact, subcontract, subtract, tact, tract, transact, unbacked, underact, untracked

Create extra rhymes for [i]
words like abstract by adding -ed
to crack etc. (see section 21.1).

- play-act • autodidact
- artefact (US artifact) • cataract
- contact
- **marked**, unremarked
- Wehrmacht
- **affect**, bisect, bull-necked, collect, confect, connect, correct, defect, deflect, deject, detect, direct, effect,

eject, elect, erect, expect, infect,
inflect, inject, inspect, interconnect,
interject, intersect, misdirect,
neglect, object, perfect, project,
prospect, protect, reflect, reject,
respect, resurrect, sect, select,
subject, suspect, transect,
unchecked, Utrecht
• prefect • abject • retroject • intellect
• genuflect • idiolect • dialect • aspect
• circumspect • retrospect • Dordrecht
• vivisect • architect • unbaked
• sun-baked

30.49

• **addict**, afflict, conflict, constrict,
contradict, convict, delict, depict,
evict, hand-picked, inflict, interdict,
Pict, predict, reconvict, strict
• edict

> Create new rhymes for words [i]
> like addict by adding -ed to lick
> etc. (see section 21.9).

• Benedict • verdict
• **imperfect**, perfect, pluperfect,
word-perfect
• object • subject • relict • district
• **concoct**, decoct
• landlocked • dreadlocked
• **unprovoked**, unsmoked
• **uncooked**, unlooked
• **abduct**, adduct, conduct, construct,
destruct, duct, instruct, misconduct,
obstruct
• ventiduct • aqueduct • product
• safe-conduct • viaduct
• **handworked**, unworked
• mulct • unthanked • sacrosanct
• **distinct**, extinct, succinct
• precinct • instinct
• **conjunct**, defunct, disjunct, injunct
• adjunct • unasked

30.50

• Kristallnacht • Gaeltacht
• **Brecht**, echt
• Fichte • Maastricht

30.51

• gestalt • asphalt
• **belt**, Celt, dealt, dwelt, felt, gelt,
knelt, melt, misdealt, pelt, Scheldt,
smelt, spelt, svelte, veld, welt
• fan belt • seat belt • lifebelt • sunbelt
• rust belt • Copperbelt • heartfelt
• underfelt • backveld • bushveld
• Roosevelt
• **atilt**, built, gilt, guilt, hilt, jilt, kilt,
lilt, quilt, silt, spilt, stilt, tilt,
upbuilt, wilt
• Vanderbilt • volte
• **assault**, Balt, exalt, fault, halt, malt,
salt, smalt, vault
• cobalt • stringhalt • basalt
• somersault • polevault
• **bolt**, colt, dolt, holt, jolt, moult
(US molt), poult, smolt, volt
• deadbolt • Humboldt • thunderbolt
• megavolt • spoilt • Iseult
• **consult**, cult, exult, indult, insult,
penult, result, ult
• adult • occult • tumult • catapult
• difficult • Hasselt

30.52

• unstamped
• **attempt**, contempt, dreamt, exempt,
kempt, pre-empt, tempt
• Klimt • prompt

30.53

• **ant**, Brabant, Brandt, brant, cant,
enceinte, extant, gallant, Kant,
levant, pant, pointe, pointes, rant,
scant
• confidant • commandant • hierophant
• Rembrandt • Amirante
• gallivant
• **aren't**, aslant, aunt, can't, chant,
courante, détente, enchant, entente,
grant, implant, Nantes, plant, shan't,
slant, supplant, transplant,
underplant
• plainchant • ashplant • eggplant
• house plant • restaurant

- **debutant**, debutante
- **absent**, accent, anent, ascent, assent, augment, bent, cement, cent, circumvent, consent, content, dent, event, extent, ferment, foment, forewent, forwent, frequent, gent, Ghent, Gwent, lament, leant, lent, meant, misrepresent, misspent, outwent, pent, percent, pigment, rent, scent, segment, sent, spent, stent, Stoke-on-Trent, Tashkent, tent, torment, Trent, underspent, underwent, vent, went

> Create extra rhymes by [i]
> adding -ing to words like absent.

- orient • comment • portent
- malcontent

30.54

- **acquaint**, ain't, attaint, complaint, constraint, distraint, faint, feint, paint, plaint, quaint, restraint, saint, taint
- spray-paint • greasepaint • warpaint
- **asquint**, bint, clint, dint, flint, glint, hint, imprint, lint, mint, misprint, print, quint, skint, splint, sprint, squint, stint, tint

> Create extra rhymes by [i]
> adding -ing to words like glint.

- Septuagint • skinflint • catmint
- varmint • spearmint • calamint
- peppermint • enprint • screen print
- offprint • blueprint • newsprint
- footprint • thumbprint • fingerprint
- monotint • mezzotint • aquatint
- pint • Geraint
- **Comte**, conte, font, fount, pont, quant, Vermont, want
- Delfont • vicomte • Frémont
- piedmont • Beaumont • Hellespont
- passant • poste restante
- **avaunt**, daunt, flaunt, gaunt, haunt, jaunt, taunt, vaunt

> Create extra rhymes by [i]
> adding -ed to words like daunt.

30.55

- **account**, amount, count, fount, miscount, mount, no-account, surmount
- headcount • viscount • paramount
- tantamount
- **don't**, won't, wont
- **anoint**, appoint, conjoint, joint, outpoint, point, point-to-point
- standpoint
- **cashpoint**, flashpoint
- checkpoint • endpoint • breakpoint
- needlepoint • midpoint • pinpoint
- vantage point • knifepoint
- strongpoint • viewpoint • gunpoint
- counterpoint • punt
- **affront**, blunt, brunt, bunt, confront, cunt, front, Granth, grunt, hunt, mahant, runt, shunt, stunt, up-front
- exeunt • manhunt • headhunt
- witch-hunt • battlefront • seafront
- beachfront • shopfront
- **forefront**, storefront

> Try rhyming one word with a [i]
> set of two: forefront, more front.

- waterfront

30.56

- **abeyant**, mayn't
- **ambient**, circumambient
- **gradient**, irradiant, radiant
- **expedient**, ingredient, mediant, obedient
- valiant • salient • resilient • emollient
- defoliant • ebullient • suppliant
- **convenient**, intervenient, lenient, prevenient
- sapient
- **impercipient**, incipient, percipient, recipient
- recreant • variant • miscreant
- Orient • nutrient
- **esurient**, luxuriant, parturient, prurient
- **nescient**, prescient
- omniscient • insouciant • renunciant

- officiant • negotiant • deviant
- subservient • transient
- **affiant**, Bryant, client, compliant, defiant, giant, pliant, reliant
- **buoyant**, clairvoyant, flamboyant
- **fluent**, pursuant, truant
- affluent • effluent • mellifluent
- confluent • circumfluent • congruent
- issuant • continuant • constituent
- lambent • absorbent
- **incumbent**, recumbent
- couchant • merchant • hadn't
- **ardent**, guardant, regardant
- pedant
- **appendant**, ascendant, attendant, codependent, defendant, descendant, descendent, intendant, interdependent, pendant, pendent, splendent, superintendent, transcendent
- **antecedent**, decedent, needn't, precedent
- didn't • diffident • confident
- accident • dissident
- **coincident**, incident
- oxidant • evident
- **improvident**, provident
- **president**, resident
- **strident**, trident
- **co-respondent**, correspondent, despondent, fondant, respondent
- **accordant**, concordant, discordant, mordant, mordent
- rodent
- **imprudent**, jurisprudent, prudent, student
- **couldn't**, shouldn't, wouldn't
- impudent
- **abundant**, redundant
- decadent • verdant • infant • elephant
- triumphant • sycophant • elegant
- fumigant • congregant • litigant
- termagant • arrogant • extravagant
- pageant
- **cotangent**, plangent, tangent
- **argent**, Sargent, sergeant
- agent • newsagent • regent
- **astringent**, contingent, stringent
- indigent • intelligent • negligent
- diligent • intransigent • exigent
- cogent

- **effulgent**, fulgent, indulgent
- pungent
- **convergent**, detergent, divergent, emergent, insurgent, resurgent, urgent
- bacchant • peccant • vacant • piquant
- predicant • mendicant • significant
- applicant • supplicant • communicant
- lubricant • desiccant • intoxicant
- **gallant**, talent
- **appellant**, propellant, propellent, repellent, water-repellent
- resemblant
- **assailant**, inhalant
- sealant • sibilant • jubilant
- flagellant • vigilant • pestilent
- silent
- **Solent**, volant
- coolant • virulent • purulent
- **ambulant**, somnambulant
- coagulant • crapulent • flatulent
- feculent • esculent • petulant
- stimulant • flocculent • opulent
- postulant • fraudulent • corpulent
- undulant
- **succulent**, truculent
- turbulent • violent • redolent
- indolent • somnolent • excellent
- insolent • nonchalant
- **benevolent**, malevolent, prevalent
- **ambivalent**, equivalent
- garment • clement • segment
- **claimant**, clamant, payment, raiment
- ailment
- **figment**, pigment
- fitment • aliment • element
- oddment
- **dormant**, informant
- moment • adamant • stagnant
- **lieutenant**, pennant, subtenant, tenant
- **pregnant**, regnant
- remnant • complainant
- **benignant**, indignant, malignant
- recombinant • contaminant
- eminent
- **discriminant**, imminent
- **dominant**, prominent
- **illuminant**, ruminant
- determinant • abstinent

- **continent**, subcontinent
- **appurtenant**, impertinent, pertinent
- revenant
- **component**, deponent, exponent, opponent, proponent
- **oppugnant**, repugnant
- immanent
- **impermanent**, permanent
- dissonant • consonant • alternant
- covenant • resonant • rampant
- discrepant • flippant • participant
- occupant • serpent
- **apparent**, arrant, transparent
- Arendt
- **aberrant**, deterrent, errant, inherent, knight-errant
- entrant
- **declarant**, parent
- grandparent • step-parent
- godparent
- **flagrant**, fragrant, vagrant
- registrant • celebrant • emigrant
- immigrant • ministrant • aspirant
- antiperspirant • recalcitrant
- integrant • tyrant • vibrant • hydrant
- **migrant**, transmigrant
- **abhorrent**, torrent, warrant
- quadrant • figurant • obscurant
- **blackcurrant**, concurrent, currant, current, occurrent, redcurrant
- white currant • cross-current
- undercurrent
- **adherent**, coherent, sederunt
- **exuberant**, protuberant
- reverberant • denaturant
- preponderant • deodorant
- **different**, vociferant
- **belligerent**, refrigerant
- accelerant • tolerant • cormorant
- itinerant • ignorant • cooperant
- expectorant • adulterant
- **irreverent**, reverent
- **nascent**, passant
- absent
- **accent**, relaxant
- **acquiescent**, adolescent, albescent, Besant, coalescent, confessant, convalescent, crescent, depressant, effervescent, erubescent, evanescent, excrescent, flavescent, fluorescent, immunosuppressant, incandescent, incessant, iridescent,

juvenescent, lactescent, liquescent, luminescent, nigrescent, obsolescent, opalescent, pearlescent, phosphorescent, pubescent, putrescent, quiescent, suppressant, tumescent, turgescent, virescent, viridescent
- **adjacent**, complacent, obeisant
- **decent**, recent
- **impuissant**, reminiscent
- Vincent • puissant
- **beneficent**, maleficent
- **magnificent**, munificent
- Millicent • concupiscent • reticent
- docent
- **lucent**, translucent
- **discussant**, mustn't
- innocent
- **conversant**, versant
- **consentient**, sentient, trenchant
- **impatient**, patient
- ancient • outpatient
- **coefficient**, deficient, efficient, proficient, sufficient
- quotient • patent
- **interactant**, reactant
- **disinfectant**, expectant, protectant
- repentant • acceptant
- **contestant**, decongestant
- sextant
- **blatant**, latent
- intermittent
- **assistant**, coexistent, consistent, distant, equidistant, existent, insistent, persistent, resistant, subsistent, water-resistant

> Create extra rhymes by adding -ly to words like consistent. | i |

- instant
- **cohabitant**, habitant
- exorbitant • militant • concomitant
- **impenitent**, penitent
- palpitant • crepitant • precipitant
- **competent**, omnicompetent
- irritant • incapacitant • Protestant
- hesitant • visitant • mightn't • octant
- remontant • constant
- **important**, oughtn't
- accountant • potent
- **mutant**, pollutant
- adjutant • executant • disputant

- reluctant
- **consultant**, exultant, resultant
- combatant • omnipotent • impotent
- inadvertent
- **Havant**, haven't, savant, savante
- advent
- **irrelevant**, relevant
- pursuivant • solvent • convent
- adjuvant
- **fervent**, observant, servant
- manservant • maidservant
- **frequent**, sequent
- delinquent • consequent
- subsequent • unguent • eloquent
- **grandiloquent**, magniloquent
- brilliant • poignant • hasn't
- **bezant**, omnipresent, peasant, pheasant, pleasant, present
- complaisant • malfeasant • isn't
- cognizant • wasn't • recusant
- doesn't

30.57

- **burnt**, learnt, weren't
- sunburnt

30.58

- **adapt**, apt, enrapt, rapt, unmapped, untapped
- periapt • snow-capped
- **accept**, crept, except, incept, inept, intercept, kept, leapt, overleaped, sept, slept, swept, upswept, wept, yclept

> Create extra rhymes for words like accept by adding -(p)ed to step etc. (see section 27.3).

- adept • housekept • transept
- precept • concept • percept
- rainswept • windswept • undraped
- pearshaped
- **conscript**, crypt, encrypt, harelipped, hipped, script, unequipped, unwhipped
- Egypt • eucalypt • transcript
- nondescript • typescript • manuscript
- subscript
- **adopt**, co-opt, Copt, opt
- unhoped
- **abrupt**, corrupt, disrupt, erupt, interrupt, irrupt

> Create new rhymes for words like abrupt by adding -(p)ed to cup etc. (see section 27.13).

- bankrupt
- **underdeveloped**, undeveloped
- excerpt • sculpt

30.59

- **unabashed**, uncashed
- unfleshed • whisht • unestablished
- unembellished • unpolished
- unpublished • unaccomplished
- unblemished
- **untarnished**, unvarnished
- **undiminished**, unfinished
- unpunished • unfurnished
- **malnourished**, undernourished
- undistinguished • unwashed
- stonewashed • borscht • unquenched

30.60

- **sawtoothed**, snaggle-toothed

Section 31: **-st**

31.1

- bast •cineaste •encomiast
- symposiast •enthusiast •bombast
- oblast •chloroplast •iconoclast
- gymnast •pederast •fantast

31.2

- **aghast**, avast, Belfast, blast, cast, caste, contrast, fast, last, mast, miscast, outlast, past, rat-arsed, unsurpassed, vast

> Create extra rhymes for words like aghast by adding -ed to class etc. (see section 28.2). [i]

- steadfast •lightfast •holdfast
- sunfast •colourfast •flabbergast
- simulcast •telecast •typecast
- forecast •broadcast •sportscast
- downcast
- **outcast**, outcaste
- newscast •roughcast •upcast
- opencast •worm cast •sandblast
- Elastoplast •counterblast •mainmast
- mizzenmast •topmast •foremast
- fly-past

31.3

- **abreast**, arrest, attest, beau geste, behest, bequest, best, blessed, blest, breast, Brest, Bucharest, Budapest, celeste, chest, contest, crest, digest, divest, guest, hest, infest, ingest, jest, lest, Midwest, molest, nest, northwest, pest, prestressed, protest, quest, rest, self-addressed, self-confessed, self-possessed, southwest, suggest, test, Trieste, unaddressed, unexpressed, unimpressed, unpressed, unstressed, vest, west, wrest, zest

> Create extra rhymes for words like abreast by adding -ed to address etc. (see section 28.3). [i]

- manifest •talkfest •Hammerfest
- Almagest •backrest •armrest
- redbreast •headrest •imprest
- chimney breast •footrest •firecrest
- incest •palimpsest •unprocessed
- road test •undervest •conquest

31.4

- **barefaced**, baste, boldfaced, chaste, haste, lambaste, paste, po-faced, red-faced, self-faced, shamefaced, smooth-faced, strait-laced, taste, unplaced, untraced, waist, waste

> Create extra rhymes for words like barefaced by adding -d to base etc. (see section 28.5). [i]

- toothpaste •foretaste •aftertaste
- shirtwaist

31.5

- **arriviste**, artiste, batiste, beast, dirigiste, east, feast, least, Mideast, modiste, northeast, piste, priest, southeast, uncreased, unreleased, yeast
- wildebeest •hartebeest •beanfeast
- **anapaest** (US anapest)

31.6

- **assist**, cist, coexist, consist, cyst, desist, enlist, exist, fist, gist, grist,

hist, insist, list, Liszt, mist, persist,
resist, schist, subsist, tryst, twist,
whist, wist, wrist
- Dadaist • deist • fideist • Hebraist
- Mithraist • essayist • prosaist
- **hobbyist**, lobbyist
- Trotskyist • boniest • copyist • veriest
- pantheist • atheist • polytheist
- monotheist
- **Maoist**, Taoist
- oboist • egoist • jingoist • banjoist
- soloist • Titoist • Shintoist
- **canoeist**, tattooist, Uist
- voodooist • altruist • casuist
- euphuist • Lamaist • vibist • cubist
- Arabist • faddist • propagandist
- contrabandist • avant-gardist • eldest
- sadist • encyclopedist
- **immodest**, modest
- Girondist • keyboardist
- harpsichordist • nudist • Buddhist
- unprejudiced • Talmudist
- psalmodist • threnodist • hymnodist
- monodist • chiropodist • parodist
- heraldist • rhapsodist • prosodist
- Methodist • absurdist

31.7

- pacifist • sophist
- **calligraphist**, epigraphist
- monographist • theosophist
- unsurfaced • druggist • collagist
- **Falangist**, phalangist
- ageist • elegist • imagist • strategist
- theurgist
- **genealogist**, metallurgist,
  mineralogist
- **apologist**, biologist, ecologist,
  geologist, ideologist, oncologist,
  ontologist, pedologist, sexologist,
  theologist, zoologist
- eulogist • suffragist • liturgist
- thaumaturgist • catechist • stockist
- Yorkist • anarchist • monarchist
- **masochist**, sadomasochist

31.8

- **backlist**, blacklist

- handlist • cabbalist • cellist • checklist
- playlist • wish-list
- **cartophilist**, necrophilist,
  oenophilist (*US* enophilist)
- nihilist • pugilist • homilist
- **bicyclist**, tricyclist
- stylist • cyclist • unicyclist
- motorcyclist • hairstylist • shortlist
- **Gaullist**, holist
- spiritualist • fabulist
- **funambulist**, noctambulist,
  somnambulist
- oculist • populist
- **idealist**, realist, surrealist
- millennialist
- **ceremonialist**, colonialist,
  neocolonialist
- aerialist
- **editorialist**, memorialist
- industrialist
- **immaterialist**, imperialist,
  materialist, serialist
- **trialist**, violist
- **loyalist**, royalist
- **dualist**, duellist (*US* duelist)
- intellectualist • conceptualist
- textualist • mutualist • individualist
- sensualist • contextualist
- **diabolist**, kabbalist
- **cymbalist**, symbolist
- tribalist
- **herbalist**, verbalist
- **medallist** (*US* medalist)
- feudalist • triumphalist • legalist
- **evangelist**, televangelist
- syndicalist • clericalist • physicalist
- vocalist • animalist • maximalist
- formalist • minimalist
- **analyst**, annalist, cryptanalyst,
  panellist (*US* panelist),
  psychoanalyst
- **nominalist**, phenomenalist
- **finalist**, semi-finalist
- communalist • regionalist
- **internationalist**, nationalist,
  rationalist
- sectionalist • conventionalist
- **Congregationalist**,
  conversationalist, educationalist,
  representationalist, sensationalist

- traditionalist • emotionalist
- constitutionalist • functionalist
- **journalist**, paternalist, photojournalist
- papalist
- **monopolist**, oligopolist
- centralist
- **amoralist**, moralist
- oralist • neutralist
- **muralist**, pluralist, ruralist
- liberalist • naturalist • structuralist
- **agriculturalist**, horticulturalist, multiculturalist
- federalist • generalist
- **multilateralist**, unilateralist
- literalist • universalist
- substantialist • specialist
- **consequentialist**, essentialist, existentialist
- racialist • provincialist • socialist
- controversialist
- **catalyst**, philatelist
- **documentalist**, environmentalist, experimentalist, fundamentalist, instrumentalist, mentalist, orientalist, ornamentalist, sentimentalist, transcendentalist
- fatalist • capitalist
- **recitalist**, vitalist
- Pentecostalist • anecdotalist
- brutalist • medievalist
- **revivalist**, survivalist
- novelist

31.9

- **alarmist**, palmist, psalmist
- **biochemist**, chemist
- extremist • animist • pessimist
- legitimist • optimist • rhymist
- **conformist**, reformist
- **bigamist**, polygamist
- misogamist • alchemist • Islamist
- columnist • dynamist
- **agronomist**, autonomist, economist, ergonomist, physiognomist
- palindromist
- **anatomist**, atomist
- epitomist • totemist • taxidermist

31.10

- Hispanist • Zenist • pyrotechnist
- Jainist • liberationist
- **machinist**, tambourinist
- hygienist • trampolinist
- **mandolinist**, violinist
- unwitnessed
- **misogynist**, philogynist
- Stalinist • Hellenist • feminist
- illuminist • determinist • Leninist
- alpinist • larcenist • Latinist
- Byzantinist • Calvinist • chauvinist
- Darwinist
- **honest**, monist
- **corniced**, hornist
- trombonist • vibraphonist
- sousaphonist
- **balloonist**, bassoonist, cartoonist, lampoonist
- opportunist • communist • pianist
- Fabianist • accordionist • alienist
- unionist • Zionist • urbanist
- hedonist • modernist • telephonist
- symphonist
- **saxophonist**, xylophonist
- **agonist**, antagonist, protagonist
- tobogganist • organist • revisionist
- **diffusionist**, exclusionist, fusionist, illusionist
- religionist • tobacconist • mechanist
- Africanist • Vaticanist • colonist
- Mammonist
- **harmonist**, shamanist
- humanist • Germanist • canonist
- expansionist • onanist • timpanist
- accompanist • ironist • Saxonist
- Jansenist • arsonist • abstractionist
- **expressionist**, impressionist, progressionist, secessionist
- **insurrectionist**, perfectionist, projectionist, protectionist, rejectionist, vivisectionist
- interventionist • receptionist
- **accommodationist**, associationist, collaborationist, conservationist, creationist, deviationist, educationist, federationist, isolationist, preservationist, representationist, restorationist, revelationist, salvationist,

situationist, vacationist
- **abolitionist**, coalitionist, demolitionist, exhibitionist, intuitionist, nutritionist, partitionist, prohibitionist, requisitionist, traditionist
- **fictionist**, restrictionist
- **abortionist**, contortionist, extortionist
- **Confucianist**, devolutionist, elocutionist, evolutionist, revolutionist
- **constructionist**, percussionist
- **obstructionist**, reductionist
- excursionist
- **Neoplatonist**, Platonist, satanist
- botanist
- **earnest**, Ernest

31.11

- Trappist • harpist • tempest
- **escapist**, papist, rapist
- landscapist • typist
- **misanthropist**, philanthropist
- **aromatherapist**, physiotherapist, psychotherapist, therapist

31.12

- tantrist
- **guitarist**, scenarist, tsarist
- sitarist • memoirist • belletrist
- centrist • Marist • sacrist
- **lyrist**, panegyrist
- equilibrist • interest
- **optometrist**, psychometrist, sociometrist
- satirist
- **afforest**, florist, forest, Forrest
- rainforest • folklorist
- **careerist**, querist, theorist
- plagiarist • meliorist • apiarist
- topiarist • diarist • psychiatrist
- **jurist**, purist, tourist
- obituarist • caricaturist • pedicurist
- manicurist • sinecurist • naturist
- miniaturist • futurist
- **agriculturist**, apiculturist, arboriculturist, horticulturist,

pisciculturist, sericulturist, silviculturist, viniculturist, viticulturist
- acupuncturist • welfarist • allegorist
- Eucharist • artillerist • secularist
- particularist
- **colourist** (*US* colorist)
- amorist • ephemerist • mesmerist
- **consumerist**, humorist
- mannerist • tenorist • seminarist
- terrorist • adventurist • detectorist
- documentarist • militarist
- monetarist • lepidopterist
- **motorist**, votarist
- scooterist • voluntarist • zitherist
- Everest • aquarist • auteurist

31.13

- saxist • classist • Marxist
- **heterosexist**, sexist
- **bassist**, racist
- solipsist • publicist
- **ceramicist**, dynamicist
- polemicist • Hispanicist • eugenicist
- technicist • esotericist
- **empiricist**, lyricist
- historicist
- **classicist**, neoclassicist
- narcissist • romanticist • geneticist
- vorticist
- **bioethicist**, ethicist
- mythicist • synthesist • physicist
- exorcist • pharmacist • supremacist
- fantasist • fascist • fetishist

31.14

- fattist
- **unpractised** (*US* unpracticed)
- **Esperantist**, obscurantist
- **Anabaptist**, Baptist
- **artist**, Chartist
- **clarinettist** (*US* clarinetist), cornetist, duettist, librettist, vignettist
- leftist • dentist • transvestist • statist
- **completist**, defeatist, Docetist, élitist, graffitist
- **pietist**, quietist, varietist

- Semitist • Sanskritist • spiritist
- syncretist • portraitist
- **anaesthetist** (*US* anesthetist)
- rightist • finitist • orthodontist
- synoptist • flautist
- **protist**, unnoticed
- **chutist**, flutist, therapeutist
- absolutist • parachutist • cultist
- contrapuntist • occultist • scientist
- egotist
- **dramatist**, epigrammatist, melodramatist
- pragmatist • stigmatist • numismatist
- systematist • dogmatist • diplomatist
- hypnotist • immanentist • nepotist
- comparatist • indifferentist
- separatist • corporatist • Adventist
- Baathist • amethyst • telepathist
- homeopathist • farthest • furthest

31.15

- harvest • recidivist • archivist
- progressivist • Bolshevist • activist
- **collectivist**, objectivist, subjectivist
- nativist • prescriptivist • primitivist
- positivist • constructivist • negativist
- relativist
- **fauvist**, Jehovist
- reservist • linguist
- **soliloquist**, ventriloquist
- pointillist

31.16

- **Christ**, heist, underpriced, unsliced
- Zeitgeist • poltergeist • Antichrist

31.17

- **accost**, cost, frost, lost, Prost, riposte

> Create extra rhymes for [i]
> words like accost by adding -ed to
> cross etc. (see section 28.14).

- teleost • Pentecost • oncost • glasnost
- compost • star-crossed • hoar frost
- permafrost

31.18

- **exhaust**, under-resourced, unforced
- hypocaust • holocaust

31.19

- **Faust**, frowst, joust, oust, roust

31.20

- **boast**, coast, ghost, host, most, oast, post, roast, toast

> Create extra rhymes by [i]
> adding -ing to words like boast.

- backmost • headmost • leftmost
- endmost • midmost • hindmost
- rightmost • topmost • foremost
- almost • northernmost • downmost
- outmost • southernmost • upmost
- utmost • rearmost • lowermost
- undermost • innermost • uppermost
- aftermost
- **centremost** (*US* centermost)
- westernmost • easternmost
- bottommost • outermost • uttermost
- nethermost • furthermost
- lamp post • bedpost • gatepost
- Freepost • impost • guidepost
- milepost • signpost • doorpost
- outpost • goalpost • newel post
- fingerpost • sternpost

31.21

- **foist**, hoist, joist, moist, unvoiced

31.22

- **boost**, langouste, mot juste, Proust, roost, self-induced, used

31.23

- August

31.24

- **adjust**, august, bust, combust, crust, dust, encrust, entrust, gust, just, lust, mistrust, must, robust, rust, thrust, trust, undiscussed

> Create extra rhymes for ⓘ
> words like adjust by adding -ed to
> fuss etc. (see section 28.21).

- stardust • sawdust • angel dust
- bloodlust • wanderlust • upthrust

31.25

- unbiased • breakfast • August
- **locust**, unfocused
- **ballast**, Sallust
- dynast • unembarrassed • provost

31.26

- **accursed**, burst, curst, erst, first, headfirst, Hurst, thirst, under-rehearsed, unrehearsed, unversed, verst, worst, wurst
- starburst • airburst • cloudburst
- outburst • sunburst • Sandhurst
- Pankhurst • Bathurst • knackwurst
- bratwurst

31.27

- **amidst**, midst
- wouldst

31.28

- **Bakst**, unrelaxed
- **next**, oversexed, sext, text, undersexed
- teletext • context • subtext
- hypertext
- **betwixt**, unmixed
- suffix

31.29

- discalced • whilst • Holst

31.30

- **against**, unfenced
- Ernst • unconvinced • unlicensed
- unannounced • uninfluenced
- valanced • fragranced • Nernst

31.31

- angst • amongst

Section 32: -θ ('-th')

32.1

- **Kath**, math, Plath, strath
- polymath • aftermath • telepath
- sociopath • homeopath • osteopath
- psychopath

32.2

- **Barth**, bath, garth, hearth, lath, path
- sand bath • hip bath • eyebath
- **bloodbath**, mudbath
- Hogarth • warpath • towpath
- footpath

32.3

- **Beth**, breath, death, Jerez, Macbeth, Seth
- megadeath • Japheth • shibboleth

32.4

- **faith**, Galbraith, inter-faith, wraith

32.5

- **beneath**, buck teeth, Hadith, heath, Keith, neath, Reith, sheath, teeth, underneath, Westmeath, wreath
- eye teeth • dog-teeth

32.6

- **myth**, outwith, pith, smith
- twentieth • seventieth • eightieth
- fiftieth • sixtieth • ninetieth
- fortieth • thirtieth • Edith • Judith
- Meredith • Griffith • Hesketh
- tallith • Delyth • Lilith • megalith
- monolith • blacksmith • Nasmyth
- tinsmith • Ladysmith • locksmith
- songsmith • goldsmith • gunsmith
- coppersmith • silversmith
- wordsmith
- **Kenneth**, zenith
- Gwyneth • Lapith • Hollerith
- Asquith • Sopwith

32.7

- Forsyth

32.8

- **broth**, cloth, froth, Goth, moth, Roth, wrath
- Sabaoth • Visigoth

This poem gives a good example of *semantic* (or, in this case, *counter-semantic*) rhyme. 'Breath' and 'death' rhyme but emphasize opposite concepts:

I am sick of singing: the bays burn deep and chafe: I am fain
To rest a little from praise and grievous pleasure and pain.
For the Gods we know not of, who give us our daily breath,
We know they are cruel as love or life, and lovely as death.

(Algernon C. Swinburne, 'Hymn to Prosperine')

- **backcloth**, sackcloth
- saddlecloth •waxcloth •grasscloth
- haircloth •J-cloth •sailcloth
- tablecloth •facecloth •cheesecloth
- dishcloth •washcloth •oilcloth
- loincloth •hawkmoth

32.9

- **forth**, fourth, henceforth, north, thenceforth

32.10

- **Louth**, mouth, mouth-to-mouth, south
- bad-mouth •bigmouth •loudmouth
- goalmouth •blabbermouth
- motormouth

32.11

- **both**, growth, loath, oath, quoth, sloth, Thoth, troth
- outgrowth •upgrowth
- undergrowth

32.12

- **buck tooth**, couth, Duluth, forsooth, Maynooth, ruth, sleuth, sooth, strewth, tooth, truth, youth
- eye tooth •dog-tooth •sawtooth
- houndstooth •sabretooth

32.13

- Goliath •Haworth •sabbath
- Elizabeth •mammoth •Dartmouth
- Weymouth •behemoth •Plymouth
- Sidmouth •bismuth •azimuth
- Monmouth •Bournemouth
- Portsmouth •vermouth
- pennyworth •Elspeth •ha'p'orth
- Morpeth •Gareth •Nazareth
- Tamworth •Hayworth •Woolworth
- Wordsworth

32.14

- **berth**, birth, dearth, earth, firth, girth, mirth, Perth, worth
- stillbirth •childbirth •afterbirth
- Edgeworth •Hepworth •Ellsworth
- Whitworth •halfpennyworth
- Bosworth •jobsworth •Iorwerth

32.15

- breadth •width •bandwidth
- hundredth

32.16

- fifth •twelfth

32.17

- **health**, stealth, wealth
- commonwealth
- **filth**, tilth
- coolth

32.18

- warmth

32.19

- amaranth
- **nth**, tenth
- **eighteenth**, fifteenth, fourteenth, nineteenth, seventeenth, sixteenth, thirteenth, umpteenth
- **plinth**, synth
- Corinth •labyrinth •jacinth
- absinthe •hyacinth •ninth
- crème de menthe •month
- twelvemonth
- **billionth**, millionth, trillionth, zillionth
- **eleventh**, seventh
- thousandth •dozenth

32.20

- **length**, strength
- wavelength

32.21

- depth

32.22

- sixth

32.23

- eighth

Section 33: -ð ('-th')

33.1

- eth • Gorsedd

33.2

- **bathe**, lathe, rathe, scathe, spathe, swathe
- sunbathe

33.3

- **bequeath**, breathe, enwreathe, Meath, seethe, sheathe, teethe, wreathe

  > Create extra rhymes by changing words like breathe to breathing.

33.4

- **forthwith**, herewith, therewith, wherewith, with
- Dafydd

33.5

- **blithe**, lithe, scythe, tithe, writhe

33.6

- mouth

33.7

- **betroth**, clothe, loathe

33.8

- **booth**, smooth, soothe
- tollbooth (*US* tolbooth)

33.9

- Gwynedd

Section 34: -v

34.1

- **have**, lav
- satnav

34.2

- **Algarve**, calve, carve, grave, Graves, halve, Slav, starve, suave, Zouave
- Wroclaw
- **Jugoslav**, Yugoslav
- moshav • Gustave

34.3

- rev • Mendeleev • Negev • maglev
- Brezhnev

34.4

- **behave**, brave, Cave, clave, concave, crave, Dave, deprave, engrave, enslave, fave, forgave, gave, grave, knave, lave, Maeve, misbehave, misgave, nave, outbrave, pave, rave, save, shave, shortwave, slave, stave, they've, waive, wave

> Create extra rhymes by changing words like behave to behaving. ℹ

- enclave • exclave • conclave
- Redgrave • architrave • Wargrave
- Palgrave • palsgrave • aftershave
- brainwave • heatwave • microwave

34.5

- **achieve**, believe, breve, cleave, conceive, deceive, eve, greave, grieve, heave, interleave, interweave, khedive, leave, misconceive, naive, Neve, peeve, perceive, reave, receive, reive, relieve, reprieve, retrieve, sheave, sleeve, steeve, Steve, Tananarive, Tel Aviv, thieve, underachieve, upheave, weave, we've, Yves

> Create extra rhymes by changing words like achieve to achieving. ℹ

- make-believe • shirtsleeve
- semibreve • Congreve

34.6

- **forgive**, give, live, misgive, outlive, shiv, sieve, spiv, Viv
- endive • gerundive • olive

34.7

- **impassive**, massive, passive
- expansive
- **aggressive**, compressive, concessive, degressive, depressive, digressive, excessive, expressive, impressive, obsessive, oppressive, possessive, progressive, recessive, regressive, repressive, retrogressive, successive, transgressive

> Create extra rhymes by adding -ly to words like aggressive. ℹ

- reflexive
- **apprehensive**, coextensive, comprehensive, defensive, expensive, extensive, intensive, offensive, ostensive, pensive, suspensive

- counteroffensive
- **abrasive**, evasive, invasive, persuasive, pervasive
- **adhesive**, cohesive
- **missive**, omissive, permissive, submissive
- **decisive**, derisive, divisive, incisive
- **irresponsive**, responsive
- **corrosive**, explosive, implosive, plosive
- **abusive**, allusive, collusive, conclusive, conducive, delusive, diffusive, effusive, elusive, exclusive, illusive, inclusive, intrusive, obtrusive, preclusive, reclusive, seclusive
- **antitussive**, percussive
- **compulsive**, convulsive, impulsive, propulsive, repulsive
- purposive
- **coercive**, cursive, excursive, subversive

34.8

- active • captive
- **festive**, restive
- **dative**, native, stative
- fictive • unitive • octave • costive
- **emotive**, motive, votive
- furtive • appraisive

34.9

- **alive**, arrive, chive, Clive, connive, contrive, deprive, dive, drive, five, gyve, hive, I've, jive, live, MI5,

revive, rive, shrive, skive, strive, survive, swive, thrive
- skydive • swan dive • nosedive
- swallow dive • scuba-dive • Argive
- beehive • archive

34.10

- **hereof**, of, thereof, whereof
- Zhukov • Nabokov • Pavlov • Asimov
- Zhdanov • Karpov • improv • Kirov
- Kasparov

34.11

- **behove**, clove, cove, dove, drove, fauve, grove, interwove, Jove, mauve, rove, shrove, stove, strove, trove, wove
- alcove • mangrove

34.12

- **approve**, groove, improve, move, prove, you've
- countermove

34.13

- **above**, dove, glove, guv, love, shove, tug-of-love
- ringdove • turtle dove • foxglove

34.14

- **conserve**, curve, Deneuve, derv,

Some rhymes look like *full rhymes* on paper but in fact the sounds are not the same. In poetry from the past one reason for this may be because pronunciation of the words has changed over time—as with 'move' and 'love' in this example:

So let us melt, and make no noise,
    No teare-floods, nor sigh-tempests move,
'Twere prophanation of our joyes
    To tell the layetie our love.

(John Donne, 'A Valediction: forbidding mourning')

hors d'oeuvre, nerve, observe, perv,
roman-fleuve, serve, subserve,
swerve, verve

34.15

- **multivalve**, salve, valve
- lipsalve • check valve • univalve

- bivalve
- **delve**, helve, shelve, twelve
- **absolve**, devolve, evolve, exsolve, involve, revolve, solve

> Create extra rhymes by   i
> changing words like absolve to
> absolving.

Section 35: -z

35.1

- **Abkhaz**, as, Baz, has, jazz, pizzazz, razz, whereas
- **Boas**, Boaz
- topaz •Shiraz •Alcatraz •razzmatazz

35.2

- **aides-mémoires**, Lamaze, Lars, Mars, parse, Paz, Stars and Bars, vase, vichyssoise

35.3

- **Fès**, fez, fraise, Kes, Les, Montez, says, sez, Varèse
- Baez •Jabez •Boulez
- **Alvarez**, Juárez
- Peres •Gutiérrez
- **Cortés**, Cortes

35.4

- **backstairs**, chargés d'affaires, downstairs, Pears, theirs, unawares, understairs, upstairs

> Create extra rhymes for
> words like backstairs by adding -s
> to affair etc. (see section 2.1). ⓘ

35.5

- **ablaze**, amaze, appraise, baize, Blaise, blaze, braise, broderie anglaise, chaise, craze, daze, écossaise, erase, faze, gaze, glaze, graze, Hayes, Hays, haze, laze, liaise, lyonnaise, maize, malaise, Marseillaise, mayonnaise, Mays, maze, phase, phrase, polonaise, praise, prase, raise, raze, upraise

> Create extra rhymes for ⓘ
> words like ablaze by adding -s to
> allay and fray etc. (see
> section 3.1).

- nowadays •polyphase •multiphase
- stargaze •amylase •periclase
- underglaze •manes •lipase
- catchphrase
- **conquistadores**, mores, señores
- polymerase •paraphrase
- chrysoprase •lactase •equites
- Gervaise •endways •edgeways
- eques •breadthways •lengthways
- leastways •widthways •anyways
- sideways •longways •crossways
- always

35.6

- **Achinese**, Ambonese, appease, Assamese, Balinese, Belize, Beninese, Bernese, bêtise, Bhutanese, breeze, Burmese, Cantonese, Castries, cerise, cheese, chemise, Chinese, Cingalese, Cleese, Congolese, Denise, Dodecanese, ease, éminence grise, expertise, Faroese, freeze, Fries, frieze, Gabonese, Genoese, Goanese, Guyanese, he's, Japanese, Javanese, jeez, journalese, Kanarese, Keys, Lebanese, lees, legalese, Louise, Macanese, Madurese, Maltese, marquise, Milanese, Nepalese, Nipponese, officialese, overseas, pease, Pekinese, Peloponnese, Piedmontese, please, Portuguese, Pyrenees, reprise, Rwandese, seise, seize, Senegalese, she's, Siamese, Sienese, Sikkimese, Sinhalese,

sleaze, sneeze, squeeze,
Stockton-on-Tees, Sudanese,
Sundanese, Surinamese, Tabriz,
Taiwanese, tease, Tees,
telegraphese, these, Timorese,
Togolese, trapeze, valise, Viennese,
Vietnamese, vocalese, wheeze

> ⓘ Create extra rhymes for words like appease by adding -s to agree etc. (see section 4.1).

• superficies •Héloïse •Averroës
• rabies • pubes • Maccabees
• headcheese

35.7

• Andes
• **Hades**, Mercedes
• Archimedes •Thucydides •aphides
• **Eumenides**, Parmenides
• **Maimonides**, Simonides
• Euripides •cantharides •Hesperides
• Hebrides
• **Aristides**, bona fides
• Culdees
• **Alcibiades**, Hyades, Pleiades
• Cyclades •antipodes •Sporades
• Ganges •Apelles
• **tales**, Thales
• **Achilles**, Antilles
• Los Angeles •Ramillies •Pericles
• isosceles •Praxiteles •Hercules
• Empedocles •Sophocles •Damocles
• Androcles •Heracles •Themistocles
• Hermes •Menes •testudines
• Diogenes •Cleisthenes
• Demosthenes
• **Aristophanes**, Xenophanes
• manganese •Holofernes •editiones principes •herpes
• **lares**, primus inter pares
• **Antares**, Ares, Aries, caries
• antifreeze •Ceres •Buenos Aires

35.8

• fasces •calces •heartsease
• **Albigenses**, amanuenses, menses, Waldenses

• syllepses
• **oases**, parabases
• **aposiopeses**, exegeses, faeces (*US* feces), theses
• radices •appendices •indices
• codices •pontifices
• **analyses** (*US* analyzes), paralyses
• helices •Ulysses •nemeses •apices
• haruspices
• **administratrices**, dominatrices, matrices, testatrices
• tortrices •executrices •diaereses
• **cortices**, vortices
• vertices •parentheses •syntheses
• **hypotheses**, protheses
• cervices
• **Anchises**, Cambyses, cicatrices, crises, Pisces
• synopses
• **apotheoses**, diagnoses, misdiagnoses, neuroses, prognoses, psychoses, scleroses, symbioses
• **anacruses**, cruces
• anabases •apodoses •emphases
• anamorphoses •periphrases
• thoraces •entases •protases
• iconostases

35.9

• **atlantes**, Cervantes
• Ecclesiastes •penates •gentes
• **Orestes**, testes, Thyestes
• **Achates**, Euphrates
• diabetes •striptease
• **pyrites**, Stylites, troglodytes
• Orontes •Boötes •Procrustes
• **Harpocrates**, Hippocrates, Isocrates, Socrates
• litotes •Surtees •Dives

35.10

• **biz**, Cadíz, Cadiz, fizz, frizz, gee-whiz, his, is, jizz, Liz, Ms, phiz, quiz, squiz, swizz, tizz, viz, whizz, wiz, zizz
• **louis**, Suez
• scabies
• **Celebes**, heebie-jeebies

- showbiz ▪ laches ▪ Marches ▪ breeches
- Indies ▪ undies ▪ hafiz ▪ Kyrgyz
- Hedges ▪ Bridges ▪ Hodges ▪ Judges
- Rockies ▪ walkies
- **Gillies**, Scillies
- pennies ▪ Benares
- **Jefferies**, Jeffreys
- Canaries
- **Delores**, Flores, furores
- series ▪ miniseries ▪ Furies
- congeries ▪ Potteries ▪ molasses
- glasses ▪ sunglasses ▪ missus ▪ suffix
- falsies ▪ fracases ▪ galluses
- Pontine Marshes ▪ species
- subspecies ▪ conches ▪ munchies
- treatise
- **civvies**, Skivvies
- Velázquez ▪ exequies ▪ obsequies
- Menzies ▪ elevenses
- **cosies** (*US* cozies), Moses
- Joneses

35.11

- **advise**, apprise, apprize, arise, assize, capsize, chastise, comprise, demise, despise, devise, downsize, excise, flies, guise, incise, low-rise, misprize, outsize, previse, prise, prize, remise, revise, rise, size, surmise, surprise, uprise, wise

> Create extra rhymes for words like advise by changing apply etc. to applies (see section 6.1). ⓘ

- archaize ▪ heroize ▪ ghettoize
- Judaize ▪ bye-byes ▪ disenfranchise
- propagandize ▪ periodize ▪ iodize
- merchandise ▪ melodize
- gourmandize ▪ methodize
- anthropomorphize ▪ apostrophize
- elegize ▪ analogize ▪ syllogize
- **anthologize**, mythologize, psychologize, tautologize, theologize
- hierarchize

35.12

- underutilize

- **tranquillize** (*US* tranquilize)
- spiritualize ▪ capsulize ▪ memorialize
- imperialize ▪ bestialize ▪ dialyse
- dualize ▪ ritualize ▪ sexualize
- sensualize ▪ contextualize
- detribalize ▪ feudalize ▪ radicalize
- theatricalize ▪ verticalize ▪ musicalize
- **delocalize**, focalize, vocalise
- animalize
- **analyse** (*US* analyze), channelize, overanalyse (*US* overanalyze), psychoanalyse (*US* psychoanalyze)
- signalize ▪ criminalize
- **phenomenalize**, pronominalize
- communalize ▪ regionalize
- depersonalize ▪ renationalize
- **factionalize**, fractionalize
- professionalize ▪ conventionalize
- sectionalize
- **operationalize**, vocationalize
- emotionalize ▪ constitutionalize
- **eternalize**, journalize, vernalize
- municipalize ▪ paralyse ▪ mongrelize
- ruralize ▪ denaturalize ▪ federalize
- overgeneralize ▪ mineralize
- literalize ▪ substantialize
- overspecialize ▪ spatialize ▪ initialize
- **catalyse** (*US* catalyze)
- cartelize
- **metallize** (*US* metalize)
- **departmentalize**, monumentalize, occidentalize, orientalize, segmentalize, transcendentalize
- devitalize ▪ totalize ▪ palatalize
- **breathalyse** (*US* breathalyze)
- medievalize ▪ novelize ▪ unequalize
- dieselize

35.13

- euphemize ▪ systemize ▪ randomize
- sodomize ▪ alchemize ▪ dynamize
- compromise ▪ anatomize
- **dichotomize**, lobotomize
- routinize ▪ platitudinize ▪ indigenize
- masculinize ▪ vitaminize ▪ gelatinize
- divinize ▪ cognize ▪ communize
- **proletarianize**, sectarianize
- suburbanize ▪ euphonize ▪ jargonize
- paganize ▪ disorganize
- **decolonize**, recolonize
- ironize ▪ satanize ▪ cosmopolitanize

- gluttonize • civilianize
- philanthropize • panegyrize
- high-rise • low-rise • moonrise
- sunrise • denuclearize • linearize
- **exteriorize**, interiorize
- diarize • barbarize • rubberize
- texturize • calendarize • slenderize
- aphorize • allegorize • subcategorize
- cicatrize • solarize • vernacularize
- secularize • singularize • formularize
- circularize • glamorize • containerize
- pauperize • mercerize • depressurize
- martyrize • vectorize • enterprise
- winterize • microenterprise
- **motorize**, notarize
- etherize

35.14

- excise • queen-size • laicize
- **Anglicise**, Anglicize
- polemicize • classicize • fanaticize
- elasticize • poeticize • parenthesize
- mythicize
- **photosynthesize**, synthesize
- synopsize • apotheosize • emphasize
- circumcise • exercise • metastasize
- hypostasize
- **affranchise**, enfranchise, franchise
- fetishize • alphabetize • concretize
- poetize • palletize • pelletize
- unitize • remonetize • syncretize
- securitize • synthetize • robotize
- narcotize
- **anagrammatize**, epigrammatize, melodramatize, overdramatize
- **emblematize**, lemmatize
- legitimatize • dogmatize • aromatize
- problematize • automatize
- bureaucratize • advertise
- telepathize • televise
- **collectivize**, objectivize
- relativize • supervise • improvise

35.15

- crabwise • slantwise • stepwise
- lengthwise • streetwise • anywise
- contrariwise • sidewise • likewise
- **clockwise**, counterclockwise
- crosswise • nowise • coastwise
- **soliloquize**, ventriloquize
- cornerwise • otherwise

35.16

- **because**, Boz, cos, Oz, Ros, Roz, schnozz, was

35.17

- **applause**, Azores, cause, clause, Dors, drawers, gauze, hawse, indoors, Laws, outdoors, pause, plus-fours, quatorze, Santa Claus, taws, tawse, yaws, yours

> Create extra rhymes for [i]
> words like applause by adding -s
> to adore etc. (see section 7.1).

- menopause

35.18

- **arouse**, blouse, browse, carouse, Cowes, dowse, drowse, espouse, house, Howes, rouse

> Create extra rhymes for [i]
> words like arouse by adding -s to
> brow and endow etc. (see
> section 8.1).

35.19

- **appose**, arose, Bose, brose, chose, close, compose, diagnose, self-diagnose, doze, enclose, expose, foreclose, froze, hose, impose, interpose, juxtapose, Montrose, noes, nose, oppose, plainclothes, pose, propose, prose, rose, suppose, those, transpose, underexpose, uprose

> Create extra rhymes for [i]
> words like arose by adding -s to
> blow etc. (see section 9.1).

- Berlioz • flambeaux • thrombose

- bandeaux •bulldoze •fricandeaux
- metamorphose •pantyhose •glucose
- **gallows**, Hallowes
- tableaux •parclose •Fellows
- bedclothes •nightclothes •rouleaux
- underclothes •misdiagnose
- Ambrose •dextrose •Faeroes
- primrose •cornrows •sucrose
- Burroughs •tuberose
- **bateaux**, gateaux, plateaux
- portmanteaux •fructose

35.20

- **avoirdupois**, noise, poise

> Create extra rhymes for
> words like noise and poise by
> adding -s to boy etc. (see
> section 10.1). ⓘ

- Anglepoise •equipoise
- counterpoise •turquoise

35.21

- **abuse**, accuse, adieux, amuse,
  bemuse, billets-doux, blues, booze,
  bruise, choose, Clews, confuse,
  contuse, cruise, cruse, Cruz, diffuse,
  do's, Druze, effuse, enthuse, excuse,
  fuse (*US* fuze), Hughes, incuse,
  interfuse, lose, Mahfouz, mews,
  misuse, muse, news, ooze, Ouse,
  perfuse, peruse, rhythm-and-blues,
  ruse, schmooze, snooze, suffuse,
  Toulouse, transfuse, trews, use,
  Vaduz, Veracruz, who's, whose,
  youse

- Andrews

> Create extra rhymes for
> words like abuse by adding -s to
> accrue and brew etc. (see
> section 11.1). ⓘ

- Matthews •circumfuse •Syracuse
- purlieux

35.22

- Hormuz •Thammuz •Soyuz

35.23

- **abuzz**, buzz, coz, does, fuzz, outdoes

35.24

- has •Sayers
- **Algiers**, cheers, Pamirs, Pears, Piers,
  Sears, Spears
- Teniers
- **Blackfriars**, Briers, pliers
- Greyfriars
- **Bowers**, Flowers, ours, Powers,
  Towers
- bejabers •Chambers •Sobers
- Scriptures •weight-watchers
- **glanders**, Landers, Randers, sanders
- **alexanders**, Flanders
- Enders •Childers •flinders
- Saunders •Bermudas •butterfingers
- Tigers •Rodgers •starkers
- Chequers •Snickers •camiknickers
- bonkers •bluchers •Moluccas
- Sellers •binoculars •Bahamas
- Summers •Marianas •Connors
- **champers**, Pampers

A standard rhyming pair is based on two single words; a *mosaic rhyme* on
the other hand uses one word with several syllables to rhyme with two or
more words, or rhymes phrases, as in the words of this song from Gilbert and
Sullivan's *Pirates of Penzance*:

About binomial theorem I'm learning a lot o' news
With interesting facts about the square of the hypotenuse

(W. S. Gilbert, 'The Modern Major-General')

• jeepers •jodhpurs •Messrs •Masters
• Peters •squitters •Winters
• **headquarters**, hindquarters, Waters
• Klosters •Butters
• **Smithers**, withers
• **Carothers**, druthers
• Travers •Havers •cleavers •Rivers
• vivers •estovers •Marquesas

35.25

• **agents provocateurs**, berceuse, chanteuse, charmeuse, chartreuse, chauffeuse, coiffeurs, danseuse, diseuse, furze, hers, messieurs, Meuse, secateurs, vendeuse
• Betelgeuse •divers

35.26

• **Babs**, dribs and drabs
• Thebes
• **Gibbs**, Hibs
• vibes •Hobbs •Forbes •Stubbs
• Jacobs •Proverbs

35.27

• **adze** (*US* adz)
• Everglades •Palisades
• Leeds •proceeds •Perseids
• Geminids
• **besides**, ides
• upsides •Mods •towards •Rhodes
• crossroads •Lloyd's •adenoids
• **goods**, Woods
• backwoods •suds •soapsuds
• Richards •innards •backwards
• Edwards •inwards •forwards
• downwards •outwards •afterwards
• **Fields**, Shields
• Bluefields •Reynolds •Sands
• badlands •odds and ends •calends
• zounds •Falklands

35.28

• moneybags •daddy-long-legs
• yellowlegs •sheer legs

• **Briggs**, Higgs
• Joe Bloggs

35.29

• Casals •Charles
• **Dardanelles**, Seychelles, Wells
• **Hales**, Swales, Wales
• entrails •telesales •cat-o'-nine-tails
• **Hills**, Mills, Sills, Wills
• **Giles**, Miles, Smiles, Stiles
• hols •consols
• **balls**, Rawls, Walls
• Fowles
• **Bowles**, Coles, Rolls
• **gules**, Jules
• collywobbles •Gorbals •Mumbles
• Goebbels •Needles •oodles •Raffles
• Engels •Gleneagles •Eccles •Pickles
• Naples •Brussels •battels •Beatles
• bristols •measles

35.30

• Abrahams •jimjams
• **alms**, Brahms, man-at-arms
• Thames
• **hames**, James
• Reims •Sims
• **betimes**, Grimes, Times
• Maritimes •oftentimes •sometimes
• Toms •telecoms •Cairngorms
• Holmes
• **Coombes**, Tombs
• Adams •diddums •Helms •doldrums
• Williams •Worms

35.31

• **banns**, glans, Prestonpans, sans
• Octans
• **Benz**, cleanse, Fens, gens, lens
• Homo sapiens •impatiens •nolens volens •delirium tremens •Serpens
• vas deferens •Cairns •Keynes
• **Jeans**, means, Queens, smithereens
• Owens •Robbins •Rubens •gubbins
• Hitchens •O'Higgins
• **Huggins**, juggins, muggins

- imagines • Jenkins • Eakins • Dickens
- Wilkins • Hopkins
- **Dawkins**, Hawkins
- Collins • Gobelins • widdershins
- matins • Martens • Athens • avens
- Heinz • confines • Apennines
- **bonze**, bronze, Johns, mod cons, Mons, St John's
- **Downs**, grounds, hash-browns, Townes
- **Jones**, nones
- lazybones • sawbones • fivestones
- **microgreens**, New Orleans, Orléans
- **Lions**, Lyons
- Gibbons • St Albans • Siddons
- shenanigans • Huygens • vengeance
- goujons • St Helens • Hollands
- Newlands • Brooklands • Netherlands
- Siemens • Symons • commons
- summons • Lorenz • Parsons
- Goossens
- **Lamentations**, United Nations
- Colossians • Sextans • Buttons
- Evans • Stevens • Ovens • Onions
- Lutyens
- **Cousins**, Cozens
- Burns

- Springs • proceedings • tidings
- pickings • feelings • filings
- Cummings • gleanings • imaginings
- earnings • belongings • trappings
- fixings • furnishings • Hastings

- beestings • hustings • underthings
- leavings • Livings • water wings
- arisings

- Stieglitz

35.34

- clothes

35.35

- haves
- **calves**, scarves
- headscarves • mooncalves • Graves
- **beeves**, eaves, Greaves, Jeeves, leaves, Reeves, thieves
- tea leaves • fig leaves • flyleaves
- Hargreaves • lives
- **Ives**, knives, wives
- jackknives • penknives • paperknives
- spaewives • alewives • midwives
- fishwives • housewives • goodwives
- **corves**, dwarves, wharves
- **Groves**, loaves
- hooves • turves
- **elves**, ourselves, selves, shelves, theirselves, themselves, yourselves
- mantelshelves • bookshelves
- wolves • aardwolves • werewolves

A *heroic couplet* is a rhyming couplet written in iambic pentameter (five pairs of unstressed and stressed beats: ti-TUM ti-TUM ti-TUM ti-TUM ti-TUM); they were often used by Chaucer and by Restoration and eighteenth-century poets, especially John Dryden and Alexander Pope:

What dire offence from am'rous causes springs,
What mighty contests rise from trivial things

(Alexander Pope, 'The Rape of the Lock')

Index

a

accommodate 30.9
accommodationist 31.10
accompanist 31.10
accompany 4.34
accomplice 28.8
accomplish 29.8
accord 16.19
accordance 28.45
accordant 30.56
according 26.5
accordion 25.37
accordionist 31.10
accost 31.17
account 30.55
accountancy 4.48
accountant 30.56
accounting 26.13
accouter 12.81
accoutre 12.81
Accra 1.1
accredit 30.21
accrete 30.18
accretion 25.49
accrual 23.25
accrue 11.1
acculturate 30.15
accumulate 30.11
accuracy 4.48
accurate 30.43
accursed 31.26
accusal 23.41
accusatorial 23.24
accusatory 4.43
accuse 35.21
accuser 12.92
accustom 24.20
ace 28.5
acedia 12.5
acer 12.69
acerb 14.15
acerbic 21.9
acerbity 4.53
acetate 30.16
acetone 25.31
acetous 28.34
acetyl 23.12
acetylene 25.10
Achaea 12.3
Achaemenid 16.10
Achates 35.9
ache 21.7
Achebe 4.10
Acheron 25.47
Acheson 25.48
Acheulian 25.37
achieve 34.5
achiever 12.85
Achilles 35.7
Achinese 35.6
achromatic 21.17

achy 4.18
acid 16.11
acidic 21.10
acidify 6.7
acidity 4.53
acidophilus 28.27
acidulate 30.11
acidulous 28.27
acini 6.13
ack-ack 21.3
ackee 4.18
acknowledge 20.6
acme 4.29
acne 4.31
acolyte 30.28
Aconcagua 12.88
acorn 25.28
acoustic 21.17
acquaint 30.54
acquaintance 28.45
acquiesce 28.3
acquiescence 28.45
acquiescent 30.56
acquire 12.13
acquirer 12.67
acquit 30.20
acquittal 23.39
acquittance 28.45
acre 12.38
acreage 20.8
acrid 16.11
acridity 4.53
Acrilan 25.2
acrimonious 28.23
acrimony 4.34
acrobat 30.1
acrobatic 21.17
acronym 24.6
acropolis 28.8
across 28.14
acrostic 21.17
acrylic 21.11
act 30.48
actable 23.26
Actaeon 25.36
actinic 21.13
actinium 24.16
action 25.49
activate 30.16
active 34.8
activewear 2.15
activist 31.15
activity 4.53
actor 12.74
actress 28.10
actressy 4.46
actual 23.25
actuarial 23.24
actuary 4.43
actuate 30.8
acuity 4.53

aculeate 30.41
acumen 25.45
acupressure 12.72
acupuncture 12.24
acupuncturist 31.12
acute 30.37
acyclic 21.11
ad 16.1
Ada 12.26
adage 20.6
adagio 9.4
Adam 24.17
adamance 28.45
adamant 30.56
adamantine 25.23
Adams 35.30
adapt 30.58
adaptor 12.74
add 16.1
addax 28.38
addenda 12.26
addendum 24.17
adder 12.25
addict 30.49
addiction 25.49
Addington 25.50
Addis Ababa 12.22
Addison 25.48
addition 25.49
additional 23.34
addle 23.28
address 28.3
addressee 4.1
addresser 12.69
adduce 28.19
adducible 23.26
adduct 30.49
Adela 12.43
Adelaide 16.6
Adele 23.3
Adelina 12.54
Adeline 25.22
Aden 25.40
Adenauer 12.16
adenoids 35.27
adept 30.58
adequacy 4.48
adequate 30.44
a deux 13.1
adhan 25.4
adhere 12.4
adherence 28.45
adherent 30.56
adhesion 25.42
adhesive 34.7
adhibit 30.20
ad hoc 21.20
adhocracy 4.48
ad hominem 24.3
Adie 4.12
adieu 11.1

adieux 35.21
ad infinitum 24.20
adiós 28.17
adit 30.21
Adivasi 4.45
adjacent 30.56
adjectival 23.40
adjoin 25.32
adjourn 25.53
adjudge 20.16
adjudicate 30.10
adjunct 30.49
adjuratory 4.43
adjure 12.20
adjust 31.24
adjuster 12.81
adjutancy 4.48
adjutant 30.56
adjuvant 30.56
Adlai 6.11
Adler 12.42
adman 25.2
admen 25.5
admin 25.17
administer 12.78
administrate 30.15
administratrices 35.8
administratrix 28.39
admiral 23.36
admiralty 4.55
admire 12.13
admirer 12.67
admissible 23.26
admit 30.20
admittance 28.45
admix 28.39
admixture 12.23
admonish 29.9
admonitory 4.43
ad nauseam 24.1
ado 11.1
adobe 4.10
adolescence 28.45
adolescent 30.56
Adonis 28.9
adopt 30.58
adoptee 4.1
adopter 12.79
adoption 25.49
adore 7.1
adorer 12.66
adorn 25.28
ad personam 24.1
adrenal 23.34
adrenalin 25.16
Adrian 25.37
Adrianne 25.1
Adriatic 21.17
Adrienne 25.5

adrift 30.47
adroit 30.36
adulate 30.11
adulatory 4.43
Adullamite 30.29
adult 30.51
adulterant 30.56
adulterate 30.15
adulterer 12.67
adulterine 25.23
adulterous 28.31
adultery 4.43
adulthood 16.26
adumbrate 30.15
ad valorem 24.3
advance 28.44
advancer 12.69
advantage 20.9
advantageous 28.25
advent 30.56
Adventist 31.14
adventitious 28.33
adventure 12.72
adventurer 12.67
adventuress 28.10
adventurist 31.12
adventurous 28.31
adverb 14.15
adverbial 23.24
adversarial 23.24
adversary 4.43
adverse 28.36
adversity 4.53
advert 30.45
advertise 35.14
advertiser 12.91
advertorial 23.24
advice 28.13
advise 35.11
adviser 12.91
advisory 4.43
advocaat 1.11
advocacy 4.48
advocate 30.10, 30.42
adware 2.15
adz 35.27
adze 35.27
adzuki 4.20
aedile 23.11
Aegean 25.36
aegis 28.7
Aegisthus 28.35
aegrotat 30.2
Aelfric 21.15
Aeneas 28.22
Aeneid 16.8
Aeolian 25.37
Aeolus 28.27
aeon 25.36
aerate 30.7
aeration 25.49

aerial 23.24
aerialist 31.8
aerie 4.43
aerobatic 21.17
aerobic 21.9
aerodrome 24.11
aerodynamic 21.12
aerofoil 23.19
aerogram 24.1
aerogramme 24.1
aeronaut 30.33
aeronautic 21.17
aeronautical 23.32
aeroplane 25.8
aerosol 23.13
aerospace 28.5
aerostat 30.2
Aeschylus 28.27
Aesop 27.8
aesthete 30.19
aesthetic 21.17
aesthetician 25.49
aestival 23.40
aetiology 4.17
afar 1.1
Afar 1.7
affable 23.26
affair 2.1
affairé 3.19
affaire 2.1
affect 30.48
affection 25.49
affectionate 30.43
affiant 30.56
affidavit 30.25
affiliate 30.8, 30.41
affined 16.42
affinity 4.53
affirm 24.22
affirmatory 4.43
affirmer 12.52
affix 28.39
afflict 30.49
affliction 25.49
affluence 28.45
affluent 30.56
afflux 28.41
afford 16.19
afforest 31.12
affranchise 35.14
affray 3.1
affright 30.26
affront 30.55
Afghan 25.1
Afghani 4.31
Afghanistan 25.4
aficionado 9.11
afield 16.35
afire 12.13
aflame 24.4
afloat 30.35

aflutter 12.81
afoot 30.39
afore 7.1
aforementioned 16.45
aforesaid 16.4
afoul 23.16
afraid 16.6
afresh 29.3
Africa 12.39
African 25.43
Africana 12.53
Africanist 31.10
Afrikaans 28.48
Afrikaner 12.53
Afro 9.21
aft 30.47
after 12.75
afterbirth 32.14
aftercare 2.7
afterdeck 21.6
afterglow 9.17
afterlife 17.7
aftermath 32.1
aftermost 31.20
afternoon 25.33
aftershave 34.4
aftershock 21.21
aftertaste 31.4
afterthought 30.33
afterward 16.30
afterwards 35.27
afterword 16.31
afterworld 16.38
Aga 12.31
Agadir 12.4
again 25.5
against 31.30
agama 12.52
Agamemnon 25.26
agapanthus 28.35
agape 3.18, 27.4
agaric 21.15
agate 30.21
Agatha 12.83
age 20.4
aged 16.10, 16.34
ageism 24.21
ageist 31.7
ageless 28.8
agency 4.48
agenda 12.26
agent 30.56
agent provocateur 13.1
agents provocateurs 35.25
Aggie 4.15
agglomerate 30.15, 30.43

agglutinate 30.13, 30.43
aggrandizer 12.91
aggravate 30.16
aggregate 30.9, 30.42
aggressive 34.7
aggressor 12.69
aggro 9.21
aghast 31.2
agile 23.11
agility 4.53
agin 25.13
Agincourt 7.10
aging 26.6
agitate 30.16
agitato 9.24
agitprop 27.8
agleam 24.5
aglet 30.22
agley 3.1
aglow 9.1
agnate 30.13
agnation 25.49
Agnes 28.9
Agni 4.31
agnostic 21.17
Agnus Dei 4.2
ago 9.1
agog 18.8
a-gogo 9.13
agonist 31.10
agony 4.34
agoraphobia 12.5
agoraphobic 21.9
agouti 4.54
Agra 12.64
agrarian 25.37
agree 4.1
Agricola 12.48
agriculturalist 31.8
agriculture 12.24
agriculturist 31.12
agrimony 4.34
Agrippa 12.62
agrochemical 23.32
agroforestry 4.40
agronomic 21.12
agronomical 23.32
agronomist 31.9
agronomy 4.30
aground 16.43
ague 11.22
ah 1.1
aha 1.1
ahead 16.3
ahem 24.3
ahimsa 1.17
ahistorical 23.32
Ahmadabad 16.1
ahoy 10.1
aid 16.6

Aida 12.26
Aidan 25.40
aide 16.6
aide-de-camp 25.24
aide-mémoire 1.1
aides-de-camp 25.24
aides-meémoires 35.2
aigrette 30.5
aiguillette 30.4
aikido 9.11
ail 23.5
Aileen 25.10
aileron 25.26
ailment 30.56
Ailsa 12.69
aim 24.4
Aimée 3.16
aimless 28.8
Ainsley 4.22
ain't 30.54
Aintree 4.39
Ainu 11.15
aïoli 4.25
air 2.1
air bag 18.1
airbase 28.5
airbed 16.3
airborne 25.28
airbrake 21.7
airbrick 21.15
airbrush 29.16
airburst 31.26
aircraft 30.47
aircrew 11.17
airdrop 27.8
Airedale 23.5
airer 12.65
airfare 2.5
airfield 16.35
airflow 9.17
airfoil 23.19
airframe 24.4
airfreight 30.15
air gun 25.35
airhead 16.3
airing 26.11
airless 28.27
airlift 30.47
airline 25.22
airliner 12.55
airlock 21.21
airmail 23.5
airman 25.45
airmen 25.45
airmiss 28.8
airmobile 23.7
airplane 25.8
airplay 3.15
airpocket 30.21
airport 30.33

airship 27.6
airsick 21.16
airside 16.16
airspace 28.5
airspeed 16.7
airstream 24.5
airstrip 27.6
airtight 30.30
airtime 24.7
airway 3.25
airwoman 25.45
airwomen 25.17
airworthy 4.57
airy 4.39
aisle 23.11
ait 30.7
aitchbone 25.30
Aix-la-Chapelle 23.3
Ajaccio 9.4
ajar 1.1
Ajax 28.38
aka 3.1
Akbar 1.4
Akhenaten 25.50
Akhetaten 25.50
akimbo 9.9
akin 25.13
Akita 12.77
Akkad 16.1
Akkadian 25.37
Akron 25.26
Aksum 24.13
Al 23.1
Alabama 12.50
Alabaman 25.45
alabaster 12.75
alack 21.1
alacrity 4.53
Aladdin 25.14
Alamo 9.18
Alan 25.44
Alana 12.53
Alar 1.12
Alaric 21.15
alarm 24.2
alarmist 31.9
alarum 24.19
alas 28.1
Alasdair 12.82
Alaska 12.37
Alaskan 25.43
alb 14.16
Alba 12.21
Albacete 4.52
Alban 25.38
Albania 12.8
Albanian 25.37
Albany 4.34
albatross 28.14
Albee 4.10
albeit 30.20

Albert 30.41
Alberta 12.82
Alberti 4.55
albescent 30.56
Albigenses 35.8
Albigensian 25.37
albino 9.19
Albinoni 4.33
Albion 25.37
albite 30.26
album 24.17
albumen 25.17
albumin 25.17
Albuquerque 4.20
Alcaeus 28.23
alcaic 21.9
alcalde 4.12
Alcatraz 35.1
Alcazar 1.1
Alcestis 28.12
alchemic 21.12
alchemical 23.32
alchemist 31.9
alchemize 35.13
alchemy 4.30
Alcibiades 35.7
alcid 36.11
Alcock 21.20
alcohol 23.13
alcoholic 21.11
Alcott 30.42
alcove 34.11
Alcuin 25.20
Aldabra 12.64
Aldebaran 25.47
Aldeburgh 12.67
al dente 4.51
alder 12.28
alderman 25.45
aldermanic 21.13
Aldermaston 25.50
aldermen 25.45
Alderney 4.34
Aldershot 30.32
alderwoman 25.45
alderwomen 25.17
Aldine 25.21
Aldiss 28.7
aldol 23.13
Aldous 28.25
Aldrin 25.18
ale 23.5
aleatoric 21.15
aleatory 4.43
Alec 21.11
alehouse 28.16
Aleksandrovsk 21.35
alembic 21.9
Aleppo 9.20
alert 30.45

Aleut 30.38
alewife 17.7
alewives 35.35
Alex 28.39
Alexa 12.69
Alexander 12.25
alexanders 35.24
Alexandra 12.64
Alexandria 12.10
Alexandrian 25.37
alexandrine 25.23
alexandrite 30.29
Alexis 28.11
alfalfa 12.30
Alfonso 9.29
Alfred 16.11
alfresco 9.16
Alfvén 25.8
alga 12.31
algae 4.17
algal 23.30
Algarve 34.2
algebra 12.65
algebraic 21.9
Algeciras 28.31
Alger 12.35
Algeria 12.10
Algerian 25.37
Algernon 25.46
Algiers 35.24
Algol 23.13
Algonquian 25.37
Algonquin 25.15
algorithm 24.20
Alhambra 12.64
Ali 4.21
alias 28.23
alibi 6.5
Alicante 4.51
Alice 28.8
Alicia 12.11
alien 25.37
alienate 30.13
alienist 31.10
aliform 24.9
alight 30.26
align 25.21
alike 21.19
aliment 30.56
alimentary 4.43
alimony 4.34
aliquot 30.32
Alison 25.48
Alissa 12.70
Alistair 12.78
alive 34.9
aliyah 12.3
alkali 6.11
alkaline 25.22
alkaloid 16.24
alkanet 30.5

all 23.14
Allah 12.42
Allahabad 16.1
allay 3.1
allege 20.3
alleged 16.10
allegiance 28.45
allegoric 21.15
allegorical 23.32
allegorist 31.12
allegorize 35.13
allegory 4.43
allegretto 9.24
allegro 9.21
allele 23.7
alleluia 12.89
allemande 16.40
Allenby 4.10
Allende 3.9
allergen 25.5
allergic 21.11
allergy 4.17
alleviate 30.8
alley 4.21
alleyway 3.25
alliance 28.45
Allie 4.21
allied 16.14
alliterate 30.15
allium 24.16
all-nighter 12.79
allocate 30.10
allocution 25.49
allophone 25.30
allot 30.31
allottee 4.1
allow 8.1
allowance 28.45
alloy 10.1,10.7
allspice 28.13
Allston 25.50
allude 16.25
allure 12.20
allusion 25.42
allusive 34.7
alluvial 23.24
alluvion 25.37
alluvium 24.16
ally 6.1, 6.11
Ally 4.21
Alma 12.50
Almagest 31.3
almanac 21.3
almandine 25.10
Almería 12.3
almighty 4.54
almond 16.45
almoner 12.58
almonry 4.43
almost 31.20
alms 35.30

almshouse 28.16
aloe 9.17
aloft 30.47
alogical 23.32
aloha 12.34
alone 25.30
along 26.15
alongshore 7.17
alongside 16.16
Alonzo 9.29
aloof 17.13
alopecia 12.11
aloud 16.22
alow 9.1
Aloysius 28.33
alp 27.16
alpaca 12.37
alpenglow 9.17
alpenhorn 25.28
alpha 12.30
alphabet 30.4
alphabetic 21.17
alphabetical 23.32
alphabetize 35.14
alphanumeric 21.15
alpine 25.23
alpinist 31.10
already 4.12
alright 30.26
Alsace 28.1
Alsatian 25.49
also 9.22
Altai 6.1
Altair 2.1
Altamira 12.67
altar 12.80
altarpiece 28.6
Altdorfer 12.30
alter 12.80
altercate 30.10
alternant 30.56
alternate 30.13, 30.23
Althea 12.12
althorn 25.28
although 9.1
Althusser 2.1
altimeter 12.77
altissimo 9.18
altitudinal 23.34
alto 9.24
altocumulus 28.27
altogether 12.84
Alton 25.50
altostratus 28.34
altruist 31.6
alum 24.18
alumina 12.55
aluminium 24.16
alumni 6.13
alumnus 28.29
Alun 25.16

Alvar 1.21
Alvarez 35.3
alveoli 6.11
alveolus 28.27
Alvin 25.19
always 35.5
Alwyn 25.20
alyssum 24.20
am 24.1
amadou 11.6
amah 12.50
Amal 23.2
Amalfi 4.14
amalgam 24.18
amalgamate 30.12
Amanda 12.25
amanuenses 35.8
amanuensis 28.11
amaranth 32.19
amaretti 4.51
amaretto 9.24
amaryllis 28.8
amass 28.1
amasser 12.69
amateur 12.82
amateurish 29.9
Amati 4.51
amatory 4.43
amaze 35.5
Amazon 25.52
Amazonia 12.8
Amazonian 25.37
ambassador 12.29
ambassadorial 23.24
ambassadress 28.10
Ambato 9.24
amber 12.21
ambergris 28.6
ambidexterity 4.53
ambidextrous 28.31
ambience 28.45
ambient 30.56
ambiguity 4.53
ambiguous 28.24
ambit 30.20
ambition 25.49
ambitious 28.33
ambivalence 28.45
ambivalent 30.56
amble 23.26
ambler 12.42
ambo 9.9
Ambonese 35.6
Ambrose 35.19
ambrosia 12.12
ambrosial 23.24
ambulance 28.45
ambulant 30.56
ambulate 30.11
ambulatory 4.43

ambuscade 16.6
ambush 29.15
ameba 12.21
amebic 21.9
ameboid 16.24
Amelia 12.6
ameliorate 30.15
amen 25.5
amend 16.41
amender 12.26
amenity 4.53
Amerasian 25.49
amerce 28.36
America 12.39
American 25.43
Americana 12.53
Americano 9.19
americium 24.16
Amerindian 25.37
Ameslan 25.2
amethyst 31.14
amethystine 25.23
Amex 28.38
Amharic 21.15
amiable 23.26
amice 28.8
amid 16.8
amidships 28.46
amidst 31.27
Amiens 25.24
amigo 9.13
Amin 25.9
Amirante 30.53
Amis 28.8
Amish 29.8
amiss 28.7
amity 4.53
Amman 25.4, 25.45
ammeter 12.77
ammo 9.18
Ammon 25.45
ammonia 12.8
ammonite 30.29
ammonium 24.16
amnesia 12.12
amnesiac 21.1
amnesic 21.18
amnesty 4.53
amniocentesis 28.11
amniotic 21.17
amoeba 12.21
amoebic 21.9
amoeboid 16.24
amok 21.20
among 26.18
amongst 31.31
amontillado 9.11
amoral 23.36
amoralist 31.8
amoretti 4.51

amoretto 9.24
amorist 31.12
Amorite 30.29
amoroso 9.22
amorous 28.31
amorphous 28.25
Amos 28.14
amount 30.55
amour 12.20
amour propre 12.65
Amoy 10.1
amp 27.17
amperage 20.8
ampere 2.10
ampersand 16.40
amphetamine 25.11
amphibian 25.37
amphibious 28.23
amphibology 4.17
amphipod 16.18
amphitheater 12.82
amphitheatre 12.82
amphora 12.67
amphorae 4.43
ample 23.35
amplifier 12.14
amplify 6.7
amplitude 16.25
amply 4.21
ampoule 23.20
ampule 23.20
ampulla 12.46
ampullae 4.26
amputate 30.16
amputee 4.1
Amritsar 12.70
Amsterdam 24.1
amtrac 21.3
Amtrak 21.3
Amu Darya 12.10
amulet 30.42
Amundsen 25.48
Amur 12.19
amuse 35.21
amusing 26.14
Amy 4.29
amyl 23.9
amylase 35.5
Amytal 23.1
an 25.1
ana 12.53
Anabaptist 31.14
anabases 35.8
anabasis 28.11
anabolic 21.11
anachronic 21.13
anacoluthic 21.18
anaconda 12.28
anacruses 35.8
anaemia 12.7
anaemic 21.12

anaesthesia 12.12
anaesthetic 21.17
anaesthetist 31.14
anaglyph 17.6
anaglyphic 21.10
anagram 24.1
anagrammatic 21.17
anagrammatical
　23.32
anagrammatize
　35.14
Anaheim 24.7
anal 23.34
analgesia 12.12
analgesic 21.18
analog 18.8
analogize 35.11
analogous 28.25
analogue 18.8
analogy 4.17
analysand 16.40
analyse 35.12
analyses 35.8
analysis 28.11
analyst 31.8
analyte 30.28
analytic 21.17
analytical 23.32
analyze 35.12
analyzes 35.8
anamnesis 28.11
anamorphic 21.10
anamorphoses 35.8
anamorphosis 28.11
Ananias 28.24
anapaest 31.5
anapest 31.5
anaphoric 21.15
anaphylactic 21.17
anaphylaxis 28.11
anarch 21.5
anarchic 21.11
anarchical 23.32
anarchist 31.7
anarchy 4.20
Anasazi 4.61
Anastasia 12.12
anastrophe 4.14
anathema 12.51
Anatolia 12.6
Anatolian 25.37
anatomical 23.32
anatomist 31.9
anatomize 35.13
anatomy 4.30
Anaxagoras 28.31
ancestor 12.78
ancestral 23.36
ancestress 28.10
ancestry 4.40
Anchises 35.8

anchor 12.37
anchorage 20.8
anchoress 28.10
anchorite 30.29
anchoritic 21.17
anchorman 25.2
anchormen 25.5
anchorwoman 25.45
anchorwomen 25.17
anchovy 4.58
ancient 30.56
ancillary 4.43
ancon 25.25
and 16.40
Andalusia 12.11
Andalusian 25.37
andante 4.51
Andean 25.37
Anderson 25.48
Andes 35.7
Andhra
　Pradesh 29.3
andiron 25.38
Andorra 12.66
Andorran 25.47
Andreé 3.19
Andrea 12.10
Andreas 28.22
Andrew 11.17
Andrews 35.21
androcentric 21.15
Androcles 35.7
androgen 25.42
androgyne 25.21
androgynous 28.29
androgyny 4.32
android 16.24
andrology 4.17
Andromache 4.20
Andromeda 12.27
Andy 4.12
anecdotage 20.9
anecdotal 23.39
anecdotalist 31.8
anecdote 30.35
anele 23.7
anemia 12.7
anemic 21.12
anemometer 12.78
anemone 4.34
anent 30.53
anesthesia 12.12
anesthetic 21.17
anesthetist 31.14
aneurysm 24.21
anew 11.1
anfractuosity 4.53
anfractuous 28.24
angel 23.31
Angela 12.43
angel dust 31.24

angelfish 29.7
angelic 21.11
angelica 12.39
angelical 23.32
Angelina 12.54
Angelo 9.17
Angelou 11.13
angelus 28.27
anger 12.31
Angers 3.1
Angharad 16.29
Angie 4.17
angina 12.55
Angkor 7.10
angle 23.30
Anglepoise 35.20
angler 12.42
Anglesey 4.45
Anglian 25.37
Anglican 25.43
anglice 4.46
Anglicise 35.14
Anglicize 35.14
Anglo 9.17
Anglophile 23.11
Anglophobe 14.11
Anglophone 25.30
Anglosphere 12.4
Angola 12.44
Angolan 25.44
angora 12.66
Angostura 12.67
angry 4.38
angst 31.31
angstrom 24.19
Anguilla 12.43
Anguillan 25.44
anguine 25.20
anguish 29.10
angular 12.46
angularity 4.53
Angus 28.25
anhedral 23.36
Anhui 4.59
ani 4.31
anilingus 28.25
anima 12.51
animadversion
　25.49
animadvert 30.45
animal 23.33
animalcule 23.20
animalist 31.8
animalize 35.12
animate 30.12, 30.43
animatronic 21.13
animeé 3.16
animist 31.9
animosity 4.53
animus 28.28
anion 25.38

a

anis 28.6
anise 28.9
aniseed 16.7
anisette 30.4
Anita 12.77
Anjou 11.1
Ankara 12.67
ankh 21.33
ankle 23.32
anklet 30.22
Anna 12.53
Annaba 12.21
Annabel 23.3
annal 23.34
annalist 31.8
Annapolis 28.8
Annapurna 12.59
annates 28.47
Anne 25.1
anneal 23.7
Anneka 12.39
annelid 16.10
Annette 30.4
annex 28.38
annexe 28.38
Annie 4.31
Annigoni 4.33
annihilate 30.11
anniversary 4.43
Anno Domini 6.13
annotate 30.16
announce 28.44
announcer 12.70
annoy 10.1
annoyance 28.45
annoyer 12.18
annoying 26.3
annual 23.25
annuity 4.53
annul 23.22
annular 12.46
annulet 30.22
annunciate 30.8
annus horribilis
 28.8
annus mirabilis
 28.8
anoa 12.17
anode 16.23
anodyne 25.21
anoint 30.55
anointer 12.81
anomalous 28.27
anomaly 4.27
anomie 4.30
anon 25.24
anonym 24.6
anonymity 4.53
anonymous 28.28
anorak 21.3
anorexia 12.11

anorexia nervosa
 12.71
anorexic 21.16
another 12.84
Anouilh 4.9
Anschluss 28.20
Anshan 25.3
answer 12.69
answerphone 25.30
ant 30.53
antacid 16.11
Antaeus 28.22
antagonist 31.10
Antakya 12.89
Antalya 12.6
Antarctic 21.17
Antarctica 12.39
Antares 35.7
ante 4.51
anteater 12.77
antebellum 24.18
antecedence 28.45
antecedent 30.56
antechamber 12.21
antedate 30.9
antediluvian 25.37
antelope 27.10
antenatal 23.39
antenna 12.53
antennae 4.31
antennal 23.34
antennary 4.43
antenuptial 23.38
anterior 12.10
anteroom 24.12
Anthea 12.12
antheap 27.5
anthelion 25.37
anthem 24.20
anthemion 25.37
anther 12.83
anthill 23.9
anthologize 35.11
anthology 4.17
Anthony 4.34
anthozoan 25.38
anthracite 30.30
anthracitic 21.17
anthrax 28.38
anthropogenic
 21.13
anthropoid 16.24
anthropology 4.17
anthropometric
 21.15
anthropomorphize
 35.11
anthropomorphous
 28.25
anthropophagous
 28.25

anti 4.51
Antibes 14.6
antibiotic 21.17
antic 21.17
Antichrist 31.16
anticipate 30.14
anticipatory 4.43
antifreeze 35.7
antigen 25.42
Antigone 4.34
Antigua 12.31
Antiguan 25.41
Antilles 35.7
antilogy 4.17
antimonious 28.23
antimony 4.34
antinomian 25.37
antinomy 4.30
Antioch 21.20
antipasto 9.24
antipathy 4.56
antiperspirant 30.56
antiphon 25.41
antiphony 4.34
antipodal 23.28
antipode 16.23
antipodean 25.37
antipodes 35.7
antiquarian 25.37
antiquary 4.43
antiquated 16.12
antique 21.8
antiquity 4.53
antirrhinum 24.19
antithetic 21.17
antitussive 34.7
antivenin 25.18
antler 12.42
Antofagasta 12.74
Antoine 25.4
Antoinette 30.4
Anton 25.26
Antonia 12.8
Antonine 25.23
Antonio 9.4
Antonioni 4.33
antonym 24.6
Antrim 24.6
antsy 4.45
Antwerp 27.15
Anubis 28.7
anus 28.29
Anvers 2.1
anvil 23.10
Anwyl 23.10
anxiety 4.53
anxious 28.33
any 4.31
anybody 4.13
anyhow 8.5
anymore 7.1

anyone 25.35
anyplace 28.5
anything 26.14
anytime 24.7
anyway 3.25
anyways 35.5
anywhere 2.15
anywise 35.15
Anzac 21.4
A-OK 3.1
aoristic 21.17
aorta 12.80
à outrance 28.44
apace 28.5
Apache 4.11
apart 30.3
apartheid 30.16
apathetic 21.17
apathy 4.56
ape 27.4
Apeldoorn 25.28
Apelles 35.7
apeman 25.2
Apennines 35.31
aperçu 11.1
aperiodic 21.10
aperitif 17.5
aperture 12.24
apery 4.43
apex 28.38
aphasia 12.12
aphasic 21.18
aphid 16.9
aphides 35.7
aphis 28.7
aphorize 35.13
Aphra 12.64
aphrodisiac 21.1
Aphrodisias 28.1
Aphrodite 4.54
Apia 12.3
apiarian 25.37
apiarist 31.12
apiary 4.43
apical 23.32
apices 35.8
apiculturist 31.12
apiece 28.6
apish 29.9
aplenty 4.51
aplomb 24.8
apnoea 12.8
apocalypse 28.46
apocalyptic 21.17
apocrypha 12.30
apocryphal 23.29
apodoses 35.8
apodosis 28.11
apogee 4.17
apolitical 23.32
Apollinaire 2.1

Apollinaris 28.10
Apollo 9.17
Apollonian 25.37
Apollonius 28.23
apologetic 21.17
apologia 12.6
apologist 31.7
apologue 18.8
apology 4.17
apophthegm 24.3
apoplectic 21.17
apoplexy 4.45
aposiopeses 35.8
apostasy 4.48
apostate 30.16
apostatical 23.32
apostle 23.37
apostolate 30.11
apostolic 21.11
apostrophe 4.14
apostrophize 35.11
apothecary 4.43
apothegm 24.3
apotheoses 35.8
apotheosis 28.11
apotheosize 35.14
appal 23.14
Appalachian 25.37
appall 23.14
Appaloosa 12.71
apparat 30.3
apparatchik 21.9
apparatus 28.34
apparel 23.36
apparent 30.56
appeal 23.7
appealer 12.43
appealing 26.8
appear 12.4
appearance 28.45
appease 35.6
appeaser 12.90
appellant 30.56
appellate 30.42
appellation
    contrôlée 3.1
appellee 4.1
append 16.41
appendage 20.6
appendant 30.56
appendices 35.8
appendicitis 28.12
appendix 28.39
appertain 25.7
appetence 28.45
appetite 30.30
appetizing 26.14
applaud 16.19
applause 35.17
apple 23.35
applejack 21.3

Appleton 25.50
appliance 28.45
applicant 30.56
applied 16.14
applier 12.13
appliquée 3.14
apply 6.1
appoint 30.55
appointee 4.1
appointer 12.81
apport 30.33
apportion 25.49
appose 35.19
apposite 30.25
appraisal 23.41
appraise 35.5
appraisee 4.1
appraiser 12.90
appraisive 34.8
appreciate 30.8
appreciatory 4.43
apprehend 16.41
apprehensible 23.26
apprehension 25.49
apprehensive 34.7
apprentice 28.12
apprise 35.11
apprize 35.11
approach 15.10
approbate 30.9
approbatory 4.43
appropriate 30.8,
    30.41
approval 23.40
approve 34.12
approving 26.14
approximate 30.12,
    30.43
appurtenance 28.45
appurtenant 30.56
apraxia 12.11
après-ski 4.1
apricot 30.31
April 23.9
apron 25.47
apropos 9.1
apse 28.46
apsidal 23.28
apt 30.58
aptitude 16.25
aptly 4.21
aptness 28.29
Apuleius 28.22
Apulia 12.6
Aqaba 12.22
aqua 12.88
aquaculture 12.24
aqualung 26.18
aquamarine 25.9
aquanaut 30.33
aquaplane 25.8

aquarelle 23.3
aquaria 12.10
Aquarian 25.37
aquarist 31.12
aquarium 24.16
Aquarius 28.23
Aquarobics 28.39
aquatic 21.17
aquatint 30.54
aquavit 30.25
aqua vitae 6.18
aqueduct 30.49
aqueous 28.23
aquifer 12.30
Aquila 12.43
aquiline 25.22
Aquinas 28.29
Aquitaine 25.8
aquiver 12.86
Arab 14.14
Arabella 12.42
arabesque 21.35
Arabia 12.5
Arabian 25.37
Arabic 21.9
arabis 28.7
Arabist 31.6
arable 23.26
Araby 4.10
Arachne 4.31
arachnid 16.10
arachnoid 16.24
Arafat 30.1
Aragon 25.41
Aramaic 21.9
Aran 25.47
Aranda 12.25
Arapaho 9.14
Arawak 21.4
arbiter 12.78
arbitral 23.36
arbitrary 4.43
arbitrate 30.15
arbitress 28.10
arbor 12.21
arboreal 23.24
arborescence 28.45
arboreta 12.77
arboretum 24.20
arboriculture 12.24
arboriculturist
    31.12
arbour 12.21
Arbus 28.24
Arbuthnot 30.43
arbutus 28.34
arc 21.5
arcade 16.6
Arcadia 12.5
Arcadian 25.37
arcading 26.5

Arcady 4.13
arcana 12.54
arcane 25.7
arcanum 24.19
Arc de Triomphe
    17.19
arch 15.2
archaeology 4.17
archaic 21.9
archaize 35.11
archangel 23.31
archangelic 21.11
archbishop 27.14
archbishopric 21.15
archdeacon 25.43
archdiocesan 25.48
archdiocese 28.11
archducal 23.32
archduchy 4.11
archduke 21.27
arch-enemy 4.29
archeology 4.17
archer 12.23
archery 4.43
archetypal 23.35
archetype 27.7
Archibald 16.36
Archiepiscopacy
    4.48
Archilochus 28.26
Archimedean 25.37
Archimedes 35.7
archipelago 9.13
architect 30.48
architecture 12.23
architrave 34.4
archival 23.40
archive 34.9
archivist 31.15
archlute 30.37
archon 25.25
archway 3.25
Arco 9.16
arctic 21.17
Arcturus 28.31
ardency 4.45
Ardennes 25.5
ardent 30.56
Ardnamurchan
    25.43
ardor 12.25
ardour 12.25
arduous 28.24
are 1.1
area 12.10
areal 23.24
areaway 3.25
arena 12.54
Arendt 30.56
aren't 30.53
areola 12.48

a

Areopagus 28.25
Arequipa 12.61
Ares 35.7
arete 30.4
argent 30.56
Argentina 12.54
Argentine 25.23
Argentinian 25.37
Argive 34.9
Argo 9.13
argol 23.13
argon 25.25
Argonaut 30.33
Argos 28.14
argosy 4.48
argot 9.13
argue 11.22
arguer 12.20
Argus 28.25
argute 30.37
argy-bargy 4.17
Argyle 23.11
Argyllshire 12.11
aria 12.10
Ariadne 4.31
Arian 25.37
arid 16.11
aridity 4.53
Aries 35.7
aright 30.26
arioso 9.29
Ariosto 9.25
arise 35.11
arisen 25.52
arisings 35.32
Aristarchus 28.26
Aristides 35.7
Aristippus 28.30
aristocracy 4.48
aristocrat 30.2
aristocratic 21.17
Aristophanes 35.7
Aristotelian 25.37
Aristotle 23.39
arithmetic 21.17
arithmetical 23.32
Arizona 12.56
Arizonan 25.46
ark 21.5
Arkansas 7.16
Arkwright 30.29
Arlene 25.10
Arles 23.2
Arlette 30.4
Arlington 25.50
arm 24.2
armada 12.25
armadillo 9.17
Armageddon 25.40
Armagh 1.1
Armagnac 21.4

Armalite 30.28
armamentaria 12.10
armamentarium
  24.16
Armand 16.45
Armani 4.31
armature 12.20
armband 16.40
armchair 2.4
Armenia 12.8
Armenian 25.37
armful 23.21
armhole 23.17
armiger 12.35
Arminian 25.37
armistice 28.12
armless 28.27
armlet 30.22
armlock 21.21
armoire 1.1
armor 12.50
armorer 12.67
armorial 23.24
Armorica 12.39
armory 4.43
armour 12.50
armourer 12.67
armoury 4.43
armpit 30.23
armrest 31.3
Armstrong 26.15
army 4.29
Arne 25.4
Arnhem 24.19
arnica 12.39
Arno 9.19
Arnold 16.38
aroma 12.52
aromatherapist
  31.11
aromatherapy 4.37
aromatic 21.17
aromatize 35.14
arose 35.19
around 16.43
arousal 23.41
arouse 35.18
Arp 27.2
arpeggio 9.4
arrack 21.30
arraign 25.7
Arran 25.47
arrange 20.19
arranger 12.35
arrant 30.56
Arras 28.31
array 3.1
arrear 12.4
arrest 31.3
arrester 12.76
arresting 26.13

arrhythmia 12.7
arris 28.10
arrival 23.40
arrive 34.9
arrivisme 24.21
arriviste 31.5
arrogance 28.45
arrogant 30.56
arrogate 30.9
arrondissements
  28.47
arrow 9.21
arrowhead 16.3
arrowroot 30.37
arrowy 4.7
arroyo 9.6
arse 28.2
arsehole 23.17
arsenal 23.34
arsenic 21.13
arson 25.48
arsonist 31.10
arsy-versy 4.49
art 30.3
art deco 9.16
artefact 30.48
artefactual 23.25
artel 23.3
Artemis 28.8
artemisia 12.12
arterial 23.24
artery 4.43
artful 23.21
arthritic 21.17
arthritis 28.12
arthropod 16.18
Arthur 12.83
Arthurian 25.37
artic 21.9
artichoke 21.24
article 23.32
articulacy 4.48
articulate 30.11,
  30.42
articulatory 4.43
artifact 30.48
artifactual 23.25
artifice 28.7
artificer 12.70
artificial 23.38
artillerist 31.12
artillery 4.43
artisan 25.1
artist 31.14
artiste 31.5
artistic 21.17
artistry 4.40
artless 28.27
art nouveau 9.1
Artois 1.1
artwork 21.31

arty 4.51
Aruba 12.21
arum 24.19
Arunta 12.81
arvo 9.27
Aryan 25.37
as 35.1
Asaph 17.1
asbestos 28.34
Ascalon 25.25
ascarid 16.11
ascend 16.41
ascendancy 4.48
ascendant 30.56
ascender 12.26
ascension 25.49
ascensional 23.34
ascent 30.53
ascertain 25.7
ascesis 28.11
ascetic 21.17
Ascham 24.18
ascidian 25.37
Asclepius 28.23
ascribe 14.8
ascription 25.49
asdic 21.10
aseptic 21.17
asexual 23.25
Asgard 16.2
ash 29.1
ashamed 16.39
Ashanti 4.51
ashcan 25.2
Ashcroft 30.47
Ashdown 25.29
Ashe 29.1
ashen 25.49
Asher 12.72
ashet 30.24
Ashkenazi 4.61
Ashkenazic 21.18
Ashkenazim 24.6
Ashkenazy 4.61
Ashley 4.21
ashore 7.1
ashplant 30.53
Ashqelon 25.25
ashram 24.1
ashrama 12.52
Ashton 25.50
ashtray 3.19
ashy 4.50
Asia 12.72
Asian 25.49
Asiatic 21.17
aside 16.14
Asimov 34.10
asinine 25.23
asininity 4.53
ask 21.35

b

Babi 4.10
babiche 29.5
babirusa 12.71
Babism 24.21
baboon 25.33
Babs 35.26
babu 11.4
babushka 12.41
baby 4.10
babycino 9.19
Babygro 9.21
babyhood 16.26
babyish 29.6
Babylon 25.25
Babylonia 12.8
Babylonian 25.37
babysat 30.2
babysit 30.24
babysitter 12.78
Bacall 23.14
baccalaureate 30.41
baccarat 1.16
Bacchae 4.18
bacchanal 23.1
bacchanalia 12.6
bacchanalian 25.37
bacchant 30.56
Bacchus 28.26
baccy 4.18
Bach 21.5
Bacharach 21.3
bachelor 12.48
bachelorhood 16.26
bacilli 6.11
bacilliform 24.9
bacillus 28.27
back 21.1
backache 21.7
backbeat 30.18
backbench 29.20
backbencher 12.72
backbiter 12.79
backblocks 28.40
backboard 16.20
backbone 25.30
backbreaking 26.7
backchat 30.1
backcloth 32.8
backcomb 24.11
backcountry 4.42
backcourt 30.33
backdate 30.7
backdraft 30.47
backdrop 27.8
backer 12.37
backfield 16.35
back-fill 23.8
backfire 12.13,12.14
backgammon 25.45
background 16.43
backhand 16.40

backhanded 16.9
backhander 12.25
backing 26.7
backlash 29.1
backlighting 26.13
backlist 31.8
backlit 30.20
backlog 18.8
backmarker 12.37
backmost 31.20
backpack 21.3
backpacker 12.37
backpedal 23.28
backrest 31.3
backroom 24.12
Backs 28.38
backscratching 26.4
backside 16.16
backslapping 26.10
backslash 29.1
backslid 16.8
backslide 16.14
backslider 12.27
backspace 28.5
backspin 25.18
backstage 20.4
backstairs 35.4
backstay 3.22
backstitch 15.6
backstop 27.8
backstreet 30.18
backstretch 15.3
backstroke 21.24
back talk 21.22
backtrack 21.3
backup 27.13
backveld 30.51
backward 16.30
backwards 35.27
backwash 29.11
backwater 12.80
backwoods 35.27
backwoodsman
    25.45
backwoodsmen
    25.45
backyard 16.2
bacon 25.43
Baconian 25.37
bacteria 12.10
bacterial 23.24
Bactria 12.10
Bactrian 25.37
bad 16.1
badass 28.2
baddish 29.6
baddy 4.12
Baden 25.40
Baden-Baden 25.40
Baden-Powell 23.25
Bader 12.25

badge 20.1
badger 12.35
badinage 19.1
badlands 35.27
badly 4.21
badminton 25.50
bad-mouth 32.10
badness 28.29
Baedeker 12.39
Baez 35.3
Baffin 25.14
baffle 23.29
bag 18.1
Baganda 12.25
bagatelle 23.3
Bagehot 30.42
bagel 23.30
bagful 23.21
baggage 20.6
baggy 4.15
Baghdad 16.1
bagman 25.2
bagmen 25.5
bagnio 9.28
bagpipe 27.7
bagpiper 12.62
baguette 30.4
bah 1.1
Baha'i 6.1
Bahamas 35.24
Bahamian 25.37
Bahawalpur 12.20
Bahia 12.3
Bahrain 25.7
Bahraini 4.31
baht 30.3
bail 23.5
bailee 4.1
bailer 12.43
bailey 4.22
bailie 4.22
bailiff 17.6
bailiwick 21.18
bailor 12.43
Bainbridge 20.8
bain-marie 4.1
Bairam 24.2
Baird 16.5
bairn 25.6
bait 30.7
baize 35.5
Bajan 25.42
bajillion 25.52
bajra 1.16
bake 21.7
bakehouse 28.16
Bakelite 30.28
baker 12.38
bakery 4.43
Bakewell 23.4
baklava 12.87

baksheesh 29.5
Bakst 31.28
Baku 11.12
Bakunin 25.18
balaclava 12.85
balafon 25.25
balalaika 12.40
balance 28.45
balancer 12.71
Balboa 12.17
Balcon 25.43
balcony 4.34
bald 16.36
baldachin 25.15
Balder 12.28
balderdash 29.1
baldish 29.6
Baldwin 25.20
baldy 4.13
bale 23.5
baleen 25.9
baler 12.43
Balfour 12.30
Bali 4.21
Balinese 35.6
Balkan 25.43
balky 4.19
ball 23.14
ballad 16.29
ballade 16.2
balladeer 12.4
balladry 4.43
Ballantyne 25.23
Ballarat 30.2
Ballard 16.2
ballast 31.25
ballbearing 26.11
ballboy 10.3
ballcock 21.20
ballerina 12.54
Ballesteros 28.14
ballet 3.15
balletic 21.17
balletomane 25.8
balletomania 12.8
Ballets Russes 28.19
ballgirl 23.42
ballgown 25.29
ballista 12.78
ballistae 4.53
ballock 21.30
balloon 25.33
balloonist 31.10
ballot 30.42
ballpark 21.5
ballroom 24.12
balls 35.29
ballsy 4.61
bally 4.21
ballyhoo 11.1
Ballymena 12.54

b

balm 24.2
Balmoral 23.36
balmy 4.29
baloney 4.33
balsa 12.70
balsam 24.20
balsamic 21.12
Balt 30.51
Balthazar 12.90
balti 4.54
Baltic 21.17
Baltimore 7.12
Baltistan 25.4
Baluchistan 25.4
baluster 12.82
balustrade 16.6
Balzac 21.4
Bamako 9.1
bambini 4.31
bambino 9.19
bamboo 11.1
bamboozle 23.41
bamboozler 12.48
Bamian 25.37
ban 25.1
banal 23.2
banality 4.53
banana 12.53
band 16.40
Banda 12.25
bandage 20.6
bandanna 12.53
Bandaranaike 12.39
bandbox 28.40
bandeau 9.11
bandeaux 35.19
banderole 23.18
bandicoot 30.37
bandit 30.21
banditry 4.40
banditti 4.53
bandleader 12.26
bandmaster 12.75
bandolier 12.4
bandore 7.1
bandstand 16.40
Bandung 26.17
bandwagon 25.41
bandwidth 32.15
bandy 4.12
bane 25.7
bang 26.1
Bangalore 7.1
banger 12.60
Bangkok 21.20
Bangladesh 29.3
Bangladeshi 4.50
bangle 23.30
bangtail 23.6
Bangui 4.1
banish 29.9

banister 12.78
banjax 28.38
banjo 9.15
banjoist 31.6
Banjul 23.20
bank 21.33
bank bill 23.8
banker 12.37
banknote 30.35
bankroll 23.18
bankrupt 30.58
bankruptcy 4.47
banksia 12.11
banner 12.53
banneret 30.24
bannock 21.30
Bannockburn 25.53
banns 35.31
banquet 30.25
banqueter 12.78
banquette 30.4
banshee 4.50
bantam 24.20
bantamweight
   30.17
banter 12.74
banterer 12.67
Banting 26.13
Bantu 11.20
Bantustan 25.4
banyan 25.3
banzai 6.22
baobab 14.1
bap 27.1
baptismal 23.33
Baptist 31.14
baptistery 4.43
bar 1.1
barb 14.2
Barbadian 25.37
Barbados 28.25
Barbara 12.67
barbarian 25.37
barbaric 21.15
barbarity 4.53
barbarize 35.13
Barbarossa 12.70
barbarous 28.31
Barbary 4.43
barbecue 11.22
barbel 23.26
barbell 23.3
barber 12.21
barberry 4.43
barbershop 27.8
barbet 30.20
barbette 30.4
barbican 25.43
Barbirolli 4.25
barbiturate 30.24
barbola 12.44

Barbour 12.21
Barbuda 12.29
barbwire 12.13
barcarole 23.17
Barcelona 12.56
Barclay 4.21
barcode 16.23
bard 16.2
bardic 21.10
Bardo 9.11
bardolater 12.82
bardolatry 4.43
Bardot 9.1
bare 2.1
bareback 21.2
barefaced 31.4
barefoot 30.39
barefooted 16.12
barège 19.3
bareheaded 16.9
Barents 28.47
barf 17.2
barfly 6.11
bargain 25.14
bargainer 12.55
barge 20.2
bargeboard 16.20
bargee 4.1
Bargello 9.17
bargepole 23.18
bar graph 17.2
Bari 4.38
Barisal 23.2
baritone 25.31
barium 24.16
bark 21.5
barker 12.37
barley 4.21
barleycorn 25.28
barm 24.2
barmaid 16.6
barman 25.45
Barmecide 16.16
barmen 25.45
barmy 4.29
barn 25.4
Barnabas 28.24
barnacle 23.32
Barnard 16.2
Barnardo 9.11
Barnet 30.23
Barney 4.31
Barnsley 4.21
barnstorm 24.9
barnstormer 12.52
Barnum 24.19
barnyard 16.2
barometer 12.78
baron 25.47
baronage 20.7
baronet 30.23

baronetage 20.9
baronetcy 4.46
baronial 23.24
barony 4.34
baroque 21.20
barouche 29.14
barque 21.5
barrack 21.30
barracks 28.41
barracuda 12.29
barrage 20.2
barramundi 4.13
barre 1.1
barrel 23.36
barrelhouse 28.16
barren 25.47
barrette 30.4
barricade 16.6
barrier 12.10
barrio 9.4
barrister 12.78
barrow 9.21
Barry 4.38
Barrymore 7.12
Barsac 21.4
Bart 30.3
bartender 12.26
barter 12.75
barterer 12.67
Barth 32.2
Barthes 30.3
Bartholomew 11.22
Bartóek 21.21
Barton 25.50
bartsia 12.11
Baruch 21.30
Baryshnikov 17.8
basalt 30.51
basaltic 21.17
base 28.5
baseball 23.14
baseboard 16.20
Basel 23.41
baseline 25.22
bash 29.1
Bashkir 12.4
Bashkiria 12.10
basho 9.23
basic 21.16
Basie 4.45
basil 23.41
basilica 12.39
basilican 25.43
basilisk 21.35
basin 25.48
basinet 30.4
basis 28.11
bask 21.35
basket 30.21
basketball 23.14
basketry 4.40

basketwork 21.31
Basle 23.2
Basotho 11.20
Basque 21.35
Basra 12.64
bas-relief 17.5
Bass 28.1
bass 28.5
basset 30.24
bassi 4.45
bassinet 30.4
bassi profundi 4.13
bassist 31.13
bassline 25.22
basso 9.22
bassoon 25.33
bassoonist 31.10
basswood 16.26
bast 31.1
bastard 16.29
bastardy 4.13
baste 31.4
Bastet 30.24
Bastia 12.12
Bastille 23.7
bastinado 9.11
bastion 25.37
Basutoland 16.40
bat 30.1
Bata 12.75
Batavian 25.37
batch 15.1
bate 30.7
bateau 9.24
bateaux 35.19
Bates 28.47
Bateson 25.48
bath 32.2
bathe 33.2
bather 12.84
bathetic 21.17
bathhouse 28.16
bathos 28.14
bathrobe 14.11
bathroom 24.12
Bathsheba 12.21
bathtub 14.13
Bathurst 31.26
bathypelagic 21.11
batik 21.8
Batista 12.77
batiste 31.5
Batman 25.2
batman 25.45
batmen 25.45
baton 25.50
batsman 25.45
batsmen 25.45
battalion 25.37
Battambang 26.1
battels 35.29

batten 25.50
Battenberg 18.13
batter 12.74
batterer 12.67
battery 4.43
battle 23.39
battleax 28.38
battleaxe 28.38
battlecruiser 12.92
battledore 7.5
battledress 28.3
battlefield 16.35
battlefront 30.55
battleground 16.43
battler 12.48
batty 4.51
batwing 26.14
bauble 23.26
Baudelaire 2.8
Bauhaus 28.16
baulk 21.22
bauxite 30.30
bauxitic 21.17
Bavaria 12.10
Bavarian 25.37
bawbee 4.1
bawd 16.19
bawdry 4.41
bawdy 4.13
bawl 23.14
Bax 28.38
Baxter 12.74
bay 3.1
Bayard 16.2
bayberry 4.43
Bayern 25.53
Baylis 28.8
bayonet 30.23
bayou 11.3
Bayreuth 30.36
Baz 35.1
bazaar 1.1
bazooka 12.41
be 4.1
Bea 4.1
beach 15.5
beachcomber 12.52
beachfront 30.55
beachhead 16.3
beachside 16.16
beachwear 2.15
beacon 25.43
bead 16.7
beadle 23.28
beadsman 25.45
beadsmen 25.45
beadwork 21.31
beady 4.12
beagle 23.30
beak 21.8
beaker 12.38

beaky 4.18
Beale 23.7
beam 24.5
beamer 12.51
beamy 4.29
bean 25.9
beanbag 18.1
beanery 4.43
beanfeast 31.5
beanie 4.31
beano 9.19
beanpole 23.18
beansprout 30.34
beanstalk 21.22
bear 2.1
beard 16.28
Beardsley 4.27
bearer 12.65
bear garden 25.40
bearing 26.11
bearish 29.9
bear pit 30.23
bearskin 25.15
beast 31.5
beastie 4.52
beastly 4.23
beat 30.18
beaten 25.50
beater 12.77
beatific 21.10
beatify 6.7
beating 26.13
beatitude 16.25
Beatles 35.29
beatnik 21.13
Beaton 25.50
Beatrice 28.10
Beatrix 28.39
Beatty 4.52
beau 9.1
beau geste 31.3
beau idéal 23.24
Beaujolais 3.15
Beaujolais Nouveau 9.1
Beaumarchais 3.21
beau monde 16.42
Beaumont 30.54
Beaune 25.30
beaut 30.37
beauteous 28.23
beautician 25.49
beautifier 12.14
beautify 6.7
beauty 4.54
beaux-arts 1.1
beaver 12.85
Beaverbrook 21.28
bebop 27.8
bebopper 12.62
becalm 24.2

became 24.4
becard 16.28
because 35.16
béchamel 23.3
bêche-de-mer 2.1
Bechstein 25.23
Bechuanaland 16.40
beck 21.6
Beckenbauer 12.16
Becker 12.37
Becket 30.21
Beckett 30.21
Beckham 24.18
Beckmann 25.45
beckon 25.43
Becky 4.18
becloud 16.22
become 24.14
becoming 26.9
bed 16.3
bedabble 23.26
bedad 16.1
bedaub 14.10
bedazzle 23.41
bedbug 18.12
bedchamber 12.21
bedclothes 35.19
bedder 12.26
Bede 16.7
bedeck 21.6
bedevil 23.40
bedew 11.1
bedfellow 9.17
Bedford 16.28
Bedfordshire 12.11
bedhead 16.3
bedight 30.26
bedim 24.6
bedizen 25.52
bedjacket 30.21
bedlam 24.18
bedlinen 25.18
bedmaker 12.38
bedmate 30.12
Bedouin 25.13
bedpan 25.3
bedplate 30.11
bedpost 31.20
bedridden 25.40
bedrock 21.21
bedroll 23.18
bedroom 24.12
bedside 16.16
bedsit 30.20
bedsock 21.21
bedsore 7.16
bedspread 16.4
bedstead 16.4
bedstraw 7.15
bedtime 24.7
bee 4.1

b

b

Beeb 14.6
beech 15.5
Beecham 24.17
beechnut 30.40
beechwood 16.26
beef 17.5
beefburger 12.32
beefcake 21.7
beefeater 12.77
beefsteak 21.7
beefy 4.14
beehive 34.9
beeline 25.22
Beelzebub 14.13
been 25.9
beep 27.5
beeper 12.61
beer 12.4
Beerbohm 24.11
beerhouse 28.16
beermoney 4.33
beery 4.43
beestings 35.32
beeswax 28.38
beeswing 26.14
beet 30.18
Beethoven 25.51
beetle 23.39
Beeton 25.50
beetroot 30.37
beeves 35.35
befall 23.14
befallen 25.44
befell 23.3
befit 30.20
befog 18.8
befool 23.20
before 7.1
beforehand 16.40
befoul 23.16
befriend 16.41
befuddle 23.28
beg 18.3
begad 16.1
began 25.1
beget 30.4
begetter 12.76
beggar 12.31
beggarly 4.27
beggary 4.43
begin 25.13
Begin 25.14
beginner 12.55
beginning 26.9
begone 25.24
begonia 12.8
begorra 12.65
begot 30.31
begotten 25.50
begrime 24.7
begrudge 20.16

beguile 23.11
beguiler 12.44
beguine 25.9
begum 24.18
begun 25.35
behalf 17.2
Behan 25.36
behave 34.4
behavior 12.89
behaviour 12.89
behavioural 23.36
behead 16.3
beheld 16.35
behemoth 32.13
behest 31.3
behind 16.42
behindhand 16.40
Behn 25.5
behold 16.37
beholden 25.40
beholder 12.28
behoof 17.13
behove 34.11
Behrens 28.45
Behring 26.11
Beiderbecke 21.6
beige 19.4
Beijing 26.3
being 26.3
Beira 12.65
Beirut 30.37
bejabers 35.24
Bekaa 1.1
belabor 12.21
belabour 12.21
Belarus 28.19
belated 16.12
belay 3.1, 3.15
belch 15.15
beldam 24.17
beleaguer 12.31
Belém 24.3
Belfast 31.2
belfry 4.38
Belgae 6.8
Belgian 25.42
Belgic 21.11
Belgium 24.18
Belgrade 16.6
Belial 23.24
belie 6.1
belief 17.5
believe 34.5
believer 12.85
Belinda 12.27
belittle 23.39
belittler 12.48
Belize 35.6
Belizean 25.37
bell 23.3
Bella 12.42

belladonna 12.56
bellboy 10.3
belle 23.3
belle époque 21.20
Bellerophon 25.25
belles-lettres 12.64
belletrist 31.12
bellflower 12.16
bellhop 27.8
bellicose 28.17
bellicosity 4.53
belligerence 28.45
belligerent 30.56
Bellini 4.31
bellman 25.45
bellmen 25.45
Belloc 21.21
bellow 9.17
bell push 29.15
bell-ringer 12.60
bell-ringing 26.10
belly 4.22
bellyache 21.7
bellyacher 12.38
bellyflop 27.8
Belmopan 25.1
belong 26.3
belongings 35.32
Belorussian 25.49
beloved 16.13
below 9.1
Bel Paese 4.61
Belsen 25.48
Belshazzar 12.90
belt 30.51
Beltane 25.8
belter 12.76
beluga 12.32
belvedere 12.5
belying 26.3
Bemba 12.21
bemire 12.13
bemoan 25.30
bemuse 35.21
Ben 25.5
Benares 35.10
Benbecula 12.46
bench 29.20
bencher 12.72
benchmark 21.5
bend 16.41
bender 12.26
Bendigo 9.13
bendy 4.12
beneath 32.5
benedicite 4.53
Benedict 30.49
Benedictine 25.12
benediction 25.49
benedictory 4.43
Benedictus 28.34

benefaction 25.49
benefactor 12.74
benefactress 28.10
benefice 28.7
beneficence 28.45
beneficent 30.56
beneficial 23.38
beneficiary 4.43
benefit 30.21
Benelux 28.41
benevolence 28.45
benevolent 30.56
Bengal 23.14
Bengali 4.25
Benghazi 4.61
Benguela 12.43
Ben-Gurion 25.37
benighted 16.12
benign 25.21
benignancy 4.48
benignant 30.56
benignity 4.53
Benin 25.9
Beninese 35.6
benison 25.52
Benito 9.24
Benjamin 25.17
Benn 25.5
Bennett 30.23
Benny 4.31
Benson 25.48
bent 30.53
Bentham 24.20
Benthamite 30.29
benthos 28.14
Bentley 4.22
bentonite 30.29
bentwood 16.26
benumb 24.14
Benz 35.31
Benzedrine 25.11
benzene 25.12
benzine 25.12
benzoin 25.13
benzol 23.13
Beowulf 17.18
bequeath 33.3
bequeather 12.84
bequest 31.3
berate 30.7
Berber 12.22
Berbera 12.67
berberis 28.10
berceuse 35.25
bereft 30.47
Berenice 28.6
beret 3.19
Berg 18.13
bergamot 30.31
Bergen 25.41
bergenia 12.8

Berger 12.32
Bergerac 21.3
Bergman 25.45
Bergson 25.48
beribboned 16.45
beriberi 4.38
Bering 26.11
berk 21.31
Berkeley 4.21, 4.28
berkelium 24.16
Berks 28.38
Berkshire 12.11
Berlin 25.13
Berliner 12.55
Berlioz 35.19
berm 24.22
Bermuda 12.29
Bermudan 25.40
Bermudas 35.24
Bermudian 25.37
Bernadette 30.4
Bernadotte 30.31
Bernard 16.2, 16.29
Berne 25.53
Bernese 35.6
Bernhardt 30.3
Bernice 28.9
Bernini 4.31
Bernstein 25.23
Berra 12.64
berry 4.38
berserk 21.31
Bert 30.45
berth 32.14
Bertha 12.83
Bertie 4.55
Bertolucci 4.11
Bertram 24.19
Bertrand 16.45
Berwickshire 12.11
beryl 23.9
beryllium 24.16
Berzelius 28.23
Besançon 25.26
Besant 30.56
beseech 15.5
beset 30.4
beside 16.14
besides 35.27
besiege 20.5
besieger 12.35
besmear 12.4
besmirch 15.14
besom 24.21
besotted 16.12
besought 30.33
bespangle 23.30
bespatter 12.74
bespeak 21.8
bespectacled 16.38
bespoke 21.24

bespoken 25.43
besprinkle 23.32
Bess 28.3
Bessarabian 25.37
Bessel 23.37
Bessemer 12.51
Bessie 4.45
best 31.3
bestial 23.24
bestialize 35.12
bestiary 4.43
bestir 13.1
bestow 9.1
bestowal 23.25
bestrew 11.1
bestrewn 25.33
bestridden 25.40
bestride 16.14
bestrode 16.23
bestseller 12.42
bet 30.4
beta 12.77
betake 21.7
betaken 25.43
Betamax 28.38
betel 23.39
Betelgeuse 35.25
bête noire 1.1
Beth 32.3
Bethany 4.34
bethink 21.33
Bethlehem 24.3
bethought 30.33
betide 16.14
betimes 35.30
bêtise 35.6
Betjeman 25.45
betoken 25.43
betony 4.34
betook 21.28
betray 3.1
betrayal 23.23
betrayer 12.2
betroth 33.7
betrothal 23.40
Betsy 4.45
Bette 30.4
better 12.76
Betterton 25.50
Betti 4.51
Bettina 12.54
bettor 12.76
Betty 4.51
between 25.9
betwixt 31.28
Bevan 25.51
bevel 23.40
beverage 20.8
Beveridge 20.8
Beverley 4.27
Bevin 25.19

bevvy 4.58
bevy 4.58
bewail 23.5
bewailer 12.43
beware 2.1
bewhiskered 16.28
Bewick 21.9
bewigged 16.33
bewilder 12.27
bewitch 15.6
bey 3.1
beyond 16.42
bezant 30.56
bezel 23.41
bezique 21.8
bezoar 7.21
Bhagavadgita 12.77
bhagwan 25.4
bhaji 4.17
bhakti 4.55
bhang 26.1
bhangra 12.64
Bhopal 23.2
Bhutan 25.4
Bhutanese 35.6
Bhutto 9.25
bi 6.1
Biafra 12.64
Biafran 25.47
Bianca 12.37
biannual 23.25
Biarritz 28.47
bias 28.24
biathlete 30.18
biathlon 25.44
biaxial 23.24
bib 14.7
bibelot 9.17
Bible 23.26
biblical 23.32
bibliographer 12.30
bibliographic 21.10
bibliography 4.14
bibliomancy 4.45
bibliomania 12.8
bibliomaniac 21.1
bibliophile 23.11
bibliophilic 21.11
bibliophily 4.24
bibliopole 23.18
bibulous 28.27
bicameral 23.36
bicarbonate 30.43
bice 28.13
bicentenary 4.43
bicentennial 23.24
biceps 28.46
bicker 12.39
bickerer 12.67
bicolored 16.29
bicoloured 16.29

bicycle 23.32
bicyclist 31.8
bid 16.8
bidder 12.27
biddy 4.12
bide 16.14
bidet 3.9
biennia 12.8
biennial 23.24
biennium 24.16
bier 12.4
Bierce 28.23
biff 17.6
biffin 25.14
bifocal 23.32
bifurcate 30.10
big 18.6
bigamist 31.9
bigamous 28.28
bigamy 4.30
biggish 29.7
bighead 16.3
bighorn 25.28
bight 30.26
bigmouth 32.10
bigness 28.9
bigot 30.42
bigotry 4.43
bigwig 18.6
Bihar 1.1
bijou 11.9
bijouterie 4.43
bike 21.19
biker 12.40
bikini 4.31
Biko 9.16
bilateral 23.36
Bilbao 8.1
bilberry 4.43
bilbo 9.9
Bildungsroman
25.4
bile 23.11
bilge 20.18
bilharzia 12.11
bilingual 23.40
bilious 28.23
bilk 21.32
bilker 12.39
bill 23.8
billabong 26.15
billboard 16.20
billet 30.22
billet-doux 11.1
billets-doux 35.21
billfold 16.37
billhook 21.28
Billie 4.24
Billingsgate 30.9
billion 25.52
billionaire 2.1

b

billionth 32.19
billow 9.17
billowy 4.7
billposter 12.80
billposting 26.13
billsticker 12.39
billy 4.24
billycan 25.2
billy-o 9.4
biltong 26.15
bimbo 9.9
bimillenary 4.43
bimonthly 4.26
bin 25.13
binary 4.43
bind 16.42
binder 12.27
bindery 4.43
bindi-eye 6.3
binding 26.5
bindweed 16.7
bin-end 16.41
Binet 3.17
bing 26.3
binge 20.19
bingo 9.13
binnacle 23.32
binocular 12.46
binoculars 35.24
binomial 23.24
bint 30.54
bio 9.5
biochemical 23.32
biochemist 31.9
biochemistry 4.40
biochip 27.6
biocompatible 23.26
bioconversion 25.49
biodiverse 28.36
biodiversity 4.53
bioethanol 23.13
bioethicist 31.13
bioethics 28.39
biogas 28.1
biographer 12.30
biographic 21.10
biography 4.14
biologist 31.7
biology 4.17
biomarker 12.37
biomass 28.1
biomaterial 23.24
biome 24.11
biomedicine 25.19
biomorph 17.9
biomorphic 21.10
bionic 21.13
biopic 21.14
biopsy 4.46
biorhythm 24.20
bioscope 27.10

biosecurity 4.53
biosignature 12.24
biosphere 12.5
biotin 25.19
bipartisan 25.1
bipartite 30.30
biped 16.3
bipedal 23.28
biplane 25.8
bipolar 12.44
bipolarity 4.53
birch 15.14
birchen 25.39
bird 16.31
birdbrain 25.8
birdcage 20.4
birder 12.29
birdie 4.13
birdlime 24.7
birdseed 16.7
bird's-eye 6.22
birdsong 26.15
birdwatcher 12.24
birdwatching 26.4
biretta 12.76
biriani 4.31
Birkenhead 16.3
birl 23.42
Birmingham 24.1,
  24.19
biro 9.21
birth 32.14
birthday 3.9
birthmark 21.5
birthplace 28.5
birth rate 30.15
birthright 30.29
birthstone 25.31
birthweight 30.17
Birtwistle 23.37
bis 28.7
Biscay 3.14
biscuit 30.21
biscuity 4.53
bisect 30.48
bisector 12.76
bisexual 23.25
bish 29.6
bishop 27.14
bishopric 21.15
Bislama 1.13
Bismarck 21.5
bismuth 32.13
bison 25.48
bisque 21.35
Bissau 8.1
bister 12.78
bistre 12.78
bistro 9.21
bit 30.20
bitch 15.6

bitchy 4.11
bite 30.26
biter 12.79
Bithynia 12.8
bitmap 27.1
bitten 25.50
bitter 12.78
bitterling 26.8
bittern 25.50
bittersweet 30.18,
  30.19
bitty 4.53
bitumen 25.17
bituminous 28.29
bivalence 28.45
bivalve 34.15
bivouac 21.1
bivvy 4.58
biweekly 4.23
biyearly 4.27
biz 35.10
bizarre 1.1
Bizerta 12.82
Bizet 3.27
blab 14.1
blabber 12.21
blabbermouth 32.10
black 21.1
blackamoor 7.12
blackball 23.14
blackbeetle 23.39
BlackBerry 4.38
blackberry 4.43
blackberrying 26.3
blackbird 16.31
blackboard 16.20
blackbuck 21.29
Blackburn 25.53
blackcap 27.1
blackcock 21.20
blackcurrant 30.56
blacken 25.43
Blackett 30.21
Blackfeet 30.18
blackfly 6.11
Blackfoot 30.39
Blackfriars 35.24
blackguard 16.2
blackguardly 4.21
blackhead 16.3
blacking 26.7
blackish 29.8
blackjack 21.3
blackleg 18.3
blacklist 31.8
blackmail 23.5
blackmailer 12.43
Blackmore 7.12
blackout 30.34
Blackpool 23.20
Blackshirt 30.45

blacksmith 32.6
blackspot 30.32
Blackstone 25.31
blackthorn 25.28
blacktop 27.8
Blackwood 16.26
bladder 12.25
bladderwort 30.45
bladderwrack 21.3
blade 16.6
blaeberry 4.43
blag 18.1
blagger 12.31
blah 1.1
blain 25.7
Blair 2.1
Blaise 35.5
Blake 21.7
Blakey 4.18
blame 24.4
blameworthy 4.57
blanch 29.20
Blanchard 16.29
Blanche 29.20
blancmange 20.19
blanco 9.16
bland 16.40
blandish 29.6
blank 21.33
blanket 30.21
blanket weed 16.7
blanquette 30.4
Blantyre 12.14
blare 2.1
blarney 4.31
blasé 3.27
blaspheme 24.5
blasphemer 12.51
blasphemous 28.28
blasphemy 4.30
blast 31.2
blaster 12.75
blatancy 4.45
blatant 30.56
blather 12.84
blatherskite 30.27
Blavatsky 4.18
blaze 35.5
blazer 12.90
blazon 25.52
blazonry 4.39
bleach 15.5
bleacher 12.23
bleak 21.8
blear 12.4
bleary 4.43
bleat 30.18
bleb 14.3
bled 16.3
Bleddyn 25.19
bleed 16.7

b

boisterous 28.31
Bokmål 23.15
bolas 28.27
bold 16.37
boldface 28.5
boldfaced 31.4
bole 23.17
bolero 9.21
boletus 28.34
Boleyn 25.13
bolide 16.14
bolivar 1.21
Bolívar 1.21
Bolivia 12.12
Bolivian 25.37
boliviano 9.19
boll 23.13
bollard 16.2
bollocking 26.7
bollocks 28.41
bolo 9.17
Bologna 12.89
boloney 4.33
Bolshevik 21.18
Bolshevist 31.15
bolshie 4.50
bolster 12.80
bolsterer 12.67
bolt 30.51
bolter 12.80
bolthole 23.17
Bolton 25.50
Boltzmann 25.45
bolus 28.27
Bolzano 9.19
bomb 24.8
bombard 16.2
bombarde 16.2
bombardier 12.4
bombardon 25.40
bombast 31.1
bombastic 21.17
Bombay 3.1
bombazine 25.12
bombe 24.8
bomber 12.51
bombshell 23.4
bombsight 30.30
bona fide 4.12
bona fides 35.7
Bonaire 2.1
bonanza 12.90
Bonaparte 30.3
Bonaventura 12.67
bon-bon 25.24
bonce 28.44
bond 16.42
bondage 20.6
bondager 12.35
Bondi 6.6
bondsman 25.45

bondsmen 25.45
bone 25.30
bonefish 29.7
bonehead 16.3
boneheaded 16.9
bonemeal 23.7
boner 12.56
boneshaker 12.38
bonfire 12.14
bong 26.15
bongo 9.13
Bonham 24.19
Bonhoeffer 12.30
bonhomie 4.30
bonhomous 28.28
bonier 12.8
boniest 31.6
Bonington 25.50
bonito 9.24
bonk 21.34
bonkers 35.24
Bonn 25.24
Bonnard 1.1
bonnet 30.23
Bonnie 4.32
bonny 4.32
bonsai 6.16
bons mots 9.1
bonspiel 23.7
bonus 28.29
bon vivant 25.24
bon viveur 13.1
bonxie 4.46
bony 4.33
bonze 35.31
bonzer 12.91
boo 11.1
boob 14.12
booboo 11.4
booby 4.10
boodle 23.28
boogie 4.15
boogie-woogie 4.15
boohoo 11.1
book 21.28
bookbinder 12.27
bookcase 28.5
bookend 16.41
booker 12.41
bookie 4.20
booking 26.7
bookish 29.8
bookkeeper 12.61
bookkeeping 26.10
booklet 30.22
bookmaker 12.38
bookmaking 26.7
bookman 25.45
bookmark 21.5
bookmen 25.45
bookmobile 23.7

bookplate 30.11
bookseller 12.42
bookshelf 17.18
bookshelves 35.35
bookshop 27.8
bookstall 23.15
booksy 4.47
bookwork 21.31
bookworm 24.22
Boole 23.20
Boolean 25.37
boom 24.12
boomer 12.52
boomerang 26.1
boomslang 26.1
boon 25.33
Boone 25.33
boor 12.20
boorish 29.9
boost 31.22
booster 12.81
boot 30.37
bootblack 21.3
bootboy 10.3
bootee 4.1
Boötes 35.9
booth 33.8
bootjack 21.3
bootlace 28.5
bootleg 18.3
bootlegger 12.31
bootlicker 12.39
bootstrap 27.1
booty 4.54
booze 35.21
boozer 12.92
boozy 4.62
bop 27.8
bopper 12.62
bora 12.66
Bora-Bora 12.66
boracic 21.16
borage 20.8
borate 30.15
borax 28.38
Bordeaux 9.1
bordello 9.17
border 12.28
borderer 12.67
borderland 16.40
borderline 25.22
Bordet 3.1
bordure 12.20
bore 7.1
boreal 23.24
boredom 24.17
borehole 23.17
borer 12.66
Borg 18.9
Borges 28.3
Borgia 12.6

boric 21.15
boring 26.11
Boris 28.10
Bork 21.22
Bormann 25.45
born 25.28
borne 25.28
Bornean 25.37
Borneo 9.4
Bornholm 24.11
Borobudur 12.20
Borodin 25.14
Borodino 9.19
boron 25.26
borough 12.66
Borromini 4.31
borrow 9.21
borrower 12.17
borrowing 26.3
Borsalino 9.19
borscht 30.59
Borstal 23.39
bort 30.33
borzoi 10.16
boscage 20.6
Bosch 29.11
Bose 35.19
bosh 29.11
Bosnia 12.8
Bosnian 25.37
bosom 24.21
bosomy 4.30
Bosporus 28.31
boss 28.14
bossy 4.46
Boston 25.50
Bostonian 25.37
bosun 25.48
Boswell 23.4
Bosworth 32.14
bot 30.31
botanic 21.13
botanical 23.32
botanist 31.10
botany 4.34
botch 15.7
botcher 12.24
both 32.11
Botha 12.80
Botham 24.20
bother 12.84
Bothwell 23.4
bothy 4.56
Botswana 12.53
Botswanan 25.46
Botticelli 4.22
bottle 23.39
bottleneck 21.6
bottler 12.48
bottom 24.20
bottommost 31.20

b

bottomry 4.43
Boucher 12.24
bouclé 3.15
Boudicca 12.39
boudoir 1.22
bouffant 25.25
Bougainville 23.10
bougainvillea 12.6
bough 8.1
bought 30.33
boughten 25.50
bouillabaisse 28.3
bouilli 4.60
bouillon 25.27
boulder 12.28
bouldery 4.43
boule 4.26, 23.20
boules 23.20
boulevard 16.2
boulevardier 3.1
Boulez 35.3
boulle 23.20
Boulogne 25.32
Boulting 26.13
bounce 28.44
bouncer 12.70
bouncy 4.47
bound 16.43
boundary 4.43
bounden 25.40
bounder 12.28
bounteous 28.23
bounty 4.54
bouquet 3.1
bouquet garni 4.1
Bourbon 25.38
bourdon 25.40
bourgeois 1.22, 28.18
bourgeoisie 4.1
Bourguiba 12.21
bourn 25.28
Bournemouth 32.13
bourrée 3.19
bout 30.34
boutique 21.8
bouzouki 4.20
bovid 16.13
bovine 25.23
Bovril 23.9
bovver 12.86
Bow 9.1
bow 8.1
bowel 23.25
Bowen 25.13
bower 12.16
bowerbird 16.31
Bowers 35.24
bowfin 25.14
bowl 23.17
bowler 12.44
Bowles 35.29

bowline 25.16
Bowman 25.45
bowmen 25.45
bowsaw 7.16
bowser 12.92
bowsprit 30.24
bowstring 26.11
bow-wow 8.1, 8.12
bowyer 12.89
box 28.40
boxcar 1.11
boxer 12.70
boxful 23.21
box room 24.12
boxy 4.46
boy 10.1
boyar 1.3
Boyce 28.18
boycott 30.31
Boyd 16.24
Boyer 12.18
boyfriend 16.41
boyhood 16.26
boyish 29.6
Boyle 23.19
boyo 9.6
Boz 35.16
bozo 9.29
bra 1.1
Brabant 30.53
Brabham 24.17
brace 28.5
bracelet 30.22
bracer 12.69
brachiosaurus 28.31
bracing 26.12
brack 21.1
bracken 25.43
bracket 30.21
brackish 29.8
bract 30.48
bradawl 23.14
Bradbury 4.43
Bradford 16.28
Bradley 4.21
Bradman 25.45
Bradshaw 7.17
Brady 4.12
brae 3.1
brag 18.1
Braga 12.31
Braganza 12.90
Bragg 18.1
braggadocio 9.4
braggart 30.42
bragger 12.31
Brahe 12.34
Brahma 12.50
Brahman 25.45
Brahmana 12.58
Brahmanic 21.13

Brahmanical 23.32
Brahmaputra 12.66
Brahmin 25.17
Brahms 35.30
braid 16.6
brail 23.5
Braille 23.5
brain 25.7
brainbox 28.40
brainchild 16.36
Braine 25.7
brainpower 12.16
brainstem 24.3
brainstorm 24.9
brainwash 29.11
brainwave 34.4
brainwork 21.31
brainy 4.31
braise 35.5
brake 21.7
brakesman 25.45
brakesmen 25.45
braless 28.27
Bram 24.1
Bramah 12.50
Bramante 4.51
bramble 23.26
brambling 26.8
brambly 4.21
Bramley 4.21
bran 25.1
Branagh 12.53
branch 29.20
branchlet 30.22
branch-like 21.19
branchy 4.50
brand 16.40
Brandenburg 18.13
brander 12.25
brandish 29.6
brandisher 12.72
brandling 26.8
Brando 9.11
Brandon 25.40
Brandt 30.53
brandy 4.12
Branigan 25.41
Branson 25.48
brant 30.53
Braque 21.5
brash 29.1
Brasília 12.6
brass 28.2
brassard 16.2
brasserie 4.43
Brassey 4.45
brassica 12.39
brassie 4.45
brassiere 12.12
Brasso 9.22
brassy 4.45

brat 30.1
Bratislava 12.85
bratty 4.51
bratwurst 31.26
Braun 25.28
Braunschweig 18.7
bravado 9.11
brave 34.4
bravery 4.43
bravo 9.1, 9.27
bravura 12.67
brawl 23.14
brawler 12.44
brawn 25.28
brawny 4.32
bray 3.1
brazen 25.52
brazier 12.12
Brazil 23.8
Brazilian 25.37
Brazzaville 23.10
breach 15.5
bread 16.3
breadbasket 30.21
breadboard 16.20
breadcrumb 24.14
breadfruit 30.37
breadline 25.22
breadth 32.15
breadthways 35.5
breadwinner 12.55
break 21.7
breakage 20.6
breakaway 3.25
breakbeat 30.18
breakdown 25.29
breaker 12.38
breakfast 31.25
breakfaster 12.82
breakneck 21.6
breakout 30.34
breakpoint 30.55
breakthrough 11.17
break-up 27.13
breakwater 12.80
bream 24.5
breast 31.3
breastbone 25.30
breastfed 16.3
breastfeed 16.7
breastplate 30.11
breaststroke 21.24
breastwork 21.31
breath 32.3
breathalyse 35.12
breathalyze 35.12
Breathalyzer 12.91
breathe 33.3
breather 12.84
breathtaking 26.7
breathy 4.56

Brecht 30.50
Brechtian 25.37
Breconshire 12.11
bred 16.3
Breda 12.26
breech 15.5
breeches 35.10
breed 16.7
breeder 12.26
breeks 28.38
breeze 35.6
breeze block 21.21
breezeway 3.25
breezy 4.61
Bremen 25.45
Bren 25.5
Brenda 12.26
Brendan 25.40
Breslau 8.7
Bresson 25.48
Brest 31.3
brethren 25.18
Breton 25.50
Brett 30.4
breve 34.5
brevet 30.25
breviary 4.43
brevity 4.53
brew 11.1
brewer 12.19
brewery 4.43
Brezhnev 34.3
Brian 25.38
briar 12.13
bribe 14.8
briber 12.21
bribery 4.43
bric-à-brac 21.3
Brice 28.13
brick 21.9
brickbat 30.1
brickfield 16.35
brickie 4.19
bricklayer 12.2
bricklaying 26.3
brickwork 21.31
brickyard 16.2
bridal 23.28
bride 16.14
bridegroom 24.12
bridesmaid 16.6
bridewell 23.4
bridge 20.6
bridgehead 16.3
Bridges 35.10
Bridget 30.21
Bridgetown 25.29
Bridgman 25.45
bridle 23.28
bridleway 3.25
bridoon 25.33

Brie 4.1
brief 17.5
briefcase 28.5
Briers 35.24
brig 18.6
brigade 16.6
brigadier 12.4
brigalow 9.17
brigand 16.45
brigandry 4.43
brigantine 25.12
Briggs 35.28
Brigham 24.18
bright 30.26
brighten 25.50
brightish 29.10
Brighton 25.50
Brigitte 30.21
brill 23.8
brilliance 28.45
brilliant 30.56
brilliantine 25.12
brim 24.6
brimstone 25.50
brindle 23.28
Brindley 4.24
brine 25.21
bring 26.3
bringer 12.60
brinjal 23.31
brink 21.33
briny 4.32
brio 9.3
brioche 29.11
Briony 4.34
briquette 30.4
Brisbane 25.38
brisk 21.35
brisken 25.43
brisket 30.21
brisling 26.8
bristle 23.37
bristletail 23.6
bristly 4.24
Bristol 23.39
bristols 35.29
Brit 30.20
Britain 25.50
Britannia 12.89
Britannic 21.13
British 29.10
Britisher 12.72
Briton 25.50
Britt 30.20
Brittany 4.34
Britten 25.50
brittle 23.39
Brno 9.19
bro 9.1
broach 15.10
broad 16.19

broadband 16.40
broadcast 31.2
broadcaster 12.75
broaden 25.40
broadleaf 17.5
broadleaved 16.49
broadloom 24.12
broadminded 16.9
Broadmoor 7.12
broadsheet 30.19
broadside 16.16
broadsword 16.21
Broadway 3.25
Brobdingnagian 25.37
brocade 16.6
broccoli 4.27
brochette 30.4
brochure 12.73
brock 21.20
Brocken 25.43
brocket 30.21
broderie anglaise 35.5
Brodsky 4.19
Brogan 25.41
brogue 18.10
broil 23.19
broiler 12.44
broke 21.24
broken 25.43
broker 12.40
brokerage 20.8
brolga 12.32
brolly 4.25
bromance 28.44
Bromberg 18.13
brome 24.11
bromide 16.14
bromine 25.11
bronchial 23.24
bronchiolar 12.44
bronchitis 28.12
bronco 9.16
Brontë 4.54
brontosaur 7.16
brontosaurus 28.31
Bronwen 25.51
Bronx 28.41
bronze 35.31
brooch 15.10
brood 16.25
brooder 12.29
broody 4.13
brook 21.28
Brooke 21.28
Brooking 26.7
Brooklands 35.31
brooklet 30.22
brooklime 24.7
Brooklyn 25.16

Brookner 12.56
Brooks 28.40
broom 24.12
broomrape 27.4
broomstick 21.17
Bros 28.14
brose 35.19
broth 32.8
brothel 23.40
brother 12.84
brotherhood 16.26
brotherly 4.27
brougham 24.17
brought 30.33
brouhaha 1.9
brow 8.1
browbeat 30.18
browbeaten 25.50
browbeater 12.77
brown 25.29
Browne 25.29
brownfield 16.35
brownie 4.32
Browning 26.9
brownish 29.9
Brownshirt 30.45
brownstone 25.31
browny 4.32
browse 35.18
browser 12.92
Brubeck 21.6
Bruce 28.19
Bruegel 23.30
Bruges 19.6
bruin 25.13
bruise 35.21
bruiser 12.92
bruit 30.37
Brum 24.14
brumby 4.10
brume 24.12
Brummagem 24.18
Brummell 23.33
Brummie 4.30
brumous 28.28
brunch 29.20
Brunei 6.13
Bruneian 25.38
Brunel 23.3
brunet 30.4
brunette 30.4
Brunhild 16.35
Bruno 9.19
Brunswick 21.18
brunt 30.55
bruschetta 12.76
brush 29.16
brushwood 16.26
brushwork 21.31
brushy 4.50
brusque 21.35

b

brusquerie 4.43
Brussels 35.29
brut 30.37
brutal 23.39
brutalist 31.8
brute 30.37
brutish 29.10
Brutus 28.34
Bryant 30.56
Brylcreem 24.5
Bryn 25.13
Brynmor 7.12
bryony 4.34
bryozoan 25.38
Brythonic 21.13
BSc 4.1
bub 14.13
bubble 23.26
bubblegum 24.14
bubbler 12.48
bubbly 4.27
bubonic 21.13
buccaneer 12.4
Buchan 25.43
Buchanan 25.46
Bucharest 31.3
Buchenwald 16.35
buck 21.29
buckaroo 11.1
buckbean 25.9
buckboard 16.20
bucket 30.21
buckeye 6.10
Buckinghamshire 12.11
Buckland 16.45
buckle 23.32
buckling 26.8
bucko 9.16
buckram 24.19
buckshee 4.1
buckshot 30.32
buckskin 25.15
buck teeth 32.5
buck tooth 32.12
buckwheat 30.19
bucolic 21.11
bud 16.27
Budapest 31.3
Buddha 12.29
Buddhist 31.6
buddleia 12.6
buddy 4.13
budge 20.16
budgerigar 1.8
budget 30.21
budgetary 4.43
budgie 4.17
Buenos Aires 35.7
buff 17.15
buffalo 9.17

buffer 12.30
buffet 3.10, 30.21
buffo 9.12
buffoon 25.33
buffoonery 4.43
buffoonish 29.9
bug 18.12
bugbear 2.3
bugger 12.32
buggery 4.43
buggy 4.15
bugle 23.30
bugler 12.45
bugloss 28.14
build 16.35
builder 12.27
building 26.5
built 30.51
Bujumbura 12.67
Bukhara 12.64
Bukovina 12.54
Bulawayo 9.2
bulb 14.16
bulbous 28.24
Bulgar 1.8
Bulgaria 12.10
Bulgarian 25.37
bulge 20.18
bulgy 4.17
bulimia 12.7
bulimia nervosa 12.71
bulimic 21.12
bulk 21.32
bulkhead 16.3
bulky 4.20
bull 23.21
bulla 12.46
bullae 4.26
bulldog 18.8
bulldoze 35.19
bulldozer 12.92
bullet 30.22
bulletin 25.19
bulletproof 17.13
bullfight 30.27
bullfighter 12.79
bullfighting 26.13
bullfinch 29.20
bullfrog 18.8
bullhead 16.3
bullhorn 25.28
bullion 25.37
bullish 29.8
bull-necked 30.48
bullock 21.30
bullocky 4.20
bullpen 25.5
bullring 26.11
bullshit 30.24
bullshitter 12.78

bullwhip 27.6
bully 4.26
bullyrag 18.1
bulrush 29.16
bulwark 21.30
bum 24.14
bumbag 18.1
bumble 23.26
bumblebee 4.10
bumbler 12.47
bumf 17.19
bummer 12.52
bump 27.17
bumper 12.63
bumpkin 25.15
bumptious 28.33
bumpy 4.37
bun 25.35
Bunbury 4.43
bunch 29.20
bunchy 4.50
bunco 9.16
bund 16.44
Bundesbank 21.33
Bundesrat 30.3
Bundestag 18.2
bundle 23.28
bundler 12.47
bung 26.18
bungalow 9.17
bungee 4.17
bunghole 23.17
bungle 23.30
bungler 12.47
bunion 25.52
bunk 21.34
bunker 12.41
bunkum 24.18
bunny 4.33
Bunsen 25.48
bunt 30.55
buntal 23.39
Bunter 12.81
bunting 26.13
buntline 25.22
Bunty 4.55
Buñuel 23.3
bunya 12.89
Bunyan 25.52
bunyip 27.6
buoy 10.1
buoyage 20.6
buoyancy 4.48
buoyant 30.56
Burbage 20.6
Burbank 21.33
Burberry 4.43
burble 23.26
burbler 12.48
burbot 30.41
burden 25.40

burdock 21.20
bureau 9.21
bureaucracy 4.48
bureaucrat 30.2
bureaucratic 21.17
bureaucratize 35.14
burg 18.13
Burgas 28.25
burgee 4.17
burgeon 25.42
burger 12.32
burgess 28.7
burgh 12.66
burghal 23.30
burgher 12.32
Burghley 4.28
burglar 12.49
burglary 4.43
burgle 23.30
burgoo 11.8
Burgoyne 25.32
Burgundian 25.37
burgundy 4.13
burial 23.24
burin 25.18
burka 12.41
Burke 21.31
Burkina 12.54
Burkinan 25.46
burl 23.42
burlap 27.1
burlesque 21.35
burlesquer 12.37
Burley 4.28
Burlington 25.50
burly 4.28
Burma 12.52
Burman 25.45
Burmese 35.6
burn 25.53
burner 12.59
burnet 30.23
Burnett 30.4
Burney 4.34
burnish 29.9
burnisher 12.72
burnous 28.19
burnout 30.34
Burns 35.31
Burnside 16.16
burnt 30.57
burp 27.15
burr 13.1
Burra 12.66
burrito 9.24
burro 9.21
Burroughs 35.19
burrow 9.21
burrower 12.17
bursar 12.71
bursarial 23.24

calamitous 28.34
calamity 4.53
calamus 28.28
calash 29.1
calcareous 28.23
calces 35.8
calcify 6.7
calcite 30.30
calcitic 21.17
calcium 24.16
calculate 30.11
calculus 28.27
Calcutta 12.81
caldaria 12.10
caldarium 24.16
Caldecott 30.31
Calder 12.28
Caldwell 23.4
Caleb 14.3
Caledonian 25.37
calendar 12.27
calendarize 35.13
calender 12.27
calendric 21.15
calendrical 23.32
calends 35.27
calendula 12.46
calf 17.2
calf-like 21.19
calfskin 25.15
Calgary 4.43
Cali 4.21
caliber 12.21
calibrate 30.15
calibre 12.21
caliche 4.11
calico 9.16
Calicut 30.42
calif 17.6
California 12.8
Californian 25.37
Caligula 12.46
caliper 12.62
caliph 17.6
caliphate 30.9
calisthenic 21.13
calk 21.22
calker 12.40
call 23.14
call-in 25.16
calla 12.42
Callaghan 25.1
Callas 28.27
callback 21.2
caller 12.44
call girl 23.42
calligrapher 12.30
calligraphic 21.10
calligraphist 31.7
calligraphy 4.14
Callimachus 28.26

calling 26.8
calliope 4.37
callipygian 25.37
callipygous 28.23
callisthenic 21.13
Callisto 9.24
callop 27.14
callous 28.27
callow 9.17
callus 28.27
calm 24.2
calorie 4.43
calorific 21.10
calque 21.32
caltrop 27.14
Calum 24.18
calumet 30.4
calumniate 30.8
calumnious 28.23
calumny 4.34
Calvados 28.14
calve 34.2
calves 35.35
Calvin 25.19
Calvinist 31.10
calx 28.41
calypso 9.22
calyx 28.39
calzone 4.33
cam 24.1
camaraderie 4.43
Camargue 18.2
camber 12.21
Cambodia 12.5
Cambodian 25.37
Cambrian 25.37
cambric 21.15
Cambridge 20.8
Cambridgeshire 12.11
Cambyses 35.8
camcorder 12.28
came 24.4
camel 23.33
camelback 21.2
cameleer 12.4
camelhair 2.6
camellia 12.6
Camelot 30.31
Camembert 2.3
cameo 9.4
camera 12.67
cameraman 25.2
cameraman 25.45
cameramen 25.5
camera obscura 12.67
cameramen 25.45
camerawork 21.31
Cameron 25.47
Cameroon 25.33

Cameroonian 25.37
camiknickers 35.24
Camilla 12.43
Camille 23.8
camisole 23.18
Camorra 12.66
camouflage 20.2
camp 27.17
campaign 25.7
campaigner 12.54
Campania 12.8
campanile 4.23
campanology 4.17
Campari 4.38
Campbell 23.26
Campeche 4.11
camper 12.61
campfire 12.14
campground 16.43
camphor 12.30
camphoric 21.15
camping 26.10
Campion 25.37
campsite 30.30
campus 28.30
campy 4.36
camshaft 30.47
Camus 11.14
can 25.1
Cana 12.54
Canaan 25.46
Canaanite 30.29
Canada 12.29
Canadian 25.37
canaille 5.1
canal 23.1
Canaletto 9.24
canape 3.18
canard 16.2
Canaries 35.10
canary 4.39
canasta 12.74
Canberra 12.67
cancan 25.2
cancel 23.37
canceller 12.43
cancer 12.69
Cancerian 25.37
cancerous 28.31
CancUn 25.33
candela 12.43
candelabra 12.64
candelabrum 24.19
Candice 28.7
candid 16.9
Candida 12.27
candidacy 4.48
candidate 30.9
candidature 12.24
candied 16.9
candle 23.28

candlelight 30.28
candlelit 30.22
Candlemas 28.1
candlestick 21.17
candlewick 21.18
candor 12.25
candour 12.25
candy 4.12
candyfloss 28.14
cane 25.7
canebrake 21.7
caner 12.54
canine 25.23
caning 26.9
canister 12.78
canker 12.37
cankerous 28.31
canna 12.53
cannabis 28.7
cannelloni 4.33
canner 12.53
cannery 4.43
Cannes 25.1
cannibal 23.26
Canning 26.9
cannon 25.46
cannonade 16.6
cannonball 23.14
cannot 30.32
canny 4.31
canoe 11.1
canoeist 31.6
canola 12.44
canon 25.46
canon 25.52
canonic 21.13
canonical 23.32
canonist 31.10
canonry 4.43
canoodle 23.28
canopied 16.10
Canopus 28.30
canopy 4.37
canorous 28.31
Canova 12.86
can't 30.53
cant 30.53
cantabile 3.15
Cantabria 12.10
Cantabrian 25.37
Cantabrigian 25.37
cantal 23.2
cantaloupe 27.11
cantankerous 28.31
cantata 12.75
canteen 25.9
canter 12.74
Canterbury 4.43
cantharides 35.7
canticle 23.32
cantilena 12.54

cantilever 12.85
cantillate 30.11
cantina 12.54
cantle 23.39
canto 9.24
Canton 25.24, 25.50
canton 25.26
cantonal 23.34
Cantonese 35.6
cantor 7.18
cantoris 28.10
cantrail 23.6
cantrip 27.6
Canuck 21.29
Canute 30.37
canvas 28.35
canvass 28.35
canvasser 12.71
canyon 25.52
canzone 4.33
caoutchouc 21.28
cap 27.1
capable 23.26
capacious 28.33
capacitance 28.45
capacitate 30.16
capacitor 12.78
capacity 4.53
caparison 25.48
cape 27.4
capelin 25.16
Capella 12.42
capellini 4.31
caper 12.61
capercaillie 4.22
caperer 12.67
Capetian 25.49
capful 23.21
capillary 4.43
capital 23.39
capitalist 31.8
capitol 23.13
capitulary 4.43
capitulate 30.11
Caplet 30.22
cap'n 25.46
capo 9.20
capoeira 12.65
capon 25.46
Capone 25.30
capot 30.31
capote 30.35
Capote 4.54
cappuccino 9.19
Capra 12.64
Capri 4.1
capriccio 9.4
capriccioso 9.22
caprice 28.6
capricious 28.33
Capricorn 25.28

Capricornian 25.37
capriole 23.17
Capsian 25.37
capsicum 24.18
capsize 35.11
capstan 25.50
capstone 25.31
capsular 12.46
capsule 23.20
capsulize 35.12
captain 25.19
captaincy 4.46
caption 25.49
captious 28.33
captivate 30.16
captive 34.8
captor 12.74
capture 12.23
capturer 12.67
Capuchin 25.19
car 1.1
car crash 29.1
carabid 16.8
carabinieri 4.39
caracal 23.1
Caracalla 12.42
Caracas 28.26
caracole 23.17
Caradoc 21.30
carafe 17.1
caragana 12.53
Carajás 28.25
caramba 12.21
carambola 12.44
caramel 23.3
carangid 16.10
carapace 28.5
carat 30.43
Caratacus 28.26
Caravaggio 9.4
caravan 25.3
caravanette 30.4
caravanner 12.53
caravanserai 6.15
caravel 23.4
caraway 3.25
carb 14.2
carbide 16.14
carbine 25.21
carbohydrate 30.15
carbolic 21.11
carbon 25.38
carbon-neutral 23.36
carbonaceous 28.33
carbonado 9.11
carbonara 12.64
carbonate 30.13
carbonic 21.13
carboniferous 28.31
Carborundum 24.17

carbuncle 23.32
carbuncular 12.46
carburetor 12.76
carburettor 12.76
carcajou 11.11
carcass 28.26
Carcassonne 25.24
Carchemish 29.8
carcinogen 25.42
carcinogenic 21.13
carcinoma 12.52
card 16.2
cardamom 24.19
cardboard 16.20
carder 12.25
cardholder 12.28
cardiac 21.1
Cardiff 17.6
cardigan 25.41
Cardin 25.1
cardinal 23.34
cardinalate 30.42
cardio 9.4
cardiogram 24.1
cardiograph 17.2
cardiography 4.14
cardiology 4.17
cardiovascular 12.46
cardoon 25.33
cardsharp 27.2
cardy 4.12
care 2.1
careen 25.9
career 12.4
careerist 31.12
carefree 4.39
carer 12.65
caress 28.3
caret 30.24
caretaker 12.38
careworn 25.28
Carey 4.39
carfare 2.5
carful 23.21
cargo 9.13
carhop 27.8
Carian 25.37
Carib 14.7
Caribbean 25.36
caribou 11.4
caricature 12.20
caricaturist 31.12
caries 35.7
carillon 25.52
caring 26.11
Carinthia 12.12
carioca 12.40
cariogenic 21.13
Carl 23.2
Carla 12.42

Carlin 25.16
carline 25.22
Carlisle 23.11
Carlo 9.17
carload 16.23
Carlton 25.50
Carly 4.21
Carlyle 23.11
Carman 25.45
Carmarthen 25.51
Carmel 23.33
Carmelite 30.28
Carmen 25.45
Carmichael 23.32
carmine 25.22
carnage 20.7
carnal 23.34
carnauba 12.21
Carné 3.1
Carnegie 4.15
carnelian 25.37
carnet 3.17
Carney 4.31
carnival 23.40
carnivore 7.20
carnivorous 28.31
Carnot 9.19
carob 14.14
carol 23.36
Carole 23.36
Carolean 25.36
caroler 12.48
Caroline 25.22
Carolingian 25.37
caroller 12.48
Carolyn 25.16
carom 24.19
carotene 25.12
Carothers 35.24
carotid 16.12
carousal 23.41
carouse 35.18
carousel 23.3
carouser 12.92
carp 27.2
Carpaccio 9.4
carpal 23.35
car park 21.5
carpe diem 24.3
carpel 23.35
carpenter 12.78
carpentry 4.40
carper 12.61
carpet 30.23
carpet bag 18.1
carpetbagger 12.31
carpeting 26.13
carport 30.33
Carr 1.1
carrack 21.30
carrageen 25.10

C

causeway 3.25
causey 4.61
caustic 21.17
caution 25.49
cautionary 4.43
cautious 28.33
Cavafy 4.14
cavalcade 16.6
cavalier 12.4
cavalry 4.38
cavalryman 25.45
cavalrymen 25.45
Cavan 25.51
Cave 34.4
caveat 30.1
caveat emptor 7.18
Cavell 23.40
caveman 25.2
cavemen 25.5
Cavendish 29.6
caver 12.85
cavern 25.51
cavernous 28.29
caviar 1.2
cavil 23.40
caviler 12.48
caviller 12.48
cavity 4.53
cavort 30.33
Cavour 12.20
cavy 4.58
caw 7.1
Cawley 4.25
Caxton 25.50
cayenne 25.5
Cayley 4.22
cayuse 28.19
cc 4.1
CD-ROM 24.8
cease 28.6
ceasefire 12.14
Cecil 23.9
cedar 12.26
cedarn 25.40
cede 16.7
cedilla 12.43
Cedric 21.15
Ceefax 28.38
ceilidh 4.22
ceiling 26.8
Ceinwen 25.5
celadon 25.40
celandine 25.21
celeb 14.3
Celebes 35.10
celebrant 30.56
celebrate 30.15
celebratory 4.43
celebrity 4.53
celeriac 21.1
celerity 4.53

celery 4.43
celeste 31.3
celestial 23.24
Celia 12.6
celibacy 4.48
celibate 30.41
cell 23.3
cellar 12.42
cellarage 20.8
cellarer 12.67
cellaret 30.24
cellarette 30.24
cellarman 25.45
cellarmen 25.45
Cellini 4.31
cellist 31.8
cello 9.17
Cellophane 25.7
cellphone 25.30
cellular 12.46
cellulite 30.28
cellulitis 28.12
celluloid 16.24
cellulose 28.17
Celsius 28.23
Celt 30.51
Celtic 21.17
cement 30.53
cementer 12.76
cemetery 4.43
cenacle 23.32
cenotaph 17.2
cense 28.44
censer 12.69
censor 12.69
censorial 23.24
censorious 28.23
censure 12.72
census 28.32
cent 30.53
centaur 7.18
centaury 4.41
centavo 9.27
centenarian 25.37
centenary 4.43
centennial 23.24
center 12.76
centerboard 16.20
centerfold 16.37
centermost 31.20
centerpiece 28.6
centigrade 16.6
centigram 24.1
centiliter 12.77
centilitre 12.77
centime 24.5
centimeter 12.77
centimetre 12.77
centimo 9.18
centipede 16.7
cento 9.24

central 23.36
centralist 31.8
centre 12.76
centreboard 16.20
centrefold 16.37
centremost 31.20
centrepiece 28.6
centric 21.15
centrifuge 20.15
centrist 31.12
centurion 25.37
century 4.41
cep 27.3
cephalic 21.11
Cephalonia 12.8
cephalopod 16.18
Cepheus 28.23
ceramic 21.12
ceramicist 31.13
Cerberus 28.31
cereal 23.24
cerebellum 24.18
cerebral 23.36
cerebrum 24.19
Ceredigion 25.24
ceremonial 23.24
ceremonialist 31.8
ceremonious 28.23
ceremony 4.34
Ceres 35.7
ceresin 25.19
Ceri 4.38
cerise 35.6
cerium 24.16
cermet 30.4
cert 30.45
certain 25.19
certainty 4.53
certificate 30.10, 30.42
certify 6.7
certiorari 6.15
certitude 16.25
cerulean 25.37
Cervantes 35.9
cervelat 30.1
cervical 23.32
cervices 35.8
cervine 25.23
cervix 28.39
Cèsar 1.24
Cesarean 25.37
cesium 24.16
cess 28.3
cession 25.49
cesspit 30.23
cesspool 23.20
cestode 16.23
cetacean 25.49
ceteris paribus 28.24

Cetshwayo 9.5
Cetus 28.34
Cèvennes 25.5
Ceylon 25.24
Cèzanne 25.1
Chablis 4.21
Chabrol 23.13
cha-cha 1.5
chaconne 25.24
Chad 16.1
Chadian 25.37
Chadic 21.10
chador 7.5
Chadwick 21.18
chafe 17.4
chafer 12.30
chaff 17.2
chaffer 12.30
chaffinch 29.20
Chagall 23.1
chagrin 25.18
Chaim 24.7
chain 25.7
chaingang 26.1
chain mail 23.5
chainsaw 7.16
chair 2.1
chairlift 30.47
chairman 25.45
chairmen 25.45
chairperson 25.48
chairwoman 25.45
chairwomen 25.17
chaise 35.5
chaise longue 26.15
chakra 12.66
Chalcedon 25.25
Chalcedonian 25.37
chalcedonic 21.13
chalcedony 4.34
Chalcis 28.11
Chaldea 12.3
Chaldean 25.36
Chaldee 4.12
chalet 3.15
chalice 28.8
chalk 21.22
chalkboard 16.20
chalky 4.19
challah 12.42
challan 25.44
challenge 20.19
challenger 12.35
challis 28.8
cham 24.1
chamber 12.21
chamberlain 25.16
chambermaid 16.6
Chambers 35.24
Chambertin 25.3
chambray 3.19

chambré 3.19
chameleon 25.37
chamfer 12.30
chamois 1.22, 4.29
chamomile 23.11
Chamonix 4.34
champ 27.17
champagne 25.7
champaign 25.7
champers 35.24
champion 25.37
Champlain 25.7
champlevé 3.24
Champs-Élysées
  3.27
chance 28.44
chancel 23.37
chancellery 4.43
chancellor 12.48
chancer 12.69
chancery 4.43
chancy 4.45
chandelier 12.4
Chandigarh 13.1
chandler 12.42
chandlery 4.43
Chandrasekhar
  12.38
Chanel 23.3
Chaney 4.31
Changchun 25.33
change 20.19
changeling 26.8
changeover 12.86
changer 12.35
Changsha 1.1
channel 23.34
channelize 35.12
chanson 25.26
chant 30.53
Chantal 23.1
chanter 12.75
chanterelle 23.3
chanteuse 35.25
chanticleer 12.6
chantry 4.38
chanty 4.51
chaos 28.14
chaotic 21.17
chap 27.1
chaparral 23.1
chapatti 4.51
chapbook 21.28
chape 27.4
chapel 23.35
chapelry 4.38
chaperone 25.30
chapfallen 25.44
chaplain 25.16
chaplaincy 4.46
chaplet 30.22

Chaplin 25.16
chapman 25.45
chapmen 25.45
chappal 23.35
Chappell 23.35
chapter 12.74
char 1.1
charabanc 26.1
characin 25.19
character 12.78
charade 16.2
charango 9.13
charas 28.31
charbroil 23.19
charcoal 23.17
charcuterie 4.43
chard 16.2
Chardonnay 3.17
charette 30.4
charge 20.2
chargé d'affaires
  2.1
chargehand 16.40
charger 12.35
chargeés d'affaires
  35.4
chariot 30.41
charioteer 12.4
charisma 12.51
charismatic 21.17
charity 4.53
charivari 4.38
charlady 4.12
charlatan 25.50
charlatanry 4.43
Charlemagne 25.8
Charlene 25.10
Charles 35.29
Charleston 25.50
Charlie 4.21
charlock 21.30
charlotte 30.42
charlotte russe
  28.19
Charlottetown
  25.29
Charlton 25.50
charm 24.2
Charmaine 25.7
charmer 12.50
charmeuse 35.25
charming 26.9
Charolais 3.15
Charon 25.47
charpoy 10.10
charr 1.1
chart 30.3
charter 12.75
charterer 12.67
Chartist 31.14
Chartres 12.64

chartreuse 35.25
charwoman 25.45
charwomen 25.17
chary 4.39
Charybdis 28.7
chase 28.5
chaser 12.69
chasm 24.21
chasmic 21.12
chassé 3.1
chasse 28.1
chassis 4.45
chaste 31.4
chasten 25.48
chastener 12.58
chastise 35.11
chastiser 12.91
chastity 4.53
chasuble 23.26
chat 30.1
chateau 9.24
chateaubriand
  25.24
châtelaine 25.8
chatline 25.22
chat show 9.23
chattel 23.39
chatter 12.74
chatterbox 28.40
chatterer 12.67
Chatterton 25.50
chattery 4.43
chatty 4.51
Chaucer 12.70
Chaucerian 25.37
chauffeur 12.30
chauffeuse 35.25
chaulmoogra 12.66
chausses 28.17
chauvinist 31.10
cheap 27.5
cheapen 25.46
cheapish 29.9
cheapjack 21.3
cheapo 9.20
cheapskate 30.10
cheat 30.18
cheater 12.77
Chechen 25.5
Chechnya 1.23
check 21.6
checker 12.37
checkerberry 4.38
checkerboard 16.20
checklist 31.8
checkmark 21.5
checkmate 30.12
checkout 30.34
checkpoint 30.55
checkrein 25.8
check-up 27.13

check valve 34.15
cheddar 12.26
cheek 21.8
cheekbone 25.30
cheeky 4.18
cheep 27.5
cheer 12.4
cheerio 9.1
cheerleader 12.26
cheers 35.24
cheery 4.43
cheese 35.6
cheeseboard 16.20
cheeseburger 12.32
cheesecake 21.7
cheesecloth 32.8
cheeseparing 26.11
cheesewood 16.26
cheesy 4.61
cheetah 12.77
chef 17.3
chef-d'œuvre 12.68
Cheka 12.37
Chekhov 17.8
Chekhovian 25.37
chelate 30.11
Chellean 25.37
Chelmsford 16.28
Chelsea 4.45
Cheltenham 24.19
Chelyabinsk 21.35
chemical 23.32
chemin de fer 2.1
chemise 35.6
chemist 31.9
chemistry 4.40
Chemnitz 28.47
chemotherapy 4.37
chenille 23.7
cheongsam 24.1
Cheops 28.46
cheque 21.6
chequebook 21.28
chequer 12.37
chequerboard 16.20
Chequers 35.24
Cher 2.1
Cherbourg 18.9
Cherenkov 17.8
cherish 29.9
chermoula 12.45
Chernobyl 23.26
Cherokee 4.20
cheroot 30.37
cherry 4.38
chert 30.45
cherub 14.14
cherubic 21.9
cherubim 24.6
Cherubini 4.31
chervil 23.10

Cherwell 23.4
Cheryl 23.9
Cheshire 12.11
chess 28.3
chessboard 16.20
chessman 25.2
chessmen 25.5
chest 31.3
Chester 12.76
chesterfield 16.35
Chesterton 25.50
chestnut 30.40
chesty 4.51
Chetnik 21.13
Chevalier 3.3
chevalier 12.4
chevet 3.1
Cheviot 30.41
chèvre 12.64
chevron 25.47
chevrotain 25.8
Chevy 4.58
chew 11.1
chewer 12.19
chewy 4.8
Cheyenne 25.1
chez 3.1
chi 6.1
Chiang Kai-shek 21.6
Chiangmai 6.1
Chianti 4.51
Chiapas 28.30
chiaroscuro 9.21
chiasmus 28.28
Chibcha 12.23
Chibchan 25.39
chibouk 21.27
chic 21.8
Chicago 9.13
Chicagoan 25.38
chicane 25.7
chicanery 4.43
chicano 9.19
Chichester 12.78
Chichewa 12.88
chichi 4.50
Chichimec 21.6
chick 21.9
chickadee 4.13
chickaree 4.43
Chickasaw 7.16
chicken 25.15
chickenfeed 16.7
chickenpox 28.40
chickpea 4.36
chickweed 16.7
chicle 23.32
chicory 4.43
chide 16.14
chider 12.27

chief 17.5
chiefdom 24.17
chieftain 25.50
chieftaincy 4.48
chiffchaff 17.1
chiffon 25.25
chiffonier 12.4
chigger 12.31
chignon 25.27
Chihuahua 12.88
chilblain 25.8
child 16.36
childbearing 26.11
childbed 16.3
childbirth 32.14
childcare 2.7
Childe 16.36
Childermas 28.1
Childers 35.24
childhood 16.26
childish 29.6
childlike 21.19
childminder 12.27
childproof 17.13
children 25.47
Chile 4.24
Chilean 25.37
chili 4.24
chiliad 16.1
chill 23.8
chiller 12.43
chilli 4.24
chillum 24.18
chilly 4.24
Chimborazo 9.29
chime 24.7
chimera 12.67
chimeric 21.15
chimerical 23.32
chimney 4.32
chimney breast 31.3
chimney piece 28.6
chimney pot 30.32
chimney stack 21.4
chimney sweep 27.5
chimp 27.17
chimpanzee 4.1
chin 25.13
china 12.55
Chinaman 25.45
Chinamen 25.45
Chinatown 25.29
chinchilla 12.43
chin-chin 25.13
Chindit 30.21
Chindwin 25.20
chine 25.21
chiné 3.1
Chinese 35.6
chink 21.33
Chinky 4.19

chino 9.19
chinoiserie 4.43
Chinook 21.28
chinstrap 27.1
chintz 28.44
chintzy 4.46
chinwag 18.1
Chios 28.14
chip 27.6
chipboard 16.20
chipmunk 21.34
chipolata 12.75
Chippendale 23.5
chipper 12.62
Chippewa 1.22
chipping 26.10
chippy 4.36
Chips 28.46
chirography 4.14
chiromancy 4.45
Chiron 25.47
chiropodist 31.6
chiropody 4.13
chiropractic 21.17
chiropractor 12.74
chirp 27.15
chirper 12.63
chirpy 4.37
chirrup 27.13
chirrupy 4.37
chisel 23.41
chiseler 12.48
chiseller 12.48
chit 30.20
chital 23.39
chitchat 30.1
chitin 25.19
chiton 25.26
Chittagong 26.15
chitterling 26.8
chitty 4.53
chivalric 21.15
chivalrous 28.31
chivalry 4.40
chive 34.9
chivvy 4.58
chloride 16.15
chlorinate 30.13
chlorine 25.11
chlorite 30.29
chlorofluorocarbon 25.38
chloroform 24.9
chlorophyll 23.8
chloroplast 31.1
chlorosis 28.11
choccy 4.19
choc ice 28.13
chock 21.20
chock-a-block 21.20
chocker 12.40

chocoholic 21.11
chocolate 30.42
chocolatey 4.55
Choctaw 7.18
choice 28.18
choir 12.13
choirboy 10.3
choirgirl 23.42
choke 21.24
chokeberry 4.43
chokecherry 4.38
choker 12.40
chokey 4.20
choler 12.44
cholera 12.67
choleraic 21.9
choleric 21.15
cholesterol 23.13
chomp 27.17
Chomskian 25.37
Chomsky 4.19
chook 21.28
choose 35.21
chooser 12.92
choosy 4.62
chop 27.8
chophouse 28.16
Chopin 25.3
chopper 12.62
choppy 4.36
chopstick 21.17
chop suey 4.8
choral 23.36
chorale 23.2
chord 16.19
chordal 23.28
chordate 30.9
chore 7.1
choreograph 17.2
choreographer 12.30
choreographic 21.10
choreography 4.14
choriambic 21.9
choriambus 28.24
choric 21.15
chorine 25.11
chorister 12.78
chorten 25.50
chortle 23.39
chorus 28.31
chose 35.19
chosen 25.52
chough 17.15
chow 8.1
chowder 12.28
chowkidar 1.6
chow mein 25.7
Chris 28.7
chrism 24.21
chrisom 24.21

Chrissie 4.46
Christ 31.16
Christabel 23.3
Christadelphian 25.37
Christchurch 15.14
christen 25.48
Christendom 24.17
christener 12.58
christening 26.9
Christian 25.39
Christiana 12.53
Christianity 4.53
Christie 4.53
Christina 12.54
Christine 25.12
Christingle 23.30
Christlike 21.19
Christly 4.25
Christmas 28.28
Christmassy 4.48
Christopher 12.30
chroma 12.52
chromatic 21.17
chromatography 4.14
chrome 24.11
chromite 30.29
chromium 24.16
chromo 9.18
chromosomal 23.33
chronic 21.13
chronicle 23.32
chronicler 12.48
chronograph 17.2
chronology 4.17
chrysalid 16.10
chrysalis 28.8
chrysanthemum 24.19
chrysoberyl 23.9
chrysolite 30.28
chrysoprase 35.5
Chrystal 23.39
chub 14.13
Chubb 14.13
chubby 4.10
chuck 21.29
chuckhole 23.17
chuckle 23.32
chucklehead 16.3
chuckler 12.48
chuff 17.15
chug 18.12
chukar 1.11
chukka 12.41
chukker 12.41
chum 24.14
chummy 4.30
chump 27.17
chunder 12.29

Chungking 26.3
chunk 21.34
chunky 4.20
Chunnel 23.34
chunter 12.81
church 15.14
churchgoer 12.17
churchgoing 26.3
Churchill 23.8
Churchillian 25.37
churchman 25.45
churchmen 25.45
churchwarden 25.40
churchwoman 25.45
churchwomen 25.17
churchy 4.11
churchyard 16.2
churinga 12.31
churl 23.42
churlish 29.8
churn 25.53
churrasco 9.16
chute 30.37
chutist 31.14
chutney 4.33
chutzpah 12.63
chypre 12.65
ciabatta 12.75
ciao 8.1
ciboria 12.10
ciborium 24.16
cicada 12.25
cicatrices 35.8
cicatrix 28.39
cicatrize 35.13
cicely 4.24
Cicero 9.21
cicerone 4.33
Ciceronian 25.37
cider 12.27
ci-devant 25.24
cigar 1.1
cigaret 30.4
cigarette 30.4
cigarillo 9.17
ciggy 4.15
cilantro 9.21
cilia 12.6
ciliary 4.43
ciliate 30.8
ciliated 16.12
cilice 28.8
Cilician 25.37
cilium 24.16
cimbalom 24.18
Cimmerian 25.37
cinch 29.20
Cincinnati 4.51
cincture 12.23
cinder 12.27

Cinderella 12.42
cindery 4.43
Cindy 4.12
cine 4.32
cineaste 31.1
cinema 12.51
CinemaScope 27.10
cinematic 21.17
cinematograph 17.2
cinematographer 12.30
cinematographic 21.10
cinematography 4.14
cinéma-verite 3.22
cinephile 23.11
cineraria 12.10
cinerarium 24.16
cinereous 28.23
Cingalese 35.6
cinnamon 25.45
cinquain 25.7
cinque 21.33
cinquecento 9.24
cinquefoil 23.19
Cinque Ports 28.47
cipher 12.30
cipolin 25.16
circa 12.41
circadian 25.37
Circassian 25.37
Circe 4.49
circle 23.32
circlet 30.22
circs 28.41
circuit 30.21
circuitous 28.34
circuitry 4.40
circular 12.46
circularity 4.53
circularize 35.13
circulate 30.11
circulatory 4.43
circumambient 30.56
circumambulate 30.11
circumambulatory 4.43
circumcise 15.14
circumcision 25.42
circumference 28.45
circumflex 28.38
circumfluent 30.56
circumfuse 35.21
circumlocution 25.49
circumlocutory 4.43

circumnavigate 30.9
circumpolar 12.44
circumscribe 14.8
circumscription 25.49
circumspect 30.48
circumspection 25.49
circumstance 28.45
circumstantial 23.38
circumvallate 30.11
circumvent 30.53
circumvention 25.49
circumvolution 25.49
circus 28.26
Cirencester 12.76
cirque 21.31
cirrhosis 28.11
cirriped 16.3
cirrocumulus 28.27
cirrostratus 28.34
cirrus 28.31
cisalpine 25.23
cisco 9.16
Ciskei 6.1
cispontine 25.23
Cissy 4.46
cist 31.6
Cistercian 25.49
cistern 25.50
cistus 28.34
citadel 23.28
citation 25.49
cite 30.26
citizen 25.52
citizenry 4.43
citole 23.18
citric 21.15
citrine 25.11
citron 25.47
citronella 12.42
citrous 28.31
citrus 28.31
cittern 25.53
city 4.53
cityscape 27.4
cityward 16.30
civet 30.25
civic 21.18
civil 23.40
civilian 25.37
civilianize 35.13
civility 4.53
civilizer 12.91
civvies 35.10
civvy 4.58
clack 21.1

clacker 12.37
clad 16.1
claim 24.4
claimant 30.56
claimer 12.50
Clair 2.1
Claire 2.1
clairvoyance 28.45
clairvoyant 30.56
clam 24.1
clamant 30.56
clambake 21.7
clamber 12.21
clammy 4.29
clamor 12.50
clamorous 28.31
clamour 12.50
clamp 27.17
clampdown 25.29
clamshell 23.4
clan 25.1
Clancy 4.45
clandestine 25.19
clandestinity 4.53
clang 26.1
clanger 12.60
clangor 12.31
clangorous 28.31
clangour 12.31
clank 21.33
clannish 29.9
clansman 25.45
clansmen 25.45
clanswoman 25.45
clanswomen 25.17
clap 27.1
clapboard 16.20
clapper 12.61
clapperboard 16.20
Clapton 25.50
claptrap 27.1
claque 21.1
claqueur 12.37
Clara 12.65
Clarabella 12.42
Clare 2.1
clarence 28.45
Clarenceux 11.18
Clarendon 25.40
claret 30.43
Clarice 28.10
clarificatory 4.43
clarifier 12.14
clarify 6.7
Clarinda 12.27
clarinet 30.4
clarinetist 31.14
clarinettist 31.14
clarion 25.37
Clarissa 12.70
clarity 4.53

Clark 21.5
clarkia 12.6
Clarrie 4.38
clart 30.3
clarty 4.51
clary 4.39
clash 29.1
clasher 12.72
clasp 27.18
clasper 12.61
class 28.2
classic 21.16
classical 23.32
classicism 31.13
classicize 35.14
classificatory 4.43
classifier 12.14
classify 6.7
classist 31.13
classmate 30.12
classroom 24.12
classy 4.45
clatter 12.74
Claude 16.19
Claudette 30.4
Claudia 12.5
Claudine 25.9
Claudius 28.23
clausal 23.41
clause 35.17
Clausewitz 28.47
claustral 23.36
claustrophobia 12.5
claustrophobic 21.9
clave 34.4
clavichord 16.21
clavicle 23.32
clavier 12.4
claw 7.1
clawback 21.2
clay 3.1
clayey 4.2
clayish 29.6
claymore 7.12
Clayton 25.50
clean 25.9
cleaner 12.54
cleanish 29.9
cleanly 4.22, 4.23
cleanse 35.31
cleanser 12.90
clean-up 27.13
clear 12.4
clearance 28.45
clearer 12.67
clearing 26.11
clearing house 28.16
clearout 30.34
clearsighted 16.12
clearstory 4.41

clearway 3.25
cleat 30.18
cleavage 20.9
cleave 34.5
cleaver 12.85
cleavers 35.24
Cledwyn 25.20
Cleese 35.6
clef 17.3
cleft 30.47
cleg 18.3
Cleisthenes 35.7
Clem 24.3
clematis 28.12
Clemence 28.45
clemency 4.48
clement 30.56
clementine 25.23
Clemmie 4.29
clench 29.20
Cleo 9.4
Cleopatra 12.64
clerestory 4.41
clergy 4.17
clergyman 25.45
clergymen 25.45
cleric 21.15
clerical 23.32
clericalist 31.8
clerihew 11.22
clerisy 4.46
clerk 21.5
clerkess 28.7
clerkish 29.8
clerkly 4.21
Cleveland 16.45
clever 12.85
clevis 28.12
clew 11.1
Clews 35.21
clianthus 28.35
cliché 3.21
click 21.9
click-clack 21.3
clicker 12.39
client 30.56
clientele 23.3
cliff 17.6
cliffhanger 12.60
cliffhanging 26.10
Clifford 16.28
clifftop 27.8
cliffy 4.14
Clifton 25.50
climacteric 21.15
climactic 21.17
climate 30.23
climatic 21.17
climatology 4.17
climax 28.38
climb 24.7

climbdown 25.29
climber 12.51
clime 24.7
clinch 29.20
clincher 12.72
cline 25.21
cling 26.3
clinger 12.60
clingfilm 24.18
clingy 4.35
clinic 21.13
clinical 23.32
clinician 25.49
clink 21.33
clinker 12.39
clint 30.54
Clinton 25.50
Clio 9.3
clip 27.6
clipboard 16.20
clip-clop 27.8
clipper 12.62
clippie 4.36
clipping 26.10
clique 21.8
cliquey 4.18
cliquish 29.8
clitoral 23.36
clitoris 28.10
Clive 34.9
cloak 21.24
cloakroom 24.12
clobber 12.21
cloche 29.11
clock 21.20
clockmaker 12.38
clockwise 35.15
clockwork 21.31
clod 16.18
Clodagh 12.28
cloddish 29.6
clodhopper 12.62
clodhopping 26.10
clog 18.8
cloggy 4.15
cloisonné 3.17
cloister 12.81
cloistral 23.36
clomp 27.17
clone 25.30
Clones 28.9
clonk 21.34
Clonmel 23.3
clop 27.8
cloqué 3.14
Close 28.17
close 35.19
closet 30.25
closish 29.9
closure 12.33
clot 30.31

cloth 32.8
clothe 33.7
clothes 35.34
clothes horse 28.15
clothesline 25.22
clothes peg 18.3
clothespin 25.18
clothier 12.12
clothing 26.14
Clotho 9.26
cloths 28.48
cloture 12.24
clou 11.1
cloud 16.22
cloudburst 31.26
cloudy 4.13
Clough 22.4
clout 30.34
clove 34.11
cloven 25.51
clover 12.86
cloverleaf 17.5
Clovis 28.12
clown 25.29
clownish 29.9
cloy 10.1
club 14.13
clubber 12.22
clubby 4.10
clubfeet 30.18
clubfoot 30.39
club-footed 16.12
clubhouse 28.16
clubland 16.40
cluck 21.29
clucky 4.20
clue 11.1
clump 27.17
clumpy 4.37
clumsy 4.62
clung 26.18
clunk 21.34
clunky 4.20
cluster 12.81
clutch 15.13
clutter 12.81
Clwyd 16.8
Clyde 16.14
Clydesdale 23.5
Clytemnestra 12.64
coach 15.10
coachbuilder 12.27
coach house 28.16
coachload 16.23
coachman 25.45
coachmen 25.45
coachwood 16.26
coachwork 21.31
coagula 12.46
coagulant 30.56
coagulate 30.11

coagulum 24.18
Coahuila 12.43
coal 23.17
coaler 12.44
coalesce 28.3
coalescence 28.45
coalescent 30.56
coalface 28.5
coalfield 16.35
coalitionist 31.10
Coalport 30.33
coaly 4.25
coaming 26.9
coarse 28.15
coarsen 25.48
coarsish 29.9
coast 31.20
coastal 23.39
coasteering 26.11
coaster 12.80
coastguard 16.2
coastline 25.22
coastwise 35.15
coat 30.35
coatee 4.54
coati 4.51
coating 26.13
Coats 28.47
coax 28.40
co-ax 28.38
coaxer 12.71
coaxial 23.24
cob 14.9
cobalt 30.51
cobaltic 21.17
cobaltous 28.34
cobber 12.21
Cobbett 30.20
cobble 23.26
cobbler 12.44
cobblestone 25.31
Cobden 25.40
coble 23.26
cobnut 30.40
cobra 12.66
cobweb 14.3
cobwebby 4.10
coca 12.40
Coca-Cola 12.44
cocaine 25.7
coccyx 28.39
Cochabamba 12.21
Cochin 25.13
cochineal 23.7
cochlea 12.6
Cochran 25.47
cock 21.20
cockade 16.6
cock-a-doodle-
doo 11.1
cock-a-hoop 27.11

cock-a-leekie 4.18
cockalorum 24.19
cockamamie 4.29
cockatiel 23.7
cockatoo 11.1
cockatrice 28.13
cockchafer 12.30
Cockcroft 30.47
cockcrow 9.21
cockerel 23.36
Cockerell 23.36
cockeyed 16.14
cockfight 30.27
cockle 23.32
cockleshell 23.4
Cockney 4.32
cockpit 30.23
cockroach 15.10
cockscomb 24.11
cocksure 7.1
cocktail 23.6
cock-up 27.13
cocky 4.19
coco 9.16
cocoa 9.16
coconut 30.40
cocoon 25.33
Cocos 28.26
cocotte 30.31
Cocteau 9.25
cod 16.18
coda 12.28
coddle 23.28
coddler 12.48
code 16.23
codeine 25.10
codependent 30.56
coder 12.28
codex 28.38
codfish 29.7
codger 12.35
codices 35.8
codicil 23.9
codicillary 4.43
codifier 12.14
codify 6.7
codpiece 28.6
codswallop 27.14
Coe 9.1
Coed 16.24
coed 16.3
coefficient 30.56
coequal 23.40
coerce 28.36
coercible 23.26
coercion 25.49
coercive 34.7
Coerdoba 12.22
Coetzee 12.4
coeval 23.40
coexist 31.6

coexistence 28.45
coexistent 30.56
coextensive 34.7
coffee 4.14
coffer 12.30
cofferdam 24.1
coffin 25.14
coffle 23.29
cog 18.8
cogency 4.48
cogent 30.56
cogitate 30.16
cogito 9.24
cognac 21.4
cognate 30.13
cognizant 30.56
cognize 35.13
cognomen 25.5
cognoscenti 4.51
cohabit 30.20
cohabitant 30.56
cohabitee 4.1
cohabiter 12.78
Cohen 25.13
cohere 12.4
coherence 28.45
coherent 30.56
cohesion 25.42
cohesive 34.7
Cohn 25.30
coho 9.14
cohort 30.33
cohosh 29.11
coif 17.2, 17.12
coiffeur 13.1
coiffeurs 35.25
coiffure 12.20
coign 25.32
coil 23.19
Coimbra 12.65
coin 25.32
coinage 20.7
coincide 16.14
coincidence 28.45
coincident 30.56
coiner 12.56
coin-op 27.8
cointreau 9.21
coital 23.39
coition 25.49
coitus 28.34
coitus interruptus
28.34
Coke 21.24, 21.28
cola 12.44
colander 12.29
Colbert 2.3, 30.45
colcannon 25.46
Colchester 12.78
Colchis 28.7
cold 16.37

cold-blooded 16.9
coldish 29.6
Colditz 28.47
coldstore 7.18
Cole 23.17
Coleman 25.45
Coleraine 25.7
Coleridge 20.8
Coles 35.29
coleslaw 7.11
Colette 30.4
coleus 28.23
coley 4.25
colic 21.11
colicky 4.19
Colima 12.51
Colin 25.16
coliseum 24.15
colitis 28.12
Coll 23.13
collaborate 30.15
collaborationist 31.10
collage 19.1
collagen 25.42
collagist 31.7
collapse 28.46
collapsible 23.26
collar 12.44
collarbone 25.30
collard 16.29
collate 30.7
collateral 23.36
colleague 18.5
collect 30.48
collectible 23.26
collection 25.49
collectivist 31.15
collectivize 35.14
collector 12.76
colleen 25.10
college 20.6
collegial 23.24
collegian 25.37
collegiate 30.41
collet 30.22
collide 16.14
collie 4.25
collier 12.6
colliery 4.43
Collins 35.31
collision 25.42
collocutor 12.81
collodion 25.37
colloid 16.24
collop 27.14
colloquia 12.12
colloquial 23.24
colloquium 24.16
colloquy 4.59
collotype 27.7

collude 16.25
colluder 12.29
collusion 25.42
collusive 34.7
collywobbles 35.29
colobus 28.24
Cologne 25.30
Colombia 12.5
Colombian 25.37
Colombo 9.9
Colón 25.24
colon 25.24, 25.44
colonel 23.34
colonelcy 4.49
colonial 23.24
colonialist 31.8
colonic 21.13
colonist 31.10
colonizer 12.91
colonnade 16.6
colonoscopy 4.37
colony 4.34
colophon 25.41
color 12.47
Coloradan 25.40
Colorado 9.11
coloratura 12.67
colorific 21.10
colorist 31.12
colorway 3.25
colossal 23.37
colossi 6.16
Colossians 35.31
colossus 28.32
colostomy 4.30
colour 12.47
colourblind 16.42
colourfast 31.2
colourist 31.12
colourway 3.25
colt 30.51
colter 12.80
coltish 29.10
Coltrane 25.7
coltsfoot 30.39
colubrine 25.23
Columba 12.22
columbaria 12.10
columbarium 24.16
Columbia 12.5
columbine 25.21
columbite 30.26
columbium 24.16
Columbus 28.24
column 24.18
columnar 12.57
columnist 31.9
coma 12.52
Comanche 4.50
comatose 28.17
comb 24.11

combat 30.1
combatant 30.56
combe 24.12
comber 12.52
combinatorial 23.24
combinatory 4.43
combine 25.21
combo 9.9
combust 31.24
combustible 23.26
combustion 25.39
come 24.14
comeback 21.2
Comecon 25.25
comedian 25.37
comedic 21.10
comedown 25.29
comedy 4.12
comely 4.26
comer 12.52
comestible 23.26
comet 30.23
comeuppance 28.45
comfit 30.21
comfort 30.41
comforter 12.82
comfrey 4.42
comfy 4.14
comic 21.11
comical 23.32
coming 26.9
Comino 9.19
Comintern 25.53
comity 4.53
comma 12.51
command 16.41
commandant 30.53
commandeer 12.4
commander 12.25
commando 9.11
comme ci
    comme ça 1.1
commedia
    dell'arte 3.22
commemorate 30.15
commence 28.44
commend 16.41
commendatory 4.43
commensurate 30.43
comment 30.53
commentary 4.43
commentate 30.16
commèrce 28.36
commercial 23.38
commere 2.9
commie 4.29
comminatory 4.43
commingle 23.30
commiserate 30.15
commissar 1.1

commissarial 23.24
commissariat 30.41
commissary 4.43
commissionaire 2.1
commissioner 12.58
commit 30.20
committal 23.39
committee 4.53
committer 12.78
commix 28.39
commixture 12.23
commode 16.23
commodify 6.7
commodious 28.23
commodity 4.53
commodore 7.5
common 25.45
commonalty 4.55
commoner 12.58
commonhold 16.37
commonplace 28.5
common room 24.12
commons 35.31
common
    sense 28.44
commonsensical
    23.32
commonwealth
    32.17
commotion 25.49
communal 23.34
communalist 31.8
communalize 35.12
communard 16.2
commune 25.33
communicant 30.56
communicate 30.10
communicatory
    4.43
communion 25.37
communiqué 3.14
communist 31.10
communitarian
    25.37
community 4.53
communize 35.13
commute 30.37
commuter 12.81
compère 2.10
comp 27.17
compact 30.48
compaction 25.49
compactor 12.74
compadre 4.38
companion 25.52
companionate 30.43
companionway 3.25
company 4.34
comparatist 31.14
compare 2.1
comparison 25.48

compass 28.30
compassionate 30.43
compatible 23.26
compatriot 30.41
compeer 12.9
compel 23.3
compendia 12.5
compendious 28.23
compendium 24.16
compensate 30.15
compensatory 4.43
Compère 2.10
compete 30.18
competence 28.45
competency 4.48
competent 30.56
competitor 12.78
compile 23.11
compiler 12.44
complacency 4.45
complacent 30.56
complain 25.7
complainant 30.56
complainer 12.54
complaint 30.54
complaisance 28.45
complaisant 30.56
compleat 30.18
complementarity 4.53
complementary 4.43
complete 30.18
completion 25.49
completist 31.14
complex 28.38
complexion 25.49
complexity 4.53
compliance 28.45
compliant 30.56
complicate 30.10
complicit 30.24
complicitous 28.34
complimentary 4.43
compline 25.16
comply 6.1
compo 9.20
component 30.56
comport 30.33
compose 35.19
composer 12.92
composite 30.25
compositor 12.78
compos
  mentis 28.12
compossible 23.26
compost 31.17
composure 12.33
compote 30.35

compound 16.43
compounder 12.28
comprador 7.1
comprehend 16.41
comprehensible 23.26
comprehension 25.49
comprehensive 34.7
compress 28.3
compressible 23.26
compressive 34.7
compressor 12.69
comprise 35.11
compromise 35.13
compromiser 12.91
Compton 25.50
comptroller 12.44
compulsion 25.49
compulsive 34.7
compulsory 4.43
compunction 25.49
compunctious 28.33
compute 30.37
computer 12.81
comrade 16.6
comradely 4.22
Comsat 30.2
Comte 30.54
con 25.24
Conakry 4.43
con amore 3.19
Conan 25.46
conation 25.49
concave 34.4
concavity 4.53
conceal 23.7
concealer 12.43
concede 16.7
conceder 12.26
conceit 30.18
conceited 16.12
conceive 34.5
concenter 12.76
concentrate 30.15
concentre 12.76
concentric 21.15
Concepcíoen 25.24
concept 30.58
conception 25.49
conceptional 23.34
conceptual 23.25
conceptualist 31.8
concern 25.53
concert 30.43, 30.45
concertante 3.22
concerted 16.12
concertina 12.54
concertino 9.19
concerto 9.24
concessionaire 2.1

concessionary 4.43
concessive 34.7
conch 29.20
concha 12.40
conchae 4.19
conches 35.10
conchie 4.50
concierge 19.3
conciliar 12.6
conciliate 30.8
conciliatory 4.43
concise 28.13
concision 25.42
conclave 34.4
conclude 16.25
conclusion 25.42
conclusive 34.7
concoct 30.49
concocter 12.79
concoction 25.49
concomitance 28.45
concomitant 30.56
concord 16.21
concordance 28.45
concordant 30.56
concordat 30.1
Concorde 16.21
concourse 28.15
concrete 30.18
concretion 25.49
concretize 35.14
concubinage 20.7
concubine 25.21
concupiscence 28.45
concupiscent 30.56
concur 13.1
concurrence 28.45
concurrent 30.56
concuss 28.21
condemn 24.3
condemnatory 4.43
condensate 30.15
condense 28.44
condescend 16.41
condescension 25.49
condign 25.21
conditioner 12.58
condo 9.11
condole 23.17
condolence 28.45
condom 24.17
condominium 24.16
condone 25.30
condoner 12.56
condor 7.5
conduce 28.19
conducive 34.7
conduct 30.49
conductance 28.45
conducti 6.18

conductible 23.26
conduction 25.49
conductor 12.81
conductress 28.10
conductus 28.34
conduit 30.21
cone 25.30
coney 4.33
confab 14.1
confabulate 30.11
confect 30.48
confection 25.49
confectioner 12.58
confectionery 4.43
confederacy 4.48
confederate 30.15, 30.43
confer 13.1
conferee 4.1
conference 28.45
conferral 23.36
confess 28.3
confessant 30.56
confessional 23.34
confessionary 4.43
confessor 12.69
confetti 4.51
confidant 30.53
confide 16.14
confidence 28.45
confident 30.56
confidential 23.38
confiding 26.5
configure 12.31
confine 25.21
confines 35.31
confirm 24.22
confirmand 16.40
confirmatory 4.43
confiscate 30.10
confiscatory 4.43
conflate 30.7
conflict 30.49
conflictual 23.25
confluence 28.45
confluent 30.56
conflux 28.41
conform 24.9
conformal 23.33
conformance 28.45
conformist 31.9
conformity 4.53
confound 16.43
confraternity 4.53
confrère 2.11
confront 30.55
Confucian 25.49
Confucianist 31.10
Confucius 28.33
confuse 35.21
confusing 26.14

Cornelius 28.23
Cornell 23.3
corner 12.56
cornerback 21.2
cornerstone 25.31
cornerwise 35.15
cornet 30.23
cornetist 31.14
cornetti 4.51
cornetto 9.24
cornfield 16.35
cornflake 21.7
cornflour 12.16
cornflower 12.16
cornice 28.9
corniced 31.10
corniche 29.5
Cornish 29.9
Cornishman 25.45
Cornishmen 25.45
cornmeal 23.7
cornrows 35.19
cornstarch 15.2
cornucopia 12.9
cornucopian 25.37
Cornwall 23.15
corny 4.32
corolla 12.44
corollary 4.43
Coromandel 23.28
corona 12.56
coronach 22.6
coronae 4.33
coronal 23.34
coronary 4.43
coroner 12.58
coronet 30.23
Corot 9.21
corpora 12.67
corporal 23.36
corporate 30.43
corporatist 31.14
corporeal 23.24
corporeity 4.53
corps 7.1
corpse 28.46
corpulence 28.45
corpulency 4.48
corpulent 30.56
corpus 28.30
Corpus Christi 4.53
corpuscle 23.37
corral 23.2
correct 30.48
correction 25.49
correctional 23.34
corrector 12.76
Correggio 9.4
correlate 30.11
correspond 16.42

correspondence
28.45
correspondent
30.56
corresponding 26.5
corrida 12.26
corridor 7.5
corrigenda 12.26
corrigendum 24.17
corrigible 23.26
corroborate 30.15
corroboratory 4.43
corroboree 4.43
corrode 16.23
corrosion 25.42
corrosive 34.7
corrugate 30.9
corrupt 30.58
corrupter 12.81
corruptible 23.26
corruption 25.49
corsage 19.1
corsair 2.12
corse 28.15
corselet 30.22
corselette 30.22
corset 30.24
corsetière 12.4
corsetry 4.40
Corsica 12.39
Corsican 25.43
Cort 30.33
cortège 19.4
Cortés 35.3
Cortes 35.3
cortex 28.38
cortices 35.8
Cortina 12.54
cortisone 25.31
corundum 24.17
Corunna 12.57
coruscate 30.10
corvée 4.26
corves 35.35
corvette 30.4
corybantic 21.17
coryphée 3.10
coryza 12.91
cos 28.14, 35.16
Cosa Nostra 12.65
cosh 29.11
cosies 35.10
cosignatory 4.43
cosine 25.23
cosmetic 21.17
cosmetician 25.49
cosmic 21.12
Cosmo 9.18
cosmogony 4.34
cosmography 4.14
cosmology 4.17

cosmonaut 30.33
cosmopolis 28.8
cosmopolitan 25.50
cosmopolitanize
35.13
cosmopolite 30.28
cosmos 28.14
cosplay 3.15
Cossack 21.4
cosset 30.24
cossie 4.61
cost 31.17
Costa 12.79
Costa Blanca 12.37
Costa Brava 12.85
co-star 1.19
Costa Rica 12.38
Costa Rican 25.43
coster 12.79
costermonger 12.32
costing 26.13
costive 34.8
costly 4.25
costume 24.12
costumier 12.7
cosy 4.61
cot 30.31
cotangent 30.56
cote 30.35
coterie 4.43
coterminous 28.29
cotillion 25.37
Cotman 25.45
Cotopaxi 4.45
Cotswold 16.37
cotta 12.79
cottage 20.9
cottager 12.35
cottagey 4.17
cottaging 26.6
cottar 12.79
cottier 12.12
cotton 25.50
cottontail 23.6
cottonwood 16.26
cottony 4.34
cotyledon 25.40
coucal 23.32
couch 15.9
couchant 30.56
couchette 30.4
cougar 12.32
cough 17.8
cougher 12.30
could 16.26
couldn't 30.56
coulée 4.26
coulisse 28.6
coulomb 24.8
coulter 12.80
council 23.37

councillor 12.43
councilman 25.45
councilmen 25.45
councilor 12.43
councilwomen
25.17
counsel 23.37
counsellor 12.43
counselor 12.43
count 30.55
countdown 25.29
countenance 28.45
counter 12.80
counteract 30.48
counteraction 25.49
counter-attack 21.4
counterbalance
28.45
counterblast 31.2
counterchange
20.19
countercharge 20.2
counterclaim 24.4
counterclockwise
35.15
counterculture
12.24
counter-
espionage 19.1
counter-
demonstration
25.49
counterfeit 30.21
counterfeiter 12.78
counterfoil 23.19
counter-intelligence
28.45
countermand 16.41
countermeasure
12.33
countermove 34.12
counteroffensive
34.7
counterpane 25.8
counterpart 30.3
counterplot 30.31
counterpoint 30.55
counterpoise 35.20
counter-
proliferation
25.49
counterproposal
23.41
counter-
revolution 25.49
counter
revolutionary
4.43
countershaft 30.47
countersign 25.23
countersink 21.33

counterstroke 21.24
countersunk 21.34
countervail 23.5
countervalue 11.22
counterweight 30.17
countess 28.12
counting
 house 28.16
countrified 16.14
country 4.42
countryman 25.45
countrymen 25.45
countryside 16.16
countrywoman
 25.45
countrywomen
 25.17
county 4.54
coup 11.1
coup de grâce 28.2
coup d'etat 1.1
coupé 3.18
couple 23.35
coupler 12.47
couplet 30.22
coupling 26.8
coupon 25.26
courage 20.8
courageous 28.25
courante 30.53
courgette 30.4
courier 12.10
Courrèges 19.2
course 28.15
courser 12.70
coursework 21.31
court 30.33
Courtauld 16.37
court-bouillon 25.27
courteous 28.23
courtesan 25.1
courtesy 4.46
courthouse 28.16
courtier 12.12
courtly 4.25
court-martial 23.38
Courtney 4.32
courtroom 24.12
courtyard 16.2
couscous 28.19
cousin 25.52
cousinhood 16.26
cousinly 4.26
Cousins 35.31
Cousteau 9.25
couth 32.12
couture 12.20
couturier 3.3
couvade 16.2
couvert 2.1
couverture 12.20

covalence 28.45
cove 34.11
coven 25.51
covenant 30.56
covenantal 23.39
covenanter 12.82
Coventry 4.41
cover 12.87
coverage 20.8
coverall 23.15
cover charge 20.2
Coverdale 23.5
covering 26.11
coverlet 30.22
covert 30.44
coverture 12.20
covet 30.25
covetous 28.34
covey 4.58
covin 25.19
coving 26.14
cow 8.1
coward 16.28
cowardice 28.7
cowardly 4.27
cowbell 23.3
cowboy 10.3
Cowdrey 4.41
cower 12.16
Cowes 35.18
cowgirl 23.42
cowherd 16.31
cowhide 16.14
cowl 23.16
cowlick 21.11
cowling 26.8
cowman 25.45
cowmen 25.45
cowpat 30.1
cowpea 4.36
Cowper 12.63
cowpoke 21.24
cowpox 28.40
cowpuncher 12.73
cowrie 4.41
cowshed 16.4
cowslip 27.6
cox 28.40
coxcomb 24.11
coxcombry 4.41
coxless 28.27
coxswain 25.48
coy 10.1
coyly 4.25
coyness 28.9
coyote 4.54
coypu 11.16
coz 35.23
cozen 25.52
cozenage 20.7
Cozens 35.31

cozies 35.10
Cozumel 23.3
cozy 4.61
crab 14.1
Crabbe 14.1
crabby 4.10
crablike 21.19
crabmeat 30.18
Crabtree 4.38
crabwise 35.15
crack 21.1
crackbrained 16.41
crackdown 25.29
cracker 12.37
cracker-barrel 23.36
crackerjack 21.3
crackle 23.32
crackling 26.8
crackly 4.21
cracknel 23.34
crackpot 30.32
cracksman 25.45
cracksmen 25.45
cracky 4.18
Cracow 17.8
cradle 23.28
craft 30.47
craftsman 25.45
craftsmen 25.45
craftswoman 25.45
craftswomen 25.17
craftwork 21.31
craftworker 12.41
crafty 4.51
crag 18.1
craggy 4.15
cragsman 25.45
cragsmen 25.45
Craig 18.4
crake 21.7
cram 24.1
crammer 12.50
cramp 27.17
crampon 25.26
cran 25.1
cranage 20.7
cranberry 4.43
crane 25.7
cranesbill 23.8
crania 12.8
cranial 23.24
craniofacial 23.38
craniology 4.17
craniometry 4.40
craniopagus 28.25
cranium 24.16
crank 21.33
crankpin 25.18
crankshaft 30.47
cranky 4.18
Cranmer 12.50

crannied 16.10
cranny 4.31
crap 27.1
crape 27.4
crapper 12.61
crappie 4.36
crappy 4.36
craps 28.46
crapulence 28.45
crapulent 30.56
crapulous 28.27
crash 29.1
crass 28.1
crassitude 16.25
Crassus 28.32
crate 30.7
crater 12.77
cravat 30.1
cravatted 16.12
crave 34.4
craven 25.51
craver 12.85
craving 26.14
craw 7.1
crawfish 29.7
Crawford 16.28
crawl 23.14
crawler 12.44
crawly 4.25
Cray 3.1
crayfish 29.7
crayon 25.24
craze 35.5
crazy 4.61
creak 21.8
creaky 4.18
cream 24.5
creamer 12.51
creamery 4.43
creamware 2.15
creamy 4.29
creance 28.45
crease 28.6
create 30.7
creation 25.49
creationist 31.10
creator 12.77
creature 12.23
creaturely 4.27
Crécy 4.45
cred 16.3
credal 23.28
credence 28.45
credential 23.38
credenza 12.90
credible 23.26
credit 30.21
creditor 12.78
credo 9.11
credulity 4.53
credulous 28.27

Cree 4.1
creed 16.7
creek 21.8
creel 23.7
creep 27.5
creeper 12.61
creepy 4.36
creepy-crawly 4.25
crema 12.50
cremate 30.7
crematoria 12.10
crematorium 24.16
crematory 4.43
crème brûlée 3.1
crème de la
  crème 24.3
crème de
  menthe 32.19
crème fraîche 29.3
Cremona 12.56
crenel 23.34
crenelate 30.11
crenellate 30.11
Creole 23.17
creosote 30.35
crêpe 27.4
crêpey 4.36
crepitant 30.56
crepitate 30.16
crepitus 28.34
crept 30.58
crepuscular 12.46
crescendo 9.11
crescent 30.56
crescentic 21.17
cress 28.3
cresset 30.24
Cressida 12.27
crest 31.3
crestfallen 25.44
Cretaceous 28.33
Cretan 25.50
Crete 30.18
cretic 21.17
cretin 25.19
cretinous 28.29
cretonne 25.24
crevasse 28.1
crevice 28.12
crew cut 30.40
crew 11.1
crew cut 30.40
Crewe 11.1
crewel 23.25
crewman 25.45
crewmen 25.45
cri de cœur 13.1
crib 14.7
cribbage 20.6
cribber 12.21
Crichton 25.50

crick 21.9
cricket 30.21
cricketer 12.78
cried 16.14
crier 12.13
crikey 4.19
crim 24.6
crime 24.7
Crimea 12.4
Crimean 25.37
crime
  passionnel 23.3
criminal 23.34
criminalize 35.12
criminology 4.17
crimp 27.17
crimper 12.62
crimplene 25.10
crimpy 4.36
crimson 25.52
cringe 20.19
cringer 12.35
cringle 23.30
crinkle 23.32
crinkly 4.24
crinoid 16.24
crinoidal 23.28
crinoline 25.16
criollo 9.17
cripes 28.46
Crippen 25.18
cripple 23.35
crippledom 24.17
crippler 12.43
crises 35.8
crisis 28.11
crisp 27.18
crispbread 16.4
crisper 12.62
Crispian 25.37
Crispin 25.18
crispy 4.36
criss-cross 28.14
criteria 12.10
criterial 23.24
criterion 25.37
critic 21.17
critical 23.32
criticizer 12.91
critique 21.8
critter 12.78
croûton 25.26
croak 21.24
croaker 12.40
croaky 4.20
Croat 30.1
Croatia 12.72
Croatian 25.49
Croce 3.8
crochet 3.21
crocheter 12.2

croci 6.10
crock 21.20
crockery 4.43
crocket 30.21
Crockett 30.21
crocodile 23.11
crocodilian 25.37
crocus 28.26
Croesus 28.32
croft 30.47
crofter 12.79
croissant 25.26
Cromarty 4.55
Crome 24.11
cromlech 22.6
Crompton 25.50
Cromwell 23.4
crone 25.30
Cronin 25.18
cronk 21.34
Cronus 28.29
crony 4.33
crook 21.28
crookback 21.2
crooked 16.10
crookery 4.43
Crookes 28.40
croon 25.33
crooner 12.56
crop 27.8
cropper 12.62
croquet 3.14
croquette 30.4
Crosby 4.10
cross 28.14
crossbar 1.4
cross-beam 24.5
crossbench 29.20
cross-
  functional 23.34
crossbill 23.8
crossbow 9.9
crossbred 16.3
crossbreed 16.7
crosscheck 21.6
cross-current 30.56
cross-cut 30.40
crosse 28.14
crossfire 12.14
crosshatch 15.1
crossing 26.12
cross-legged 16.9
crossover 12.86
crosspatch 15.1
crosspiece 28.6
crossroads 35.27
crosstalk 21.22
crosstie 6.18
crosswalk 21.22
crossways 35.5
crosswind 16.42

crosswise 35.15
crossword 16.31
crotch 15.7
crotchet 30.20
crotchety 4.53
croton 25.50
crouch 15.9
croup 27.11
croupier 3.3
croupy 4.37
croustade 16.2
croûton 25.26
crow 9.1
crowbar 1.4
crowberry 4.43
crowd 16.22
crowd-pleaser 12.90
crowfoot 30.39
crown 25.29
crozier 12.12
cru 11.1
cruces 35.8
crucial 23.38
cruciate 30.41
crucible 23.26
crucifer 12.30
cruciferous 28.31
crucifier 12.14
crucifix 28.39
crucifixion 25.49
cruciform 24.9
crucify 6.7
cruck 21.29
crud 16.27
cruddy 4.13
crude 16.25
crudités 3.1
crudity 4.53
cruel 23.25
cruelty 4.55
cruet 30.20
Cruikshank 21.33
cruise 35.21
cruiser 12.92
cruller 12.47
crumb 24.14
crumble 23.26
crumbly 4.26
crumby 4.30
crummy 4.30
crump 27.17
crumpet 30.23
crumple 23.35
crumply 4.26
crunch 29.20
cruncher 12.73
crunchy 4.50
crupper 12.63
crural 23.36
crusade 16.6
crusader 12.26

C

Cyclades 35.7
Cycladic 21.10
cyclamen 25.45
cycle 23.32
cyclic 21.11
cyclist 31.8
cyclone 25.30
cyclonic 21.13
Cyclopean 25.36
cyclopedic 21.10
Cyclops 28.46
cyclorama 12.50
cycloramic 21.12
cyclostome 24.11
cyclostyle 23.12
cyclotron 25.26
cygnet 30.23
Cygnus 28.29
cylinder 12.27
cylindrical 23.32
cymbal 23.26
cymbalist 31.8
Cymbeline 25.10
cymbidium 24.16
Cymric 21.15
Cymru 4.42
cynic 21.13
cynical 23.32
cynosure 12.20
Cynthia 12.12
cypress 28.10
cy-press 3.1
Cypriot 30.41
Cyprus 28.31
Cyrenaic 21.9
Cyrenaica 12.39
Cyrene 4.31
Cyril 23.9
Cyrillic 21.11
Cyrus 28.31
cyst 31.6
cystic 21.17
cystitis 28.12
Cytherea 12.3
cytoplasm 24.21
cytoplasmic 21.12
Czech 21.6
Czechoslovak 21.4
Czechoslovakia
  12.6
Czechoslovakian
  25.37
Czerny 4.34

D

Da Nang 26.1
Daéil 23.19
dab 14.1

dabber 12.21
dabble 23.26
dabbler 12.48
dabbling 26.8
dabchick 21.9
dace 28.5
dacha 12.23
Dachau 8.6
dachshund 16.45
Dacia 12.11
Dacian 25.37
dacite 30.30
dacoit 30.36
Dacron 25.26
dactyl 23.9
dactylic 21.11
dad 16.1
Dada 1.6
Dadaist 31.6
daddy-long-
  legs 35.28
daddy 4.12
dado 9.11
Daedalus 28.27
daemon 25.45
daemonic 21.13
daffodil 23.8
daffy 4.14
daft 30.47
Dafydd 33.4
dag 18.1
Dagestan 25.4
dagga 12.31
dagger 12.31
Dagmar 1.13
Dagon 25.25
Daguerre 2.1
daguerreotype 27.7
Dagwood 16.26
dahlia 12.6
Dai 6.1
Dáil Eireann 25.47
daily 4.22
Daimler 12.43
dainty 4.52
daiquiri 4.40
Dairen 25.5
dairy 4.39
dairying 26.3
dairymaid 16.6
dairyman 25.45
dairymen 25.45
dais 28.7
daisy 4.61
Dakar 1.11
Dakota 12.80
Dakotan 25.50
dalasi 4.45
dale 23.5
Dalek 21.6
Daley 4.22

Dalglish 29.5
Dalhousie 4.61
Dali 4.21
Dalian 25.37
Dallas 28.27
dalliance 28.45
dally 4.21
Dalmatia 12.72
Dalmatian 25.49
dalmatic 21.17
Dalriada 12.25
dal segno 9.28
Dalton 25.50
Daly 4.22
dam 24.1
damage 20.7
Damara 12.64
Damaraland 16.40
damascene 25.11
Damascus 28.26
damask 21.35
dame 24.4
Damian 25.37
dammit 30.23
damn 24.1
damnatory 4.43
damnify 6.7
damnum 24.19
Damocles 35.7
Damon 25.45
damp 27.17
dampen 25.46
dampener 12.58
damper 12.61
Dampier 12.3
dampish 29.9
damsel 23.41
damselfish 29.7
damselfly 6.11
damson 25.52
dan 25.1
Dana 12.53
Danae 4.3
Danakil 23.9
Da Nang 26.1
dance 28.44
dancer 12.69
dandelion 25.38
dander 12.25
dandle 23.28
dandruff 17.15
dandy 4.12
dandyish 29.6
Dane 25.7
Danelaw 7.11
dang 26.1
danger 12.35
dangerous 28.31
dangle 23.30
dangler 12.42
dangly 4.21

Daniel 23.40
Daniela 12.42
Danish 29.9
dank 21.33
Danny 4.31
danseur 13.1
danseuse 35.25
Dante 4.51
Dantean 25.37
Dantesque 21.35
Danton 25.26
Danube 14.12
Danubian 25.37
Danzig 18.6
dap 27.1
daphne 4.31
Daphnis 28.9
dapper 12.61
dapple 23.35
Darby 4.10
Darcy 4.45
Dardanelles 35.29
dare 2.1
daredevil 23.40
daredevilry 4.38
darer 12.65
Darfur 13.1
dargah 12.31
Dari 4.39
Darien 25.37
daring 26.1
dariole 23.17
Darius 28.23, 28.24
Darjeeling 26.8
dark 21.5
darken 25.43
darkener 12.58
darkish 29.8
darkroom 24.12
Darlene 25.10
darling 26.8
Darlington 25.50
Darmstadt 30.2
darn 25.4
darner 12.53
Darnley 4.21
Darrell 23.36
Darren 25.47
Darryl 23.36
dart 30.3
dartboard 16.20
darter 12.75
Dartmoor 12.20
Dartmouth 32.13
Darwin 25.20
Darwinian 25.37
Darwinist 31.10
dash 29.1
dashboard 16.20
dashing 26.12
dashpot 30.32

de rigueur 13.1
derision 25.42
derisive 34.7
derisory 4.43
derma 12.52
dermatitis 28.12
dermatology 4.17
dermis 28.8
Dermot 30.43
dernier cri 4.1
derogate 30.9
derogatory 4.43
derrick 21.15
Derrida 12.26
Derridean 25.37
derrière 2.1
derring-do 11.1
derringer 12.35
derris 28.10
Derry 4.38
derv 34.14
dervish 29.10
Descartes 30.3
descendant 30.56
descendent 30.56
descender 12.26
descendible 23.26
description 25.49
Desdemona 12.56
desecrate 30.15
desert 30.44, 30.45
deserter 12.82
desertion 25.49
deserts 28.47
déshabillé
desiccant 30.56
desiccate 30.10
desiderata 12.75
desiderate 30.15,
    30.43
desideratum 24.20
designate 30.13,
    30.43
desire 12.13
Desirée 3.19
desirous 28.31
desist 31.6
desk 21.35
deskilled 16.35
deskilling 26.8
desktop 27.8
desman 25.45
desmid 16.10
Des Moines
    25.32
Desmond 16.45
desolate 30.11, 30.42
despair 2.1
desperado 9.11
desperate 30.43
despise 35.11

despiser 12.91
despond 16.42
despondence 28.45
despondency 4.48
despondent 30.56
despot 30.32
despotic 21.17
Dessau 8.11
dessert 30.45
dessertspoon 25.33
De Stijl 23.11
destine 25.19
destiny 4.32
destitute 30.38
destitution 25.49
destrier 12.10
destroy 10.1
destroyer 12.18
destruct 30.49
destructible 23.26
destruction 25.49
destructor 12.81
desultory 4.43
detach 15.1
detail 23.6
detain 25.7
detainee 4.1
detainer 12.54
detect 30.48
detection 25.49
detector 12.76
detectorist 31.12
detente 30.53
detention 25.49
deter 13.1
detergent 30.56
deteriorate 30.15
determinant 30.56
determinate 30.43
determine 25.17
determiner 12.55
determinist 31.10
deterrence 28.45
deterrent 30.56
detonate 30.13
detour 12.20
detox 28.40
detoxify 6.7
detribalize 35.12
detritus 28.34
Detroit 30.36
Dettol 23.13
Deucalion 25.37
deuce 28.19
deuced 16.11
deus ex machina
    12.54
Deuteronomy 4.30
Deutschmark 21.5
deva 12.85
devastate 30.16

develop 27.14
developer 12.63
Devereux 9.21
Devi 4.58
deviance 28.45
deviancy 4.48
deviant 30.56
deviate 30.8
deviationist 31.10
devil 23.40
devilfish 29.7
devilish 29.8
devilry 4.38
devious 28.23
devise 35.11
devisee 4.1
deviser 12.91
devitalize 35.12
devoir 1.1
devolutionary 4.43
devolutionist 31.10
devolve 34.15
Devon 25.51
Devonian 25.37
Devonshire 12.11
devotee 4.1
devotion 25.49
devotional 23.34
devour 12.16
devourer 12.67
devout 30.34
dew 11.1
dewan 25.4
Dewar 12.19
dewberry 4.43
dewdrop 27.8
Dewey 4.8
dewfall 23.15
Dewi 4.59
dewlap 27.1
dewpond 16.42
Dewsbury 4.43
dewy 4.8
Dexedrine 25.11
dexter 12.76
dexterity 4.53
dexterous 28.31
dextral 23.36
dextrin 25.18
dextrose 35.19
Dhaka 12.37
dhal 23.2
dharma 12.50
dhobi 4.10
Dhofar 1.1
dhole 23.17
dhoti 4.54
dhow 8.1
dhurrie 4.42
Di 6.1
diabetes 35.9

diabetic 21.17
diablerie 4.43
diabolic 21.11
diabolical 23.32
diabolist 31.8
diabolo 9.17
diacritic 21.17
diacritical 23.32
diadem 24.3
Diadochi 6.10
diaereses 35.8
diaeresis 28.11
Diaghilev 17.3
diagnose 35.19
diagnoses 35.8
diagnosis 28.11
diagnostic 21.17
diagnostician 25.49
diagonal 23.34
diagram 24.1
diagrammatic 21.17
dial 23.25
dialect 30.48
dialectal 23.39
dialectic 21.17
dialectical 23.32
dialectician 25.49
dialog 18.8
dialogic 21.11
dialogue 18.8
dialyse 35.12
dialysis 28.11
diamanté 3.22
diamantine 25.12
diameter 12.78
diametric 21.15
diametrical 23.32
diamond 16.45
diamondback 21.2
Diana 12.53
Diane 25.1
Dianetics 28.39
dianthus 28.35
diapason 25.48
diaper 12.63
diaphanous 28.29
diaphragm 24.1
diaphragmatic
    21.17
diarchal 23.32
diarchy 4.18
diarist 31.12
diarize 35.13
diarrhea 12.4
diarrhoea 12.4
diary 4.43
Diaspora 12.67
diatom 24.20
diatonic 21.13
diatribe 14.8
diazepam 24.1

d

dib 14.7
dibber 12.21
dibble 23.26
dice 28.13
dicer 12.70
dicey 4.46
dichotomize 35.13
dichotomous 28.28
dichotomy 4.30
dick 21.9
Dickens 35.31
Dickensian 25.37
dicker 12.39
dickerer 12.67
dickhead 16.3
Dickie 4.19
Dickinson 25.48
dickybird 16.31
dicotyledon 25.40
dicta 12.78
dictaphone 25.30
dictate 30.7, 30.16
dictatorial 23.24
diction 25.49
dictionary 4.43
dictum 24.20
did 16.8
didactic 21.17
diddle 23.28
diddler 12.48
diddly-squat 30.32
diddums 35.30
diddy 4.12
Diderot 9.21
didgeridoo 11.1
didicoi 10.6
didn't 30.56
Dido 9.11
die 6.1
dieback 21.2
Diego 9.13
diehard 16.2
Dieppe 27.3
dieresis 28.11
diesel 23.41
dieselize 35.12
Dies Irae 3.19
diesis 28.11
diet 30.41
dietary 4.43
Dieter 12.77
dietetic 21.17
dietitian 25.49
Dietrich 21.15
differ 12.30
difference 28.45
different 30.56
differentia 12.11
differentiae 4.3
differential 23.38
differentiate 30.8

difficult 30.51
difficulty 4.53
diffidence 28.45
diffident 30.56
diffract 30.48
diffraction 25.49
diffuse 28.19, 35.21
diffuser 12.92
diffusion 25.42
diffusionist 31.10
diffusive 34.7
dig 18.6
Digby 4.10
digest 31.3
digestible 23.26
digestion 25.39
digger 12.31
digging 26.6
dight 30.26
digit 30.21
digital 23.39
digitalis 28.8
dignified 16.14
dignify 6.7
dignitary 4.43
dignity 4.53
digress 28.3
digresser 12.69
digressive 34.7
dihedral 23.36
Dijon 25.25
dik-dik 21.10
diktat 30.2
dilapidate 30.9
dilate 30.7
dilation 25.49
dilatory 4.43
dildo 9.11
dilemma 12.50
dilettante 4.51
Dili 4.24
diligence 28.45
diligent 30.56
dill 23.8
Dillon 25.44
dilly 4.24
dillybag 18.1
dilly-dally 4.21
dilute 30.37
dilution 25.49
diluvial 23.24
diluvian 25.37
Dilwyn 25.20
Dilys 28.8
dim 24.6
DiMaggio 9.4
Dimbleby 4.10
dime 24.7
dimension 25.49
diminish 29.9
diminuendo 9.11

diminution 25.49
dimissory 4.43
dimity 4.53
dimly 4.24
dimmer 12.51
dimmish 29.8
dimness 28.9
dimple 23.35
dimply 4.27
dimwit 30.25
din 25.13
Dinah 12.55
dinar 1.14
dine 25.21
diner 12.55
dinero 9.21
dinette 30.4
ding 26.3
dingaling 26.3
dingbat 30.1
dingdong 26.15
dinghy 4.35
dingle 23.30
dingo 9.13
dingus 28.25
dingy 4.17
dink 21.33
dinkum 24.18
dinky 4.19
dinner 12.55
dinosaur 7.16
dint 30.54
diocesan 25.48
diocese 28.11
Diocletian 25.49
diode 16.23
Diogenes 35.7
Dione 25.30
Dionysiac 21.1
Dionysius 28.23
Dionysus 28.32
Diophantus 28.34
diopside 16.16
dioptre 12.79
Dior 7.2
diorama 12.50
diorite 30.29
dioritic 21.17
dioxide 16.16
dip 27.6
diphtheria 12.10
diphthong 26.15
diphthongal 23.30
diplodocus 28.26
diploma 12.52
diplomacy 4.48
diplomat 30.1
diplomate 30.12
diplomatic 21.17
diplomatist 31.14
dipper 12.62

dippy 4.36
dipso 9.22
dipsomania 12.8
dipsomaniac 21.1
dipstick 21.17
dipswitch 15.6
dipteral 23.36
dipteran 25.47
diptych 21.17
Dirac 21.1
dire 12.13
direct 30.48
direction 25.49
directional 23.34
directly 4.22
Directoire 1.1
director 12.76
directorate 30.43
directorial 23.24
directory 4.43
directress 28.10
dirge 20.17
dirham 24.1
dirigible 23.26
dirigisme 24.21
dirigiste 31.5
dirk 21.31
dirndl 23.28
dirt 30.45
dirty 4.55
disaffected 16.12
disappointing 26.13
disapprover 12.87
disarmer 12.50
disarming 26.9
disastrous 28.31
disbursal 23.37
disburser 12.71
disc 21.35
discalced 31.29
discarnate 30.43
discern 25.53
discerner 12.59
discernible 23.26
discerning 26.9
discerptible 23.26
disciple 23.35
disciplinal 23.34
disciplinarian 25.37
disciplinary 4.43
discipline 25.16
discloser 12.92
disco 9.16
discoboli 6.11
discobolus 28.27
discography 4.14
discoid 16.24
discombobulate
   30.11
discomfiture 12.23
disconcerting 26.13

disconcertion 25.49
disconnected 16.12
disconsolate 30.42
discontented 16.12
discord 16.21
discordance 28.45
discordancy 4.47
discordant 30.56
discothèque 21.6
discouraging 26.6
discourtesy 4.48
discoverer 12.67
discovery 4.43
discreet 30.18
discrepancy 4.45
discrepant 30.56
discrete 30.18
discretion 25.49
discretionary 4.43
discriminant 30.56
discriminate 30.13,
   30.43
discriminatory 4.43
discus 28.26
discussant 30.56
discusser 12.71
disdain 25.7
disembodied 16.9
disembogue 18.10
disembowel 23.25
disenfranchise 35.11
diseuse 35.25
disgruntled 16.38
disgusting 26.13
dish 29.6
dishcloth 32.8
dishevel 23.40
dishrag 18.1
dishwasher 12.73
dishwater 12.80
dishy 4.50
disinfectant 30.56
disjunct 30.49
disk 21.35
diskette 30.4
Disko 9.16
dislocate 30.10
dismal 23.33
dismantler 12.48
dismissible 23.26
Disney 4.32
disorganize 35.13
disparage 20.8
disparate 30.43
dispel 23.3
dispeller 12.42
dispensary 4.43
dispense 28.44
dispenser 12.69
dispersal 23.37
dispersion 25.49

dispirit 30.24
disposal 23.41
disputant 30.56
disputatious 28.33
dispute 30.37
disputer 12.81
disquieting 26.13
Disraeli 4.22
disrupt 30.58
disrupter 12.81
disruption 25.49
Diss 28.7
dissemble 23.26
dissembler 12.42
disseminate 30.13
dissension 25.49
dissenter 12.76
dissidence 28.45
dissident 30.56
dissimilate 30.11
dissipate 30.14
dissociate 30.8
dissolute 30.37
dissonance 28.45
dissonant 30.56
dissuade 16.6
dissuader 12.26
distaff 17.2
distance 28.45
distant 30.56
distensible 23.26
distich 21.17
distil 23.8
distill 23.8
distillate 30.42
distillery 4.43
distinct 30.49
distinction 25.49
distingueé 3.11
distingueée 3.1
distinguish 29.10
distortion 25.49
distracted 16.12
distraint 30.54
distraite 30.7
distraught 30.33
distressing 26.12
distribution 25.49
distributor 12.81
district 30.49
disturb 14.15
disturbance 28.45
disturber 12.22
disyllabic 21.9
dit 30.20
ditch 15.6
ditcher 12.23
dither 12.84
ditherer 12.67
dithery 4.43
dithyramb 24.1

dithyrambic 21.9
dittany 4.34
ditto 9.24
ditty 4.53
ditzy 4.46
diuretic 21.17
diurnal 23.34
diva 12.85
divan 25.1
divaricate 30.10
dive 34.9
diver 12.86
diverge 20.17
divergence 28.45
divergent 30.56
divers 35.25
diverse 28.36
diversify 6.7
diversion 25.49
diversionary 4.43
diversity 4.53
divert 30.45
diverticula 12.46
divertimenti 4.51
divertimento 9.24
Dives 35.9
divest 31.3
divestiture 12.23
divesture 12.23
divide 16.14
dividend 16.41
divider 12.27
divine 25.21
diviner 12.55
diving board 16.20
divinity 4.53
divinize 35.13
Divis 28.12
divisible 23.26
division 25.42
divisional 23.34
divisive 34.7
divisor 12.91
divorce 28.15
divorcee 4.1
divot 30.44
divulge 20.18
divulgence 28.45
divvy 4.58
Diwali 4.21
dixie 4.46
Dixieland 16.40
dizzy 4.61
djellaba 12.22
Djerba 12.22
Djibouti 4.54
Djiboutian 25.37
Dnieper 12.61
Dniester 12.77
do 11.1
doable 23.26

dob 14.9
dobbin 25.13
dobe 4.10
Dobermann 25.45
doc 21.20
docent 30.56
Docetist 31.14
doch-an-
   dorris 28.10
docile 23.11
docility 4.53
dock 21.20
dockage 20.6
docker 12.40
docket 30.21
dockland 16.45
dockside 16.16
dockyard 16.2
doctor 12.79
doctoral 23.36
doctorate 30.43
doctorly 4.27
doctrinaire 2.1
doctrinal 23.34
doctrine 25.18
docudrama 12.50
documentalist 31.8
documentarist
   31.12
documentary 4.43
dodder 12.28
dodderer 12.67
doddery 4.43
doddle 23.28
dodecagon 25.25
dodecahedron 25.47
Dodecanese 35.6
dodge 20.11
dodgem 24.18
dodger 12.35
dodgy 4.17
dodo 9.11
doe 9.1
doer 12.19
does 35.23
doeskin 25.15
doesn't 30.56
doff 17.8
dog 18.8
dogberry 4.43
dogcart 30.3
doge 20.14
dogfight 30.27
dogfighter 12.79
dogfighting 26.13
dogfish 29.7
dogged 16.9
dogger 12.32
doggerel 23.36
dogging 26.6
doggish 29.7

doggo 9.13
doggone 25.25
doggy 4.15
doghouse 28.16
dogie 4.15
dogleg 18.3
doglike 21.19
dogma 12.51
dogmatic 21.17
dogmatist 31.14
dogmatize 35.14
dogsbody 4.13
dogshore 7.17
dog tag 18.1
dog-teeth 32.5
dog-tooth 32.12
dogtrot 30.32
dogwatch 15.7
dogwood 16.26
doh 9.1
Doha 1.9
doily 4.25
doing 26.3
doit 30.36
dojo 9.15
Dolby 4.10
dolce vita 12.77
Dolcelatte 4.51
doldrums 35.30
dole 23.17
dolerite 30.29
Dolin 25.16
doll 23.13
dollar 12.44
Dollfuss 28.25
dollhouse 28.16
dollop 27.14
dolly 4.25
dolma 12.51
dolman 25.45
dolmen 25.45
dolomite 30.29
dolomitic 21.17
dolor 12.44
Dolores 28.10
dolorous 28.31
dolour 12.44
dolphin 25.14
dolphinarium 24.16
dolt 30.51
doltish 29.10
dom 24.8
domain 25.7
domaine 25.7
dome 24.11
domelike 21.19
Domesday 3.9
domestic 21.17
domesticate 30.10
domicile 23.11
domiciliary 4.43

dominance 28.45
dominant 30.56
dominate 30.13
dominatrices 35.8
dominatrix 28.39
domineer 12.4
Domingo 9.13
Dominic 21.13
Dominica 12.38
dominical 23.32
Dominican 25.43
dominie 4.32
dominion 25.37
Dominique 21.8
domino 9.19
Domitian 25.49
Don Quixote 30.43
don't 30.55
don 25.24
Donal 23.34
Donald 16.38
Donat 30.1
donate 30.7
Donatello 9.17
donation 25.49
Donatus 28.34
Donau 8.9
Donbas 28.1
Doncaster 12.82
done 25.35
Donegal 23.14
Donetsk 21.35
dong 26.15
donga 12.32
Donizetti 4.51
donjon 25.42
donkey 4.19
donkeywork 21.31
Donkin 25.15
donna 12.56
Donne 25.35
donnée 3.17
donnish 29.9
donnybrook 21.28
donor 12.56
Donovan 25.51
donut 30.40
doodad 16.1
doodah 1.6
doodle 23.28
doodlebug 18.12
doodler 12.48
doodling 26.8
doohickey 4.19
Doolittle 23.39
doom 24.12
doomsday 3.9
doomster 12.81
door 7.1
doorbell 23.3
doorcase 28.5

doorframe 24.4
doorknob 14.9
doorman 25.45
doormat 30.1
doormen 25.45
doornail 23.6
doorpost 31.20
doorstep 27.3
doorstop 27.8
doorstopper 12.62
doorway 3.25
doozy 4.62
dop 27.8
dopamine 25.11
dope 27.10
doper 12.63
dopey 4.36
dopiaza 12.90
doppelganger 12.60
Dopper 12.62
Doppler 12.44
Doré 3.19
Dora 12.66
Dorado 9.11
Doran 25.47
Dorcas 28.26
Dorchester 12.76
Dordogne 25.32
Dordrecht 30.48
Doreen 25.11
Dorian 25.37
Doric 21.15
Dorinda 12.27
Doris 28.10
dork 21.22
dorm 24.9
dormancy 4.48
dormant 30.56
dormer 12.52
dormice 28.13
dormitory 4.43
Dormobile 23.7
dormouse 28.16
dormy 4.29
Dorothea 12.4
Dorothy 4.56
dorp 27.9
Dors 35.17
dorsal 23.37
Dorset 30.24
Dortmund 16.45
dory 4.41
do's 35.21
dos-à-dos 9.1
dosage 20.9
dose 28.17
dosh 29.11
do-si-do 9.1
Dos Passos 28.14
dois 35.21
doss 28.14

dossal 23.37
dosser 12.70
dosshouse 28.16
dossier 12.11
Dostoevsky 4.18
dot 30.31
dotage 20.9
dotard 16.29
dote 30.35
doter 12.80
dotter 12.79
dotterel 23.36
dottle 23.39
dotty 4.54
Douala 12.42
double entendre
    12.65
double 23.26
doubler 12.47
doublespeak 21.8
doublet 30.22
doublethink 21.33
doubleton 25.50
doubloon 25.33
doublure 12.20
doubt 30.34
doubter 12.80
douce 28.19
douche 29.14
Doug 18.12
Dougal 23.30
dough 9.1
doughboy 10.3
doughnut 30.40
doughty 4.54
doughy 4.7
Douglas 28.27
Doulton 25.50
dour 12.20
Douro 9.21
douse 28.16
dove 34.11, 34.13
dovecote 30.31
dovelike 21.19
Dover 12.86
dovetail 23.6
Dow 8.1
dowager 12.35
Dowding 26.5
dowdy 4.13
dowel 23.25
dower 12.16
down 25.29
down-and-out 30.34
downbeat 30.18
downcast 31.2
downer 12.56
downfall 23.15
downgrade 16.6
downhearted 16.12
downhill 23.8

downhiller 12.43
Downing 26.9
downlighter 12.79
download 16.23
downmarket 30.21
downmost 31.20
downplay 3.1
downpour 7.14
downright 30.29
downriver 12.86
Downs 35.31
downscale 23.5
downshift 30.47
downside 16.16
downsize 35.11
downstage 20.4
downstairs 35.4
downstate 30.7
downstream 24.5
downstroke 21.24
downswing 26.14
downtempo 9.20
downtime 24.7
downtown 25.29
downtrodden 25.40
downward 16.30
downwards 35.27
downwind 16.42
downy 4.32
dowry 4.43
dowse 28.16, 35.18
dowser 12.70, 12.92
Dowsing 26.14
doxy 4.46
doyen 25.38
Doyle 23.19
doze 35.19
dozen 25.52
dozenth 32.19
dozer 12.92
dozy 4.61
drab 14.1
drabble 23.26
drachm 24.1
drachma 12.50
drachmae 4.29
drack 21.1
Draco 9.16
draconian 25.37
draconic 21.13
Dracula 12.46
draft 30.47
draftee 4.1
drafter 12.75
drafts 28.47
draftsman 25.45
draftsmen 25.45
drafty 4.51
drag 18.1
draggle 23.30
draggy 4.15

dragline 25.22
dragnet 30.5
dragoman 25.45
dragon 25.41
dragonet 30.23
dragonfly 6.11
dragoon 25.33
dragster 12.74
drail 23.5
drain 25.7
drainage 20.7
drainboard 16.20
drainer 12.54
drainpipe 27.7
drake 21.7
Dralon 25.25
dram 24.1
drama 12.50
dramatic 21.17
dramatist 31.14
dramaturge 20.17
dramaturgic 21.11
dramaturgical 23.32
dramaturgy 4.17
Drambuie 4.8
Drammen 25.45
drank 21.33
drape 27.4
draper 12.61
drapery 4.43
drastic 21.17
drat 30.1
dratted 16.12
draught 30.47
draughtboard 16.20
draughts 28.47
draughtsman 25.45
draughtsmen 25.45
draughtswoman 25.45
draughtswomen 25.17
draughty 4.51
Dravidian 25.37
draw 7.1
drawback 21.2
drawbridge 20.8
drawcord 16.21
drawer 7.1,12.15
drawers 35.17
drawing 26.3
drawl 23.14
drawler 12.44
drawn 25.28
drawstring 26.11
dray 3.1
dread 16.3
dreadlocked 30.49
dreadlocks 28.40
dreadnought 30.33
dream 24.5

dreamboat 30.35
dreamer 12.51
dreamland 16.40
dreamlike 21.19
dreamt 30.52
dreamtime 24.7
dreamworld 16.38
dreamy 4.29
drear 12.4
dreary 4.43
dreck 21.6
dredge 20.3
dredger 12.35
dree 4.1
dreggy 4.15
Dreiser 12.91
drench 29.20
Dresden 25.40
dress 28.3
dressage 20.2
dresser 12.69
dressing 26.12
dressmaker 12.38
dressmaking 26.7
dressy 4.45
drew 11.1
Dreyfus 28.25
dribble 23.26
dribbler 12.48
dribbly 4.27
driblet 30.22
dribs and
    drabs 35.26
dried 16.14
drier 12.13
drift 30.47
drifter 12.78
driftnet 30.5
driftwood 16.26
drill 23.8
driller 12.43
drily 4.25
drink 21.33
drinker 12.39
drip 27.6
dripfed 16.3
dripfeed 16.7
dripping 26.10
drippy 4.36
drive 34.9
drivel 23.40
driveler 12.48
driveller 12.48
driven 25.51
driver 12.86
driveshaft 30.47
driveway 3.25
drizzle 23.41
drizzly 4.24
Drogheda 12.27
drogue 18.10

droid 16.24
droit 30.36
droll 23.17
drollery 4.43
dromedary 4.43
dromoi 10.8
drone 25.30
drongo 9.13
droob 14.12
drookit 30.21
drool 23.20
droop 27.11
droopy 4.37
drop 27.8
drophead 16.3
dropkick 21.11
drop-leaf 17.5
droplet 30.22
dropout 30.34
dropper 12.62
dropping 26.10
dropsy 4.46
droshky 4.19
drosophila 12.43
dross 28.14
drought 30.34
Drouzhba 12.21
drove 34.11
drover 12.86
drown 25.29
drowning 26.9
drowse 35.18
drowsy 4.61
drub 14.13
drudge 20.16
drudgery 4.43
drug 18.12
drugget 30.21
druggist 31.7
druggy 4.15
drugstore 7.18
Druid 16.8
Druidic 21.10
Druidical 23.32
drum 24.14
drumbeat 30.18
drumhead 16.3
drummer 12.52
drumstick 21.17
drunk 21.34
drunkard 16.28
drunken 25.43
drupe 27.11
Drusilla 12.43
druthers 35.24
Druze 35.21
dry 6.1
dryad 16.1
dryas 28.24
Dryden 25.40
dryer 12.13

d

dryish 29.6
dryland 16.45
dryness 28.9
drystone 25.31
drysuit 30.38
drywall 23.14
Du Maurier 3.3
dual 23.25
dualist 31.8
duality 4.53
dualize 35.12
Duane 25.7
dub 14.13
Dubai 6.1
dubbin 25.13
Dubcek 21.6
dubiety 4.53
dubious 28.23
Dublin 25.16
Du Bois 1.1
Dubonnet 3.17
Dubrovnik 21.13
ducal 23.32
ducat 30.42
Duce 3.8
Duchamp 25.24
duchess 28.7
duchesse 28.3
duchy 4.11
duck 21.29
duckbill 23.8
duckboard 16.20
ducker 12.41
duckling 26.8
duckweed 16.7
ducky 4.20
duct 30.49
ductile 23.12
dud 16.27
dude 16.25
dudgeon 25.42
Dudley 4.26
due 11.1
duel 23.25
dueler 12.48
duelist 31.8
dueller 12.48
duellist 31.8
duende 3.9
duenna 12.53
duet 30.4
duettist 31.14
Dufay 3.1
duff 17.15
duffel 23.29
duffer 12.30
Dufy 4.14
dug 18.12
dugout 30.34
duiker 12.40
Duisburg 18.13

duke 21.27
dukedom 24.17
dulcet 30.24
Dulcie 4.47
dulcify 6.7
dulcimer 12.51
dulcitone 25.31
dulia 12.6
dull 23.22
dullard 16.29
Dulles 28.8
dullish 29.8
dully 4.26
dulse 28.42
Duluth 32.12
duly 4.26
Duma 12.52
Dumas 1.1
Du Maurier 3.3
dumb 24.14
Dumbarton 25.50
dumbfound 16.43
dumbo 9.9
dumbshow 9.23
dumbstruck 21.29
dumbwaiter 12.77
dumdum 24.14
Dumfries 28.6
dummy 4.30
dump 27.17
dumper 12.63
dumpling 26.8
dumpster 12.81
dumpy 4.37
dun 25.35
Dunbar 1.1
Duncan 25.43
dunce cap 27.1
dunce 28.44
Dundalk 21.22
Dundee 4.1
dunderhead 16.3
dune 25.33
Dunedin 25.14
Dunfermline 25.16
dung 26.18
dungaree 4.1
Dungarvan 25.51
dungeon 25.42
dunghill 23.9
dunk 21.34
Dunkirk 21.31
Dun Laoghaire 4.43
dunlin 25.16
Dunlop 27.8
dunnage 20.7
dunny 4.33
Duns Scotus 28.34
Dunstan 25.50
duo 9.7
duodecimo 9.18

duodena 12.54
duodenum 24.19
duologue 18.8
duomo 9.18
duotone 25.31
dupable 23.26
dupe 27.11
duper 12.63
dupery 4.43
dupion 25.24
duple 23.35
duplex 28.38
duplicate 30.10, 30.42
duplicitous 28.34
duppy 4.37
durable 23.26
Duralumin 25.17
durance 28.45
Durango 9.13
duration 25.49
durational 23.34
Durban 25.38
durbar 1.4
Dürer 12.67
duress 28.3
Durex 28.38
Durham 24.19
durian 25.37
during 26.11
Durkheim 24.7
durra 12.67
Durrell 23.36
durzi 4.62
Dushanbe 3.1
dusk 21.35
dusky 4.20
Düsseldorf 17.9
dust 31.24
dustbin 25.13
dustbowl 23.17
dustcart 30.3
duster 12.81
Dustin 25.19
dustman 25.45
dustmen 25.45
dustpan 25.3
dust sheet 30.19
dusty 4.55
Dutch 15.13
Dutchman 25.45
Dutchmen 25.45
Dutchwoman 25.45
duteous 28.23
duty 4.54
duumvirate 30.43
Duvalier 3.3
duvet 3.24
dux 28.41
dwale 23.5
Dwane 25.7
dwarf 17.9

dwarves 35.35
dweeb 14.6
dwell 23.3
dweller 12.42
dwelling 26.8
dwelt 30.51
Dwight 30.26
dwindle 23.28
dyad 16.1
dybbuk 21.28
dye 6.1
dyeable 23.26
dyer 12.13
Dyfed 16.13
dying 26.3
dyke 21.19
Dylan 25.44
dynamic 21.12
dynamical 23.32
dynamicist 31.13
dynamist 31.9
dynamite 30.29
dynamize 35.13
dynamo 9.18
dynast 31.25
dynastic 21.17
dyne 25.21
dysentery 4.43
dysfunction 25.49
dysfunctional 23.34
dyslexia 12.11
dyslexic 21.16
dyspepsia 12.11
dyspeptic 21.17
dysphasia 12.12
dysplasia 12.12
dyspraxia 12.11
dystopia 12.9
dystopian 25.37
dystrophic 21.10
dystrophy 4.14
Dzerzhinsky 4.19
dzo 9.1
Dzongkha 12.40

each 15.5
eager 12.31
eagle 23.30
eaglet 30.22
Eakins 35.31
Eamon 25.45
ear 12.4
earache 21.7
earbash 29.1
eardrum 24.14
earful 23.21
Earhart 30.3

e

egress 28.3
egret 30.24
Egypt 30.58
Egyptian 25.49
eh 3.1
Ehrlich 21.11
Eichmann 25.45
Eid 16.7
eider 12.27
eiderdown 25.29
eidola 12.44
eidolon 25.25
Eiffel 23.29
Eiger 12.31
Eigg 18.3
eight 30.7
eighteen 25.9
eighteenth 32.19
eightfold 16.37
eighth 32.23
eightieth 32.6
eighty 4.52
Eilat 30.3
Eileen 25.10
Eilidh 4.22
Eindhoven 25.51
einkorn 25.28
Einstein 25.23
Éire 12.65
Eisenhower 12.16
Eisenstadt 30.2
Eisenstein 25.23
eisteddfod 16.18
eisteddfodau 6.6
either 12.84
ejaculate 30.11,
    30.42
ejaculatory 4.43
eject 30.48
ejection 25.49
ejector 12.76
eke 21.8
el 23.3
elaborate 30.15,
    30.43
Elaine 25.7
Elam 24.1
Elamite 30.29
élan 25.1
Elan 25.1, 25.44
eland 16.45
elapse 28.46
elastane 25.8
elastic 21.17
elasticated 16.12
elasticize 35.14
Elastoplast 31.2
elate 30.7
elated 16.12
elation 25.49
Elba 12.21

Elbe 14.16
elbow 9.9
elbow room 24.12
Elche 3.8
eld 16.35
elder 12.26
elderberry 4.38
elderflower 12.16
elderly 4.27
eldest 31.6
Eldon 25.40
eldorado 9.11
eldritch 15.6
Eleanor 12.58
elect 30.48
election 25.49
electioneer 12.4
electioneering
    26.11
elector 12.76
electoral 23.36
electorate 30.43
Electra 12.64
Electress 28.10
electric 21.15
electrical 23.32
electrician 25.49
electrify 6.7
electro 9.21
electrocardiogram
    24.1
electrocute 30.38
electrocution 25.49
electrode 16.23
electrolysis 28.11
electrolyte 30.28
electromagnetic
    21.17
electron 25.26
electronic 21.13
electronica 12.39
electroplate 30.11
electrotype 27.7
electuary 4.43
elegance 28.45
elegant 30.56
elegiac 21.30
elegist 31.7
elegize 35.11
elegy 4.17
element 30.56
elementary 4.43
Eleonora 12.66
elephant 30.56
elephantiasis 28.11
elephantine 25.23
elevate 30.16
elevatory 4.43
eleven 25.51
elevenfold 16.37
elevenses 35.10

eleventh 32.19
elf 17.18
elfin 25.14
elfish 29.7
Elfreda 12.26
Elgar 1.8
El Giza 12.90
El Greco 9.6
Eli 6.11
Elia 12.6
Elias 28.24
elicit 30.24
elicitor 12.78
elide 16.14
eligible 23.26
Elijah 12.35
eliminate 30.13
eliminatory 4.43
Elinor 12.55
Eliot 30.41
Elisabethville 23.10
Elisha 12.72
elision 25.42
élite 30.18
élitist 31.14
elixir 12.11
Eliza 12.91
Elizabeth 32.13
Elizabethan 25.51
elk 21.32
Elkie 4.18
ell 23.3
Ella 12.42
Ellen 25.44
Ellie 4.22
Ellington 25.50
ellipse 28.46
ellipsis 28.11
elliptic 21.17
Ellis 28.8
Ellsworth 32.14
elm 24.18
Elmer 12.50
Elmo 9.18
Elmwood 16.26
elmy 4.29
El Niño 9.28
elocution 25.49
elocutionary 4.43
elocutionist 31.10
Elohim 24.6
elongate 30.9
elope 27.10
eloper 12.63
eloquence 28.45
eloquent 30.56
El Paso 9.22
Elroy 10.11
Elsa 12.69
else 28.42
elsewhere 2.1

Elsie 4.45
Elsinore 7.13
Elspeth 32.13
Elton 25.50
elucidate 30.9
elucidatory 4.43
elude 16.25
Elul 23.22
elusive 34.7
elver 12.85
elves 35.35
Elvira 12.67
Elvis 28.12
elvish 29.10
Ely 4.23, 6.11
Elysian 25.37
Elysium 24.16
Elzevir 12.12
em 24.3
email 23.5
emanate 30.13
emancipate 30.14
emancipatory 4.43
Emanuel 23.25
emasculate 30.11
emasculatory 4.43
embalm 24.2
embalmer 12.50
embank 21.33
embargo 9.13
embark 21.5
embarras de choix
    1.1
embarrass 28.31
embarrassing 26.12
embassy 4.48
embattle 23.39
embattled 16.38
embay 3.1
embed 16.3
embellish 29.8
embellisher 12.72
ember 12.21
embezzle 23.41
embezzler 12.42
embitter 12.78
emblazon 25.52
emblem 24.18
emblematic 21.17
emblematical 23.32
emblematize 35.14
embody 4.13
embolden 25.40
embolic 21.11
emboss 28.14
embosser 12.70
embouchure 12.20
embower 12.16
embrace 28.5
embracer 12.69
embrasure 12.33

embrittle 23.39
embroider 12.28
embroiderer 12.67
embroidery 4.43
embroil 23.19
embryo 9.4
embryology 4.17
embryonal 23.34
embryonic 21.13
emcee 4.1
emend 16.41
Emeny 4.34
emerald 16.38
emerge 20.17
emergence 28.45
emergency 4.48
emergent 30.56
emeritus 28.34
emersion 25.49
Emerson 25.48
emery 4.43
emetic 21.17
emigrant 30.56
emigrate 30.15
émigré 3.19
Emile 23.7
Emily 4.24
eminence 28.45
éminence grise 35.6
eminent 30.56
emir 12.4
emirate 30.43
emissary 4.43
emission 25.49
emit 30.20
emitter 12.78
Emlyn 25.16
Emma 12.50
Emmanuel 23.25
Emmeline 25.10
Emmental 23.2
emmer 12.50
emmet 30.23
Emmy 4.29
emo 9.18
emollience 28.45
emollient 30.56
emote 30.35
emoter 12.80
emoticon 25.25
emotion 25.49
emotional 23.34
emotionalist 31.8
emotionalize 35.12
emotive 34.8
empathy 4.56
Empedocles 35.7
emperor 12.67
emphases 35.8
emphasis 28.11
emphasize 35.14

emphatic 21.17
emphysema 12.51
empire 12.14
empiric 21.15
empirical 23.32
empiricist 31.13
employ 10.1
employee 4.1
employer 12.18
emporia 12.10
emporium 24.16
empower 12.16
empress 28.10
Empson 25.48
empty 4.51
empyreal 23.23
empyrean 25.36
Emrys 28.10
emu 11.22
emulate 30.11
emulous 28.27
emulsifier 12.14
emulsify 6.7
emulsion 25.49
Emyr 12.7
en brosse 28.14
en famille 4.1
en masse 28.1
en 25.5
Ena 12.54
enable 23.26
enact 30.48
enaction 25.49
enactor 12.74
enamel 23.33
enameler 12.48
enameling 26.8
enameller 12.48
enamelling 26.8
enamored 16.29
en brosse 28.14
encamp 27.17
encapsulate 30.11
encase 28.5
encash 29.1
enceinte 30.53
Enceladus 28.25
encephalic 21.11
encephalitis 28.12
encephalogram 24.1
encephalopathy 4.56
enchant 30.53
enchanter 12.75
enchanting 26.13
enchantress 28.10
enchase 28.5
enchilada 12.25
enchiridion 25.37
encipher 12.30
encircle 23.32

enclave 34.4
enclitic 21.17
enclose 35.19
enclosure 12.33
encode 16.23
encomia 12.7
encomiast 31.1
encomiastic 21.17
encomium 24.16
encompass 28.30
encore 7.10
encounter 12.80
encourage 20.8
encourager 12.35
encroach 15.10
encroacher 12.24
encrust 31.24
encrypt 30.58
encryption 25.49
encumber 12.22
encumbrance 28.45
encyclical 23.32
encyclopedia 12.5
encyclopedic 21.10
encyclopedist 31.6
end 16.41
endanger 12.35
endear 12.4
endeavor 12.85
endeavour 12.85
endemic 21.12
Enders 35.24
endgame 24.4
ending 26.5
endive 34.6
endless 28.27
endmost 31.20
endnote 30.35
endocrine 25.23
endogamous 28.28
endogamy 4.30
endogenous 28.29
endorphin 25.14
endorse 28.15
endorsee 4.1
endorser 12.70
endosperm 24.22
endow 8.1
endower 12.16
endpaper 12.61
endplay 3.15
endpoint 30.55
endrun 25.35
endue 11.1
endurance 28.45
endure 12.20
enduro 9.21
endways 35.5
Endymion 25.37
endzone 25.31
enema 12.51

enemy 4.29
energetic 21.17
energumen 25.45
energy 4.17
enervate 30.16
en famille 4.1
enfant
  terrible 12.43
enfeeble 23.26
enfeoff 17.5
enfilade 16.6
enfold 16.37
enforce 28.15
enforcer 12.70
enfranchise 35.14
engage 20.4
engagé 3.1
engaging 26.6
Engelbert 30.45
Engels 35.29
engender 12.26
engine 25.14
engineer 12.4
engineering 26.11
engird 16.31
engirdle 23.28
England 16.45
English 29.8
Englishman 25.45
Englishmen 25.45
Englishwoman 25.45
Englishwomen 25.17
engorge 20.12
engraft 30.47
engrave 34.4
engraver 12.85
engraving 26.14
engross 28.17
engulf 17.18
enhance 28.44
enhancer 12.69
Enid 16.10
enigma 12.51
enigmatic 21.17
enigmatical 23.32
enjoin 25.32
enjoy 10.1
enjoyer 12.18
enlace 28.5
enlarge 20.2
enlarger 12.35
enlighten 25.50
enlightener 12.58
enlist 31.6
enlister 12.78
enliven 25.51
enlivener 12.58
en masse 28.1
enmesh 29.3

erect 30.48
erectile 23.12
erection 25.49
erector 12.76
eremite 30.29
eremitic 21.17
eremitical 23.32
erg 18.13
ergo 9.13
ergonomic 21.12
ergonomist 31.9
ergot 30.42
Eric 21.15
erica 12.39
Ericsson 25.48
Eridanus 28.29
Erin 25.18
Erinys 28.9
Eritrea 12.2
Eritrean 25.36
erk 21.31
Erlanger 12.31
Erle 23.42
erl-king 26.7
ermine 25.17
Ermintrude 16.25
Ernest 31.10
Ernie 4.34
Ernst 31.30
erode 16.23
erogenous 28.29
Eros 28.14
erosion 25.42
erotic 21.17
erotica 12.39
erotogenic 21.13
erotomania 12.8
err 13.1
errand 16.45
errant 30.56
errata 12.75
erratic 21.17
erratum 24.20
Errol 23.36
erroneous 28.23
error 12.64
ersatz 28.47
Erse 28.36
erst 31.26
erstwhile 23.12
erubescent 30.56
erudite 30.26
erupt 30.58
eruption 25.49
Erzgebirge 12.32
Esau 7.16
Esbjerg 18.13
escadrille 23.9
escalate 30.11
escallop 27.14
escalope 27.14

escapade 16.6
escape 27.4
escapee 4.1
escaper 12.61
escapist 31.11
escargot 9.13
eschaton 25.26
escheat 30.18
eschew 11.1
eschewal 23.25
Escorial 23.2
escort 30.33
escritoire 1.1
escrow 9.21
escudo 9.11
esculent 30.56
escutcheon 25.39
escutcheoned 16.45
Esdras 28.1
Eskimo 9.18
Esky 4.18
Esmeralda 12.25
Esmond 16.45
esophagus 28.25
esoteric 21.15
esotericist 31.13
espadrille 23.9
espalier 12.6
esparto 9.24
especial 23.38
Esperantist 31.14
Esperanto 9.24
espial 23.25
espionage 20.2
esplanade 16.6
espousal 23.41
espouse 35.18
espouser 12.92
espresso 9.22
esprit 4.1
espy 6.1
esquire 12.13
essay 3.1, 3.20
essayist 31.6
Essen 25.48
essence 28.45
Essene 25.11
essential 23.38
essentialist 31.8
Essex 28.39
establish 29.8
establisher 12.72
establishmentarian 25.37
estaminet 3.17
estancia 12.11
estate 30.7
esteem 24.5
Estelle 23.3
ester 12.76

Esther 12.76
esthete 30.19
esthetic 21.17
esthetician 25.49
estimate 30.12, 30.43
estival 23.40
Estonia 12.8
Estonian 25.37
estop 27.8
Estoril 23.8
estovers 35.24
estrange 20.19
estreat 30.18
Estremadura 12.67
estrogen 25.42
estuarine 25.23
estuary 4.41
esurient 30.56
eta 12.77
et cetera 12.67
etch 15.3
etcher 12.23
etching 26.4
eternal 23.34
eternalize 35.12
eternity 4.53
eth 33.1
Ethan 25.51
ethane 25.8
ethanol 23.13
Ethel 23.40
Etheldreda 12.26
ethene 25.12
ether 12.83
ethereal 23.24
etherize 35.13
Ethernet 30.5
ethic 21.18
ethical 23.32
ethicist 31.13
Ethiopia 12.9
Ethiopian 25.37
Ethiopic 21.14
ethnic 21.13
ethnocentric 21.15
ethnologic 21.11
ethos 28.14
ethyl 23.9
etiology 4.17
etiquette 30.4
Etna 12.53
Etonian 25.37
Etruria 12.10
Etruscan 25.43
étude 16.25
etymology 4.17
Euboea 12.3
eucalypt 30.58
eucalyptus 28.34
Eucharist 31.12

euchre 12.41
Euclid 16.10
Euclidean 25.37
Eudora 12.66
Eugene 25.10
eugenic 21.13
eugenicist 31.13
Eugénie 4.31
Euler 12.44
eulogia 12.6
eulogist 31.7
eulogy 4.17
Eumenides 35.7
Eunice 28.9
eunuch 21.30
Euphemia 12.7
euphemize 35.13
euphonic 21.13
euphonious 28.23
euphonium 24.16
euphonize 35.13
euphony 4.34
euphorbia 12.5
euphoria 12.10
euphoric 21.15
Euphrates 35.9
euphuist 31.6
Eurasian 25.42
Euratom 24.20
eureka 12.38
eurhythmic 21.12
Euripides 35.7
euro 9.21
Eurobond 16.42
Eurocentric 21.15
Eurocrat 30.2
Euromarket 30.21
Europa 12.63
Europe 27.14
European 25.36
europium 24.16
Eurovision 25.42
Eurydice 4.46
Eusebius 28.23
Eustace 28.34
euthanasia 12.12
Eva 12.85
evacuate 30.8
evacuee 4.1
evade 16.6
evader 12.26
Evadne 4.31
evaluate 30.8
Evan 25.51
evanesce 28.3
evanescence 28.45
evanescent 30.56
evangel 23.31
evangelic 21.11
evangelical 23.32
Evangeline 25.10

evangelist 31.8
evangelizer 12.91
Evans 35.31
evaporate 30.15
evasion 25.42
evasive 34.7
eve 34.5
Evelyn 25.16
even 25.51
evening 26.9
evensong 26.15
event 30.53
eventer 12.76
eventide 16.17
eventual 23.25
eventuate 30.8
ever 12.85
Everard 16.2
Everest 31.12
Everett 30.24
Everglades 35.27
evergreen 25.11
everlasting 26.13
evermore 7.1
Evert 30.44
every 4.38
everybody 4.13
everyday 3.1
everyman 25.2
everyone 25.35
everyplace 28.5
everything 26.14
everywhere 2.15
evict 30.49
eviction 25.49
evictor 12.78
evidence 28.45
evident 30.56
evidential 23.38
evidentiary 4.43
evil 23.40
evil-doer 12.19
evil-doing 26.3
evince 28.44
eviscerate 30.15
Evita 12.77
evoke 21.24
evoker 12.40
evolution 25.49
evolutional 23.34
evolutionary 4.43
evolutionist 31.10
evolve 34.15
Evonne 25.24
Ewan 25.38
Ewart 30.41
ewer 12.19
ex cathedra 12.65
ex gratia 12.72
ex libris 28.10
ex officio 9.4

ex parte 4.51
ex-directory 4.43
ex 28.38
exacerbate 30.9
exact 30.48
exacting 26.13
exaction 25.49
exactitude 16.25
exactor 12.74
exaggerate 30.15
exalt 30.51
exam 24.1
examine 25.17
examinee 4.1
examiner 12.55
example 23.35
exarch 21.5
exasperate 30.15
Excalibur 12.21
excavate 30.16
exceed 16.7
exceeding 26.5
excel 23.3
excellence 28.45
excellency 4.48
excellent 30.56
excelsior 7.3
except 30.58
excepting 26.13
exception 25.49
exceptional 23.34
excerpt 30.58
excerption 25.49
excess 28.3
excessive 34.7
exchange 20.19
exchanger 12.35
exchequer 12.37
excise 35.11, 35.14
exciseman 25.45
excisemen 25.45
excision 25.42
excite 30.26
exclaim 24.4
exclamatory 4.43
exclave 34.4
exclude 16.25
excluder 12.29
exclusion 25.42
exclusionary 4.43
exclusionist 31.10
exclusive 34.7
excogitate 30.16
excommunicate
 30.10
excommunicatory
 4.43
excoriate 30.8
excrescence 28.45
excrescent 30.56
excreta 12.77

excrete 30.18
excretion 25.49
excretory 4.43
excruciate 30.8
exculpate 30.14
exculpatory 4.43
excursion 25.49
excursionist 31.10
excursive 34.7
excursus 28.32
excusatory 4.43
excuse 28.19, 35.21
excuse-me 4.30
ex-directory 4.43
exeat 30.1
exec 21.6
execrate 30.15
execratory 4.43
executant 30.56
execute 30.38
execution 25.49
executioner 12.58
executor 12.81
executorial 23.24
executory 4.43
executrices 35.8
executrix 28.39
exegeses 35.8
exegesis 28.11
exegete 30.18
exegetic 21.17
exempla 12.42
exemplar 12.42
exemplary 4.43
exemplify 6.7
exemplum 24.18
exempt 30.52
exemption 25.49
exequies 35.10
exercise 35.14
exerciser 12.91
exergue 18.13
exert 30.45
exertion 25.49
Exeter 12.78
exeunt 30.55
exfiltrate 30.15
exfoliate 30.8
ex gratia 12.72
exhale 23.5
exhaust 31.18
exhauster 12.80
exhaustible 23.26
exhaustion 25.39
exhibit 30.20
exhibitioner 12.58
exhibitionist 31.10
exhibitor 12.78
exhilarate 30.15
exhort 30.33
exhortatory 4.43

exhorter 12.80
exhume 24.12
exigence 28.45
exigency 4.48
exigent 30.56
exigible 23.26
exiguity 4.53
exiguous 28.24
exile 23.12
exilic 21.11
exist 31.6
existence 28.45
existent 30.56
existential 23.38
existentialist 31.8
exit 30.24
Exmoor 12.20
Exocet 30.5
exodus 28.25
ex officio 9.4
exogamy 4.30
exogenous 28.29
exon 25.26
exonerate 30.15
exorbitance 28.45
exorbitant 30.56
exorcist 31.13
exordial 23.24
exordium 24.16
exoskeleton 25.50
exoteric 21.15
exotic 21.17
exotica 12.39
expand 16.40
expander 12.25
expanse 28.44
expansible 23.26
expansion 25.49
expansionary 4.43
expansionist 31.10
expansive 34.7
expat 30.1
expatiate 30.8
expatriate 30.8,
 30.41
expect 30.48
expectancy 4.48
expectant 30.56
expectorant 30.56
expectorate 30.15
expedience 28.45
expediency 4.48
expedient 30.56
expedite 30.26
expediter 12.79
expeditionary 4.43
expeditious 28.33
expel 23.3
expellee 4.1
expeller 12.42
expend 16.41

expenditure 12.23
expense 28.44
expensive 34.7
experience 28.45
experiential 23.38
experimentalist 31.8
experimenter 12.76
expert 30.45
expertise 35.6
expiate 30.8
expiatory 4.43
expire 12.13
expiry 4.43
explain 25.7
explainer 12.54
explanatory 4.43
explicate 30.10
explicatory 4.43
explicit 30.24
explode 16.23
exploder 12.28
exploit 30.36
exploiter 12.81
exploratory 4.43
explore 7.1
explorer 12.66
explosion 25.42
explosive 34.7
Expo 9.20
exponent 30.56
exponential 23.38
export 30.33
exporter 12.80
expose 35.19
exposé 3.27
exposer 12.92
expositor 12.78
expository 4.43
expostulate 30.11
expostulatory 4.43
exposure 12.33
expound 16.43
expounder 12.28
express 28.3
expressional 23.34
expressionist 31.10
expressive 34.7
expressway 3.25
expropriate 30.8
expulsion 25.49
expunction 25.49
expunge 20.19
expunger 12.36
expurgate 30.9
expurgatory 4.43
exquisite 30.25
exsolve 34.15
extant 30.53
extemporaneous 28.23

extemporary 4.43
extempore 4.43
extend 16.41
extender 12.26
extendible 23.26
extensible 23.26
extensile 23.11
extension 25.49
extensive 34.7
extent 35.53
extenuate 30.8
extenuatory 4.43
exterior 12.10
exteriorize 35.13
exterminate 30.13
exterminatory 4.43
extern 25.53
external 23.34
extinct 30.49
extinction 25.49
extinguish 29.10
extinguisher 12.72
extirpate 30.14
extol 23.17
extoller 12.44
extort 30.33
extorter 12.80
extortion 25.49
extortionate 30.43
extortioner 12.58
extortionist 31.10
extra 12.64
extract 30.48
extraction 25.49
extractor 12.74
extradite 30.26
extrados 28.14
extraneous 28.23
extraordinaire 2.1
extrapolate 30.11
extravagance 28.45
extravagancy 4.48
extravagant 30.56
extravaganza 12.90
extreme 24.5
extremist 31.9
extremity 4.53
extricate 30.10
extrinsic 21.16
extroversion 25.49
extrovert 30.45
extroverted 16.12
extrude 16.25
extrusion 25.42
exuberance 28.45
exuberant 30.56
exude 16.25
exult 30.51
exultancy 4.48

exultant 30.56
exurb 14.15
exurban 25.38
exurbanite 30.29
exurbia 12.5
exuviate 30.8
eyas 28.24
eye 6.1
eyeball 23.14
eyebath 32.2
eyeblack 21.3
eyebright 30.29
eyebrow 8.10
eyeful 23.21
eyeglass 28.2
eyehole 23.17
eyelash 29.1
eyeless 28.8
eyelet 30.22
eye level 23.40
eyelid 16.10
eyeliner 12.55
eyepatch 15.1
eyeshade 16.6
eyeshadow 9.11
eyeshot 30.32
eyesight 30.30
eyesore 7.16
eye teeth 32.5
eye tooth 32.12
eyewash 29.11
Eyre 2.1
eyrie 4.43
Eysenck 21.33
Ezekiel 23.24
Ezra 12.64

fab 14.1
Fabergé 3.12
Fabian 25.37
Fabianist 31.10
Fabius 28.23
fable 23.26
fabler 12.43
Fablon 25.25
fabric 21.15
fabricate 30.10
fabulist 31.8
fabulosity 4.53
fabulous 28.27
facade 16.2
face 28.5
facecloth 32.8
facelift 30.47
facemask 21.35
faceplate 30.11
facer 12.69

facet 30.24
facetiae 4.3
facetious 28.33
facial 23.38
facile 23.11
facilitate 30.16
facility 4.53
facing 26.12
facsimile 4.24
fact 30.48
faction 25.49
factional 23.34
factionalize 35.12
factious 28.33
factitious 28.33
factoid 16.24
factor 12.74
factorage 20.8
factory 4.43
factotum 24.20
factual 23.25
factum 24.20
facture 12.23
facula 12.46
faculty 4.51
fad 16.1
faddish 29.6
faddist 31.6
faddy 4.12
fade 16.6
fader 12.26
faecal 23.32
faeces 35.8
Faenza 12.69
faerie 4.39
Faeroe 9.21
Faeroes 35.19
faff 17.1
fag 18.1
faggot 30.42
faggoty 4.55
fagot 30.42
fah 1.1
Fahrenheit 30.27
faience 28.44
fail 23.5
failing 26.8
faille 23.5
failure 12.89
fain 25.7
faint 30.54
fair 2.1
Fairbanks 28.41
Fairfax 28.38
fairground 16.43
fairing 26.11
fairish 29.9
fairway 3.25
fairy 4.39
fairyland 16.40
Faisalabad 16.1

fait accompli 4.25
faith 32.4
fake 21.7
faker 12.38
fakery 4.43
fakir 12.6
falafel 23.29
Falange 20.19
Falangist 31.7
Falasha 12.72
falcon 25.43
falconer 12.58
falconet 30.23
falconry 4.43
Faldo 9.11
faldstool 23.20
Falk 21.22
Falkirk 21.31
Falkland 16.45
Falklands 35.27
fall 23.14
fallacious 28.33
fallacy 4.48
fallback 21.2
fallen 25.44
faller 12.44
fallible 23.26
fallout 30.34
fallow 9.17
false 28.42
falsehood 16.26
falsetto 9.24
falsework 21.31
falsies 35.10
falsify 6.7
falsity 4.53
Falstaffian 25.37
falter 12.80
falterer 12.67
faltering 26.11
fame 24.4
familial 23.24
familiar 12.6
familiarity 4.53
famille noire 1.1
famille verte 30.6
family 4.24
famine 25.17
famish 29.8
famous 28.28
famulus 28.27
fan 25.1
fanatic 21.17
fanatical 23.32
fanaticize 35.14
fan belt 30.51
fancier 12.11
fancy 4.45
fandangle 23.30
fandango 9.13
fandom 24.17

fane 25.7
fanfare 2.5
fang 26.1
fanlight 30.28
fanlike 21.19
fanner 12.53
fanny 4.31
fantail 23.6
fantasia 12.12
fantasist 31.13
fantast 31.1
fantastic 21.17
fantastical 23.32
fantasy 4.48
Fante 4.51
fanzine 25.12
far 1.1
farad 16.1
faraday 3.9
farandole 23.17
faraway 3.1
farce 28.2
farceur 13.1
farcical 23.32
farcy 4.45
fare 2.1
farewell 23.3
farfalle 4.21
farfetched 30.46
farina 12.54
farinaceous 28.33
farl 23.2
farm 24.2
farmer 12.50
farmhand 16.40
farmhouse 28.16
farmland 16.40
farmstead 16.4
farmyard 16.2
Farnborough 12.67
Farne 25.4
Farnese 4.61
Faro 9.21
Faroese 35.6
far-off 17.8
farouche 29.14
Farouk 21.27
Farquhar 1.11
farraginous 28.29
farrago 9.13
Farrell 23.36
farrier 12.10
farriery 4.43
farrow 9.21
farruca 12.41
far-seeing 26.3
Farsi 4.45
fart 30.3
farther 12.84
farthest 31.14
farthing 26.14

farthingale 23.5
fartlek 21.6
fasces 35.8
fascia 12.11
fascial 23.38
fascicle 23.32
fascicule 23.20
fascinate 30.13
fascinator 12.77
fascine 25.9
fascist 31.13
fashion 25.49
fashioner 12.58
Fassbinder 12.27
fast 31.2
fastback 21.2
fasten 25.48
fastener 12.58
fastening 26.9
faster 12.75
fastidious 28.23
fasting 26.13
Fastnet 30.5
fat 30.1
fatal 23.39
fatalist 31.8
fatality 4.53
fatback 21.2
fat cat 30.1
fate 30.7
Fates 28.47
fathead 16.3
fatheaded 16.9
father 12.84
fatherhood 16.26
fatherland 16.40
fatherlike 21.19
fatherly 4.27
fathom 24.20
fatigue 18.5
Fatiha 12.34
Fatima 12.51
Fatimid 16.10
Fatimite 30.29
fatless 28.27
fatling 26.8
fatly 4.21
fatness 28.29
fatso 9.22
fatstock 21.21
fatted 16.12
fatten 25.50
fattish 29.10
fattist 31.14
fatty 4.51
fatuity 4.53
fatuous 28.24
fatwa 1.22
faucet 30.24
Faulkner 12.56
fault 30.51

faulty 4.54
faun 25.28
fauna 12.56
Fauntleroy 10.11
Faunus 28.29
Faure 3.19
Faust 31.19
Faustian 25.37
faute de mieux 13.1
fauteuil 5.3
fauve 34.11
fauvist 31.15
Faux 28.40
fave 34.4
favela 12.42
favor 12.85
favorer 12.67
favorite 30.24
favour 12.85
favourer 12.67
favourite 30.24
Fawkes 28.40
fawn 25.28
fax 28.38
fay 3.1
fayre 2.1
faze 35.5
fazenda 12.26
fealty 4.55
fear 12.4
feasible 23.26
feast 31.5
feaster 12.77
feat 30.18
feather 12.84
featherbed 16.3
featherbrained
   16.41
featherweight 30.17
feathery 4.43
feature 12.23
febrile 23.11
February 4.43
fecal 23.32
feces 35.8
feculence 28.45
feculent 30.56
fecund 16.45
fecundate 30.9
fecundity 4.53
fed 16.3
fedayeen 25.9
federal 23.36
federalist 31.8
federalize 35.12
federate 30.15
federationist 31.10
fedora 12.66
fee 4.1
feeble 23.26
feed 16.7

feedback 21.2
feeder 12.26
feedstock 21.21
feedstuff 17.15
feel 23.7
feeler 12.43
feeling 26.8
feelings 35.32
feet 30.18
feign 25.7
feint 30.54
feisty 4.54
feldspar 1.15
Felicia 12.11
felicitate 30.16
felicitous 28.34
felicity 4.53
feline 25.22
Felix 28.39
Felixstowe 9.24
fell 23.3
fella 12.42
fellah 12.42
fellate 30.7
fellatio 9.4
feller 12.42
Fellini 4.31
fellow 9.17
Fellows 35.19
felon 25.44
felonious 28.23
felony 4.34
felt 30.51
felty 4.51
felucca 12.41
female 23.5
femineity 4.53
feminine 25.18
femininity 4.53
feminist 31.10
femme 24.1
femme fatale 23.2
femoral 23.36
femur 12.51
fen 25.5
fence 28.44
fencer 12.69
fend 16.41
fender 12.26
Fenella 12.42
feng shui 4.8
Fenian 25.37
fenland 16.40
fennec 21.13
fennel 23.34
fenny 4.31
Fens 35.31
Fenton 25.50
fenugreek 21.8
feoffor 12.30
feral 23.36

Ferdinand 16.40
Fergal 23.30
Fergus 28.25
Ferguson 25.48
ferial 23.24
Fermanagh 12.53
Fermat 1.13
ferment 30.53
fermenter 12.76
fermentor 12.76
fermium 24.16
fern 25.53
fernery 4.43
ferny 4.34
ferocious 28.33
ferocity 4.53
Ferranti 4.51
Ferrara 12.64
Ferrari 4.38
Ferrer 12.64
ferret 30.24
ferreter 12.78
ferrety 4.53
ferriage 20.6
ferric 21.15
Ferrier 12.10
ferrous 28.31
ferruginous 28.29
ferrule 23.20
ferry 4.38
ferryman 25.45
ferrymen 25.45
fertile 23.12
fertility 4.53
ferule 23.20
fervency 4.49
fervent 30.56
fervid 16.13
fervor 12.87
fervour 12.87
Fés 35.3
fess 28.3
festal 23.39
fester 12.76
festival 23.40
festive 34.8
festoon 25.33
Festschrift 30.47
Festschriften 25.50
Festus 28.34
feta 12.76
fetal 23.39
fetch 15.3
fetcher 12.23
fête 30.7
fetid 16.12
fetish 29.10
fetishist 31.13
fetishize 35.14
fetlock 21.21
fetor 12.77

fetter 12.76
fetterlock 21.21
fettle 23.39
fettler 12.48
fettuccine 4.31
fetus 28.34
feu 11.1
feud 16.25
feudal 23.28
feudalist 31.8
feudalize 35.12
feu de joie 1.1
feuilleton 25.26
fever 12.85
feverish 29.9
feverous 28.31
few 11.1
fey 3.1
Feydeau 9.11
feyly 4.22
feyness 28.9
Feynman 25.45
fez 35.3
fiacre 12.64
fiancé 3.20
fiancée 3.20
Fianna Fáil 23.19
fiasco 9.16
fiat 30.1
fib 14.7
fibber 12.21
fiber 12.21
fiberboard 16.20
fiberfill 23.8
fiberglass 28.2
fibre 12.21
fibreboard 16.20
fibrefill 23.8
fibreglass 28.2
fibril 23.9
fibrillar 12.43
fibrillary 4.43
fibrillate 30.11
fibro 9.21
fibrous 28.31
fibula 12.46
fiche 29.5
Fichte 30.50
fichu 11.19
fickle 23.32
fictile 23.12
fiction 25.49
fictional 23.34
fictionist 31.10
fictitious 28.33
fictive 34.8
fiddle 23.28
fiddle-de-dee 4.1
fiddler 12.43
fiddlestick 21.17
fiddly 4.27

fideist 31.6
Fidel 23.3
Fidelis 28.8
fidelity 4.53
fidget 30.21
fidgety 4.53
Fido 9.11
fiducial 23.38
fiduciary 4.43
fie 6.1
fief 17.5
fiefdom 24.17
field 16.35
fielder 12.26
fieldfare 2.5
Fielding 26.5
fieldmice 28.13
field mouse 28.16
Fields 35.27
fieldsman 25.45
fieldsmen 25.45
fieldwork 21.31
fieldworker 12.41
fiend 16.41
fiendish 29.6
fiendlike 21.19
fierce 28.23
fiery 4.43
fiesta 12.76
fife 17.7
fifer 12.30
Fifi 4.14
fifteen 25.9
fifteenth 32.19
fifth 32.16
fiftieth 32.6
fifty 4.53
fifty-fifty 4.53
fig 18.6
fight 30.26
fightback 21.2
fighter 12.79
fig leaf 17.5
fig leaves 35.35
figment 30.56
figtree 4.40
figura 12.67
figural 23.36
figurant 30.56
figure 12.31
figurehead 16.3
figurine 25.9
Fiji 4.17
Fijian 25.36
filaria 12.10
filariae 4.3
filarial 23.24
filature 12.24
filbert 30.41
filch 15.15
filcher 12.23

f

flameproof 17.13
flamingo 9.13
flamy 4.29
flan 25.1
Flanders 35.24
flâneur 13.1
flange 20.19
flank 21.33
flanker 12.37
flannel 23.34
flannelette 30.4
flap 27.1
flapjack 21.3
flapper 12.61
flappy 4.36
flare 2.1
flash 29.1
flashback 21.2
flashbulb 14.16
flashcard 16.2
flasher 12.72
flashgun 25.35
flashing 26.12
flashlight 30.28
flashpoint 30.55
flashy 4.50
flask 21.35
flat 30.1
flatbed 16.3
flatboat 30.35
flatbread 16.4
flatfeet 30.18
flatfish 29.7
flatfoot 30.39
Flathead 16.3
flatiron 25.38
flatland 16.40
flatlet 30.22
flatmate 30.12
flatten 25.50
flattener 12.58
flatter 12.74
flatterer 12.67
flattery 4.43
flattie 4.51
flattish 29.10
flat-top 27.8
flatulence 28.45
flatulent 30.56
flatware 2.15
flatwater 12.80
flatworm 24.22
Flaubert 2.3
flaunt 30.54
flaunter 12.80
flaunty 4.54
flautist 31.14
flavescent 30.56
Flavia 12.12
Flavian 25.37
flavone 25.31

flavor 12.85
flavoring 26.11
flavour 12.85
flavouring 26.11
flaw 7.1
flax 28.38
flaxen 25.48
Flaxman 25.45
flaxseed 16.7
flay 3.1
flayer 12.2
flea 4.1
fleabag 18.1
fleapit 30.23
flèche 29.4
fleck 21.6
Flecker 12.37
fled 16.3
fledge 20.3
fledgling 26.8
flee 4.1
fleece 28.6
fleecy 4.45
fleer 12.4
fleet 30.18
fleeting 26.13
Fleming 26.9
Flemish 29.8
flesh 29.3
flesher 12.72
fleshly 4.22
fleshpot 30.32
fleshy 4.50
fletcher 12.23
Fleur 13.1
fleur-de-lis 4.1
fleuron 25.26
flew 11.1
flex 28.38
flexible 23.26
flexile 23.11
flexility 4.53
flexitime 24.7
flexor 12.69
flexuous 28.24
flibbertigibbet 30.20
flick 21.9
flicker 12.39
flickering 26.11
flies 35.11
flight 30.26
flighty 4.54
flimflam 24.1
flimflammer 12.50
flimflammery 4.43
flimsy 4.61
flinch 29.20
flincher 12.72
flinders 35.24
fling 26.3

flinger 12.60
flint 30.54
flintlock 21.21
Flintshire 12.5
flinty 4.53
flip 27.6
flipflop 27.8
flippancy 4.48
flippant 30.56
flipper 12.62
flirt 30.45
flirtatious 28.33
flirty 4.55
flit 30.20
flitch 15.6
flitter 12.78
Flo 9.1
float 30.35
floater 12.80
floaty 4.54
floc 21.20
flocci 6.16
flocculate 30.11
floccule 23.20
flocculent 30.56
flocculi 6.11
flocculus 28.27
floccus 28.26
flock 21.20
flocky 4.19
floe 9.1
Floella 12.42
flog 18.8
flogger 12.32
flood 16.27
floodgate 30.9
floodlight 30.28
floodlit 30.22
floor 7.1
floorboard 16.20
flooring 26.11
floozie 4.62
flop 27.8
flophouse 28.16
floppy 4.36
flora 12.66
floral 23.36
floreat 30.1
Florence 28.45
Florentine 25.23
Flores 35.10
florescence 28.45
floret 30.24
Florey 4.41
florid 16.11
Florida 12.27
Floridian 25.37
florilegia 12.6
florin 25.18
Florio 9.4
florist 31.12

floristry 4.40
Florrie 4.41
floruit 30.20
flory 4.41
floss 28.14
Flossie 4.46
flossy 4.46
flotilla 12.43
flotsam 24.20
flounce 28.44
flounder 12.28
flounderer 12.67
flour 12.16
flourish 29.9
flourisher 12.72
floury 4.43
flout 30.34
flow 9.1
flow chart 30.3
flower 12.16
flowerer 12.67
floweret 30.24
flower-like 21.19
flowerpot 30.32
Flowers 35.24
flowery 4.43
flowing 26.3
flown 25.30
flowsheet 30.19
Floyd 16.24
flu 11.1
flub 14.13
fluctuate 30.8
flue 11.1
fluence 28.45
fluency 4.48
fluent 30.56
fluff 17.15
fluffy 4.14
Flügelhorn 25.28
fluid 16.8
fluidity 4.53
fluid ounce 28.44
fluke 21.27
fluky 4.20
flume 24.12
flummery 4.43
flummox 28.41
flump 27.17
flung 26.18
flunk 21.34
flunkey 4.20
fluoresce 28.3
fluorescence 28.45
fluorescent 30.56
fluoridate 30.9
fluoride 16.15
fluorine 25.11
fluorite 30.29
fluorspar 1.15
flurry 4.42

flush 29.16
flusher 12.73
Flushing 26.12
fluster 12.81
flute 30.37
flutist 31.14
flutter 12.81
flutterer 12.67
fluttery 4.43
fluty 4.54
fluvial 23.24
fluviatile 23.12
flux 28.41
fluxional 23.34
fly 6.1
flyable 23.26
flyaway 3.25
flyblown 25.30
flycatcher 12.23
flyer 12.13
flyleaf 17.5
flyleaves 35.35
flyness 28.9
Flynn 25.13
flyover 12.86
flypaper 12.61
fly-past 31.2
flysheet 30.19
flyweight 30.17
flywheel 23.7
foal 23.17
foam 24.11
foamy 4.29
fob 14.9
fobwatch 15.7
focaccia 12.23
focal 23.32
focalize 35.12
Foch 29.11
foci 6.10
fo'c's'le 23.37
focus 28.26
fodder 12.28
foe 9.1
fog bank 21.33
fog 18.8
fogbound 16.43
fogey 4.15
fogeydom 24.17
fogeyish 29.6
foggy 4.15
foghorn 25.28
fohn 25.53
foible 23.26
foie gras 1.1
foil 23.19
foist 31.21
Fokker 12.40
fold 16.37
foldaway 3.25
folder 12.28

folderol 23.13
Foley 4.25
foliaceous 28.33
foliage 20.6
foliate 30.8, 30.41
Folies-Bergere 2.1
folio 9.4
folk 21.24
Folkestone 25.50
folkie 4.20
folkish 29.8
folklore 7.11
folkloric 21.15
folklorist 31.12
folksy 4.47
folktale 23.6
folky 4.20
follicle 23.32
follow 9.17
follower 12.17
following 26.3
follow-my-leader
  12.26
folly 4.25
Folsom 24.20
foment 30.53
fomenter 12.76
fond 16.42
Fonda 12.28
fondant 30.56
fondle 23.28
fondler 12.48
fondue 11.6
font 30.54
fontal 23.39
fontanelle 23.3
Fonteyn 25.8
Foochow 8.1
food 16.25
foodie 4.13
foodstuff 17.15
fool 23.20
foolery 4.43
foolhardy 4.12
foolish 29.8
foolproof 17.13
foolscap 27.1
foot 30.39
footage 20.9
football 23.14
footballer 12.44
footbed 16.3
footbrake 21.7
footbridge 20.8
footer 12.81
footfall 23.15
foothill 23.9
foothold 16.37
footing 26.13
footle 23.39
footlights 28.47

footlocker 12.40
footloose 28.19
footman 25.45
footmark 21.5
footmen 25.45
footnote 30.35
footpad 16.1
footpath 32.2
footplate 30.11
footprint 30.54
footrest 31.3
footsie 4.47
footslog 18.8
footslogger 12.32
footsore 7.16
footstep 27.3
footstool 23.20
footway 3.25
footwear 2.15
footwork 21.31
footy 4.55
foozle 23.41
fop 27.8
foppery 4.43
foppish 29.9
for 7.1
fora 12.66
forage 20.8
forager 12.35
foray 3.19
forbade 16.1
forbear 2.1, 2.3
forbearance 28.45
Forbes 35.26
forbid 16.8
forbidden 25.40
forbidding 26.5
forbore 7.1
forborne 25.28
forbye 6.1
force 28.15
force majeure 13.1
forcemeat 30.18
forceps 28.46
forcer 12.70
forcible 23.26
ford 16.19
fore 7.1
forearm 24.2
forebear 2.3
forebode 16.23
foreboding 26.5
forecast 31.2
forecaster 12.75
forecastle 23.37
foreclose 35.19
foreclosure 12.33
forecourt 30.33
foredeck 21.6
foredoom 24.12
forefather 12.84

forefeet 30.18
forefinger 12.31
forefoot 30.39
forefront 30.55
foregather 12.84
foregoer 12.17
foregoing 26.3
foregone 25.24
foreground 16.43
forehand 16.40
forehead 16.11
forehock 21.20
foreign 25.18
foreigner 12.55
foreknew 11.1
foreknow 9.1
foreknowledge 20.6
foreknown 25.30
foreland 16.45
foreleg 18.3
forelimb 24.6
forelock 21.21
foreman 25.45
foremast 31.2
foremen 25.45
foremost 31.20
forename 24.4
forenoon 25.33
forensic 21.18
forepart 30.3
forepaw 7.14
forepeak 21.8
foreplay 3.15
foreran 25.1
forerun 25.35
forerunner 12.57
foresail 23.6
foresaw 7.1
foresee 4.1
foreseen 25.9
foreseer 12.3
foreshadow 9.11
foresheets 28.47
foreshore 7.17
foreshorten 25.50
foreshow 9.1
foreshown 25.30
foresight 30.30
foresighted 16.12
foreskin 25.15
forest 31.12
forestall 23.14
forestaller 12.44
forestay 3.22
forester 12.78
forestry 4.40
foretaste 31.4
foretell 23.3
foreteller 12.42
forethought 30.33
foretoken 25.43

foretold 16.37
foretop 27.8
forever 12.85
forevermore 7.1
forewarn 25.28
forewarner 12.56
forewent 30.53
forewing 26.14
forewoman 25.45
forewomen 25.17
foreword 16.31
foreyard 16.2
Forfar 12.30
Forfarshire 12.11
forfeit 30.21
forfeiter 12.78
forfeiture 12.23
forfend 16.41
forgave 34.4
forge 20.12
forger 12.35
forgery 4.43
forget 30.4
forget-me-not 30.32
forgetter 12.76
forgive 34.6
forgiven 25.51
forgiver 12.86
forgo 9.1
forgot 30.31
forgotten 25.50
fork 21.22
forlorn 25.28
form 24.9
formal 23.33
formaldehyde 16.14
formalin 25.16
formalist 31.8
format 30.1
Formby 4.10
forme 24.9
former 12.52
Formica 12.40
Formosa 12.71
formula 12.46
formulae 4.26
formulaic 21.9
formularize 35.13
formulary 4.43
formulate 30.11
formwork 21.31
fornicate 30.10
Forrest 31.12
forsake 21.7
forsaken 25.43
forsaker 12.38
forsook 21.28
forsooth 32.12
Forster 12.80
forswear 2.1
forswore 7.1

Forsyth 32.7
forsythia 12.12
fort 30.33
forte 3.22
Fortean 25.37
forth 32.9
forthcoming 26.9
forthright 30.29
forthwith 33.4
fortieth 32.6
fortifier 12.14
fortify 6.7
fortissimo 9.18
fortitude 16.25
fortnight 30.29
fortnightly 4.25
fortress 28.10
fortuitous 28.34
fortuity 4.53
fortunate 30.43
fortune 25.33
forty 4.54
forty-niner 12.55
forum 24.19
forward 16.30
forwarder 12.29
forwards 35.27
forwent 30.53
Fosbury 4.43
fossa 12.70
fosse 28.14
fossick 21.16
fossicker 12.39
fossil 23.37
foster 12.79
fosterage 20.8
fosterer 12.67
Foucault 9.1
fouetté 3.22
fought 30.33
foul 23.16
foulard 1.12
foumart 30.43
found 16.43
founder 12.28
foundling 26.8
foundry 4.41
fount 30.54, 30.55
fountain 25.19
fountainhead 16.3
fountain pen 25.5
four 7.1
fourfold 16.37
Fourier 12.10
fourscore 7.1
foursquare 2.1
fourteen 25.9
fourteenth 32.19
fourth 32.9
fowl 23.16
fowler 12.44

Fowles 35.29
fowling 26.8
fox 28.40
Foxe 28.40
foxglove 34.13
foxhole 23.17
foxhound 16.43
foxlike 21.19
foxtail 23.6
foxtrot 30.32
foxy 4.46
foyer 3.4
Fra 1.1
frabjous 28.25
fracas 1.11
fracases 35.10
fractal 23.39
fraction 25.49
fractional 23.34
fractionalize 35.12
fractionate 30.13
fractious 28.33
fracture 12.23
fragile 23.11
fragility 4.53
fragmentary 4.43
Fragonard 1.14
fragrance 28.45
fragranced 31.30
fragrancy 4.48
fragrant 30.56
frail 23.5
frailty 4.52
fraise 35.3
Fraktur 12.20
frame 24.4
framer 12.50
framework 21.31
Fran 25.1
franc 21.33
France 28.44
Frances 28.11
Francesca 12.37
franchise 35.14
franchisee 4.1
franchiser 12.91
Francine 25.9
Francis 28.11
Franciscan 25.43
francium 24.16
Franck 21.33
Franco 9.16
François 1.22
Françoise 1.22
francolin 25.16
Francophile 23.11
francophone 25.30
frangible 23.26
frangipane 25.8
frangipani 4.31
franglais 3.15

frank 21.33
Frankenstein 25.23
franker 12.37
Frankfort 30.41
Frankfurt 30.45
frankfurter 12.82
Frankie 4.18
frankincense 28.44
Frankish 29.8
franklin 25.16
Franks 28.41
frantic 21.17
frap 27.1
frappé 3.18
Frascati 4.51
Fraser 12.90
frat 30.1
fraternal 23.34
fraternity 4.53
fratricidal 23.28
fratricide 16.16
Frau 8.1
fraud 16.19
fraudster 12.80
fraudulence 28.45
fraudulent 30.56
fraught 30.33
Fräulein 25.22
Fraunhofer 12.30
fray 3.1
Frazier 12.12
frazil 23.10
frazzle 23.41
freak 21.8
freakish 29.8
freaky 4.18
freckle 23.32
freckly 4.22
Fred 16.3
Freddie 4.12
Frederica 12.38
Frederick 21.15
Fredericton 25.50
free 4.1
freebase 28.5
freebie 4.10
freeboard 16.20
freeboot 30.37
freebooter 12.81
freeborn 25.28
freedman 25.2
freedmen 25.5
freedom 24.17
Freefone 25.30
freegan 25.41
freehand 16.40
freehold 16.37
freeholder 12.28
freelance 28.44
freeload 16.23
freeloader 12.28

Freeman 25.45
Freemason 25.48
freemasonry 4.39
freemen 25.45
freemium 24.16
Freeport 30.33
Freepost 31.20
freer 12.3
Freer 12.4
freesia 12.12
freestanding 26.5
freestone 25.31
freestyle 23.12
freestyler 12.44
freethinker 12.39
freethinking 26.7
Freetown 25.29
freeware 2.15
freeway 3.25
freewheel 23.7
freewill 23.8
freeze 35.6
freezer 12.90
Freiburg 18.13
freight 30.7
freightage 20.9
freighter 12.77
Fremantle 23.39
Frémont 30.54
French 29.20
Frenchman 25.45
Frenchmen 25.45
Frenchwoman 25.45
Frenchwomen 25.17
Frenchy 4.50
frenetic 21.17
frenzied 16.13
frenzy 4.61
frequency 4.48
frequent 30.53, 30.56
frequenter 12.76
fresco 9.16
fresh 29.3
freshen 25.49
fresher 12.72
freshman 25.45
freshmen 25.45
freshwater 12.80
Fresnel 23.3
Fresno 9.19
fret 30.4
fretboard 16.20
fretsaw 7.16
fretwork 21.31
Freud 16.24
Freudian 25.37
Frey 3.1
Freya 12.2
friable 23.26
friar 12.13
friary 4.43

fribble 23.26
fricandeau 9.11
fricandeaux 35.19
fricassee 4.48
friction 25.49
Friday 3.9
fridge 20.6
Friedan 25.1
Friedman 25.45
Friedrich 21.15
friend 16.41
friendly 4.22
Fries 35.6
Friesian 25.42
Friesland 16.45
frieze 35.6
frig 18.6, 20.6
frigate 30.21
Frigga 12.31
fright 30.26
frighten 25.50
frightener 12.58
frigid 16.10
frigidaria 12.10
frigidarium 24.16
frigidity 4.53
frill 23.8
frilly 4.24
fringe 20.19
fringy 4.17
Frink 21.33
frippery 4.43
frisbee 4.10
Frisch 29.6
frisée 3.27
Frisian 25.37
frisk 21.35
frisker 12.39
frisket 30.21
frisky 4.19
frisson 25.26
frit 30.20
fritillary 4.43
fritter 12.78
fritto misto 9.24
Fritz 28.47
Friuli 4.26
Friulian 25.37
frivolity 4.53
frivolous 28.27
frizz 35.10
frizzle 23.41
frizzly 4.27
frizzy 4.61
Frobisher 12.72
frock 21.20
froe 9.1
Froebel 23.26
frog 18.8
frogging 26.6
froggy 4.15

frogman 25.45
frogmarch 15.2
frogmen 25.45
frogspawn 25.28
frolic 21.11
frolicker 12.39
from 24.8
fromage blanc 25.24
fromage frais 3.1
frond 16.42
front 30.55
frontage 20.9
frontager 12.35
frontal 23.39
frontbench 29.20
front-bencher 12.72
frontier 12.12
frontiersman 25.45
frontiersmen 25.45
frontierswoman
   25.45
frontierswomen
   25.17
frontispiece 28.6
frontlet 30.22
frontline 25.21
frontman 25.2
frontmen 25.5
fronton 25.50
front-runner 12.57
frontward 16.30
frost 31.17
frostbite 30.26
frosting 26.13
frosty 4.54
froth 32.8
frothy 4.56
frottage 19.1
froufrou 11.17
froward 16.28
frown 25.29
frowst 31.19
frowsty 4.54
frowzy 4.61
froze 35.19
frozen 25.52
fructify 6.7
fructose 35.19
fructuous 28.24
frugal 23.30
fruit 30.37
fruitarian 25.37
fruitbat 30.1
fruitcake 21.7
fruiterer 12.67
fruition 25.49
fruitlet 30.22
fruitwood 16.26
fruity 4.54
frump 27.17
frumpish 29.9

frumpy 4.37
frustrate 30.7
frustrater 12.77
fry 6.1
Frye 6.1
fryer 12.13
frypan 25.3
fry-up 27.13
fubsy 4.47
Fuchs 28.40
fuchsia 12.73
fuci 6.16
fuck 21.29
fucker 12.41
fucus 28.26
fuddle 23.28
fuddy-duddy 4.13
fudge 20.16
fuel 23.25
Fuentes 28.5
fug 18.12
fugacious 28.33
fugacity 4.53
fugal 23.30
fuggy 4.15
fugu 11.8
fugue 18.11
Führer 12.67
Fujairah 12.65
Fuji 4.17
Fujian 25.37
Fulani 4.31
Fulbright 30.29
fulcra 12.66
fulcrum 24.19
fulfil 23.8
fulfill 23.8
fulfiller 12.43
fulgent 30.56
fuliginous 28.29
full 23.21
fullback 21.2
fuller 12.46
fully 4.26
fulmar 12.52
fulminate 30.13
fulness 28.29
fulsome 24.20
Fulton 25.50
fulvous 28.35
fumarole 23.18
fumble 23.26
fumbler 12.48
fume 24.12
fumigant 30.56
fumigate 30.9
fumitory 4.43
fumy 4.30
fun 25.35
funambulist 31.8
Funchal 23.2

f
g

gamma 12.50
gammon 25.45
gammy 4.29
Gamow 9.18
gamp 27.17
gamut 30.43
gamy 4.29
gander 12.25
Gandhi 4.12
gang 26.1
gangboard 16.20
gangbuster 12.81
ganger 12.60
Ganges 35.7
gangland 16.40
gangling 26.8
ganglion 25.37
gangly 4.21
gangplank 21.33
gangrene 25.11
gangsta 12.74
gangster 12.74
gangway 3.25
ganja 12.35
gannet 30.23
gantlet 30.22
gantry 4.38
Ganymede 16.7
gap 27.1
gape 27.4
gaper 12.61
gappy 4.36
gar 1.1
garage 20.2
garb 14.2
garbage 20.6
garbanzo 9.29
garble 23.26
garbler 12.42
Garbo 9.9
garçon 25.26
Garda 12.25
Gardaí 4.1
garden 25.40
gardener 12.58
gardenia 12.8
Gardner 12.53
Gareth 32.13
Garfield 16.35
garfish 29.7
garganey 4.34
gargantuan 25.38
gargle 23.30
gargoyle 23.19
Garibaldi 4.13
garish 29.9
garland 16.45
garlic 21.11
garlicky 4.19
garment 30.56
garnacha 12.23

garner 12.53
garnet 30.23
garnish 29.9
garnishee 4.1
garnishing 26.12
garniture 12.23
Garonne 25.24
garpike 21.19
garret 30.43
Garrick 21.15
garrison 25.48
garrote 30.31
garrotte 30.31
garrulity 4.53
garrulous 28.27
garter 12.75
garth 32.2
Garvey 4.58
Gary 4.38
gas 28.1
gasbag 18.1
Gascogne 25.32
Gascon 25.43
Gascony 4.34
gaseous 28.23
gash 29.1
Gaskell 23.32
gasket 30.21
gaskin 25.15
gaslight 30.28
gasman 25.2
gasmen 25.5
gasoline 25.10
gasometer 12.78
gasp 27.18
gasper 12.61
Gassendi 4.12
gasser 12.69
gassy 4.45
Gasthaus 28.16
gastric 21.15
gastroenteritis
   28.12
gastronome 24.11
gastronomic 21.12
gastronomical 23.32
gastronomy 4.30
gastropod 16.18
gasworks 28.41
gat 30.1
gate 30.7
gateau 9.24
gateaux 35.19
gatecrash 29.1
gatecrasher 12.72
gatefold 16.37
gatehouse 28.16
gatekeeper 12.61
gatelegged 16.33
gatepost 31.20
Gates 28.47

Gateshead 16.3
gateway 3.25
gather 12.84
gatherer 12.67
gathering 26.11
Gatling 26.8
Gatwick 21.18
gauche 29.13
gaucherie 4.43
gaucho 9.10
gaud 16.19
Gaudí 4.13
gaudy 4.13
gauge 20.4
gauger 12.35
Gauguin 25.1
Gaul 23.14
Gaulish 29.8
Gaullist 31.8
gaunt 30.54
gauntlet 30.22
gaur 12.16
Gauss 28.16
Gaussian 25.37
gauze 35.17
gauzy 4.61
gave 34.4
gavel 23.40
Gavin 25.19
gavotte 30.31
Gawain 25.8
Gawd 16.19
gawk 21.22
gawky 4.19
gawp 27.9
gawper 12.62
gay 3.1
gayal 23.2
Gaye 3.1
gayety 4.53
gayness 28.9
Gaynor 12.54
gaze 35.5
gazebo 9.9
gazelle 23.3
gazer 12.90
gazette 30.4
gazetteer 12.4
gazpacho 9.10
gazump 27.17
gazumper 12.63
Gdansk 21.35
Gdynia 12.8
gean 25.9
gear 12.4
gearbox 28.40
gearing 26.11
gearstick 21.17
gearwheel 23.7
Geber 12.21
gecko 9.16

gee 4.1
gee-gee 4.17
geek 21.8
Geelong 26.15
geese 28.6
gee-string 26.11
gee-whiz 35.10
geezer 12.90
Gehrig 18.6
Geikie 4.18
geisha 12.72
gel 23.3
gelada 12.25
gelatin 25.19
gelatinize 35.13
gelatinous 28.29
gelato 9.24
geld 16.35
gelding 26.5
gelid 16.10
gelignite 30.29
Gell-Mann 25.1
gelsemium 24.16
gelt 30.51
gem 24.3
Gemara 12.64
gematria 12.10
Gemini 4.32, 6.13
Geminian 25.38
Geminids 35.27
gem-like 21.19
gemsbok 21.20
gemstone 25.31
gemütlich 21.11
gen 25.5
gendarme 24.2
gendarmerie 4.43
gender 12.26
gene 25.9
genealogist 31.7
genealogy 4.17
genera 12.67
general 23.36
generalissimo 9.18
generalist 31.8
generalizer 12.91
generate 30.15
generic 21.15
generosity 4.53
generous 28.31
genesis 28.11
genet 30.23
Genet 3.1
genetic 21.17
geneticist 31.13
Geneva 12.85
genial 23.23, 23.24
genie 4.31
genii 6.3
genital 23.39
genitalia 12.6

genitival 23.40
genius 28.23
genoa 12.17
genocidal 23.28
genocide 16.16
Genoese 35.6
genome 24.11
genotype 27.7
Genova 12.87
genre 12.65
gens 35.31
gent 30.53
genteel 23.7
gentes 35.9
gentian 25.49
gentile 23.12
gentility 4.53
gentle 23.39
gentlefolk 21.24
gentleman 25.45
gentlemanly 4.27
gentlemen 25.45
gentlewoman 25.45
gentlewomen 25.17
gentoo 11.20
gentrifier 12.14
gentrify 6.7
gentry 4.38
genuflect 30.48
genuflection 25.49
genuflector 12.76
genuine 25.13
genus 28.29
geocentric 21.15
geode 16.23
geodesic 21.16
geodic 21.10
geoengineering 26.11
Geoff 17.3
Geoffrey 4.38
geographer 12.30
geographic 21.10
geography 4.14
geoid 16.24
geolocation 25.49
geologist 31.7
geology 4.17
geomancy 4.45
geomantic 21.17
geometer 12.78
geometric 21.15
geometrical 23.32
geometry 4.40
geopolitical 23.32
geopolitics 28.39
Geordie 4.13
George 20.12
Georgetown 25.29
Georgette 30.4
Georgia 12.35

Georgian 25.42
Georgiana 12.53
georgic 21.11
Georgie 4.17
Georgina 12.54
geotagging 26.6
geotechnical 23.32
geothermal 23.33
Geraint 30.54
Gerald 16.38
Geraldine 25.10
Geraldton 25.50
geranium 24.16
Gerard 16.2
gerbera 12.67
gerbil 23.8
Gerda 12.29
geriatric 21.15
germ 24.22
Germaine 25.7
German 25.45
germander 12.25
germane 25.7
Germanic 21.13
Germanist 31.10
germanium 24.16
Germany 4.34
germicidal 23.28
germicide 16.16
germinal 23.34
germinate 30.13
Germiston 25.50
Geronimo 9.18
gerontocracy 4.48
Gerry 4.38
gerrymander 12.25
gerrymanderer 12.67
Gershwin 25.20
Gertrude 16.25
gerund 16.45
gerundive 34.6
Gervaise 35.5
gesso 9.22
gestalt 30.51
Gestapo 9.20
gestate 30.7
gesticulate 30.11
gesticulatory 4.43
gesture 12.23
gesundheit 30.27
get 30.4
getaway 3.25
Gethin 25.19
getter 12.76
Getty 4.51
Gettysburg 18.13
gewgaw 7.7
geyser 12.90
Ghana 12.53
Ghanaian 25.36

ghastly 4.21
ghat 30.3
Ghazi 4.61
ghee 4.1
Ghent 30.53
gherkin 25.15
ghetto 9.24
ghettoize 35.11
ghost 31.20
ghostlike 21.19
ghostly 4.25
ghostwriter 12.79
ghoul 23.20
ghoulish 29.8
Giacometti 4.51
giant 30.56
giantess 28.12
gibber 12.21
gibberish 29.9
gibbet 30.20
gibbon 25.38
Gibbons 35.31
gibbous 28.24
Gibbs 35.26
giblets 28.47
Gibraltar 12.80
Gibraltarian 25.37
Gibson 25.48
giclee 3.1
giddy 4.12
Gide 16.7
Gideon 25.37
Gielgud 16.26
gift 30.47
giftware 2.15
giftwrap 27.1
gig 18.6
gigabyte 30.26
gigaflop 27.8
giganotosaurus 28.31
gigantic 21.17
giggle 23.30
giggler 12.48
giggly 4.24
Gigli 4.23
gigolo 9.17
gigot 30.42
Gilbert 30.41
Gilbertian 25.37
gild 16.35
Giles 35.29
gilet 3.1
gilgai 6.8
Gilgamesh 29.3
Gill 23.8
Gillespie 4.36
Gillian 25.37

gillie 4.24
Gillies 35.10
Gillingham 24.19
Gilly 4.24
Gilroy 10.11
gilt-edged 16.34
gilt 30.51
giltwood 16.26
gimbal 23.26
gimcrack 21.3
gimcrackery 4.43
gimlet 30.22
gimme 4.29
gimmick 21.12
gimmickry 4.40
gimmicky 4.19
gimp 27.17
gimpy 4.36
gin 25.13
Gina 12.54
ginger 12.35
gingerbread 16.4
gingerly 4.27
gingery 4.43
gingham 24.19
gingivitis 28.12
gink 21.33
ginkgo 9.16
Ginny 4.32
Gino 9.19
ginormous 28.28
Ginsberg 18.13
ginseng 26.2
Giorgione 4.33
Giotto 9.25
Giovanni 4.31
giraffe 17.2
girandole 23.17
girasol 23.13
gird 16.31
girder 12.29
girdle 23.28
girl 23.42
girlfriend 16.41
girlhood 16.26
girlie 4.28
girlish 29.8
giro 9.21
Gironde 16.42
Girondin 25.14
Girondist 31.6
girt 30.45
girth 32.14
Gisborne 25.53
Giselle 23.3
Gish 29.6
Gissing 26.12
gist 31.6
git 30.20
gittern 25.53
Giuseppe 4.36

g

give 34.6
giveaway 3.25
given 25.51
giver 12.86
gizmo 9.18
gizzard 16.30
glacé 3.20
glacial 23.38
glaciated 16.12
glacier 12.11
glacis 28.11
glad 16.1
gladden 25.40
gladdon 25.40
glade 16.6
gladiatorial 23.24
gladioli 6.11
gladiolus 28.27
Gladstone 25.50
Gladwin 25.20
Gladys 28.7
glair 2.1
glairy 4.39
glam 24.1
glamor 12.50
Glamorgan 25.41
glamorize 35.13
glamorous 28.31
glamour 12.50
glamping 26.10
glance 28.44
gland 16.40
glanders 35.24
glandular 12.46
glans 35.31
glare 2.1
glary 4.39
Glasgow 9.13
glasnost 31.17
glass 28.2
glasses 35.10
glasshouse 28.16
glassine 25.11
glass-like 21.19
glassware 2.15
glassy 4.45
Glastonbury 4.43
Glaswegian 25.42
glaucoma 12.52
glaucous 28.26
glaze 35.5
glazer 12.90
glazier 12.12
glazy 4.61
gleam 24.5
gleamy 4.29
glean 25.9
gleaner 12.54
gleanings 35.32
glebe 14.6
glee 4.1

glen 25.5
Glenda 12.26
Glendower 12.16
Gleneagles 35.29
glengarry 4.38
Glenn 25.5
Glenrothes 28.12
Glenys 28.9
glib 14.7
glide 16.14
glider 12.27
glim 24.6
glimmer 12.51
glimmering 26.11
glimpse 28.43
Glinka 12.39
glint 30.54
glissade 16.2
glissandi 4.12
glissando 9.11
glissé 3.1
glisten 25.48
glister 12.78
glitch 15.6
glitter 12.78
glitterati 4.51
glittery 4.43
glitz 28.47
glitzy 4.46
gloaming 26.9
gloat 30.35
gloater 12.80
glob 14.9
global 23.26
globe 14.11
globe-like 21.19
globetrotter 12.79
globoid 16.24
globose 28.17
globular 12.46
globule 23.20
globulin 25.16
glocalization 25.49
Glockenspiel 23.7
glom 24.8
gloom 24.12
gloomy 4.30
glop 27.8
Gloria 12.10
Gloriana 12.53
glorifier 12.14
glorify 6.7
gloriole 23.17
glorious 28.23
glory 4.41
gloss 28.14
glossal 23.37
glossary 4.43
glosser 12.70
glossy 4.46
glottal 23.39

glottis 28.12
Gloucester 12.79
glove 34.13
Glover 12.87
glow 9.1
glower 12.16
gloxinia 12.8
Gluck 21.28
glucose 35.19
glue 11.1
gluey 4.8
glug 18.12
Gluühwein 25.23
glum 24.14
gluon 25.24
glut 30.40
glutamate 30.12
gluteal 23.24
gluten 25.19
glutinous 28.29
glutton 25.50
gluttonize 35.13
gluttonous 28.29
gluttony 4.34
glycerin 25.11
glycerine 25.11
glycine 25.11
glycogen 25.42
glycol 23.13
Glyn 25.13
Glynis 28.9
glyph 17.6
glyptic 21.17
gnamma 12.50
gnarl 23.2
gnarly 4.21
gnash 29.1
gnat 30.1
gnaw 7.1
gneiss 28.13
gnocchi 4.19
gnome 24.11
gnomic 21.12
gnomish 29.8
gnomon 25.25
gnostic 21.17
gnu 11.1
go 9.1
goad 16.23
go-ahead 16.3
goal 23.17
goalball 23.14
goalie 4.25
goalkeeper 12.61
goalkeeping 26.10
goalmouth 32.10
goalpost 31.20
goalscorer 12.66
goalscoring 26.11
goaltending 26.5
Goan 25.38

Goanese 35.6
goat 30.35
goatee 4.1
goatherd 16.31
goatish 29.10
goatskin 25.15
goaty 4.54
gob 14.9
gobbet 30.20
Gobbi 4.10
gobble 23.26
gobbledegook 21.27
gobbler 12.44
Gobelins 35.31
go-between 25.12
Gobineau 9.19
goblet 30.22
goblin 25.16
go-by 6.5
god 16.18
Godard 1.6
godchild 16.36
godchildren 25.47
goddam 24.1
Goddard 16.2
goddess 28.7
Gödel 23.28
godet 30.4
godetia 12.11
godets 28.47
godfather 12.84
God-fearing 26.11
godforsaken 25.43
Godfrey 4.41
Godgiven 25.51
godhead 16.3
Godiva 12.86
godless 28.27
godlike 21.19
godly 4.25
Godman 25.45
godmother 12.84
godown 25.29
godparent 30.56
godsend 16.41
godship 27.6
godson 25.35
Godspeed 16.7
Godunov 17.8
Godwin 25.20
Godwottery 4.43
Godzilla 12.43
Goebbels 35.29
goer 12.17
Goering 26.11
Goethe 12.82
Goethean 25.37
gofer 12.30
goffer 12.30
go-getter 12.46
goggle 23.30

go-go 9.13
Gogol 23.13
going 26.3
goiter 12.81
goitre 12.81
go-kart 30.3
Golan Heights 28.47
Golconda 12.28
gold 16.37
golden 25.40
golden-ager 12.35
goldeneye 6.13
goldenrod 16.18
goldfield 16.35
goldfinch 29.20
goldfish 29.7
Goldie 4.13
Goldilocks 28.40
Golding 26.5
Goldman 25.45
Goldmark 21.5
goldmine 25.22
Goldschmidt 30.23
goldsmith 32.6
Goldwyn 25.20
golem 24.18
golf 17.18
golfer 12.30
Golgotha 12.83
Goliath 32.13
Gollancz 28.41
golliwog 18.8
gollop 27.14
golly 4.25
gombeen 25.9
Gomorrah 12.65
gonad 16.1
gondola 12.48
gondolier 12.4
Gondwanaland 16.40
gone 25.24
goner 12.56
gonfalon 25.44
gong 26.15
gonna 12.56
gonorrhea 12.4
gonorrhoea 12.4
gonzo 9.29
goo 11.1
good 16.26
Goodall 23.14
goodby 6.1
goodbye 6.1
good-hearted 16.12
goodish 29.6
goodly 4.26
good-natured 16.28
goodnight 30.26
good-oh 9.1
goods 35.27
goodwife 17.7

goodwill 23.8
Goodwin 25.20
goodwives 35.35
Goodwood 16.26
goody 4.13
Goodyear 12.12
gooey 4.8
goof 17.13
goofball 23.14
goofy 4.14
google 23.30
googly 4.26
googol 23.13
gook 21.27
goolie 4.26
goon 25.33
goop 27.11
goopy 4.37
goosander 12.25
goose 28.19
gooseberry 4.43
goosebumps 28.46
gooseflesh 29.3
goosefoot 30.39
goosegrass 28.2
goosestep 27.3
goosey 4.47
Goossens 35.31
gopher 12.30
goral 23.36
Gorbachev 17.8
Gorbals 35.29
gorblimey 4.29
gorcock 21.20
Gordimer 12.51
Gordium 24.16
Gordon 25.40
gore 7.1
Gore-tex 28.38
gorge 20.12
gorgeous 28.25
gorger 12.35
Gorgio 9.15
gorgon 25.41
gorgonian 25.37
Gorgonzola 12.44
gorilla 12.43
Goring 26.11
Gorky 4.19
Goronwy 4.59
gorse 28.15
Gorsedd 33.1
gorsy 4.47
gory 4.41
gosh 29.11
goshawk 21.22
gosling 26.8
go-slow 9.1
gospel 23.35
gospeler 12.48
gospeller 12.48

Goss 28.14
gossamer 12.52
gossamery 4.43
gossip 27.6
gossiper 12.62
gossipy 4.36
got 30.31
gotcha 12.24
Goth 32.8
Gotha 12.83
Gotham 24.20
Gothenburg 18.13
Gothic 21.18
gotta 12.79
gouache 29.2
Gouda 12.28
gouge 20.13
gouger 12.35
goujons 35.31
goulash 29.1
Gould 16.37
Gounod 9.19
gourami 4.29
gourd 16.28
gourmand 16.45
gourmandize 35.11
gourmet 3.16
gout 30.34
govern 25.51
governance 28.45
governess 4.46
governor 12.58
gowan 25.38
gowk 21.23
gown 25.29
Goya 12.18
goyim 24.6
Gozo 9.29
grab 14.1
grabber 12.21
grabble 23.26
grabby 4.10
graben 25.38
Gracchus 28.26
grace 28.5
Gracie 4.45
gracile 23.9
gracious 28.33
grackle 23.32
grad 16.1
gradate 30.7
grade 16.6
grader 12.26
gradient 30.56
gradine 25.10
grading 26.5
gradual 23.25
graduand 16.40
graduate 30.8, 30.41
Graeme 24.15
Graf 17.2

graffiti 4.52
graffitist 31.14
graffito 9.24
graft 30.47
grafter 12.75
Grafton 25.50
graham 24.15
Grail 23.5
grain 25.7
grainer 12.54
Grainger 12.35
grainy 4.31
gram 24.1
grammar 12.50
grammarian 25.37
grammatical 23.32
Grammy 4.29
gramophone 25.30
Grampian 25.37
grampus 28.30
Gramsci 4.50
gran 25.1
Granada 12.25
granary 4.43
Gran Canaria 12.10
Gran Chaco 9.16
grand 16.40
grandad 16.1
grandam 24.1
grandchild 16.36
grandchildren 25.47
granddaughter 12.80
grandee 4.1
grandeur 12.35
grandfather 12.84
grandfatherly 4.27
grandiloquence
  28.45
grandiloquent 30.56
grandiose 28.17
grandiosity 4.53
grandma 1.13
grandmal 23.1
grandmama 1.13
grandmaster 12.75
grandmother 12.84
grandmotherly 4.27
grandpa 1.15
grandpapa 1.15
grandparent 30.56
Grand prix 4.1
grandson 25.35
grandstand 16.40
grange 20.19
granita 12.77
granite 30.23
granny 4.31
granola 12.44
grant 30.53
grantee 4.1
granter 12.75

g

Granth 30.55
Grantha 12.81
grantor 7.1
grant turismo 9.18
granular 12.46
granularity 4.53
granulate 30.11
granule 23.20
Granville 23.10
grape 27.4
grapefruit 30.37
grapeshot 30.32
grapevine 25.23
graph 17.2
graphic 21.10
graphical 23.32
graphite 30.27
grapnel 23.34
grappa 12.61
Grappelli 4.22
grapple 23.35
grappler 12.48
Grasmere 12.7
grasp 27.18
grasper 12.61
grass 28.2
grasscloth 32.8
Grasse 28.2
grasshopper 12.62
grassland 16.40
grass-like 21.19
grassy 4.45
grate 30.7
grater 12.77
graticule 23.20
gratifier 12.14
gratify 6.7
gratin 25.3
gratiné 3.17
grating 26.13
gratis 28.12
gratitude 16.25
gratuitous 28.34
gratuity 4.53
graunch 29.20
gravadlax 28.38
grave 34.2, 34.4
gravedigger 12.31
gravel 23.40
gravelly 4.27
graven 25.51
graver 12.85
Graves 34.2, 35.35
graveside 16.16
gravestone 25.31
graveyard 16.2
gravitas 28.1
gravitate 30.16
gravity 4.53
gravlax 28.38
gravure 12.20

gravy 4.58
gray 3.1
graybeard 16.28
grayish 29.6
grayling 26.8
grayness 28.9
Graz 28.47
graze 35.5
grazer 12.90
grazier 12.12
grease 28.6
greasepaint 30.54
greaseproof 17.13
greaser 12.69
greasy 4.45
great 30.7
greatcoat 30.35
greave 34.5
Greaves 35.35
grebe 14.6
grebo 9.9
Grecian 25.49
Greece 28.6
greed 16.7
greedy 4.12
Greek 21.8
green 25.9
Greenaway 3.25
greenback 21.2
greenbottle 23.39
Greene 25.9
greenery 4.43
greenfeed 16.7
Greenfield 16.35
greenfinch 29.20
greenfly 6.11
greengage 20.4
greengrocer 12.71
greengrocery 4.43
greenhead 16.3
greenheart 30.3
greenhorn 25.28
greenhouse 28.16
greening 26.9
greenish 29.9
greenkeeper 12.61
greenkeeping 26.10
Greenland 16.45
Greenlander 12.29
Greenock 21.30
Greenpeace 28.6
green room 24.12
greensand 16.40
greenshank 21.33
greenskeeper 12.61
greenstone 25.31
greenstuff 17.15
greensward 16.21
Greenwich 15.6
greenwood 16.26
greeny 4.31

Greer 12.4
greet 30.18
greeter 12.77
greeting 26.13
Greg 18.3
gregarious 28.23
Gregor 12.31
Gregory 4.43
greisen 25.52
gremlin 25.16
Grenada 12.26
grenade 16.6
Grenadian 25.37
grenadier 12.4
grenadine 25.10
Grendel 23.28
Grenfell 23.3
Grenoble 23.26
Grenville 23.10
Gresham 24.20
Greta 12.76
Greville 23.10
grew 11.1
grey 3.1
greybeard 16.28
Greyfriars 35.24
greyhound 16.43
greyish 29.6
greylag 18.1
greyness 28.9
Gribble 23.26
gricer 12.70
grid 16.8
griddle 23.28
gridiron 25.38
gridlock 21.21
grief 17.5
Grieg 18.5
Grierson 25.48
grievance 28.45
grieve 34.5
griever 12.85
grievous 28.35
griffin 25.14
Griffith 32.6
griffon 25.41
grift 30.47
grifter 12.78
grig 18.6
grill 23.8
grillade 16.6
grillage 20.6
grille 23.8
griller 12.43
grilling 26.8
grilse 28.42
grim 24.6
grimace 28.28
grimacer 12.71
Grimaldi 4.13
grimalkin 25.15

grime 24.7
Grimes 35.30
Grimm 24.6
Grimond 16.45
Grimsby 4.10
grimy 4.29
grin 25.13
grind 16.42
grinder 12.27
grindstone 25.31
gringo 9.13
grinner 12.55
grip 27.6
gripe 27.7
griper 12.62
gripper 12.62
grippy 4.36
Griqua 12.38
grisaille 23.5
Griselda 12.26
grisette 30.4
griskin 25.15
grisly 4.24
grison 25.52
grissini 4.31
grist 31.6
gristle 23.37
gristly 4.24
gristmill 23.9
grit 30.20
gritter 12.78
gritty 4.53
grizzle 23.41
grizzler 12.43
grizzly 4.24
groan 25.30
groaner 12.56
groat 30.35
grocer 12.71
grocery 4.43
grockle 23.32
Grodno 9.19
grog 18.8
groggy 4.15
grogram 24.19
groin 25.32
grommet 30.23
Gromyko 9.16
Groningen 25.46
groom 24.12
groove 34.12
groovy 4.58
grope 27.10
groper 12.63
Gropius 28.23
grosbeak 21.8
groschen 25.49
grosgrain 25.8
gross 28.17
Grosz 28.17
grot 30.31

grotesque 21.35
grotesquerie 4.43
Grotius 28.23
grotto 9.25
grotty 4.54
grouch 15.9
grouchy 4.11
ground 16.43
grounder 12.28
groundhog 18.8
grounding 26.5
groundling 26.8
groundnut 30.40
grounds 35.31
groundsel 23.37
groundsheet 30.19
groundsman 25.45
groundsmen 25.45
groundswell 23.4
groundwork 21.31
group 27.11
groupage 20.7
grouper 12.63
groupie 4.37
grouping 26.10
grouse 28.16
grouser 12.70
grout 30.34
grouter 12.80
grove 34.11
grovel 23.40
groveler 12.48
groveller 12.48
Grover 12.86
Groves 35.35
grovy 4.58
grow 9.1
growbag 18.1
grower 12.17
growl 23.16
growler 12.44
Growmore 7.12
grown 25.30
grown-up 27.13
growth 32.11
groyne 25.32
Grozny 4.32
grub 14.13
grubber 12.22
grubby 4.10
grubstake 21.7
grudge 20.16
grudger 12.36
gruel 23.25
grueling 26.8
gruelling 26.8
gruff 17.15
grumble 23.26
grumbler 12.47
grumbling 26.8
grumbly 4.26

grump 27.17
grumpish 29.9
grumpy 4.37
grunge 20.19
grungy 4.17
grunion 25.52
grunt 30.55
grunter 12.81
Gruyère 2.16
grysbok 21.20
guacamole 4.25
guacharo 9.21
Guadalajara 12.64
Guadalcanál 23.1
Guadeloupe 27.11
Guadeloupian 25.37
Guam 24.2
guan 25.4
guanaco 9.16
Guangdong 26.15
guano 9.19
guar 1.1
Guarani 4.1
guarantee 4.1
guarantor 7.1
guaranty 4.55
guard 16.2
guardant 30.56
guardhouse 28.16
Guardi 4.12
guardian 25.37
guard rail 23.6
guardroom 24.12
guardsman 25.45
guardsmen 25.45
Guarneri 4.39
Guatemala 12.42
Guatemalan 25.44
guava 12.85
Guayaquil 23.7
gubbins 35.31
gubernatorial 23.24
gudgeon 25.42
Gudrun 25.34
Guelphic 21.10
guenon 25.24
guerdon 25.40
Guernica 12.39
Guernsey 4.62
guerrilla 12.43
guess 28.3
guesser 12.69
guesstimate 30.12, 30.43
guesswork 21.31
guest 31.3
guestbook 21.26
guesthouse 28.16
Guevara 12.64
guff 17.15
guffaw 7.1

Guggenheim 24.7
Guiana 12.53
guidance 28.45
guide 16.14
guidebook 21.28
guideline 25.22
guidepost 31.20
Guider 12.27
guideway 3.25
Guido 9.11
guidon 25.40
Guignol 23.13
guild 16.35
guilder 12.27
Guildford 16.28
guildhall 23.15
guildsman 25.45
guildsmen 25.45
guile 23.11
Guillaume 24.11
guillemot 30.31
guilloche 29.13
guillotine 25.12
guilt 30.51
guilty 4.53
guinea 4.32
Guinean 25.37
Guinevere 12.12
guise 35.11
guitar 1.1
guitarist 31.12
Gujarat 30.3
Gujarati 4.51
Gujranwala 12.42
Gujrat 30.3
gulag 18.1
gulch 15.15
gulden 25.40
gules 35.29
gulf 17.18
gull 23.22
gullet 30.22
gulley 4.26
gullible 23.26
gully 4.26
gulp 27.16
gulper 12.63
gulpy 4.37
gum 24.14
gumbo 9.9
gumboot 30.37
gumdrop 27.8
gummy 4.30
gumption 25.49
gumshield 16.35
gumshoe 11.19
gun 25.35
gunboat 30.35
gundog 18.8
gunfight 30.27
gunfighter 12.79

gunfire 12.14
gung-ho 9.1
gunge 20.19
gungy 4.17
gunk 21.34
gunless 28.27
gunlock 21.21
gunman 25.45
gunmen 25.45
gunmetal 23.39
Gunn 25.35
gunnel 23.34
gunner 12.57
gunnera 12.67
gunnery 4.43
gunny 4.33
gunplay 3.15
gunpoint 30.55
gunpowder 12.28
gunroom 24.12
gunrunner 12.57
gunrunning 26.9
gunsel 23.37
gunship 27.6
gunshot 30.32
gun-shy 6.17
gunsight 30.30
gunslinger 12.60
gunslinging 26.10
gunsmith 32.6
gunstock 21.21
Gunter 12.81
Gunther 12.83
gunwale 23.34
gunyah 12.89
guppy 4.37
Gupta 12.81
gurdwara 12.64
gurgle 23.30
Gurkha 12.41
Gurkhali 4.21
gurnard 16.29
gurney 4.34
guru 11.17
Gus 28.21
gush 29.16
gusher 12.73
gushing 26.12
gushy 4.50
gusset 30.24
gust 31.24
gustatory 4.43
Gustave 34.2
gusto 9.25
gusty 4.55
gut 30.40
Gutenberg 18.13
Guthrie 4.42
Gutiéirrez 35.3
gutless 28.27
gutsy 4.47

gutter 12.81
guttersnipe 27.7
gutty 4.55
guv 34.13
guv'nor 12.57
guy 6.1
Guyana 12.53
Guyanese 35.6
Guyenne 25.5
guzzle 23.41
guzzler 12.48
Gwalior 7.3
Gwen 25.5
Gwenda 12.26
Gwendolen 25.16
Gwent 30.53
Gwyn 25.13
Gwynedd 33.9
Gwyneth 32.6
Gwynfor 7.20
gybe 14.8
gym 24.6
gymkhana 12.53
gymnasia 12.12
gymnasial 23.24
gymnasium 24.16
gymnast 31.1
gymnastic 21.17
gymnosophy 4.14
gymnosperm 24.22
gymslip 27.6
gynaecea 12.3
gynaecocracy 4.48
gynaecology 4.17
gynandrous 28.31
gynecocracy 4.48
gynecology 4.17
gyp 27.6
gypsum 24.20
Gypsy 4.46
Gypsyish 29.6
gyrate 30.7
gyration 25.49
gyrator 12.77
gyratory 4.43
gyre 12.13
gyrfalcon 25.43
gyro 9.21
gyropilot 30.42
gyroplane 25.8
gyroscope 27.10
gyroscopic 21.14
gyve 34.9

H

ha 1.1
Haarlem 24.18
Habakkuk 21.29

habanera 12.65
haberdasher 12.72
haberdashery 4.43
habilitate 30.16
habit 30.20
habitant 30.56
habitat 30.2
habitual 23.25
habituate 30.8
habitude 16.25
habitué 3.6
Habsburg 18.13
hacek 21.6
hacienda 12.26
hack 21.1
hackberry 4.43
hacker 12.37
hackery 4.43
hackle 23.32
hackney 4.31
hacksaw 7.16
had 16.1
haddock 21.30
Hadean 25.37
Hades 35.7
Hadith 32.5
Hadlee 4.21
hadn't 30.56
Hadrian 25.37
haematology 4.17
haemocyte 30.30
haemoglobin 25.13
haemophilia 12.6
haemophiliac 21.1
haemorrhage 20.8
haemorrhoid 16.24
haemostat 30.2
hafiz 35.10
haft 30.47
hag 18.1
Hagar 1.8
Haggadah 12.25
Haggadic 21.10
Haggadoth 30.35
Haggai 6.8
haggard 16.28
haggis 28.7
haggish 29.7
haggle 23.30
haggler 12.48
Hagiographa 12.30
hagiographer 12.30
hagiographic 21.10
hagiography 4.14
hagiolatry 4.43
hagiology 4.17
hagridden 25.40
Hague 18.4
hah 1.1
ha-ha 1.1, 1.9
Hahn 25.4

Haida 12.27
Haifa 12.30
Haig 18.4
haik 21.19
haiku 11.12
hail 23.5
hailer 12.43
Haile Selassie 4.45
hailstone 25.31
Hailwood 16.26
Haiphong 26.15
hair 2.1
hairbrush 29.16
haircare 2.7
haircloth 32.8
haircut 30.40
hairdo 11.6
hairdresser 12.69
hairdressing 26.12
hairdryer 12.14
hairgrip 27.6
hairline 25.22
hairnet 30.56
hairpiece 28.6
hairpin 25.18
hairspray 3.19
hairstreak 21.8
hairstyle 23.12
hairstyling 26.8
hairstylist 31.8
hairy 4.39
Haiti 4.52
Haitian 25.49
haji 4.17
hajj 20.1
haka 12.37
hake 21.7
Hakenkreuz 28.47
hakim 24.5
Hakka 12.37
Hakluyt 30.37
Hal 23.1
Halacha 1.1
Halafian 25.37
halal 23.2
halation 25.49
halberd 16.28
halcyon 25.37
Haldane 25.7
hale 23.5
Hales 35.29
Haley 4.22
half 17.2
halfback 21.2
halfpence 28.45
halfpenny 4.31
halfpennyworth 32.14
half-time 24.7
half-tone 25.30
half-track 21.3

halfway 3.1
halfwit 30.25
half-witted 16.12
halibut 30.41
Halicarnassus 28.32
Halifax 28.38
halite 30.28
halitosis 28.11
hall 23.14
Hallé 3.15
hallelujah 12.89
Haller 12.42
Halley 4.21
Halliday 3.9
hallmark 21.5
halloo 11.1
hallow 9.17
Halloween 25.9
Hallowes 35.19
hallstand 16.40
Hallstatt 30.3
hallucinate 30.13
hallucinatory 4.43
hallucinogen 25.42
hallucinogenic 21.13
hallway 3.26
halma 12.50
Halmahera 12.65
halo 9.17
halogen 25.42
Hals 28.42
halt 30.51
halter 12.80
halterneck 21.6
halva 12.85
halve 34.2
halyard 16.30
ham 24.1
Hamada 12.25
hamadryad 16.28
hamadryas 28.24
hamartia 12.12
Hamas 28.1
hambone 25.30
Hamburg 18.13
hamburger 12.32
Hamelin 25.16
hames 35.30
Hamilcar 1.11
Hamilton 25.50
Hamish 29.8
Hamite 30.29
hamlet 30.22
hammer 12.50
Hammerfest 31.3
hammerhead 16.3
hammering 26.12
hammerlock 21.21
Hammerstein 25.23
Hammett 30.23

hammock 21.30
Hammond 16.45
hammy 4.29
Hamnett 30.23
hamper 12.61
Hampshire 12.11
Hampstead 16.12
Hampton 25.50
hamster 12.74
hamstring 26.11
hamstrung 26.18
Han 25.1
Hancock 21.20
hand 16.40
hand-rear 12.4
handbag 18.1
handball 23.14
handbasin 25.48
handbell 23.3
handbill 23.8
handbook 21.28
handbrake 21.7
handcart 30.3
handclap 27.1
handcraft 30.47
handcuff 17.15
Handel 23.28
handgrip 27.6
handgun 25.35
handhold 16.37
handicap 27.1
handicapper 12.61
handicraft 30.47
handiwork 21.31
handkerchief 17.6
handkerchiefs 28.37
handle 23.28
handlebar 1.4
handler 12.42
handlist 31.8
handmade 16.6
handmaid 16.6
handmaiden 25.40
handout 30.34
handover 12.86
hand-pick 21.9
hand-picked 30.49
handpump 27.17
handrail 23.6
handset 30.5
handshake 21.7
handspike 21.19
handspring 26.11
handstand 16.40
handwork 21.31
handworked 30.49
handwriting 26.13
handwritten 25.50
handy 4.12
handyman 25.2
handymen 25.5

hang 26.1
hangar 12.60
hangdog 18.8
hanger 12.60
hangi 4.35
hanging 26.10
hangman 25.45
hangmen 25.45
hangnail 23.6
hangout 30.34
hangover 12.86
hang-up 27.13
Hangzhou 8.1
hank 21.33
hanker 12.37
hankerer 12.67
hankering 26.11
Hanks 28.41
hanky 4.18
hanky-panky 4.18
Hannah 12.53
Hannibal 23.26
Hanoi 10.1
Hanover 12.86
Hanoverian 25.37
Hans 28.44
Hansard 16.2
Hanse 28.44
hansel 23.37
Hänsel 23.37
hansom 24.20
Hants 28.47
Hanukkah 12.41
Hanuman 25.4
Haonsel 23.37
hap 27.1
haphazard 16.30
hapless 28.27
ha'p'orth 32.13
happen 25.46
happening 26.9
happenstance 28.44
happi 4.36
happy 4.36
happy-go-lucky 4.20
hara-kiri 4.40
harangue 26.1
haranguer 12.60
Harare 4.38
harass 28.31
harasser 12.71
harbinger 12.35
harbor 12.21
harborage 20.8
harbour 12.21
harbourage 20.8
harbourmaster (US
  harbormaster)
  12.75
hard 16.2
hardback 21.2

hardball 23.14
hardbitten 25.50
hardboard 16.20
hard-core 7.1
hardcore 7.10
hardcover 12.87
harden 25.40
hardener 12.58
hard hat 30.1
hard-heated 16.9
hard-hearted 16.12
Hardie 4.12
Harding 26.5
hardish 29.6
hardline 25.21
hardliner 12.55
hardstanding 26.5
hard track 21.4
hardtop 27.8
Hardwar 1.22
hardware 2.15
hardwearing 26.11
hardwood 16.26
hardworking 26.7
hardy 4.12
hare 2.1
harebell 23.3
harebrained 16.41
harelip 27.6
harelipped 30.58
harem 24.19
Harewood 16.26
Hargreaves 35.35
haricot 9.16
Harijan 25.42
hark 21.5
Harlech 22.6
Harlem 24.18
harlequin 25.20
harlequinade 16.6
harlot 30.42
harlotry 4.43
Harlow 9.17
harm 24.2
harmattan 25.50
harmonic 21.13
harmonica 12.39
harmonious 28.23
harmonist 31.10
harmonium 24.16
harmony 4.34
harness 28.9
harnesser 12.70
Harold 16.38
harp 27.2
harper 12.61
harpist 31.11
Harpocrates 35.9
harpoon 25.33
harpooner 12.56
harpsichord 16.21

harpsichordist 31.6
harpy 4.36
harridan 25.40
harrier 12.10
Harries 28.10
Harriet 30.41
Harrington 25.50
Harris 28.10
Harrison 25.48
Harrod 16.29
Harrovian 25.37
harrow 9.21
harrower 12.17
harrumph 17.19
harry 4.38
harsh 29.2
harshen 25.49
hart 30.3
hartal 23.2
Harte 30.3
hartebeest 31.5
Hartford 16.28
Hartlepool 23.20
Hartley 4.21
hartshorn 25.28
harum-scarum
  24.19
haruspex 28.38
haruspices 35.8
Harvard 16.29
harvest 31.15
harvester 12.78
harvestman 25.45
harvestmen 25.45
Harvey 4.58
Harwich 20.8
Haryana 12.53
has 35.1, 35.24
Hasdrubal 23.26
Hasek 21.6
hash 29.1
hash-browns 35.31
Hashemite 30.29
hashish 29.5
hashtag 18.1
Hasid 16.11
hasidic 21.10
Hasidim 24.6
haslet 30.22
Hasmonean 25.36
hasn't 30.56
hasp 27.18
Hasselt 30.51
hassle 23.37
hassock 21.30
haste 31.4
hasten 25.48
Hastings 35.32
hasty 4.52
hat 30.1
hatable 23.26

hatband 16.40
hatbox 28.40
hatch 15.1
hatchback 21.2
hatchery 4.43
hatchet 30.20
hatching 26.4
hatchling 26.8
hatchway 3.25
hate 30.7
hater 12.77
hatful 23.21
Hathaway 3.25
Hathor 7.19
hatless 28.27
hatpin 25.18
hatred 16.11
Hatshepsut 30.38
hatstand 16.40
hatter 12.74
Hattie 4.51
Haugh 7.1
haughty 4.54
haul 23.14
haulage 20.6
hauler 12.44
haulier 12.6
haulm 24.9
haunch 29.20
haunt 30.54
haunter 12.80
Hauptmann 25.45
Hausa 12.70
Hausfrau 8.10
hautboy 10.3
haute école 23.13
hauteur 13.1
haut monde 16.42
Havana 12.53
Havant 30.56
have 34.1
Havel 23.40
haven't 30.56
haver 12.85
Havers 35.24
haversack 21.4
haves 35.35
havildar 1.6
havoc 21.30
haw 7.1
Hawaii 4.4
Hawaiian 25.38
hawfinch 29.20
hawk 21.22
Hawke 21.22
hawker 12.40
Hawking 26.7
Hawkins 35.31
hawkish 29.8
hawkmoth 32.8
Hawksmoor 12.20

Haworth 32.13
hawse 35.17
hawser 12.91
hawthorn 25.28
hay 3.1
haybox 28.40
haycock 21.20
Haydn 25.40
Hayek 21.6
Hayes 35.5
Hayley 4.22
hayloft 30.47
haymaker 12.38
haymaking 26.7
hayrick 21.15
hayride 16.15
Hays 35.5
hayseed 16.7
haystack 21.4
haywire 12.14
Hayworth 32.13
hazard 16.30
hazardous 28.25
haze 35.5
hazel 23.41
hazelnut 30.40
Hazlitt 30.22
hazy 4.61
he 4.1
head 16.3
headache 21.7
headachy 4.18
headage 20.6
headband 16.40
headbanger 12.60
headbanging 26.10
headboard 16.20
headcheese 35.6
headcount 30.55
headdress 28.3
header 12.26
headfirst 31.26
headgear 12.5
headhunt 30.55
headhunter 12.81
heading 26.5
headlamp 27.17
headland 16.45
headlight 30.28
headline 25.22
headliner 12.55
headlock 21.21
headlong 26.15
headman 25.45
headmaster 12.75
headmasterly 4.27
headmen 25.45
headmistress 28.10
headmost 31.20
headnote 30.35
headphone 25.30

headpiece 28.6
headquarter 12.80
headquarters 35.24
headrest 31.3
headroom 24.12
headsail 23.6
headscarf 17.2
headscarves 35.35
headset 30.5
headshrinker 12.39
headsman 25.45
headsmen 25.45
headspring 26.11
headsquare 2.15
headstall 23.15
headstand 16.40
headstock 21.21
headstone 25.31
headstrong 26.15
headteacher 12.23
headward 16.30
headway 3.25
headwear 2.15
headwind 16.42
headword 16.31
headwork 21.31
heady 4.12
heal 23.7
healer 12.43
health 32.17
healthy 4.56
Heaney 4.31
heap 27.5
hear 12.4
Heard 16.31
hearer 12.67
hearing-
   impaired 16.5
hearken 25.43
hearsay 3.20
hearse 28.36
heart 30.3
heartache 21.7
heartbeat 30.18
heartbreak 21.7
heartbreaker 12.38
heartbreaking 26.7
heartbroken 25.43
heartburn 25.53
hearten 25.50
heartfelt 30.51
hearth 32.2
hearthrug 18.12
hearthstone 25.31
heartland 16.45
heartrending 26.5
heartsearching 26.4
heartsease 35.8
heartsick 21.16
heartsore 7.16
heartthrob 14.9

heart-to-heart 30.3
heartwarming 26.9
heartwood 16.26
hearty 4.51
heat 30.18
heater 12.77
heath 32.5
heathen 25.51
heathendom 24.17
heathenish 29.9
heather 12.84
heathery 4.43
heathland 16.45
Heathrow 9.1
heathy 4.56
heatproof 17.13
heatstroke 21.24
heatwave 34.4
heave 34.5
heave-ho 9.1
heaven 25.51
heavenly 4.22
heavenward 16.30
heaver 12.85
heavy 4.58
heavy-handed 16.9
heavy-hearted 16.12
heavyish 29.6
heavyset 30.4
heavyweight 30.17
Hebe 4.10
hebetude 16.25
Hebraic 21.9
Hebraist 31.6
Hebrew 11.17
Hebridean 25.36
Hebrides 35.7
Hebron 25.26
Hecate 4.55
hecatomb 24.12
heck 21.6
heckelphone 25.30
heckle 23.32
heckler 12.48
hectarage 20.8
hectare 2.14
hectic 21.17
hector 12.76
Hecuba 12.21
he'd 16.7
heddle 23.28
hedge 20.3
hedgehog 18.8
hedgehop 27.8
hedger 12.35
hedgerow 9.21
Hedges 35.10
Hedley 4.22
hedonist 31.10
heebie-jeebies 35.10
heed 16.7

hee-haw 7.8
heel 23.7
heelball 23.14
heelbar 1.4
heeltap 27.1
heft 30.47
hefty 4.51
Hegel 23.30
Hegelian 25.37
hegemonic 21.13
hegemony 4.34
Hegira 12.65
Heidegger 12.31
Heidelberg 18.13
Heidi 4.12
heifer 12.30
heigh-ho 9.1
heigh 3.1
height 30.26
heighten 25.50
Heilbronn 25.26
Heilong 26.15
Heine 4.32
heinous 28.29
Heinz 35.31
heir 2.1
heirdom 24.17
heiress 28.10
heirloom 24.12
Heisenberg 18.13
heist 31.16
Hekla 12.42
held 16.35
Helen 25.16
Helena 12.55
helenium 24.16
Helga 12.31
Helgoland 16.40
helianthemum 24.19
helianthus 28.35
helical 23.32
helices 35.8
Helicon 25.43
helicopter 12.79
Heligoland 16.40
Heliogabalus 28.27
heliogram 24.1
heliograph 17.2
Heliopolis 28.8
Helios 28.14
heliotrope 27.10
heliotropic 21.14
helipad 16.1
heliport 30.33
helium 24.16
helix 28.39
he'll 23.7
hell 23.3
hellacious 28.33
Helladic 21.10

Hellas 28.1
hellcat 30.1
hellebore 7.4
helleborine 25.11
Hellene 25.10
Hellenic 21.13
Hellenist 31.10
Heller 12.42
Hellespont 30.54
hellfire 12.13
hellhole 23.17
hellhound 16.43
hellion 25.52
hellish 29.8
Hellman 25.45
hello 9.1
hellraiser 12.90
hellraising 26.14
helluva 12.87
hellward 16.30
helm 24.18
helmet 30.23
Helmholtz 28.47
Helms 35.30
helmsman 25.45
helmsmen 25.45
Hélo'ise 35.6
Helot 30.42
helotry 4.43
help 27.16
helper 12.61
helping 26.10
helpline 25.22
Helpmann 25.45
helpmate 30.12
Helsingborg 18.9
Helsingor 12.60
Helsinki 4.19
helter-skelter 12.76
helve 34.15
Helvetia 12.11
Helvetian 25.49
Helvetic 21.17
hem 24.3
he-man 25.2
hematology 4.17
Hemel
   Hempstead 16.4
he-men 25.5
Hemingway 3.25
hemipteran 25.47
hemisphere 12.5
hemispheric 21.15
hemispherical 23.32
hemistich 21.17
hemline 25.22
hemlock 21.21
hemoglobin 25.13
hemophilia 12.6
hemophiliac 21.1
hemorrhage 20.8

hemorrhoid 16.24
hemp 27.17
hempen 25.46
hemstitch 15.6
hen 25.5
Henan 25.46
hence 28.44
henceforth 32.9
henceforward 16.30
henchman 25.45
henchmen 25.45
hendiadys 28.7
Hendrix 28.39
Hendry 4.38
henge 20.19
henna 12.53
henpeck 21.6
Henri 4.38
Henrietta 12.76
henry 4.38
Henze 12.69
hep 27.3
hepatic 21.17
hepatica 12.39
hepatitis 28.12
Hepburn 25.53
Hephaestus 28.34
Hepplewhite 30.30
heptad 16.1
heptagon 25.41
heptagonal 23.34
heptameter 12.78
heptarchic 21.11
heptathlete 30.18
heptathlon 25.44
Hepworth 32.14
her 13.1
Hera 12.67
Heracles 35.7
Heraclitus 28.34
Heraklion 25.37
herald 16.38
heraldic 21.10
heraldist 31.6
heraldry 4.43
herb 14.15
herbaceous 28.33
herbage 20.6
herbal 23.26
herbalist 31.8
herbaria 12.10
herbarium 24.16
Herbert 30.41
herbicide 16.16
herbivore 7.20
herbivorous 28.31
herby 4.10
Herculaneum 24.16
Herculean 25.36
Hercules 35.7
herd 16.31

herder 12.29
herdsman 25.45
herdsmen 25.45
Herdwick 21.18
here 12.4
hereabout 30.34
hereafter 12.75
hereat 30.1
hereby 6.1
hereditary 4.43
heredity 4.53
Hereford 16.28
Herefordshire 12.11
herein 25.13
hereof 34.10
heresy 4.46
heretic 21.17
heretical 23.32
hereto 11.1
hereunder 12.29
hereunto 11.20
hereupon 25.24
herewith 33.4
heriot 30.41
heritage 20.9
herky-jerky 4.20
herl 23.42
herm 24.22
Herman 25.45
hermaphrodite 30.26
Hermes 35.7
hermetic 21.17
Hermia 12.7
Hermione 4.34
hermit 30.23
hermitage 20.9
Hermitian 25.49
hermitic 21.17
hernia 12.8
Herning 26.9
hero 9.21
Herod 16.29
Herodotus 28.34
heroic 21.9
heroin 25.13
heroine 25.13
heroize 35.11
heron 25.47
herpes 35.7
Herr 2.1
Herrick 21.15
herring 26.11
herringbone 25.30
Herriot 30.41
herself 17.18
Herschel 23.38
hers 35.25
Hertford 16.28
Hertfordshire 12.11
Hertz 28.47

h

h

Herzegovina 12.55
Herzl 23.37
Herzog 18.8
he's 35.6
hesitance 28.45
hesitancy 4.48
hesitant 30.56
hesitate 30.16
hesitater 12.77
Hesketh 32.6
Hesperian 25.37
Hesperides 35.7
Hesperus 28.31
Hesse 28.3
Hessian 25.37
hest 31.3
Hester 12.76
Hesvan 25.51
hetaera 12.67
heteroclite 30.28
heterodox 28.40
heterodoxy 4.46
heterogamy 4.30
heterogeneity 4.53
heterogeneous 28.23
heteronomous 28.28
heteronomy 4.30
heterosexist 31.13
heterosexual 23.25
Hettie 4.51
heuchera 12.67
hew 11.1
hewer 12.19
hex 28.38
hexad 16.1
hexagon 25.41
hexagonal 23.34
hexameter 12.78
hexastyle 23.12
hey 3.1
heyday 3.9
Heyerdahl 23.2
Hezbollah 12.44
hi 6.1
hiatal 23.39
hiatus 28.34
Hiawatha 12.83
hibachi 4.11
hibernate 30.13
Hibernian 25.37
hibiscus 28.26
Hibs 35.26
hic 21.9
hiccup 27.13
hiccupy 4.37
hic jacet 30.5
hick 21.9
hickey 4.19
Hickok 21.20

hickory 4.43
Hicks 28.39
hid 16.8
Hidalgo 9.13
hidden 25.40
hide 16.14
hide-and-seek 21.8
hideaway 3.25
hidebound 16.43
hideous 28.23
hideout 30.34
hider 12.27
hidey-hole 23.17
hiding 26.5
hie 6.1
hierarch 21.5
hierarchic 21.11
hierarchical 23.32
hierarchize 35.11
hierarchy 4.18
hieratic 21.17
hierocracy 4.48
hieroglyph 17.6
hieroglyphic 21.10
Hieronymus 28.28
hierophant 30.53
hi-fi 6.7
higgle 23.30
higgledy-
  piggledy 4.12
Higgs 35.28
high 6.1
highball 23.14
highbinder 12.27
highborn 25.28
highbrow 8.10
highfalutin 25.19
high-handled 16.9
high-hat 30.1
highland 16.45
Highlander 12.29
Highlandman 25.45
Highlandmen 25.45
highlight 30.28
highlighter 12.79
high-rise 35.13
highroad 16.23
hightail 23.6
highway 3.25
highwayman 25.45
highwaymen 25.45
hijab 14.2
hijack 21.3
hijacker 12.37
hike 21.19
hiker 12.40
hilarious 28.23
hilarity 4.53
Hilary 4.43
Hilda 12.27
hill 23.8

hillbilly 4.24
Hillel 23.3
Hillier 12.6
Hillman 25.45
hillock 21.30
hillocky 4.20
Hills 35.29
hillside 16.16
hilltop 27.8
hillwalker 12.40
hillwalking 26.7
hilly 4.24
hilt 30.51
hilum 24.18
Hilversum 24.20
him 24.6
Himalayan 25.36
himation 25.37
Himmler 12.43
himself 17.18
hind 16.42
Hindemith 30.23
Hindenburg 18.13
hinder 12.27
Hindi 4.12
hindmost 31.20
hindquarters 35.24
hindrance 28.45
hindsight 30.30
Hindu 11.1
Hindu Kush 29.15
Hindustan 25.4
Hindustani 4.31
hinge 20.19
hinny 4.32
hint 30.54
hinterland 16.40
hip 27.6
hip bath 32.2
hip bone 25.30
hiphop 27.8
hipness 28.9
Hipparchus 28.26
hipped 30.58
hipper 12.62
hippo 9.20
hippocampus 28.30
hippocras 28.1
Hippocrates 35.9
Hippocrene 25.11
hippodrome 24.11
hippogriff 17.6
Hippolytus 28.34
hippopotamus 28.28
hippy 4.36
Hiram 24.19
hircine 25.23
hire 12.13
hireling 26.8
hirer 12.67

Hirohito 9.24
Hiroshima 12.51
hirsute 30.38
his 35.10
Hispanic 21.13
Hispanicist 31.13
Hispaniola 12.44
Hispanist 31.10
hiss 28.7
hist 31.6
histamine 25.11
historian 25.37
historiated 16.12
historic 21.15
historical 23.32
historicist 31.13
historiographic 21.10
historiography 4.14
history 4.43
histrionic 21.13
hit 30.20
hitch 15.6
Hitchcock 21.20
Hitchens 35.31
hitcher 12.23
hitchhike 21.19
hitech 21.6
hither 12.84
hitherto 11.1
Hitler 12.43
Hitlerian 25.37
Hitlerite 30.29
hitmaker 12.38
hitman 25.2
hitmen 25.5
hitter 12.78
Hittite 30.30
hive 34.9
hiya 12.13
HMRC 4.1
ho 9.1
hoagie 4.15
hoar 7.1
hoard 16.19
hoarder 12.28
hoarding 26.5
hoar frost 31.17
hoarse 28.15
hoarsen 25.48
hoary 4.41
hoax 28.40
hoaxer 12.71
hob 14.9
Hobart 30.3
hobbit 30.20
hobble 23.26
hobbledehoy 10.4
hobbler 12.48
Hobbs 35.26
hobby 4.10

hobby horse 28.15
hobbyist 31.6
Hobday 3.9
hobgoblin 25.16
hobnail 23.6
hobnob 14.9
hobo 9.9
Ho Chi Minh 25.13
hock 21.20
hockey 4.19
hocus 28.26
hocus-pocus 28.26
hod 16.18
hodden 25.40
Hodge 20.11
hodgepodge 20.11
Hodges 35.10
Hodgkin 25.15
hodman 25.45
hodmen 25.45
hoe 9.1
hoedown 25.29
hoer 12.17
Hoffman 25.45
Hofmannsthal 23.2
hog 18.8
hogan 25.41
Hogarth 32.2
Hogarthian 25.37
Hogg 18.8
Hoggar 12.32
hogger 12.32
hoggery 4.43
hogget 30.21
hoggin 25.14
hoggish 29.7
Hogmanay 3.17
hogshead 16.3
hogtie 6.18
hogwash 29.11
Hohenzollern 25.44
ho-ho 9.1
ho-hum 24.14
hoick 21.25
hoi polloi 10.1
hoist 31.21
hoister 12.81
hoity-toity 4.54
hokey 4.20
hokey-cokey 4.20
hoki 4.20
Hokkaido 9.11
hokum 24.18
Holbein 25.21
hold 16.37
holdall 23.14
holder 12.28
Hölderlin 25.10
holdfast 31.2
holding 26.5
hold-up 27.13

hole 23.17
holey 4.25
Holi 4.25
holiday 3.9
holidaymaker 12.38
Holinshed 16.4
holism 24.21
holist 31.8
holistic 21.17
Holland 16.45
Hollander 12.29
Hollands 35.31
holler 12.44
Hollerith 32.6
hollow 9.17
hollow-eyed 16.14
holly 4.25
hollyhock 21.20
Hollywood 16.26
holm 24.11
Holme 24.11
Holmes 35.30
Holmesian 25.37
holmium 24.16
holmoak 21.24
holocaust 31.18
Holocene 25.11
Holofernes 35.7
hologram 24.1
holograph 17.2
holographic 21.10
holothurian 25.37
hols 35.29
Holst 31.29
Holstein 25.8
holster 12.80
holt 30.51
holus-bolus 28.27
holy 4.25
Holyhead 16.3
Holyoake 21.24
holystone 25.31
hom 24.11
homage 20.7
hombre 3.19
homburg 18.13
home 24.11
homebody 4.13
homeboy 10.3
homebuyer 12.13
homecoming 26.9
home-grown 25.30
homeland 16.40
homelike 21.19
homely 4.25
homemade 16.6
homemaker 12.38
home-making 26.7
homeopath 32.1
homeopathic 21.18
homeopathist 31.14

homeopathy 4.56
homeowner 12.56
Homer 12.52
Homeric 21.15
homeschool 23.20
homesick 21.16
homespun 25.35
homestay 3.22
homestead 16.4
homesteader 12.26
homestyle 23.12
hometown 25.29
homeward 16.30
homework 21.31
homeworker 12.41
homey 4.29
homicidal 23.28
homicide 16.16
homiletic 21.17
homilist 31.8
homily 4.24
homing 26.9
hominid 16.10
hominoid 16.24
hominy 4.32
Homo 9.18
homoerotic 21.17
homogamy 4.30
homogeneity 4.53
homogeneous 28.23
homogenizer 12.91
homogenous 28.29
homogeny 4.32
homologous 28.25
homonym 24.6
homophobe 14.11
homophobia 12.5
homophobic 21.9
homophone 25.30
homophonic 21.13
homophonous 28.29
homophony 4.34
Homo sapiens 35.31
homosexual 23.25
homunculus 28.27
hon 25.35
honcho 9.10
Honda 12.28
Honduran 25.47
Honduras 28.31
hone 25.30
Honecker 12.39
Honegger 12.31
honest 31.10
honesty 4.53
honey 4.33
honeybee 4.10
honeybun 25.35
honeybunch 29.20
honeycomb 24.11
honeydew 11.22

honeymoon 25.33
honeymooner 12.56
honeysuckle 23.32
Hong Kong 26.15
Honiara 12.64
honied 16.10
honk 21.34
honky 4.19
honky-tonk 21.34
Honolulu 11.13
honor 12.56
honorand 16.40
honoraria 12.10
honorarium 24.16
honorary 4.43
honorific 21.10
honour 12.56
Honshu 11.19
hooch 15.11
hood 16.26
hoodie 4.13
hood-like 21.19
hoodlum 24.18
hoodoo 11.6
hoodwink 21.33
hooey 4.8
hoof 17.13
hoofer 12.30
Hooghly 4.26
hoo-ha 1.9
hook 21.28
hookah 12.41
hooker 12.41
hookey 4.20
hooklet 30.22
hook-like 21.19
hook-up 27.13
hookworm 24.22
hooky 4.20
Hooley 4.26
hooligan 25.41
hoon 25.33
hoop 27.11
Hooper 12.63
hoopla 1.12
hoopoe 11.16
hooray 3.1
hoosegow 8.4
Hoosier 12.33
hoot 30.37
hootenanny 4.31
hooter 12.81
hoover 12.87
hooves 35.35
hop 27.8
hope 27.10
hoper 12.63
hophead 16.3
Hopi 4.36
Hopkin 25.15
Hopkins 35.31

h

hopper 12.62
hopple 23.35
hopscotch 15.7
Horace 28.10
horary 4.43
Horatian 25.49
Horatio 9.4
horde 16.19
Hordern 25.40
horizon 25.52
horizontal 23.39
Horlicks 28.39
hormonal 23.34
hormone 25.30
Hormuz 35.22
horn 25.28
hornbeam 24.5
hornbill 23.8
hornbook 21.28
hornet 30.23
hornist 31.10
hornpipe 27.7
hornswoggle 23.30
Hornung 26.17
horny 4.32
horologe 20.11
horology 4.17
horoscope 27.10
horoscopic 21.14
horoscopy 4.37
Horowitz 28.47
horrendous 28.25
horrible 23.26
horrid 16.11
horrific 21.10
horrify 6.7
horror 12.65
hors d'oeuvre 34.14
horse 28.15
horseback 21.2
horsebox 28.40
horseflesh 29.3
horsefly 6.11
horsehair 2.6
horseleech 15.5
horselike 21.19
horseman 25.45
horsemen 25.45
horseplay 3.15
horsepower 12.16
horseradish 29.6
horseshoe 11.19
horsetail 23.6
horsewhip 27.6
horsewoman 25.45
horsewomen 25.17
horsey 4.47
Horta 12.80
hortatory 4.43
Hortense 28.44
horticulturalist 31.8

horticulture 12.24
horticulturist 31.12
Horus 28.31
hosanna 12.53
hose 35.19
Hosea 12.4
hosepipe 27.7
hosier 12.12
hosiery 4.43
hospice 28.9
hospital 23.39
hospitaler 12.48
hospitaller 12.48
host 31.20
hostage 20.9
hostel 23.39
hosteler 12.48
hosteller 12.48
hostelry 4.41
hostess 28.34
hostile 23.12
hostility 4.53
hot 30.31
hotbed 16.3
hot-blooded 16.9
hotchpotch 15.7
hotdog 18.8
hotel 23.3
hotelier 12.6
hotfoot 30.39
hothead 16.3
hot-headed 16.9
hothouse 28.16
hotline 25.22
hotly 4.25
hotness 28.29
hotplate 30.11
hotpot 30.32
hotrod 16.18
hot-rodder 12.28
hot-rodding 26.5
hotshot 30.31
hotspot 30.32
hotspur 13.4
Hottentot 30.32
hotter 12.79
hottie 4.54
hottish 29.10
Houdini 4.31
Hough 8.1
hough 21.20
hound 16.43
houndstooth 32.12
hour 12.16
hourglass 28.2
houri 4.43
hourly 4.27
house husband
   16.45
house lights 28.47
house plant 30.53

house-sitter 12.78
house 28.16, 35.18
houseboat 30.35
housebound 16.43
houseboy 10.3
housebreaker 12.38
housebreaking 26.7
housecarl 23.2
housecoat 30.35
housefly 6.11
household 16.37
householder 12.28
househusband
   16.45
housekeep 27.5
housekeeper 12.61
housekeeping 26.10
housekept 30.58
houseleek 21.8
houselights 28.47
housemaid 16.6
housemaster 12.75
housemate 30.12
housemistress 28.10
housemother 12.84
house Plant 30.53
houseroom 24.12
house-sitter 12.78
house-warming
   26.9
housewife 17.7
housewifely 4.25
housewifery 4.43
housewives 35.35
housework 21.31
housey-housey 4.61
housing 26.14
Housman 25.45
Houston 25.50
hovel 23.40
hover 12.86
hovercraft 30.47
hoverer 12.67
hoverfly 6.11
hoverport 30.33
how-do-you-do 11.1
how 8.1
Howard 16.28
howbeit 30.20
howdah 12.28
howdy 4.13
Howe 8.1
Howell 23.25
Howes 35.18
however 12.85
howitzer 12.70
howl 23.16
howler 12.44
howsoever 12.85
howzat 30.1
hoy 10.1

hoya 12.18
hoyden 25.40
hoydenish 29.9
Hoyle 23.19
Huascarán 25.4
hub 14.13
Hubble 23.26
hubbub 14.13
hubby 4.10
hubcap 27.1
Hubei 3.1
Hubert 30.41
hubris 28.10
huckaback 21.2
huckleberry 4.43
huckster 12.81
Huddersfield 16.35
huddle 23.28
Hudson 25.48
hue 11.1
Hué 3.1
huff 17.15
huffish 29.7
huffy 4.14
hug 18.12
huge 20.15
hugger-mugger
   12.32
hugger 12.32
Huggins 35.31
Hugh 11.1
Hughes 35.21
Hughie 4.8
Hugo 9.13
Huguenot 9.19
huh 12.1
hula 12.45
hula-hoop 27.11
hulk 21.32
hull 23.22
hullabaloo 11.1
hum 24.14
human 25.45
humane 25.7
humanist 31.10
humanitarian 25.37
humanity 4.53
humankind 16.42
humanoid 16.24
Humber 12.22
Humberside 16.16
Humbert 30.41
humble 23.26
Humboldt 30.51
humbug 18.12
humbuggery 4.43
humdinger 12.60
humdrum 24.14
Hume 24.12
humeral 23.36
humerus 28.31

h

humic 21.12
humid 16.10
humidifier 12.14
humidify 6.7
humidity 4.53
humidor 7.5
humify 6.7
humiliate 30.8
humility 4.53
hummer 12.52
hummingbird 16.31
hummock 21.30
hummocky 4.20
hummus 28.28
humongous 28.25
humor 12.52
humoresque 21.35
humorist 31.12
humorous 28.31
humour 12.52
humous 28.28
hump 27.17
humpback 21.2
humpbacked 30.48
Humperdinck 21.33
humph 17.19
Humphrey 4.42
humpty-dumpty 4.55
humpy 4.37
humus 28.28
Hun 25.35
Hunan 25.1
hunch 29.20
hunchback 21.2
hunchbacked 30.48
hundred 16.29
hundredfold 16.37
hundredth 32.15
hundredweight 30.17
hung 26.18
Hungarian 25.37
Hungary 4.43
hunger 12.32
hungry 4.42
hunk 21.34
hunker 12.41
hunky 4.20
hunky-dory 4.41
Hunnish 29.9
hunt 30.55
hunter 12.81
Huntingdon 25.40
Huntington 25.50
huntress 28.10
huntsman 25.45
huntsmen 25.45
Huntsville 23.10
hurdle 23.28
hurdler 12.48

hurdy-gurdy 4.13
hurl 23.42
hurley 4.28
hurly-burly 4.28
Huron 25.26
hurrah 1.1
hurray 3.1
Hurri 4.41
hurricane 25.43
hurried 16.11
hurry 4.42
Hurst 31.26
Hurston 25.50
hurt 30.45
hurtle 23.39
Husák 21.4
husband 16.45
husbander 12.29
husbandhood 16.26
husbandly 4.27
husbandry 4.43
hush 29.16
hushaby 6.5
husk 21.35
hush-hush 29.16
husky 4.20
huss 28.21
hussar 1.1
Hussein 25.7
Husserl 23.42
Hussite 30.30
hussy 4.47
hustings 35.32
hustle 23.37
hustler 12.47
hut 30.40
hutch 15.13
Hutterite 30.29
Hutton 25.50
Hutu 11.20
Huxley 4.26
Huygens 35.31
huzza 1.1
Hwange 4.15
hwyl 23.8
hyacinth 32.19
hyacinthine 25.23
Hyacinthus 28.35
Hyades 35.7
hybrid 16.11
hybridity 4.53
Hyderabad 16.1
Hydra 12.65
hydrangea 12.35
hydrant 30.56
hydrate 30.7, 30.15
hydraulic 21.11
hydric 21.15
hydrocarbon 25.38
hydrodynamic 21.12

hydrodynamical 23.32
hydroelectric 21.15
hydrofoil 23.19
hydrogen 25.42
hydrogenous 28.29
hydrographic 21.10
hydrography 4.14
hydroid 16.24
hydrologic 21.11
hydrology 4.17
hydromechanics 28.39
hydrophobia 12.5
hydrophobic 21.9
hydroplane 25.8
hydrostatic 21.17
hydrous 28.31
hydroxide 16.16
hydrozoan 25.38
hyena 12.54
hygiene 25.10
hygienic 21.13
hygienist 31.10
Hyksos 28.14
Hyman 25.45
hymen 25.5
hymeneal 23.23
hymn 24.6
hymnal 23.34
hymnary 4.43
hymnic 21.13
hymnodist 31.6
hymnody 4.13
hypaethral 23.36
hypallage 4.17
Hypatia 12.11
hype 27.7
hyperbola 12.48
hyperbole 4.27
hyperbolic 21.11
hyperbolical 23.32
Hyperborean 25.37
hypercritical 23.32
hypergamy 4.30
hypericum 24.18
Hyperion 25.37
hypermarket 30.21
hypersonic 21.13
hyperspace 28.5
hypersthene 25.12
hypertension 25.49
hypertext 31.28
hyperthermia 12.7
hyperventilate 30.11
hypethral 23.36
hyphen 25.41
hyphenate 30.13

Hypnos 28.14
hypnosis 28.11
hypnotherapy 4.37
hypnotic 21.17
hypnotist 31.14
hypo 9.20
hypo-allergenic 21.13
hypocaust 31.18
hypochondria 12.10
hypochondriac 21.1
hypocrisy 4.48
hypocrite 30.24
hypocritical 23.32
hypodermic 21.12
hypoglycaemia 12.7
hypoid 16.24
hypolimnion 25.37
hypostasis 28.11
hypostasize 35.14
hypostatic 21.17
hypostyle 23.12
hypotension 25.49
hypotenuse 28.19
hypothalamus 28.28
hypothecate 30.10
hypothermia 12.7
hypotheses 35.8
hypothesis 28.11
hypothetical 23.32
hyrax 28.38
hysterectomy 4.30
hysteria 12.10
hysteric 21.15
hysterical 23.32
Hywel 23.40

I

I 6.1
iamb 24.1
iambic 21.9
iambus 28.24
Ian 25.36
Iapetus 28.34
Ibadan 25.40
Iban 25.4
Iberia 12.10
Iberian 25.37
ibex 28.38
ibid 16.8
ibis 28.7
Ibiza 12.83
Ibsen 25.48
ibuprofen 25.41
Icarus 28.31
ice 28.13
iceberg 18.13

infancy 4.48
infant 30.56
infanta 12.74
infante 4.51
infanticidal 23.28
infanticide 16.16
infantile 23.12
infantility 4.53
infantine 25.23
infantry 4.43
infantryman 25.45
infantrymen 25.45
infatuate 30.8
infect 30.48
infection 25.49
infectious 28.33
infer 13.1
inference 28.45
inferior 12.10
inferiority 4.53
infernal 23.34
inferno 9.19
infest 31.3
infibulate 30.11
infidel 23.3
infighting 26.13
infinite 30.43
infinitesimal 23.33
infinitival 23.40
infinity 4.53
infirmary 4.43
infirmity 4.53
inflammatory 4.43
inflate 30.7
inflationary 4.43
inflect 30.48
inflection 25.49
inflict 30.49
inflicter 12.78
infliction 25.49
inflow 9.17
influencer 12.71
influential 23.38
influenza 12.90
info 9.12
infomercial 23.38
informant 30.56
informatics 28.39
informatory 4.43
infotech 21.6
infractor 12.74
infrared 16.3
infrastructure 12.24
infringer 12.35
infuriate 30.8
infuser 12.92
ingeminate 30.13
ingenious 28.23
ingénue 11.15
ingenuity 4.53
ingenuous 28.24

ingest 31.3
ingestion 25.39
inglenook 21.28
ingot 30.42
ingrain 25.8
ingrained 16.41
Ingram 24.19
ingrate 30.15
ingratiate 30.8
ingredient 30.56
Ingres 12.64
ingress 28.3
Ingrid 16.11
ingurgitate 30.16
inhalant 30.56
inhaler 12.43
inherence 28.45
inherent 30.56
inherit 30.24
inheritance 28.45
inhibit 30.20
inhibitor 12.78
inhibitory 4.43
inhume 24.12
inimical 23.32
iniquitous 28.34
iniquity 4.53
initial 23.38
initialize 35.12
initiate 30.8, 30.41
initiatory 4.43
inject 30.48
injection 25.49
injector 12.76
Injun 25.42
injunct 30.49
injure 12.35
injurer 12.67
injurious 28.23
ink 21.33
Inkatha 12.75
inker 12.39
inkhorn 25.28
inkling 26.8
inkstand 16.40
inkwell 23.4
inky 4.19
inlander 12.25
in-law 7.11
inlay 3.15
inlet 30.22
in loco
 parentis 28.12
inly 4.24
inmate 30.12
in memoriam 24.1
inn 25.13
innards 35.27
innate 30.7
inner 12.55
innermost 31.20

Innes 28.9
inning 26.9
innit 30.23
innkeeper 12.61
innocence 28.45
innocency 4.48
innocent 30.56
innominate 30.43
innovate 30.16
innovatory 4.43
Innsbruck 21.28
innuendo 9.11
inoculate 30.11
inordinate 30.43
inquirer 12.67
inquiry 4.43
inquisitor 12.78
inrushing 26.12
inscription 25.49
inscriptional 23.34
insecticidal 23.28
insecticide 16.16
insectile 23.12
insectivore 7.20
insectivorous 28.31
inseminate 30.13
insert 30.45
inserter 12.82
insertion 25.49
inset 30.5
inshallah 12.42
insider 12.27
insidious 28.23
insight 30.30
insignia 12.8
insignificancy 4.48
insinuate 30.8
insipid 16.10
insipidity 4.53
insist 31.6
insistence 28.45
insistency 4.48
insistent 30.56
insitu 11.22
insofar 1.1
insole 23.18
insolence 28.45
insolent 30.56
insomnia 12.8
insomniac 21.1
insomuch 15.13
insouciance 28.45
insouciant 30.56
inspan 25.3
inspect 30.48
inspection 25.49
inspector 12.76
inspectorate 30.43
installer 12.44
instance 28.45
instancy 4.48

instant 30.56
instantaneous 28.23
instantiate 30.8
instigate 30.9
instil 23.8
instinct 30.49
instinctual 23.25
institute 30.38
institution 25.49
institutional 23.34
instruct 30.49
instruction 25.49
instructional 23.34
instructor 12.81
instructress 28.10
instrumentalist
 31.8
insufflate 30.11
insular 12.46
insularity 4.53
insulate 30.11
insulin 25.16
insult 30.51
insulter 12.81
insurance 28.45
insurer 12.67
insurgence 28.45
insurgency 4.48
insurgent 30.56
insurrection 25.49
insurrectionary
 4.43
insurrectionist
 31.10
intaglio 9.4
intarsia 12.11
integer 12.35
integral 23.36
integrant 30.56
integrate 30.15
integrity 4.53
intellect 30.48
intellectual 23.25
intellectualist 31.8
intelligentsia 12.11
intelligence 28.45
intelligent 30.56
intelligential 23.38
intelligentsia 12.11
intelligible 23.26
intendancy 4.48
intendant 30.56
intended 16.9
intensifier 12.14
intensify 6.7
intensive 34.7
intention 25.49
intentional 23.34
inter 13.1
interact 30.48
interactant 30.56
interaction 25.49

iPod 16.18
Ipoh 9.20
ipso facto 9.24
Ipswich 15.6
Iqbal 23.1
Iran 25.4
Irangate 30.9
Iranian 25.37
Iraq 21.5
Iraqi 4.18
irascible 23.26
irate 30.7
ire 12.13
Ireland 16.45
Irene 25.11
Irgun 25.33
iridescence 28.45
iridescent 30.56
iridium 24.16
iridology 4.17
iris 28.10
Irish 29.9
Irishman 25.45
Irishmen 25.45
Irishwoman 25.45
Irishwomen 25.17
irk 21.31
irksome 24.20
Irkutsk 21.35
Irma 12.52
iron 25.38
ironbark 21.5
ironclad 16.1
ironer 12.58
ironic 21.13
ironical 23.32
ironist 31.10
ironize 35.13
ironmonger 12.32
ironmongery 4.43
ironstone 25.31
ironware 2.15
ironwood 16.26
ironwork 21.31
irony 4.34
Iroquoian 25.38
Iroquois 10.14
irradiance 28.45
irradiant 30.56
irradiate 30.8
irrational 23.34
Irrawaddy 4.13
irreducible 23.26
irregular 12.46
irregularity 4.53
irrelevance 28.45
irrelevancy 4.48
irrelevant 30.56
irreligion 25.42
irreligious 28.25
irremissible 23.26

irrepressible 23.26
irresistible 23.26
irresolute 30.37
irresolution 25.49
irresponsible 23.26
irresponsive 34.7
irreverence 28.45
irreverent 30.56
irreverential 23.38
irreversible 23.26
irrigate 30.9
irritant 30.56
irritate 30.16
irrupt 30.58
Irving 26.14
Irvingite 30.29
Irwin 25.20
is 35.10
Isaac 21.30
Isabel 23.3
Isadora 12.66
isagogic 21.11
Isaiah 12.13
Ischia 12.6
Iseult 30.51
Isfahan 25.4
Isherwood 16.26
Ishiguro 9.21
Ishmael 23.5
Ishmaelite 30.28
Ishtar 1.19
Isidore 7.5
Isis 28.11
Isla 12.44
Islam 24.2
Islamabad 16.1
Islamic 21.12
Islamist 31.9
island 16.45
islander 12.29
isle 23.11
islet 30.22
Islwyn 25.13
ism 24.21
Ismaili 4.23
isn't 30.56
isobar 1.4
Isobel 23.3
isochromatic 21.17
Isocrates 35.9
isogeotherm 24.22
isolate 30.11, 30.42
isolationist 31.10
Isolde 12.28
isomer 12.52
isometric 21.15
isopod 16.18
isopropyl 23.11
isosceles 35.7
isothermal 23.33
isotonic 21.13

isotope 27.10
isotopic 21.14
isotropic 21.14
I-spy 6.1
Israel 23.6
Israeli 4.22
Israelite 30.28
Issachar 1.11
Issigonis 28.9
issuance 28.45
issuant 30.56
issue 11.19
issuer 12.19
Istanbul 23.21
isthmian 25.37
isthmus 28.28
it 30.20
Italian 25.52
Italianate 30.13
italic 21.11
Italy 4.27
itch 15.6
itchy 4.11
it'd 16.29
item 24.6
itemizer 12.91
iterate 30.15
Ithaca 12.41
itinerancy 4.48
itinerant 30.56
itinerary 4.43
itinerate 30.15
it'll 23.39
Ito 9.24
it's 28.47
its 28.47
itself 17.18
itsy-bitsy 4.46
Ivan 25.1, 25.51
I've 34.9
Ives 35.35
ivied 16.13
Ivor 12.86
ivory 4.43
ivy 4.58
Iwo Jima 12.51
ixia 12.11
Ixion 25.38
Iyyar 1.23
izard 16.30
Izmir 12.4
Iznik 21.13
Izvestia 12.12
Izzy 4.61

J

jab 14.1
Jabalpur 12.20

jabber 12.21
jabberwocky 4.19
Jabez 35.3
jabot 9.9
jacana 12.58
jacaranda 12.25
Jacinta 12.78
jacinth 32.19
jack 21.1
jackal 23.32
jackanapes 28.46
jackaroo 11.1
jackass 28.1
jackboot 30.37
jackdaw 7.5
jacket 30.21
jackfruit 30.37
jackhammer 12.50
Jackie 4.18
jackknife 17.7
jackknives 35.35
Jacklin 25.16
jackpot 30.32
jackrabbit 30.20
Jackson 25.48
Jacksonville 23.10
jackstaff 17.2
jackstone 25.31
jackstraw 7.15
Jacob 14.14
Jacobean 25.36
Jacobi 4.10
Jacobin 25.13
Jacobinic 21.13
Jacobinical 23.32
Jacobite 30.26
Jacobs 35.26
jaconet 30.5
Jacquard 16.2
Jacqueline 25.10
jacquerie 4.43
Jacques 28.38
jacuzzi 4.62
jade 16.6
j'adoube 14.12
jadeite 30.26
Jaeger 12.31
Jaffa 12.30
Jaffna 12.53
jag 18.1
jagged 16.9, 16.33
Jagger 12.31
jaggy 4.15
Jago 9.13
jaguar 12.20
jail 23.5
jailbait 30.9
jailbird 16.31
jailbreak 21.7
jailer 12.43
jailhouse 28.16

Jain 25.7
Jainist 31.10
Jaipur 12.20
Jakarta 12.75
Jake 21.7
Jalalabad 16.1
jalapeno 9.28
jalopy 4.36
jalousie 4.62
jam 24.1
Jamaica 12.38
Jamaican 25.43
jamb 24.1
jambalaya 12.13
jamboree 4.1
James 35.30
Jamestown 25.29
Jamie 4.29
jammer 12.50
Jammu 11.14
jammy 4.29
Jamshid 16.7
Jan 25.1
Jancis 28.11
Jane 25.7
Janet 30.23
Janey 4.31
jangle 23.30
Janice 28.9
Janine 25.9
janissary 4.43
janitor 12.78
janitorial 23.24
Jansen 25.48
Jansenist 31.10
January 4.43
Janus 28.29
Jap 27.1
Japan 25.1
Japanese 35.6
jape 27.4
japery 4.43
Japheth 32.3
japonica 12.39
jar 1.1
jardinière 2.1
jargon 25.41
jargonize 35.13
jarrah 12.64
Jarrow 9.21
Jarvis 28.12
jasmine 25.17
Jason 25.48
jaspé 3.18
jasper 12.61
Jat 30.3
Jataka 12.41
jaundice 28.7
jaunt 30.54
jaunty 4.54
Java 12.85

Javan 25.51
Javanese 35.6
javelin 25.16
jaw 7.1
jawbone 25.30
jawbreaker 12.38
jawline 25.22
jay 3.1
Jaycee 4.1
jaywalk 21.22
jaywalker 12.40
jazz 35.1
jazzer 12.90
jazzman 25.2
jazzmen 25.5
jazzy 4.61
J-cloth 32.8
jealous 28.27
jealousy 4.48
Jean 25.9, 25.24
Jeanette 30.4
Jeanie 4.31
Jeannine 25.9
Jeans 35.31
Jeep 27.5
jeepers 35.24
jeer 12.4
Jeeves 35.35
jeez 35.6
Jeff 17.3
Jefferies 35.10
Jefferson 25.48
Jeffreys 35.10
Jehoshaphat 30.1
Jehovah 12.86
Jehovist 31.15
Jehu 11.22
jejune 25.33
Jekyll 33.32
Jellicoe 9.16
jellify 6.7
jello 9.17
jelly 4.22
jellyfish 29.7
Jem 24.3
Jemima 12.51
Jemma 12.50
jemmy 4.29
Jena 12.54
je ne sais quoi 1.1
Jenkin 25.15
Jenkins 35.31
Jenna 12.53
Jenner 12.53
jennet 30.23
Jennifer 12.30
jenny 4.31
jeopardy 4.13
jerboa 12.17
jeremiad 16.28
Jeremiah 12.13

Jeremy 4.29
Jerez 32.3
Jericho 9.16
jerk 21.31
jerker 12.41
jerkin 25.15
jerky 4.20
Jermaine 25.7
jeroboam 24.17
Jerome 24.11
jerry 4.38
jerrycan 25.2
jersey 4.62
Jerusalem 24.18
Jervis 28.12
Jespersen 25.48
jess 28.3
Jessica 12.39
Jessie 4.45
jest 31.3
jester 12.76
Jesu 11.22
Jesuit 30.20
Jesus 28.35
jet 30.4
jeté 3.22
jetfoil 23.19
Jethro 9.21
jetlag 18.1
jetliner 12.55
jetsam 24.20
jet stream 24.5
jettison 25.48
jetton 25.50
jetty 4.51
jeu d'esprit 4.1
jeunesse dorée 3.1
Jew 11.1
jewel 23.25
jeweler 12.48
jeweller 12.48
jewellery 4.43
jewelry 4.43
Jewess 28.3
Jewish 29.6
Jewry 4.43
Jezebel 23.3
jib 14.7
jibba 12.21
jibber 12.21
jibe 14.8
Jiddah 12.27
jiffy 4.14
jig 18.6
jigger 12.31
jiggery-pokery 4.43
jiggle 23.30
jiggly 4.27
jigsaw 7.16
jihad 16.1
jihadi 4.12

jillion 25.52
jilt 30.51
Jim 24.6
jim-dandy 4.12
jimjams 35.30
Jin 25.13
Jinan 25.1
jingle 23.30
jingly 4.24
jingo 9.13
jingoist 31.6
jink 21.33
jinker 12.39
jinks 28.41
jinn 25.13
Jinnah 12.55
jinx 28.41
jitney 4.32
jitter 12.78
jitterbug 18.12
jittery 4.43
Jivaro 9.21
jive 34.9
jiver 12.86
jizz 35.10
jo 9.1
Joachim 24.6
Joan 25.30
Joanna 12.53
Joanne 25.1
job 14.9
Job 14.11
jobber 12.21
jobbery 4.43
jobcentre 12.76
jobless 28.27
Jo'burg 18.13
jobsworth 32.14
jobseeker 12.38
Jocasta 12.74
Jocelyn 25.16
jock 21.20
jockey 4.19
jockstrap 27.1
jocose 28.17
jocosity 4.53
jocular 12.46
jocularity 4.53
jocund 16.45
jocundity 4.53
Jodhpur 12.20
jodhpurs 35.24
Jodie 4.13
Joe 9.1
Joe Bloggs 35.28
Joel 23.17
joey 4.7
jog 18.8
jogger 12.32
joggle 23.30
jogtrot 30.32

j

Johannesburg 18.13
john 25.24
johnny 4.32
johnnycake 21.7
John o'Groats 28.47
Johns 35.31
Johnson 25.48
Johnsonian 25.37
Johor 7.1
joie de vivre 12.65
join 25.32
joinder 12.28
joiner 12.56
joinery 4.43
joint 30.55
jointer 12.81
jointress 28.10
jointure 12.24
joist 31.21
jojoba 12.21
joke 21.24
joker 12.40
jokey 4.20
Jolene 25.9
jollity 4.53
jolly 4.25
Jolson 25.48
jolt 30.51
jolty 4.54
Jolyon 25.37
Jomon 25.25
Jon 25.24
Jonah 12.56
Jonas 28.29
Jonathan 25.51
Jones 35.31
Joneses 35.10
Jong 26.15
jongleur 13.1
jonquil 23.10
Jonson 25.48
Joplin 25.16
Joppa 12.62
Jordan 25.40
Jordanian 25.37
jorum 24.19
José 3.1
Joseph 17.6
Josephine 25.10
Josephus 28.25
josh 29.11
josher 12.73
Joshua 12.20
Josiah 12.13
Josie 4.61
joss 28.14
josser 12.70
jostle 23.37
jot 30.31
jotter 12.79
Joule 23.20

jounce 28.44
journal 23.34
journalese 35.6
journalist 31.8
journalize 35.12
journey 4.34
journeyer 12.8
journeyman 25.45
journeymen 25.45
journo 9.19
joust 31.19
jouster 12.80
Jove 34.11
jovial 23.24
Jovian 25.37
jowl 23.16
jowly 4.25
joy 10.1
Joyce 28.18
Joycean 25.37
joyful 23.21
joyless 28.8
joyous 28.24
joyride 16.15
joyrider 12.27
joystick 21.17
Juan 25.4
Juanita 12.77
Juárez 35.3
jube 4.10, 14.12
jubilance 28.45
jubilant 30.56
Jubilate 3.22
jubilate 30.11
jubilee 4.24
Judaea 12.4
Judaean 25.37
Judah 12.29
Judaic 21.9
Judaize 35.11
Judas 28.25
Judas Iscariot 30.41
Judas
  Maccabaeus 28.22
Judd 16.27
judder 12.29
Jude 16.25
judge 20.16
Judges 35.10
judicatory 4.43
judicature 12.24
judicial 23.38
judiciary 4.43
judicious 28.33
Judith 32.6
judo 9.11
judoka 12.40
Judy 4.13
jug 18.12
Jugendstil 23.7
jugful 23.21

juggernaut 30.33
juggins 35.31
juggle 23.30
juggler 12.47
jugglery 4.43
Jugoslav 34.2
jugular 12.46
Jugurtha 12.83
Jugurthine 25.23
juice 28.19
juicer 12.71
juicy 4.47
ju-jitsu 11.18
juju 11.11
jujube 14.12
jukebox 28.40
Jukes 28.40
julep 27.6
Jules 35.29
Julia 12.6
Julian 25.37
Julie 4.26
Julien 25.37
julienne 25.5
Juliet 30.41
Julius 28.23
July 6.1
jumble 23.26
jumbo 9.9
jump 27.17
jumper 12.63
jumpsuit 30.38
jumpy 4.37
junco 9.16
junction 25.49
juncture 12.24
June 25.33
Juneau 9.19
Jung 26.17
Jungfrau 8.10
Jungian 25.37
jungle 23.30
jungly 4.26
junior 12.8
juniority 4.53
juniper 12.62
junk 21.34
Junker 12.41
junket 30.21
junkie 4.20
junky 4.20
junkyard 16.2
Juno 9.19
Junoesque 21.35
junta 12.81
Jupiter 12.78
Jura 12.67
jural 23.36
Jurassic 21.16
jurat 30.2
juridical 23.32

jurisdiction 25.49
jurisdictional 23.34
jurisprudence 28.45
jurisprudent 30.56
jurisprudential
  23.38
jurist 31.12
juristic 21.17
juror 12.67
jury 4.43
jurywoman 25.45
jurywomen 25.17
just 31.24
justice 28.12
justiciar 12.72
justiciary 4.43
justificatory 4.43
justifier 12.14
justify 6.7
Justin 25.19
Justine 25.12
Justinian 25.37
jut 30.40
jute 30.37
Jutish 29.10
Jutland 16.45
Juvenal 23.34
juvenescence 28.45
juvenescent 30.56
juvenile 23.11
juvenilia 12.6
juvenility 4.53
juxtapose 35.19

ka 1.1
Kaaba 12.21
kabaddi 4.12
Kabaka 12.37
kabbala 12.42
kabbalist 31.8
kabuki 4.20
Kabul 23.21
Kabwe 3.25
Kabyle 23.11
kachina 12.54
kaddish 29.6
kafir 12.30
Kafka 12.37
Kafkaesque 21.35
kaftan 25.3
Kagoshima 12.51
Kahlua 12.19
kai 6.1
Kaifeng 26.2
kaiseki 4.18
Kaiser 12.91
kaizen 25.52

kaka 1.11
kala-azar 1.1
Kalahari 4.38
Kalashnikov 17.8
kale 23.5
kaleidoscope 27.10
kaleidoscopic 21.14
Kali 4.21
Kalinin 25.18
Kalmar 1.13
Kalmyk 21.12
kalpa 12.63
Kaluga 12.32
Kama 12.50
Kamchatka 12.37
kamikaze 4.61
Kampala 12.42
kampong 25.26
Kampuchea 12.3
Kampuchean 25.36
Kanarese 35.6
kanban 25.1
Kandahar 1.1
Kandinsky 4.19
Kandy 4.12
Kandyan 25.37
Kane 25.7
kangaroo 11.1
Kannada 12.29
Kano 9.19
Kansan 25.52
Kansas 28.35
Kant 30.53
Kantian 25.37
kaolin 25.16
kaolinite 30.29
kapok 21.21
kappa 12.61
kaput 30.39
Karachi 4.11
Karajan 25.4
Karakoram 24.19
Karakorum 24.19
Kara Kum 24.14
karaoke 4.20
karat 30.43
karate 4.51
Karelia 12.6
Karelian 25.37
Karen 25.5, 25.47
Karin 25.18
Karl 23.2
Karloff 17.8
Karlsruhe 12.20
karma 12.50
karmic 21.12
Karnak 21.3
Karnataka 12.41
Karpov 34.10
Karroo 11.1
Kars 28.2

kart 30.3
kasbah 1.4
Kashmir 12.4
Kashmiri 4.43
Kasparov 34.10
Kassel 23.37
Katanga 12.31
Kate 30.7
Kath 32.1
Kathleen 25.10
Kathmandu 11.1
Kathryn 25.18
Katowice 12.23
Kattegat 30.1
Katy 4.52
Katya 12.89
katydid 16.9
Kauffmann 25.45
Kaunas 28.29
Kaunda 12.29
kauri 4.41
kava 12.85
Kawasaki 4.18
Kay 3.1
kayak 21.1
Kaye 3.1
kayo 9.1
Kazakh 21.1
Kazakhstan 25.4
Kazan 25.1
kazoo 11.1
kea 12.3
Kean 25.9
Keating 26.13
Keaton 25.50
Keats 28.47
Keatsian 25.37
kebab 14.1
Keble 23.26
keck 21.6
ked 16.3
Kedah 12.26
kedge 20.3
kedgeree 4.43
Keegan 25.41
keek 21.8
keel 23.7
keelboat 30.35
Keeler 12.43
Keeley 4.23
keelhaul 23.15
Keeling 26.8
keelson 25.48
keen 25.9
Keene 25.9
keep 27.5
keeper 12.61
keepnet 30.5
keepsake 21.7
Keflavik 21.18
keg 18.3

Keighley 4.23
Keir 12.4
keiretsu 11.18
keirin 25.18
keister 12.77
Keith 32.5
Keller 12.42
Kellogg 18.8
Kelly 4.22
kelp 27.16
kelpie 4.36
kelvin 25.19
Kemble 23.26
kemp 27.17
kempt 30.52
kempy 4.36
ken 25.5
Kendall 23.28
kendo 9.11
Kendrick 21.15
Keneally 4.23
Kenelm 24.18
Kennedy 4.12
kennel 23.34
Kenneth 32.6
kenning 26.9
Kenny 4.31
keno 9.19
kenosis 28.11
Kensington 25.50
Kentish 29.10
Kenton 25.50
Kentuckian 25.37
Kentucky 4.20
Kenya 12.89
Kenyan 25.52
Kenyatta 12.74
kepi 4.36
Kepler 12.42
kept 30.58
Kerala 12.48
keratin 25.19
kerb 14.15
kerbside 16.16
kerbstone 25.31
kerchief 17.6
kerfuffle 23.29
kermis 28.8
Kermit 30.23
kern 25.53
kernel 23.34
kerosene 25.11
Kerouac 21.1
Kerr 13.1
Kerry 4.38
kersey 4.62
Kes 35.3
Kesey 4.61
Kesh 29.3
kesh 29.4
kestrel 23.36

Keswick 21.18
ketch 15.3
ketchup 27.14
Kettering 26.11
kettle 23.39
kettledrum 24.14
kettling 26.8
kevel 23.40
Kevin 25.19
key 4.1
keyboard 16.20
keyboarder 12.28
keyboardist 31.6
keyer 12.3
keyholder 12.28
keyhole 23.17
keyless 28.8
Keynes 35.31
Keynesian 25.37
keynote 30.35
keypad 16.1
keypunch 29.20
keyring 26.11
Keys 35.6
keystone 25.31
keystroke 21.24
keyway 3.25
keyword 16.31
Khabarovsk 21.35
Khachaturian 25.37
khaddar 12.25
khaki 4.18
khan 25.4
khanate 30.13
Khartoum 24.12
khazi 4.61
Khedival 23.40
khedive 34.5
khimar 1.1
Khíos 28.14
Khmer 2.1
Khoikhoi 10.6
Khoisan 25.4
Khomeini 4.31
Khorramshahr 1.1
khoum 24.12
Khrushchev 17.8
Khufu 11.7
kiang 26.1
Kiangsu 11.1
Kia-Ora 12.66
kibble 23.26
kibbutz 28.47
kibbutzim 24.6
kibbutznik 21.13
kibitka 12.39
kibitzer 12.70
kiblah 12.43
kibosh 29.11
kick 21.9
kick-ass 28.2

k

kickback 21.2
kick-boxing 26.12
kick-down 25.29
kicker 12.39
kick-off 17.8
kick-pleat 30.18
kickshaw 7.17
kickstand 16.40
kick-start 30.3
kid 16.8
Kidd 16.8
kidder 12.27
Kidderminster 12.78
kiddie 4.12
kiddiewink 21.33
kiddle 23.28
kiddush 29.15
kidnap 27.1
kidnaping 26.10
kidnapper 12.61
kidnapping 26.10
kidney 4.32
kidology 4.17
Kiel 23.7
Kielce 12.69
Kieran 25.47
Kierkegaard 16.2
Kiev 17.3
kif 17.6
Kigali 4.21
kike 21.19
Kikuyu 11.22
Kildare 2.1
kilim 24.5
Kilimanjaro 9.21
Kilkenny 4.31
kill 23.8
Killarney 4.31
killer 12.43
killifish 29.7
killing 26.8
killjoy 10.5
Kilmarnock 21.30
kiln 25.44
kilo 9.17
kilobyte 30.26
kilocalorie 4.43
kilogram 24.1
kilohertz 28.47
kilojoule 23.20
kiloliter 12.77
kilolitre 12.77
kilometer 12.77
kilometre 12.77
kilometric 21.15
kiloton 25.35
kilowatt 30.32
Kilroy 10.11
kilt 30.51
kilter 12.78

kiltie 4.53
Kim 24.6
Kimberley 4.27
kimono 9.19
kin 25.13
kina 12.54
kind 16.42
kinda 12.27
Kinder 12.27
kindergarten 25.50
kind-hearted 16.12
kindle 23.28
kindler 12.43
kindling 26.8
kindly 4.25
kindred 16.11
kine 25.21
kinesics 28.39
kinetic 21.17
king 26.3
kingcraft 30.47
kingdom 24.17
kingfish 29.7
kingfisher 12.72
kinghood 16.26
King Kong 26.15
kinglet 30.22
kingly 4.24
kingmaker 12.38
kingpin 25.18
Kingsley 4.24
Kingston 25.50
Kingstown 25.29
kink 21.33
kinkajou 11.11
Kinki 4.19
kinky 4.19
kinless 28.8
Kinsey 4.61
kinsfolk 21.24
Kinshasa 12.69
kinship 27.6
kinsman 25.45
kinsmen 25.45
kinswoman 25.45
kinswomen 25.17
Kintyre 12.13
kiosk 21.35
kip 27.6
Kipling 26.8
kipper 12.62
kir 12.4
kirby grip 27.6
Kirchhoff 17.8
Kirghizia 12.12
Kiribati 4.51
Kirin 25.18
kirk 21.31
Kirkcaldy 4.13
Kirkcudbright 4.41
kirkman 25.45

kirkmen 25.45
Kirkwall 23.15
Kirov 34.10
kirsch 29.17
Kirsten 25.19
Kirstie 4.55
kirtle 23.39
Kirundi 4.13
Kislev 17.3
kismet 30.23
kiss 28.7
kisser 12.70
Kissinger 12.35
kissogram 24.1
kissy 4.46
kit 30.20
kitbag 18.1
kitchen 25.13
Kitchener 12.55
kitchenette 30.4
kitchenware 2.15
kite 30.26
Kitemark 21.5
kitsch 15.6
kitschy 4.11
kitten 25.50
kittenish 29.9
kittiwake 21.7
kittle 23.39
kitty 4.53
Kitwe 3.25
Kiwanis 28.9
kiwi 4.59
Klan 25.1
Klansman 25.45
Klansmen 25.45
Klaus 28.16
klaxon 25.48
Klee 3.1
Kleenex 28.38
kleftiko 9.16
Klein 25.21
Klemperer 12.67
klepht 30.47
kleptomania 12.8
kleptomaniac 21.1
Klerksdorp 27.9
Klimt 30.52
klipspringer 12.60
Klondike 21.19
Klosters 35.24
kludge 20.15
klutz 28.47
klutzy 4.62
K-meson 25.27
knack 21.1
knacker 12.37
knackwurst 31.26
knap 27.1
knapper 12.61
knapsack 21.4

knapweed 16.7
knar 1.1
knave 34.4
knavery 4.43
knavish 29.10
knawel 23.25
knead 16.7
kneader 12.26
knee 4.1
kneecap 27.1
kneecapping 26.10
kneehole 23.17
kneel 23.7
kneeler 12.43
knee-trembler 12.42
knell 23.3
knelt 30.51
Knesset 30.24
knew 11.1
Knickerbocker 12.40
knick-knack 21.3
knick-knackery 4.43
knife 17.7
knifepoint 30.55
knifer 12.30
knight 30.26
knight-errant 30.56
knight-errantry 4.43
knighthood 16.26
knightly 4.25
Knightsbridge 20.8
knish 29.6
knit 30.20
knitter 12.78
knitwear 2.15
knives 35.35
knob 14.9
knobble 23.26
knobbly 4.25
knobby 4.10
knobkerrie 4.38
knob-like 21.19
knobstick 21.17
knock 21.20
knockabout 30.34
knocker 12.40
knockout 30.34
knoll 23.17
knop 27.8
Knossos 28.14
knot 30.31
knotgrass 28.2
knothole 23.17
knotter 12.79
knotting 26.13
knotty 4.54
knotwork 21.31
knout 30.34
know 9.1

knower 12.17
know-how 8.5
knowing 26.3
knowledge 20.6
known 25.30
Knox 28.40
Knoxville 23.10
knuckle 23.32
knuckle bone 25.30
knucklehead 16.3
knuckly 4.27
knurl 23.42
koala 12.42
koan 25.1
Koch 21.24
koel 23.25
Koestler 12.49
Koh-i-noor 12.20
kohl 23.17
kohlrabi 4.10
koi 10.1
kola 12.44
Kolhapur 12.20
kolinsky 4.19
Köln 25.44
Komodo 9.11
Komsomolsk 21.35
Kongo 9.13
Kon-Tiki 4.18
Koönigsberg 18.13
kook 21.27
kookaburra 12.66
kooky 4.20
kop 27.8
kopek 21.6
Koran 25.4
Koranic 21.13
Korda 12.28
Kordofan 25.1
Korea 12.4
Korean 25.37
korfball 23.14
Korinthos 28.14
korma 12.52
koruna 12.56
Kos 28.14
kosher 12.73
Kosovo 9.27
Kostroma 1.13
Kosygin 25.14
Kota 12.80
Kotka 12.40
koto 9.25
Kowloon 25.33
kowtow 8.1
kraal 23.2
kraft 30.47
Krakatoa 12.17
kraken 25.43
Kraków 8.6
Krasnodar 1.1

Krasnoyarsk 21.35
Kraut 30.34
Kray 3.1
Kreisler 12.44
Kremlin 25.16
kriegspiel 23.7
krill 23.8
Krio 9.3
kris 28.6
Krishna 12.55
Krishnamurti 4.55
Kristallnacht 30.50
kroner 12.56
Kronstadt 30.2
Kropotkin 25.15
Kru 11.1
Kruger 12.32
Krugerrand 16.40
Krupp 27.12
krypton 25.26
Kshatriya 12.10
K2 11.1
Kuala Lumpur 12.20
Kubrick 21.15
kuccha 12.24
kudos 28.14
kudu 11.6
kudzu 11.23
Kufic 21.10
kukri 4.41
kulak 21.3
kulan 25.44
Kultur 12.20
Kulturkampf 17.19
Kumamoto 9.25
kumara 12.67
Kömmel 23.33
kumquat 30.32
Kundera 12.67
Kung 26.17
kung fu 11.1
Kunming 26.3
Kuomintang 26.1
kurbash 29.1
Kurd 16.31
Kurdish 29.6
Kurdistan 25.4
Kurgan 25.1
Kurosawa 12.88
Kursaal 23.2
Kurt 30.45
kurta 12.82
kurus 29.15
Kuwait 30.7
Kuwaiti 4.52
kvass 28.2
kvetch 15.3
Kwa 1.1
kwacha 12.23
KwaNdebele 4.23
kwanza 12.90

kwashiorkor 7.10
KwaZulu 11.13
Kweilin 25.13
Kweiyang 26.1
kyat 30.3
kyle 23.11
kylie 4.25
kylin 25.16
kylix 28.39
kyloe 9.17
Kyoto 9.25
Kyrgyz 35.10
Kyrgyzstan 25.4
Kyrie 3.3
Kyushu 11.19

L

laager 12.31
lab 14.1
Laban 25.38
labarum 24.19
label 23.26
labeler 12.48
labeller 12.48
labia 12.5
labial 23.24
labiate 30.8
labile 23.11
labor 12.21
laboratory 4.43
laborer 12.67
laborious 28.23
Laborite 30.29
labour 12.21
labourer 12.67
Labourite 30.29
Labrador 7.5
La Bruyère 2.1
Labuan 25.38
laburnum 24.19
labyrinth 32.19
labyrinthine 25.23
Lacan 25.1
lace 28.5
lacemaker 12.38
lacemaking 26.7
lacerate 30.15
lacewing 26.14
lacewood 16.26
lacework 21.31
laches 35.10
Lachesis 28.11
Lachlan 25.44
lachrymal 23.33
lachrymatory 4.43
lachrymose 28.17
lacing 26.12
lack 21.1

lackadaisical 23.32
lackey 4.18
lackluster 12.81
lacklustre 12.81
Laconia 12.8
Laconian 25.37
laconic 21.13
La Coruña 12.89
lacquer 12.37
lacquerer 12.67
lacrosse 28.14
lactase 35.5
lactate 30.7, 30.16
lacteal 23.24
lactescent 30.56
lactic 21.17
lactose 28.17
lacuna 12.56
lacunae 4.33
lacunar 12.56
lacustrine 25.23
lacy 4.45
lad 16.1
Ladakh 21.5
ladanum 24.19
ladder 12.25
laddie 4.12
laddish 29.6
lade 16.6
laden 25.40
la-di-da 1.1
Ladin 25.9
lading 26.5
Ladino 9.19
ladle 23.28
ladler 12.48
lady 4.12
ladybird 16.31
ladybug 18.12
lady-fern 25.53
ladyfinger 12.31
ladyfy 6.7
ladykiller 12.43
ladylike 21.19
Ladysmith 32.6
Lae 3.1
Laetitia 12.72
La Fayette 30.4
La Fontaine 25.7
lag 18.1
lagan 25.41
lager 12.31
Lagerlöf 17.11
laggard 16.28
laggardly 4.27
lagger 12.31
lagging 26.6
lagoon 25.33
lagoonal 23.34
Lagos 28.14
Lagrange 20.19

lah 1.1
Lahnda 12.25
Lahore 7.1
Lahu 11.1
laical 23.32
laicize 35.14
laid 16.6
lain 25.7
Laing 26.1
lair 2.1
laird 16.5
lairy 4.39
laissez-faire 2.1
laissez-passer 3.20
laity 4.53
Laius 28.22
lake 21.7
Lakeland 16.45
lakelet 30.22
Laker 12.38
lakeside 16.16
lakh 21.1
Lakshmi 4.29
Lalage 4.15
Lalique 21.8
lam 24.1
lama 12.50
Lamaist 31.6
Lamarck 21.5
Lamaze 35.2
lamb 24.1
lambada 12.25
lambaste 31.4
lambda 12.25
lambent 30.56
lamber 12.50
lambert 30.41
lambkin 25.15
lamblike 21.19
Lambrusco 9.16
lambskin 25.15
lambswool 23.21
lame 24.4
lamé 3.16
lamebrain 25.8
lamellae 4.22
lament 30.53
Lamentations 35.31
lamenter 12.76
laminate 30.13, 30.43
lamington 25.50
Lammas 28.28
lammergeier 12.14
lamp 27.17
lampern 25.46
lamplight 30.28
lamplighter 12.79
lamplit 30.22
lampoon 25.33
lampooner 12.56
lampoonist 31.10

lamp post 31.20
lamprey 4.38
lampshade 16.6
Lana 12.53
Lancashire 12.11
Lancaster 12.82
Lancastrian 25.37
lance 28.44
lancelet 30.22
Lancelot 30.31
lanceolate 30.11
lancer 12.69
lancet 30.24
lancewood 16.26
Lancing 26.12
land 16.40
landau 7.5
landaulet 30.4
landbanking 26.7
Länder 12.26
Landers 35.24
landfall 23.15
landfill 23.8
landform 24.9
landholding 26.5
landing 26.5
landlady 4.12
ländler 12.42
landline 25.22
landlocked 30.49
landlord 16.21
landlubber 12.22
landmark 21.5
landmass 28.1
landmine 25.22
Landor 7.5
landowner 12.56
landowning 26.9
landrail 23.6
landscape 27.4
landscapist 31.11
Landseer 12.11
landslide 16.14
landslip 27.6
landsman 25.45
landsmen 25.45
Landsteiner 12.55
landward 16.30
lane 25.7
Langland 16.45
langlauf 17.10
Langley 4.21
Langmuir 12.20
langouste 31.22
langoustine 25.9
Langton 25.50
Langtry 4.38
language 20.9
langue d'oc 21.20
Languedoc 21.20
languid 16.13

languish 29.10
languisher 12.72
languor 12.31
languorous 28.31
langur 13.3
lank 21.33
lanky 4.18
lanner 12.53
lanneret 30.24
lanolin 25.16
Lansing 26.12
lantana 12.53
lantern 25.50
lanthanum 24.14
lanyard 16.30
Lanzarote 4.54
Lanzhou 11.1
Lao 8.1
Laocoon 25.24
Laodicean 25.36
Laois 29.5
Laos 28.14
Laotian 25.49
Lao-tzu 11.1
lap 27.1
lapdog 18.8
lapel 23.3
lapful 23.21
lapidary 4.43
lapis lazuli 6.11
Lapith 32.6
Laplace 28.2
Lapland 16.40
Laplander 12.25
Lapp 27.1
Lappish 29.9
lapse 28.46
lapsus linguae 6.21
laptop 27.8
lapwing 26.14
Lara 12.64
Laramie 4.30
larcener 12.55
larcenist 31.10
larcenous 28.29
larceny 4.32
larch 15.2
lard 16.2
lardass 28.2
larder 12.25
lardon 25.40
lardy 4.12
lares 35.7
large 20.2
largesse 28.3
larghetto 9.24
largish 29.7
largo 9.13
lari 4.38
lariat 30.41
Larissa 12.70

lark 21.5
Larkin 25.15
larkspur 13.4
larky 4.18
Larousse 28.19
larrikin 25.15
larrup 27.14
Larry 4.38
Lars 35.2
larva 12.85
larvae 4.58
larval 23.40
Larwood 16.26
laryngitis 28.12
larynx 28.41
lasagne 12.89
La saue 23.1
La scala 12.42
lascar 12.37
lascivious 28.23
laser 12.90
laserdisc 21.35
LaserVision 25.42
lash 29.1
lasher 12.72
lashing 26.12
Las Palmas 28.28
lass 28.1
lassie 4.45
lassitude 16.25
lasso 11.1
lassoer 12.19
Lassus 28.32
last 31.2
lasting 26.13
Las Vegas 28.25
lat 30.1
Latakia 12.3
latch 15.1
latchet 30.20
latchkey 4.18
late 30.7
latecomer 12.52
latency 4.48
latent 30.56
later 12.77
lateral 23.36
Lateran 25.47
laterite 30.29
latex 28.38
lath 32.2
lathe 33.2
lather 12.84
lathery 4.43
lathi 4.51
Latimer 12.51
Latin 25.19
Latinate 30.13
Latinist 31.10
Latino 9.19
latish 29.10

latitude 16.25
latitudinal 23.34
latitudinarian 25.37
Latium 24.16
latke 12.41
latria 12.13
latrine 25.9
latte 3.22
latter 12.74
lattice 28.12
Latvia 12.12
Latvian 25.37
laud 16.19
Lauda 12.28
laudanum 24.19
laudatory 4.43
laugh 17.2
laugher 12.30
laughing stock 21.21
laughter 12.75
Laughton 25.50
Launceston 25.50
launch 29.20
launcher 12.73
launch pad 16.1
launder 12.28
launderer 12.67
launderette 30.4
laundress 28.10
laundromat 30.1
laundry 4.41
Laura 12.66
laureate 30.41
laurel 23.36
Lauren 25.47
Laurie 4.41
Laurier 12.10
Lausanne 25.1
lav 34.1
lava 12.85
lavabo 9.9
lavation 25.49
lavatorial 23.24
lavatory 4.43
lave 34.4
lavender 12.27
laver 12.85
Lavinia 12.8
lavish 29.10
Lavoisier 3.3
law 7.1
lawful 23.21
lawgiver 12.86
lawless 28.27
lawmaker 12.38
lawman 25.2
lawmen 25.5
lawn 25.28
lawnmower 12.17
lawny 4.32

Lawrence 28.45
lawrencium 24.16
Laws 35.17
lawsuit 30.38
lawyer 12.18
lawyerly 4.27
lax 28.38
laxity 4.53
lay 3.1
layabout 30.34
Layamon 25.45
lay-by 6.5
layer 12.2
layette 30.4
layman 25.45
laymen 25.45
lay-off 17.8
layout 30.34
layover 12.86
layperson 25.48
layshaft 30.47
laywoman 25.45
laywomen 25.17
lazaret 30.4
Lazarus 28.31
laze 35.5
Lazio 9.4
lazy 4.61
lazybones 35.31
L-dopa 12.63
Lea 4.1
leach 15.5
Leacock 21.20
lead 16.3, 16.7
leaden 25.40
leader 12.26
lead-in 25.14
leading 26.5
leaf 17.5
leaflet 30.22
leaf-like 21.19
leafy 4.14
league 18.5
leaguer 12.31
Leah 12.3
leak 21.8
leakage 20.6
leaker 12.38
Leakey 4.18
leaky 4.18
leal 23.7
lean 25.9
Leander 12.25
leaning 26.9
Leanne 25.1
leant 30.53
lean-to 11.20
leap 27.5
leaper 12.61
leapfrog 18.8
leapt 30.58

Lear 12.4
learn 25.53
learned 16.10, 16.46
learner 12.59
learnt 30.57
lease 28.6
leaseback 21.2
leasehold 16.37
leaseholder 12.28
leash 29.5
least 31.5
leastways 35.5
leat 30.18
leather 12.84
leatherette 30.4
leatherjacket 30.21
leathern 25.51
leatherneck 21.6
leathery 4.43
leave 34.5
leaven 25.51
leaver 12.85
leaves 35.35
leavings 35.32
Leavis 28.12
Lebanese 35.6
Lebanon 25.46
Lebensraum 24.10
lebkuchen 25.43
Leblanc 21.34
Lebowa 12.17
Le Carré 3.19
lech 15.3
lecher 12.23
lecherous 28.31
lechery 4.43
lecithin 25.19
Le Corbusier 3.3
lectern 25.50
lection 25.49
lectionary 4.43
lector 7.18
lecture 12.23
lecturer 12.67
lecythi 6.19
led 16.3
Leda 12.26
Lederhosen 25.52
ledge 20.3
ledger 12.35
lee 4.1
leech 15.5
Leeds 35.27
Lee-Enfield 16.35
leek 21.8
leer 12.4
leery 4.43
lees 35.6
leet 30.18
leeward 16.28,16.30
leeway 3.25

left 30.47
leftish 29.10
leftist 31.14
leftmost 31.20
left-over 12.86
leftover 12.86
leftward 16.30
lefty 4.51
leg 18.3
legacy 4.48
legal 23.30
legalese 35.6
legalist 31.8
legality 4.53
legate 30.42
legatee 4.1
legatine 25.19
legation 25.49
legato 9.24
legator 12.77
legend 16.45
legendary 4.43
legerdemain 25.7
legged 16.9
legging 26.6
leggy 4.15
leghorn 25.28
legible 23.26
legion 25.42
legionary 4.43
legionnaire 2.1
legislate 30.11
legislature 12.24
legit 30.20
legitimacy 4.48
legitimate 30.43
legitimatize 35.14
legitimist 31.9
legless 28.27
legman 25.2
legmen 25.5
Lego 9.13
legroom 24.12
legume 24.12
leguminous 28.29
legwork 21.31
Lehár 1.1
Le Havre 12.64
lei 3.1
Leibniz 28.47
Leibnizian 25.37
Leicester 12.76
Leicestershire 12.11
Leichhardt 30.3
Leiden 25.40
Leif 17.5
Leigh 4.1
Leighton 25.50
Leila 12.43
Leinster 12.76
Leipzig 18.6

leister 12.77
leisure 12.33
leisurely 4.27
leisurewear 2.15
leitmotif 17.5
Leitrim 24.6
lek 21.6
Leland 16.45
Lely 4.23
leman 25.45
Le Mans 25.24
lemma 12.50
lemmatize 35.14
lemme 4.29
lemming 26.9
Lemmon 25.45
Lemnos 28.14
lemon 25.45
lemonade 16.6
lemony 4.34
lempira 12.67
Lemuel 23.25
lemur 12.51
Len 25.5
Lena 12.54
lend 16.41
lender 12.26
Lendl 23.28
length 32.20
lengthen 25.51
lengthener 12.58
lengthways 35.5
lengthwise 35.15
lengthy 4.56
lenience 28.45
leniency 4.48
lenient 30.56
Lenin 25.18
Leninakan 25.2
Leningrad 16.1
Leninist 31.10
Leninite 30.29
lenity 4.53
Lennon 25.46
Lennox 28.41
Lenny 4.31
Leno 9.19
Le Notre 12.65
lens 35.31
lensman 25.45
lensmen 25.45
lent 30.53
Lenten 25.50
lenticular 12.46
lentil 23.9
lento 9.24
Leo 9.3
Leoan 25.24
León 25.24
Leona 12.56
Leonard 16.29

Leonardo 9.11
leone 25.30
Léonid 16.10
leonine 25.23
Leonora 12.66
leopard 16.29
Leopold 16.37
Léopoldville 23.10
leotard 16.2
leper 12.61
lepidopteran 25.47
lepidopterist 31.12
Lepidus 28.25
leprechaun 25.28
leprosy 4.48
leprous 28.31
lepton 25.26
Lepus 28.30
Leroy 10.11
Lerwick 21.18
Les 35.3
Lesage 19.1
lesbian 25.37
Lesbos 28.14
lesion 25.42
Lesley 4.22
Leslie 4.22
Lesotho 11.20
less 28.3
lessee 4.1
lessen 25.48
Lesseps 28.46
lesser 12.69
Lessing 26.12
lesson 25.48
lessor 7.1
lest 31.3
Lester 12.76
let 30.4
letdown 25.29
lethal 23.40
lethargic 21.11
lethargy 4.17
Lethe 4.56
Lethean 25.37
Leticia 12.11
Lett 30.4
letter 12.76
letter box 28.40
letterhead 16.3
letterpress 28.3
Lettice 28.12
letting 26.13
lettuce 28.12
let-up 27.13
leu 11.2
leucocyte 30.30
leukaemia 12.7
leukemia 12.7
Leuven 25.5
levant 30.53

levanter 12.74
Levantine 25.23
levee 4.58
level 23.40
leveler 12.48
leveller 12.48
lever 12.85
leverage 20.8
leveret 30.24
Leverhulme 24.12
Le Verrier 3.3
Levi 4.58, 6.20
leviathan 25.51
levin 25.19
levirate 30.43
levitate 30.16
Levite 30.30
Leviticus 28.26
levity 4.53
levy 4.58
lewd 16.25
Lewes 28.7
lewis 28.7
lexical 23.32
lexicographer 12.30
lexicography 4.14
lexicon 25.43
Lexington 25.50
Ley 4.1
leylandii 6.3
Leyte 4.52
Lhasa 12.69
liability 4.53
liable 23.26
liaise 35.5
liaison 25.52
Liam 24.15
liana 12.53
Liao 8.1
liar 12.13
Lias 28.24
lib 14.7
libation 25.49
libber 12.21
Libby 4.10
LibDem 24.3
libel 23.26
libeler 12.48
libeller 12.48
libellous 28.27
libelous 28.27
Liberace 4.11
liberal 23.36
liberalist 31.8
liberalizer 12.91
liberate 30.15
liberationist 31.10
Liberia 12.10
Liberian 25.37
libertarian 25.37
libertinage 20.7

libertine 25.12
liberty 4.55
libidinal 23.34
libidinous 28.29
libido 9.11
Libra 12.65
Libran 25.47
librarian 25.37
library 4.43
librettist 31.14
libretto 9.24
Librium 24.16
Libya 12.5
Libyan 25.37
lice 28.13
licence 28.45
license 28.45
licensee 4.1
licenser 12.71
licensor 12.71
licentiate 30.41
licentious 28.33
lichen 25.13
Lichfield 16.35
Lichtenstein 25.23
licit 30.24
lick 21.9
lickerish 29.9
lickety-split 30.20
licking 26.7
lickspittle 23.39
licorice 29.9
lid 16.8
Liddell 23.28
lidless 28.8
lido 9.11
lie 6.1
Liebfraumilch 21.32
Liebig 18.6
Liechtenstein 25.23
Liechtensteiner 12.55
lied 16.14
Lieder 12.26
lief 17.5
liege 20.5
Liège 19.4
liegeman 25.45
liegemen 25.45
lie-in 25.13
lien 25.36
lieu 11.1
lieutenancy 4.48
lieutenant 30.56
life 17.7
lifebelt 30.51
lifeblood 16.27
lifeboat 30.35
lifeboatman 25.45
lifeboatmen 25.45

lifebuoy 10.3
lifeguard 16.2
lifejacket 30.21
lifelike 21.19
lifeline 25.22
lifelong 26.15
lifer 12.30
lifesaver 12.85
lifespan 25.3
lifestyle 23.12
lifetime 24.7
Liffey 4.14
lift 30.47
lifter 12.78
lig 18.6
ligand 16.45
ligature 12.24
liger 12.31
ligger 12.31
light 30.26
lighten 25.50
lightening 26.9
lighter 12.79
lightfast 31.2
light-footed 16.12
light-headed 16.9
light-hearted 16.12
lighthouse 28.16
lighting 26.13
lightish 29.10
lightning 26.9
lightweight 30.17
ligneous 28.23
lignite 30.29
lignitic 21.17
Liguria 12.10
Ligurian 25.37
likable 23.26
like 21.19
likelihood 16.26
likely 4.25
like-minded 16.9
liken 25.43
likewise 35.15
liking 26.7
Likud 16.26
lilac 21.30
Lilian 25.37
Lilienthal 23.2
Lilith 32.6
Lille 23.7
Lillee 4.24
Lilliputian 25.49
lilo 9.17
lilt 30.51
lily 4.24
lily-livered 16.29
Lima 12.51
Limassol 23.13
limb 24.6
limber 12.21,12.51

limbo 9.9
Limburger 12.32
lime 24.7
limeade 16.6
limekiln 25.44
limelight 30.28
limepit 30.23
limerick 21.15
limestone 25.31
limewash 29.11
limey 4.29
liminal 23.34
limit 30.23
limitary 4.43
limited 16.12
limiter 12.78
limn 24.6
limner 12.51
limo 9.18
Limoges 19.5
Limousin 25.1
limousine 25.9
limp 27.17
limpet 30.23
limpid 16.10
limpidity 4.53
limpkin 25.15
limp-wristed 16.12
Limpopo 9.20
Linacre 12.41
linage 20.7
linchpin 25.18
Lincoln 25.43
Lincolnshire 12.11
linctus 28.34
Lind 16.42
Linda 12.27
Lindbergh 18.13
linden 25.40
Lindisfarne 25.4
Lindon 25.40
Lindsay 4.61
Lindy 4.12
line 25.21
lineage 20.6
lineal 23.24
linear 12.8
linearity 4.53
linearize 35.13
linebacker 12.37
Lineker 12.39
lineman 25.45
linemen 25.45
linen 25.18
liner 12.55
linesman 25.45
linesmen 25.45
line-up 27.13
Linford 16.28
ling 26.3
Lingala 12.42

lingam 24.18
linger 12.31
lingerer 12.67
lingerie 4.43
lingo 9.13
lingua franca 12.37
lingual 23.40
linguine 4.31
linguist 31.15
linguistician 25.49
lining 26.9
link 21.33
linkage 20.6
linkman 25.2
linkmen 25.5
link-up 27.13
linn 25.13
Linnaean 25.36
Linnaeus 28.22
Linnean 25.36
linnet 30.23
lino 9.19
linocut 30.40
linocutting 26.13
linoleum 24.16
linotype 27.7
linsang 26.1
linseed 16.7
lint 30.54
lintel 23.39
Linton 25.50
linty 4.53
Linus 28.29
liny 4.32
Linz 28.44
lion 25.38
Lionel 23.34
lion-hearted 16.12
lionizer 12.91
lion-like 21.19
Lions 35.31
lip 27.6
lipase 35.5
lipid 16.10
Lipizzaner 12.53
lipless 28.8
lip-like 21.19
liposuction 25.49
Lippi 4.36
Lippmann 25.45
lippy 4.36
lipsalve 34.15
lipstick 21.17
lip-sync 21.33
lip-syncer 12.39
liquefaction 25.49
liquefier 12.14
liquefy 6.7
liquescent 30.56
liqueur 12.20
liquid 16.13

liquidate 30.9
liquidity 4.53
liquor 12.39
liquorice 29.9
lira 12.67
lire 12.67
Lisa 12.69
Lisbon 25.38
Lisburn 25.53
lisente 4.51
lisle 23.11
lisp 27.18
lissom 24.20
list 31.6
listen 25.48
listener 12.58
lister 12.78
listeria 12.10
listing 26.13
Liston 25.50
Liszt 31.6
lit 30.20
litany 4.34
lite 30.26
liter 12.77
literacy 4.48
literage 20.8
literal 23.36
literalist 31.8
literalize 35.12
literary 4.43
literate 30.43
literati 4.51
literatim 24.6
literature 12.23
lithe 33.5
lithium 24.16
litho 9.26
lithograph 17.2
lithographer 12.30
lithographic 21.10
lithography 4.14
Lithuania 12.8
Lithuanian 25.37
litigant 30.56
litigate 30.9
litigious 28.25
litmus 28.28
litotes 35.9
litre 12.77
litreage 20.8
litter 12.78
littérateur 13.1
litter lout 30.34
litterbug 18.12
little 23.39
Little Englander 12.29
Littler 12.43
Littlewood 16.26
littoral 23.36

Littré 3.1
liturgical 23.32
liturgist 31.7
liturgy 4.17
livable 23.26
live 34.6, 34.9
livelihood 16.26
livelong 26.15
lively 4.25
liven 25.51
Liver 12.86
liveried 16.11
liverish 29.9
Liverpool 23.20
Liverpudlian 25.37
liverwort 30.45
livery 4.43
liveryman 25.45
liverymen 25.45
lives 35.35
livestock 21.21
Livia 12.12
livid 16.13
lividity 4.53
living 26.14
Livings 35.32
Livingstone 25.50
Livonia 12.8
Livorno 9.19
Livy 4.58
Liz 35.10
Liza 12.91
lizard 16.30
Lizzie 4.61
Ljubljana 12.53
llama 12.50
Llandudno 9.19
llano 9.19
Llewelyn 25.16
Lloyd's 35.27
Lloyd 16.24
lo 9.1
loach 15.10
load 16.23
loader 12.28
loading 26.5
loaf 17.11
loafer 12.30
loam 24.11
loamy 4.29
loan 25.30
loanee 4.1
loaner 12.56
loan shark 21.5
loanword 16.31
loath 32.11
loathe 33.7
loather 12.84
loaves 35.35
lob 14.9
lobby 4.10

lobbyist 31.6
lobe 14.11
lobo 9.9
lobotomize 35.13
lobotomy 4.30
lobscouse 28.16
lobster 12.79
lobster pot 30.32
lobster thermidor 7.5
lobworm 24.22
local 23.32
locale 23.2
locality 4.53
Locarno 9.19
locate 30.7
location 25.49
locational 23.34
loch 22.4
lochan 25.43
loci 6.16
lock 21.20
lockage 20.6
Locke 21.20
locker 12.40
Lockerbie 4.10
locket 30.21
lockjaw 7.9
locknut 30.40
lockout 30.34
locksmith 32.6
lock-up 27.13
Lockyer 12.89
loco 9.16
locomotion 25.49
locum 24.18
locus 28.26
locust 31.25
locution 25.49
lode 16.23
loden 25.40
lodestar 1.19
lodestone 25.31
lodge 20.11
lodger 12.35
lodging 26.6
loess 28.7
loft 30.47
lofty 4.54
log 18.8
Logan 25.41
loganberry 4.43
logarithm 24.20
logarithmic 21.12
logbook 21.28
loge 19.5
logger 12.32
loggerhead 16.3
loggia 12.6
logia 12.5
logic 21.11

logical 23.32
logician 25.49
logion 25.37
logistic 21.17
logistical 23.32
logjam 24.1
logo 9.13
logomachy 4.20
logon 25.25
logorrheic 21.9
logorrhoeic 21.9
logos 28.14
logotype 27.7
logroller 12.44
logwood 16.26
Lohengrin 25.18
loin 25.32
loincloth 32.8
Loire 1.1
Lois 28.7
loiter 12.81
loiterer 12.67
Loki 4.20
Lola 12.44
Lolita 12.77
loll 23.13
lollapalooza 12.92
Lollard 16.29
Lollardy 4.13
lollipop 27.8
lollop 27.14
lolly 4.25
Lombard 16.2
Lombardic 21.10
Lombardy 4.13
Lombok 21.20
Lomé 3.16
London 25.40
Londonderry 4.38
Londoner 12.58
lone 25.30
lonely 4.25
loner 12.56
long 26.15
longboat 30.35
longbow 9.9
longevity 4.53
Longfellow 9.17
Longford 16.28
longhair 2.6
longhand 16.40
longhorn 25.28
longing 26.10
Longinus 28.29
longish 29.9
longitude 16.25
longitudinal 23.34
longshore 7.17
longshoreman 25.45
longshoremen 25.45
longstop 27.8

Longton 25.50
longueur 13.1
longways 35.5
Lonnie 4.32
loo 11.1
loofah 12.30
look 21.28
lookalike 21.19
lookbook 21.28
looker 12.41
lookout 30.34
look-see 4.47
lookup 27.13
loom 24.12
loon 25.33
loony 4.33
loop 27.11
looper 12.63
loophole 23.17
loopy 4.37
loose 28.19
loosen 25.48
loosener 12.58
loot 30.37
looter 12.81
lop 27.8
lope 27.10
lopsided 16.9
loquacious 28.33
loquacity 4.53
loquat 30.32
loquitur 12.78
lor 7.1
loran 25.47
Lorca 12.40
Lorcan 25.43
lord 16.19
lord-like 21.19
lordling 26.8
lordly 4.25
Lordy 4.13
lore 7.1
Lorelei 6.11
Loren 25.5
Lorentz 28.45
Lorenz 35.31
Lorenzo 9.29
Loreto 9.24
Loretta 12.76
lorgnette 30.4
lorikeet 30.18
loris 28.10
lorn 25.28
Lorna 12.56
Lorraine 25.7
lorry 4.41
lory 4.41
Los Alamos 28.14
Los Angeles 35.7
lose 35.21
loser 12.92

loss 28.14
lost 31.17
lot 30.31
Lothario 9.4
Lothian 25.37
lotion 25.49
lottery 4.43
Lottie 4.54
lotto 9.25
lotus 28.34
Lou 11.1
louche 29.14
loud 16.22
louden 25.40
loudhailer 12.43
loudmouth 32.10
loudmouthed 16.48
loudspeaker 12.38
Louella 12.42
lough 22.4
Loughborough 12.67
Loughlin 25.16
Lough Neagh 3.1
Louie 4.8
Louis 4.8
louis 35.10
Louisa 12.90
Louise 35.6
Louisiana 12.53
Louisianan 25.46
Louisville 23.10
lounge 20.19
lounger 12.35
loungewear 2.15
lour 12.16
Lourdes 16.28
Lourenço Marques 28.38
loury 4.43
louse 28.16
lousy 4.61
lout 30.34
Louth 32.10
loutish 29.10
Louvain 25.1
louver 12.87
Louvre 12.66
louvre 12.87
lovable 23.26
lovage 20.9
lovat 30.44
love 34.13
lovebird 16.31
love bite 30.26
lovechild 16.36
Lovelace 28.5
Lovell 23.40
lovelock 21.21
lovelorn 25.28
lovely 4.26

lover 12.87
lovesick 21.16
lovey 4.58
lovey-dovey 4.58
low 9.1
lowball 23.14
lowboy 10.3
lowbrow 8.10
low-down 25.29
Lowell 23.25
lower 12.16, 12.17
lowermost 31.20
Lowestoft 30.47
lowish 29.6
lowland 16.45
lowlander 12.29
lowlife 17.7
lowlight 30.28
lowly 4.25
lowness 28.29
low-rise 35.11, 35.13
Lowry 4.41
lox 28.40
loyal 23.25
loyalist 31.8
loyalty 4.55
lozenge 20.19
Lualaba 12.21
Luanda 12.25
Luang Prabang 26.1
luau 8.2
lubber 12.22
lubberly 4.27
Lubbock 21.30
lube 14.12
Lübeck 21.6
Lublin 25.16
lubricant 30.56
lubricate 30.10
lubricious 28.33
Lubumbashi 4.50
Lubyanka 12.37
Lucan 25.43
Lucas 28.26
luce 28.19
lucency 4.47
lucent 30.56
Lucerne 25.53
Lucia 12.3, 12.11
Lucian 25.37
lucid 16.11
lucidity 4.53
Lucifer 12.30
Lucille 23.7
Lucinda 12.27
Lucius 28.23
luck 21.29
Lucknow 8.9
lucky 4.20
lucre 12.41
Lucrece 28.6

Lucretia 12.72
Lucretius 28.33
Lucy 4.47
Luda 12.29
Luddite 30.26
Ludendorff 17.9
ludic 21.10
ludicrous 28.31
ludo 9.11
Ludovic 21.18
Ludwig 18.6
luff 17.15
Luftwaffe 12.30
lug 18.12
Lugano 9.19
luge 20.15
Luger 12.32
luggage 20.6
lugger 12.32
lughole 23.17
lugsail 23.6
lugubrious 28.23
lugworm 24.22
Lukács 15.1
Luke 21.27
lukewarm 24.9
lull 23.22
lullaby 6.5
Lully 4.26
lulu 11.13
lum 24.14
lumbago 9.13
lumbar 12.22
lumber 12.22
lumberer 12.67
lumberjack 21.3
lumbermen 25.45
lumen 25.17
luminaire 2.1
luminary 4.43
luminescence 28.45
luminescent 30.56
luminosity 4.53
luminous 28.29
lumme 4.30
lummox 28.41
lump 27.17
lumpen 25.46
lumpenproletariat 30.41
lumper 12.63
lumpfish 29.7
lumpish 29.9
lumpy 4.37
Luna 12.56
lunacy 4.48
lunar 12.56
lunate 30.13
lunatic 21.17
lunation 25.49
lunch 29.20

luncheon 25.49
luncheonette 30.4
luncher 12.73
lunchtime 24.7
Lund 16.43, 16.44
Lundy 4.13
lunette 30.4
lung 26.18
lunge 20.19
lungfish 29.7
lungi 4.15
lungworm 24.22
lungwort 30.45
lunisolar 12.44
lunker 12.41
Luo 9.7
Lupercalia 12.6
lupin 25.18
lupine 25.18, 25.23
lupus 28.30
lurch 15.14
lurcher 12.24
lure 12.20
Lurex 28.38
lurgy 4.15
lurid 16.11
lurk 21.31
lurker 12.41
Lusaka 12.37
luscious 28.33
lush 29.16
Lusitania 12.8
lust 31.24
luster 12.81
lustral 23.36
lustrate 30.7
lustre 12.81
lustrous 28.31
lustrum 24.19
lusty 4.55
lute 30.37
lutein 25.13
lutetium 24.16
Luther 12.83
Lutheran 25.47
Luton 25.50
Lutyens 35.31
Lutz 28.47
luvvy 4.58
lux 28.41
luxe 28.41
Luxembourg 18.13
Luxembourger 12.32
Luxor 7.16
luxuriance 28.45
luxuriant 30.56
luxuriate 30.8
luxurious 28.23
luxury 4.43
Luzon 25.24

lwei 3.1
Lyall 23.25
lycanthrope 27.10
lycanthropy 4.37
lycée 3.20
lyceum 24.15
lychee 4.1
lychgate 30.9
lychnis 28.9
Lycia 12.11
Lycian 25.37
lycopene 25.11
Lycra 12.65
Lycurgus 28.25
lyddite 30.26
Lydgate 30.9
Lydia 12.5
Lydian 25.37
lye 6.1
lying 26.3
Lyle 23.11
Lyly 4.24
lymph 17.19
lymphangitis 28.12
lymphatic 21.17
lymphoma 12.52
lynch 29.20
lyncher 12.72
lynching 26.12
Lynette 30.4
Lynn 25.13
Lynsey 4.61
lynx 28.41
Lyon 25.38
lyonnaise 35.5
Lyons 25.24, 35.31
Lyra 12.65
lyre 12.13
lyrebird 16.31
lyric 21.15
lyrical 23.32
lyricist 31.13
lyrist 31.12
Lysander 12.25
Lysenko 9.16
Lysippus 28.30
Lysol 23.13
Lytton 25.50

M

Málaga 12.32
mésalliance 28.45
ma'am 24.2
ma 1.1
Maas 28.2
Maastricht 30.50
Maat 30.3
Mabel 23.26

Mabinogion 25.24
macédoine 25.4
mac 21.1
macabre 12.64
macadam 24.17
macadamia 12.7
Macanese 35.6
Macao 8.1
macaque 21.5
macaroni 4.33
macaronic 21.13
macaroon 25.33
MacArthur 12.83
macassar 12.69
Macau 8.1
Macaulay 4.25
macaw 7.1
Macbeth 32.3
Maccabean 25.36
Maccabees 35.6
MacDiarmid 16.10
Macdonald 16.38
mace 28.5
Macedon 25.40
Macedonia 12.8
Macedonian 25.37
macer 12.69
macerate 30.15
mach 21.1
machete 4.51
Machiavelli 4.22
Machiavellian 25.37
machinate 30.13
machine 25.9
machinery 4.43
machinist 31.10
machismo 9.18
Machmeter 12.77
macho 9.10
Machu Picchu 11.5
Mackay 6.1
Mackenzie 4.61
mackerel 23.36
mackinaw 7.13
mackintosh 29.11
mackle 23.32
Maclean 25.9
Macleod 16.22
Macmillan 25.44
MacNeice 28.6
Macquarie 4.41
macramé 4.29
macro 9.21
macrobiotic 21.17
macrocosm 24.21
macrocosmic 21.12
macron 25.26
macropod 16.18
macroscopic 21.14
mad 16.1
Madagascan 25.43

Madagascar 12.37
madam 24.17
Madame 24.17
madcap 27.1
madden 25.40
madder 12.25
made 16.6
Madeira 12.67
Madeiran 25.47
madeleine 25.16
mademoiselle 23.3
made-to-measure 12.33
Madge 20.1
madhouse 28.16
Madhya Pradesh 29.3
Madison 25.48
madly 4.21
madman 25.45
madmen 25.45
madness 28.29
Madras 28.2
madrasa 12.69
Madrid 16.8
madrigal 23.30
madrigalian 25.37
Madura 12.67
Madurese 35.6
madwomen 25.17
Mae 3.1
Maecenas 28.29
maelstrom 24.19
maenad 16.1
maenadic 21.10
maestro 9.21
Maeterlinck 21.33
Maeve 34.4
Mafeking 26.7
Mafia 12.5
mafiosi 4.61
mafioso 9.29
mag 18.1
magazine 25.9
Magdalen 25.16
Magdalena 12.54
Magdalenian 25.37
Magdeburg 18.13
mage 20.4
Magellan 25.44
magenta 12.76
Maggie 4.15
maggot 30.42
maggoty 4.55
Maghrib 14.6
magi 6.9
magian 25.37
magic 21.11
magical 23.32
magician 25.49
magisterial 23.24

magisterium 24.16
magistracy 4.48
magistrate 30.15
magistrature 12.23
maglev 34.3
magma 12.50
Magna Carta 12.75
magna cum laude 3.9
magnanimity 4.53
magnanimous 28.28
magnate 30.13
magnesia 12.72
magnesite 30.30
magnesium 24.16
magnet 30.23
magnetic 21.17
magnetite 30.30
magneto 9.24
magneton 25.26
Magnificat 30.1
magnificence 28.45
magnificent 30.56
magnifico 9.16
magnifier 12.14
magnify 6.7
magniloquence 28.45
magniloquent 30.56
magnitude 16.25
magnolia 12.6
Magnox 28.40
magnum 24.19
Magnus 28.29
magpie 6.14
Magritte 30.18
maguey 3.1
magus 28.25
Magyar 1.23
Mahabharata 12.82
Mahalia 12.6
mahant 30.55
maharaja 12.35
maharani 4.31
Maharashtra 12.64
Maharashtrian 25.37
maharishi 4.50
mahatma 12.50
Mahaweli 4.22
Mahayana 12.53
Mahdi 4.12
Mahfouz 35.21
mah-jong 26.15
Mahler 12.42
mahogany 4.34
Mahon 25.4
mahonia 12.8
mahout 30.34
mahseer 12.11
Maia 12.13

maid 16.6
maidan 25.4
maiden 25.40
maidenhair 2.6
maidenhead 16.3
maidenhood 16.26
maidenish 29.9
maidenly 4.22
maidservant 30.56
Maidstone 25.50
maigre 12.31
mail 23.5
mailbag 18.1
mailboat 30.35
mailbox 28.40
mailer 12.43
mailing 26.8
maillot 9.1
mailman 25.2
mailmen 25.5
mailshot 30.32
maim 24.4
Maimonides 35.7
main 25.7
Main 25.21
Maine 25.7
mainframe 24.4
mainland 16.45
mainlander 12.29
mainline 25.22
mainliner 12.55
mainmast 31.2
mainplane 25.8
mainsail 23.37
mainsheet 30.19
mainspring 26.11
mainstay 3.22
mainstream 24.5
maintain 25.7
maintainer 12.54
maintenance 28.45
Maintenon 25.26
maintop 27.8
Mainz 28.47
maiolica 12.39
Maisie 4.61
maisonette 30.4
Maithili 4.24
maître d'hôtel 23.3
maize 35.5
majestic 21.17
majesty 4.53
Majlis 28.7
majolica 12.39
major 12.35
Majorca 12.40
Majorcan 25.43
majordomo 9.18
majorette 30.4
majoritarian 25.37
majority 4.53

majuscular 12.46
majuscule 23.20
Makassar 12.69
make 21.7
make-believe 34.5
makeover 12.86
maker 12.38
makeshift 30.47
make-up 27.13
making 26.7
mako 9.16
Malabo 9.9
Malachi 6.10
malachite 30.27
Malachy 4.20
maladjusted 16.12
maladminister 12.78
maladroit 30.36
malady 4.13
mala fide 4.12
Málaga 12.32
Malagasy 4.45
malaise 35.5
Malamud 16.26
malamute 30.38
malapert 30.45
malaprop 27.8
malapropos 9.1
malaria 12.10
malarial 23.24
malarkey 4.18
Malawi 4.59
Malawian 25.37
Malay 3.1
Malaya 12.2
Malayalam 24.18
Malayan 25.36
Malaysia 12.12
Malaysian 25.37
Malcolm 24.18
malcontent 30.53
malcontented 16.12
mal de mer 2.1
Maldivian 25.37
male 23.5
malediction 25.49
maledictory 4.43
malefaction 25.49
malefactor 12.74
malefic 21.10
maleficence 28.45
maleficent 30.56
malevolence 28.45
malevolent 30.56
malfeasance 28.45
malfeasant 30.56
malformed 16.39
malfunction 25.49
Malherbe 14.4
Mali 4.21

Malian 25.37
Malibu 11.4
malice 28.8
malice
  aforethought
  30.33
malicious 28.33
malign 25.21
malignancy 4.48
malignant 30.56
maligner 12.55
malignity 4.53
Malin 25.16
Malines 25.9
malinger 12.31
malingerer 12.67
Malinowski 4.19
malison 25.52
mall 23.1
mallam 24.18
mallard 16.2
Mallarmé 3.1
mallee 4.21
mallet 30.22
mallow 9.17
malm 24.2
Malmö 9.18
malnourished 30.59
malodorous 28.31
Malory 4.43
Malpighi 4.15
Malplaquet 3.14
malpractice 28.12
malt 30.51
Malta 12.80
Maltese 35.6
malthouse 28.16
Malthus 28.35
Malthusian 25.37
malting 26.13
maltreat 30.18
maltreater 12.77
Malvinas 28.29
mam 24.1
mama 1.1
mamaguy 6.8
mamba 12.21
mambo 9.9
Mamet 30.23
Mamie 4.29
mamilla 4.43
mamma 1.1, 12.50
mammae 4.29
mammal 23.33
mammalian 25.37
mammary 4.43
mammee 4.29
mammogram 24.1
Mammon 25.45
Mammonist 31.10
mammoth 32.13

mammy 4.29
man 25.1
mana 12.53
manacle 23.32
manage 20.7
manager 12.35
manageress 28.3
managerial 23.24
managing 26.6
Managua 12.20
manakin 25.15
mañana 12.53
Manasseh 4.45
man-at-arms 35.30
manatee 4.1
Manaus 28.16
Manawatu 11.20
manbag 18.1
Manchester 12.78
manchineel 23.7
Manchu 11.1
Manchuria 12.10
manciple 23.35
Mancunian 25.37
Mandaean 25.36
mandala 12.48
Mandalay 3.1
mandarin 25.18
mandatary 4.43
mandate 30.7, 30.9
mandatory 4.43
Mandean 25.36
Mandela 12.42
Mandeville 23.10
mandible 23.26
mandola 12.44
mandolin 25.13
mandoline 25.13
mandolinist 31.10
mandrake 21.7
mandrel 23.9
mandrill 23.9
manducate 30.10
Mandy 4.12
mane 25.7
manège 19.4
manes 35.5
Manet 3.17
maneuver 12.87
maneuverer 12.67
maneuvering 26.11
Manfred 16.11
manful 23.21
manga 12.31
manganese 35.7
manganic 21.13
manganite 30.29
mange 20.19
mangel 23.30
mangel-wurzel
  23.41

m

manger 12.35
mangetout 11.1
mangle 23.30
mangler 12.48
mango 9.13
mangold 16.37
mangosteen 25.12
mangrove 34.11
mangy 4.17
manhandle 23.28
Manhattan 25.50
manhole 23.17
manhood 16.26
man-hour 12.16
manhunt 30.55
mania 12.8
maniac 21.1
maniacal 23.32
manic 21.13
Manichee 4.1
manicure 12.20
manicurist 31.12
manifest 31.3
manifesto 9.24
manifold 16.37
manikin 25.15
Manila 12.43
manilla 12.43
manioc 21.20
maniple 23.35
manipulate 30.11
manipulatory 4.43
Manipur 12.20
Manipuri 4.43
Manitoba 12.21
Manitoban 25.38
manitou 11.20
mankind 16.42
mankini 4.31
manky 4.18
manless 28.27
Manley 4.21
manlike 21.19
manly 4.21
man-made 16.6
Mann 25.1
manna 12.53
manned 16.40
mannequin 25.15
manner 12.53
mannerist 31.12
mannerly 4.27
Mannheim 24.7
Manning 26.9
mannish 29.9
Mano 9.19
manoeuvre 12.87
manoeuvrer 12.67
manoeuvring 26.11
manometer 12.78
manor 12.53

manorial 23.24
man-o'-war 7.1
manpower 12.16
manqué 3.14
mansard 16.2
Mansart 30.3
manse 28.44
Mansell 23.37
manservant 30.56
Mansfield 16.35
mansion 25.49
manslaughter 12.80
Manson 25.48
manta 12.74
manteau 9.24
Mantegna 12.89
mantel 23.39
mantelletta 12.76
mantellette 3.22
mantelpiece 28.6
mantelshelf 17.18
mantelshelves 35.35
mantic 21.17
manticore 7.10
mantilla 12.43
mantis 28.12
mantle 23.39
mantlet 30.22
mantling 26.8
mantra 12.64
mantrap 27.1
mantua 12.20
Manu 11.15
manual 23.25
Manuel 23.3
manufactory 4.43
manufacture 12.23
manufacturer 12.67
manuka 12.41
manumit 30.20
manure 12.20
manuscript 30.58
Manx 28.41
many 4.31
manyfold 16.37
Manzoni 4.33
Maoism 24.21
Maoist 31.6
Maori 4.41
Mao Zedong 26.15
map 27.1
maple 23.35
mapless 28.27
Mappa Mundi 4.13
mapper 12.61
Maputo 9.25
maquette 30.4
maquillage 19.1
maquis 4.1
mar 1.1
marabou 11.4

marabout 11.4, 30.37
maraca 12.37
Maracaibo 9.9
Maradona 12.56
Maramba 12.21
maraschino 9.19
Marat 1.16
Maratha 12.75
Marathi 4.51
marathon 25.51
marathoner 12.58
maraud 16.19
marauder 12.28
Marbella 12.2
marble 23.26
marbling 26.8
marbly 4.27
marc 21.5
Marcan 25.43
marcasite 30.30
Marceau 9.1
marcel 23.3
march 15.2
marcher 12.23
Marches 35.10
Marcia 12.11
Marciano 9.19
Marconi 4.33
Marcos 28.14
Marcus 28.26
Marcuse 12.92
Mardi Gras 1.1
Marduk 21.30
mardy 4.12
mare 2.1, 3.19
maremma 12.50
Marengo 9.13
Margaret 30.24
margarine 25.9
margarita 12.77
Margate 30.9
margate 30.21
marge 20.2
margin 25.14
marginal 23.34
marginalia 12.6
Margot 9.13
marguerite 30.18
Mari 4.38
Maria 12.4
Marian 25.37
Marianas 35.24
Marianne 25.1
Marie 4.1
Marie-Antoinette 30.4
marigold 16.37
marijuana 12.53
Marilyn 25.16
marimba 12.21
marina 12.54

marinade 16.6
marinara 12.64
marinate 30.13
marine 25.9
mariner 12.55
Marinetti 4.51
Mario 9.4
marionette 30.4
Marisa 12.70
Marist 31.12
marital 23.39
maritime 24.7
Maritimes 35.30
Maritsa 12.70
Marius 28.23
marjoram 24.19
Marjorie 4.43
mark 21.5
markdown 25.29
marked 30.48
marker 12.37
market 30.21
marketeer 12.4
marketer 12.78
marketing 26.13
marketplace 28.5
marking 26.7
markka 1.11
Markova 12.86
Marks 28.38
marksman 25.45
marksmen 25.45
markup 27.13
marl 23.2
Marlborough 12.67
Marlene 12.54, 25.10
Marley 4.21
marlin 25.16
marline 25.16
marlinspike 21.19
Marlon 25.44
Marlowe 9.17
marly 4.21
Marmaduke 21.27
marmalade 16.6
marmite 30.29
marmoreal 23.24
marmoset 30.5
marmot 30.43
Marne 25.4
marocain 25.7
Maronite 30.29
maroon 25.33
marque 21.5
marquee 4.1
Marquesas 35.24
marquess 28.12
marquetry 4.40
Marquette 30.4
marquis 28.12
marquisate 30.43

marquise 35.6
marquisette 30.4
Marrakesh 29.3
Marrano 9.19
marriage 20.8
married 16.11
marrow 9.21
marrowbone 25.30
marry 4.38
Marryat 30.41
Mars 35.2
Marsala 12.42
Marseillaise 35.5
Marseilles 3.1
marsh 29.2
Marsha 12.72
marshal 23.38
marshland 16.40
marshmallow 9.17
marshy 4.50
marsupial 23.24
mart 30.3
martello 9.17
marten 25.19
Martens 35.31
Martha 12.83
martial 23.38
Martian 25.49
martin 25.19
Martina 12.54
Martineau 9.19
martinet 30.4
martingale 23.5
martini 4.31
Martinique 21.8
Martinmas 28.1
martlet 30.22
martyr 12.75
martyrdom 24.17
martyrize 35.13
martyry 4.43
marvel 23.40
marveler 12.48
Marvell 23.40
marveller 12.48
marvellous 28.27
marvelous 28.27
Marvin 25.19
Marx 28.38
Marxist 31.13
Mary 4.39
Maryland 16.45
Mary Magdalene 25.16
marzipan 25.3
Masada 12.25
Masai 6.16
masala 12.42
Masaryk 21.15
Mascagni 4.60
mascara 12.64

Mascarene 25.9
mascarpone 4.33
mascle 23.32
mascot 30.31
masculine 25.16
masculinity 4.53
masculinize 35.13
Masefield 16.35
Maseru 11.17
mash 29.1
masher 12.72
mashie 4.50
Mashona 12.56
Mashonaland 16.40
mask 21.35
masker 12.37
masochist 31.7
mason 25.48
Masonic 21.13
masonry 4.39
masque 21.35
masquerade 16.6
masquerader 12.26
mass 28.1
Massachusetts 28.47
massacre 12.41
massage 20.2
massager 12.36
Massawa 12.88
massé 4.45
masseur 13.1
massif 17.5
Massine 25.9
Massinger 12.35
massive 34.7
Masson 25.48
massy 4.45
mast 31.2
mastaba 12.22
mastectomy 4.30
master 12.75
masterclass 28.2
masterly 4.27
mastermind 16.42
masterpiece 28.6
Masters 35.24
masterstroke 21.24
masterwork 21.31
mastery 4.43
masthead 16.3
mastic 21.17
masticate 30.10
masticatory 4.43
mastiff 17.6
mastodon 25.25
mastoid 16.24
masturbate 30.9
masturbatory 4.39
mat 30.1
Matabele 4.23

Matabeleland 16.40
matador 7.5
Mata Hari 4.38
matamata 12.74
match 15.1
matchbox 28.40
matchlock 21.21
matchmaker 12.38
matchmaking 26.7
matchplay 3.15
matchstick 21.17
matchwood 16.26
mate 30.7
maté 3.22
matelot 9.17
matelote 30.35
mater 12.77
materfamilias 28.1
material 23.24
materialist 31.8
matériel 23.3
maternal 23.34
maternity 4.53
matey 4.52
math 32.1
mathematical 23.32
mathematician 25.49
mathematics 28.39
Mathias 28.24
maths 28.48
Matilda 12.27
matinée 3.17
matins 35.31
Matisse 28.6
Mato Grosso 9.22
matriarch 21.5
matriarchal 23.32
matriarchy 4.18
matrices 35.8
matricidal 23.28
matricide 16.16
matriculate 30.11
matrilineal 23.24
matrimonial 23.24
matrimony 4.34
matrix 28.39
matron 25.47
matronly 4.27
matsuri 4.41
Matsuyama 12.50
matt 30.1
matte 30.1
matted 16.12
matter 12.74
Matterhorn 25.28
matter-of-fact 30.48
Matthew 11.22
Matthews 35.21
matting 26.13
mattock 21.30

mattress 28.10
mature 12.20
maturity 4.53
matzo 12.70
maudlin 25.16
Maugham 24.9
maul 23.14
mauler 12.44
Mau Mau 8.8
maunder 12.28
maundering 26.11
Maundy 4.13
Maupassant 25.26
Maura 12.66
Maureen 25.11
Mauriac 21.1
Maurice 28.10
Mauritania 12.8
Mauritanian 25.37
Mauritian 25.49
Mauritius 28.33
Maury 4.41
Maurya 12.10
Mauser 12.92
mausoleum 24.15
mauve 34.11
maven 25.51
maverick 21.15
mavis 28.12
maw 7.1
mawkish 29.8
max 28.38
maxi 4.45
maxillary 4.43
maxim 24.6
maxima 12.51
maximal 23.33
maximalist 31.8
Maximilian 25.37
maximizer 12.91
maximum 24.19
Maxine 25.9
maxixe 28.38
Maxwell 23.4
may 3.1
Maya 12.2, 12.13
Mayan 25.38
maybe 4.10
mayday 3.9
Mayer 12.2, 12.13
Mayfair 2.5
mayflower 12.16
mayfly 6.11
mayhap 27.1
mayhem 24.3
Maynard 16.2
Maynooth 32.12
mayn't 30.56
Mayo 9.2
mayonnaise 35.5
mayor 2.1

m

m

mayoral 23.36
mayoralty 4.55
mayoress 28.31
Mayotte 30.31
maypole 23.18
Mays 35.5
Mazar-e-Sharif 17.5
Mazarin 25.18
maze 35.5
mazer 12.90
mazurka 12.41
mazy 4.61
mazzard 16.30
Mazzini 4.31
Mbabane 4.31
McAleese 28.6
McCarthy 4.56
McCarthyite 30.26
McCartney 4.31
McEnroe 9.21
McEwan 25.38
McGonagall 23.30
McIntosh 29.11
McKinlay 4.24
McLuhan 25.38
me 4.1
mea culpa 12.63
mead 16.7
meadow 9.11
meadowlark 21.5
meadowsweet 30.19
meadowy 4.7
meager 12.31
meagre 12.31
meal 23.7
mealie 4.23
mealtime 24.7
mealworm 24.22
mealy 4.23
mealy-mouthed
16.48
mean 25.9
meander 12.25
meandering 26.11
meanie 4.31
meaning 26.9
means 35.31
meant 30.53
meantime 24.7
meanwhile 23.12
measles 35.29
measly 4.23
measure 12.33
meat 30.18
meatball 23.14
Meath 33.3
meathead 16.3
meaty 4.52
mecca 12.37
meccano 9.19
mechanic 21.13

mechanical 23.32
mechanician 25.49
mechanist 31.10
mechanizer 12.91
mechatronics 28.39
Mechlin 25.16
Mecklenburg
18.13
Med 16.3
medal 23.28
medalist 31.8
medallic 21.11
medallion 25.37
medallist 31.8
Medawar 12.88
meddle 23.28
meddler 12.48
Mede 16.7
Medea 12.4
Medellín 25.9
Medevac 21.4
media 12.5
medial 23.24
median 25.37
mediant 30.56
mediate 30.8
mediatory 4.43
medic 21.10
Medicaid 16.6
medical 23.32
Medicare 2.7
medicate 30.10
Medicean 25.36
Medici 4.11
medicinal 23.34
medicine 25.19
medick 21.10
medieval 23.40
medievalist 31.8
medievalize 35.12
Medina 12.54, 12.55
mediocre 12.40
mediocrity 4.53
meditate 30.16
Mediterranean
25.37
medium 24.16
medlar 12.42
medley 4.22
Médoc 21.20
medulla 12.47
medusa 12.92
medusae 4.62
meed 16.7
meek 21.8
meerkat 30.1
meerschaum 24.20
Meerut 30.43
meet 30.18
meet-and-
greet 30.18

meeting 26.13
meeting house
28.16
meetup 27.13
Meg 18.3
mega 12.31
megabuck 21.29
megabyte 30.26
megacity 4.53
megadeath 32.3
Megaera 12.67
megaflop 27.8
megahertz 28.47
megalith 32.6
megalithic 21.18
megalomania 12.8
megalomaniac 21.1
megalomaniacal
23.32
megalopolis 28.8
megalopolitan 25.50
megalosaurus 28.31
Megan 25.41
megaphone 25.30
megastar 1.19
megastore 7.18
megaton 25.35
megavolt 30.51
megawatt 30.32
Megger 12.31
megohm 24.11
megrim 24.6
meiosis 28.11
meiotic 21.17
Meir 12.4
Meissen 25.48
Mekong 26.15
melamine 25.22
melancholia 12.6
melancholic 21.11
melancholy 4.27
Melanchthon 25.51
Melanesia 12.89
Melanesian 25.52
mélange 19.7
Melanie 4.34
melanin 25.18
melanoma 12.52
Melbourne 25.38
Melchior 7.3
meld 16.35
Meleager 12.31
melee 3.15
melic 21.11
melick 21.11
Melilla 12.4
melilot 30.31
Melinda 12.27
meliorate 30.15
meliorist 31.12
Melissa 12.70

melliferous 28.31
mellifluence 28.45
mellifluent 30.56
mellifluous 28.24
Mellon 25.44
mellotron 25.26
mellow 9.17
melodeon 25.37
melodic 21.10
melodica 12.39
melodious 28.23
melodize 35.11
melodrama 12.50
melodramatic 21.17
melodramatist
31.14
melodramatize
35.14
melody 4.13
melon 25.44
Melos 28.14
Melpomene 4.32
melt 30.51
meltdown 25.29
melter 12.76
melton 25.50
Melville 23.10
Melvin 25.19
member 12.21
membrane 25.8
membranous 28.29
meme 24.5
memento 9.24
memento mori 6.15
Memnon 25.26
memo 9.18
memoir 1.22
memoirist 31.12
memorabilia 12.6
memoranda 12.25
memorandum 24.17
memorial 23.24
memorialist 31.8
memorialize 35.12
memorizer 12.91
memory 4.43
Memphis 28.7
memsahib 14.7
men 25.5
menace 28.9
menacer 12.70
ménage 19.1
ménage à trois 1.1
menagerie 4.43
Menander 12.25
menarche 4.18
Mencken 25.43
mend 16.41
mendacious 28.33
mendacity 4.53
Mendel 23.28

Mendeleev 34.3
Mendelian 25.37
Mendelssohn 25.48
mender 12.26
mendicancy 4.48
mendicant 30.56
Mendoza 12.92
Menelaus 28.22
Menes 35.7
menfolk 21.24
menhir 12.5
menial 23.24
meningitis 28.12
meniscus 28.26
Mennonite 30.29
menopausal 23.41
menopause 35.17
menorah 12.66
Mensa 12.69
menses 35.8
Menshevik 21.18
menstrual 23.25
menstruate 30.8
menswear 2.15
mental 23.39
mentalist 31.8
menthol 23.13
mentholated 16.12
mention 25.49
mentor 7.18
menu 11.22
Menuhin 25.13
Menzies 35.10
mephedrone 25.30
Mephistophelian 25.37
mephitic 21.17
mercantile 23.12
Mercedes 35.7
mercenary 4.43
mercer 12.71
mercerize 35.13
mercury 4.43
merchandise 28.13, 35.11
merchandiser 12.91
merchant 30.56
Mercia 12.11
Mercian 25.37
Merckx 28.41
mercurial 23.24
mercury 4.41
mercy 4.49
mere 12.4
Meredith 32.6
meretricious 28.33
merge 20.17
merger 12.36
Mérida 12.27
meridian 25.37
meridional 23.34

Meriel 23.24
meringue 26.1
merino 9.19
merit 30.24
meritocracy 4.48
meritocratic 21.17
meritorious 28.23
merkin 25.15
merle 23.42
merlin 25.16
merlon 25.44
Merlot 30.42
mermaid 16.6
merman 25.2
mermen 25.5
Merovingian 25.37
Merrill 23.9
merry 4.38
merry-go-round 16.43
merrymaker 12.38
merrymaking 26.7
Mersey 4.62
Merseyside 16.16
Merthyr Tydfil 23.10
Mervyn 25.19
mesa 12.69
mésalliance 28.45
mescal 23.1
mescaline 25.16
mesdames 24.1
mesdemoiselles 23.3
mesh 29.3
mesic 21.18
Mesmer 12.50
mesmeric 21.15
mesmerist 31.12
mesmerizer 12.91
mesne 25.9
mesocephalic 21.11
Mesolithic 21.18
Mesopotamia 12.7
Mesopotamian 25.37
Mesozoic 21.9
mesquite 30.18
mess 28.3
message 20.9
Messalina 12.54
messenger 12.35
Messiaen 25.27
messiah 12.13
messianic 21.13
messieurs 35.25
Messina 12.54
messmate 30.12
Messrs 35.24
messy 4.45
met 30.4

metabolic 21.11
metacarpus 28.30
metal 23.39
metalize 35.12
metallic 21.11
metallize 35.12
metallurgical 23.32
metallurgist 31.7
metallurgy 4.17
metalwork 21.31
metalworker 12.41
metalworking 26.7
metamorphic 21.10
metamorphose 35.19
metamorphosis 28.11
metaphor 12.30
metaphoric 21.15
metaphorical 23.32
metaphysic 21.18
metaphysical 23.32
metaphysician 25.49
metastasize 35.14
metatarsal 23.37
metathesis 28.11
metathetical 23.32
metaverse 28.36
mete 30.18
metempsychosis 28.11
meteor 12.12
meteoric 21.15
meteorite 30.29
meteoroid 16.24
meteorology 4.17
meter 12.77
meterage 20.8
methadone 25.30
methane 25.8
methanol 23.13
Methedrine 25.11
methinks 28.41
method 16.29
methodic 21.10
methodical 23.32
Methodist 31.6
methodize 35.11
methodizer 12.91
methodology 4.17
methought 30.33
meths 28.48
methuselah 12.48
metic 21.17
metical 23.32
meticulous 28.27
métier 3.3
metol 23.13
metonym 24.6
metonymy 4.30

metre 12.77
metreage 20.8
metric 21.15
metrical 23.32
metricate 30.10
metro 9.21
metronome 24.11
metronomic 21.12
metronymic 21.12
Metropole 23.18
metropolis 28.8
metropolitan 25.50
Metternich 21.13
mettle 23.39
Metz 28.47
meunière 2.1
Meurig 18.6
Meuse 35.25
mew 11.1
mewl 23.20
mews 35.21
Mexicali 4.21
Mexican 25.43
Mexico 9.16
Meyerhof 17.8
mezuzah 12.92
mezuzoth 30.35
mezzanine 25.11
mezza voce 3.8
mezzo 9.22
Mezzogiorno 9.19
mezzotint 30.54
mho 9.1
Mia 12.4
Miami 4.29
miaow 8.1
miasma 12.50
miasmal 23.33
miasmatic 21.17
miasmic 21.12
miaul 23.14
mic 21.19
mica 12.40
Micawber 12.21
Micawberish 29.9
mice 28.13
Michael 23.32
Michaelmas 28.28
Michel 23.3
Michelangelo 9.17
Michelin 25.16
Michelle 23.3
Michelson 25.48
Michigan 25.41
Michoacéan 25.4
mick 21.9
mickey 4.19
mickle 23.32
micro 9.21
microbe 14.11
microbial 23.24

m

microblogging 26.6
microchip 27.6
microcline 25.22
microcosm 24.21
microcosmic 21.12
microdot 30.31
microenterprise 35.13
microfiche 29.5
microfilm 24.18
microfinance 28.44
microform 24.9
microgram 24.1
micrograph 17.2
microgreens 35.31
microlending 26.5
microlight 30.28
micromesh 29.3
micrometer 12.77, 12.78
micrometre 12.77
micrometry 4.40
micron 25.26
Micronesia 12.89
Micronesian 25.52
microphone 25.30
microprocessor 12.69
microscope 27.10
microscopic 21.14
microscopy 4.37
microsecond 16.45
microsite 30.30
microsurgery 4.43
microtone 25.31
microwave 34.4
mid 16.8
mid-air 2.1
Midas 28.25
midday 3.1
midden 25.40
middle 23.28
middlebrow 8.10
middleman 25.2
middlemen 25.5
middle-of-the-road 16.23
Middlesbrough 12.65
Middlesex 28.38
Middleton 25.50
middleweight 30.17
middling 26.8
middy 4.12
Mideast 31.5
midfield 16.35
midfielder 12.26
Midgard 16.2
midge 20.6
midget 30.21
midgut 30.40

Midi 4.1
midi 4.12
midiron 25.38
midland 16.45
midlander 12.29
midlife 17.7
Midlothian 25.37
midmost 31.20
midnight 30.29
midpoint 30.55
Midrash 29.1
Midrashim 24.6
midriff 17.6
midship 27.6
midshipman 25.45
midshipmen 25.45
midships 28.46
midst 31.27
midstream 24.5
midsummer 12.52
midterm 24.22
midtown 25.29
Midway 3.25
midway 3.1
midweek 21.8
Midwest 31.3
Midwestern 25.50
midwicket 30.21
midwife 17.7
midwifery 4.43
midwinter 12.78
midwives 35.35
mien 25.9
miff 17.6
MI5 34.9
might 30.26
mightn't 30.56
mighty 4.54
migraine 25.8
migrant 30.56
migrate 30.7
migratory 4.43
Miguel 23.3
mihrab 14.2
Mikado 9.11
mike 21.19
Mikhail 23.11
mil 23.8
milady 4.12
Milan 25.1
Milanese 35.6
milch 29.19
mild 16.36
mildew 11.22
mildewy 4.8
mildish 29.6
Mildred 16.11
mile 23.11
mileage 20.6
milepost 31.20
miler 12.44

Miles 35.29
Milesian 25.37
milestone 25.31
Miletus 28.34
milfoil 23.19
Milhaud 9.3
milieu 13.5
militancy 4.48
militant 30.56
militarist 31.12
military 4.43
militate 30.16
militia 12.72
militiaman 25.45
militiamen 25.45
milk 21.32
milker 12.39
milkmaid 16.6
milkman 25.45
milkmen 25.5
milkshake 21.7
milksop 27.8
milkwort 30.45
milky 4.19
mill 23.8
Millais 3.15
millefeuille 5.2
millenarian 25.37
millenary 4.43
millennial 23.24
millennialist 31.8
millennium 24.16
millepore 7.14
miller 12.43
millet 30.22
millhand 16.40
milliampere 2.10
millibar 1.4
Millicent 30.56
Milligan 25.41
milligram 24.1
Millikan 25.43
milliliter 12.77
millilitre 12.77
millimeter 12.77
millimetre 12.77
milliner 12.55
millinery 4.43
million 25.52
millionaire 2.1
millionfold 16.37
millionth 32.19
millipede 16.7
millisecond 16.45
millpond 16.42
millrace 28.5
Mills 35.29
millstone 25.31
millstream 24.5
millwheel 23.7
millwright 30.29

Milne 25.44
milo 9.17
milometer 12.78
milord 16.19
Milton 25.50
Miltonian 25.37
Miltonic 21.13
Milwaukee 4.19
Mimas 28.28
mime 24.7
mimer 12.51
mimesis 28.11
mimetic 21.17
Mimi 4.29
mimic 21.12
mimicker 12.39
mimicry 4.40
mimosa 12.92
mimulus 28.27
Min 25.13
minaret 30.4
minareted 16.12
mince 28.44
mincemeat 30.18
mincer 12.70
Minch 29.20
mind 16.42
Mindanao 8.1
minder 12.27
mind-numbing 26.9
Mindoro 9.21
mind-reader 12.26
mindset 30.5
mine 25.21
minefield 16.35
minelayer 12.2
minelaying 26.3
miner 12.55
mineral 23.36
mineralize 35.12
mineralogist 31.7
mineralogy 4.17
Minerva 12.87
minestrone 4.33
minesweeper 12.61
minesweeping 26.10
Ming 26.3
mingle 23.30
Mingus 28.25
mingy 4.17
mini 4.32
miniature 12.23
miniaturist 31.12
minibar 1.4
minibus 28.21
minicab 14.1
minicam 24.1
minidress 28.3
minikin 25.15
minim 24.6

minima 12.51
minimal 23.33
minimalist 31.8
minimax 28.38
minimizer 12.91
minimum 24.19
minion 25.52
mini-pill 23.9
miniseries 35.10
miniskirt 30.45
minister 12.78
ministerial 23.24
ministrant 30.56
ministry 4.40
minivan 25.3
miniver 12.86
mink 21.33
minke 4.19
Minkowski 4.19
Minneapolis 28.8
Minnesinger 12.31
Minnesota 12.80
Minnesotan 25.50
Minnie 4.32
minnow 9.19
Minoan 25.38
minor 12.55
Minorca 12.40
Minorcan 25.43
Minorite 30.29
minority 4.53
Minos 28.14
Minotaur 7.18
Minsk 21.35
minster 12.78
minstrel 23.36
minstrelsy 4.48
mint 30.54
mintage 20.9
Minter 12.78
Minton 25.50
minty 4.53
minuet 30.4
minus 28.29
minuscular 12.46
minuscule 23.20
minute 30.23, 30.37
minutiae 6.3
minx 28.41
minxish 29.9
Miocene 25.11
Mir 12.4
Mirabeau 9.9
mirabelle 23.3
miracle 23.32
miraculous 28.27
mirador 7.1
mirage 19.1
Miranda 12.25
mire 12.13
mirepoix 1.1

Miriam 24.16
mirid 16.11
mirk 21.31
mirky 4.20
Miró 9.1
mirror 12.65
mirth 32.14
miry 4.43
misadventure 12.23
misalliance 28.45
misanthrope 27.10
misanthropic 21.14
misanthropical 23.32
misanthropist 31.11
misanthropy 4.37
misapply 6.1
misapprehend 16.41
misapprehension 25.49
misappropriate 30.8
misbegotten 25.50
misbehave 34.4
misbehavior 12.89
misbehaviour 12.89
misbelief 17.5
miscalculate 30.11
miscall 23.14
miscarriage 20.8
miscarry 4.38
miscast 31.2
miscellanea 12.8
miscellaneous 28.23
miscellany 4.34
mischance 28.44
mischief 17.6
mischievous 28.35
miscible 23.26
misconceive 34.5
misconception 25.49
misconduct 30.49
misconstruction 25.49
misconstrue 11.1
miscount 30.55
miscreant 30.56
miscue 11.1, 11.22
misdate 30.7
misdeal 23.7
misdealt 30.51
misdeed 16.7
misdemeanor 12.54
misdemeanour 12.54
misdescription 25.49
misdiagnose 35.19
misdiagnoses 35.8
misdiagnosis 28.11
misdirect 30.48

misdirection 25.49
misdoing 26.3
misdoubt 30.34
mise en scène 25.7
miser 12.91
misère 2.1
miserere 4.39
misericord 16.21
miserly 4.27
misery 4.43
misfield 16.35
misfire 12.13, 12.14
misfit 30.21
misfortune 25.33
misgave 34.4
misgive 34.6
misgiven 25.51
misgiving 26.14
misgovern 25.51
misguidance 28.45
misguide 16.14
misguided 16.9
mishandle 23.28
mishap 27.1
mishear 12.4
misheard 16.31
mishit 30.20
mishmash 29.1
Mishnah 12.55
Mishnaic 21.9
misidentify 6.7
misinform 24.9
misinterpret 30.24
misinterpreter 12.78
MI6 28.39
misjudge 20.16
miskick 21.9
Miskito 9.24
mislay 3.1
mislead 16.7
misleader 12.26
misleading 26.5
misled 16.3
mislike 21.19
mismanage 20.7
mismatch 15.1
mismated 16.12
misname 24.4
misnomer 12.52
misogamist 31.9
misogamy 4.30
misogynist 31.10
misogynous 28.29
misogyny 4.32
misplace 28.5
misplay 3.1, 3.15
misprint 30.54
misprision 25.42
misprize 35.11
mispronounce 28.44

misquote 30.35
misread 16.3, 16.7
misreport 30.33
misrepresent 30.53
misrule 23.20
miss 28.7
missal 23.37
misshape 27.4
misshapen 25.46
missile 23.11
mission 25.49
missionary 4.43
missioner 12.58
Mississippi 4.36
Mississippian 25.37
missive 34.7
Missolonghi 4.35
Missouri 4.43
Missourian 25.37
misspell 23.3
misspelling 26.8
misspend 16.41
misspent 30.53
misstate 30.7
misstep 27.3
missus 35.10
missy 4.46
mist 31.6
mistake 21.7
mistaken 25.43
mister 12.78
mistime 24.7
mistitle 23.39
mistletoe 9.24
mistook 21.28
mistranslate 30.7
mistreat 30.18
mistress 28.10
mistrial 23.25
mistrust 31.24
misty 4.53
mistype 27.7
misunderstand 16.40
misunderstanding 26.5
misunderstood 16.26
misusage 20.9
misuse 28.19, 35.21
misuser 12.92
Mitch 15.6
Mitchell 23.23
Mitchum 24.17
mite 30.26
miter 12.79
Mitford 16.28
Mithraic 21.9
Mithraist 31.6
Mithras 28.1
mitigate 30.9

m

mitigatory 4.43
Mitla 12.43
mitochondria 12.10
mitre 12.79
mitt 30.20
mitten 25.50
Mitterrand 25.26
Mitzi 4.46
mitzvah 12.86
mitzvoth 30.35
mix 28.39
mixable 23.26
mixed-race 28.5
mixer 12.70
Mixtec 21.6
mixture 12.23
Mizoram 24.19
mizuna 12.56
mizzen 25.52
mizzenmast 31.2
mizzle 23.41
mnemonic 21.13
mo 9.1
moa 12.17
Moab 14.1
Moabite 30.26
moan 25.30
moaner 12.56
moat 30.35
mob 14.9
mobber 12.21
mobile 23.11
mobility 4.53
mobilizer 12.91
mobocracy 4.48
mobster 12.79
Mobutu 11.20
moccasin 25.19
mocha 12.40
mock 21.20
mocker 12.40
mockery 4.43
mockingbird 16.31
mocktail 23.5
mod 16.18
modal 23.28
modality 4.53
mod cons 35.31
mode 16.23
model 23.28
modeler 12.48
modeller 12.48
modem 24.3
Modena 12.55
moderate 30.15,
   30.43
moderato 9.24
modern 25.40
modernist 31.10
modernity 4.53
modernizer 12.91

modest 31.6
modesty 4.53
modicum 24.18
modificatory 4.43
modifier 12.14
modify 6.7
Modigliani 4.31
modillion 25.52
modish 29.6
modiste 31.5
Mods 35.27
modular 12.46
modulate 30.11
module 23.20
modulo 9.17
modus operandi
   4.12
modus vivendi 4.12
Mogadishu 11.19
Mogadon 25.25
moggie 4.15
mogul 23.30
mohair 2.6
Mohammedan
   25.40
mohawk 21.22
Mohican 25.43
Moho 9.14
Mohs 9.1
moiety 4.53
moil 23.19
Moira 12.66
moire 1.1
moist 31.21
moisten 25.48
moisture 12.24
Mojave 4.58
mojo 9.15
moke 21.24
moko 9.16
moksha 12.73
mol 23.17
molar 12.44
molasses 35.10
mold 16.37
Moldau 8.3
Moldavia 12.12
Moldavian 25.37
moldboard 16.20
molder 12.28
molding 26.5
Moldova 12.86
moldy 4.13
mole 23.17
molecular 12.46
molecule 23.20
molehill 23.9
moleskin 25.15
molest 31.3
molester 12.76
Molière 2.2

moline 25.21
Moline 25.9
moll 23.13
Mollie 4.25
mollifier 12.14
mollify 6.7
mollusc 21.35
molluscan 25.43
mollusk 21.35
molluskan 25.43
molly 4.25
mollycoddle 23.28
Molotov 17.8
molt 30.51
molten 25.50
molto 9.25
Moluccas 35.24
moly 4.25
molybdenum 24.19
mom 24.8
Mombasa 12.69
moment 30.56
momentary 4.43
momentous 28.34
momentum 24.20
momma 12.51
Mommsen 25.48
mommy 4.29
momo 9.18
Mon 25.30
Mona 12.56
Monaco 9.16
monad 16.1
Monaghan 25.42
monarch 21.30
monarchal 23.32
monarchial 23.24
monarchic 21.11
monarchical 23.32
monarchist 31.7
monarchy 4.20
monastery 4.43
monastic 21.17
Monck 21.34
mondaine 25.7
Monday 3.9
mondial 23.24
Monégasque 21.35
Monel 23.34
Monet 3.17
monetarist 31.12
monetary 4.43
money 4.33
moneybags 35.28
moneychanger
   12.35
moneymaker 12.38
moneymaking 26.7
Mongol 23.30
Mongolia 12.6
Mongolian 25.37

mongoloid 16.24
mongoose 28.19
mongrel 23.36
mongrelize 35.12
monial 23.24
Monica 12.39
moniker 12.39
monism 24.21
monist 31.10
monistic 21.17
monition 25.49
monitor 12.78
monitorial 23.24
monitory 4.43
monk 21.34
monkey 4.20
monkeyish 29.6
monkfish 29.7
Mon-Khmer 2.1
monkish 29.8
Monks 28.41
Monmouth 32.13
Monmouthshire
   12.11
Mono 9.19
monocausal 23.41
Monoceros 28.31
monochord 16.21
monochromatic
   21.17
monochrome 24.11
monochromic 21.12
monocle 23.32
monocoque 21.20
monocotyledon
   25.40
monocracy 4.48
monocratic 21.17
monocycle 23.32
monodic 21.10
monodist 31.6
monofil 23.8
monogamous 28.28
monogamy 4.30
monogenean 25.36
monoglot 30.31
monogram 24.1
monogrammatic
   21.17
monograph 17.2
monographic 21.10
monographist 31.7
monohull 23.22
monokini 4.31
monolingual 23.40
monolith 32.6
monolithic 21.18
monologic 21.11
monologue 18.8
monomania 12.8
monomaniac 21.1

m

monomer 12.52
mononucleosis 28.11
Monophysite 30.30
monoplane 25.8
monopod 16.18
Monopole 23.18
monopolist 31.8
monopolizer 12.91
monopoly 4.27
monopteros 28.14
monorail 23.6
monosyllabic 21.9
monotheist 31.6
Monothelite 30.28
monotint 30.54
monotone 25.31
monotonic 21.13
monotonous 28.29
monotony 4.34
monotreme 24.5
Monotype 27.7
monoxide 16.16
Monroe 9.1
Monrovia 12.12
Mons 35.31
Monseigneur 13.1
monsieur 13.1
Monsignor 12.89
monsignori 4.41
monsoon 25.33
monsoonal 23.34
monster 12.79
monstera 12.67
monstrance 28.45
monstrosity 4.53
monstrous 28.31
montage 19.1
Montagna 12.89
Montagnard 16.2
Montague 11.22
Montaigne 25.7
Montana 12.53
Montanan 25.46
montane 25.8
Mont Blanc 25.24
Montcalm 24.2
Monte 4.54
Monte Cassino 9.19
Montenegrin 25.18
Montenegro 9.21
Monterrey 3.1
Montesquieu 13.1
Montessori 4.41
Monteverdi 4.12
Montevideo 9.2
Montez 35.3
Montgolfier 12.5
Montgomery 4.43
month 32.19
monthly 4.26

Montmartre 12.64
Montmorency 4.45
Montpelier 12.6
Montpellier 12.6
Montreal 23.14
Montreux 13.1
Montrose 35.19
Montserrat 30.1
Montserratian 25.37
Monty 4.54
monumentalize 35.12
moo 11.1
mooch 15.11
moocher 12.24
mood 16.25
moody 4.13
moolah 12.45
mooli 4.26
moon 25.33
moonbeam 24.5
mooncalf 17.2
mooncalves 35.35
Moonie 4.33
moonlight 30.28
moonlighter 12.79
moonlit 30.22
moonquake 21.7
moonrise 35.13
moonscape 27.4
moonset 30.5
moonshine 25.23
moonshiner 12.55
moonstone 25.51
moonstruck 21.29
moony 4.33
moor 12.20
moorage 20.8
moorcock 21.20
Moore 12.20
moorfowl 23.16
moorhen 25.5
mooring 26.11
Moorish 29.9
moorland 16.45
moory 4.43
moose 28.19
moot 30.37
mop 27.8
mope 27.10
moped 16.3
moper 12.63
mophead 16.3
moppet 30.23
moppy 4.36
moquette 30.4
mor 7.1
Morag 18.1
moraine 25.7
moral 23.36

morale 23.2
moralist 31.8
morality 4.53
moralizer 12.91
Moran 25.1
morass 28.1
moratoria 12.10
moratorium 24.16
Moravia 12.12
Moravian 25.37
moray 3.19
morbid 16.8
morbidity 4.53
mordacious 28.33
mordancy 4.47
mordant 30.56
Mordecai 6.10
mordent 30.56
Mordred 16.11
more 7.1
moreen 25.9
moreish 29.9
morel 23.3
morello 9.17
moreover 12.86
mores 35.5
Moresque 21.35
Morgan 25.41
morgen 25.41
morgue 18.9
moribund 16.44
moribundity 4.53
morion 25.37
Morisco 9.16
Morley 4.25
Mormon 25.45
morn 25.28
Morna 12.56
Mornay 3.17
morning 26.9
Moro 9.21
Moroccan 25.43
Morocco 9.16
moron 25.26
Moroni 4.33
moronic 21.13
morose 28.17
Morpeth 32.13
morph 17.9
morpheme 24.5
Morpheus 28.23
morphine 25.10
morphing 26.6
Morrison 25.48
morrow 9.21
morse 28.15
morsel 23.37
mort 30.33
mortadella 12.42
mortal 23.39
mortar 12.80

mortar board 16.20
mortgage 20.6
mortgagee 4.1
mortgagor 7.1
mortician 25.49
mortify 6.7
Mortimer 12.51
mortise 28.12
Morton 25.50
mortuary 4.43
Morwenna 12.53
mosaic 21.9
moschatel 23.3
Moscow 9.16
Moseley 4.25
Moselle 23.3
Moses 35.10
mosey 4.61
mosh 29.11
moshav 34.2
Moskva 12.86
mosque 21.35
mosquito 9.24
moss 28.14
Mossad 16.1
mossie 4.61
mossy 4.46
most 31.20
Mostyn 25.19
Mosul 23.37
mot 9.1
mote 30.35
motel 23.3
motet 30.4
moth 32.8
mothball 23.14
mother 12.84
motherboard 16.20
motherfucker 12.41
motherfucking 26.7
motherhood 16.26
motherland 16.40
motherly 4.27
mothproof 17.13
mothy 4.56
motif 17.5
motion 25.49
motional 23.34
motivate 30.16
motive 34.8
mot juste 31.22
motley 4.25
motmot 30.31
moto perpetuo 9.8
motor 12.80
motorbike 21.19
motorboat 30.35
motorcade 16.6
motorcar 1.11
motorcycle 23.32
motorcycling 26.8

m

motorcyclist 31.8
motorhome 24.11
motorist 31.12
motorize 35.13
motorman 25.2
motormen 25.5
motormouth 32.10
motorway 3.25
Motown 25.29
motte 30.31
mottle 23.39
motto 9.25
Motu 11.20
moue 11.1
mouflon 25.25
mould 16.37
mouldboard 16.20
moulder 12.28
moulding 26.5
mouldy 4.13
moulin 25.16
Moulmein 25.8
moult 30.51
mound 16.43
mount 30.55
mountain 25.19
mountaineer 12.4
mountainous 28.29
mountainside 16.16
mountainy 4.32
Mountbatten 25.50
mountebank 21.33
mountebankery
  4.43
mounter 12.80
Mountie 4.54
mounting 26.13
Mount Isa 12.91
mourn 25.28
mourner 12.56
mourning 26.9
mouse 28.16
mouser 12.70
mousetrap 27.1
moussaka 12.37
mousse 28.19
mousseline 25.10
moustache 29.2
mousy 4.47
mouth 32.10, 33.6
mouthbrooder 12.29
mouthfeel 23.7
mouther 12.84
mouthpiece 28.6
mouth-to-mouth
  32.10
mouthwash 29.11
mouthy 4.57
movable 23.26
move 34.12
mover 12.87

movie 4.58
mow 8.1, 9.1
mower 12.17
mowing 26.3
mown 25.30
moxie 4.46
Mozambican 25.43
Mozambique 21.8
Mozarabic 21.9
Mozart 30.3
Mozartian 25.37
mozzarella 12.42
mph 15.4
Ms 35.10
MSc 4.1
MS-DOS 28.14
mu 11.1
Mubarak 21.3
much 15.13
mucilage 20.6
muck 21.29
mucker 12.41
muckle 23.32
muckrake 21.7
muckraker 12.38
mucky 4.20
mucous 28.26
mucus 28.26
mud 16.27
mudbank 21.33
mudbath 32.2
muddle 23.28
muddler 12.48
muddy 4.13
Mudéjar 1.9
Mudéjares 28.3
mudfish 29.7
mudflap 27.1
mudflat 30.1
mudflow 9.17
mudguard 16.2
mudlark 21.5
mudpack 21.3
mudskipper 12.62
mud-slinger 12.60
mud-slinging 26.10
mudstone 25.31
muesli 4.26
muezzin 25.20
muff 17.15
muffin 25.14
muffle 23.29
muffler 12.47
mufti 4.55
mug 18.12
Mugabe 4.10
mugful 23.21
mugger 12.32
mugging 26.6
muggins 35.31
muggy 4.15

Mughal 23.30
mugshot 30.32
mugwump 27.17
Muhammad 16.29
Muir 12.20
mujahedin 25.9
Mukden 25.40
mulatto 9.24
mulberry 4.43
mulch 29.19
mulct 30.49
Muldoon 25.33
mule 23.20
muleteer 12.4
mulga 12.32
mulish 29.8
mull 23.22
mullah 12.47
mullein 25.16
Müller 12.46
Muller 12.47
mullet 30.22
mulligan 25.41
mulligatawny 4.32
mullion 25.37
mulloway 3.25
Mulroney 4.33
multibillion 25.52
multichannel 23.34
multicolor 12.47
multicolored 16.29
multicolour 12.47
multicoloured 16.29
multiculturalist
  31.8
multi-ethnic 21.13
multifaceted 16.12
multifarious 28.23
multifoil 23.19
multiform 24.9
multiformity 4.53
multifunction 25.49
multifunctional
  23.34
multigrade 16.6
multihull 23.22
multilateral 23.36
multilateralist 31.8
multi-layered 16.28
multilingual 23.40
multimedia 12.5
multimillion 25.52
multimillionaire
  2.1
multipartite 30.30
multiphase 35.5
multi-platform 24.9
multiple 23.35
multiplex 28.38
multiplier 12.14
multiply 6.11

multipolar 12.44
multipurpose 28.30
multiracial 23.38
multistage 20.4
multistorey 4.41
multitalented 16.12
multitude 16.25
multitudinous
  28.29
multivalve 34.15
multum in
  parvo 9.27
mum 24.14
mumble 23.26
mumbler 12.48
Mumbles 35.29
mumbling 26.8
mumbo-jumbo 9.9
mummer 12.52
mummery 4.43
mummify 6.7
mumming 26.9
mummy 4.30
mumps 28.46
Munch 21.34
munch 29.20
München 25.49
munchies 35.10
Munda 12.29
mundane 25.7
mundanity 4.53
mungo 9.13
Munich 21.13
municipal 23.35
municipalize 35.12
munificence 28.45
munificent 30.56
munition 25.49
munitioner 12.58
Munro 9.1
munshi 4.50
Münster 12.81
Munster 12.81
mural 23.36
muralist 31.8
murder 12.29
murderer 12.67
murderess 28.3
murderous 28.31
Murdo 9.11
Murdoch 21.20
mure 12.20
murex 28.38
Murgatroyd 16.24
Muriel 23.24
Murillo 9.17
murk 21.31
murky 4.20
Murmansk 21.35
murmur 12.52
murmurer 12.67

murmurous 28.31
murphy 4.14
murrain 25.18
Murray 4.42
murre 13.1
Murrumbidgee 4.17
Mururoa 12.17
Muscadet 3.9
muscadine 25.21
muscat 30.1
muscatel 23.3
muscle 23.37
muscly 4.27
muscovado 9.11
Muscovite 30.30
Muscovy 4.58
muscular 12.46
musculature 12.24
muse 35.21
musette 30.4
museum 24.15
mush 29.15, 29.16
mushroom 24.12
mushroomy 4.30
mushy 4.50
music 21.18
musical 23.32
musicale 23.2
musicalize 35.12
musician 25.49
musicianly 4.24
musicology 4.17
musing 26.14
musk 21.35
musket 30.21
musketeer 12.4
Muskogean 25.37
muskrat 30.2
musky 4.20
Muslim 24.6
muslin 25.16
muso 9.29
musquash 29.11
muss 28.21
mussel 23.37
Mussolini 4.31
Mussorgsky 4.19
mussy 4.47
must 31.24
mustache 29.2
mustang 26.1
mustard 16.29
muster 12.81
musterer 12.67
Mustique 21.8
mustn't 30.56
musty 4.55
Mut 30.40
mutable 23.26
mutant 30.56
mutate 30.7

mutation 25.49
mutch 15.13
mute 30.37
mutilate 30.11
mutineer 12.4
mutinous 28.29
mutiny 4.32
mutt 30.40
mutter 12.81
mutterer 12.67
muttering 26.11
mutton 25.50
muttonhead 16.3
muttony 4.34
mutual 23.25
mutualist 31.8
mutule 23.20
muumuu 11.14
Muzak 21.4
muzhik 21.11
muzzle 23.41
muzzy 4.62
my 6.1
myalgia 12.6
myall 23.25
Mycenae 4.31
Mycenaean 25.37
Mycenean 25.37
Myfanwy 4.59
Mykonos 28.14
Mylar 1.12
mynah 12.55
myope 27.10
myopia 12.9
myopic 21.14
myosotis 28.12
Myra 12.65
myriad 16.28
myriapod 16.18
Myrmidon 25.40
Myrna 12.59
myrobalan 25.44
Myron 25.47
myrrh 13.1
myrtle 23.39
myself 17.18
Mysia 12.11
Mysian 25.37
Mysore 7.1
mysterious 28.23
mystery 4.43
mystic 21.17
mystical 23.32
mystify 6.7
mystique 21.8
myth 32.6
mythi 6.19
mythic 21.18
mythical 23.32
mythicist 31.13
mythicize 35.14

mythologer 12.36
mythologic 21.11
mythologize 35.11
mythologizer 12.91
mythology 4.17
mythopoeic 21.9
Mytilene 25.10
myxomatosis 28.11

N'Djamena 12.54
nab 14.1
Nabataean 25.36
Nabatean 25.36
Nablus 28.27
nabob 14.9
Nabokov 34.10
nacelle 23.3
nacho 9.10
nacre 12.38
Na-Dene 3.1
Nader 12.26
Nadia 12.5
Nadine 25.9
nadir 12.5
naff 17.1
nag 18.1
naga 12.31
Nagaland 16.40
Nagasaki 4.18
nagger 12.31
N agorno-
  Karabakh 21.1
Nagoya 12.18
Nagpur 12.20
Nahuatl 23.39
Nahum 24.18
naiad 16.1
naif 17.5
nail 23.5
nailer 12.43
nailery 4.43
nainsook 21.28
Naipaul 23.14
naira 12.65
Nairobi 4.10
naive 34.5
naivety 4.53
Najaf 17.1
naked 16.10
Nakuru 11.17
nam pla 1.1
Namaqualand 16.40
namby-pamby 4.10
name 24.4
namedrop 27.8
name-dropper 12.62
nameplate 30.11

namesake 21.7
Namibia 12.5
Namibian 25.37
Namur 12.20
nan 25.1
nana 12.53
Nanak 21.3
nance 28.44
Nanchang 26.1
Nancy 4.45
Nandi 4.12
Nanette 30.4
Nanga Parbat 30.1
Nanjing 26.3
nankeen 25.9
nanny 4.31
nanny goat 30.35
nanometer 12.77
nanometre 12.77
nanoparticle 23.32
nanosecond 16.45
Nansen 25.48
Nantes 30.53
Nantucket 30.21
naoi 10.2
Naomi 4.29
nap 27.1
napalm 24.2
nape 27.4
napery 4.43
Naphtali 6.11
naphtha 12.83
naphthalene 25.10
Napier 12.9
napkin 25.15
Naples 35.29
napoleon 25.37
Napoleonic 21.13
nappa 12.61
nappe 27.1
napper 12.61
nappy 4.36
Nara 12.64
Narayan 25.38
Narbonne 25.24
narc 21.5
narcissi 6.16
narcissist 31.13
narcissus 28.32
narcolepsy 4.45
narcotic 21.17
narcotize 35.14
nard 16.2
nardoo 11.1
nark 21.5
narky 4.18
Narragansett 30.24
narrate 30.7
narrow 9.21
narrowcasting 26.13
narrowish 29.6

Narvik 21.18
narwhal 23.40
nary 4.39
nasal 23.41
nascent 30.56
Naseby 4.10
Nash 29.1
Nashville 23.10
Nasmyth 32.6
Nassau 7.16, 8.11
Nasser 12.69
nasturtium 24.20
nasty 4.51
Nat 30.1
natal 23.39
Natal 23.1
Natalie 4.27
natality 4.53
Natasha 12.72
natation 25.49
natatorial 23.24
natatorium 24.14
natatory 4.43
natch 15.1
Nathan 25.51
Nathaniel 23.24
nation 25.49
national 23.34
nationalist 31.8
nationalizer 12.91
nationhood 16.26
nationwide 16.14
native 34.8
nativist 31.15
nativity 4.53
natron 25.26
natter 12.74
natterer 12.67
natty 4.51
natural 23.36
naturalist 31.8
nature 12.23
naturist 31.12
naught 30.33
Naughton 25.50
naughty 4.54
Nauru 11.17
nausea 12.11
nauseate 30.8
nauseous 28.23
nautch 15.8
nautical 23.32
nautilus 28.27
Navajo 9.14
naval 23.40
navarin 25.18
Navarino 9.19
Navarre 1.1
nave 34.4
navel 23.40
navicular 12.46

navigate 30.9
Navrátilová 12.86
navvy 4.58
navy 4.58
nawab 14.2
nay 3.1
naysay 3.20
naysayer 12.2
Nazarene 25.9
Nazareth 32.13
Nazi 4.45
Nazify 6.7
Nazirite 30.29
Nazism 24.21
Ndebele 4.23
N'Djamena 12.54
Ndola 12.44
neé 3.1
neanderthal 23.2
neap 27.5
Neapolitan 25.50
near 12.4
nearby 6.1
nearish 29.9
nearside 16.16
neat 30.18
neaten 25.50
neath 32.5
Neaxos 28.14
nebbish 29.6
Nebraska 12.37
Nebraskan 25.43
Nebuchadnezzar
  12.90
nebula 12.46
nebulosity 4.53
nebulous 28.27
nebuly 4.26
necessarian 25.37
necessary 4.43
necessitarian 25.37
necessitate 30.16
necessitous 28.34
necessity 4.53
neck 21.6
Neckar 12.37
neckband 16.40
Necker 12.37
neckerchief 17.6
necklace 28.8
necklet 30.22
neckline 25.22
necktie 6.18
neckwear 2.15
necrology 4.17
necromancer 12.69
necromancy 4.45
necromantic 21.17
necrophile 23.11
necrophilia 12.6
necrophiliac 21.1

necrophilic 21.11
necrophilist 31.8
necropolis 28.8
necrosis 28.11
nectar 12.76
nectarine 25.11
nectarous 28.31
Ned 16.3
neddy 4.12
née 3.1
need 16.7
Needham 24.17
needle 23.28
needlecord 16.21
needlecraft 30.47
needlepoint 30.55
Needles 35.29
needlework 21.31
needn't 30.56
needy 4.12
neep 27.5
ne'er 2.1
ne'er-do-well 23.4
nefarious 28.23
Nefertiti 4.52
negate 30.7
negation 25.49
negativist 31.15
negator 12.77
negatory 4.43
negligee 3.12
negligence 28.45
negligent 30.56
negligible 23.26
Negombo 9.9
negotiant 30.56
negotiate 30.8
Negrillo 9.17
Negro 9.21
negus 28.25
Nehemiah 12.13
Nehru 11.17
neigh 3.1
neighbor 12.21
neighborhood 16.26
neighborly 4.27
neighbour 12.21
neighbourhood
  16.26
neighbourly 4.27
Neil 23.7
neither 12.84
Nell 23.3
nelly 4.22
Nelson 25.48
nematode 16.23
Nembutal 23.1
nemertean 25.37
nemertine 25.23

nemeses 35.8
nemesia 12.5
nemesis 28.11
Nene 25.5, 25.9
Nennius 28.23
neoclassic 21.16
neoclassical 23.32
neoclassicist 31.13
neocolonial 23.24
neocolonialist 31.8
neocon 25.25
neolithic 21.18
neon 25.24
neonatal 23.39
neonate 30.13
neophyte 30.27
neoplastic 21.17
Neoplatonist 31.10
Nepal 23.14
Nepalese 35.6
Nepali 4.25
nepheline 25.10
nephew 11.22
nephrite 30.29
nephritis 28.12
nepotist 31.14
Neptune 25.33
Neptunian 25.37
neptunium 24.16
nerd 16.31
nerdy 4.13
nereid 16.8
Nereus 28.23
Nerissa 12.69
Nernst 31.30
Nero 9.21
Neruda 12.29
Nerva 12.87
nerve 34.14
nerve-racking 26.7
Nervi 4.58
nervous 28.35
nervy 4.58
Nerys 28.10
Nesbit 30.20
nescience 28.45
nescient 30.56
nesh 29.3
ness 28.3
Nessie 4.45
nest 31.3
Nestlé 3.15
nestle 23.37
nestling 26.8
Nestor 12.76
Nestorian 25.37
net 30.4
netball 23.14
netbook 21.28
nether 12.84
Netherlander 12.25

Netherlandish 29.6
Netherlands 35.31
nethermost 31.20
netherworld 16.38
netsuke 4.20
Nettie 4.51
nettle 23.39
network 21.31
networker 12.41
neume 24.12
neural 23.36
neuralgia 12.35
neuralgic 21.11
neurasthenia 12.8
neuritis 28.12
neurology 4.17
neuron 25.26
neuroscience 28.45
neuroses 35.8
neurosis 28.11
neurotic 21.17
neuter 12.81
neutral 23.36
neutralist 31.8
neutralizer 12.91
neutrino 9.19
neutron 25.26
Neva 12.85
Nevada 12.25
Nevadan 25.40
Névé 34.5
never 12.85
nevermore 7.1
never-never 12.85
Neville 23.10
Nevis 28.12
New Orleans 35.31
new 11.1
Newark 21.5, 21.30
newbie 4.10
newborn 25.28
Newby 4.10
Newcastle 23.37
Newcomen 25.45
newcomer 12.52
newel 23.25
newel post 31.20
newfangled 16.38
Newfoundland
  16.45
Newfoundlander
  12.29
Newgate 30.9
newish 29.6
newlaid 16.6
Newlands 35.31
newly 4.26
newly-wed 16.4
Newman 25.45
Newmarket 30.21
newness 28.29

New Orleans 35.31
Newport 30.33
Newry 4.43
news 35.21
newsagent 30.56
newsboy 10.3
newscast 31.2
newscaster 12.75
newsflash 29.1
newshound 16.43
newsletter 12.76
newsman 25.2
newsmen 25.5
newspaper 12.61
newspaperman 25.2
newspapermen 25.5
newspeak 21.8
newsprint 30.54
newsreader 12.26
newsreel 23.7
newsroom 24.12
news sheet 30.19
news stand 16.40
newsvendor 12.26
newsworthy 4.57
newsy 4.62
newt 30.37
newton 25.50
Newtonian 25.37
Newtown 25.29
next 31.28
nexus 28.32
Ney 3.1
ngaio 9.5
Ngamiland 16.40
Nguni 4.33
niacin 25.19
Niagara 12.64
Niall 23.25
Niamey 3.16
nib 14.7
nibble 23.26
nibbler 12.48
Nibelung 26.17
Nibelungenlied
  16.7
niblick 21.11
nicad 16.1
Nicaea 12.3
Nicam 24.1
Nicaragua 12.20
Nicaraguan 25.38
nice 28.13
Nice 28.6
niceish 29.9
nicety 4.53
niche 29.5
Nicholas 28.27
Nicholson 25.48
Nichrome 24.11
nick 21.9

nickel 23.32
nickelodeon 25.37
nicker 12.39
Nicklaus 28.27
nickname 24.4
Nicky 4.19
Nicobar 1.4
Nicola 12.48
Nicole 23.17
Nicosia 12.3
nicotine 25.12
nide 16.14
nidi 6.6
nidus 28.25
niece 28.6
niello 9.17
Nielsen 25.48
Niemeyer 12.14
Niersteiner 12.55
Nietzsche 12.23
Nietzschean 25.37
niff 17.6
niffy 4.14
nifty 4.53
Nigel 23.31
Nigella 12.42
Niger 2.1, 12.35
Nigeria 12.10
Nigerian 25.37
niggard 16.28
niggardly 4.27
niggle 23.30
niggly 4.24
nigh 6.1
night light 30.28
night 30.26
nightbird 16.31
nightcap 27.1
nightclothes 35.19
nightclub 14.13
nightdress 28.3
nightfall 23.15
nightgown 25.29
nighthawk 21.22
nightie 4.54
nightingale 23.5
nightjar 1.10
nightlife 17.7
nightly 4.25
nightmare 2.9
nightmarish 29.9
nightshade 16.6
nightshirt 30.45
nightspot 30.32
nightstick 21.17
nighttime 24.7
nightwear 2.15
nigrescent 30.56
nihilist 31.8
nihility 4.53
Nijinsky 4.19

Nijmegen 25.41
Nike 4.19
nil 23.8
nil desperandum
  24.17
Nile 23.11
Nilsson 25.48
nim 24.6
nimbi 6.5
nimble 23.26
nimbostratus 28.34
nimbus 28.24
nimby 4.10
Nimes 24.5
niminy-piminy 4.32
Nimrod 16.18
Nina 12.54
nincompoop 27.11
nine 25.21
ninefold 16.37
nineteen 25.9
nineteenth 32.19
ninetieth 32.6
ninety 4.54
Nineveh 12.86
Ninian 25.37
ninja 12.35
ninny 4.32
ninon 25.26
ninth 32.19
Niobe 4.10
nip 27.6
nipper 12.62
nipple 23.35
nipplewort 30.45
Nippon 25.26
Nipponese 35.6
nippy 4.36
nirvana 12.53
Nisan 25.4
nisi 6.16
nit 30.20
nite 30.26
niterie 4.43
nitpick 21.14
nitrate 30.15
nitric 21.15
nitrite 30.29
nitrogen 25.42
nitroglycerin 25.11
nitroglycerine 25.11
nitty-gritty 4.53
nitwit 30.25
nitwitted 16.12
Niue 3.5
Niven 25.51
niveous 28.23
nix 28.39
Nixon 25.48
Nkomo 9.18
Nkrumah 12.52

n

no 9.1
no-account 30.55
Noah 12.17
Noam 24.17
nob 14.9
no-ball 23.14
nobble 23.26
nobbler 12.48
Nobel 23.3
nobelium 24.16
nobility 4.53
noble 23.26
nobleman 25.45
noblemen 25.45
noblesse 28.3
noblewomen 25.17
nobly 4.25
nobody 4.13
nock 21.20
noctambulist 31.8
noctuid 16.8
noctule 23.20
nocturn 25.53
nocturnal 23.34
nocturne 25.53
nocuous 28.24
nod 16.18
noddle 23.28
noddy 4.13
node 16.23
nodular 12.46
nodule 23.20
Noel 23.3, 23.25
noes 35.19
nog 18.8
noggin 25.14
nogging 26.6
Noh 9.1
no-hoper 12.63
nohow 8.5
noil 23.19
noir 1.1
noise 35.20
noisette 30.4
noisome 24.20
noisy 4.61
Nolan 25.44
nolens volens 35.31
nomad 16.1
nomadic 21.10
no-man's land 16.40
nombril 23.9
nollie 4.25
nom de guerre 2.1
Nome 24.11
nomen 25.5
nomenclature 12.24
nomenklatura 12.67
nominal 23.34
nominalist 31.8
nominate 30.13

nominee 4.1
nonage 20.7
nonagenarian 25.37
nonaligned 16.42
nonce 28.44
nonchalance 28.45
nonchalant 30.56
non sequitur 12.78
non-com 24.8
nonda 12.28
nondescript 30.58
none 25.35
nones 35.31
nonesuch 15.13
nonet 30.4
nong 26.15
nonpareil 23.5
nonsense 28.45
nonsensical 23.32
non-U 11.1
non-polluting 26.13
noodle 23.28
nook 21.28
nooky 4.20
noon 25.33
noonday 3.9
noontide 16.17
noontime 24.7
noose 28.19
nopal 23.35
nope 27.10
nor 7.1
Nora 12.66
noradrenalin 25.16
Norbert 30.41
Nordic 21.10
Noreen 25.11
Norfolk 21.30
Noriega 12.31
nork 21.22
norm 24.9
Norma 12.52
normal 23.33
normalcy 4.47
Norman 25.45
Normandy 4.13
Norn 25.28
Norris 28.10
Norroy 10.11
Norse 28.15
Norseman 25.45
Norsemen 25.45
north 32.9
Northampton 25.50
Northamptonshire 12.11
Northants 28.47
northbound 16.43
Northcliffe 17.6
northeast 31.5

northeastern 25.50
northeastward 16.30
northerly 4.27
northern 25.51
northerner 12.58
northernmost 31.20
northing 26.14
Northland 16.45
Northumberland 16.45
Northumbria 12.10
Northumbrian 25.37
northward 16.30
northwest 31.3
northwestern 25.50
northwestward 16.30
Norway 3.25
Norwegian 25.42
Norwich 20.8
nose 35.19
nosebag 18.1
noseband 16.40
nosebleed 16.7
nosedive 34.9
nosegay 3.11
nosh 29.11
noshery 4.43
no-show 9.1
nosh-up 27.13
nostalgia 12.6
nostalgic 21.11
nostoc 21.21
Nostradamus 28.28
nostril 23.9
nostrum 24.19
nosy 4.61
nosy parker 12.37
not 30.31
nota bene 3.17
notable 23.26
notarial 23.24
notarize 35.13
notary 4.43
notate 30.7
notation 25.49
notch 15.7
notchy 4.11
note 30.35
notebook 21.28
notecase 28.5
notelet 30.22
notepad 16.1
notepaper 12.61
noteworthy 4.57
nothing 26.14
notice 28.12
noticeboard 16.20
notify 6.7

notion 25.49
notional 23.34
notoriety 4.53
notorious 28.23
Notre-Dame 24.2
Nottingham 24.19
Nottinghamshire 12.11
notwithstanding 26.5
nougat 1.8
nougatine 25.9
nought 30.33
Nouméa 12.2
noumena 12.55
noumenal 23.34
noumenon 25.26
noun 25.29
nounal 23.34
nourish 29.9
nourisher 12.72
nous 28.16
nouveau riche 29.5
nova 12.86
Nova Scotian 25.49
novel 23.40
novelette 30.4
novelist 31.8
novelize 35.12
novella 12.42
Novello 9.17
novelty 4.54
November 12.21
novena 12.54
Novgorod 16.18
novice 28.12
novitiate 30.41
novocaine 25.7
Novokuznetsk 21.35
Novosibirsk 21.35
Novotný 4.32
now 8.1
nowadays 35.5
noway 3.1
nowhere 2.15
no-win 25.13
nowise 35.15
nowt 30.34
noxious 28.33
nozzle 23.41
nth 32.19
nu 11.1
nuance 28.44
nub 14.13
Nuba 12.21
nubble 23.26
nubbly 4.26
nubby 4.10
Nubia 12.5
Nubian 25.37

nubile 23.11
nubility 4.53
nuclear 12.6
nucleate 30.8
nuclei 6.3
nucleon 25.24
nucleotide 16.17
nucleus 28.23
nuddy 4.13
nude 16.25
nudge 20.16
nudger 12.36
nudism 24.21
nudist 31.6
nudity 4.53
nudnik 21.13
Nuer 12.19
Nuffield 16.35
nugatory 4.43
nugget 30.21
nuisance 28.45
nuke 21.27
Nuku'alofa 12.30
null 23.22
nullah 12.47
nullifier 12.14
nullify 6.7
nullity 4.53
numb 24.14
numbat 30.1
number 12.22
number plate 30.11
number 12.22
numbskull 23.22
numdah 12.29
numen 25.45
numeracy 4.48
numeral 23.36
numerate 30.43
numeric 21.15
numerical 23.32
numerology 4.17
numerous 28.31
Numidia 12.5
Numidian 25.37
numina 12.55
numinous 28.29
numismatic 21.17
numismatist 31.14
nun 25.35
nunciature 12.20
nuncio 9.4
Nuneaton 25.50
nunlike 21.19
nunnery 4.43
nunnish 29.9
Nupe 3.18
nuptial 23.38
nurdle 23.28
Nuremberg 18.13
Nureyev 17.3

Nurofen 25.5
nurse 28.36
nurseling 26.8
nursemaid 16.6
nursery 4.43
nurseryman 25.45
nurserymen 25.45
nursling 26.8
nurture 12.24
nurturer 12.67
nut 30.40
nutation 25.49
nutcase 28.5
nutcracker 12.37
nuthouse 28.16
nutmeg 18.3
nutrient 30.56
nutritionist 31.10
nutritious 28.33
nutshell 23.3
nutter 12.81
Nutting 26.13
nutty 4.55
nuzzle 23.41
nyala 12.42
Nyasaland 16.40
Nye 6.1
Nyerere 4.39
nylon 25.25
nymph 17.19
nymphal 23.29
nymphean 25.37
nymphet 30.4
nympho 9.12
nympholepsy 4.45
nympholeptic 21.17
nymphomania 12.8
nymphomaniac 21.1
Nynorsk 21.35
Nyree 4.40
Nyx 28.39

O

oaf 17.11
oafish 29.7
Oahu 11.10
oak 21.24
oaken 25.43
Oakland 16.45
Oakley 4.25
Oaks 28.40
oakum 24.18
oar 7.1
oarless 28.27
oarlock 21.21
oarsman 25.45
oarsmen 25.45

oarswoman 25.45
oarswomen 25.17
oases 35.8
oasis 28.11
oast 31.20
oast house 28.16
oat 30.35
oatcake 21.7
oaten 25.50
Oates 28.47
oath 32.11
oatmeal 23.7
oaty 4.54
Oaxaca 12.37
Obadiah 12.13
obbligati 4.51
obbligato 9.24
obduracy 4.48
obdurate 30.43
obedience 28.45
obedient 30.56
obeisance 28.45
obeisant 30.56
obelisk 21.35
obelus 28.27
Oberammergau 8.4
Oberon 25.26
obese 28.6
obesity 4.53
obey 3.1
obeyer 12.2
obfuscate 30.10
obfuscatory 4.43
obi 4.10
obit 30.20
obituarist 31.12
obituary 4.43
object 30.48, 30.49
objection 25.49
objectivist 31.15
objectivize 35.14
objector 12.76
objet d'art 1.1
objurgate 30.9
objurgatory 4.43
oblast 31.1
oblate 30.11
oblation 25.49
oblational 23.34
obligati 30.9
obligati 4.51
obligato 9.24
obligatory 4.43
oblige 20.10
obligee 4.1
obliger 12.35
obliging 26.6
obligor 7.1
oblique 21.8
obliquity 4.53

obliterate 30.15
oblivion 25.37
oblivious 28.23
oblong 26.15
obloquy 4.59
obnoxious 28.33
oboe 9.9
oboist 31.6
obol 23.13
O'Brion 25.38
obscene 25.9
obscenity 4.53
obscurant 30.56
obscurantist 31.14
obscure 12.20
obscurity 4.53
obsequies 35.10
obsequious 28.23
observance 28.45
observant 30.56
observatory 4.43
observe 34.14
observer 12.87
obsess 28.3
obsessional 23.34
obsessive 34.7
obsidian 25.37
obsolescence 28.45
obsolescent 30.56
obsolete 30.18
obstacle 23.32
obstetric 21.15
obstetrician 25.49
obstinacy 4.48
obstinate 30.43
obstreperous 28.31
obstruct 30.49
obstruction 25.49
obstructionist 31.10
obstructor 12.81
obtain 25.7
obtainer 12.54
obtention 25.49
obtrude 16.25
obtruder 12.29
obtrusion 25.42
obtrusive 34.7
obtuse 28.19
obverse 28.36
obviate 30.8
obvious 28.23
ocarina 12.54
O'Casey 4.45
Occam 24.18
occasion 25.42
occasional 23.34
occidentalize 35.12
Occitan 25.50
occlude 16.25
occlusion 25.42
occult 30.51

occultist 31.14
occupancy 4.48
occupant 30.56
occupier 12.14
occupy 6.14
occur 13.1
occurrence 28.45
occurrent 30.56
ocean 25.49
Oceania 12.8
Oceanian 25.37
oceanic 21.13
Oceanid 16.10
oceanographer 12.30
oceanography 4.14
Oceanus 28.29
oceanward 16.30
ocelot 30.31
och 22.4
oche 4.19
ocher 12.40
ocherish 29.9
ocherous 28.31
ochery 4.41
ochone 25.30
ochre 12.40
ochreish 29.9
ochrous 28.31
ochry 4.41
ocker 12.40
o'clock 21.20
O'Connell 23.34
O'Connor 12.56
octad 16.1
octagon 25.41
octagonal 23.34
octahedron 25.47
octane 25.8
Octans 35.31
octant 30.56
octave 34.8
Octavia 12.12
Octavian 25.37
Octavius 28.23
octavo 9.27
octet 30.4
October 12.21
octodecimo 9.18
octogenarian 25.37
octopus 28.30
octuple 23.35
ocular 12.46
oculist 31.8
od 16.18
odalisque 21.35
odd 16.18
oddball 23.14
Oddfellow 9.17
oddish 29.6
oddity 4.53

oddly 4.25
oddment 30.56
oddness 28.29
odds and ends 35.27
odds-on 25.24
ode 16.23
O'Dea 3.1
odea 12.5
Odense 12.71
Odeon 25.37
Oder 12.28
Odessa 12.69
Odets 28.47
Odette 30.4
odeum 24.16
Odin 25.14
odious 28.23
odium 24.16
Odonata 12.75
odonate 30.13
odor 12.28
odoriferous 28.31
odorous 28.31
odour 12.28
Odyssean 25.37
Odysseus 28.19
odyssey 4.46
oedema 12.51
Oedipal 23.35
Oedipus 28.30
Oenone 25.30
oenophilist 31.8
o'er 12.17
oesophagus 28.25
oestrogen 25.42
oeuvre 12.68
of 34.10
off 17.8
Offa 12.30
offal 23.29
Offaly 4.27
offbeat 30.18
offcut 30.40
Offenbach 21.5
offence 28.44
offend 16.41
offender 12.26
offense 28.44
offensive 34.7
offer 12.30
offerer 12.67
offering 26.11
offertory 4.43
offhand 16.40
offhanded 16.9
office 28.7
officer 12.70
official 23.38
officialdom 24.17
officialese 35.6
officiant 30.56

officiate 30.8
officinal 23.34
officious 28.33
offing 26.6
offish 29.7
offload 16.23
offprint 30.54
off-putting 26.13
offset 30.5
offshoot 30.38
offshore 7.1
offside 16.14
offspring 26.11
offstage 20.4
Ofgas 28.1
oft 30.47
Oftel 23.4
often 25.41
oftentimes 35.30
Ofwat 30.32
Ogaden 25.5
ogee 4.17
ogham 24.18
ogle 23.30
ogler 12.44
ogre 12.32
ogreish 29.9
oh 9.1
O'Higgins 35.31
Ohio 9.5
Ohioan 25.38
ohm 24.11
ohmic 21.12
oho 9.1
oi 10.1
oik 21.25
oil 23.19
oilcake 21.7
oilcan 25.2
oilcloth 32.8
oiler 12.44
oilfield 16.35
oilman 25.2
oilmen 25.5
oilrig 18.6
oilseed 16.7
oilskin 15.15
oily 4.25
oink 21.34
Oireachtas 28.34
Ojibwa 12.88
okapi 4.36
Okavango 9.13
okay 3.1
O'Keeffe 17.5
okey-doke 21.24
okey-dokey 4.20
Okie 4.20
Okinawa 12.88
Oklahoma 12.52
Oklahoman 25.45

okra 12.66
Olaf 17.1
Ölard 16.40
old 16.37
olden 25.40
olde worlde 4.13
old-fashioned 16.45
Oldham 24.17
oldie 4.13
oldish 29.6
old-maidish 29.6
oldness 28.29
old-stager 12.35
old-timer 12.51
oldster 12.80
oleaginous 28.29
oleander 12.25
oleaster 12.74
olé 3.1
Oleg 18.3
olfactometer 12.78
olfactory 4.43
Olga 12.32
oligarch 21.5
oligarchic 21.11
oligarchical 23.32
oligarchy 4.18
oligopolist 31.8
oligopoly 4.27
olio 9.4
olive 34.6
Oliver 12.86
Olivia 12.12
Olivier 3.3
olivine 25.12
Ollie 4.25
olm 24.18
Olmec 21.6
oloroso 9.22
Olwen 25.20
Olympia 12.9
Olympiad 16.28
Olympian 25.37
Olympic 21.14
Olympus 28.30
om 24.11
Omagh 12.52
Omaha 1.9
Oman 25.4, 25.45
Omani 4.31
Omar Khayyám 24.1
ombree 3.19
ombré 12.21
ombudsman 25.45
ombudsmen 25.45
Omdurman 25.45
omega 12.31
omelet 30.22
omelette 30.22
omen 25.45

ominous 28.29
omissible 23.26
omission 25.49
omissive 34.7
omit 30.20
omnibus 28.24
omnicompetence 28.45
omnicompetent 30.56
omnifarious 28.23
omnipotence 28.45
omnipotent 30.56
omnipresence 28.45
omnipresent 30.56
omniscience 28.45
omniscient 30.56
omnivore 7.20
omnivorous 28.31
omphalos 28.14
Omsk 21.35
on 25.24
on-trend 16.41
onager 12.36
onanist 31.10
Onassis 28.11
once 28.44
once-over 12.86
oncer 12.71
oncologist 31.7
oncology 4.17
oncoming 26.9
oncost 31.17
one 25.35
Oneida 12.27
O'Neill 23.7
oneiric 21.15
oneness 28.29
oner 12.57
onerous 28.31
oneself 17.18
one-sided 16.9
one-step 27.3
one-time 24.7
one-to-one 25.35
ongoing 26.3
onion 25.52
Onions 35.31
oniony 4.34
on-line 25.21
onlooker 12.41
onlooking 26.7
only 4.25
onomatopoeia 12.3
onomatopoeic 21.9
Onondaga 12.31
onrush 29.16
onrushing 26.12
onset 30.5
onshore 7.1
onside 16.14
onslaught 30.33

onstage 20.4
Ontario 9.4
onto 11.20
ontologist 31.7
ontology 4.17
onus 28.29
onward 16.30
onyx 28.39
oodles 35.29
ooh 11.1
oolong 26.15
oompah 1.15
oomph 17.19
Oona 12.56
oops 28.46
oops-a-daisy 4.61
Oort 30.33
Oostende 16.41
ooze 35.21
oozy 4.62
op 27.8
opacity 4.53
opah 12.63
opal 23.35
opalescence 28.45
opalescent 30.56
opaline 25.22
opaque 21.7
ope 27.10
Opel 23.35
open 25.46
opencast 31.2
opener 12.58
opening 26.9
openwork 21.31
opera 12.67
opera buffa 12.30
opéra comique 21.8
operate 30.15
operatic 21.17
operationalize 35.12
operetta 12.76
Ophelia 12.6
Ophir 12.30
Ophiuchus 28.26
ophthalmic 21.12
ophthalmology 4.17
opiate 30.41
Opie 4.36
opine 25.21
opinion 25.52
opinionated 16.12
opium 24.16
Oporto 9.25
opossum 24.20
Oppenheimer 12.51
oppo 9.20
opponent 30.56
opportune 25.33
opportunist 31.10

opportunity 4.53
oppose 35.19
opposer 12.92
opposite 30.25
oppress 28.3
oppressive 34.7
oppressor 12.69
opprobrious 28.23
opprobrium 24.16
oppugn 25.33
oppugnant 30.56
oppugner 12.56
Oprah 12.66
opt 10.58
optic 21.17
optical 23.32
optician 25.49
optima 12.51
optimal 23.33
optimist 31.9
optimum 24.19
option 25.49
optional 23.34
optometer 12.78
optometrist 31.12
optometry 4.40
opulence 28.45
opulent 30.56
opus 28.30
opuscule 23.20
or 7.1
oracle 23.32
oracular 12.46
oral 23.36
oralist 31.8
orality 4.53
Oran 25.1
orange 20.19
orangeade 16.6
Orangeman 25.45
Orangemen 25.45
orangery 4.43
orang-utan 25.3
orate 30.7
oration 25.49
orator 12.82
oratorial 23.24
oratorian 25.37
oratorical 23.32
oratorio 9.4
oratory 4.43
orb 14.10
orbit 30.20
orbital 23.39
orc 21.22
orca 12.40
Orcadian 25.37
orchard 16.28
orchestra 12.65
orchestral 23.36
orchestrate 30.15

orchid 16.10
orchil 23.9
Orczy 4.47
ordain 25.7
ordainer 12.54
ordeal 23.7
order 12.28
ordering 26.11
orderly 4.27
ordinal 23.34
ordinance 28.45
ordinand 16.40
ordinary 4.43
ordnance 28.45
ordonnance 28.45
Ordovician 25.37
ordure 12.20
ore 7.1
oread 16.1
oregano 9.19
Oregon 25.41
Oregonian 25.37
Orenburg 18.13
Oreo 9.4
Orestes 35.9
orfe 17.9
Orff 17.9
organ 25.41
organdie 4.13
organdy 4.13
organelle 23.3
organic 21.13
organist 31.10
organizer 12.91
organon 25.26
organum 24.19
organza 12.90
organzine 25.12
orgasm 24.21
orgasmic 21.12
orgastic 21.17
orgeat 30.41
orgiastic 21.17
orgy 4.17
Oriana 12.53
oribi 4.10
oriel 23.24
Orient 30.56
orient 30.53
Oriental 23.39
orientalist 31.8
orientalize 35.12
orientate 30.16
orienteer 12.4
orienteering 26.11
orifice 28.7
oriflamme 24.1
origami 4.29
origanum 24.19
Origen 25.5
origin 25.14

o

outsider 12.27
outsit 30.20
outsize 35.11
outskirts 28.47
outsmart 30.3
outsold 16.37
outsource 28.15
outspan 25.1, 25.3
outspoken 25.43
outspread 16.3
outstanding 26.5
outstare 2.1
outstay 3.1
outstep 27.3
outstretch 15.3
outstretched 30.46
outstrip 27.6
outswing 26.14
outvote 30.35
outwalk 21.22
outward 16.30
outwards 35.27
outwatch 15.7
outwear 2.1
outweigh 3.1
outwent 30.53
outwit 30.20
outwith 32.6
outwore 7.1
outwork 21.31
outworker 12.41
outworking 26.7
outworn 25.28
ouzel 23.41
ouzo 9.29
ova 12.86
oval 23.40
ovarian 25.37
ovary 4.43
ovate 30.16
ovation 25.49
oven 25.51
ovenproof 17.13
oven-ready 4.12
Ovens 35.31
ovenware 2.15
over 12.86
overage 20.8
overall 23.15
overanalyse 35.13
overcall 23.15
overcomplicate
    30.10
overconsumption
    25.49
overdependence
    28.45
overdramatize 35.14
overeaten 25.50
overeducated 16.12
overfall 23.15

overflight 30.28
overflow 9.17
overgeneralize
    35.12
overhaul 23.15
overheard 16.31
overinflated 16.12
overjoyed 16.24
overkill 23.9
overlander 12.25
overlay 3.15
overleaped 30.58
overlord 16.21
overnighter 12.79
overparted 16.12
overqualified 16.14
overseas 35.6
overseer 12.11
oversexed 31.28
overshoe 11.19
overside 16.16
oversight 30.30
oversoul 23.18
overspecialize 35.12
overspill 23.9
overt 30.45
overthrow 9.21
overtone 25.31
overtrick 21.15
overture 12.20
overview 11.22
overweening 26.9
overwhelm 24.18
Ovid 16.13
Oviedo 9.11
oviform 24.9
oviraptor 12.74
ovoid 16.24
ovulate 30.11
ovum 24.20
ow 8.1
owe 9.1
Owen 25.13
Owens 35.31
owl 23.16
owlet 30.22
owlish 29.8
own 25.30
owner 12.56
owt 30.34
ox 28.40
ox tongue 26.18
oxbow 9.9
Oxbridge 20.8
oxen 25.48
Oxfam 24.1
Oxford 16.28
Oxfordshire 12.11
oxhide 16.14
oxidant 30.56
oxide 16.16

oxlip 27.6
Oxon 25.26
Oxonian 25.37
oxtail 23.6
oxter 12.79
ox tongue 26.18
oxygen 25.42
oxygenate 30.13
oxygenous 28.29
oxymoron 25.26
oxytocin 25.19
oyez 3.1
oyster 12.81
oystercatcher 12.23
Oz 35.16
Ozalid 16.10
ozone 25.31

P

pa 1.1
Pablo 9.17
Pablum 24.18
pabulum 24.18
paca 12.37
pacarana 12.53
pace 4.45, 28.5
pacemaker 12.38
pacemaking 26.7
pacer 12.69
pace-setting 26.13
Pachelbel 23.3
pachyderm 24.22
pachydermal 23.33
pacific 21.10
pacificatory 4.43
pacifier 12.14
pacifist 31.7
pacify 6.7
Pacino 9.19
pack 21.1
package 20.6
packager 12.35
packer 12.37
packet 30.21
packhorse 28.15
packice 28.13
packing case 28.5
packing 26.7
packman 25.2
packmen 25.5
packsaddle 23.28
Pac-man 25.2
pact 30.48
pacy 4.45
pad 16.1
paddle 23.28
paddler 12.48
paddock 21.30

paddy 4.12
Paderewski 4.18
padlock 21.21
Padma 12.50
padre 3.19
padrone 4.33
Padua 12.20
Paduan 25.38
paean 25.36
paediatric 21.15
paediatrician 25.49
paedophile 23.11
paedophilia 12.6
paella 12.42
paeon 25.36
Pagalu 11.13
pagan 25.41
Paganini 4.31
paganish 29.9
paganize 35.13
page 20.4
pageant 30.56
pageantry 4.43
pageboy 10.3
pager 12.35
paginal 23.34
paginate 30.13
pagoda 12.28
pah 1.1
Pahang 26.1
Pahlavi 4.58
paid 16.6
Paige 20.4
Paignton 25.50
pail 23.5
pain 25.7
Paine 25.7
painkiller 12.43
painkilling 26.8
painstaking 26.7
paint 30.54
paintball 23.14
paintbox 28.40
paintbrush 29.16
painter 12.77
painterly 4.27
painting 26.13
paintwork 21.31
painty 4.52
pair 2.1
pairing 26.11
paisa 1.17
paise 12.70
paisley 4.22
Paiute 30.37
pakeha 1.9
Pakistan 25.4
Pakistani 4.31
pakora 12.66
pal 23.1
palace 28.8

o

p

paladin 25.14
Palaeocene 25.11
palaeographer 12.30
palaeographic 21.10
palaeography 4.14
Palaeolithic 21.18
Palaeozoic 21.9
palaestra 12.65
palais 3.15
palanquin 25.9
palatalize 35.12
palate 30.42
palatial 23.38
Palatinate 30.43
Palatine 25.23
Palau 8.1
palaver 12.85
Palawan 25.38
pale 23.5
paleface 28.5
Palekh 21.6
Palembang 26.1
Palenque 4.18
Paleocene 25.11
paleographer 12.30
paleographic 21.10
paleography 4.14
Paleolithic 21.18
Paleozoic 21.9
Palermo 9.18
Palestine 25.23
Palestinian 25.37
palestra 12.65
Palestrina 12.54
palette 30.22
palfrey 4.41
Palgrave 34.4
Pali 4.21
palimony 4.34
palimpsest 31.3
palindrome 24.11
palindromic 21.12
palindromist 31.9
paling 26.8
palisade 16.6
Palisades 35.27
palish 29.8
pall 23.14
Palladian 25.37
Palladio 9.4
palladium 24.16
Pallas 28.27
pallbearer 12.65
pallet 30.22
palletize 35.14
pallia 12.6
pallial 23.24
palliasse 28.1
palliate 30.8
pallid 16.10
pallium 24.16

pall-mall 23.1
pallor 12.42
pally 4.21
palm 24.2
Palma 12.50
Palmerston 25.50
palmist 31.9
palmistry 4.40
palmtop 27.8
palmy 4.29
palmyra 12.65
palomino 9.19
palooka 12.41
Palouse 28.19
palpate 30.14
palpitant 30.56
palpitate 30.16
palsgrave 34.4
palsied 16.13
palsy 4.61
palsy-walsy 4.61
palter 12.80
palterer 12.67
paltry 4.41
Paludrine 25.18
Pam 24.1
Pamela 12.43
Pamirs 35.24
pampas 28.30
pamper 12.61
Pampers 35.24
pamphlet 30.22
pamphleteer 12.4
Pamphylian 25.37
Pamplona 12.56
Pan 25.1
pan 25.4
panacea 12.4
panache 29.1
panada 12.25
Panadol 23.13
Panaji 4.17
Panama 1.1
Panamanian 25.37
panatella 12.42
pancake 21.7
panchromatic 21.17
Pancras 28.31
pancreas 28.23
pancreatic 21.17
panda 12.25
pandanus 28.29
Pandarus 28.31
pandemic 21.12
pandemonium 24.16
pander 12.25
pandit 30.21
Pandora 12.66
pane 25.7
paneer 12.4
panegyric 21.15

panegyrical 23.32
panegyrist 31.12
panegyrize 35.13
panel 23.34
panelist 31.8
panellist 31.8
panettone 3.17
panettoni 4.33
panforte 3.22
pan-fried 16.14
panfry 6.15
panful 23.21
pang 26.1
panga 12.31
Pangaea 12.3
pangolin 25.16
pangram 24.1
panhandle 23.28
panhandler 12.48
panic 21.13
panicky 4.19
Panini 4.31, 4.32
panjandrum 24.19
Pankhurst 31.26
panlike 21.19
pannage 20.7
panne 25.1
pannier 12.8
pannikin 25.15
panoply 4.27
panoptic 21.17
panorama 12.50
panoramic 21.12
panstick 21.17
pansy 4.61
pant 30.53
pantalets 28.47
pantalettes 28.47
pantechnicon 25.43
Pantelleria 12.9
pantheist 31.6
pantheon 25.37
panther 12.83
pantile 23.12
panto 9.24
pantomime 24.7
pantomimic 21.12
pantry 4.38
pants 28.47
pantsuit 30.38
pantyhose 35.19
Panzer 12.90
pap 27.1
papa 1.1
papacy 4.48
papal 23.35
papalist 31.8
paparazzi 4.45
paparazzo 9.22
papaya 12.13
paper 12.61

paperback 21.2
paperboy 10.3
paperchase 28.5
paperclip 27.6
paperer 12.67
paperhanger 12.60
paperknife 17.7
paperknives 35.35
paperweight 30.17
paperwork 21.31
papery 4.43
papier-mâché 3.21
papillae 4.24
papillon 25.25
papism 24.21
papist 31.11
papistical 23.32
papistry 4.40
papoose 28.19
pappardelle 3.15
pappy 4.36
paprika 12.39
Papua 12.20
Papuan 25.38
papyri 6.15
papyrus 28.31
par avion 25.27
Paréa 1.1
par 1.1
pará 12.64
parabases 35.8
paraben 25.5
parable 23.26
parabola 12.48
parabolic 21.11
Paracelsus 28.32
paracetamol 23.13
parachute 30.38
parachutist 31.14
paraclete 30.18
parade 16.6
parader 12.26
paradiddle 23.28
paradigm 24.7
paradigmatic 21.17
paradisal 23.37
paradise 28.13
paradisiacal 23.32
parador 7.5
paradox 28.40
paradoxical 23.32
paraffin 25.14
paraglide 16.14
paraglider 12.27
paragliding 26.5
paragon 25.41
paragraph 17.2
Paraguay 6.21
Paraguayan 25.38
parakeet 30.18
paralegal 23.30

paralipsis 28.11
parallax 28.38
parallel 23.3
parallelogram 24.1
Paralympian 25.37
Paralympics 28.39
paralyse 35.12
paralyses 35.8
paralysis 28.11
paralytic 21.17
paramedic 21.10
paramedical 23.32
parameter 12.78
paramilitary 4.43
paramo 9.18
paramount 30.55
paramountcy 4.47
paramour 12.20
Paraná 1.1
parang 26.1
paranoia 12.18
paranoid 16.24
paranormal 23.33
parapet 30.23
paraph 17.1
paraphernalia 12.6
paraphrase 35.5
paraplegia 12.35
paraplegic 21.11
paraquat 30.32
parasailing 26.8
parascend 16.41
parascender 12.26
parasite 30.30
parasitic 21.17
parasiticide 16.16
parasitology 4.17
parasol 23.13
parathion 25.24
paratrooper 12.63
paravane 25.8
par avoin 25.27
parboil 23.19
parbuckle 23.32
parcel 23.37
parch 15.2
Parcheesi 4.61
parclose 35.19
pard 16.2
pardon 25.40
pardoner 12.58
pare 2.1
paren 25.5
parent 30.56
parentage 20.9
parental 23.39
parentheses 35.8
parenthesis 28.11
parenthesize 35.14
parenthetic 21.17
parenthetical 23.32

parenthood 16.26
parer 12.65
parfait 3.10
parfleche 29.3
parfumerie 4.43
parfumier 12.7
pariah 12.13
Parian 25.37
paring 26.11
Paris 28.10
parish 29.9
parishioner 12.58
Parisian 25.37
parity 4.53
park 21.5
parka 12.37
parkin 25.15
parkland 16.45
parkour 12.20
Parks 28.38
parkway 3.25
parky 4.18
parlance 28.45
parlay 3.15
parley 4.21
parliamentarian
   25.37
parliamentary 4.43
parlor 12.42
parlormaid 16.6
parlour 12.42
parlourmaid 16.6
parlous 28.27
Parma 12.50
Parmenides 35.7
Parmentier 12.12
parmesan 25.1
Parnassian 25.37
Parnell 23.3
parochial 23.24
parodic 21.10
parodist 31.6
parody 4.13
parol 23.17
parole 23.17
parolee 4.1
paroxysm 24.21
paroxysmal 23.33
parpen 25.46
parquet 3.14
parquetry 4.40
parricidal 23.28
parricide 16.16
parrot 30.43
parrotfish 29.7
parry 4.38
parse 35.2
Parsee 4.1
parser 12.90
Parsifal 23.1
parsimonious 28.23

parsimony 4.34
parsnip 27.6
parson 25.48
parsonage 20.7
Parsons 35.31
part 30.3
partake 21.7
partaken 25.43
partaker 12.38
parterre 2.1
part-exchange 20.19
parthenogenesis
   28.11
Parthenon 25.46
Parthia 12.12
Parthian 25.37
parti pris 4.1
partial 23.38
partible 23.26
participant 30.56
participate 30.14
participatory 4.43
participial 23.24
participle 23.35
particle 23.32
particolored 16.29
particoloured 16.29
particular 12.46
particularist 31.12
particularity 4.53
parting 26.13
parti pris 4.1
partisan 25.1
partite 30.30
partitioner 12.58
partitionist 31.10
partner 12.53
Parton 25.50
partook 21.28
partridge 20.8
part song 26.15
part-time 24.7
part-timer 12.51
parturient 30.56
part-way 3.1
part-work 21.31
party 4.51
party-pooper 12.63
parvenu 11.15
parvis 28.12
pas 1.1
Pasadena 12.54
pasanda 12.25
Pascal 23.2
paschal 23.32
pas de deux 13.1
pash 29.1
pasha 12.72
Pashto 9.25
paso doble 3.15
paspalum 24.18

pasquinade 16.6
pass 28.2
passage 20.9
passageway 3.25
Passamaquoddy
   4.13
passant 30.54, 30.56
passata 12.75
passbook 21.28
Passchendaele 23.5
passé 3.20
passel 23.37
passementerie 4.43
passenger 12.35
passe-partout 11.20
passer 12.69
passer-by 6.1
passerine 25.23
pas seul 23.42
passible 23.26
passim 24.6
passing 26.12
passion 25.49
passional 23.34
passionate 30.43
passion flower 12.16
passion fruit 30.37
passive 34.7
passkey 4.18
Passover 12.86
passport 30.33
password 16.31
past 31.2
pasta 12.74
paste 31.4
pasteboard 16.20
pastel 23.39
pastern 25.50
Pasternak 21.3
Pasteur 13.1
pasticcio 9.10
pastiche 29.5
pastie 4.52
pastille 23.9
pastime 24.7
pasting 26.13
pastis 28.12
pastmaster 12.75
pastor 12.75
pastoral 23.36
pastorale 23.2
pastorate 30.43
pastrami 4.29
pastry 4.39
pasturage 20.8
pasture 12.23
pasty 4.51, 4.52
pat 30.1
pat-a-cake 21.7
Patagonia 12.8
Patagonian 25.37

p

patball 23.14
patch 15.1
patcher 12.23
patchouli 4.26
patchwork 21.31
patchy 4.11
pâté 3.22
Pate 30.7
paté de foie gras 1.1
patella 12.42
paten 25.50
patency 4.45
patent 30.56
patentee 4.1
pater 12.77
paterfamilias 28.1
paternal 23.34
paternalist 31.8
paternity 4.53
paternoster 12.79
path 32.2
Pathan 25.4
Pathé 3.23
pathetic 21.17
pathfinder 12.27
pathogenesis 28.11
pathologic 21.11
pathology 4.17
pathos 28.14
pathway 3.25
patience 28.45
patient 30.56
patina 12.55
patio 9.4
pâtisserie 4.43
patly 4.21
Pátmos 28.14
Patna 12.53
patness 28.29
patois 1.22
Paton 25.50
patrial 23.24
patriarch 21.5
patriarchal 23.32
patriarchate 30.42
patriarchy 4.18
Patricia 12.72
patrician 25.49
patriciate 30.41
patricidal 23.28
patricide 16.16
Patrick 21.15
patrilineal 23.24
patrimonial 23.24
patrimony 4.34
patriot 30.41
patriotic 21.17
Patroclus 28.27
patrol 23.17
patroller 12.44
patrolman 25.2

patrolmen 25.5
patron 25.47
patronage 20.7
patronal 23.34
patronizer 12.91
patronymic 21.12
patsy 4.45
pattée 3.22
patten 25.50
patter 12.74
pattern 25.50
patty 4.51
patulous 28.27
paucity 4.53
Paul 23.14
Paula 12.44
Paulette 30.4
Pauli 4.25
Pauline 25.10, 25.22
Pauling 26.8
paunch 29.20
paunchy 4.50
pauper 12.62
pauperdom 24.17
pauperize 35.13
Pausanias 28.23
pause 35.17
pavage 20.9
pavane 25.1
Pavarotti 4.54
paveé 3.24
pave 34.4
paver 12.85
pavilion 25.37
paving 26.14
pavior 12.12
paviour 12.12
Pavlov 34.10
Pavlova 12.86
Pavlovian 25.37
pavonine 25.23
paw 7.1
pawky 4.19
pawl 23.14
pawn 25.28
pawnbroker 12.40
pawnbroking 26.7
Pawnee 4.1
pawnshop 27.8
pawpaw 7.14
pax 28.38
Paxton 25.50
pay 3.1
payable 23.26
payback 21.2
payday 3.9
pay dirt 30.45
payee 4.1
payer 12.2
payload 16.23
paymaster 12.75

payment 30.56
paynim 24.6
payoff 17.8
payola 12.44
payout 30.34
payphone 25.30
payroll 23.18
paysage 19.1
payslip 27.6
paywall 23.15
Paz 35.2
pea 4.1
peace 28.6
peacekeeper 12.61
peacekeeping 26.10
peacemaker 12.38
peacemaking 26.7
peacenik 21.13
peacetime 24.7
peach 15.5
peachick 21.9
peachy 4.11
peacock 21.20
peafowl 23.16
peahen 25.5
peak 21.8
Peake 21.8
peakload 16.23
peaky 4.18
peal 23.7
pean 25.36
peanut 30.40
pear 2.1
Pearce 28.23
pearl 23.42
pearler 12.49
pearlescent 30.56
Pearl Harbor 12.21
pearlite 30.28
pearlized 16.50
pearly 4.28
Pears 35.4, 35.24
pearshaped 30.58
Pearson 28.23
peart 30.41
peasant 30.56
peasantry 4.38
peasanty 4.51
pease 35.6
peasepudding 26.5
peashooter 12.81
pea-souper 12.63
peat 30.18
peatland 16.40
peatmoss 28.14
peaty 4.52
peau-de-soie 1.1
pebble 23.26
pebbledash 29.1
pebbly 4.27
pecan 25.1

peccadillo 9.17
peccant 30.56
peccary 4.43
peck 21.6
pecker 12.37
peckish 29.8
pecorino 9.19
pecten 25.19
pectin 25.19
pectinate 30.43
pectoral 23.36
peculiar 12.6
peculiarity 4.53
pecuniary 4.43
pedagogic 21.11
pedagogue 18.8
pedagogy 4.17
pedal 23.28
pedalo 9.17
pedant 30.56
pedantic 21.17
pedantry 4.38
peddle 23.28
pederast 31.1
pederastic 21.17
pederasty 4.51
pedestal 23.39
pedestrian 25.37
pediatric 21.15
pediatrician 25.49
pedicab 14.1
pedicure 12.20
pedicurist 31.12
pedigree 4.40
pedlar 12.42
pedlary 4.43
pedologist 31.7
pedometer 12.78
pedophile 23.11
pedophilia 12.6
Pedro 9.21
peduncle 23.32
pee 4.1
peek 21.8
peekaboo 11.1
peel 23.7
peeler 12.43
peeling 26.8
Peelite 30.28
peen 25.9
peep 27.5
peep-bo 9.20
peeper 12.61
peephole 23.17
peep show 9.23
peepul 23.35
peer 12.4
peerage 20.8
peeress 28.10
peer group 27.11
peeve 34.5

peevish 29.10
peewee 4.59
peewit 30.25
peg 18.3
Pegasus 28.32
Peg-board 16.20
pegboard 16.20
Peggy 4.15
peg-leg 18.3
Pegu 11.22
Pei 3.1
peignoir 1.22
Peirce 28.23
pekan 25.43
Pekinese 35.6
Peking 26.3
pekoe 9.16
Pelagian 25.37
Pelagius 28.23
pelargonium 24.16
Pelé 3.15
Peleus 28.35
pelham 24.18
pelican 25.43
Pelion 25.37
pelisse 28.6
pelite 30.28
pellagra 12.64
pellet 30.22
pelletize 35.14
pell-mell 23.3
pellucid 16.11
pelmet 30.23
Peloponnese 35.6
Pelops 28.46
pelorus 28.31
pelota 12.79
peloton 25.26
pelt 30.51
pelta 12.76
peltate 30.16
peltry 4.38
pelvic 21.18
pelvis 28.12
Pemba 12.21
Pembroke 21.28
pen 25.5
penal 23.34
penalty 4.51
penance 28.45
Penang 26.1
penates 35.9
pence 28.44
penchant 25.26
pencil 23.37
penciler 12.48
penciller 12.48
pendant 30.56
pendency 4.48
pendent 30.56
pendragon 25.41

pendulous 28.27
pendulum 24.18
Penelope 4.37
penetrate 30.15
penfriend 16.41
penguin 25.20
penicillin 25.16
penile 23.11
peninsula 12.46
penis 28.9
Penistone 25.50
penitence 28.45
penitent 30.56
penitential 23.38
penitentiary 4.43
penknife 17.7
penknives 35.35
penlight 30.28
penman 25.45
penmen 25.45
Penn 25.5
pennant 30.56
penne 4.31
penniua 1.2
pennies 35.10
pennon 25.46
Pennsylvania 12.8
Pennsylvanian
  25.37
penny 4.31
pennyfarthing
  26.14
pennyweight 30.17
pennyworth 32.13
penpusher 12.73
pensée 3.20
pension 25.27, 25.49
pensioner 12.58
pensive 34.7
penstock 21.21
pent 30.53
pentachord 16.21
pentacle 23.32
pentad 16.1
pentagon 25.41
pentagram 24.1
pentameter 12.78
pentangle 23.30
Pentateuch 21.27
pentateuchal 23.32
pentathlete 30.18
pentathlon 25.44
Pentecost 31.17
Pentecostal 23.39
Pentecostalist 31.8
penthouse 28.16
Pentothal 23.1
penult 30.51
penultimate 30.43
penumbra 12.66
penumbrae 4.42

penurious 28.23
penury 4.41
Penza 12.90
Penzance 28.44
peon 25.36
peony 4.34
people 23.35
pep 27.3
Pepe 3.18
peplum 24.18
pepper 12.61
pepperbox 28.40
peppercorn 25.28
peppermint 30.54
pepperminty 4.53
pepperoni 4.33
pepperpot 30.32
peppery 4.43
peppy 4.36
peptalk 21.22
peptic 21.17
peptide 16.17
Pepäs 28.46
per 13.1
peradventure 12.23
Perak 12.65
perambulate 30.11
perambulatory 4.43
per annum 24.19
per capita 12.78
per caput 30.39
perceive 34.5
perceiver 12.85
percent 30.53
percentage 20.9
percentile 23.12
percept 30.58
perceptible 23.26
perception 25.49
perceptional 23.34
perceptual 23.25
perch 15.14
perchance 28.44
percher 12.24
Percheron 25.26
percipience 28.45
percipient 30.56
Percival 23.40
percolate 30.11
percussionist 31.10
percussive 34.7
Percy 4.49
per diem 24.3
Perdita 12.78
père 2.1
peregrinate 30.13
peregrine 25.18
Perelman 25.45
peremptory 4.43
perennial 23.24
Peres 35.3

perestroika 12.39
perfect 30.48, 30.49
perfecter 12.76
perfectible 23.26
perfection 25.49
perfectionist 31.10
perfecto 9.24
perfervid 16.13
perfidious 28.23
perfidy 4.12
perfin 25.14
perforate 30.15,
  30.43
perforce 28.15
perform 24.9
performance 28.45
performer 12.52
perfume 24.12
perfumer 12.52
perfumery 4.43
perfumy 4.30
perfunctory 4.43
perfuse 35.21
Pergamum 24.19
pergola 12.48
perhaps 28.46
peri 4.43
periapt 30.58
pericarditis 28.12
periclase 35.5
Periclean 25.36
Pericles 35.7
pericope 4.37
peridot 30.31
peril 23.9
perilous 28.27
perimeter 12.78
period 16.28
periodic 21.10
periodical 23.32
periodize 35.11
peripatetic 21.17
peripeteia 12.13
peripheral 23.36
periphery 4.43
periphrases 35.8
periphrasis 28.11
periphrastic 21.17
peripteral 23.36
periscope 27.10
perish 29.9
perisher 12.72
peristyle 23.12
peritoneal 23.23
peritoneum 24.15
peritonitis 28.12
periwig 18.6
periwinkle 23.32
perjure 12.36
perjurer 12.67
perjurious 28.23

p

perjury 4.43
perk 21.31
Perkin 25.15
Perks 28.41
perky 4.20
perlite 30.28
perlocution 25.49
perm 24.22
permafrost 31.17
permanence 28.45
permanency 4.48
permanent 30.56
permeate 30.8
Permian 25.37
permissible 23.26
permissive 34.7
permit 30.20, 30.23
permittee 4.1
permitter 12.78
permutate 30.16
permute 30.37
pernicious 28.33
pernickety 4.53
pernoctate 30.16
Pernod 9.19
perorate 30.15
peroxide 16.16
perpend 16.41
perpendicular 12.46
perpetrate 30.15
perpetual 23.25
perpetuance 28.45
perpetuate 30.8
perpetuity 4.53
perplex 28.38
perplexity 4.53
perquisite 30.25
Perrault 9.1
Perrin 25.3, 25.18
perron 25.47
perry 4.38
per se 3.1
perse 28.36
persecute 30.38
persecution 25.49
persecutor 12.81
persecutory 4.43
Perseids 35.27
Persephone 4.34
Persepolis 28.8
Perseus 28.23
perseverance 28.45
persevere 12.4
Persia 12.73
Persian 25.49
persiflage 19.1
persimmon 25.45
persist 31.6
persistence 28.45
persistency 4.48

persistent 30.56
person 25.48
persona 12.56
personae 6.13
personage 20.7
personal 23.34
personalty 4.55
persona non
  grata 12.75
personate 30.13
personifier 12.14
personify 6.7
personnel 23.3
perspectival 23.40
perspex 28.38
perspicacious 28.33
perspicacity 4.53
perspicuity 4.53
perspicuous 28.24
perspiratory 4.43
perspire 12.13
persuade 16.6
persuader 12.26
persuasible 23.26
persuasion 25.42
persuasive 34.7
pert 30.45
pertain 25.7
Perth 32.14
pertinacious 28.33
pertinacity 4.53
pertinence 28.45
pertinency 4.48
pertinent 30.56
perturb 14.15
Peru 11.1
Perugia 12.6
peruke 21.27
perusal 23.41
peruse 35.21
peruser 12.92
Perutz 28.47
Peruvian 25.37
perv 34.14
pervade 16.6
pervasion 25.42
pervasive 34.7
perverse 28.36
perversion 25.49
perversity 4.53
pervert 30.45
perverter 12.82
pervious 28.23
Pesach 21.5
peseta 12.77
pesky 4.18
peso 9.22
pessary 4.43
pessimist 31.9
pest 31.3
pester 12.76

pesterer 12.67
pesticidal 23.28
pesticide 16.16
pestiferous 28.31
pestilence 28.45
pestilent 30.56
pestilential 23.38
pestle 23.37
pesto 9.24
pet 30.4
Peta 12.77
Pétain 25.1
petal 23.39
pétanque 21.34
petard 16.2
petasus 28.32
petcock 21.20
Pete 30.18
peter 12.77
Peterborough 12.67
Peters 35.24
petersham 24.20
Peterson 25.48
petit 4.51
petite 30.18
petition 25.49
petitionary 4.43
petitioner 12.58
petit mal 23.1
Petra 12.64
Petrarch 21.5
Petrarchan 25.43
petrel 23.36
Petrie 4.39
petrifaction 25.49
petrify 6.7
petrochemical 23.32
Petrograd 16.1
petrol 23.36
petrolatum 24.20
petroleum 24.16
Petronius 28.23
petter 12.76
petticoat 30.35
pettifog 18.8
pettifogger 12.32
pettifoggery 4.43
pettish 29.10
petty 4.51
Petula 12.45
petulance 28.45
petulant 30.56
petunia 12.8
Pevsner 12.53
pew 11.1
pewter 12.81
peyote 4.54
Pfennig 18.6
pH 15.4
Phaedra 12.65
Phaethon 25.51

phaeton 25.50
phagocyte 30.30
phalanger 12.35
phalangist 31.7
phalanx 28.41
phalli 6.11
phallic 21.11
phallocentric 21.15
phallus 28.27
phantasm 24.21
phantasmagoria
  12.10
phantasmagoric
  21.15
phantasmagorical
  23.32
phantasmal 23.33
phantasmic 21.12
phantasy 4.48
phantom 24.20
pharaoh 9.21
Pharisaic 21.9
Pharisaical 23.32
Pharisee 4.46
pharmaceutical 23.32
pharmacist 31.13
pharmacology 4.17
pharmacopoeia 12.3
pharmacy 4.48
pharming 26.9
pharos 28.14
pharyngitis 28.12
pharynx 28.41
phase 35.5
phasic 21.18
Phasmida 12.27
pheasant 30.56
pheasantry 4.38
phenobarbital 23.39
phenomena 12.55
phenomenal 23.34
phenomenalist 31.8
phenomenalize
  35.12
phenomenon 25.46
phenotype 27.7
pheromone 25.30
phi 6.1
phial 23.25
Phidias 28.1
Phil 23.8
Philadelphia 12.5
Philadelphian 25.37
philander 12.25
philanderer 12.67
philanthrope 27.10
philanthropic 21.14
philanthropist
  31.11
philanthropize
  35.13

philanthropy 4.37
philatelic 21.11
philatelist 31.8
philately 4.27
Philby 4.10
Philemon 25.45
philharmonic 21.13
philhellene 25.10
Philip 27.6
Philippa 12.62
Philippi 6.14
philippic 21.14
Philippine 25.11
Philistine 25.23
Phillida 12.27
Phillips 28.46
Philly 4.24
philogynist 31.10
philologian 25.37
Philomela 12.43
Philomena 12.54
philosopher 12.30
philosophic 21.10
philosophizer
12.91
philosophy 4.14
philter 12.78
philtre 12.78
philtrum 24.14
Phineas 28.23
phiz 35.10
phizog 18.8
phlegm 24.3
phlegmatic 21.17
phlox 28.40
Phnom Penh 25.5
pho 9.1
phobia 12.5
phobic 21.9
Phobos 28.14
phoebe 4.10
Phoebus 28.24
Phoenicia 12.72
Phoenician 25.49
phoenix 28.39
phon 25.24
phone 25.30
phonecard 16.2
phone-in 25.18
phoneme 24.5
phonetic 21.17
phoney 4.33
phonic 21.13
phono 9.19
phonograph 17.2
phonolite 30.28
phooey 4.8
phosgene 25.10
phosphate 30.9
phosphor 12.30
phosphoresce 28.3

phosphorescence
28.45
phosphorescent
30.56
phosphoric 21.15
phosphorite 30.29
phosphorous 28.31
phosphorus 28.31
photic 21.17
Photius 28.23
photo 9.25
photocall 23.15
photochemical
23.32
photochemistry
4.40
photochromic 21.12
photocopier 12.9
photocopy 4.36
photoelectric 21.15
photofit 30.21
photogenic 21.13
photogram 24.1
photograph 17.2
photographer 12.30
photographic 21.10
photography 4.14
photogravure 12.20
photojournalist
31.8
photometer 12.78
photomontage 19.1
photon 25.26
photoset 30.5
photosetter 12.76
photosetting 26.13
photostat 30.2
photostatic 21.17
photosynthesis
28.11
photosynthesize
35.14
photosynthetic
21.17
phototropic 21.14
phrasal 23.41
phrase 35.5
phrase book 21.28
phraseology 4.17
phrasing 26.14
phrenology 4.17
Phrygia 12.6
Phrygian 25.37
Phuket 30.4
phut 30.40
phylactery 4.43
Phyllis 28.8
phyllite 30.28
phylum 24.18
physical 23.32
physicalist 31.8

physician 25.49
physicist 31.13
physio 9.4
physiognomic 21.12
physiognomical
23.32
physiognomist 31.9
physiognomy 4.30
physiology 4.17
physiotherapist
31.11
physiotherapy 4.37
physique 21.8
phytoplankton
25.50
pi 6.1
Piaf 17.1
piaffe 17.1
Piaget 3.12
pianissimo 9.18
pianist 31.10
piano 9.19
pianoforte 4.54
pianola 12.44
piaster 12.74
piastre 12.74
piazza 12.69
pibroch 21.21
pic 21.9
pica 12.40
picador 7.5
Picard 16.2
Picardy 4.13
picaresque 21.35
Picasso 9.22
picayune 25.33
Piccadilly 4.24
piccalilli 4.24
piccolo 9.17
pick 21.9
pickaback 21.2
pickax 28.38
pickaxe 28.38
picker 12.39
pickerel 23.36
Pickering 26.11
picket 30.21
picketer 12.78
Pickford 16.28
pickings 35.32
pickle 23.32
pickler 12.48
Pickles 35.29
pick-me-up 27.13
pickpocket 30.21
pickpocketing 26.13
pickup 27.13
Pickwickian 25.37
picky 4.19
picnic 21.13
picnicker 12.39

picot 9.16
picquet 30.4, 30.21
Pict 30.49
Pictish 29.10
pictograph 17.2
pictographic 21.10
pictorial 23.24
picture 12.23
picture book 21.28
picturesque 21.35
piddle 23.28
piddler 12.48
piddock 21.30
pidgin 25.14
pie 6.1
piebald 16.36
piece 28.6
pièce de
résistance 28.44
piecemeal 23.7
piecer 12.69
piecework 21.31
pied-à-terre 2.1
pied 16.14
piedmont 30.54
Piedmontese 35.6
pie-eyed 16.14
pier 12.4
pierce 28.23
piercer 12.71
Pierre 2.1, 12.4
Pierrot 9.21
Piers 35.24
pietà 1.1
pietist 31.14
piety 4.53
piffle 23.29
piffling 26.8
pig 18.6
pigeon 25.14
pigeonhole 23.17
piggery 4.43
piggish 29.7
Piggott 30.42
piggy 4.15
piggyback 21.2
piggy bank 21.33
pig-headed 16.9
piglet 30.22
piglike 21.19
pigment 30.53, 30.56
pigpen 25.5
pigskin 25.15
pigsty 5.18
pigswill 23.10
pigtail 23.6
pika 12.40
pike 21.19
pikelet 30.22
pikeperch 15.14
piker 12.40

p

pikestaff 17.2
pilaf 17.1
pilaster 12.74
Pilate 30.42
pilchard 16.28
pile 23.11
piledriver 12.86
piledriving 26.14
pile-up 27.13
pilfer 12.30
pilferage 20.8
pilferer 12.67
pilgrim 24.6
pilgrimage 20.7
piling 26.8
pill 23.8
pillage 20.6
pillager 12.35
pillar 12.43
pillar box 28.40
pillaret 30.4
pillbox 28.40
Pilling 26.8
pillion 25.52
pillock 21.30
pillory 4.43
pillow 9.17
pillowcase 28.5
pillowslip 27.6
pillowy 4.7
pillwort 30.45
pilot 30.42
pilotage 20.9
Pilsen 25.52
Pilsner 12.55
Pima 12.51
pimiento 9.24
pimp 27.17
pimpernel 23.3
pimple 23.35
pimply 4.24
pin-up 27.13
pin 25.13
piña colada 12.25
pinafore 7.6
pinball 23.14
pince-nez 3.1
pincer 12.70
pincette 30.4
pinch 29.20
pinchbeck 21.6
pinchpenny 4.31
pincushion 25.49
Pindar 1.6
Pindaric 21.15
pine 25.21
pineapple 23.35
pine cone 25.30
Pinero 9.21
pinery 4.43
pinetree 4.40

pinewood 16.26
pinfold 16.37
ping 26.3
pinger 12.60
pingpong 26.15
pinhead 16.3
pinheaded 16.9
pinhole 23.17
pinion 25.52
pink 21.33
Pinkerton 25.50
pink-eye 6.10
pinkie 4.19
pinkish 29.8
pinko 9.16
pinky 4.19
pinnace 28.9
pinnacle 23.32
pinny 4.32
Pinochet 3.21
pinochle 23.32
pinole 4.25, 23.17
piñon 25.24
Pinot Blanc 25.24
Pinot Noir 1.1
pinpoint 30.55
pinprick 21.15
pinstripe 27.7
pint 30.54
Pinta 12.78
pintail 23.6
Pinter 12.78
pintle 23.39
pinto 9.24
pin-up 27.13
pinwheel 23.7
piny 4.32
Pinyin 25.13
pioneer 12.4
pious 28.24
pip 27.6
pipe 27.7
pipeclay 3.15
pipecleaner 12.54
pipefish 29.7
pipeline 25.22
piper 12.62
pipette 30.4
pipistrelle 23.3
pipit 30.23
pipkin 25.15
Pippa 12.62
pippin 25.18
pipsqueak 21.8
pipy 4.36
piquancy 4.48
piquant 30.56
piqué 3.14
pique 21.8
piquet 30.4, 30.21
piquillo 9.28

piracy 4.48
Piraeus 28.22
Pirandello 9.17
Piranesi 4.61
piranha 12.53
pirate 30.43
piratic 21.17
piratical 23.32
piripiri 4.40
pirog 18.10
pirogue 18.10
pirouette 30.4
Pisa 12.90
pis aller 3.15
Pisano 9.19
piscatorial 23.24
piscatory 4.43
piscean 25.36
Piscean 25.37
Pisces 35.8
pisciculture 12.24
pisciculturist 31.12
piscina 12.54
piscine 25.11, 25.23
pisco 9.16
pish 29.6
Pisidian 25.37
piss 28.7
Pissarro 9.21
pissoir 1.22
piss-taker 12.38
piss-taking 26.7
piss-up 27.13
pistachio 9.4
piste 31.5
pisteur 13.1
pistil 23.9
pistol 23.39
pistole 23.18
pistoleer 12.4
piston 25.50
pistou 11.20
pit 30.20
pit-a-pat 30.1
pitch 15.6
pitchblack 21.1
pitcher 12.23
pitchfork 21.22
pitchman 25.45
pitchmen 25.45
pitchpine 25.23
pitchpipe 27.7
pitchside 16.14
pitchstone 25.31
pitchy 4.11
piteous 28.23
pitfall 23.15
pith 32.6
pithead 16.3
pithy 4.56
pitman 25.45

pitmen 25.45
piton 25.26
Pitt 30.20
pitta 12.78
pittance 28.45
pitter-patter 12.74
Pitti 4.53
pittosporum 24.19
Pittsburgh 18.13
pity 4.53
pivot 30.44
pivotal 23.39
pix 28.39
pixel 23.37
pixie 4.46
pixilated 16.12
Pizarro 9.21
pizza 12.69
pizzazz 35.1
pizzeria 12.3
pizzicato 9.24
pizzle 23.41
placard 16.2
placate 30.7
placatory 4.43
place 28.5
placebo 9.9
placenta 12.76
placer 12.69
placet 30.5
placid 16.11
placidity 4.53
placing 26.12
placket 30.21
plafond 25.24
plage 19.1
plagiarist 31.12
plagiarizer 12.91
plague 18.4
plaguy 4.15
plaice 28.5
plaid 16.1
plaided 16.9
plain 25.7
plainchant 30.53
plainclothes 35.19
plainsman 25.45
plainsmen 25.45
plainsong 26.15
plain-spoken 25.43
plaint 30.54
plaintiff 17.6
plait 30.1
plan 25.1
planar 12.54
planarian 25.37
planchet 30.24
planchette 30.4
Planck 21.33
plane 25.7
planer 12.54

p

planet 30.23
planetarium 24.16
planetary 4.43
planetoid 16.24
plangency 4.48
plangent 30.56
planisphere 12.5
plank 21.33
plankton 25.50
planner 12.53
plant 30.53
Plantagenet 30.23
plantain 25.19
planter 12.75
planting 26.13
plantlet 30.22
plant-like 21.19
plaque 21.1
plash 29.1
plashy 4.50
plasma 12.50
plasmodia 12.5
plasmodial 23.24
plasmodium 24.16
plaster 12.75
plasterboard 16.20
plasterer 12.67
plasterwork 21.31
plastery 4.43
plastic 21.17
Plasticine 25.11
plasticky 4.19
plastral 23.36
plastron 25.47
plat 30.1
plat du jour 12.20
plate 30.7
plateau 9.24
plateaux 35.19
platelet 30.22
platen 25.50
plater 12.77
plateresque 21.35
platform 24.9
Plath 32.1
plating 26.13
platinum 24.19
platitude 16.25
platitudinize 35.13
platitudinous 28.29
Plato 9.24
Platonic 21.13
Platonist 31.10
platoon 25.33
platteland 16.40
platter 12.74
platypus 28.30
plaudit 30.21
plausible 23.26
Plautus 28.34
play 3.1

playa 12.13
play-act 30.48
playback 21.2
playbill 23.8
playbook 21.28
playboy 10.3
player 12.2
Playfair 2.5
playfellow 9.17
playground 16.43
playgroup 27.11
playhouse 28.16
playlet 30.22
playlist 31.8
playmaker 12.38
playmate 30.12
playoff 17.8
playpen 25.5
playroom 24.12
playschool 23.20
playsuit 30.38
plaything 26.14
playtime 24.7
playwright 30.29
plaza 12.90
plc 4.1
plea 4.1
pleach 15.5
plead 16.7
pleader 12.26
pleading 26.5
pleasance 28.45
pleasant 30.56
pleasantry 4.38
please 35.6
pleasure 12.33
pleat 30.18
pleb 14.3
plebby 4.10
plebe 14.6
plebeian 25.36
plebiscitary 4.43
plebiscite 30.24
plectra 12.64
plectrum 24.19
pledge 20.3
pledgee 4.1
pledger 12.35
Pleiades 35.7
plein-air 2.1
Pleistocene 25.11
plenary 4.43
plenipotentiary
4.43
plenitude 16.25
plenteous 28.23
plenty 4.51
plenum 24.19
pleonasm 24.21
pleonastic 21.17
plesiosaur 7.16

plethora 12.67
pleurisy 4.48
Pleven 25.51
plew 11.1
plexus 28.32
pliable 23.26
pliancy 4.48
pliant 30.56
plié 3.2
pliers 35.24
plight 30.26
plimsoll 23.37
plink 21.33
plinth 32.19
Pliny 4.32
Pliocene 25.11
plissé 3.20
plod 16.18
plodder 12.28
plonk 21.34
plonker 12.40
plop 27.8
plosive 34.7
plot 30.31
Plotinus 28.29
plotter 12.79
plough 8.1
plougher 12.16
ploughman 25.45
ploughmen 25.45
ploughshare 2.13
plover 12.87
plow 8.1
plower 12.16
plowman 25.45
plowmen 25.45
plowshare 2.13
ploy 10.1
pluck 21.29
plucker 12.41
plucky 4.20
plug 18.12
plugger 12.32
plughole 23.17
plug-ugly 4.26
plum 24.14
plumage 20.7
plumb 24.14
plumber 12.52
plumb line 25.22
plume 24.12
plummet 30.23
plummy 4.30
plump 27.17
plumpish 29.9
plumpy 4.37
plumy 4.30
plunder 12.29
plunderer 12.67
plundering 26.11
plunge 20.19

plunger 12.36
plunk 21.34
pluperfect 30.49
plural 23.36
pluralist 31.8
plus 28.21
plus-fours 35.17
plus-one 25.35
plush 29.16
plushy 4.50
Plutarch 21.5
Pluto 9.25
plutocracy 4.48
plutocrat 30.2
plutocratic 21.17
Plutonian 25.37
Plutonic 21.13
plutonium 24.16
pluvial 23.24
ply 6.1
Plymouth 32.13
plywood 16.26
pneumatic 21.17
pneumonia 12.8
Pnyx 28.39
po 9.1
poach 15.10
poacher 12.24
poblano 9.19
Pocahontas 28.34
pochard 16.28
pochette 30.4
pock 21.20
pocket 30.21
pocketbook 21.28
pockmark 21.5
pocky 4.19
poco 9.16
pod 16.18
podgy 4.17
podia 12.5
podiatry 4.43
podium 24.16
Poe 9.1
poem 24.6
poesy 4.61
poet 30.20
poetaster 12.74
poetess 28.12
poetic 21.17
poetical 23.32
poeticize 35.14
poetize 35.14
poetry 4.40
po-faced 31.4
pogo 9.13
pogonia 12.8
pogrom 24.19
poi 10.1
poignance 28.45
poignancy 4.48

p

poignant 30.56
poind 16.43
Poindexter 12.76
poinsettia 12.12
point 30.55
point-blank 21.33
pointe 30.53
pointer 12.81
pointes 30.53
pointillist 31.15
point-to-point 30.55
pointy 4.54
poise 35.20
poison 25.52
poisoner 12.58
poisoning 26.9
poisonous 28.29
Poitier 3.3
Poitiers 3.3
Poitou 11.1
poke 21.24
poker 12.40
pokey 4.20
poky 4.20
pol 23.13
Poland 16.45
Polanski 4.18
polar 12.44
Polaris 28.10
polarity 4.53
Polaroid 16.24
polder 12.28
pole 23.17
poleaxe 28.38
polecat 30.1
polemic 21.12
polemical 23.32
polemicist 31.13
polemicize 35.14
polenta 12.76
polevault 30.51
pole-vaulter 12.80
poleward 16.30
police 28.6
policeman 25.45
policemen 25.45
policewoman 25.45
policewomen 25.17
policy 4.46
policyholder 12.28
polio 9.4
polis 28.8
Polisario 9.4
Polish 29.8
polisher 12.72
Politburo 9.21
polite 30.26
politesse 28.3
politic 21.17
political 23.32
politician 25.49

politicking 26.7
politico 9.16
polity 4.53
polka 12.40
polka dot 30.31
poll 23.13, 23.17
pollack 21.30
pollan 25.44
pollard 16.29
pollee 4.1
pollen 25.44
pollinate 30.13
polliwog 18.8
pollock 21.30
pollster 12.80
pollutant 30.56
pollute 30.37
polluter 12.81
pollution 25.49
Pollux 28.41
polly 4.25
Pollyanna 12.53
Pollyannaish 29.6
polo 9.17
polonaise 35.5
polonium 24.16
polony 4.33
poltergeist 31.16
poltroon 25.33
poltroonery 4.43
poly 4.25
polyamide 16.14
polyandrous 28.31
polyandry 4.38
polyanthus 28.35
Polybius 28.23
polychaete 30.18
polychromatic 21.17
polychrome 24.11
polychromy 4.29
Polyclitus 28.34
polycyclic 21.11
polyester 12.76
Polyfilla 12.43
polygamist 31.9
polygamous 28.28
polygamy 4.30
polygeny 4.32
polyglot 30.31
polygon 25.41
polygonum 24.19
polygraph 17.2
polygynous 28.29
polygyny 4.32
polyhedron 25.47
polymath 32.1
polymathic 21.18
polymathy 4.56
polymer 12.51
polymerase 35.5
polymorphic 21.10

polymorphous 28.25
Polynesia 12.89
Polynesian 25.52
polyp 27.6
polyphase 35.5
Polyphemus 28.28
polyphonic 21.13
polyphonous 28.29
polyphony 4.34
polyptych 21.17
polystyrene 25.11
polysyllabic 21.9
polytechnic 21.13
polytheist 31.6
polythene 25.12
polytonal 23.34
polyunsaturate 30.15
polyunsaturates 28.47
polyurethane 25.8
pom 24.8
pomace 28.8
pomade 16.2
pomander 12.25
pomatum 24.20
pomegranate 30.23
pomelo 9.17
Pomerania 12.8
Pomeranian 25.37
pomfret 30.24
pommel 23.33
pommie 4.29
pommy 4.29
pomp 27.17
Pompadour 12.20
pompano 9.19
Pompeii 4.2
Pompey 4.36
Pompidou 11.6
pompom 24.8
pomposity 4.53
pompous 28.30
ponce 28.44
poncey 4.46
poncho 9.23
pond 16.42
ponder 12.28
pondering 26.11
ponderosa 12.92
ponderosity 4.53
ponderous 28.31
Pondicherry 4.38
pondweed 16.7
pone 25.30
pong 26.15
ponga 12.60
pongal 23.30
pongo 9.13
pongy 4.35

poniard 16.30
pons asinorum 24.19
pont 30.54
Pontianak 21.3
pontifex 28.38
pontiff 17.6
pontifical 23.32
pontificate 30.10, 30.42
pontifices 35.8
Pontine Marshes 35.10
pontoon 25.33
Pontormo 9.18
Pontus 28.34
pony 4.33
ponytail 23.6
pooch 15.11
poodle 23.28
pooh 11.1
pooh-bah 1.1
pooh-pooh 11.1
pooka 12.41
pool 23.20
Poole 23.20
poolroom 24.12
poolside 16.16
poon 25.33
Poona 12.56
poop 27.11
pooper-scooper 12.63
poor 7.1
poorhouse 28.16
poorly 4.25
Pooterish 29.9
pootle 23.39
pop 27.8
popcorn 25.28
pope 27.10
popedom 24.17
Popemobile 23.7
popery 4.43
popeyed 16.14
popgun 25.35
popinjay 3.13
poplar 12.44
poplin 25.16
Popocatépetl 23.39
popover 12.86
poppa 12.62
poppadom 24.17
popper 12.62
poppet 30.23
poppied 16.10
popple 23.35
poppy 4.36
poppycock 21.20
Popsicle 23.32
popsy 4.46

populace 28.27
popular 12.46
popularity 4.53
popularizer 12.91
populate 30.11
populist 31.8
populous 28.27
porbeagle 23.30
porcelain 25.16
porcellaneous 28.23
porcellanous 28.29
porch 15.8
porcine 25.23
porcini 4.31
porcupine 25.23
pore 7.1
porgy 4.15
Pori 4.41
pork 21.22
porker 12.40
porkling 26.8
porky 4.19
porn 25.28
porno 9.19
pornographer 12.30
pornographic 21.10
pornography 4.14
porosity 4.53
porous 28.31
porphyry 4.40
porpoise 28.30
porridge 20.8
porridgy 4.17
porringer 12.35
Porsche 29.12
Porsena 12.55
port 30.33
portage 20.9
Portakabin 25.13
portal 23.39
portamenti 4.51
portamento 9.24
Port-au-Prince 28.44
portcullis 28.8
Porte 30.33
portend 16.41
portent 30.53
portentous 28.34
porter 12.80
porterage 20.8
porterhouse 28.16
portfolio 9.4
Port Harcourt 30.33
porthole 23.17
Portia 12.73
portico 9.16
portion 25.49
Portland 16.45
portly 4.25
portmanteau 9.24

portmanteaux 35.19
Port Moresby 4.10
Porto 9.25
Porto Alegre 12.64
Portobello 9.17
Port-of-Spain 25.7
portolan 25.44
Porto Novo 9.27
portrait 30.15
portraitist 31.14
portraiture 12.23
portray 3.1
portrayal 23.23
portrayer 12.2
Portsmouth 32.13
Portugal 23.30
Portuguese 35.6
pose 35.19
Poseidon 25.40
poser 12.92
poseur 13.1
posey 4.61
posh 29.11
posit 30.25
position 25.49
positional 23.34
positioner 12.58
positivist 31.15
positron 25.26
posse 4.46
possess 28.3
possessive 34.7
possessor 12.69
possessory 4.43
posset 30.24
possible 23.26
possum 24.20
post 31.20
postage 20.9
postal 23.39
postcolonial 23.24
poste restante 30.54
poster 12.80
posterior 12.10
posterity 4.53
postern 25.50
post hoc 21.20
postie 4.54
postil 23.9
postilion 25.37
posting 26.13
postlude 16.25
postman 25.45
postmen 25.45
postmortem 24.20
post-partum 24.20
postponer 12.56
postulant 30.56
postulate 30.11,
    30.42
posture 12.24

posturer 12.67
posturing 26.11
posy 4.61
pot 30.31
potable 23.26
potage 19.1
potager 12.36
potash 29.1
potassic 21.16
potassium 24.16
potation 25.49
potato 9.24
pot-au-feu 13.1
potboiler 12.44
poteen 25.9
Potemkin 25.15
potence 28.45
potency 4.47
potent 30.56
potentate 30.16
potential 23.38
potentiate 30.8
potful 23.21
pother 12.84
potherb 14.15
pothole 23.17
potholer 12.44
pothouse 28.16
potion 25.49
Potiphar 12.30
Potomac 21.3
potoroo 11.1
potpourri 4.41
Potsdam 24.1
potsherd 16.31
potshot 30.32
pottage 20.9
potter 12.79
potterer 12.67
Potteries 35.10
pottery 4.43
pottle 23.39
potty 4.54
pouch 15.9
pouchy 4.11
pouffe 17.13, 17.14
Poulenc 21.33
poult 30.51
poult-de-soie 1.1
poulterer 12.67
poultice 28.12
poultry 4.41
pounce 28.44
pouncer 12.70
pound 16.43
poundage 20.6
poundal 23.28
pounder 12.28
pour 7.1
pourboire 1.22
pourer 12.66

pousada 12.25
Poussin 25.3
pout 30.34
pouter 12.80
pouty 4.54
poverty 4.55
pow 8.1
powder 12.28
powder puff 17.15
powdery 4.43
Powell 23.25
power 12.16
powerboat 30.35
powerhouse 28.16
power pack 21.3
Powers 35.24
powwow 8.12
Powys 28.7
pox 28.40
poxy 4.46
Poznan 25.2
practical 23.32
practice 28.12
practicer 12.70
practicum 24.18
practise 28.12
practiser 12.70
practitioner 12.58
Prado 9.11
praecipe 4.36
praemunire 4.43
praenomen 25.5
praetor 12.77
praetorian 25.37
pragmatic 21.17
pragmatist 31.14
Prague 18.2
Praha 1.9
Praia 12.13
prairie 4.39
praise 35.5
praiser 12.90
praiseworthy 4.57
Prakrit 30.24
praline 25.10
pram 24.1
prana 12.53
pranayama 12.50
prance 28.44
prancer 12.69
prandial 23.24
Prandtl 23.39
prang 26.1
prank 21.33
prankish 29.8
prankster 12.74
prase 35.5
prat 30.1
prate 30.7
pratfall 23.15
pratie 4.52

p

pratique 21.8
prattle 23.39
prattler 12.48
Pravda 12.25
prawn 25.28
praxis 28.11
Praxiteles 35.7
pray 3.1
prayer 2.1, 12.2
preach 15.5
preacher 12.23
preachify 6.7
preaching 26.4
preachy 4.11
preambular 12.46
prebend 16.45
prebendal 23.28
prebendary 4.43
prebiotic 21.17
precarious 28.23
precatory 4.43
precedence 28.45
precedent 30.56
precentor 12.76
precept 30.58
preceptor 12.76
precinct 30.49
preciosity 4.53
precious 28.33
precipice 28.9
precipitancy 4.48
precipitant 30.56
precipitate 30.16,
   30.43
precipitous 28.34
precis 4.45
precise 28.13
precisian 25.42
precision 25.42
preclude 16.25
preclusion 25.42
preclusive 34.7
precocial 23.38
precocious 28.33
precocity 4.53
predatory 4.43
predecessor 12.69
predella 12.42
predestinarian
   25.37
predestinate 30.13
predicant 30.56
predicate 30.10,
   30.42
predict 30.49
predictor 12.78
predigested 16.12
predilection 25.49
preemie 4.29
pre-empt 30.52
pre-emption 25.49

pre-emptor 12.76
preen 25.9
preface 28.7
prefatory 4.43
prefect 30.48
prefectoral 23.36
prefectorial 23.24
prefecture 12.20
prefer 13.1
preference 28.45
preferential 23.38
pregnancy 4.48
pregnant 30.56
prehensile 23.11
prehension 25.49
prejudice 28.7
prelacy 4.48
prelapsarian 25.37
prelate 30.42
prelatic 21.17
prelatical 23.32
prelature 12.24
prelim 24.6
preliminary 4.43
prelude 16.25
preludial 23.24
premature 12.24
premed 16.3
premier 12.7
première 2.2
premise 28.8
premium 24.16
prentice 28.12
pre-owned 16.43
prep 27.3
preparatory 4.43
prepense 28.44
preponderance
   28.45
preponderant 30.56
preponderate 30.15
preposterous 28.31
preppy 4.36
prequel 23.40
Pre-Raphaelite
   30.28
presage 20.9
presager 12.35
presbyter 12.78
presbyteral 23.36
presbyterate 30.43
presbyterial 23.24
Presbyterian 25.37
presbytery 4.43
pre-schooler 12.45
prescient 30.56
prescind 16.42
prescription 25.49
prescriptivist 31.15
presence 28.45
present 30.56

presentee 4.1
presenter 12.76
preservationist
   31.10
preset 30.5
presidency 4.48
president 30.56
presidential 23.38
Presley 4.22
press 28.3
Pressburg 18.13
pressgang 26.1
pressing 26.12
pressman 25.45
pressmen 25.45
press-up 27.13
pressure 12.72
prestige 20.5
prestigious 28.25
presto 9.24
Preston 25.50
Prestonpans 35.31
prestressed 31.3
Prestwick 21.18
presume 24.12
presumption 25.49
prêt-à-porter 3.22
pretence 28.44
pretense 28.44
pretentious 28.33
preterit 30.24
preterite 30.24
pretermit 30.20
pretor 12.77
Pretoria 12.10
pretorian 25.37
prettifier 12.14
prettify 6.7
pretty 4.53
prettyish 29.6
pretzel 23.37
prevalent 30.56
prevaricate 30.10
prevenient 30.56
preventer 12.76
prevention 25.49
preview 11.22
Previn 25.19
previous 28.23
previse 35.11
prexy 4.45
prey 3.1
preyer 12.2
prezzie 4.61
Priam 24.1
priapic 21.14
Priapus 28.30
price 28.13
pricer 12.70
pricey 4.46
prick 21.9

pricker 12.39
pricket 30.21
prickle 23.32
prickly 4.24
pride 16.14
prie-dieu 13.1
priest 31.5
priestcraft 30.47
priestess 28.3
priesthood 16.26
Priestley 4.23
priestly 4.23
prig 18.6
priggery 4.43
priggish 29.7
prim 24.6
primacy 4.48
prima donnaish
   29.6
prima facie 4.3
primal 23.33
primary 4.43
primate 30.12, 30.43
primatial 23.38
primavera 12.65
prime 24.7
primer 12.51
primeval 23.40
primitivist 31.15
primo 9.18
primogenital 23.39
primogenitary 4.43
primogenitor 12.78
primogeniture
   12.23
primordial 23.24
primp 27.17
primrose 35.19
primula 12.46
primus 28.28
primus inter
   pares 35.7
prince 28.44
princedom 24.17
princelike 21.19
princeling 26.8
princely 4.24
princess 28.3
principal 23.35
principate 30.43
principe 3.18
principle 23.35
prink 21.33
print 30.54
printer 12.78
printery 4.43
printing 26.13
printmaker 12.38
printmaking 26.7
printout 30.34
printworks 28.41

p

prion 25.24, 25.38
prior 12.13
priorate 30.43
priority 4.53
priory 4.43
Priscian 25.37
Priscilla 12.43
prise 35.11
prism 24.21
prismatic 21.17
prismoid 16.24
prison 25.52
prisoner 12.55
prissy 4.46
Pristina 12.55
pristine 25.12
Pritchett 30.20
prithee 4.57
privacy 4.48
private 30.25
privateer 12.4
privateering 26.11
privateersman
   25.45
privateersmen
   25.45
privatizer 12.91
privet 30.25
privilege 20.6
privileged 16.34
privy 4.58
prix fixe 28.39
prize 35.11
prizefight 30.27
prizefighter 12.79
prizefighting 26.13
prizewinner 12.55
prizewinning 26.9
pro-am 24.1
pro 9.1
proa 12.17
proaction 25.49
probate 30.9
probationary 4.43
probationer 12.58
probe 14.11
probing 26.4
probit 30.20
probity 4.53
problem 24.18
problematic 21.17
problematical 23.32
problematize 35.14
proboscis 28.11
procedure 12.35
proceed 16.7
proceedings 35.32
proceeds 35.27
process 28.3
processional 23.34
processor 12.69

procès-verbal 23.2
pro-choice 28.18
proclaim 24.4
proclaimer 12.50
proclamatory 4.43
Procne 4.32
proconsul 23.37
proconsulate 30.42
Procopius 28.23
procrastinate 30.13
procrastinatory
   4.43
procreate 30.8
Procrustean 25.37
Procrustes 35.9
proctor 12.79
procure 12.20
procurer 12.67
procuress 28.3
prod 16.18
prodder 12.28
prodigal 23.30
prodigious 28.25
prodigy 4.17
produce 28.19
producer 12.71
producible 23.26
product 30.49
production 25.49
proem 24.3
proemial 23.24
profane 25.7
profaner 12.54
profanity 4.53
profess 28.3
professional 23.34
professionalize
   35.12
professor 12.69
professorate 30.43
professorial 23.24
professoriate 30.41
proffer 12.30
proficiency 4.46
proficient 30.56
profile 23.11
profiler 12.44
profit 30.21
profiteer 12.4
profiterole 23.18
profligacy 4.48
profligate 30.42
pro-forma 12.52
profound 16.43
Profumo 9.18
profundity 4.53
profuse 28.19
profusion 25.42
prog 18.8
progenitor 12.78
progeniture 12.23

progeny 4.32
progesterone 25.30
prognoses 35.8
prognosis 28.11
prognostic 21.17
prognosticate 30.10
prognosticatory
   4.43
program 24.1
programmatic 21.17
programme 24.1
programmer 12.50
progress 28.3
progressional 23.34
progressionist 31.10
progressive 34.7
progressivist 31.15
prohibit 30.20
prohibiter 12.78
prohibitionary 4.43
prohibitionist 31.10
prohibitory 4.43
project 30.48
projectile 23.12
projection 25.49
projectionist 31.10
projector 12.76
Prokofiev 17.3
prolapse 28.46
prole 23.17
prolegomena 12.55
prolegomenon
   25.46
prolepsis 28.11
proleptic 21.17
proletarian 25.37
proletarianize 35.13
proletariat 30.41
pro-life 17.7
proliferate 30.15
prolific 21.10
prolificacy 4.48
prolix 28.39
prolixity 4.53
prolog 18.8
prologue 18.8
prolong 26.15
prolonger 12.60
prolusion 25.42
prom 24.8
promenade 16.2
promenader 12.25
Promethean 25.37
Prometheus 28.23
promethium 24.16
prominence 28.45
prominency 4.48
prominent 30.56
promiscuity 4.53
promiscuous 28.24
promise 28.8

promisee 4.1
promiser 12.70
promissory 4.43
prommer 12.51
promo 9.18
promontory 4.43
promote 30.35
promoter 12.80
promotion 25.49
promotional 23.34
prompt 30.52
prompter 12.79
prompting 26.13
promptitude 16.25
promulgate 30.9
promulge 20.18
pronaoi 10.2
prone 25.30
prong 26.15
pronominal 23.34
pronominalize
   35.12
pronoun 25.29
pronounce 28.44
pronouncer 12.70
pronto 9.25
proof 17.13
proofread 16.4, 16.7
proofreader 12.26
prop 27.8
propaganda 12.25
propagandist 31.6
propagandize 35.11
propagate 30.9
propane 25.8
propel 23.3
propellant 30.56
propellent 30.56
propeller 12.42
propensity 4.53
proper 12.62
propertied 16.12
Propertius 28.23
property 4.55
prophecy 4.46
prophesier 12.14
prophesy 6.16
prophet 30.21
prophetess 28.3
prophetic 21.17
prophetical 23.32
prophylactic 21.17
propinquity 4.53
propitiate 30.8
propitiatory 4.43
propitious 28.33
propjet 30.4
proponent 30.56
proportion 25.49
proportional 23.34
proportionate 30.43

p

proposal 23.41
propose 35.19
proposer 12.92
propound 16.43
propounder 12.28
proprietary 4.43
proprietor 12.82
proprietorial 23.24
propriety 4.55
propulsion 25.49
propulsive 34.7
propulsor 12.71
propyla 12.43
propylaeum 24.15
propylon 25.25
prorate 30.7
prorogue 18.10
prosaic 21.9
prosaist 31.6
proscenia 12.8
proscenium 24.16
prosciutto 9.25
proscribe 14.8
proscription 25.49
prose 35.19
prosecute 30.38
prosecution 25.49
prosecutor 12.81
proselyte 30.28
proselytizer 12.91
proser 12.92
prosimian 25.37
prosodic 21.10
prosodist 31.6
prosody 4.13
prospect 30.48
prospector 12.76
prospectus 28.34
prosper 12.62
prosperity 4.53
Prospero 9.21
prosperous 28.31
Prost 31.17
prostate 30.16
prosthesis 28.11
prostitute 30.38
prostitution 25.49
prostitutor 12.81
prostrate 30.7, 30.15
prosy 4.61
protagonist 31.10
protases 35.8
protasis 28.11
protea 12.12
protean 25.37
protect 30.48
protectant 30.56
protection 25.49
protectionist 31.10
protector 12.76
protectoral 23.36

protectorate 30.43
protectress 28.3
protégé 3.12
protein 25.12
proteinous 28.29
pro tem 24.3
protest 31.3
Protestant 30.56
protester 12.76
Proteus 28.23
prothalamium 24.16
protheses 35.8
prothesis 28.11
prothetic 21.17
protist 31.14
protium 24.16
protocol 23.13
proton 25.26
protonotary 4.43
prototypal 23.35
prototype 27.7
prototypic 21.14
prototypical 23.32
protozoa 12.17
protozoan 25.38
protozoon 25.38
protract 30.48
protracted 16.12
protraction 25.49
protractor 12.74
protrude 16.25
protrusion 25.42
protuberance 28.45
protuberant 30.56
proud 16.22
Proudhon 25.25
Proust 31.22
Prout 30.34
prove 34.12
proven 25.51
provenance 28.45
Provençal 23.2
Provence 28.44
provender 12.27
provenience 28.45
proverb 14.15
proverbial 23.24
Proverbs 35.26
provide 16.14
providence 28.45
provident 30.56
providential 23.38
provider 12.27
province 28.44
provincial 23.38
provincialist 31.8
provision 25.42
provisional 23.34
provisioner 12.58
proviso 9.29
provisor 12.91

provisory 4.43
Provo 9.27
provoke 21.24
provoker 12.40
provost 31.25
prow 8.1
prowess 28.7
prowl 23.16
prowler 12.44
proximate 30.43
proximity 4.53
proximo 9.18
proxy 4.46
Prozac 21.4
prude 16.25
prudence 28.45
prudent 30.56
prudential 23.38
prudery 4.43
prudish 29.6
prune 25.33
pruner 12.56
prurience 28.45
pruriency 4.48
prurient 30.56
Prussia 12.73
Prussian 25.49
pry 6.1
psalm 24.2
psalmic 21.12
psalmist 31.9
psalmodic 21.10
psalmodist 31.6
psalmody 4.13
psalter 12.80
psaltery 4.43
pseud 16.25
pseudo 9.11
pseudoephedrine 25.11
pseudomorph 17.9
pseudonym 24.6
pseudonymity 4.53
pseudonymous 28.28
psi 6.1
psittacosis 28.11
psoriasis 28.11
psych 21.19
psyche 4.19, 21.19
psychedelia 12.6
psychedelic 21.11
psychiatric 21.15
psychiatrist 31.12
psychiatry 4.43
psychic 21.11
psychical 23.32
psycho 9.16
psychoanalyse 35.12

psychoanalysis 28.11
psychoanalyst 31.8
psychoanalytic 21.17
psychoanalyze 35.12
psychobabble 23.26
psychodynamic 21.12
psychokinesis 28.11
psychokinetic 21.17
psychologize 35.11
psychology 4.17
psychometric 21.15
psychometrist 31.12
psychometry 4.40
psychopath 32.1
psychopathic 21.18
psychoses 35.8
psychosexual 23.25
psychosis 28.11
psychosocial 23.38
psychosomatic 21.17
psychotherapeutic 21.17
psychotherapist 31.11
psychotherapy 4.37
psychotic 21.17
psyllium 24.16
ptarmigan 25.41
pteranodon 25.25
pterodactyl 23.9
Ptolemaic 21.9
Ptolemy 4.30
pub 14.13
pub crawl 23.15
puberty 4.55
pubes 35.6
pubescence 28.45
pubescent 30.56
pubic 21.9
pubis 28.7
public 21.11
publican 25.43
publicist 31.13
publish 29.8
publisher 12.72
Puccini 4.31
puccoon 25.33
puce 28.19
puck 21.29
pucker 12.41
puckery 4.43
puckish 29.8
pud 16.26
pudding 26.5
puddingy 4.35
puddle 23.28

p

puddler 12.48
puddly 4.27
pudenda 12.26
pudeur 13.1
pudge 20.16
pudgy 4.17
pudic 21.10
Puebla 12.42
pueblo 9.17
puerile 23.11
puerility 4.53
Puerto Rican 25.43
Puerto Rico 9.16
puff 17.15
puffball 23.14
puffer 12.30
puffery 4.43
puffin 25.14
puffy 4.14
pug 18.12
puggish 29.7
puggy 4.15
pugilist 31.8
Pugin 25.14
pugnacious 28.33
pugnacity 4.53
puissance 28.45
puissant 30.56
puja 12.35
puke 21.27
pukey 4.20
pukka 12.41
pul 23.20
pula 12.46
Pulaski 4.18
pulchritude 16.25
pulchritudinous
 28.29
pule 23.20
puli 4.26
Pulitzer 12.70
pull 23.21
puller 12.46
pullet 30.22
pulley 4.26
Pullman 25.45
pull-out 30.34
pullover 12.86
pull-up 27.13
pulmonaria 12.10
pulmonary 4.43
pulmonate 30.43
pulp 27.16
pulper 12.63
pulpit 30.23
pulpy 4.37
pulsar 1.17
pulsate 30.7
pulsatory 4.43
pulse 28.42
pultrude 16.25

pulverizer 12.91
puma 12.52
pumice 28.8
pummel 23.33
pump 27.17
pumpernickel 23.32
pumpkin 25.15
pumpkinseed 16.7
pun 25.35
puna 12.56
punch 29.20
punchbag 18.1
punchball 23.14
punchbowl 23.17
punch-drunk 21.34
puncher 12.73
Punchinello 9.17
punchline 25.22
punch-up 27.13
punchy 4.50
punctilio 9.4
punctilious 28.23
punctual 23.25
punctuate 30.8
puncture 12.24
pundit 30.21
punditry 4.40
pungency 4.48
pungent 30.56
Punic 21.13
punish 29.9
punisher 12.72
Punjab 14.2
Punjabi 4.10
punk 21.34
punkah 12.41
punkish 29.8
punky 4.20
punner 12.57
punnet 30.23
punster 12.81
punt 30.55
Punta Arenas 28.29
punter 12.81
puny 4.33
pup 27.13
pupa 12.63
pupae 4.37
pupal 23.35
pupate 30.7
pupil 23.35
pupilage 20.6
pupillage 20.6
puppet 30.23
puppeteer 12.4
puppeteering 26.11
puppetry 4.40
puppy 4.37
puppyhood 16.26
puppyish 29.6
Purana 12.53

Puranic 21.13
purblind 16.42
Purcell 23.37
purchase 28.7
purchaser 12.70
purdah 1.6
pure 12.20
pure-bred 16.3, 16.4
puree 3.19
purgatory 4.43
purge 20.17
purger 12.36
purificatory 4.43
purifier 12.14
purify 6.7
Purim 24.6
purism 24.21
purist 31.12
puristic 21.17
puritan 25.50
puritanical 23.32
purity 4.53
purl 23.42
purler 12.49
purlieu 11.22
purlieux 35.21
purlin 25.16
purloin 25.32
purloiner 12.56
purple 23.35
purplish 29.8
purply 4.27
purport 30.33
purpose 28.30
purposive 34.7
purpure 12.20
purr 13.1
purse 28.36
purser 12.71
purslane 25.16
pursuance 28.45
pursuant 30.56
pursue 11.1
pursuer 12.19
pursuit 30.37
pursuivant 30.56
pursy 4.49
purulent 30.56
purvey 3.1
purveyance 28.45
purveyor 12.2
purview 11.22
pus 28.21
Pusan 25.1
Pusey 4.62
push 29.15
pushbike 21.19
pushcart 30.3
pushchair 2.4
pusher 12.73
Pushkin 25.15

pushover 12.86
pushpin 25.18
push-pull 23.21
pushrod 16.18
push-start 30.3
pushy 4.50
pusillanimity 4.53
pusillanimous 28.28
puss 28.20
pussy 4.47
pussycat 30.1
pussyfoot 30.39
pussyfooter 12.81
pustular 12.46
pustulate 30.11
pustule 23.20
put 30.39
put-down 25.29
putrefaction 25.49
putrefy 6.7
putrescence 28.45
putrescent 30.56
putrid 16.11
putridity 4.53
putsch 15.12
putt 30.40
puttee 4.55
putter 12.81
putti 4.55
putting green 25.11
Puttnam 24.19
putto 9.25
putty 4.55
putz 28.47
puzzle 23.41
puzzler 12.47
puzzling 26.8
pya 1.1
Pygmalion 25.37
pygmy 4.29
pyknic 21.13
pylon 25.44
Pyongyang 26.1
pyramid 16.10
pyramidal 23.28
Pyramus 28.28
pyre 12.13
Pyrenean 25.36
Pyrenees 35.6
pyrethrin 25.18
pyrethrum 24.19
Pyrex 28.38
pyrite 30.29
pyrites 35.9
pyritic 21.17
pyrogenic 21.13
pyromania 12.8
pyromaniac 21.1
pyrometer 12.78
pyrometric 21.15
pyrometry 4.40

p

pyrophoric 21.15
pyrotechnic 21.13
pyrotechnical 23.32
pyrotechnist 31.10
pyrotechny 4.31
pyroxene 25.11
Pyrrhic 21.15
Pyrrho 9.21
Pyrrhus 28.31
Pythagoras 28.31
Pythagorean 25.36
Pythia 12.12
Pythian 25.37
python 25.51
Pythonesque 21.35
pyx 28.39

Q

Qatar 1.19
Qatari 4.38
Qinghai 6.1
qua 3.1
Quaalude 16.25
quack 21.1
quackery 4.43
quackish 29.8
quad 16.18
quadragenarian 25.37
quadrangle 23.30
quadrangular 12.46
quadrant 30.56
quadraphonic 21.13
quadrat 30.43
quadrate 30.7, 30.15
quadratic 21.17
quadrennia 12.8
quadriceps 28.46
quadrilateral 23.36
quadrille 23.8
quadripartite 30.30
quadriplegia 12.6
quadriplegic 21.11
quadruped 16.3
quadruple 23.35
quadruplet 30.22
quadruplicate 30.10, 30.42
quadrupole 23.18
quaestor 12.77
quaff 17.8
quaffer 12.30
quag 18.1
quagga 12.31
quaggy 4.15
quagmire 12.14
quaich 22.2

Quai d'Orsay 3.1
quail 23.5
quaint 30.54
quake 21.7
Quaker 12.38
Quakerish 29.9
quaky 4.18
qualificatory 4.43
qualifier 12.14
qualify 6.7
quality 4.53
qualm 24.2
quandary 4.43
quango 9.13
quant 30.54
quantifier 12.14
quantify 6.7
quantity 4.53
quantum 24.20
quarantine 25.12
quark 21.5
quarrel 23.36
quarreler 12.48
quarreller 12.48
quarry 4.41
quarryman 25.45
quarrymen 25.45
quart 30.33
quartan 25.50
quarte 30.3
quarter 12.80
quarterage 20.8
quarterback 21.2
quarterdeck 21.6
quarterfinal 23.34
quartering 26.11
quarterly 4.27
quartermaster 12.75
quartern 25.50
quartet 30.4
quarto 9.25
quartz 28.47
quartzite 30.30
quasar 1.24
quash 29.11
Quasimodo 9.11
quassia 12.11
quaternary 4.43
quatorze 35.17
quatrain 25.8
quaver 12.85
quavery 4.43
quay 4.1
quayage 20.6
quayside 16.16
quean 25.9
queasy 4.61
Québec 21.6
Quebecker 12.37
Quechua 12.88
Quechuan 25.51

queen 25.9
queendom 24.17
queenie 4.31
queen-like 21.19
queenly 4.23
Queens 35.31
queen-size 35.14
Queensland 16.45
Queenslander 12.29
queer 12.4
queerish 29.9
quell 23.3
queller 12.42
quench 29.20
quenelle 23.3
Quentin 25.19
querist 31.12
quern 25.53
querulous 28.27
query 4.43
quest 31.3
Quested 16.12
quester 12.76
question 25.39
questioner 12.58
questionnaire 2.1
Quetta 12.76
queue 11.1
quibble 23.26
quibbler 12.48
quiche 29.5
quick 21.9
quicken 25.43
quickie 4.19
quicklime 24.7
quicksand 16.40
quickset 30.4
quicksilver 12.86
quickstep 27.3
quick-witted 16.12
quid 16.8
quiddity 4.53
quidnunc 21.34
quid pro quo 9.1
quiescence 28.45
quiescent 30.56
quiet 30.41
quieten 25.50
quietist 31.14
quietude 16.25
quietus 28.34
quiff 17.6
quill 23.8
quilling 26.8
quilt 30.51
quilter 12.78
quim 24.6
quin 25.13
quinary 4.43
quince 28.44
quincunx 28.41

quinella 12.42
quinine 25.11
quinquagenarian 25.37
quinquennia 12.8
quint 30.54
quintain 25.19
quintal 23.39
quintessence 28.45
quintessential 23.38
quintet 30.4
quintile 23.9
Quintilian 25.37
Quinton 25.50
quintuple 23.35
quintuplet 30.22
quintuplicate 30.10
Quintus 28.34
quip 27.6
quipster 12.78
quipu 11.16
quire 12.13
quirk 21.31
quirkish 29.8
quirky 4.20
quirt 30.45
quisling 26.8
quit 30.20
quitch 15.6
quite 30.26
Quito 9.24
quittance 28.45
quitter 12.78
quiver 12.86
quivering 26.11
quivery 4.43
quixotic 21.17
quixotry 4.41
quiz 35.10
quizmaster 12.75
quizzer 12.90
quizzical 23.32
Qum 24.13
Qumran 25.4
quod 16.18
quodlibet 30.4
quodlibetarian 25.37
quoin 25.32
quoit 30.36
quokka 12.40
quondam 24.1
Quonset 30.24
quorate 30.15
Quorn 25.28
quorum 24.19
quota 12.80
quote 30.35
quoth 32.11
quotidian 25.37

p
q

quotient 30.56
Qwaqwa 12.88

Rabat 30.1
Rabaul 23.16
rabbet 30.20
rabbi 6.5
Rabbie 4.10
rabbinate 30.43
rabbinic 21.13
rabbinical 23.32
rabbit 30.20
rabbity 4.53
rabble 23.26
rabble-rouser 12.92
Rabelais 3.15
Rabelaisian 25.37
rabid 16.8
rabidity 4.53
rabies 35.6
Rabin 25.9
raccoon 25.33
race 28.5
racecard 16.2
racecourse 28.15
racegoer 12.17
racehorse 28.15
raceme 24.5
racer 12.69
racetrack 21.3
Rachel 23.27
Rachmaninov 17.8
racial 23.38
racialist 31.8
Racine 25.9
racism 24.21
racist 31.13
rack 21.1
racket 30.21
racketeer 12.4
rackety 4.53
Rackham 24.18
racon 25.25
raconteur 13.1
racquetball 23.14
racy 4.45
rad 16.1
radar 1.6
Radcliffe 17.6
radial 23.24
radian 25.37
radiance 28.45
radiancy 4.48
radiant 30.56
radiate 30.8
radical 23.32
radicalize 35.12

radicchio 9.4
radices 35.8
radii 6.3
radio 9.4
radiocarbon 25.38
radiogenic 21.13
radiogram 24.1
radiograph 17.2
radiographer 12.30
radiography 4.14
radioisotope 27.10
radiology 4.17
radio-telephone 25.30
radiotherapy 4.37
radish 29.6
radium 24.16
radius 28.23
radix 28.39
radome 24.11
radon 25.25
Rae 3.1
Raeburn 25.53
Raelene 25.10
Rafe 17.4
raffia 12.5
raffish 29.7
raffle 23.29
Raffles 35.29
Rafsanjani 4.31
raft 30.47
rafter 12.75
raftsman 25.45
raftsmen 25.45
rag 18.1
raga 12.31
ragamuffin 25.14
ragbag 18.1
rage 20.4
ragged 16.9
raggedy 4.12
raggle-taggle 23.30
raglan 25.44
ragman 25.2
ragmen 25.5
Ragnarök 21.21
ragout 11.8
ragstone 25.31
ragtag 18.1
ragtime 24.7
ragtop 27.8
ragweed 16.7
ragworm 24.22
ragwort 30.45
rah 1.1
rah-rah 1.16
rai 6.1
raid 16.6
raider 12.26
rail 23.5
railage 20.6
railcar 1.11

railcard 16.2
railer 12.43
railhead 16.3
railing 26.8
raillery 4.43
railman 25.45
railmen 25.45
railroad 16.23
railway 3.25
railwayman 25.45
railwaymen 25.45
raiment 30.56
rain 25.7
rainbow 9.9
raincoat 30.35
raindrop 27.8
Raine 25.7
rainfall 23.15
rainforest 31.12
Rainier 3.3, 12.8
rainmaker 12.38
rainproof 17.13
rainstorm 24.9
rainswept 30.58
rainwater 12.80
rainwear 2.15
rainy 4.31
Raisa 12.69
raise 35.5
raisin 25.52
raisiny 4.34
raison d'être 12.64
raj 20.2
raja 12.35
Rajasthan 25.4
Rajasthani 4.31
Rajneesh 29.5
Rajput 30.39
Rajshahi 4.16
rake 21.7
raker 12.38
raki 4.18
rakish 29.8
raku 11.12
Raleigh 4.21
rallier 12.6
rally 4.21
rallycross 28.14
Ralph 17.18
ram 24.1
Rama 12.50
Ramadan 25.1
Ramakrishna 12.55
Ramayana 12.58
Rambert 2.3
ramble 23.26
rambler 12.42
rambling 26.8
Rambo 9.9
rambunctious 28.33
rambutan 25.50

Rameau 9.18
ramekin 25.15
ramen 25.5
rami 6.12
ramie 4.29
ramify 6.7
Ramillies 35.7
ramin 25.9
ramjet 30.4
rammer 12.50
rammy 4.29
Ramón 25.24
Ramona 12.56
ramp 27.17
rampage 20.4
rampageous 28.25
rampager 12.35
rampancy 4.48
rampant 30.56
rampart 30.3
rampion 25.37
ram raid 16.6
ramrod 16.18
Ramsay 4.61
ramshackle 23.32
ran 25.1
ranch 29.20
rancher 12.72
ranchero 9.21
Ranchi 4.50
rancid 16.11
rancidity 4.53
rancor 12.37
rancorous 28.31
rancour 12.37
rand 16.40
Randall 23.28
Randers 35.24
Randolph 17.18
random 24.17
randomize 35.13
Randstad 30.2
randy 4.12
rang 26.1
rangatira 12.67
range 20.19
rangé 3.1
rangefinder 12.27
ranger 12.35
Rangoon 25.33
rangy 4.17
rani 4.31
rank 21.33
rank-and-file 23.11
ranker 12.37
ranking 26.7
rankle 23.32
ransack 21.4
ransacker 12.37
ransom 24.20
Ransome 24.20

rant 30.53
ranter 12.74
ranting 26.13
Ranulf 17.18
ranunculi 6.11
ranunculus 28.27
Raoul 23.20
rap 27.1
rapacious 28.33
rapacity 4.53
rape 27.4
raper 12.61
rapeseed 16.7
Raphael 23.23
rapid 16.10
rapidity 4.53
rapier 12.9
rapine 25.23
rapini 4.31
rapist 31.11
rappel 23.3
rapper 12.61
rapport 7.1
rapporteur 13.1
rapscallion 25.37
rapt 30.58
raptor 12.74
rapture 12.23
rapturous 28.31
Raquel 23.3
rare 2.1
rarebit 30.20
rarefy 6.7
raring 26.11
rarity 4.53
Rarotonga 12.32
rascal 23.32
rascally 4.27
rash 29.1
rasher 12.72
rasp 27.18
raspberry 4.43
rasper 12.61
Rasputin 25.19
raspy 4.36
Rasta 12.74
Rastafari 4.38
Rastafarian 25.37
Rastus 28.34
rat 30.1
rata 12.75
ratafia 12.4
rataplan 25.1
rat-arsed 31.2
ratatouille 4.1
ratbag 18.1
ratchet 30.20
rate 30.7
ratel 23.39
ratepayer 12.2
rathe 33.2

rather 12.84
rathole 23.17
ratifier 12.14
ratify 6.7
rating 26.13
ratio 9.4
ration 25.49
rational 23.34
rationale 23.2
rationalist 31.8
rationalizer 12.91
ratline 25.16
ratoon 25.33
ratrace 28.5
rat's-tail 23.6
rattan 25.1
rat-tat 30.1
ratter 12.74
Rattigan 25.41
rattle 23.39
rattler 12.48
rattlesnake 21.7
rattling 26.8
rattly 4.27
ratty 4.51
raucous 28.26
raunch 29.20
raunchy 4.50
ravage 20.9
ravager 12.35
rave 34.4
Ravel 23.3
ravel 23.40
ravelin 25.16
raven 25.51
Ravenna 12.53
ravenous 28.29
raver 12.85
rave-up 27.13
ravin 25.19
ravine 25.9, 25.19
raving 26.14
ravioli 4.25
ravish 29.10
ravisher 12.72
ravishing 26.12
raw 7.1
Rawalpindi 4.12
rawhide 16.14
Rawlplug 18.12
Rawls 35.29
rawly 4.25
rawness 28.29
ray 3.1
Rayleigh 4.22
rayless 28.8
Raymond 16.45
Rayner 12.54
rayon 25.24
raze 35.5
razor 12.90

razorback 21.2
razorbill 23.8
razor blade 16.6
razorshell 23.4
razz 35.1
razzle 23.41
razzle-dazzle 23.41
razzmatazz 35.1
reésumeé 3.16
reésumeé 3.16
Reéunion 25.37
re 3.1
reach 15.5
reactant 30.56
reactionary 4.43
read 16.3, 16.7
reader 12.26
Reading 26.5
readout 30.34
ready 4.12
ready-to-wear 2.1
Reagan 25.41
real 23.2, 23.24
realgar 12.31
realist 31.8
reality 4.53
really 4.27
realm 24.18
Realpolitik 21.8
realtor 12.82
realty 4.55
ream 24.5
reamer 12.51
reap 27.5
reaper 12.61
rear 12.4
rearer 12.67
rearguard 16.2
rearmost 31.20
rearward 16.30
reason 25.52
reasoner 12.58
reasoning 26.9
reassuring 26.11
reave 34.5
reb 14.3
rebar 1.4
rebate 30.9
rebbe 12.21
rebbetzin 25.19
Rebecca 12.37
rebel 23.3, 23.26
rebellion 25.52
rebellious 28.35
rebirthing 26.14
rebuke 11.27
rebuker 12.41
rebus 28.24
rebuttal 23.39
rec 21.6
recalcitrance 28.45

recalcitrant 30.56
recalibrate 30.15
recall 23.15
recce 4.18
receipt 30.18
receive 34.5
receiver 12.85
recension 25.49
recent 30.56
receptacle 23.32
reception 25.49
receptionist 31.10
receptor 12.76
recessional 23.34
recessive 34.7
Rechabite 30.26
recherchee 3.21
recidivist 31.15
recipe 4.36
recipiency 4.48
recipient 30.56
reciprocal 23.32
reciprocate 30.10
reciprocity 4.53
recital 23.39
recitalist 31.8
reciter 12.79
reck 21.6
reckon 25.43
reckoner 12.58
reckoning 26.9
recliner 12.55
recluse 28.19
reclusion 25.42
reclusive 34.7
recognizance 28.45
recognizer 12.91
recolonize 35.13
recombinant 30.56
recommender 12.26
recompense 28.44
recompense 28.44
reconcile 23.11
reconcile 23.11
recondite 30.26
recondite 30.26
reconnaissance 28.45
reconnoiter 12.81
reconnoitre 12.81
reconvict 30.49
record 16.21
recorder 12.28
recording 26.5
record-player 12.2
recoup 27.11
recoverer 12.67
recovery 4.43
recreancy 4.48
recreant 30.56
recreate 30.8

r

recriminate 30.13
recriminatory 4.43
recruit 30.37
recruiter 12.81
rectal 23.39
rectangle 23.30
rectangular 12.46
rectify 6.7
rectilinear 12.8
rectitude 16.25
recto 9.24
rector 12.76
rectorate 30.43
rectorial 23.24
rectory 4.43
rectum 24.20
recumbency 4.48
recumbent 30.56
recuperate 30.15
recurrence 28.45
recusance 28.45
recusant 30.56
recycler 12.44
red 16.3
redact 30.48
redaction 25.49
redactional 23.34
redactor 12.74
redback 21.2
red-blooded 16.9
redbreast 31.3
red-brick 21.15
redbud 16.27
redbush 29.15
redcap 27.1
redcoat 30.35
redcurrant 30.56
redd 16.3
redden 25.40
reddish 29.6
Redditch 15.6
reddy 4.12
rede 16.7
redeemer 12.51
redemption 25.49
redesignate 30.13
red-eye 6.6
red-faced 31.4
redfish 29.7
Redford 16.28
Redgrave 34.4
red-handed 16.9
redhead 16.3
redingote 30.35
redivivus 28.35
redline 25.22
redly 4.22
Redmond 16.45
redneck 21.6
redness 28.29
redolence 28.45

redolent 30.56
redound 16.43
redpoll 23.18
redressal 23.37
redshank 21.33
redshirt 30.45
redskin 25.15
reduce 28.19
reducer 12.71
reducible 23.26
reductio ad
    absurdum 24.17
reduction 25.49
reductionist 31.10
redundancy 4.48
redundant 30.56
redwing 26.14
redwood 16.26
reed 16.7
reed bed 16.3
reedbuck 21.29
reeded 16.9
reeding 26.5
reedling 26.8
reed-warbler 12.44
reedy 4.12
reef 17.5
reefer 12.30
reek 21.8
reeky 4.18
reel 23.7
reeler 12.43
Rees 28.6
Reeves 35.35
ref 17.3
refection 25.49
refectory 4.43
refer 13.1
referee 4.1
reference 28.45
referenda 12.26
referendum 24.17
referential 23.38
referral 23.36
referrer 12.68
refiner 12.55
refit 30.21
reflect 30.48
reflection 25.49
reflector 12.76
reflet 3.1
reflexive 34.7
reflexology 4.17
reformatory 4.43
reformist 31.9
refract 30.48
refractor 12.74
refractory 4.43
refrain 25.7
refrigerant 30.56
refrigerate 30.15

refrigeratory 4.43
reft 30.47
refuge 20.15
refugee 4.1
refulgence 28.45
refusal 23.41
refuse 28.19
refusenik 21.13
refuser 12.92
refutal 23.39
refute 30.37
refuter 12.81
reg 20.3
regal 23.30
regalia 12.6
regality 4.53
Regan 25.41
regard 16.2
regardant 30.56
regatta 12.74
regency 4.48
regenerate 30.43
regent 30.56
reggae 3.11
regicidal 23.28
regicide 16.16
regime 24.5
regimen 25.45
Regina 12.55
Reginald 16.38
region 25.42
regional 23.34
regionalist 31.8
regionalize 35.12
register 12.78
registrant 30.56
registrar 1.1
registrary 4.43
registry 4.40
reglet 30.22
regnal 23.34
regnant 30.56
regress 28.3
regressive 34.7
regret 30.4
regular 12.46
regularity 4.53
regulate 30.11
regulatory 4.43
reguli 6.11
regulo 9.17
regulus 28.27
regurgitate 30.16
rehab 14.1
reheard 16.31
rehearsal 23.37
rehearser 12.71
Reich 22.3
Reichstag 18.2
Reid 16.7
reificatory 4.43

reify 6.7
reign 25.7
reimburse 28.36
Reims 35.30
rein 25.7
reindeer 12.5
reinforce 28.15
reinforcer 12.70
Reinhardt 30.3
reinvestigate 30.9
Reith 32.5
reive 34.5
reiver 12.85
reject 30.48
rejection 25.49
rejectionist 31.10
rejector 12.76
rejoice 28.18
rejoicer 12.71
rejoicing 26.12
rejuvenate 30.13
relatable 23.26
relation 25.49
relational 23.34
relatival 23.40
relativist 31.15
relativize 35.14
relaxant 30.56
relaxer 12.69
relay 3.15
releasee 4.1
releaser 12.69
relegate 30.9
relevance 28.45
relevancy 4.48
relevant 30.56
releve 3.1
reliance 28.45
reliant 30.56
relic 21.11
relict 30.49
relieve 34.5
reliever 12.85
relievo 9.27
religion 25.42
religionist 31.10
religiose 28.17
religiosity 4.53
religious 28.25
relinquish 29.10
reliquary 4.43
reliquiae 4.3
relish 29.8
reluctance 28.45
reluctant 30.56
rely 6.1
rem 24.3
remainder 12.26
remand 16.41
Rembrandt 30.53
remedy 4.12

r

rememberer | retroussé

rememberer 12.67
remembrance 28.45
remembrancer 12.71
reminisce 28.7
reminiscence 28.45
reminiscent 30.56
reminiscer 12.70
remise 35.11
remissible 23.26
remit 30.20, 30.23
remittal 23.39
remittance 28.45
remitter 12.78
remnant 30.56
remonetize 35.14
remonstrate 30.15
remontant 30.56
remora 12.67
removal 23.40
remunerate 30.15
Remus 28.28
Renaissance 28.45
renal 23.34
renascence 28.45
Renata 12.75
renationalize 35.12
Renault 9.19
rend 16.41
Rendell 23.28
render 12.26
renderer 12.67
rendering 26.11
rendezvous 11.21
René 3.17
renegade 16.6
renegado 9.11
renege 18.5
reneger 12.31
renewal 23.25
renewer 12.19
renminbi 4.10
Rennes 25.5
rennet 30.23
Rennie 4.31
Reno 9.19
Renoir 1.22
renounce 28.44
renouncer 12.70
renovate 30.16
renown 25.29
rent 30.53
rental 23.39
rentboy 10.3
renter 12.76
renunciant 30.56
renunciatory 4.43
renvoi 1.22
rep 27.3
repairer 12.65
repairman 25.2
repairmen 25.5

repartee 4.1
repatriate 30.8
repeater 12.77
repêchage 19.1
repel 23.3
repellence 28.45
repellency 4.48
repellent 30.56
repeller 12.42
repentance 28.45
repentant 30.56
repenter 12.76
repertoire 1.22
repertory 4.43
repetend 16.41
repetitious 28.33
replay 3.15
replenish 29.9
replenisher 12.72
replete 30.18
repletion 25.49
replevin 25.19
replica 12.39
replicate 30.10
replier 12.13
repo 9.20
reportage 20.2
reportorial 23.24
repository 4.43
repoussé 3.20
reprehend 16.41
reprehensible 23.26
representationalist 31.8
representationist 31.10
represser 12.69
repressible 23.26
repressive 34.7
reprieve 34.5
reprimand 16.41
reprisal 23.41
reprise 35.6
repro 9.21
reproach 15.10
reproacher 12.24
reprographic 21.10
reprography 4.14
reprover 12.87
reproving 26.14
reptile 23.12
reptilian 25.37
Repton 25.50
repudiate 30.8
repugnance 28.45
repugnant 30.56
repulsion 25.49
repulsive 34.7
repute 30.37
requiem 24.16
requiescat 30.1

requirer 12.67
requisite 30.25
requisitioner 12.58
requisitionist 31.10
requital 23.39
reredos 28.14
resale 23.6
rescind 16.42
rescue 11.22
rescuer 12.19
resemblant 30.56
resemble 23.26
reservist 31.15
reservoir 1.22
reshow 9.1
residence 28.45
residency 4.48
resident 30.56
residential 23.38
residentiary 4.43
residua 12.20
residual 23.21
residuary 4.41
residue 11.22
residuum 24.17
resigned 16.42
resile 23.11
resilience 28.45
resiliency 4.48
resilient 30.56
resin 25.20
resinate 30.13
resinous 28.29
resist 31.6
resistance 28.45
resistant 30.56
resistible 23.26
resistor 12.78
resit 30.24
resolute 30.37
resonance 28.45
resonant 30.56
resonate 30.13
respect 30.48
respecter 12.76
respiratory 4.43
respite 30.29
resplendence 28.45
resplendency 4.48
respond 16.42
respondent 30.56
responder 12.28
response 28.44
responsible 23.26
responsive 34.7
responsory 4.43
respray 3.19
res publica 12.39
rest 31.3
restaurant 30.53
restaurateur 13.1

restitution 25.49
restive 34.8
restorationist 31.10
restraint 30.54
restriction 25.49
restrictionist 31.10
restroom 24.12
restructuring 26.11
result 30.51
resultant 30.56
résumé 3.16, 24.12
resumption 25.49
resurgence 28.45
resurgent 30.56
resurrect 30.48
resurrection 25.49
resuscitate 30.16
ret 30.4
retail 23.6
retailer 12.43
retain 25.7
retainer 12.54
retaliate 30.8
retaliatory 4.43
retard 16.2
retarded 16.9
retarder 12.25
retch 15.3
retention 25.49
retiarius 28.23
reticence 28.45
reticent 30.56
reticle 23.32
reticule 23.20
retiform 24.9
retina 12.55
retinue 11.22
retiral 23.36
retiree 4.1
retiring 26.11
retortion 25.49
retread 16.4
retribution 25.49
retributory 4.43
retrieval 23.40
retrieve 34.5
retriever 12.85
retro 9.21
retroact 30.48
retroaction 25.49
retrocede 16.7
retrochoir 12.14
retrofit 30.20
retrograde 16.6
retrogress 28.3
retrogressive 34.7
retroject 30.48
retrospect 30.48
retrospection 25.49
retroussé 3.20

r

rinse 28.44
rinser 12.70
Rio 9.3
Rio de Janeiro 9.21
Rio de la Plata 12.75
Río Grande 4.12
Rioja 12.40
Riordan 25.40
riot 30.41
rioter 12.82
riotous 28.34
rip-off 17.8
rip 27.6
riparian 25.37
ripcord 16.21
ripe 27.7
ripen 25.46
ripieno 9.19
rip-off 17.8
riposte 31.17
ripper 12.62
ripple 23.35
ripplet 30.22
ripply 4.27
riproaring 26.11
ripsaw 7.16
ripsnorter 12.80
ripsnorting 26.13
ripstop 27.8
riptide 16.17
rise 35.11
risen 25.52
riser 12.91
risible 23.26
rising 26.14
risk 21.35
risky 4.19
ristretto 9.24
Risorgimento 9.24
risotto 9.25
risqué 3.14
rissole 23.18
Rita 12.77
Ritalin 25.16
rite 30.26
ritenuto 9.25
ritual 23.25
ritualize 35.12
Ritz 28.47
ritzy 4.46
rival 23.40
rivalry 4.40
rive 34.9
riven 25.51
river 12.86
Rivera 12.65
riverbank 21.33
riverboat 30.35
riverine 25.23
Rivers 35.24
riverside 16.16

rivet 30.25
riveter 12.78
Riviera 12.65
rivière 2.1
rivulet 30.22
Riyadh 16.1
riyal 23.2
roach 15.10
road 16.23
roadbed 16.3
roadblock 21.21
roadhog 18.8
roadholding 26.5
roadhouse 28.16
roadie 4.13
roadkill 23.9
roadroller 12.44
roadrunner 12.57
roadshow 9.23
roadside 16.16
roadstead 16.4
roadster 12.80
road test 31.3
roadway 3.25
roadwork 21.31
roadworthy 4.57
Roald 16.38
roam 24.11
roamer 12.52
roan 25.30
roar 7.1
roarer 12.66
roaring 26.11
roast 31.20
roaster 12.80
roasting 26.13
rob 14.9
robber 12.21
robbery 4.43
Robbins 35.31
robe 14.11
Robert 30.41
Roberts 28.47
Robeson 25.48
Robespierre 2.2
Robey 4.10
Robin Goodfellow
9.17
Robinson 25.48
Robinson Crusoe
9.22
robot 30.31
robotic 21.17
robotize 35.14
Robsart 30.3
Robson 25.48
robust 31.24
roc 21.20
rocaille 6.1
rocambole 23.17
Rocco 9.16

Rochelle 23.3
Rochester 12.78
rochet 30.20
rock 21.20
rockabilly 4.24
Rockall 23.15
rock-bottom 24.20
rock cake 21.7
Rockefeller 12.42
rocker 12.40
rockery 4.43
rocket 30.21
rocketeer 12.4
rocketry 4.40
rockfall 23.15
rockfish 29.7
Rockhampton 25.50
Rockies 35.10
rock-like 21.19
rockling 26.8
Rockwell 23.4
rocky 4.19
rococo 9.16
rod 16.18
Roddenberry 4.43
Roddick 21.10
rode 16.23
rodent 30.56
rodeo 9.4
Roderick 21.15
Rodgers 35.24
rodham 24.17
Rodin 25.1
rodless 28.27
rodlet 30.22
rod-like 21.19
Rodney 4.32
rodomontade 16.2
roe 9.1
roebuck 21.29
Roedean 25.10
roe-deer 12.5
roentgen 25.52
rogation 25.49
roger 12.35
Roget 3.12
rogue 18.10
roguery 4.43
roguish 29.7
roil 23.19
roister 12.81
roisterer 12.67
roistering 26.11
roisterous 28.31
Roland 16.45
rôle 23.17
Rolf 17.18
roll 23.17
rollaway 3.25
rollback 21.2
rollbar 1.4

rollcall 23.15
roller 12.44
rollerball 23.14
rollerblade 16.6
rollerblader 12.26
rollick 21.11
rollmop 27.8
Rollo 9.17
roll-on 25.25
roll-on roll-off 17.8
Rolls 35.29
roly-poly 4.25
Rom 24.8
Roma 12.52
Romaic 21.9
romaine 25.7
Roman 25.45
Romance 28.44
roman-à-clef 3.1
romancer 12.69
Romanesque 21.35
roman-fleuve 34.14
Romania 12.8
Romanian 25.37
Romanic 21.13
Romano 9.19
Romanov 17.8
Romansh 29.20
romantic 21.17
romanticist 21.13
Romany 4.34
Romberg 18.13
Rome 24.11
Romeo 9.4
romer 12.52
Rommel 23.33
Romney 4.32
romp 27.17
Romulus 28.27
Ronald 16.38
Ronan 25.46
Roncesvalles 23.2
rondavel 23.40
ronde 16.42
rondeau 9.11
rondel 23.28
rondo 9.11
Rondônia 12.8
rone 25.30
ronin 25.18
Ronnie 4.32
roo 11.1
rood 16.25
rood screen 25.11
roof 17.13
roofer 12.30
roofing 26.6
roofscape 27.4
rooftop 27.8
rooibos 28.14
rook 21.28

r

rookery 4.43
rookie 4.20
room 24.12
roomer 12.52
roomette 30.4
roomie 4.30
room-mate 30.12
roomy 4.30
Rooney 4.33
Roosevelt 30.51
roost 31.22
rooster 12.81
root 30.37
rootbeer 12.5
rooter 12.81
rootle 23.39
root-like 21.19
rootstock 21.21
rootsy 4.47
rooty 4.54
rope 27.10
rope-walk 21.22
roping 26.10
ropy 4.36
roque 21.24
Roquefort 7.6
rorqual 23.40
rort 30.33
rorty 4.54
Rory 4.41
Ros 35.16
Rosa 12.92
rosace 28.5
Rosaleen 25.10
Rosalie 4.27
Rosalind 16.42
rosaline 25.10
Rosalyn 25.16
Rosamund 16.44
Rosanna 12.53
Rosanne 25.1
rosaria 12.10
rosarian 25.37
Rosario 9.4
rosarium 24.16
rosary 4.43
Roscius 28.23
roscoe 9.16
Roscommon 25.45
rose 35.19
rosé 3.27
roseate 30.41
rosebay 3.7
Rosebery 4.43
rosehip 27.6
rose-like 21.19
rosella 12.42
rosemary 4.43
rosette 30.4
rosetted 16.12
rosewater 12.80

rosewood 16.26
Rosh Hashana 12.53
Rosicrucian 25.49
Rosie 4.61
rosin 25.20
Roskilde 16.35
Ross 28.14
Rossellini 4.31
Rossetti 4.51
Rossini 4.31
Rosslare 2.1
roster 12.79
Rostock 21.21
rostra 12.65
rostral 23.36
rostrum 24.19
Roswell 23.4
rosy 4.61
rot 30.31
rota 12.80
Rotarian 25.37
rotary 4.43
rotate 30.7
rotation 25.49
rotational 23.34
rotator 12.77
rotatory 4.43
rotavate 30.16
rote 30.35
rotgut 30.40
Roth 32.8
Rotherham 24.19
Rothko 9.16
Rothschild 16.36
roti 4.54
rotisserie 4.43
rotogravure 12.20
rotor 12.80
rotten 25.50
rotter 12.79
Rotterdam 24.1
Rottweiler 12.44
rotund 16.44
rotunda 12.29
rotundity 4.53
Rouault 9.1
rouble 23.26
roué 3.5
Rouen 25.24
rouge 19.6
rough 17.15
roughage 20.6
rough-and-
   tumble 23.26
roughcast 31.2
roughen 25.41
roughie 4.14
roughish 29.7
roughneck 21.6
roughrider 12.27
roughshod 16.18

roughy 4.14
rouille 4.8
roulade 16.2
rouleau 9.17
rouleaux 35.19
roulette 30.4
round 16.43
roundabout 30.34
roundel 23.28
roundelay 3.15
rounder 12.28
Roundhead 16.3
roundish 29.6
roundsman 25.45
roundsmen 25.45
round-up 27.13
roundworm 24.22
roup 27.11
roupy 4.37
Rouse 28.16
rouse 35.18
rouser 12.92
Rousse 28.19
Rousseau 9.22
Roussillon 25.27
roust 31.19
roustabout 30.34
rout 30.34
route 30.37
routine 25.9
routinize 35.13
roux 11.1
rove 34.11
rover 12.86
row 8.1, 9.1
rowan 25.38
rowboat 30.35
rowdy 4.13
Rowe 9.1
rowel 23.25
rowen 25.38
Rowena 12.54
rower 12.17
Rowlandson 25.48
Rowley 4.25
rowlock 21.30
Rowntree 4.41
Roy 10.1
royal 23.25
royalist 31.8
royalty 4.55
Royce 28.18
Royle 23.19
Royston 25.50
Roz 35.16
rozzer 12.91
rub 14.13
rubato 9.24
rubber 12.22
rubberize 35.13
rubberneck 21.6

rubbery 4.43
rubbing 26.4
rubbish 29.6
rubbishy 4.50
rubble 23.26
rubbly 4.27
Rubbra 12.66
rube 14.12
rubella 12.42
rubellite 30.28
Rubens 35.31
rubeola 12.48
Rubicon 25.43
rubicund 16.45
rubicundity 4.53
rubidium 24.16
rubiginous 28.29
Rubinstein 25.23
rubric 21.15
rubrical 23.32
rubricate 30.10
ruby 4.10
ruche 29.14
ruck 21.29
ruckle 23.32
rucksack 21.4
ruckus 28.26
ruction 25.49
rudbeckia 12.6
rudd 16.27
rudder 12.29
ruddle 23.28
ruddy 4.13
rude 16.25
rudery 4.43
Rudi 4.13
rudimentary 4.43
Rudolph 17.18
rue 11.1
rueful 23.21
ruff 17.15
ruffian 25.37
ruffle 23.29
rufous 28.25
Rufus 28.25
rug 18.12
rugby 4.10
Rügen 25.42
rugged 16.9
rugger 12.32
Ruhr 12.20
ruin 25.13
ruinous 28.29
rule 23.20
ruler 12.45
ruling 26.8
rum 24.14
rumba 12.22
rumble 23.26
rumbler 12.48
rumbling 26.8

r

rumbustious 28.24
ruminant 30.56
ruminate 30.13
rumly 4.26
rummage 20.7
rummager 12.35
rummer 12.52
rummy 4.30
rumness 28.29
rumor 12.52
rumour 12.52
rump 27.17
rumple 23.35
rumply 4.27
rumpus 28.30
rumpy-pumpy 4.37
run 25.35
runabout 30.34
runaround 16.43
runaway 3.25
Runcorn 25.28
rundown 25.29
run-down 25.29
rune 25.33
rung 26.18
runic 21.13
run-in 25.18
runlet 30.22
runnel 23.34
runner 12.57
running board 16.20
runny 4.33
Runnymede 16.7
runt 30.55
run-through 11.17
runty 4.55
run-up 27.13
runway 3.25
Runyon 25.52
rupee 4.1
Rupert 30.43
rupiah 12.3
rupture 12.24
rural 23.36
ruralist 31.8
rurality 4.53
ruralize 35.12
Rurik 21.15
Ruritania 12.8
Ruritanian 25.37
rusa 12.71
ruse 35.21
rush 29.16
Rushdie 4.13
rusher 12.73
rush hour 12.16
rushlight 30.28
rushy 4.50
rusk 21.35
Ruskin 25.15
Russ 28.21

Russell 23.37
russet 30.24
russety 4.53
Russia 12.73
Russian 25.49
Russophile 23.11
rust 31.24
rust belt 30.51
rust bucket 30.21
rustic 21.17
rusticate 30.10
rustle 23.37
rustler 12.47
rustling 26.8
rustproof 17.13
rusty 4.55
rut 30.40
rutabaga 12.31
ruth 32.12
ruthenium 24.16
Rutherford 16.28
rutherfordium
   24.16
rutile 23.12
Rutland 16.45
rutty 4.55
Rwanda 12.25
Rwandan 25.40
Rwandese 35.6
Ryan 25.38
Ryder 12.27
rye 6.1
ryegrass 28.2
Ryle 23.11
ryokan 25.43
ryot 30.41

Saadi 4.12
Saar 1.1
Saarbrücken 25.43
Saarland 16.40
Saba 12.21
Sabaean 25.36
Sabah 12.21
Sabaoth 32.8
sabayon 25.27
sabbatarian 25.37
sabbath 32.13
sabbatical 23.32
Sabellian 25.37
saber 12.21
Sabian 25.37
Sabine 25.9, 25.21
sable 23.26
sabot 9.9
sabotage 20.2
saboteur 13.1

sabra 12.64
sabre 12.21
sabretooth 32.12
sabreur 13.1
Sabrina 12.54
sac 21.1
saccade 16.2
saccharide 16.15
saccharin 25.18
saccharine 25.18
sacerdotal 23.39
sachem 24.17
sachet 3.21
Sacheverell 23.36
Sachs 28.38
Sachsen 25.48
sack 21.1
sackbut 30.40
sackcloth 32.8
sacking 26.7
sacra 12.65
sacral 23.36
Sacramento 9.24
sacraria 12.10
sacred 16.11
sacrifice 28.13
sacrificial 23.38
sacrilege 20.6
sacrilegious 28.25
sacrist 31.12
sacristan 25.50
sacristy 4.53
sacroiliac 21.1
sacrosanct 30.49
sacrosanctity 4.53
sacrum 24.19
sad 16.1
Sadat 30.1
sadden 25.40
saddish 29.6
saddle 23.28
saddleback 21.2
saddlebag 18.1
saddlecloth 32.8
saddler 12.42
saddlery 4.43
Sadducean 25.36
Sadducee 4.47
Sade 16.2
sadhu 11.6
Sadie 4.12
sadism 24.21
sadist 31.6
sadistic 21.17
sadly 4.21
sadness 28.29
sadomasochist 31.7
safari 4.38
safe 17.4
safebreaker 12.38
safe-conduct 30.49

safecracker 12.37
safeguard 16.2
safekeeping 26.10
safety 4.52
safflower 12.16
saffron 25.47
saffrony 4.34
sag 18.1
saga 12.31
sagacious 28.33
sagacity 4.53
sagamore 7.12
Sagan 25.1
Sagar 12.31
sage 20.4
sagebrush 29.16
saggar 12.31
saggy 4.15
sagittal 23.39
Sagittarian 25.37
Sagittarius 28.23
sago 9.13
Sahara 12.64
Saharan 25.47
Sahel 23.3
Sahelian 25.37
sahib 14.2
Said 16.14
said 16.3
Saida 12.27
saiga 12.31
Saigon 25.24
sail 23.5
sailboard 16.20
sailboarder 12.28
sailboarding 26.5
sailboat 30.35
sailcloth 32.8
sailer 12.43
sail-fluke 21.27
sailing 26.8
sailmaker 12.38
sailor 12.43
sailorly 4.27
sailplane 25.8
Sainsbury 4.43
saint 30.54
saintdom 24.17
sainted 16.12
sainthood 16.26
saintly 4.22
Saint-Saëns 25.24
Saipan 25.1
sake 21.7
saké 4.18
saker 12.38
Sakhalin 25.10
Sakharov 17.8
saki 4.18
sal 23.1
salaam 24.2

salable 23.26
salacious 28.33
salad 16.29
salade 16.2
Saladin 25.14
Salamanca 12.37
salamander 12.25
salamandrine 25.23
salami 4.29
Salamis 28.8
salariat 30.41
salary 4.43
salat 30.3
Salazar 1.1
sale 23.5
Salem 24.18
Salerno 9.19
saleroom 24.12
salesclerk 21.5
salesgirl 23.42
Salesian 25.37
saleslady 4.12
salesman 25.45
salesmen 25.45
salesperson 25.48
salesroom 24.12
saleswoman 25.45
saleswomen 25.17
Salford 16.28
Salian 25.37
Salic 21.11
salience 28.45
saliency 4.48
salient 30.56
Salieri 4.39
Salina 12.55
Salinas 28.29
saline 25.22
Salinger 12.35
salinity 4.53
Salisbury 4.43
Salish 29.8
saliva 12.86
salivary 4.43
salivate 30.16
sallow 9.17
sallowish 29.6
sallowy 4.7
Sallust 31.25
sally 4.21
salmanazar 12.90
salmon 25.45
salmonella 12.42
salmonid 16.10
salmony 4.34
Salome 4.29
salon 25.25
Salonica 12.39
saloon 25.33
Salop 27.14
Salopian 25.37

salsa 12.69
salsify 4.14
salt 30.51
salt-and-pepper
  12.61
saltbox 28.40
saltbush 29.15
saltcellar 12.42
salter 12.80
saltern 25.50
saltimbocca 12.40
saltine 25.9
salting 26.13
saltire 12.14
saltish 29.10
saltlick 21.11
Saltmarsh 29.2
saltpan 25.3
saltpeter 12.77
saltpetre 12.77
saltus 28.34
saltwater 12.80
salty 4.54
salubrious 28.23
salubrity 4.53
saluki 4.20
salutary 4.43
salutatorian 25.37
salutatory 4.43
salute 30.37
saluter 12.81
Salvador 7.5
Salvadorean 25.37
salvage 20.9
salvager 12.35
salvationist 31.10
salve 34.15
salver 12.85
salvia 12.12
salvo 9.27
salvor 12.85
Salyut 30.37
Salzburg 18.13
Sam 24.1
samadhi 4.12
Samantha 12.83
Samar 12.50
Samara 12.64
Samaria 12.10
Samaritan 25.50
Samarkand 16.40
samba 12.21
sambar 12.21
sambhar 12.21
same 24.4
samey 4.29
samfu 11.7
Samhain 25.13
Samian 25.37
samisen 25.5
samite 30.29

samizdat 30.1
Sammy 4.29
Samnite 30.29
Samoa 12.17
Samoan 25.38
Sámos 28.14
samosa 12.71
samovar 1.21
samoyed 16.3
Samoyedic 21.10
samp 27.17
sampan 25.3
sample 23.35
sampler 12.42
sampling 26.8
samsara 12.64
samsaric 21.15
samskara 12.64
Samson 25.48
Samuel 23.25
samurai 6.15
Sana'a 1.1
sanatoria 12.10
sanatorium 24.16
Sancho 9.23
sanctifier 12.14
sanctify 6.7
sanctimonious 28.23
sanctimony 4.34
sanction 25.49
sanctitude 16.25
sanctity 4.53
sanctuary 4.43
sanctum 24.20
Sanctus 28.34
sand 16.40
Sand 25.24
sandal 23.28
sandalwood 16.26
sandarac 21.3
sandbag 18.1
sandbagger 12.31
sandbank 21.33
sandbar 1.4
sand bath 32.2
sandblast 31.2
sandblaster 12.75
sandbox 28.40
sandboy 10.3
sandcastle 23.37
sander 12.25
sanderling 26.8
sanders 35.24
sandfly 6.11
Sandford 16.28
sandglass 28.2
sandhi 4.12
sandhog 18.8
Sandhurst 31.26
Sandinista 12.78
sandlot 30.31

sandman 25.2
sandpaper 12.61
sandpiper 12.62
sandpit 30.23
Sandra 12.64
Sands 35.27
sandshoe 11.19
sandstone 25.31
sandstorm 24.9
sandwich
  board 16.20
Sandwich 15.6
sandwich 20.9
sandy 4.12
sandyish 29.6
sane 25.7
Sanford 16.28
San Francisco 9.16
sang 26.1
sangar 12.31
sang-froid 1.1
sangeet 30.18
Sanger 12.60
sangha 12.32
Sango 9.13
sangrail 23.5
sangria 12.3
sanguinary 4.43
sanguine 25.20
sanguineous 28.23
Sanhedrin 25.18
sanicle 23.32
sanidine 25.10
sanitarian 25.37
sanitarium 24.16
sanitary 4.43
sanitizer 12.91
sanity 4.53
sank 21.33
San Marino 9.19
sans 35.31
sans-culotte 30.31
Sanskrit 30.24
Sanskritic 21.17
Sanskritist 31.14
Sansovino 9.19
Santa 12.74
Santa Claus 35.17
Santa Fé 3.1
Santander 2.1
Santayana 12.53
Santiago de
  Compostela 12.42
Santiago 9.13
santonica 12.39
santonin 25.18
Santoríni 4.31
Santos 28.14
São Paulo 9.17
sap 27.1
sapele 4.23

S

sapid 16.10
sapient 30.56
sapiential 23.38
Sapir 12.4
sapling 26.8
sapodilla 12.43
saponaceous 28.33
sapper 12.61
Sapphic 21.10
sapphire 12.14
sapphirine 25.23
Sappho 9.12
Sapporo 9.21
sappy 4.36
saprophyte 30.27
saprophytic 21.17
sapwood 16.26
saraband 16.40
Saracen 25.48
Saragossa 12.70
Sarah 12.65
Sarajevo 9.27
saran 25.1
sarangi 4.15
Saransk 21.35
Saranwrap 27.1
Saratoga 12.32
Sarawak 21.4
sarcasm 24.21
sarcastic 21.17
sarcoma 12.8
sarcopenia 12.8
sarcophagi 6.8
sarcophagus 28.25
sard 16.2
Sardanapalus 28.27
Sardegna 12.89
sardelle 23.3
sardine 25.9, 25.21
Sardinia 12.8
Sardinian 25.37
Sardis 28.7
sardonic 21.13
sardonyx 28.39
Sargasso 9.22
sarge 20.2
Sargent 30.56
Sargodha 12.28
Sargon 25.25
sari 4.38
sarin 25.9
sark 21.5
sarking 26.7
sarky 4.18
Sarmatian 25.49
sarnie 4.31
sarod 16.23
sarong 26.15
Saros 28.14
sarrusophone 25.30
sarsaparilla 12.43

sarsen 25.48
sartorial 23.24
Sartre 12.64
Sarum 24.19
sash 29.1
Sasha 12.72
sashay 3.21
sashimi 4.29
sasine 25.19
Saskatchewan 25.38
Saskatoon 25.33
Saskia 12.6
sasquatch 15.1
sass 28.1
sassafras 28.1
Sassanian 25.37
Sassanid 16.10
Sassenach 22.1
Sassoon 25.33
sassy 4.45
sastrugi 4.15
sat 30.1
Satan 25.50
satang 26.1
satanic 21.13
satanist 31.10
satanize 35.13
satay 3.22
satchel 23.27
sate 30.7
sateen 25.9
satellite 30.28
satiate 30.8, 30.41
Satie 4.51
satiety 4.53
satin 25.19
satinette 30.4
satinized 16.50
satinwood 16.26
satiny 4.32
satire 12.14
satiric 21.15
satirical 23.32
satirist 31.12
satisfaction 25.49
satisfactory 4.43
satisfy 6.7
satnav 34.1
satori 4.41
satrap 27.14
satrapy 4.37
satsuma 12.52
saturate 30.15
Saturday 3.9
Saturn 25.50
Saturnalia 12.6
saturnalian 25.37
Saturnian 25.37
saturnine 25.23
satyr 12.74
satyric 21.15

sauce 28.15
sauceboat 30.35
saucepan 25.46
saucer 12.70
saucy 4.47
Saudi 4.13
sauerkraut 30.34
Saul 23.14
Saumur 12.20
sauna 12.56
saunter 12.80
saunterer 12.67
sauropod 16.18
saury 4.41
sausage 20.9
Saussure 12.20
sauté 3.22
Sauternes 25.53
Sauveterrian 25.37
Sauvignon 25.27
savable 23.26
savage 20.9
savagery 4.43
savannah 12.53
savant 30.56
savante 30.56
savarin 25.18
savate 30.3
save 34.4
saveloy 10.7
saver 12.85
Savery 4.43
savin 25.19
saving 26.14
savior 12.89
saviour 12.89
savoir faire 2.1
Savonarola 12.44
savor 12.85
savory 4.43
savour 12.85
savoury 4.43
savoy 10.1
Savoyard 16.2
savvy 4.58
saw 7.1
sawbill 23.8
sawbones 35.31
sawbuck 21.29
sawdust 31.24
sawgrass 28.2
sawhorse 28.15
sawmill 23.9
sawn 25.28
sawtooth 32.12
sawtoothed 30.60
sawyer 12.89
sax 28.38
saxe 28.38
saxifrage 20.4

saxist 31.13
Saxon 25.48
Saxonist 31.10
saxony 4.34
saxophone 25.30
saxophonic 21.13
saxophonist 31.10
say 3.1
sayable 23.26
Sayers 35.24
saying 26.3
says 35.3
say-so 9.22
scab 14.1
scabbard 16.28
scabby 4.10
scabies 35.10
scabious 28.23
scabrous 28.31
scad 16.1
scaffold 16.37
scaffolder 12.25
scaffolding 26.5
scagliola 12.44
scald 16.36
scale 23.5
scalene 25.10
scaler 12.43
Scaliger 12.35
scallawag 18.1
scallion 25.37
scallop 27.14
scalloper 12.63
scallywag 18.1
scalp 27.16
scalpel 23.35
scalper 12.61
scaly 4.22
scam 24.1
scammony 4.34
scamp 27.17
scamper 12.61
scampi 4.36
scampish 29.9
scan 25.1
scandal 23.28
scandalmonger 12.32
scandalous 28.27
Scandinavia 12.12
Scandinavian 25.37
scandium 24.16
scanner 12.53
scansion 25.49
scant 30.53
scantling 26.8
scanty 4.51
scapegoat 30.35
scapula 12.46
scapulary 4.43
scar 1.1

scarab 14.14
scarabaeid 16.8
scaramouch 29.14
Scarborough 12.67
scarce 28.4
scarcity 4.53
scare 2.1
scarecrow 9.21
scaredy-cat 30.1
scaremonger 12.32
scaremongering 26.11
scarer 12.65
scarf 17.2
scarifier 12.14
scarify 6.7
scarlatina 12.54
Scarlatti 4.51
scarlet 30.22
Scarlett 30.22
scarp 27.2
scarper 12.61
Scart 30.3
scarves 35.35
scary 4.39
scat 30.1
scathe 33.2
scathing 26.14
scatology 4.17
scatter 12.74
scatterbrain 25.8
scatterer 12.67
scattergun 25.35
scatty 4.51
scaup 27.9
scaur 7.1
scavenge 20.19
scavenger 12.35
scena 12.54
scenario 9.4
scenarist 31.12
scene 25.9
scenery 4.43
scenester 12.77
scenic 21.13
scent 30.53
scepter 12.76
sceptic 21.17
sceptical 23.32
sceptre 12.76
Schadenfreude 12.28
schappe 27.1
schedule 23.21
scheduler 12.46
Scheele 12.43
Scheherazade 12.25
Scheldt 30.51
schema 12.51
schemata 12.82
schematic 21.17

scheme 24.5
schemer 12.51
scheming 26.9
scherzo 9.22
Schiaparelli 4.22
Schiele 12.43
Schiller 12.43
Schilling 26.8
schism 24.21
schismatic 21.17
schist 31.6
schizo 9.22
schizoid 16.24
schizophrenia 12.8
schizophrenic 21.13
Schlegel 23.30
schlemiel 23.7
schlepp 27.3
Schleswig 18.6
Schliemann 25.45
schlieren 25.47
schlock 21.20
schlocky 4.19
schmaltz 28.47
schmaltzy 4.47
schmooze 35.21
schmuck 21.29
schnapps 28.46
schnauzer 12.70
schnitzel 23.37
schnook 21.28
schnozz 35.16
Schoenberg 18.13
scholar 12.44
scholarly 4.27
scholastic 21.17
scholiastic 21.17
school 23.20
schoolbook 21.28
schoolboy 10.3
schoolchild 16.36
schoolchildren 25.47
schoolfellow 9.17
schoolgirl 23.42
schoolhouse 28.16
schoolie 4.26
schooling 26.8
schoolman 25.2
schoolmarm 24.2
schoolmarmish 29.8
schoolmaster 12.75
schoolmastering 26.11
schoolmasterly 4.27
schoolmate 30.12
schoolmistress 28.10
schoolroom 24.12
schoolteacher 12.23
schoolteaching 26.4

schooner 12.56
Schopenhauer 12.16
schorl 23.14
schottische 29.5
Schroder 12.28
Schrüodinger 12.60
schtuck 21.28
Schubert 30.41
Schulz 28.47
Schumacher 12.37
Schumann 25.45
schuss 28.20
Schütz 28.47
schwa 1.1
Schwann 25.24
Schwarzkopf 17.8
Schwarzwald 16.35
Schweitzer 12.70
sciatic 21.17
sciatica 12.39
science 28.45
sciential 23.38
scientific 21.10
scientist 31.14
Scientology 4.17
sci-fi 6.7
scilicet 30.5
scilla 12.43
Scillies 35.10
scimitar 12.78
scintilla 12.43
scintillate 30.11
scion 25.38
Scipio 9.4
scissel 23.37
scission 25.42
scissor 12.90
scleroses 35.8
sclerosis 28.11
sclerotic 21.17
scoff 17.8
scoffer 12.30
scold 16.37
scolder 12.28
scolding 26.5
scollop 27.14
sconce 28.44
Scone 25.33
scone 25.24
scoop 27.11
scooper 12.63
scoot 30.37
scooter 12.81
scooterist 31.12
scope 27.10
scorch 15.8
scorcher 12.24
score 7.1
scoreboard 16.20
scorebook 21.28
scorecard 16.2

scorekeeper 12.61
scorer 12.66
scoring 26.11
scorn 25.28
scorner 12.56
scorp 27.9
Scorpian 25.37
Scorpio 9.4
scorpion 25.37
Scorpius 28.23
scorzonera 12.67
Scot 30.31
scotch 15.7
scoter 12.80
scot-free 4.1
Scotia 12.73
Scotland 16.45
Scots 28.47
Scotsman 25.45
Scotsmen 25.45
Scotswoman 25.45
Scotswomen 25.17
Scott 30.31
Scottie 4.54
Scottish 29.10
scoundrel 23.36
scoundrelly 4.27
scour 12.16
scourer 12.67
scourge 20.17
scourger 12.36
Scouser 12.70
scout 30.34
scouter 12.80
Scoutmaster 12.75
scow 8.1
scowl 23.16
scowler 12.44
scrabble 23.26
scrag 18.1
scrag-end 16.41
scraggly 4.21
scraggy 4.15
scram 24.1
scramble 23.26
scrambler 12.42
scramjet 30.4
scran 25.1
Scranton 25.50
scrap 27.1
scrapbook 21.28
scrapbooking 26.7
scrape 27.4
scraper 12.61
scraperboard 16.20
scrapheap 27.5
scrapie 4.36
scraping 26.10
scrappage 20.7
scrapper 12.61
scrapple 23.35

S

scrappy 4.36
scrapyard 16.2
scratch 15.1
scratchboard 16.20
scratcher 12.23
scratch pad 16.1
scratchy 4.11
scrawl 23.14
scrawly 4.25
scrawny 4.32
scream 24.5
screamer 12.51
scree 4.1
screech 15.5
screecher 12.23
screechy 4.11
screed 16.7
screen 25.9
screener 12.54
screening 26.9
screenplay 3.15
screen print 30.54
screenwriter 12.79
screenwriting 26.13
screw 11.1
screwball 23.14
screwdriver 12.86
screwer 12.19
screwtop 27.8
screw-top 27.8
screw worm 24.22
screwy 4.8
Scriabin 25.13
scribal 23.26
scribble 23.26
scribbler 12.48
scribbling 26.8
scribbly 4.27
scribe 14.8
scriber 12.21
scrim 24.6
scrimmage 20.7
scrimmager 12.35
scrimp 27.17
scrimshank 21.33
scrimshanker 12.37
scrimshaw 7.17
scrip 27.6
script 30.58
scriptoria 12.10
scriptorial 23.24
scriptorium 24.16
scripture 12.23
Scriptures 35.24
scriptwriter 12.79
scriptwriting 26.13
scrivener 12.58
scrod 16.18
scrofulous 28.27
scroll 23.17
scroller 12.44

scrooge 20.15
scrotum 24.20
scrounge 20.19
scrounger 12.35
scrub 14.13
scrubber 12.22
scrubby 4.10
scrubland 16.40
scruff 17.15
scruffy 4.14
scrum 24.14
scrum half 17.2
scrummage 20.7
scrummager 12.35
scrummy 4.30
scrump 27.17
scrumple 23.35
scrumptious 28.33
scrumpy 4.37
scrunch 29.20
scruple 23.35
scrupulosity 4.53
scrupulous 28.27
scrutineer 12.4
scrutinizer 12.91
scrutiny 4.32
scry 6.1
scryer 12.13
scuba 12.21
scuba-dive 34.9
scud 16.27
scuff 17.15
scuffle 23.29
scull 23.22
sculler 12.47
scullery 4.43
scullion 25.37
sculpt 30.58
sculptor 12.81
sculpture 12.24
sculpturesque 21.35
scum 24.14
scumbag 18.1
scumble 23.26
scummy 4.30
scuncheon 25.49
scunge 20.19
scungy 4.17
scunner 12.57
Scunthorpe 27.9
scup 27.13
scupper 12.63
scurf 17.17
scurfy 4.14
scurrilous 28.27
scurry 4.42
scurvy 4.58
scut 30.40
Scutari 4.38
scutch 15.13
scutcheon 25.39

scutcher 12.24
scutter 12.81
scuttle 23.39
scuttlebutt 30.40
scuzzy 4.62
scythe 33.5
Scythia 12.12
Scythian 25.37
sea 4.1
seabed 16.3
seabird 16.31
seaboard 16.20
seaborne 25.28
seacock 21.20
seadog 18.8
seafarer 12.65
seafaring 26.11
seafood 16.25
seafront 30.55
seagoing 26.3
seagull 23.22
sea horse 28.15
seal 23.7
sealant 30.56
sealer 12.43
sealskin 25.15
Sealyham 24.16
seam 24.5
seaman 25.45
seamanlike 21.19
seamanly 4.27
seamark 21.5
seamen 25.45
seamer 12.51
seamstress 28.10
Seamus 28.28
seamy 4.29
Sean 25.28
Seanad 16.29
séance 28.44
seaplane 25.8
seaport 30.33
seaquake 21.7
sear 12.4
search 15.14
searcher 12.24
searchlight 30.28
Searle 23.42
Sears 35.24
seascape 27.4
seashell 23.4
seashore 7.17
seasick 21.16
seaside 16.16
season 25.52
seasonal 23.34
seasoning 26.9
seat belt 30.51
seat 30.18
Seattle 23.39
seawall 23.14

seaward 16.30
seawater 12.80
seaway 3.25
seaweed 16.7
seaworthy 4.57
sebaceous 28.33
Sebastian 25.37
Sebastopol 23.13
Sebat 30.1
sec 21.6
secateurs 35.25
secco 9.16
secede 16.7
seceder 12.26
secessional 23.34
secessionist 31.10
seclude 16.25
seclusion 25.42
seclusive 34.7
second 16.42, 16.45
secondary 4.43
secondee 4.1
seconder 12.29
secondi 4.13
secondo 9.11
secrecy 4.46
secret 30.24
secretaire 2.1
secretarial 23.24
secretariat 30.41
secretary 4.43
secrete 30.18
secretion 25.49
secretor 12.77
sect 30.48
sectarian 25.37
sectarianize 35.13
section 25.49
sectional 23.34
sectionalist 31.8
sectionalize 35.12
sector 12.76
sectorial 23.24
secular 12.46
secularist 31.12
secularity 4.53
secularize 35.13
secure 12.20
securitize 35.14
security 4.53
sedan 25.1
sedate 30.7
sedation 25.49
sedentary 4.43
Seder 12.26
sederunt 30.56
sedge 20.3
Sedgemoor 7.12
Sedgwick 21.18
sedgy 4.17
sedilia 12.6

sedimentary 4.43
sedition 25.49
seditious 28.33
seduce 28.19
seducer 12.71
seducible 23.26
seduction 25.49
seductress 28.10
sedulity 4.53
sedulous 28.27
see 4.1
seeable 23.26
seed 16.7
seedbed 16.3
seedcake 21.7
seedcorn 25.28
seeder 12.26
seedling 26.8
seedsman 25.45
seedsmen 25.45
seedy 4.12
Seeger 12.31
seek 21.8
seeker 12.38
seel 23.7
seem 24.5
seemly 4.23
seen 25.9
seep 27.5
seepage 20.7
seer 12.3,12.4
seersucker 12.41
seesaw 7.16
seethe 33.3
see-through 11.17
segment 30.53, 30.56
segmentalize 35.12
segmentary 4.43
Segovia 12.12
segregate 30.9
segue 3.25
seguidilla 12.89
sei 3.1
seif 17.5
seigneur 13.1
seigneurial 23.24
Seine 25.7
seiner 12.54
seise 35.6
seisin 25.20
seismic 21.12
seismical 23.32
seismograph 17.2
seismology 4.17
seize 35.6
seizer 12.90
seizure 12.33
seldom 24.17
select 30.48
selection 25.49
selector 12.76

Selene 4.31
selenide 16.14
selenite 30.29
selenium 24.16
Seleucid 16.11
self 17.18
self-absorbed 16.32
self-addressed 31.3
self-adjusting 26.13
self-aggrandizing
  26.14
self-appointed 16.12
self-assured 16.28
self-catering 26.11
self-centered 16.29
self-centred 16.29
self-cocking 26.7
self-colored 16.29
self-coloured 16.29
self-confessed 31.3
self-contained 16.41
self-controlled
  16.37
self-deceiving 26.14
self-defeating 26.13
self-denying 26.3
self-deprecating
  26.13
self-educated 16.12
self-effacing 26.12
self-employed 16.24
self-faced 31.4
self-feeding 26.5
self-fulfilling 26.8
self-governed 16.45
self-governing 26.9
self-imposed 16.50
self-induced 31.22
self-inflicted 16.12
self-interested
  16.12
selfish 29.7
self-mocking 26.7
self-motivated 16.12
self-perpetuating
  26.13
self-pitying 26.3
self-possessed 31.3
self-proclaimed
  16.39
self-propelled 16.35
self-propelling 26.8
self-regarding 26.5
self-regulating
  26.13
self-respecting
  26.13
self-restrained
  16.41
Selfridge 20.8
self-righting 26.13

self-sacrificing
  26.12
self-satisfied 16.14
self-sealing 26.8
self-seeking 26.7
self-selecting 26.13
self-styled 16.36
self-supporting
  26.13
self-sustained 16.41
self-sustaining 26.9
self-willed 16.35
self-diagnose 35.19
self-storage 20.8
Selima 12.51
Selina 12.54
Seljuk 21.27
Selkirk 21.31
sell 23.3
Sellafield 16.35
seller 12.42
Sellers 35.24
sellotape 27.4
sell-out 30.34
Selma 12.50
Selous 11.1
seltzer 12.69
Selvas 28.35
selvedge 20.9
selves 35.35
Selwyn 25.20
Selznick 21.13
semantic 21.17
semaphore 7.6
semaphoric 21.15
Semarang 26.1
semblance 28.45
Semele 4.24
semen 25.45
semester 12.76
semi 4.29
semi-automatic
  21.17
semibreve 34.5
semicircle 23.32
semicircular 12.46
semicolon 25.44
semiconductor 12.81
semifreddo 9.11
semi-detached 30.46
semi-final 23.34
semi-finalist 31.8
Semillon 25.27
seminal 23.34
seminar 1.14
seminarian 25.37
seminarist 31.12
seminary 4.43
Seminole 23.17
semiology 4.17
semiotic 21.17

semi-precious 28.33
semiquaver 12.85
semi-retired 16.28
Semite 30.29
Semitic 21.17
Semitist 31.14
semitone 25.31
semi-tropical 23.32
semi-tropics 28.39
semivowel 23.25
semmit 30.23
semolina 12.54
sempervivum 24.20
semplice 4.11
sempre 3.19
sempstress 28.10
Semtex 28.38
senarius 28.23
senary 4.43
senate 30.23
senator 12.78
senatorial 23.24
send 16.41
Sendai 6.6
sendal 23.28
sender 12.26
Seneca 12.39
Senegal 23.14
Senegalese 35.6
seneschal 23.38
senhor 7.1
senhora 12.66
Senhorita 12.77
senile 23.11
senility 4.53
senior 12.8
seniority 4.53
senna 12.53
Sennacherib 14.7
sennet 30.23
sennight 30.29
sennit 30.23
señor 7.1
señora 12.66
senores 35.5
senorita 12.77
sensate 30.15
sensationalist 31.8
sense 28.44
sensible 23.26
sensitizer 12.91
sensor 12.69
sensory 4.43
sensual 23.25
sensualist 31.8
sensualize 35.12
sensum 24.20
sensuous 28.24
sent 30.53
sente 4.51
sentence 28.45

S

S

shalwar 1.21
shaly 4.22
sham 24.1
shaman 25.45
shamanic 21.13
shamanist 31.10
shamateur 12.82
shamble 23.26
shambolic 21.11
shame 24.4
shamefaced 31.4
Shamir 12.4
shammer 12.50
shammy 4.29
shampoo 11.1
shamrock 21.21
shamus 28.28
Shan 25.4
shandy 4.12
Shane 25.7
Shang 26.1
shanghai 6.1
Shangri-La 1.1
shank 21.33
Shankar 1.11
Shankly 4.21
Shanks 28.41
Shannon 25.46
shan't 30.53
shantung 26.18
shanty town 25.29
shanty 4.51
Shanxi 4.1
shape 27.4
shapely 4.22
shaper 12.61
shaping 26.10
shard 16.2
share 2.1
sharecrop 27.8
sharecropper 12.62
shareholder 12.28
shareholding 26.5
sharer 12.65
shareware 2.15
shapewear 2.15
sharia 12.3
Sharif 17.5
Sharjah 1.10
shark 21.5
sharkskin 25.15
Sharman 25.45
Sharon 25.47
sharp 27.2
Shar Pei 3.1
sharpen 25.46
sharpener 12.58
sharpening 26.9
sharper 12.61
sharpie 4.36
sharpish 29.9

sharpshooter 12.81
sharpshooting 26.13
Shastra 12.64
shat 30.1
Shatt al-Arab 14.14
shatter 12.74
shatterer 12.67
shatterproof 17.13
shave 34.4
shaven 25.51
shaver 12.85
Shavian 25.37
shaving 26.14
Shavuoth 28.24
shaw 7.1
shawl 23.14
shawm 24.9
Shawnee 4.1
shay 3.1
shchi 4.1
she 4.1
shea 4.1
sheading 26.5
sheaf 17.5
shear 12.4
shearer 12.67
shearing 26.11
shearling 26.8
shearwater 12.80
sheath 32.5
sheathe 33.3
sheathing 26.14
sheave 34.5
Sheba 12.21
shebang 26.1
shebeen 25.9
shed 16.3
she'd 16.7
shedder 12.26
she-devil 23.40
sheen 25.9
Sheena 12.54
sheeny 4.31
sheep 27.5
sheepdip 27.6
sheepdog 18.8
sheepfold 16.37
sheepish 29.9
sheeplike 21.19
sheep run 25.35
sheepshank 21.33
sheepskin 25.15
sheep walk 21.22
sheer 12.4
sheer legs 35.28
sheet 30.18
Sheetrock 21.21
Sheffield 16.35
sheikh 21.7
sheikhdom 24.17
sheila 12.43

shekel 23.32
Shekinah 12.55
Shelagh 12.43
Sheldon 25.40
shelduck 21.29
shelf 17.18
shelf-life 17.7
she'll 23.7
shell shock 21.21
shell 23.3
shellac 21.1
shellback 21.2
Shelley 4.22
shellfire 12.14
shellfish 29.7
shelly 4.22
Shelta 12.76
shelter 12.76
shelterer 12.67
sheltie 4.51
shelve 34.15
shelves 35.35
Shem 24.3
Shema 12.50
shemozzle 23.41
Shenandoah 12.17
shenanigans 35.31
Shenyang 26.1
Shenzhen 25.5
shepherd 16.29
shepherdess 28.3
Sher 13.1
Sheraton 25.50
sherbet 30.41
shereef 17.5
Sheridan 25.40
sheriff 17.6
Sherman 25.45
sherpa 12.63
Sherrington 25.50
sherry 4.38
Sheryl 23.9
she's 35.6
Shetland 16.45
Shetlander 12.29
Shevardnadze 12.90
shew 9.1
Shia 12.3
shiatsu 11.18
shibboleth 32.3
shicker 12.39
shied 16.14
shield 16.35
Shields 35.27
shieling 26.8
shift 30.47
shifter 12.78
shifty 4.53
shih-tzu 11.1
Shiism 24.21
Shiite 30.26

shikar 1.1
shikara 12.64
shikari 4.38
Shikoku 11.12
shill 23.8
shillelagh 12.43
shilling 26.8
Shillong 26.15
Shilluk 21.28
shilly-shally 4.21
shilly-shallyer 12.6
Shilton 25.50
shim 24.6
shimmer 12.51
shimmery 4.43
shimmy 4.29
shin 25.13
shin bone 25.30
shindig 18.6
shindy 4.12
shine 25.21
shiner 12.55
shingle 23.30
shingly 4.24
shinny 4.32
shin splints 28.47
Shinto 9.24
Shintoist 31.6
shinty 4.53
shiny 4.32
ship 27.6
shipboard 16.20
shipbroker 12.40
shipbuilder 12.27
shipbuilding 26.5
Shipley 4.24
shipload 16.23
shipmate 30.12
shipowner 12.56
shipper 12.62
ship-rigged 16.33
shipshape 27.4
ship-to-shore 7.1
shipway 3.25
shipwreck 21.6
shipwright 30.29
shipyard 16.2
Shiraz 35.1
shire 12.13
shire horse 28.15
shirk 21.31
shirker 12.41
Shirley 4.28
shirr 13.1
shirt 30.45
shirtdress 28.3
shirting 26.13
shirtsleeve 34.5
shirt tail 23.6
shirtwaist 31.4
shirtwaister 12.77

S

shirty 4.55
shit 30.20
shite 30.26
shit-scared 16.5
shitty 4.53
shiv 34.6
Shiva 12.85
shiver 12.86
shiverer 12.67
shivery 4.43
shoal 23.17
shoaly 4.25
shoat 30.35
shock 21.20
shocker 12.40
shocking 26.7
shockproof 17.13
shod 16.18
shoddy 4.13
shoe 11.1
shoebill 23.8
shoeblack 21.3
shoebox 28.40
shoehorn 25.28
shoelace 28.5
shoemaking 26.7
shoeshine 25.23
shoestring 26.11
shoetree 4.41
shofar 12.30
shofroth 30.35
shogun 25.35
Sholto 9.25
Shona 12.56
shone 25.24
shonky 4.19
shoo 11.1
shoo-in 25.13
shook 21.28
shoot 30.37
shooter 12.81
shooting 26.13
shoot-out 30.34
shop 27.8
shopaholic 21.11
shopfitter 12.78
shopfitting 26.13
shop-floor 7.1
shopfront 30.55
shopkeeper 12.61
shopkeeping 26.10
shoplift 30.47
shoplifter 12.78
shopper 12.62
shopsoiled 16.37
shopwalker 12.40
shopworker 12.41
shopworn 25.28
shore 7.1
shorebird 16.31
shoreline 25.22

shoreward 16.30
shoring 26.11
shorn 25.28
short 30.33
shortage 20.9
short weight 30.7
short-arm 24.2
shortbread 16.4
shortcake 21.7
short-change 20.19
short-circuit 30.21
short-handed 16.9
shortcoming 26.9
shortcut 30.40
shorten 25.50
shortfall 23.15
shorthair 2.6
shorthand 16.40
short handed 16.9
shorthaul 23.15
shorthold 16.37
shorthorn 25.28
shortish 29.10
shortlist 31.8
shortsighted 16.12
shortstop 27.8
shortwave 34.4
short weight 30.7
shorty 4.54
Shoshone 4.33
Shostakovich 15.6
shot 30.31
shotgun 25.35
should 16.26
shoulder 12.28
shouldn't 30.56
shout 30.34
shouter 12.80
shove 34.13
shove-halfpenny
   4.31
shovel 23.40
shovelboard 16.20
shoveler 12.48
shoveller 12.48
show 9.1
show-and-tell 23.3
showband 16.40
showbiz 35.10
showboat 30.35
showcard 16.2
showcase 28.5
showdown 25.29
shower 12.16, 12.17
showerproof 17.13
showery 4.43
showgirl 23.42
showground 16.43
showing 26.3
showjump 27.17
showjumper 12.63

showjumping 26.10
showman 25.45
showmen 25.45
shown 25.30
show-off 17.8
showpiece 28.6
showplace 28.5
showroom 24.12
show-stopper 12.62
show-stopping 26.10
showy 4.7
shoyu 11.22
shrank 21.33
shrapnel 23.34
shred 16.3
shredder 12.26
Shreveport 30.33
shrew 11.1
shrewd 16.25
shrewish 29.6
Shrewsbury 4.43
shriek 21.8
shrieker 12.38
shrieval 23.40
shrift 30.47
shrike 21.19
shrill 23.8
shrimp 27.17
shrimper 12.62
shrine 25.21
shrink 21.33
shrinkage 20.6
shrinker 12.39
shrinking 26.7
shrive 34.9
shrivel 23.40
shriven 25.51
Shropshire 12.11
shroud 16.22
shrove 34.11
Shrovetide 16.17
shrub 14.13
shrubbery 4.43
shrubby 4.10
shrug 18.12
shrunk 21.34
shrunken 25.43
shtick 21.9
shuck 21.29
shucker 12.41
shudder 12.29
shuddery 4.43
shuffle 23.29
shuffleboard 16.20
shuffler 12.48
shuffling 26.8
shufti 4.55
shul 23.20
Shula 12.45
Shumen 25.5
shun 25.35

shunt 30.55
shunter 12.81
shush 29.16
shut 30.40
shutdown 25.29
Shute 30.37
shut-eye 6.18
shut-out 30.34
shutter 12.81
shutterbug 18.12
shuttle 23.39
shuttlecock 21.20
shy 6.1
shyer 12.13
Shylock 21.21
shyly 4.25
shyness 28.9
shyster 12.79
si 4.1
Siam 24.1
Siamese 35.6
Siân 25.4
sib 14.7
Sibelius 28.23
Siberia 12.10
Siberian 25.37
sibilance 28.45
sibilant 30.56
sibilate 30.11
sibling 26.8
sibyl 23.8
sibylline 25.22
sic 21.9
sice 28.13
Sichuan 25.4
Sicilian 25.37
siciliano 9.19
Sicily 4.24
sick 21.9
sickbay 3.7
sickbed 16.3
sicken 25.43
sickener 12.58
Sickert 30.42
sickie 4.19
sickish 29.8
sickle 23.32
sickly 4.24
sicko 9.16
sickroom 24.12
Siddons 35.31
side 16.14
sidearm 24.2
sidebar 1.4
sideboard 16.20
sideburn 25.53
sidecar 1.11
sidehill 23.9
sidekick 21.11
sidelamp 27.17
sidelight 30.28

sideline 25.22
sidelong 26.15
side-on 25.24
sidereal 23.24
side-saddle 23.28
sideshow 9.23
side-slip 27.6
side-splitting 26.13
sidestep 27.3
sidestepper 12.61
sidestroke 21.24
sideswipe 27.7
sidetrack 21.3
sidewalk 21.22
sideward 16.30
sideways 35.5
sidewinder 12.27
sidewise 35.15
siding 26.5
sidle 23.28
Sidmouth 32.13
Sidney 4.32
Sidon 25.40
siege 20.5
Siegfried 16.7
Sieg Heil 23.11
Siemens 35.31
Siena 12.53
Sienese 35.6
sienna 12.53
sierra 12.64
Sierra Madre 3.19
siesta 12.76
sieve 34.6
sievert 30.44
sifaka 12.37
sift 30.47
sifter 12.78
sigh 6.1
sight 30.26
sighter 12.79
sighting 26.13
sight line 25.22
sightly 4.25
sight-reader 12.26
sight screen 25.11
sightsee 4.46
sightseeing 26.3
sightseer 12.3
sigil 23.9
Sigismund 16.45
sigla 12.43
sigma 12.51
Sigmund 16.45
sign 25.21
signal 23.34
signaler 12.48
signalize 35.12
signaller 12.48
signalman 25.45
signalmen 25.45

signatory 4.43
signature 12.24
signboard 16.20
signer 12.55
signet 30.23
significance 28.45
significant 30.56
signified 16.14
signifier 12.14
signify 6.7
signing 26.9
signor 7.1
signora 12.66
signorina 12.54
signpost 31.20
signwriter 12.79
signwriting 26.13
Sigurd 16.31
Sihanouk 21.28
sika 12.38
Sikh 21.8
Sikkim 24.6
Sikkimese 35.6
Sikorsky 4.19
silage 20.6
Silas 28.27
Silchester 12.78
sild 16.35
silence 28.45
silencer 12.71
silent 30.56
Silesia 12.12
Silesian 25.37
silex 28.38
silhouette 30.4
silica 12.39
silicate 30.42
siliceous 28.33
silicon 25.43
silicone 25.30
siliqua 12.88
siliquose 28.17
silk 21.32
silken 25.43
silkscreen 25.11
silkworm 24.22
silky 4.19
sill 23.8
Sillitoe 9.24
Sills 35.29
silly 4.24
silo 9.17
Siloam 24.17
silt 30.51
siltstone 25.31
silty 4.53
Silurian 25.37
Silvanus 28.29
silver 12.86
silverfish 29.7
silvern 25.51

silverside 16.16
silversmith 32.6
silversmithing 26.14
Silverstone 25.31
silverware 2.15
silverweed 16.7
silvery 4.43
silviculture 12.24
silviculturist 31.12
Sim 24.6
simcha 12.23
significance 28.45
Simenon 25.26
Simeon 25.37
simian 25.37
similar 12.43
similarity 4.53
simile 4.24
similitude 16.25
Simla 12.43
simmer 12.51
simoleon 25.37
Simon 25.45
Simone 25.30
Simonides 35.7
simon-pure 12.20
simony 4.34
simp 27.17
simpatico 9.16
simper 12.62
simple 23.35
simple-minded 16.9
simpleton 25.50
simplex 28.38
simplify 6.7
Simplon 25.25
Simpson 25.48
Sims 35.30
simulacra 12.65
simulacrum 24.19
simulate 30.11
simulcast 31.2
simultaneity 4.53
simultaneous 28.23
sin 25.13
Sinai 6.3
Sinatra 12.64
Sinbad 16.1
sin bin 25.13
since 28.44
sincere 12.4
sincerity 4.53
Sinclair 2.8
Sind 16.42
Sindebele 4.23
Sindhi 4.12
Sindy 4.12
sine 25.21
Sinéad 16.6
sinecure 12.20
sinecurist 31.12

sine qua non 25.24
sinew 11.22
sinewy 4.8
sinfonia 12.8
sinfonietta 12.76
sinful 23.21
sing 26.3
singalong 26.15
Singapore 7.1
Singaporean 25.37
singe 20.19
singer 12.60
Singh 26.3
single 23.30
single-minded 16.9
singlet 30.22
singleton 25.50
singsong 26.15
singular 12.46
singularity 4.53
singularize 35.13
Sinhala 12.42
Sinhalese 35.6
sinister 12.78
sinistral 23.36
sink 21.33
sinkage 20.6
sinker 12.39
sinkhole 23.17
sinking 26.7
sinless 28.8
sinner 12.55
sinnet 30.23
Sinn Fein 25.7
Sinn Feiner 12.54
Sintra 12.65
sinuosity 4.53
sinuous 28.24
sinus 28.29
sinusitis 28.12
Siouan 25.38
Sioux 11.1
sip 27.6
sipe 27.7
siphon 25.41
siphonic 21.13
sipper 12.62
sippet 30.23
sir 13.1
sirdar 1.6
sire 12.13
siren 25.47
Sirius 28.23
sirloin 25.32
sirocco 9.16
sirrah 12.65
sirree 4.1
sirup 27.14
sirupy 4.37
sis 28.7
sisal 23.37

S

siskin 25.15
Sisley 4.24
sissified 16.14
sissy 4.46
sissyish 29.6
sister 12.78
sisterhood 16.26
sister-in-law 7.11
sisterly 4.27
Sistine 25.12
sistra 12.65
sistrum 24.19
Sisyphean 25.36
Sisyphus 28.25
sit 30.20
Sita 12.77
sitar 1.19
sitarist 31.12
sitcom 24.8
sit-down 25.29
site 30.26
sit-in 25.19
Sitka 12.39
Sittang 26.1
sitter 12.78
sitting 26.13
situate 30.8, 30.41
situationist 31.10
sit-up 27.13
Sitwell 23.4
Sitzkrieg 18.5
Sivaite 30.26
Sivan 25.51
Siwash 29.11
six 28.39
sixain 25.8
sixer 12.70
sixfold 16.37
sixgun 25.35
sixpence 28.45
sixpenny 4.34
six-shooter 12.81
sixteen 25.9
sixteenth 32.19
sixth 32.22
sixth-former 12.52
sixtieth 32.6
sixty 4.53
sizable 23.26
size 35.11
sizer 12.91
Sizewell 23.4
sizzle 23.41
sizzler 12.48
sjambok 21.20
ska 1.1
Skagerrak 21.3
Skanda 12.25
skarn 25.4
skat 30.1
skate 30.7

skateboard 16.20
skateboarder 12.28
skatepark 21.5
skater 12.77
skean 25.36
skean dhu 11.1
sked 16.3
skedaddle 23.28
skeet 30.18
skeeter 12.77
skeg 18.3
skein 25.7
skeletal 23.39
skeleton 25.50
Skelton 25.50
skep 27.3
skeptic 21.17
skeptical 23.32
skerrick 21.15
sketch 15.3
sketchbook 21.28
sketcher 12.23
sketch pad 16.1
sketchy 4.11
skew 11.1
skewbald 16.36
skewer 12.19
skew-whiff 17.6
ski 4.1
skiable 23.26
skibob 14.9
skid 16.8
skidlid 16.10
skidoo 11.1
skidpan 25.3
skier 12.3
skiff 17.6
skiffle 23.29
ski-jump 27.17
skilift 30.47
skill 23.8
skillet 30.22
skilly 4.24
skim 24.6
skimmer 12.51
skimp 27.17
skimpy 4.36
skin 25.13
skincare 2.7
skin-deep 27.5
skinflick 21.11
skinflint 30.54
skinhead 16.3
skink 21.33
skinner 12.55
skinny 4.32
skinny-dip 27.6
skint 30.54
skintight 30.26
skip 27.6
skipjack 21.3

ski-plane 25.8
skipper 12.62
skippet 30.23
skipping-rope 27.10
skirl 23.42
skirmish 29.8
skirmisher 12.72
skirr 13.1
skirret 30.24
skirt 30.45
skirting 26.13
skit 30.20
skite 30.26
skitter 12.78
skittery 4.43
skittish 29.10
skittle 23.39
skivo 34.9
skiver 12.86
Skivvies 35.10
skivvy 4.58
skoal 23.17
skol 23.13
skua 12.19
skulduggery 4.43
skulk 21.32
skulker 12.41
skull 23.22
skullcap 27.1
skunk 21.34
sky 6.1
skydive 34.9
skydiver 12.86
skydiving 26.14
Skye 6.1
skyer 12.13
skyey 4.4
sky-high 6.1
skyhook 21.28
skyjack 21.3
skyjacker 12.37
Skylab 14.1
skylark 21.5
skyless 28.8
skylight 30.28
skyline 25.22
Skype 27.7
skyrocket 30.21
skysail 23.6
skyscape 27.4
skyscraper 12.61
skywalk 21.22
skyward 16.30
skywatch 15.7
skyway 3.25
skywriting 26.13
slab 14.1
slack 21.1
slacken 25.43
slacker 12.37
slag 18.1

slaggy 4.15
slagheap 27.5
slain 25.7
sláinte 12.35
slake 21.7
slalom 24.18
slam 24.1
slambang 26.1
slammer 12.50
slander 12.25
slanderer 12.67
slanderous 28.31
slang 26.1
slangy 4.35
slant 30.53
slantwise 35.15
slap 27.1
slapdash 29.1
slap-happy 4.36
slapshot 30.32
slapstick 21.17
slap-up 27.13
slash 29.1
slasher 12.72
slat 30.1
slate 30.7
slater 12.77
slather 12.84
slating 26.13
slattern 25.50
slatternly 4.21
slaty 4.52
slaughter 12.80
slaughterer 12.67
slaughterhouse 28.16
slaughterous 28.31
Slav 34.2
slave 34.4
slave-driver 12.86
slaver 12.85
slavery 4.43
slavey 4.58
Slavic 21.18
slavish 29.10
Slavonic 21.13
slay 3.1
slayer 12.2
slaying 26.3
sleaze 35.6
sleazy 4.61
sled 16.3
sledge 20.3
sledgehammer 12.50
sleek 21.8
sleeky 4.18
sleep 27.5
sleeper 12.61
sleepover 12.86
sleepwalk 21.22

sleepwalker 12.40
sleepwalking 26.7
sleepwear 2.15
sleepy 4.36
sleepyhead 16.3
sleet 30.18
sleety 4.52
sleeve 34.5
sleigh 3.1
sleight 30.26
slender 12.26
slenderize 35.13
slept 30.58
sleuth 32.12
slew 11.1
sley 3.1
slice 28.13
slicer 12.70
slick 21.9
slicker 12.39
slid 16.8
slide 16.14
slider 12.27
slight 30.26
slightish 29.10
Sligo 9.13
slim 24.6
slime 24.7
slimline 25.22
slimmer 12.51
slimy 4.29
sling 26.3
slingback 21.2
slinger 12.60
slingshot 30.32
slink 21.33
slinky 4.19
slip 27.6
slipcase 28.5
slipcover 12.87
slip knot 30.32
slipover 12.86
slippage 20.7
slipper 12.62
slippery 4.43
slippy 4.36
slipshod 16.18
slipstream 24.5
slipway 3.25
slit 30.20
slither 12.84
slithery 4.43
slitter 12.78
slitty 4.53
sliver 12.86
slivovitz 28.47
slo-mo 9.18
Sloane 25.30
Sloaney 4.33
slob 14.9
slobber 12.21

slobbery 4.43
slobbish 29.6
sloe 9.1
sloe-eyed 16.14
slog 18.8
slogan 25.41
slogger 12.32
sloop 27.11
sloosh 29.14
sloot 30.37
slop 27.8
slope 27.10
sloppy 4.36
slosh 29.11
sloshy 4.50
slot 30.31
sloth 32.11
slouch 15.9
slouchy 4.11
slough 17.15
Slough 8.1
Slovak 21.4
Slovakia 12.6
sloven 25.51
Slovene 25.12
Slovenia 12.8
Slovenian 25.37
slovenly 4.26
slow 9.1
slowcoach 15.10
slowdown 25.29
slowish 29.6
slowpoke 21.24
slow-worm 24.22
slub 14.13
sludge 20.16
sludgy 4.17
slug 18.12
sluggard 16.28
sluggardly 4.27
slugger 12.32
sluggish 29.7
sluice 28.19
sluicegate 30.9
sluiceway 3.25
slum 24.14
slumber 12.22
slumberer 12.67
slumberous 28.31
slumgullion 25.52
slumlord 16.21
slummock 21.30
slummy 4.30
slump 27.17
slung 26.18
slunk 21.34
slur 13.1
slurp 27.15
slurry 4.42
slush 29.16
slushy 4.50

slut 30.40
sluttish 29.10
sly 6.1
slyboots 28.47
slyly 4.25
slyness 28.9
slype 27.7
smack 21.1
smacker 12.37
small 23.14
smallholder 12.28
smallholding 26.5
smallish 29.8
small-minded 16.9
smallpox 28.40
small talk 21.22
smalt 30.51
smarm 24.2
smarmy 4.29
smart 30.3
smart-alecky 4.19
smart-arse 28.2
smarten 25.50
smartish 29.10
smarty-pants 28.47
smash 29.1
smash-and-grab
  14.1
smasher 12.72
smatter 12.74
smattering 26.11
smear 12.4
smearer 12.67
smeary 4.43
smell 23.3
smeller 12.42
smelly 4.22
smelt 30.51
Smersh 29.18
Smetana 12.58
smew 11.1
smidgen 25.14
smile 23.11
smiler 12.44
Smiles 35.29
smiley 4.25
Smily 4.25
smirch 15.14
smirk 21.31
smirker 12.41
smirky 4.20
smite 30.26
smiter 12.79
smith 32.6
smithereens 35.31
Smithers 35.24
Smithfield 16.35
smithy 4.57
smitten 25.50
smock 21.20
smog 18.8

smoggy 4.15
smoke 21.24
smokehouse 28.16
smoker 12.40
smokescreen 25.11
smokestack 21.4
smoky 4.20
smolder 12.28
Smolensk 21.35
Smollett 30.22
smolt 30.51
smooch 15.11
smoocher 12.24
smoochy 4.11
smoodge 20.15
smooth 33.8
smoother 12.84
smooth-faced 31.4
smoothie 4.57
smoothish 29.10
smooth-talk 21.22
smooth-tongued
  16.47
smorgasbord 16.20
smote 30.35
smother 12.84
smoulder 12.28
smriti 4.53
smudge 20.16
smudgy 4.17
smug 18.12
smuggle 23.30
smuggler 12.48
smut 30.40
Smuts 28.47
smutty 4.55
Smyrna 12.59
snack 21.1
snaffle 23.29
snafu 11.1
snag 18.1
snaggle-toothed
  30.60
snaggy 4.15
snail 23.5
snake 21.7
snakebite 30.26
snake-charmer
  12.50
snakeroot 30.37
snakeskin 25.15
snaky 4.18
snap 27.1
snapdragon 25.41
snapper 12.61
snappish 29.9
snappy 4.36
snapshot 30.32
snare 2.1
snarer 12.65
snark 21.5

S

solstitial 23.38
Solti 4.54
soluble 23.26
solus 28.27
solution 25.49
solve 34.15
solvency 4.48
solvent 30.56
solver 12.86
Solzhenitsyn 25.19
soma 12.52
Somali 4.21
Somalia 12.6
Somalian 25.37
somatic 21.17
somber 12.21
sombre 12.21
sombrero 9.21
some 24.14
somebody 4.13
someday 3.9
somehow 8.5
someone 25.35
someplace 28.5
somersault 30.51
Somerset 30.5
something 26.14
sometime 24.7
sometimes 35.30
someway 3.25
somewhat 30.32
somewhen 25.5
somewhere 2.15
Somme 24.8
sommelier 12.6
somnambulant
  30.56
somnambulist 31.8
somniferous 28.31
somnolence 28.45
somnolent 30.56
Somoza 12.92
son 25.35
sonar 1.14
sonata 12.75
sonatina 12.54
Sondheim 24.7
sone 25.30
son et lumière 2.2
song thrush 29.16
song 26.15
songbird 16.31
songbook 21.28
songsmith 32.6
songster 12.79
songwriter 12.79
songwriting 26.13
Sonia 12.8
sonic 21.13
son-in-law 7.11
sonnet 30.23

sonneteer 12.4
sonny 4.33
sonogram 24.1
Sonora 12.66
sonority 4.53
sonorous 28.31
sonsy 4.46
Sontag 18.1
sool 23.20
soon 25.33
soonish 29.9
soot 30.39
sooth 32.12
soothe 33.8
soother 12.84
soothsayer 12.2
sooty 4.55
sop 27.8
Sophia 12.13
Sophie 4.14
sophist 31.7
sophisticate 30.10
sophistry 4.40
Sophocles 35.7
sophomore 7.12
sophomoric 21.15
soporific 21.10
sopping 26.10
soppy 4.36
soprano 9.19
Sopwith 32.6
sora 12.66
sorb 14.10
sorbet 3.7
Sorbian 25.37
sorbitol 23.13
Sorbonne 25.24
sorcerer 12.67
sorcerous 28.31
sorcery 4.43
sordid 16.9
sordor 12.28
sore 7.1
sorehead 16.3
sorel 23.36
sorghum 24.18
sori 6.15
sorority 4.53
sorption 25.49
sorrel 23.36
Sorrento 9.24
sorrow 9.21
sorry 4.41
sort 30.33
sorter 12.80
sortie 4.54
sortilege 20.6
sorus 28.31
so-so 9.22
sostenuto 9.25
sot 30.31

Sothic 21.18
Sotho 11.20
sottish 29.10
sotto voce 4.11
sou 11.1
soubrette 30.4
souchong 26.15
soufflé 3.15
Soufrière 2.1
sough 8.1
sought 30.33
sought-after 12.75
souk 21.27
soukous 28.26
soul 23.17
soulmate 30.12
soulster 12.80
sound 16.43
soundalike 21.19
soundbite 30.26
soundboard 16.20
soundbox 28.40
soundcheck 21.6
sounder 12.28
soundhole 23.17
sounding 26.5
soundproof 17.13
soundtrack 21.3
soup 27.11
soupçon 25.26
soupspoon 25.33
soupy 4.37
sour 12.16
source 28.15
sourcebook 21.28
sourdough 9.11
sourish 29.9
sourpuss 28.20
Sousa 12.92
sousaphone 25.30
sousaphonist 31.10
souse 28.16
souslik 21.11
Sousse 28.19
soutache 29.1
soutane 25.4
souteneur 13.1
souter 12.81
south 32.10
Southampton 25.50
southbound 16.43
South Carolina
  12.55
Southdown 25.29
southeast 31.5
southeastern 25.50
southeastward
  16.30
southerly 4.27
southern 25.51
southerner 12.58

southernmost 31.20
Southey 4.57
southing 26.14
southpaw 7.14
southward 16.30
southwest 31.3
southwestern 25.50
southwestward
souvenir 12.4
souvlaki 4.18
souvlakia 12.6
sou'wester 12.76
sovereign 25.18
sovereignty 4.53
soviet 30.41
sow 8.1, 9.1
sowbread 16.4
sower 12.17
Sowetan 25.50
Soweto 9.24
sowing 26.3
sown 25.30
soy 10.1
soya 12.18
soybean 25.9
Soyinka 12.39
Soyuz 35.22
sozzled 16.38
spa 1.1
space 28.5
space-age 20.4
spacecraft 30.47
spaceman 25.2
spacer 12.69
spacesuit 30.38
space walk 21.22
spacey 4.45
spacing 26.12
spacious 28.33
spade 16.6
spadework 21.31
spadille 23.8
spae 3.1
spaewife 17.7
spaewives 35.35
spaghetti 4.51
spaghettini 4.31
spahi 4.16
Spain 25.7
spalpeen 25.11
Spam 24.1
span 25.1
spanakopita 12.78
spandrel 23.36
spang 26.1
spangle 23.30
Spanglish 29.8
spangly 4.27
Spaniard 16.30
spaniel 23.40
Spanish 29.9

S

spank 21.33
spanker 12.37
spanking 26.7
spanner 12.53
spar 1.1
spare 2.1
sparer 12.65
sparerib 14.7
sparge 20.2
sparing 26.11
spark 21.5
sparkish 29.8
sparkle 23.32
sparkler 12.42
sparkly 4.21
Sparks 28.38
sparky 4.18
sparling 26.8
sparrow 9.21
sparrowhawk 21.22
sparry 4.38
sparse 28.2
sparsity 4.53
Sparta 12.75
Spartacus 28.26
spartan 25.50
spasm 24.21
spasmodic 21.10
spastic 21.17
spat 30.1
spatchcock 21.20
spate 30.7
spathe 33.2
spatial 23.38
spatialize 35.12
spatio-temporal 23.36
Spätlesen 25.52
spatter 12.74
spatterdash 29.1
spatula 12.46
spatulate 30.42
spavin 25.19
spawn 25.28
spawning 26.9
spay 3.1
speak 21.8
speakeasy 4.61
speaker 12.38
speakerphone 25.30
spear 12.4
spearfish 29.7
speargun 25.35
spearhead 16.3
spearmint 30.54
Spears 35.24
spec 21.6
special 23.38
specialist 31.8
specialty 4.51
species 35.10

specific 21.10
specifier 12.14
specify 6.7
specimen 25.17
specious 28.33
speck 21.6
speckle 23.32
specs 28.38
spectacle 23.32
spectacular 12.46
spectate 30.7
specter 12.76
Spector 12.76
spectra 12.64
spectral 23.36
spectre 12.76
spectrograph 17.2
spectrum 24.19
specular 12.46
speculate 30.11
speculum 24.18
sped 16.3
speech 15.5
speechifier 12.14
speechify 6.7
speed 16.7
speedball 23.14
speedboat 30.35
speeder 12.26
speedo 9.11
speedometer 12.78
speedster 12.77
speedway 3.25
speedwell 23.4
speedy 4.12
speiss 28.13
Speke 21.8
spell 23.3
spellbind 16.42
spellbinder 12.27
spellbound 16.43
speller 12.42
spelling 26.8
spelt 30.51
spelunker 12.41
spelunking 26.7
spence 28.44
spend 16.41
spender 12.26
spendthrift 30.47
Spenser 12.69
Spenserian 25.37
spent 30.53
sperm 24.22
spermatozoa 12.17
spermatozoid 16.8
spermatozoon 25.38
spermicide 16.16
spew 11.1
spewer 12.19
Spey 3.1

sphenoid 16.24
spheral 23.36
sphere 12.4
spheric 21.15
spherical 23.32
spheroid 16.24
sphincter 12.78
sphinx 28.41
spic 21.9
spice 28.13
spicebush 29.15
spick-and-span 25.1
spicy 4.46
spider 12.27
spiderish 29.9
spidery 4.43
spiel 23.7
Spielberg 18.13
spieler 12.43
spiffing 26.6
spifflicate 30.10
spiffy 4.14
spignel 23.34
spigot 30.42
spike 21.19
spiky 4.19
spile 23.11
spill 23.8
spillage 20.6
Spillane 25.7
spiller 12.43
spillikin 25.15
spillover 12.86
spilt 30.51
spin 25.13
spina bifida 12.27
spinach 20.7
spinal 23.34
spindle 23.28
spindleshanks 28.41
spindly 4.24
spindrift 30.47
spin-dry 6.1
spine 25.21
spinel 23.3
spinet 30.4
spinifex 28.38
spinnaker 12.41
spinner 12.55
spinneret 30.4
spinney 4.32
spin-off 17.8
spin-out 30.34
Spinoza 12.92
spinster 12.78
spinsterhood 16.26
spinsterish 29.9
spiny 4.32
spiraea 12.3
spiral 23.36
spire 12.13

spirea 12.3
spirit 30.24
spiritist 31.14
spiritous 28.34
spiritual 23.25
spiritualist 31.8
spiritualize 35.12
spirituous 28.24
spirogyra 12.65
spirt 30.45
spiry 4.43
spit 30.20
spit-and-polish 29.8
spitball 23.14
spite 30.26
spitfire 12.14
Spithead 16.3
Spitsbergen 25.41
spitter 12.78
spittle 23.39
spittoon 25.33
spitty 4.53
spitz 28.47
spiv 34.6
spivvish 29.10
spivvy 4.58
splake 21.7
splash 29.1
splashback 21.2
splashy 4.50
splat 30.1
splatter 12.74
splay 3.1
splay-feet 30.18
splay-foot 30.39
splay-footed 16.12
spleen 25.9
splendent 30.56
splendid 16.9
splendiferous 28.31
splendor 12.26
splendour 12.26
splenetic 21.17
splice 28.13
splicer 12.70
spliff 17.6
spline 25.21
splint 30.54
splint bone 25.30
splinter 12.78
splintery 4.43
split 30.20
split-level 23.40
split-second 16.45
splitter 12.78
splodge 20.11
splodgy 4.17
splosh 29.11
splotch 15.7
splotchy 4.11
splurge 20.17

splutter 12.81
splutterer 12.67
Spock 21.20
Spode 16.23
spoil 23.19
spoilage 20.6
spoiler 12.44
spoilsport 30.33
spoilt 30.51
Spokane 25.1
spoke 21.24
spoken 25.43
spokesman 25.45
spokesmen 25.45
spokesperson 25.48
spokeswoman 25.45
spokeswomen 25.17
spondaic 21.9
spondee 4.13
spondulicks 28.39
sponge 20.19
sponge-like 21.19
sponger 12.36
spongiform 24.9
spongy 4.17
sponson 25.48
sponsor 12.70
spontaneity 4.53
spontaneous 28.23
spoof 17.13
spoofer 12.30
spoofery 4.43
spook 21.27
spooky 4.20
spool 23.20
spoon 25.33
spoonbill 23.8
spooner 12.56
spoonfed 16.3
spoonfeed 16.7
spoony 4.33
spoor 12.20
Sporades 35.7
sporadic 21.10
sporangia 12.6
spore 7.1
sporran 25.47
sport 30.33
sporter 12.80
sportif 17.5
sportscast 31.2
sportscaster 12.75
sportsman 25.45
sportsmanlike 21.19
sportsmen 25.45
sportspeople 23.35
sportsperson 25.48
sportswear 2.15
sportswoman 25.45
sportswomen 25.17
sporty 4.54

spot 30.31
spot-check 21.6
spotlamp 27.17
spotlight 30.28
spot-on 25.24
spotter 12.79
spotty 4.54
spot-weld 16.35
spot-welder 12.26
spousal 23.41
spouse 28.16
spout 30.34
spouter 12.80
sprag 18.1
sprain 25.7
sprang 26.1
sprat 30.1
sprawl 23.14
spray 3.1
spray-dry 6.15
sprayer 12.2
spray-paint 30.54
spread 16.3
spread eagle 23.30
spreader 12.26
spreadsheet 30.19
spree 4.1
sprig 18.6
spriggy 4.15
sprightly 4.25
spring 26.3
springboard 16.20
springbok 21.20
spring-clean 25.9,
    25.10
spring-cleaning 26.9
springe 20.19
springer 12.60
Springfield 16.35
springlet 30.22
springlike 21.19
spring-loaded 16.9
Springs 35.32
Springsteen 25.12
springtail 23.6
springtide 16.17
springtime 24.7
springy 4.35
sprinkle 23.32
sprinkler 12.43
sprinkling 26.8
sprint 30.54
sprinter 12.78
sprit 30.20
sprite 30.26
spritsail 23.37
spritz 28.47
spritzer 12.70
sprocket 30.21
sprog 18.8
sprout 30.34

spruce 28.19
sprucer 12.71
sprue 11.1
spruik 21.27
spruit 30.7
sprung 26.18
spry 6.1
spud 16.27
spumante 4.51
spume 24.12
spumous 28.28
spumy 4.30
spun 25.35
spunk 21.34
spunky 4.20
spur 13.1
spurge 20.17
spurious 28.23
spurn 25.53
spurner 12.59
spurrier 12.10
spurt 30.45
sputnik 21.13
sputter 12.81
sputum 24.20
spy 6.1
spyglass 28.2
spyhole 23.17
spymaster 12.75
squab 14.9
squabble 23.26
squabbler 12.48
squad 16.18
squaddie 4.13
squadron 25.47
squalid 16.10
squall 23.14
squally 4.25
squalor 12.44
squander 12.28
squanderer 12.67
square 2.1
square-bashing
    26.12
square dance 28.44
square-eyed 16.14
squarer 12.65
square-rigged 16.33
squarish 29.9
squash 29.11
squashy 4.50
squat 30.31
squatter 12.79
squaw 7.1
squawk 21.22
squawker 12.40
squeak 21.8
squeaker 12.38
squeaky 4.18
squeal 23.7
squealer 12.43

squeamish 29.8
squeegee 4.17
squeeze 35.6
squeezebox 28.40
squeezer 12.90
squelch 15.15
squelchy 4.11
squib 14.7
squid 16.8
squidgy 4.17
squiffed 30.47
squiffy 4.14
squiggle 23.30
squiggly 4.27
squill 23.8
squillion 25.52
squinch 29.20
squint 30.54
squire 12.13
squirearch 21.5
squireen 25.9
squirl 23.42
squirm 24.22
squirmer 12.52
squirmy 4.30
squirrel 23.36
squirrelly 4.27
squirt 30.45
squish 29.6
squishy 4.50
squit 30.20
squitters 35.24
squiz 35.10
Sri Lanka 12.37
Sri Lankan 25.43
Srinagar 12.32
St Albans 35.31
St Helens 35.31
St Helier 12.6
St John's 35.31
St Kilda 12.27
St Kitts 28.47
St Leger 12.35
St Petersburg 18.13
stab 14.1
stabber 12.21
stabbing 26.4
stabile 23.11
stability 4.53
stable 23.26
stablemate 30.12
stablish 29.8
staccato 9.24
Stacey 4.45
stack 21.1
stacker 12.37
staddle 23.28
stadia 12.5
stadium 24.16
staff 17.2
Staffa 12.30

S

staffage 20.6
staffer 12.30
Stafford 16.28
Staffordshire 12.11
staffroom 24.12
stag 18.1
stage-manage 20.7
stage 20.4
stagecoach 15.10
stagecraft 30.47
stagehand 16.40
stager 12.35
stagestruck 21.29
stagger 12.31
staggerer 12.67
staging 26.6
stagnancy 4.48
stagnant 30.56
stagnate 30.7
stagy 4.17
staid 16.6
stain 25.7
stained-glass 28.2
stair 2.1
staircase 28.5
stairhead 16.3
stairlift 30.47
stairway 3.25
stairwell 23.4
stake 21.7
stakeholder 12.28
stakeout 30.34
staker 12.38
stalactite 30.30
Stalag 18.1
stalagmite 30.29
St Albans 35.31
stale 23.5
stalemate 30.12
Stalin 25.16
Stalingrad 16.1
Stalinist 31.10
stalk 21.22
stalker 12.40
stall 23.14
stallage 20.6
stallholder 12.28
stallion 25.52
stalwart 30.44
Stamboul 23.20
stamen 25.45
stamina 12.55
stammer 12.50
stammerer 12.67
stamp 27.11
stampede 16.7
stampeder 12.26
stamper 12.61
stance 28.44
stanchion 25.49
stand 16.40

standard 16.28
standardizer 12.91
standby 6.5
standee 4.1
stander 12.25
stand-in 25.14
standing 26.5
Standish 29.6
stand-off 17.8
standoffish 29.7
standout 30.34
standpipe 27.7
standpoint 30.55
standstill 23.9
stand-to 11.20
Stanford 16.28
Stanhope 27.14
Stanislas 28.1
Stanislavsky 4.18
stank 21.33
Stanley 4.21
Stanleyville 23.10
Stansted 16.4
stanza 12.90
stanzaic 21.9
staple 23.35
stapler 12.48
star 1.1
starboard 16.28
starburst 31.26
starch 15.2
starcher 12.23
starchy 4.11
star-crossed 31.17
stardom 24.17
stardust 31.24
stare 2.1
starer 12.65
starfish 29.7
stargaze 35.5
stargazer 12.90
stargazing 26.14
stark 21.5
starkers 35.24
starlet 30.22
starlight 30.28
starlike 21.19
starling 26.8
starlit 30.22
Starr 1.1
starry 4.38
starry-eyed 16.14
Stars and Bars 35.2
Stars and
    Stripes 28.46
start 30.3
starter 12.75
startle 23.39
startler 12.48
start-up 27.13
starve 34.2

starveling 26.8
stash 29.1
Stasi 4.61
stasis 28.11
stat 30.1
state 30.7
statecraft 30.47
statehood 16.26
statehouse 28.16
statelet 30.22
stately 4.22
stater 12.77
stateroom 24.12
stateside 16.16
statesman 25.45
statesmanlike 21.19
statesmen 25.45
stateswoman 25.45
stateswomen 25.17
statewide 16.14
static 21.17
statice 4.46

station 25.49
stationary 4.43
stationer 12.58
stationery 4.43
station-keeping
    26.10
statist 31.14
statistician 25.49
Statius 28.23
stative 34.8
stats 28.47
statuary 4.43
statue 11.5
statuesque 21.35
statuette 30.4
stature 12.23
status 28.34
status quo 9.1
statute 30.37
statutory 4.43
staunch 29.20
Stavanger 12.60
stave 34.4
stavesacre 12.38
stay 3.1
staycation 25.49
stayer 12.2
staysail 23.37
stead 16.3
steadfast 31.2
steadier 12.5
steading 26.5
steady 4.12
steak 21.7
steakhouse 28.16
steal 23.7
stealer 12.43
stealth 32.17

stealthy 4.56
steam 24.5
steamboat 30.35
steamer 12.51
steaming 26.9
steamroller 12.44
steamy 4.29
stearin 25.18
Stedman 25.45
steed 16.7
steel 23.7
Steele 23.7
steelworks 28.41
steely 4.23
steelyard 16.30
Steen 25.9
steenbok 21.20
steep 27.5
steepen 25.46
steepish 29.9
steeple 23.35
steeplechase 28.5
steeplechaser 12.69
steeplechasing
    26.12
steeplejack 21.3
steer 12.4
steerage 20.8
steerageway 3.25
steerer 12.67
steersman 25.45
steersmen 25.45
steeve 34.5
stegosaur 7.16
stegosaurus 28.31
stein 25.21
Steinbeck 21.6
Steiner 12.55
Steinway 3.25
Stella 12.42
stellar 12.42
stem 24.3
stemma 12.50
stemple 23.35
stench 29.20
stencil 23.37
Stendhal 23.2
steno 9.19
stenographer 12.30
stenographic 21.10
stenography 4.14
stenotype 27.7
stent 30.53
stentor 7.18
stentorian 25.37
step 27.3
stepbrother 12.84
stepchild 16.36
stepchildren 25.47
stepdaughter 12.80
stepfamily 4.24

S

stepfather 12.84
Stephanie 4.34
stepladder 12.25
stepmother 12.84
step-parent 30.56
steppe 27.3
stepping stone 25.31
stepsister 12.78
stepson 25.35
stepwise 35.15
steradian 25.37
stere 12.4
stereo 9.4
stereobate 30.9
stereophonic 21.13
stereopticon 25.25
stereoscope 27.10
stereoscopy 4.37
stereotype 27.7
stereotypic 21.14
stereotypical 23.32
sterile 23.11
sterility 4.53
sterling 26.8
stern 25.53
Sterne 25.53
Sterno 9.19
sternpost 31.20
sternum 24.19
sternway 3.25
steroid 16.24
stertorous 28.31
stet 30.4
stethoscope 27.10
Stetson 25.48
Steve 34.5
stevedore 7.5
Steven 25.51
Stevenage 20.7
Stevens 35.31
Stevenson 25.48
stew 11.1
steward 16.28
stewardess 28.7
Stewart 30.41
stewpot 30.32
St Helens 35.31
St Helier 12.6
stichomythia 12.12
stick 21.9
stickball 23.14
sticker 12.39
stick-in-the-mud 16.27
stickleback 21.2
stickler 12.43
stickpin 25.18
stickum 24.18
stick-up 27.13
sticky 4.19

stickybeak 21.8
Stieglitz 35.33
stifado 9.11
stiff 17.6
stiffen 25.41
stiffener 12.58
stiffening 26.9
stiffish 29.7
stiffy 4.14
stifle 23.29
stifler 12.44
stigma 12.51
stigmata 12.82
stigmatic 21.17
stigmatist 31.14
stilb 14.16
stile 23.11
Stiles 35.29
stiletto 9.24
still 23.8
stillage 20.6
stillbirth 32.14
stillborn 25.28
still-life 17.7
Stillson 25.48
stilly 4.24
stilt 30.51
stilted 16.12
Stilton 25.50
stimulant 30.56
stimulate 30.11
stimuli 6.11
stimulus 28.27
sting 26.3
stinger 12.60
stingray 3.19
stingy 4.17, 4.35
stink 21.33
stink bomb 24.8
stinker 12.39
stinko 9.16
stinkpot 30.32
stinkweed 16.7
stinkwood 16.26
stinky 4.19
stint 30.54
stipend 16.41
stipendiary 4.43
stipple 23.35
stippler 12.48
stipulate 30.11
stir 13.1
stir-crazy 4.61
stir-fry 6.15
stirk 21.31
Stirling 26.8
stirrer 12.68
stirring 26.11
stirrup 27.14
stitch 15.6
stitcher 12.23

stitchery 4.43
St John's 35.31
St Kilda 12.27
St Kitts 28.47
St Leger 12.35
stoat 30.35
stob 14.9
stock 21.20
stockade 16.6
stockbreeder 12.26
stockbreeding 26.5
stockbroker 12.40
stockcar 1.11
stocker 12.40
Stockhausen 25.52
stockholder 12.28
Stockholm 24.11
stockinet 30.4
stocking 26.7
stock-in-trade 16.6
stockist 31.7
stockman 25.45
stockmen 25.45
stockpile 23.11
stockpiler 12.44
Stockport 30.33
stockpot 30.32
stockroom 24.12
Stocks 28.40
stock-still 23.8
stocktake 21.7
stocktaking 26.7
Stockton-on-Tees 35.6
stocky 4.19
stockyard 16.2
stodge 20.11
stodgy 4.17
stoep 27.11
stogy 4.15
Stoic 21.9
stoical 23.32
stoke 21.24
stokehole 23.17
Stoke-on-Trent 30.53
Stoker 12.40
stokes 28.40
Stokowski 4.19
stole 23.17
stolen 25.44
stolid 16.10
stolidity 4.53
Stollen 25.44
stomach 21.30
stomacher 12.41
stomp 27.17
stomper 12.62
stone 25.30
stone-broke 21.24
stonecrop 27.8

stonefish 29.7
stoneground 16.43
Stonehenge 20.19
stonemason 25.48
stonemasonry 4.39
stoner 12.56
stonewall 23.14
stonewaller 12.44
stoneware 2.15
stonewashed 30.59
stonework 21.31
stoneworker 12.41
stonker 12.40
stonking 26.7
stony 4.33
stony-broke 21.24
stood 16.26
stooge 20.15
stook 21.27
stool 23.20
stoolball 23.14
stoolie 4.26
stool pigeon 25.14
stoop 27.11
stop 27.8
stopcock 21.20
Stopes 28.46
stopgap 27.1
stopover 12.86
stoppage 20.7
Stoppard 16.2
stopper 12.62
stopping 26.10
stopple 23.35
stopwatch 15.7
storage 20.8
storax 28.38
store 7.1
storefront 30.55
storehouse 28.16
storekeeper 12.61
storeman 25.45
storemen 25.45
storer 12.66
storeroom 24.12
storey 4.41
storiated 16.12
storied 16.11
stork 21.22
storksbill 23.8
storm 24.9
stormbound 16.43
stormdoor 7.5
stormer 12.52
stormproof 17.13
stormy 4.29
Stornoway 3.25
story 4.41
storyboard 16.20
storybook 21.28
storyline 25.22

S

S

stupefy 6.7
stupendous 28.25
stupid 16.10
stupidity 4.53
stupor 12.63
stuporous 28.31
sturdy 4.13
sturgeon 25.42
Sturm und
   Drang 26.1
Sturt 30.45
stutter 12.81
stutterer 12.67
Stuttgart 30.3
sty 6.1
Stygian 25.37
style 23.11
styler 12.44
stylet 30.22
styli 6.11
stylish 29.8
stylist 31.8
stylite 30.28
Stylites 35.9
stylobate 30.9
stylograph 17.2
stylus 28.27
stymie 4.29
styptic 21.17
Styria 12.10
Styrofoam 24.11
Styx 28.39
suable 23.26
suasion 25.42
suave 34.2
suavity 4.53
sub judice 4.46
sub 14.13
subacute 30.37
subaltern 25.50
subantarctic 21.17
sub-aqua 12.88
sub-aquatic 21.17
sub-prime 24.7
subaqueous 28.23
subarctic 21.17
subatomic 21.12
Subbuteo 9.4
subcategorize 35.13
subcategory 4.43
subclass 28.2
subcommittee 4.53
subconscious 28.33
subcontinent 30.56
subcontract 30.48
subcontractor 12.74
subcritical 23.32
subculture 12.24
subcutaneous 28.23
subdivide 16.14
subdivision 25.42

subdue 11.1
subedit 30.21
subeditor 12.78
subfamily 4.24
subfloor 7.11
subframe 24.4
subfusc 21.35
subgroup 27.11
sub-head 16.3
sub-heading 26.5
sub judice 4.46
subhuman 25.45
subject 30.48, 30.49
subjection 25.49
subjectivist 31.15
subjoin 25.32
subjugate 30.9
sublease 28.6
sublet 30.4
sublimate 30.12
sublime 24.7
subliminal 23.34
sublunary 4.43
submarginal 23.34
submarine 25.9
submariner 12.55
submerge 20.17
submergence 28.45
submergible 23.26
submerse 28.36
submersible 23.26
submersion 25.49
submissive 34.7
submit 30.20
submitter 12.78
subnormal 23.33
subordinary 4.43
subordinate 30.13,
   30.43
suborn 25.28
suborner 12.56
sub-plot 30.31
subpoena 12.54
subrogate 30.9
subscribe 14.8
subscriber 12.21
subscript 30.58
subscription 25.49
subsection 25.49
subsequence 28.45
subsequent 30.56
subserve 34.14
subservience 28.45
subserviency 4.48
subservient 30.56
subset 30.5
subside 16.14
subsidence 28.45
subsidiarity 4.53
subsidiary 4.43
subsidizer 12.91

subsidy 4.12
subsist 31.6
subsistence 28.45
subsistent 30.56
subsoil 23.19
subsonic 21.13
subspecies 35.10
substance 28.45
sub-standard 16.28
substantial 23.38
substantialist 31.8
substantialize 35.12
substantiate 30.8
substantival 23.40
substitute 30.38
substitution 25.49
substitutional 23.34
substitutionary
   4.43
substrata 12.75
substrate 30.15
substratum 24.20
substructure 12.24
subsume 24.12
subsystem 24.6
subtenancy 4.48
subtenant 30.56
subtend 16.41
subterfuge 20.15
subterranean 25.37
subtext 31.28
subtitle 23.39
subtle 23.39
subtlety 4.55
subtonic 21.13
subtopia 12.9
subtopian 25.37
subtotal 23.39
subtract 30.48
subtraction 25.49
subtropical 23.32
subtropics 28.39
subtype 27.7
suburb 14.15
suburban 25.38
suburbanite 30.29
suburbanize 35.13
suburbia 12.5
subvention 25.49
subversion 25.49
subversive 34.7
subvert 30.45
subverter 12.82
subway 3.25
sub-zero 9.21
succeed 16.7
succeeder 12.26
success 28.3
successional 23.34
successive 34.7
successor 12.69

succinct 30.49
succor 12.41
succory 4.43
succotash 29.1
Succoth 30.35
succour 12.41
succubi 6.5
succubus 28.24
succulence 28.45
succulent 30.56
succumb 24.14
succursal 23.37
such 15.13
suchlike 21.19
suck 21.29
sucker 12.41
suckle 23.32
suckler 12.47
Suckling 26.8
sucre 3.19
sucrose 35.19
suction 25.49
Sudan 25.4
Sudanese 35.6
sudarium 24.16
sudatoria 12.10
sudatorium 24.16
Sudbury 4.43
sudd 16.27
sudden 25.40
Sudetenland 16.40
Sudra 12.66
suds 35.27
sudsy 4.62
sue 11.1
suede 16.6
suer 12.19
suet 30.20
Suetonius 28.23
suety 4.53
Suez 35.10
suffer 12.30
sufferance 28.45
sufferer 12.67
suffering 26.11
suffice 28.13
sufficiency 4.46
sufficient 30.56
suffix 28.39, 31.28,
   35.10
suffocate 30.10
suffocating 26.13
Suffolk 21.30
suffrage 20.8
suffragette 30.4
suffragist 31.7
suffuse 35.21
suffusion 25.42
Sufi 4.14
Sufic 21.10
Sufism 24.21

S

sugar 12.32
sugar beet 30.18
sugar cane 25.7
sugarcoated 16.12
sugarloaf 17.11
sugarplum 24.14
sugary 4.43
suggest 31.3
suggester 12.76
suggestible 23.26
suggestion 25.39
Sui 3.1
suicidal 23.28
suicide 16.16
suit 30.37
suitcase 28.5
suite 30.18
suiting 26.13
suitor 12.01
Sukarno 9.19
Sukhotai 6.1
Sukie 4.20
sukiyaki 4.18
Sukkur 12.41
Sulawesi 4.45
sulfur 12.30
sulfureous 28.23
sulfuric 21.15
sulfurous 28.31
sulfury 4.43
sulk 21.32
sulker 12.41
sulky 4.20
Sulla 12.47
sullen 25.44
Sullivan 25.51
sully 4.26
sulphur 12.30
sulphureous 28.23
sulphuric 21.15
sulphurous 28.31
sulphury 4.43
sultan 25.50
sultana 12.53
sultanate 30.43
sultry 4.42
sum 24.14
sumac 21.3
Sumatra 12.64
Sumatran 25.47
Sumer 12.52
Sumerian 25.37
summa 12.52
summa cum
    laude 3.9
summarizer 12.91
summary 4.43
summer 12.52
summerhouse 28.16
Summers 35.24
summertime 24.7

summery 4.43
summing-up 27.13
summit 30.23
summiteer 12.4
summon 25.45
summoner 12.58
summons 35.31
summum bonum
    24.19
sumo 9.18
sump 27.17
sumptuary 4.43
sumptuosity 4.53
sumptuous 28.24
sun 25.35
sun-baked 30.48
sunbathe 33.2
sunbather 12.84
sunbeam 24.5
sunbed 16.3
sunbelt 30.51
sunblind 16.42
sunblock 21.21
sunburn 25.53
sunburnt 30.57
sunburst 31.26
sundae 3.9
Sundanese 35.6
Sunday 3.9
sundeck 21.6
sunder 12.29
Sunderland 16.45
sundial 23.25
sundown 25.29
sundowner 12.56
sundress 28.3
sun-dried 16.15
sundry 4.42
sunfast 31.2
sunflower 12.16
sung 26.18
sunglasses 35.10
sun hat 30.1
sunk 21.34
sunken 25.43
sunlamp 27.17
sunless 28.27
sunlight 30.28
sunlike 21.19
sunlit 30.22
sunlounger 12.35
Sunna 12.56
Sunni 4.33
Sunnite 30.29
sunny 4.33
sunray 3.19
sunrise 35.13
sunroof 17.13
sunroom 24.12
sunscreen 25.11
sunset 30.5

sunshade 16.6
sunshine 25.23
sunshiny 4.32
sunspot 30.32
sunstar 1.19
sunstone 25.31
sunstroke 21.24
suntan 25.3
suntrap 27.1
sunup 27.13
sunward 16.30
Sun Yat-sen 25.5
sup 27.13
super 12.63
superannuate 30.8
superb 14.15
supercilious 28.23
supererogatory 4.43
superficial 23.38
superficies 35.6
superfluity 4.53
superfluous 28.24
superglue 11.13
superintendence
    28.45
superintendency
    4.48
superintendent
    30.56
superior 12.10
superiority 4.53
superlunary 4.43
Superman 25.2
supernal 23.34
supernumerary
    4.43
superordinate 30.43
superscription
    25.49
supersede 16.7
superstar 1.19
superstate 30.16
superstitious 28.33
superstore 7.18
supervene 25.9
supervention 25.49
supervise 35.14
supervisory 4.43
supine 25.23
supper 12.63
supplant 30.53
supplanter 12.75
supple 23.35
supplementary 4.43
suppletion 25.49
suppliant 30.56
supplicant 30.56
supplicate 30.10
supplicatory 4.43
supplier 12.13
supply 6.1

support 30.33
supporter 12.80
suppose 35.19
suppositious 28.33
suppository 4.43
suppress 28.3
suppressant 30.56
suppurate 30.15
supra 12.66
supremacist 31.13
supremacy 4.48
supreme 24.5
supremo 9.18
sura 12.67
Surabaya 12.13
surah 12.67
surahi 4.16
Surat 30.1
surcease 28.6
surcharge 20.2
surcingle 23.30
surcoat 30.35
sure 12.20
surefire 12.14
sure-footed 16.12
surely 4.27
surety 4.53
surf 17.17
surface 28.7
surfacer 12.70
surface-to-air 2.1
surface-to-
    surface 28.7
surfboard 16.20
surfeit 30.21
surfer 12.30
surfy 4.14
surge 20.17
surgeon 25.42
surgery 4.43
surgical 23.32
Suriname 24.1
Surinamer 12.50
Surinamese 35.6
surly 4.28
surmise 35.11
surmount 30.55
surname 24.4
surpass 28.2
surpassing 26.12
surplice 28.8
surplus 28.27
surprise 35.11
surprising 26.14
surreal 23.24
surrealist 31.8
surrebuttal 23.39
surrender 12.26
surreptitious 28.33
surrey 4.42
surrogacy 4.48

surrogate 30.42
surround 16.43
surrounding 26.5
surtax 28.38
Surtees 35.9
surtitle 23.39
surtout 11.20
surveil 23.5
surveillance 28.45
survey 3.1, 3.24
surveyor 12.2
survival 23.40
survivalist 31.8
survive 34.9
survivor 12.86
Surya 12.10
sus 28.21
Susan 25.52
Susanna 12.53
susceptible 23.26
sushi 4.50
Susie 4.62
suspect 30.48
suspend 16.41
suspender 12.26
suspense 28.44
suspension 25.49
suspensive 34.7
suspensory 4.43
suspicion 25.49
suspicious 28.33
suspire 12.13
suss 28.21
Sussex 28.39
sustain 25.7
sustainer 12.54
sustenance 28.45
Sutherland 16.45
sutra 12.66
suttee 4.1
Sutton Coldfield 16.35
suture 12.24
Suva 12.87
Suwannee 4.32
Suzanne 25.1
suzerain 25.8
suzerainty 4.52
Suzette 30.4
Suzuki 4.20
Svalbard 16.2
svelte 30.51
Svengali 4.21
Sverdlovsk 21.35
swab 14.9
swabbie 4.10
Swabia 12.5
Swabian 25.37
swaddle 23.28
swag 18.1
swage 20.4

swagger 12.31
swaggerer 12.67
swagman 25.2
swagmen 25.5
Swahili 4.23
swain 25.7
swale 23.5
Swales 35.29
swallow 9.17
swallow dive 34.9
swallower 12.17
swallowtail 23.6
swam 24.1
swami 4.29
swamp 27.17
swampland 16.40
swampy 4.36
swan 25.24
swan dive 34.9
swank 21.33
swanky 4.18
swanlike 21.19
swan-neck 21.6
Swansea 4.61
Swanson 25.48
swansong 26.15
swap 27.8
swapper 12.62
Swaraj 20.2
sward 16.19
swarf 17.9
swarm 24.9
swart 30.33
swarthy 4.57
swash 29.11
swashbuckler 12.47
swashbuckling 26.8
swastika 12.39
swat 30.31
swatch 15.7
swathe 33.2
sway 3.1
Swazi 4.61
Swaziland 16.40
swear 2.1
swearer 12.65
swear word 16.31
sweat 30.4
sweatband 16.40
sweater 12.76
sweatpants 28.47
sweatshirt 30.45
sweatshop 27.8
sweatsuit 30.38
sweaty 4.51
Swede 16.7
Sweden 25.40
Swedenborg 18.9
Swedenborgian 25.37
Swedish 29.6

Sweeney 4.31
sweep 27.5
sweepback 21.2
sweeper 12.61
sweeping 26.10
sweepstake 21.7
sweet 30.18
sweet-and-sour 12.16
sweetbread 16.4
sweetcorn 25.28
sweeten 25.50
sweetener 12.54
sweetening 26.9
sweetheart 30.3
sweetie 4.52
sweetie-pie 6.14
sweeting 26.13
sweetish 29.10
sweetmeal 23.7
sweetmeat 30.18
sweetsop 27.8
sweet-talk 21.22
swell 23.3
swelling 26.8
swelter 12.76
swept 30.58
swerve 34.14
swerver 12.87
swift 30.47
swiftie 4.53
swig 18.6
swigger 12.31
swill 23.8
swiller 12.43
swim 24.6
swimmer 12.51
swimsuit 30.38
swimwear 2.15
Swinburne 25.53
swindle 23.28
swindler 12.43
Swindon 25.40
swine 25.21
swineherd 16.31
swing 26.3
swingbin 25.13
swinge 20.19
swinger 12.60
swingle 23.30
swingometer 12.78
swingy 4.35
swinish 29.9
swipe 27.7
swiper 12.62
swirl 23.42
swirly 4.28
swish 29.6
swishy 4.50
Swiss 28.7
switch 15.6

switchback 21.2
switchblade 16.6
switchboard 16.20
switcheroo 11.1
switchgear 12.5
swither 12.84
Switzerland 16.45
swive 34.9
swivel 23.40
swizz 35.10
swizzle 23.41
swollen 25.44
swoon 25.33
swoop 27.11
swoosh 29.14
sword 16.19
swordbearer 12.65
swordfish 29.7
swordplay 3.15
swordsman 25.45
swordstick 21.17
swore 7.1
sworn 25.28
swot 30.31
swum 24.14
swung 26.18
sybarite 30.29
sybaritic 21.17
sycamore 7.12
syce 28.13
sycophancy 4.48
sycophant 30.56
sycophantic 21.17
Sydney 4.32
syenitic 21.17
syllabi 6.5
syllabic 21.9
syllabub 14.13
syllabus 28.24
syllepses 35.8
syllepsis 28.11
syllogize 35.11
sylph 17.18
sylphlike 21.19
sylvan 25.51
sylvatic 21.17
Sylvester 12.76
Sylvia 12.12
Sylvie 4.58
symbioses 35.8
symbiosis 28.11
symbiotic 21.17
symbol 23.26
symbolic 21.11
symbolical 23.32
symbolist 31.8
symbology 4.17
symmetrical 23.32
symmetry 4.40
Symons 35.31
sympathetic 21.17

S

sympathizer 12.91
sympathy 4.56
symphonic 21.13
symphonist 31.10
symphony 4.34
symposia 12.12
symposiast 31.1
symposium 24.16
symptom 24.20
symptomatic 21.17
synaesthesia 12.12
synagogal 23.30
synagogue 18.8
synapse 28.46
synapsis 28.11
synaptic 21.17
synarchy 4.18
sync 21.33
synchro 9.21
synchromesh 29.3
synchronizer 12.91
synchronous 28.29
synchrony 4.34
syncopal 23.35
syncopate 30.14
syncope 4.37
syncretic 21.17
syncretist 31.14
syncretize 35.14
syndetic 21.17
syndic 21.10
syndical 23.32
syndicalist 31.8
syndicate 30.10,
  30.42
syndrome 24.11
syne 25.21
synecdoche 4.20
synecdochic 21.11
synergy 4.17
Synge 26.3
synod 16.29
synodal 23.28
synodical 23.32
synonym 24.6
synonymous 28.28
synonymy 4.29
synopses 35.8
synopsis 28.11
synopsize 35.14
synoptic 21.17
synoptical 23.32
synoptist 31.14
synovial 23.24
syntactic 21.17
syntactical 23.32
syntax 28.38
synth 32.19
syntheses 35.8
synthesis 28.11
synthesist 31.13

synthesize 35.14
synthetic 21.17
synthetical 23.32
synthetize 35.14
syphilis 28.8
syphilitic 21.17
Syracuse 28.19,
  35.21
Syria 12.10
Syriac 21.1
Syrian 25.37
syringe 20.19
syrup 27.14
syrupy 4.37
system 24.6
systematic 21.17
systematist 31.14
systematizer 12.91
systemic 21.12
systemize 35.13
systemizer 12.91
systole 4.27
Szeged 16.3

T

ta 1.1
Taal 23.2
tab 14.1
tabard 16.28
Tabasco 9.16
tabby 4.10
tabernacle 23.32
Tabitha 12.83
tabla 12.42
tablature 12.24
table 23.26
tableau 9.17
tableau vivant 25.26
tableaux 35.19
tablecloth 32.8
table d'hote 30.35
tablespoon 25.33
tablet 30.22
tabletop 27.8
tableware 2.15
tablier 3.3
tabloid 16.24
taboo 11.1
tabor 12.21
Tabriz 35.6
tabular 12.46
tabula rasa 12.90
tabulate 30.11
tacet 30.24
tach 21.1
tacho 9.16
tachograph 17.2
tachometer 12.78

tachycardia 12.5
tachygraphy 4.14
tacit 30.24
taciturn 25.53
taciturnity 4.53
Tacitus 28.34
tack 21.1
tacker 12.37
tackle 23.32
tackler 12.42
tacky 4.18
taco 9.16
tact 30.48
tactic 21.17
tactical 23.32
tactician 25.49
tactile 23.12
tactility 4.53
tactual 23.25
tad 16.1
tadpole 23.18
Taff 17.1
taffeta 12.78
taffy 4.14
tafia 12.5
Taft 30.47
tag 18.1
Taganrog 18.8
tagliatelle 4.22
Tagore 7.1
Tagus 28.25
Tahiti 4.52
Tahitian 25.49
tahr 1.1
Tai 6.1
Tai'an 25.4
t'ai chi ch'uan
  25.4
Taichung 26.17
taig 18.4
taiga 12.31
tail 23.5
tailback 21.2
tailboard 16.20
tail bone 25.30
tailcoat 30.35
tail end 16.41
tailgate 30.9
tailgater 12.77
tailing 26.8
Tailleferre 2.1
tail light 30.28
tailor 12.43
tailor-made 16.6
tailpiece 28.6
tailpipe 27.7
tailplane 25.8
tailspin 25.18
tailstock 21.21
tailwind 16.42
Tainan 25.1

taint 30.54
taipan 25.3
Taipei 3.1
Taiwan 25.4
Taiwanese 35.6
taj 20.2
Tajik 21.11
Tajikistan 25.4
Taj Mahal 23.2
Tajo 9.14
taka 1.11
takable 23.26
takahe 4.16
take 21.7
takeaway 3.25
takedown 25.29
taken 25.43
take-off 17.8
takeout 30.34
takeover 12.86
taker 12.38
take-up 27.13
taking 26.7
Taklimakan 25.4
tala 12.42
talapoin 25.32
talc 21.32
talcy 4.18
tale 23.5
talebearing 26.11
talent 30.56
tales 35.7
talipot 30.32
talisman 25.45
talismanic 21.13
talk 21.22
talkathon 25.26
talkback 21.2
talker 12.40
talkfest 31.3
talkie 4.19
tall 23.14
tallage 20.6
Tallahassee 4.45
tallboy 10.3
Talleyrand 16.40
Tallinn 25.16
Tallis 28.8
tallish 29.8
tallith 32.6
tallow 9.17
tallowy 4.7
Tallulah 12.45
tally 4.21
tally-ho 9.1
tallyman 25.45
tallymen 25.45
Talmud 16.26
Talmudic 21.10
Talmudical 23.32
Talmudist 31.6

talon 25.44
talus 28.27
tam 24.1
tamale 4.21
tamandua 12.20
Tamar 1.13
Tamara 12.64
tamarack 21.3
tamari 4.38
tamarillo 9.17
tamarin 25.18
tamarind 16.42
tamarisk 21.35
tambala 12.42
Tambo 9.9
tambour 12.20
tamboura 12.67
tambourin 25.18
tambourine 25.9
tambourinist
    31.10
tame 24.4
tamer 12.50
Tamerlane 25.8
Tamil 23.9
Tamilian 25.37
Tamil Nadu 11.6
Tammany 4.34
tam-o'-shanter
    12.74
tamp 27.17
Tampa 12.61
tamper 12.61
Tampere 12.67
tamperer 12.67
tampering 26.11
Tampico 9.16
tampion 25.37
tampon 25.26
tam-tam 24.1
Tamworth 32.13
tan 25.1
tanager 12.36
Tanagra 12.67
Tananarive 34.5
tanbark 21.5
tandem 24.17
tandoor 12.20
tandoori 4.43
tang 26.1
tanga 12.31
Tanganyika 12.38
tangelo 9.17
tangent 30.56
tangential 23.38
tangerine 25.9
tangible 23.26
Tangier 12.4
tangle 23.30
tangly 4.21
tango 9.13

tangram 24.1
tangy 4.35
tank 21.33
tanka 12.37
tankage 20.6
tankard 16.28
tanker 12.37
tanktop 27.8
tanner 12.53
tannery 4.43
Tannhäuser 12.92
tannin 25.18
tannish 29.9
tannoy 10.9
tansy 4.61
tantalic 21.11
tantalite 30.28
tantalizer 12.91
tantalum 24.18
tantalus 28.27
tantamount 30.55
tant mieux 13.1
tant pis 4.1
tantra 12.64
tantric 21.15
tantrist 31.12
tantrum 24.19
Tanya 12.8
Tanzania 12.3
Tanzanian 25.36
Tao 8.1
Taoiseach 21.30
Taoism 24.21
Taoist 31.6
Taoistic 21.17
Taormina 12.54
tap 27.1
tapas 28.30
tap-dance 28.44
tape 27.4
tape-record 16.21
taper 12.61
tapestry 4.40
tapeworm 24.22
tapioca 12.40
tapir 12.9
tapis 4.36
tapper 12.61
tapping 26.10
taproom 24.12
tapu 11.16
taqueria 12.3
tar 1.1
Tara 12.64
taradiddle 23.28
tarakihi 4.16
taramasalata 12.75
tarantass 28.1
tarantella 12.42
tarantula 12.46
tarboosh 29.14

Tardis 28.7
tardy 4.12
tare 2.1
target 30.21
Targum 24.18
tariff 17.6
Tarmac 21.3
tarmacadam 24.17
tarn 25.4
tarnish 29.9
taro 9.21
tarot 9.21
tarp 27.2
tarpan 25.3
tarpaulin 25.16
Tarpeia 12.3
tarpon 25.46
Tarquin 25.20
tarragon 25.41
Tarrasa 12.69
tarrier 12.10
tarry 4.38
tarsal 23.37
tarsier 12.11
tarsus 28.32
tart 30.3
tartan 25.50
tartar 12.75
tartare 1.1
Tartarus 28.31
Tartary 4.43
tartlet 30.22
Tartuffe 17.13
tarty 4.51
Tarzan 25.52
taser 12.90
Tashkent 30.53
task 21.35
taskmaster 12.75
Tasman 25.45
Tasmania 12.8
Tasmanian 25.37
tass 28.1
tassel 23.37
Tasso 9.22
taste 31.4
taster 12.77
tasting 26.13
tasty 4.52
tat 30.1
tata 1.1
Tatar 12.75
Tatarstan 25.4
Tate 30.7
tater 12.77
Tati 4.51
Tatiana 12.53
Tatras 28.31
tatsoi 10.1
tatterdemalion
    25.37

tattersall 23.15
tattery 4.43
tattie 4.51
tattle 23.39
tattler 12.48
tattletale 23.6
tattoo 11.1
tattooer 12.19
tattooist 31.6
tatty 4.51
Tatum 24.20
tau 7.1
taught 30.33
taunt 30.54
taunter 12.80
Taunton 25.50
taupe 27.10
Tauranga 12.31
Taurean 25.37
taurine 25.11,
    25.23
Taurus 28.31
taut 30.33
tauten 25.50
tautog 18.8
tautologize 35.11
tautologous 28.25
tautology 4.17
tavern 25.51
taverna 12.59
Taverner 12.58
taw 7.1
tawdry 4.41
tawer 12.15
tawny 4.32
taws 35.17
tawse 35.17
tax 28.38
taxable 23.26
taxation 25.49
tax-deductible 23.26
taxi 4.45
taxicab 14.1
taxidermal 23.33
taxidermic 21.12
taxidermist 31.9
taxidermy 4.30
taxis 28.11
taxiway 3.25
taxman 25.2
taxmen 25.5
taxonomic 21.12
taxonomy 4.30
taxpayer 12.2
Tay 3.1
Taylor 12.43
Tayside 16.16
tazza 12.69
Tbilisi 4.45
Tchaikovsky 4.19
tea 4.1

tea bag 18.1
tea garden 25.40
tea leaf 17.5
tea leaves 35.35
tea 4.1
teabread 16.4
teacake 21.7
teach 15.5
teacher 12.23
teacherly 4.27
teaching 26.4
teacup 27.13
teak 21.8
teal 23.7
team 24.5
teammate 30.12
teamster 12.77
teamwork 21.31
teapot 30.32
teapoy 10.10
tear 2.1, 12.4
tearaway 3.25
teardrop 27.8
tearer 12.65
teargas 28.1
tearjerker 12.41
tear-jerking 26.7
tearoom 24.12
tearstained 16.41
teary 4.43
tease 35.6
teasel 23.41
teaser 12.90
teaset 30.5
Teasmade 16.6
teaspoon 25.33
teat 30.18
teatime 24.7
tec 21.6
tech 21.6
techie 4.18
technetium 24.16
technic 21.13
technical 23.32
technician 25.49
technicist 31.13
technicolor 12.47
technique 21.8
techno 9.19
technobabble 23.26
technocracy 4.48
technocrat 30.2
technocratic 21.17
technology 4.17
technophile 23.11
technophobe 14.11
technophobia 12.5
technophobic 21.9
technospeak 21.8
tectonic 21.13
ted 16.3

tedder 12.26
teddy 4.12
Te Deum 24.15
tedious 28.23
tedium 24.16
tee 4.1
tee-hee 4.1
teem 24.5
teen 25.9
teenage 20.4
teenager 12.35
teensy 4.61
teeny 4.31
teenybopper 12.62
teeny-weeny 4.31
Tees 35.6
Teesside 16.16
teeter 12.77
teeth 32.5
teethe 33.3
teetotal 23.39
teetotaler 12.44
teetotaller 12.44
teetotum 24.20
teff 17.3
Teflon 25.25
teg 18.3
Tehran 25.4
Teilhard de
    Chardin 25.1
Te Kanawa 12.88
telamon 25.45
Tel Aviv 34.5
telecast 31.2
telecaster 12.75
telecine 4.32
Telecom 24.8
telecommute 30.37
telecommuter 12.81
telecoms 35.30
Telefax 28.38
telefilm 24.18
telegenic 21.13
telegram 24.1
telegraph 17.2
telegrapher 12.30
telegraphese 35.6
telegraphic 21.10
telekinesis 28.11
telekinetic 21.17
Telemachus 28.26
Telemann 25.2
telemark 21.5
telemarketing 26.13
teleologic 21.11
teleost 31.17
telepath 32.1
telepathic 21.18
telepathist 31.14
telepathize 35.14
telepathy 4.56

telephone 25.30
telephonist 31.10
telephony 4.34
teleplay 3.15
teleport 30.33
teleprinter 12.78
teleprompter 12.79
telerecord 16.21
telerecording 26.5
telesales 35.29
telescope 27.10
telescopic 21.14
teletext 31.28
telethon 25.26
televangelist 31.8
televise 35.14
television 25.42
televisual 23.25
telework 21.31
teleworker 12.41
Telex 28.38
Telford 16.28
tell 23.3
teller 12.42
telling 26.8
telling-off 17.8
telltale 23.6
tellurian 25.37
telluric 21.15
telluride 16.15
tellurium 24.16
telly 4.22
telnet 30.5
telos 28.14
Telstar 1.19
Telugu 11.8
temerarious 28.23
temerity 4.53
temp 27.17
temper 12.61
tempera 12.67
temperance 28.45
temperate 30.43
temperature 12.23
temperer 12.67
tempest 31.11
tempestuous 28.24
tempi 4.36
Templar 12.42
template 30.11
temple 23.35
tempo 9.20
temporal 23.36
temporary 4.43
temporizer 12.91
tempt 30.52
tempter 12.76
tempting 26.13
temptress 28.10
tempura 12.67
ten 25.5

tenable 23.26
tenace 28.5
tenacious 28.33
tenacity 4.53
tenancy 4.48
tenant 30.56
tenantry 4.43
tench 29.20
tend 16.41
tendance 28.45
tendency 4.48
tendentious 28.33
tender 12.26
tenderer 12.67
tenderfoot 30.39
tender-
    hearted 16.12
tenderizer 12.91
tenderloin 25.32
tendon 25.40
tendresse 28.3
tendril 23.9
tenebrae 4.40
tenebrous 28.31
Tenerife 17.5
tenet 30.23
tenfold 16.37
Teniers 35.24
tenner 12.53
Tennessee 4.1
Tennesseean 25.36
Tenniel 23.24
tennis 28.9
tenno 9.19
Tennyson 25.48
Tennysonian 25.37
Tenochtitlan 25.4
tenon 25.46
tenor 12.53
tenorist 31.12
tenpin 25.18
tense 28.44
tensile 23.11
tension 25.49
tensional 23.34
tensioner 12.58
tensity 4.53
tent 30.53
tentacle 23.32
tenter 12.76
tenterhook 21.28
tenth 32.19
tenuity 4.53
tenuous 28.24
tenure 12.89
tenurial 23.24
tenuto 9.25
Tenzing
    Norgay 3.11
tepee 4.36
tepid 16.10

t

tepidaria 12.10
tepidarium 24.16
tepidity 4.53
tequila 12.43
teraflop 27.8
teraphim 24.6
terawatt 30.32
terbium 24.16
terce 28.36
tercel 23.37
tercet 30.24
teredo 9.11
Terence 28.45
Teresa 12.90
tergiversate 30.15
teriyaki 4.18
term 24.22
termagant 30.56
terminal 23.34
terminate 30.13
termini 6.13
terminology 4.17
terminus 28.29
termite 30.29
termly 4.28
tern 25.53
ternary 4.43
terne 25.53
Terpsichore 4.43
Terpsichorean 25.36
terra firma 12.52
terra incognita 12.77
terrace 28.10
terracotta 12.79
terrain 25.7
terramare 4.38
Terramycin 25.19
terrapin 25.18
terraria 12.10
terrarium 24.16
terrazzo 9.22
Terre Haute 30.35
terrene 25.11
terreplein 25.8
terrestrial 23.24
terre-verte 30.6
terrible 23.26
terrier 12.10
terrific 21.10
terrifier 12.14
terrify 6.7
terrine 25.9
territorial 23.24
territory 4.43
terror 12.64
terrorist 31.12
terrorizer 12.91
terry 4.38
terse 28.36
tertian 25.49

tertiary 4.43
Tertullian 25.37
terylene 25.10
terza rima 12.51
tesla 12.42
tessellate 30.11
tessera 12.67
tesserae 4.43
tesseral 23.36
test 31.3
testamentary 4.43
testate 30.16
testatrices 35.8
testee 4.1
tester 12.76
testes 35.9
testicle 23.32
testicular 12.46
testifier 12.14
testify 6.7
testimonial 23.24
testimony 4.34
testis 28.12
testosterone 25.30
testudines 35.7
testudo 9.11
testy 4.51
tetanus 28.29
tetchy 4.11
tête-à-tête 30.7
tether 12.84
Tethys 28.12
Teton 25.26
tetra 12.64
tetrad 16.1
tetragonal 23.34
tetrahedral 23.36
tetrahedron 25.47
tetralogy 4.17
tetrameter 12.78
tetrarch 21.5
tetrastyle 23.12
tetrathlon 25.44
Teuton 25.50
Teutonic 21.13
Tevet 30.5
Tex 28.38
Texan 25.48
Texas 28.32
Texel 23.37
Tex-Mex 28.38
text 31.28
textbook 21.28
textbookish 29.8
textile 23.12
textspeak 21.8
textual 23.25
textualist 31.8
texture 12.23
texturize 35.13
Thackeray 4.43

Thaddeus 28.23
Thai 6.1
Thailand 16.40
thalamus 28.28
Thales 35.7
Thalia 12.6
thalidomide 16.14
thallium 24.16
thalweg 18.3
Thames 35.30
Thammuz 35.22
than 25.1
thane 25.7
thanedom 24.17
thang 26.1
thank 21.33
thanksgiving 26.14
that 30.1
thatch 15.1
thatcher 12.23
Thatcherite 30.29
thaumatrope 27.10
thaumaturge 20.17
thaumaturgist 31.7
thaw 7.1
the 4.1
Thea 12.3
theater 12.82
theatergoer 12.17
theater-in-the-round 16.43
theatre 12.82
theatregoer 12.17
theatregoing 26.3
theatre-in-the-round 16.43
theatric 21.15
theatrical 23.32
theatricalize 35.12
Theban 25.38
thebe 3.7
Thebes 35.26
theca 12.38
thee 4.1
theft 30.47
their 2.1
theirs 35.4
theirselves 35.35
theism 24.21
theistic 21.17
Thelma 12.50
them 24.3
thematic 21.17
theme 24.5
Themistocles 35.7
themself 17.18
themselves 35.35
then 25.5
thence 28.44
thenceforth 32.9
thenceforward 16.30

Theo 9.3
Theobald 16.36
theocentric 21.15
theocracy 4.48
theocrat 30.2
theocratic 21.17
Theocritus 28.34
theodicean 25.36
theodicy 4.46
Theodora 12.66
Theodorakis 28.7
Theodore 7.5
theogony 4.34
theologian 25.42
theologist 31.7
theologize 35.11
theology 4.17
theomachy 4.20
theophany 4.34
Theophilus 28.27
theophoric 21.15
Theophrastus 28.34
theorem 24.19
theoretic 21.17
theoretical 23.32
theoretician 25.49
theorist 31.12
theorizer 12.91
theory 4.43
theosopher 12.30
theosophic 21.10
theosophist 31.7
theosophy 4.14
Thera 12.67
therapeutic 21.17
therapeutical 23.32
therapeutist 31.14
therapist 31.11
therapy 4.37
Theravada 12.25
there 2.1
thereabout 30.34
thereabouts 28.47
thereafter 12.75
thereat 30.1
thereby 6.1
therefore 7.6
therefrom 24.8
therein 25.13
thereinto 11.20
theremin 25.17
thereof 34.10
thereon 25.24
thereout 30.34
Theresa 12.90
thereto 11.1
thereunder 12.29
thereunto 11.20
thereupon 25.24
therewith 33.4
therewithal 23.15

t

theriac 21.1
therm 24.22
thermae 4.30
thermal 23.33
thermic 21.12
thermionic 21.13
thermite 30.29
thermodynamic 21.12
thermometer 12.78
thermonuclear 12.6
Thermos 28.28
thermosphere 12.5
thermostat 30.2
thermostatic 21.17
thesauri 6.15
thesaurus 28.31
these 35.6
theses 35.8
Theseus 28.23
thesis 28.11
thespian 25.37
Thespis 28.9
Thessalian 25.37
Thessaloníki 4.18
Thessaly 4.27
theta 12.77
Thetis 28.12
theurgist 31.7
thew 11.1
they'd 16.6
they'll 23.5
they're 2.1
they've 34.4
they 3.1
thiamine 25.11
thick 21.9
thicken 25.43
thickener 12.58
thickening 26.9
thicket 30.21
thickhead 16.3
thickheaded 16.9
thickish 29.8
thicko 9.16
thickset 30.4
thick-skulled 16.37
thief 17.5
thieve 34.5
thievery 4.43
thieves 35.35
thievish 29.10
thigh 6.1
thigh bone 25.30
thill 23.8
thimble 23.26
thimblerig 18.6
thin 25.13
thine 25.21
thing 26.3
thingamabob 14.9

thingamajig 18.6
thingummy 4.30
thingy 4.35
think 21.33
thinker 12.39
think tank 21.33
thinner 12.55
thinning 26.9
thinnish 29.9
third 16.31
thirdhand 16.40
thirst 31.26
thirsty 4.55
thirteen 25.9
thirteenth 32.19
thirtieth 32.6
thirty 4.55
this 28.7
Thisbe 4.10
thistle 23.37
thistledown 25.29
thistly 4.27
thither 12.84
thole 23.17
tholos 28.14
Thom 24.8
Thomas 28.28
Thompson 25.48
thong 26.15
Thor 7.1
thoraces 35.8
thoracic 21.16
thorax 28.38
Thoreau 9.21
thorn 25.28
Thorndike 21.19
thorny 4.32
thorough 12.66
thoroughbred 16.4
thoroughfare 2.5
thoroughgoing 26.3
Thorpe 27.9
those 35.19
Thoth 32.11
thou 8.1
though 9.1
thought 30.33
thought-provoking 26.7
thousand 16.45
thousandfold 16.37
thousandth 32.19
Thrace 28.5
Thracian 25.49
thraldom 24.17
thrall 23.14
thrash 29.1
thrasher 12.72
thrashing 26.12
thrawn 25.28
thread 16.3

threadbare 2.3
threader 12.26
thread-like 21.19
threadworm 24.22
thready 4.12
threat 30.4
threaten 25.50
threatener 12.58
three 4.1
three-dimensional 23.34
threefold 16.37
threepence 28.45
threepenny 4.34
three-quarter 12.80
threescore 7.1
threnodic 21.10
threnodist 31.6
threnody 4.13
thresh 29.3
thresher 12.72
threshold 16.37
threw 11.1
thrice 28.13
thrift 30.47
thrifty 4.53
thrill 23.8
thriller 12.43
thrips 28.46
thrive 34.9
thriven 25.51
thro 11.1
throat 30.35
throaty 4.54
throb 14.9
thrombose 35.19
thrombosis 28.11
throne 25.30
throng 26.15
throstle 23.37
throttle 23.39
throttler 12.48
through 11.1
throughout 30.34
throughput 30.39
throughway 3.25
throw 9.1
throwaway 3.25
throwback 21.2
thrower 12.17
throw-in 25.13
thrown 25.30
thru 11.1
thrum 24.14
thrush 29.16
thrust 31.24
thruster 12.81
thrutch 15.13
Thucydides 35.7
thud 16.27
thug 18.12

thuggee 4.1
thuggery 4.43
thuggish 29.7
Thule 4.26, 23.20
thulium 24.16
thumb 24.14
thumbnail 23.6
thumbprint 30.54
thumbscrew 11.17
thumbtack 21.4
thump 27.17
thumper 12.63
thunder 12.29
thunderbird 16.31
thunderbolt 30.51
thunderbox 28.40
thunderbug 18.12
thunderclap 27.1
thundercloud 16.22
thunderer 12.67
thunderflash 29.1
thundering 26.11
thunderous 28.31
thunderstorm 24.9
thunderstruck 21.29
thundery 4.43
thunk 21.34
Thurber 12.22
thurible 23.26
thurifer 12.30
Thuringia 12.6
Thursday 3.9
Thurso 9.22
thus 28.21
thwack 21.1
Thwaite 30.7
thwart 30.33
thy 6.1
Thyestean 25.37
Thyestes 35.9
thylacine 25.23
thyme 24.7
thymus 28.28
thymy 4.29
thyroid 16.24
thyrsi 6.16
thyrsus 28.32
thyself 17.18
tiara 12.64
Tiber 12.21
Tiberius 28.23
Tibet 30.4
Tibetan 25.50
tibia 12.5
Tibullus 28.27
tic 21.9
tick 21.9
ticker 12.39
ticker tape 27.4
ticket 30.21

tickety-boo 11.1
ticking 26.7
tickle 23.32
tickler 12.48
ticklish 29.8
tickly 4.27
tick-tock 21.21
ticky-tacky 4.18
tic-tac 21.4
tic-tac-toe 9.1
tidal 23.28
tidbit 30.20
tiddledywink 21.33
tiddler 12.48
tiddly 4.24
tiddlywink 21.33
tide 16.14
tideline 25.22
tidemark 21.5
tidewater 12.80
tideway 3.25
tidings 35.32
tidy 4.12
tie 6.1
tieback 21.2
tiebreak 21.7
tie-breaker 12.38
tie-dye 6.6
tieless 28.8
Tientsin 25.13
tiepin 25.18
tier 12.4, 12.13
tierce 28.23
Tierney 4.34
Tierra del Fuego 9.13
tiff 17.6
tiffany 4.34
tiffin 25.14
tig 18.6
tiger 12.31
tigerish 29.9
Tigers 35.24
tiger's-eye 6.22
tight 30.26
tighten 25.50
tight-fisted 16.12
tightrope 27.10
tightwad 16.18
tigon 25.41
Tigray 3.19
Tigrayan 25.36
tigress 28.10
Tigrinya 12.89
Tigris 28.10
Tijuana 12.53
tiki 4.18
tikka 12.38
Tilburg 18.13
tilbury 4.43
Tilda 12.27

tilde 12.27
tile 23.11
tiler 12.44
tiling 26.8
till 23.8
tillage 20.6
tiller 12.43
Tilly 4.24
Tilsit 30.24
tilt 30.51
tilter 12.78
tilth 32.17
Tim 24.6
Timaru 11.17
timbal 23.26
timbale 23.2
timber 12.21
timberland 16.40
timberline 25.22
timbre 12.21
timbrel 23.36
Timbuktu 11.1
time 24.7
timekeeper 12.61
timekeeping 26.10
timely 4.25
timeous 28.28
timeout 30.34
timepiece 28.6
timer 12.51
Times 35.30
timescale 23.5
time-server 12.87
time-serving 26.14
timeshare 2.13
time-sharing 26.11
time sheet 30.19
time-worn 25.28
timid 16.10
timidity 4.53
timing 26.9
Timmy 4.29
Timor 7.12
Timorese 35.6
timorous 28.31
timothy 4.56
timpani 4.34
timpanist 31.10
tin 25.13
tinamou 11.14
tincture 12.23
tinder 12.27
tinderbox 28.40
tindery 4.43
tine 25.21
tinfoil 23.19
ting 26.3
tinge 20.19
tingle 23.30
tingly 4.24
tinhorn 25.28

tinker 12.39
tinkerer 12.67
tinkering 26.11
tinkle 23.32
tinkling 26.8
tinkly 4.24
tinnitus 28.34
tinny 4.32
tinpot 30.32
tinsel 23.37
tinselly 4.27
Tinseltown 25.31
tinsmith 32.6
tint 30.54
Tintagel 23.31
tinter 12.78
Tintoretto 9.24
tinware 2.15
tiny 4.32
tip 27.6
tipper 12.62
Tipperary 4.39
tippet 30.23
Tippett 30.23
Tipp-Ex 28.38
tipple 23.35
tippler 12.48
tippy 4.36
tipstaff 17.2
tipster 12.78
tipsy 4.46
tipsy cake 21.7
tiptoe 9.24
tiptop 27.8
tirade 16.6
tiramisu 11.1
Tirana 12.53
tire 12.13
Tiree 4.1
Tiresias 28.23
Tirol 23.17
tisane 25.1
Tishri 4.40
tissue 11.19
tit 30.20
titan 25.50
Titania 12.8
titanic 21.13
titanium 24.16
titbit 30.20
titch 15.6
titchy 4.11
titfer 12.30
tit-for-tat 30.1
tithe 33.5
tithing 26.14
Tithonus 28.29
titi 4.52
Titian 25.49
titillate 30.11
titivate 30.16

titlark 21.5
title 23.39
titling 26.8
titmice 28.13
titmouse 28.16
Tito 9.24
Titograd 16.1
Titoist 31.6
titter 12.78
titterer 12.67
tittle 23.39
tittle-tattle 23.39
tittup 27.14
titty 4.53
titular 12.46
Titus 28.34
tizz 35.10
tizzy 4.61
T-junction 25.49
Tlemcen 25.5
Tlingit 30.21
to 11.1
toad 16.23
toadflax 28.38
toad-in-the-
  hole 23.17
toadish 29.6
toadlet 30.22
toadstool 23.20
toady 4.13
toadyish 29.6
to-and-fro 9.1
toast 31.20
toaster 12.80
toastie 4.54
toastmaster 12.75
toastmistress 28.10
toasty 4.54
tobacco 9.16
tobacconist 31.10
Tobago 9.13
Tobagonian 25.37
Tobias 28.24
Tobit 30.20
toboggan 25.41
tobogganer 12.58
tobogganist 31.10
Tobruk 21.28
tocsin 25.19
tod 16.18
today 3.1
Todd 16.18
toddle 23.28
toddler 12.48
toddlerhood 16.26
toddy 4.13
todger 12.35
to-do 11.1
tody 4.13
toe 9.1
toecap 27.1

toehold 16.37
toeless 28.27
toenail 23.6
toey 4.7
toff 17.8
toffee 4.14
toffee-nosed 16.50
toft 30.47
tofu 11.7
tog 18.8
toga 12.32
together 12.84
toggery 4.43
toggle 23.30
Togo 9.13
Togolese 35.6
toil 23.19
toile 23.2
toiler 12.44
toilet 30.22
toilette 30.4
toilworn 25.28
toing and
    froing 26.3
Tojo 9.15
tokay 3.1
toke 21.24
Tokelau 8.7
token 25.43
Tokugawa 12.88
Tokyo 9.4
tolbooth 33.8
told 16.37
Toledo 9.11
tolerance 28.45
tolerant 30.56
tolerate 30.15
Tolkien 25.10
toll 23.17
tollbridge 20.8
tollbooth 33.8
toll gate 30.9
Tolstoy 10.12
Toltec 21.6
tom 24.8
tomahawk 21.22
tomato 9.24
tomatoey 4.7
tomb 24.12
Tombaugh 7.4
tombola 12.44
tombolo 9.17
tomboy 10.3
tomboyish 29.6
Tombs 35.30
tombstone 25.31
tomcat 30.1
tome 24.11
tomfool 23.20
tomfoolery 4.43
tommy 4.29

tommyrot 30.32
tomorrow 9.21
Toms 35.30
Tomsk 21.35
tomtit 30.24
tomtom 24.8
ton 25.24, 25.35
tonal 23.34
tonality 4.53
tondi 4.13
tondo 9.11
tone 25.30
tonearm 24.2
tone-deaf 17.3
toner 12.56
tong 26.15
tonga 12.60
Tongan 25.46
tongue 26.18
tongue-in-cheek
    21.8
tongue-lashing 26.12
tongue-tie 6.18
tonguing 26.10
Toni 4.33
tonic 21.13
tonight 30.26
Tonkin 25.13, 25.15
Tonks 28.41
tonnage 20.7
tonne 25.35
tonneau 9.19
tonsil 23.37
tonsillectomy 4.30
tonsillitis 28.12
tonsorial 23.24
tonsure 12.73
tontine 25.12
Tonton Macoute
    30.37
ton-up 27.13
tony 4.33
too 11.1
toodle-oo 11.1
toodle-pip 27.6
took 21.28
tool 23.20
toolbox 28.40
toolkit 30.21
toolmaking 26.7
toot 30.37
tooter 12.81
tooth 32.12
toothache 21.7
toothbrush 29.16
toothcomb 24.11
toothglass 28.2
tooth-like 21.19
toothpaste 31.4
toothpick 21.14
toothy 4.56

Tooting 26.13
tootle 23.39
tootsie 4.47
Toowoomba 12.21
top 27.8
topaz 35.1
top boot 30.37
topcoat 30.35
top-dress 28.3
tope 27.10
Topeka 12.38
toper 12.63
top-heavy 4.58
Tophet 30.21
topi 4.36
topiarian 25.37
topiarist 31.12
topiary 4.43
topic 21.14
topical 23.32
topknot 30.32
topless 28.27
topmast 31.2
topmost 31.20
topnotch 15.7
top-notcher 12.24
topo 9.20
topographer 12.30
topography 4.14
topoi 10.10
topology 4.17
topos 28.14
topper 12.62
topping 26.10
topple 23.35
topsail 23.6
topside 16.16
top-slice 28.13
topsoil 23.19
topspin 25.18
topstitch 15.6
topsy-turvy 4.58
top-up 27.13
toque 21.24
tor 7.1
Torah 12.66
Torbay 3.1
torc 21.22
torch 15.8
torch-bearer 12.65
torchlight 30.28
torchlit 30.22
torchon 25.26
tore 7.1
toreador 7.5
torero 9.21
torgoch 22.4
tori 6.15
torii 4.3
Torino 9.19
torment 30.53

tormentil 23.9
tormentor 12.76
torn 25.28
tornado 9.11
Tornio 9.4
Toronto 9.25
torpedo 9.11
torpid 16.10
torpidity 4.53
torpor 12.62
Torquay 4.1
torque 21.22
Torquemada 12.25
torr 7.1
torrent 30.56
torrential 23.38
Torricelli 4.22
torrid 16.11
torridity 4.53
torse 28.15
Tórshavn 25.51
torsion 25.49
torso 9.22
tort 30.33
torte 12.80
Tortelier 3.3
tortellini 4.31
torten 25.50
tortilla 12.89
tortious 28.33
tortoise 28.34
tortoiseshell 23.4
Tortola 12.44
tortrices 35.8
tortrix 28.39
tortuous 28.24
torture 12.24
torturer 12.67
torturous 28.31
torulae 4.26
torus 28.31
Tory 4.41
Toscanini 4.31
tosh 29.11
Tosk 21.35
toss 28.14
tosser 12.70
tosspot 30.32
toss-up 27.13
tostada 12.25
tostone 6.13
tot 30.31
total 23.39
totalitarian 25.37
totality 4.53
totalize 35.12
totalizer 12.91
tote 30.35
totem 24.20
totemic 21.12
totemist 31.9

t'other 12.84
totter 12.79
totterer 12.67
tottery 4.43
totting-up 27.13
totty 4.54
toucan 25.43
touch 15.13
touch-and-go 9.1
touchback 21.2
touchdown 25.29
touché 3.21
toucher 12.24
touchline 25.22
touch-me-not 30.32
touch pad 16.1
touchstone 25.31
touchy 4.11
Tough 17.15, 22.5
toughen 25.41
toughener 12.58
toughie 4.14
toughish 29.7
tough-minded 16.9
Toulon 25.24
Toulouse 35.21
Toulouse-
  Lautrec 21.6
toupée 3.18
tour 12.20
tourer 12.67
tourist 31.12
touristy 4.53
tourmaline 25.10
Tournai 3.1
tournedos 9.11
tourney 4.34
tourniquet 3.14
Tours 12.20
tousle 23.41
tout 30.34
touter 12.80
tow 9.1
towable 23.26
towage 20.6
toward 16.19
towards 35.27
towbar 1.4
towel 23.25
toweling 26.8
towelling 26.8
tower 12.16, 12.17
Towers 35.24
towery 4.43
towhee 4.16
towline 25.22
town 25.29
town house 28.16
Townes 35.31
townie 4.32
townish 29.9

townlet 30.22
townscape 27.4
townsfolk 21.24
townsman 25.45
townsmen 25.45
townspeople 23.35
Townsville 23.10
townswoman 25.45
townswomen 25.17
townward 16.30
towpath 32.2
towplane 25.8
towrope 27.10
towy 4.7
Towy 4.6
toxic 21.16
toxicity 4.53
toxicology 4.17
toxin 25.19
toxophily 4.24
toxoplasmosis 28.11
toy 10.1
toyboy 10.3
toylike 21.19
Toynbee 4.10
toyshop 27.8
toytown 25.29
trace 28.5
tracer 12.69
tracery 4.43
trachea 12.3
tracheotomy 4.30
tracing 26.12
track 21.1
trackage 20.6
trackbed 16.3
tracker 12.37
tracking 26.7
tracklayer 12.2
trackman 25.45
trackmen 25.45
trackside 16.16
tracksuit 16.16
trackway 3.25
tract 30.48
tractate 30.16
traction 25.49
tractor 12.74
Tracy 4.45
trad 16.1
trade 16.6
trademark 21.5
trader 12.26
tradesman 25.45
tradesmen 25.45
tradespeople 23.35
tradewind 16.42
traditionalist 31.8
traditionary 4.43
traditionist 31.10
traduce 28.19

traducer 12.71
Trafalgar 12.31
traffic 21.10
trafficker 12.39
tragedian 25.37
tragedy 4.12
tragic 21.11
tragical 23.32
tragicomedy 4.12
tragicomic 21.12
tragopan 25.3
Traherne 25.53
trail 23.5
trailblazer 12.90
trailblazing 26.14
trailer 12.43
train 25.7
trainee 4.1
trainer 12.54
trainload 16.23
traipse 28.46
trait 3.1
traitor 12.77
traitorous 28.31
Trajan 25.42
trajectory 4.43
tra-la 1.1
Tralee 4.1
tram 24.1
tramcar 1.11
tramline 25.22
trammel 23.33
tramontana 12.53
tramp 27.17
tramper 12.61
trampish 29.9
trample 23.35
trampler 12.42
trampoline 25.10
trampolinist 31.10
tramway 3.25
trance 28.44
tranche 29.20
tranny 4.31
tranquil 23.10
tranquility 4.53
tranquilize 35.12
tranquillity 4.53
tranquillize 35.12
transact 30.48
transaction 25.49
transactional 23.34
transactor 12.74
transatlantic 21.17
transaxle 23.41
transcend 16.41
transcendence
  28.45
transcendency
  4.48
transcendent 30.56

transcendentalist
  31.8
transcendentalize
  35.12
transcribe 14.8
transcriber 12.21
transcript 30.58
transcription 25.49
transect 30.48
transection 25.49
transept 30.58
transeptal 23.39
trans-fat 30.1
transfer 13.1,13.2
transferee 4.1
transference 28.45
transferor 12.68
transferral 23.36
transferrer 12.68
transfigure 12.31
transfinite 30.29
transfix 28.39
transfixion 25.49
transform 24.9
transformer 12.52
transfuse 35.21
transfusion 25.42
transgress 28.3
transgressive 34.7
transgressor 12.69
transience 28.45
transiency 4.48
transient 30.56
transistor 12.78
transit 30.24
transitionary 4.43
transitory 4.43
Transkei 6.1
translate 30.7
transliterate 30.15
translocate 30.7
translucence 28.45
translucency 4.47
translucent 30.56
transmarine 25.9
transmigrant 30.56
transmigrate 30.7
transmigratory 4.43
transmissible 23.26
transmit 30.20
transmitter 12.78
transmogrify 6.7
transmute 30.37
transmuter 12.81
transoceanic 21.13
transom 24.20
transonic 21.13
transpacific 21.10
transparence 28.45
transparency 4.48
transparent 30.56

t

transpersonal 23.34
transpire 12.13
transplant 30.53
transplanter 12.75
transpontine 25.23
transport 30.33
transporter 12.80
transpose 35.19
transsexual 23.25
transubstantiate 30.8
transude 16.25
Transvaal 23.2
transversal 23.37
transverse 28.36
transvestist 31.14
transvestite 30.30
Transylvania 12.8
Transylvanian 25.37
trap 27.1
trapdoor 7.1
trapes 28.46
trapeze 35.6
trapezium 24.16
trapezoid 16.24
trap-like 21.19
trapper 12.61
trappings 35.32
Trappist 31.11
trash 29.1
trash can 25.2
trashy 4.50
trattoria 12.3
trauma 12.52
traumata 12.82
traumatic 21.17
travail 23.6
travel 23.40
traveler 12.48
traveller 12.48
travelogue 18.8
Travers 35.24
traversal 23.37
traverse 28.35
traverser 12.71
travertine 25.12
travesty 4.53
Travis 28.12
trawl 23.14
trawler 12.44
trawlerman 25.45
tray 3.1
treacherous 28.31
treachery 4.43
treacle 23.32
treacly 4.27
tread 16.3
treader 12.26
treadle 23.28
treadmill 23.9
treadwheel 23.7

treason 25.52
treasonous 28.29
treasure 12.33
treasurer 12.67
treasury 4.43
treat 30.18
treater 12.77
treatise 35.10
treaty 4.52
Trebizond 16.42
treble 23.26
Treblinka 12.39
trebly 4.22
trebuchet 30.5
tree 4.1
treecreeper 12.61
treehouse 28.16
treeline 25.22
treen 25.9
treenail 23.6
treetop 27.8
trefa 12.30
trefoil 23.19
trek 21.6
trekker 12.37
trellis 28.8
trematode 16.23
tremble 23.26
trembler 12.42
trembling 26.8
trembly 4.22
tremendous 28.25
tremolo 9.17
tremor 12.50
tremulous 28.27
trench 29.20
trenchancy 4.48
trenchant 30.56
Trenchard 16.2
trencher 12.72
trencherman 25.45
trenchermen 25.45
trend 16.41
trendsetter 12.76
trendsetting 26.13
trendy 4.12
Trent 30.53
Trento 9.24
Trenton 25.50
trepan 25.1
trepang 26.1
trespass 28.30
trespasser 12.71
tress 28.3
tressy 4.45
trestle 23.37
tret 30.4
Trevelyan 25.37
Trevino 9.19
Trevor 12.85
trews 35.21

trey 3.1
triable 23.26
triacetate 30.16
triad 16.1
triadic 21.10
triage 19.1
trial 23.25
trialist 31.8
triangle 23.30
triangular 12.46
triangulate 30.11, 30.42
Trianon 25.26
Trias 28.1
Triassic 21.16
triathlete 30.18
triathlon 25.44
triaxial 23.24
tribade 16.28
tribal 23.26
tribalist 31.8
tribe 14.8
tribesman 25.45
tribesmen 25.45
tribeswoman 25.45
tribeswomen 25.17
triblet 30.22
tribrach 21.3
tribunal 23.34
tribunate 30.43
tribune 25.33
tributary 4.43
tribute 30.38
tricar 1.11
trice 28.13
Tricel 23.3
triceps 28.46
triceratops 28.46
trichinosis 28.11
trichomonad 16.1
trichotomous 28.28
trichotomy 4.30
Tricia 12.72
trick 21.9
tricker 12.39
trickery 4.43
trickle 23.32
trickster 12.78
tricksy 4.46
tricky 4.19
triclinia 12.8
tricolor 12.48
tricolour 12.48
tricorne 25.28
tricot 9.16
tricycle 23.32
tricyclist 31.8
trident 30.56
Tridentine 25.23
triduum 24.17
tried 16.14

triennia 12.8
triennial 23.24
Trier 12.4
trier 12.13
Trieste 31.3
triffid 16.9
trifle 23.29
trifler 12.44
trifoliate 30.41
triform 24.9
trig 18.6
trigamous 28.28
trigamy 4.30
trigger 12.31
triglyphic 21.10
trigon 25.41
trigonal 23.34
trigonometry 4.40
trike 21.19
trilateral 23.36
trilby 4.10
trill 23.8
Trilling 26.8
trillion 25.52
trillionth 32.19
trillium 24.16
trilogy 4.17
trim 24.6
trimaran 25.3
trimester 12.76
trimetrical 23.32
trimmer 12.51
trimming 26.9
Trimurti 4.55
Trincomalee 4.1
trine 25.21
Trini 4.31
Trinidad 16.1
Trinidadian 25.37
Trinitarian 25.37
trinity 4.53
trinket 30.21
trinketry 4.40
trio 9.3
triode 16.23
triolet 30.4
trip 27.6
tripartite 30.30
tripe 27.7
Tripitaka 12.41
triplane 25.8
triple 23.35
triplet 30.22
triplex 28.38
triplicate 30.10, 30.42
tripod 16.18
tripodal 23.28
tripoli 4.27
Tripolitanian 25.37
tripos 28.14

t

tripper 12.62
trippy 4.36
triptych 21.17
Tripura 12.66
tripwire 12.14
trishaw 7.17
triskelion 25.37
Tristan da
  Cunha 12.56
tristesse 28.3
Tristram 24.19
trite 30.26
triton 25.50
tritone 25.31
triturate 30.15
triumph 17.19
triumphal 23.29
triumphalist 31.8
triumphant 30.56
triumvir 12.87
triumviral 23.36
triumvirate 30.43
triune 25.33
trivet 30.25
trivia 12.12
trivial 23.24
Trixie 4.46
trochaic 21.9
trochee 4.20
trod 16.18
trodden 25.40
trog 18.8
troglodyte 30.26
troglodytes 35.9
troglodytic 21.17
troika 12.40
Troilus 28.27
Trojan 25.42
troll 23.13, 23.17
troller 12.44
trolley 4.25
trolleybus 28.21
trollop 27.14
Trollope 27.14
trombone 25.30
trombonist 31.10
tromp 27.17
trompe l'œil 10.1
tronc 21.34
Trondheim 24.7
Troon 25.33
troop 27.11
trooper 12.63
trope 27.10
trophic 21.10
trophy 4.14
tropic 21.14
tropical 23.32
troppo 9.20
Trossachs 28.41
trot 30.31

troth 32.11
Trotsky 4.19
Trotskyist 31.6
Trotskyite 30.26
trotter 12.79
troubadour 7.5
trouble 23.26
troublemaker 12.38
troublemaking 26.7
troubler 12.47
troubleshoot 30.38
troubleshooter
  12.81
troubleshot 30.32
troublous 28.27
trough 17.8
trounce 28.44
trouncer 12.70
troupe 27.11
trouper 12.63
trouser 12.92
trousseau 9.22
trout 30.34
trove 34.11
trover 12.86
trow 9.4
Trowbridge 20.8
trowel 23.25
troy 10.1
truancy 4.48
truant 30.56
truce 28.19
Trucial States 28.47
truck 21.29
truckage 20.6
trucker 12.41
truckle 23.32
truckload 16.23
truculence 28.45
truculent 30.56
Trudeau 9.11
trudge 20.16
trudgen 25.42
trudger 12.36
Trudy 4.13
true 11.1
true-blue 11.1
Trueman 25.45
Truffaut 9.12
truffle 23.29
trug 18.12
truism 24.21
truistic 21.17
Trujillo 9.28
trull 23.22
truly 4.26
trump 27.17
trumpery 4.43
trumpet 30.23
trumpeter 12.78
trumpeting 26.13

truncate 30.7
truncheon 25.49
trundle 23.28
trunk 21.34
trunking 26.7
Truro 9.21
truss 28.21
trusser 12.71
trust 31.24
trustee 4.1
truster 12.81
trusting 26.13
trustworthy 4.57
trusty 4.55
truth 32.12
try 6.1
trysail 23.37
tryst 31.6
tryster 12.78
tsar 1.1
tsardom 24.17
tsarevich 15.6
tsarina 12.54
tsarist 31.12
tsessebi 4.10
tsetse 4.45
T-shirt 30.45
T-square 2.15
tsunami 4.29
Tsushima 12.51
Tswana 12.53
tub 14.13
tuba 12.21
tubby 4.10
tube 14.12
tuber 12.21
tubercular 12.46
tuberculosis 28.11
tuberose 35.19
tuberous 28.31
tubful 23.21
tubifex 28.38
tubing 26.4
tubular 12.46
tuck 21.29
tucker 12.41
tucket 30.21
Tucson 25.26
Tudor 12.29
Tuesday 3.9
tufa 12.30
tuff 17.15
tuffet 30.21
tuft 30.47
tufty 4.55
tug 18.12
tugboat 30.35
tugger 12.32
tug-of-love 34.13
tug-of-war 7.1
tugrik 21.8

Tuileries 4.43
tuition 25.49
tuitional 23.34
Tula 12.45
tulip 27.6
Tull 23.22
Tullamore 7.12
tulle 23.20
Tulsa 12.71
tum 24.14
tumble 23.26
tumbledown 25.29
tumble-dry 6.1
tumble-dryer 12.13
tumbler 12.47
tumbleweed 16.7
tumbril 23.9
tumefaction 25.49
tumefy 6.7
tumescence 28.45
tumescent 30.56
tumid 16.10
tummy 4.30
tumor 12.52
tumour 12.52
tump 27.17
tumult 30.51
tumultuous 28.24
tumulus 28.27
tun 25.35
tuna 12.56
tunable 23.26
tundra 12.66
tune 25.33
tuner 12.56
tungsten 25.50
tunic 21.13
tunicate 30.10
tunicle 23.32
tuning 26.9
Tunis 28.9
Tunisia 12.12
Tunisian 25.37
tunnel 23.34
tunneler 12.48
tunneller 12.48
tunny 4.33
tup 27.13
Tupamaro 9.21
tupelo 9.17
Tupi 4.37
tuppence 28.45
tuppenny 4.34
Tupperware 2.15
tuque 21.27
turaco 9.16
Turanian 25.37
turban 25.38
turbary 4.43
turbid 16.8
turbine 25.21

t

uglify 6.7
ugly 4.26
Ugrian 25.37
Ugric 21.15
uh-huh 12.1
Uist 31.6
Ujjain 25.7
ukiyo-e 3.1
Ukraine 25.7
Ukrainian 25.37
ukulele 4.22
Ulanova 12.87
ulcer 12.71
ulema 12.51
Ulfilas 28.1
Ulm 24.18
Ulster 12.81
Ulsterman 25.45
Ulstermen 25.45
Ulsterwoman 25.45
Ulsterwomen 25.17
ult 30.51
ulterior 12.10
ultimacy 4.48
ultimata 12.77
ultimate 30.43
ultimatum 24.20
ultimo 9.18
ultra 12.66
ultramarine 25.9
ultramundane 25.7
ultrasonic 21.13
ultrasound 16.43
ultraviolet 30.42
ululate 30.11
Ulysses 35.8
um 24.15
umbel 23.26
umbellifer 12.30
umbelliferous 28.31
umber 12.22
umbilical 23.32
umbilicus 28.26
umbo 9.9
umbonate 30.43
umbra 12.66
umbrage 20.8
umbrageous 28.25
umbrella 12.42
Umbria 12.10
Umbrian 25.37
Umbriel 23.24
umiak 21.1
umlaut 30.34
ump 27.17
umpirage 20.8
umpire 12.14
umpteen 25.9
umpteenth 32.19
Una 12.56
unabashed 30.59

unabated 16.12
unabridged 16.34
unaccented 16.12
unaccommodating 26.13
unaccompanied 16.10
unaccomplished 30.59
unaccounted 16.12
unaccredited 16.12
unaccustomed 16.39
unacknowledged 16.34
unacquainted 16.12
unadapted 16.12
unaddressed 31.3
unadopted 16.12
unadorned 16.42
unadulterated 16.12
unadvertised 16.50
unaffected 16.12
unaffiliated 16.12
unaided 16.9
unaligned 16.42
unalleviated 16.12
unallocated 16.12
unalloyed 16.24
unaltered 16.29
unamended 16.9
unamused 16.50
unanalysed 16.50
unanalyzed 16.50
unaneled 16.35
unanimity 4.53
unanimous 28.28
unannounced 31.30
unanswered 16.29
unanticipated 16.12
unappeased 16.50
unappreciated 16.12
unapprehended 16.9
unappropriated 16.12
unapproved 16.49
unarmed 16.39
unarticulated 16.12
unascertained 16.41
unasked 30.49
unaspirated 16.12
unassigned 16.42
unassimilated 16.12
unassisted 16.12
unassociated 16.12
unassuaged 16.34
unattached 30.46
unattended 16.9

unattributed 16.12
unavailing 26.8
unavowed 16.22
unawares 35.4
unawed 16.19
unbacked 30.48
unbaked 30.48
unbefitting 26.13
unbeknown 25.30
unbelieving 26.14
unbiased 31.25
unbidden 25.40
unblemished 30.59
unblended 16.9
unblinking 26.7
unblushing 26.12
unbothered 16.29
unbounded 16.9
unbowed 16.22
unbranded 16.9
unbrotherly 4.27
unbruised 16.50
unburied 16.11
uncalled 16.36
uncarpeted 16.12
uncashed 30.59
unceasing 26.12
uncelebrated 16.12
uncensored 16.29
uncertain 25.50
uncertainty 4.55
uncertified 16.14
unchallenged 16.34
unchallenging 26.6
unchanged 16.34
unchanging 26.6
unchaperoned 16.43
uncharged 16.34
uncharted 16.12
unchartered 16.29
unchastened 16.45
unchecked 30.48
unchristian 25.39
uncial 23.24
unciform 24.9
uncircumcised 16.50
unclaimed 16.39
unclassified 16.14
uncle 23.32
unclimbed 16.39
unclouded 16.9
uncluttered 16.29
unco 9.16
uncollected 16.12
uncolored 16.29
uncoloured 16.29
uncombed 16.39
uncommercialized 16.50
uncommitted 16.12

uncompensated 16.12
uncomplaining 26.9
uncompleted 16.12
uncomplicated 16.12
uncomprehending 26.5
uncompromising 26.14
unconcealed 16.35
unconditioned 16.45
unconfined 16.42
unconfirmed 16.39
unconnected 16.12
unconquered 16.28
unconsecrated 16.12
unconsenting 26.13
unconsidered 16.28
unconstrained 16.41
unconstricted 16.12
unconsumed 16.39
unconsummated 16.12
uncontaminated 16.12
uncontested 16.12
uncontrived 16.49
uncontrolled 16.37
uncontroverted 16.12
unconverted 16.12
unconvinced 31.30
unconvincing 26.12
uncooked 30.49
uncoordinated 16.12
uncorrected 16.12
uncorroborated 16.12
uncorrupted 16.12
uncounted 16.12
uncovenanted 16.12
uncreased 31.5
uncredited 16.12
uncrowded 16.9
uncrumpled 16.38
unction 25.49
unctuous 28.24
uncultivated 16.12
uncultured 16.28
uncured 16.28
uncurtained 16.42
undamaged 16.34
undated 16.12
undaunted 16.12
undecided 16.9
undeclared 16.5

u

undecorated 16.12
undefeated 16.12
undefended 16.9
undefiled 16.36
undefined 16.42
undelivered 16.29
undemanding 26.5
undented 16.12
under 12.29
underachieve 34.5
underachiever 12.85
underact 30.48
under-age 20.4
underarm 24.2
underbelly 4.22
underbid 16.8
underbred 16.3
undercarriage 20.8
undercharge 20.2
underclass 28.2
underclothes 35.19
underclothing 26.14
undercoat 30.35
undercook 21.28
undercover 12.87
undercroft 30.47
undercurrent 30.56
undercut 30.40
underdeveloped 30.58
underdog 18.8
underdone 25.35
underdrawing 26.3
underdress 28.3
undereducated 16.12
underemphasis 28.11
underemployed 16.24
underestimate 30.12, 30.43
underexpose 35.19
underfed 16.3
underfelt 30.51
underfloor 7.1
underflow 9.17
underfoot 30.39
underframe 24.4
underfunded 16.9
underfunding 26.5
undergird 16.31
underglaze 35.5
undergo 9.1
undergone 25.24
undergrad 16.1
undergraduate 30.41
underground 16.43
undergrowth 32.11

underhand 16.40
underhanded 16.9
underlain 25.7
underlay 3.1, 3.15
underlease 28.6
underlet 30.4
underlie 6.1
underline 25.21, 25.22
underlinen 25.18
underling 26.8
undermanned 16.40
undermanning 26.9
undermentioned 16.45
undermine 25.21
undermost 31.20
underneath 32.5
undernourished 30.59
underpaid 16.6
underpainting 26.13
underpants 28.44
underpart 30.3
underpass 28.2
underperform 24.9
underpin 25.13
underpinning 26.9
underplant 30.53
underpopulated 16.12
underpowered 16.28
underprepared 16.5
underprice 28.13
underpriced 31.16
underprivileged 16.34
underproduction 25.49
underproof 17.13
underprop 27.8
underrate 30.7
under-rehearsed 31.26
under-represented 16.12
under-resourced 31.18
underscore 7.1, 7.10
undersea 4.1
underseal 23.7
undersecretary 4.43
undersell 23.3
undersexed 31.28
undershirt 30.45
undershoot 30.37
undershorts 28.47
undershot 30.31
underside 16.16

undersigned 16.42
undersized 16.50
underskirt 30.45
underslung 26.18
undersold 16.37
undersow 9.1
undersown 25.30
underspend 16.41
underspent 30.53
understaffed 30.47
understaffing 26.6
understairs 35.4
understand 16.40
understander 12.25
understanding 26.5
understate 30.7
understater 12.77
understood 16.26
understorey 4.41
understudy 4.13
undersubscribed 16.32
undersurface 28.7
undertake 21.7
undertaker 12.38
undertaking 26.7
underthings 35.32
undertone 25.31
undertook 21.28
undertow 9.25
undertrained 16.41
undertrick 21.15
underused 16.50
underutilize 35.12
undervalue 11.22
undervest 31.3
underwater 12.80
underwear 2.15
underweight 30.7
underwent 30.53
underwhelm 24.18
underwing 26.14
underwire 12.14
underwired 16.28
underwood 16.26
underwork 21.31
underworld 16.38
underwrite 30.26
underwriter 12.79
underwritten 25.50
undeserved 16.49
undesigned 16.42
undesired 16.28
undetected 16.12
undetermined 16.42
undeterred 16.31
undeveloped 30.58
undeviating 26.13
undiagnosed 16.50
undies 35.10

undifferentiated 16.12
undigested 16.12
undiluted 16.12
undiminished 30.59
undimmed 16.39
undine 25.10
undirected 16.12
undischarged 16.34
undisclosed 16.50
undiscovered 16.29
undiscriminating 26.13
undiscussed 31.24
undisguised 16.50
undismayed 16.6
undisputed 16.12
undissolved 16.49
undistinguished 16.12
undistorted 16.12
undistributed 16.12
undisturbed 16.32
undivided 16.9
undocumented 16.12
undomesticated 16.12
undoubted 16.12
undrained 16.41
undraped 30.58
undreamed 16.39
undulant 30.56
undulate 30.11
undy 4.13
undyed 16.14
unearned 16.46
uneaten 25.50
unedifying 26.3
unedited 16.12
uneducated 16.12
unelected 16.12
unembarrassed 31.25
unembellished 30.59
unemployed 16.24
unenclosed 16.50
unencrypted 16.12
unencumbered 16.28
unendowed 16.22
unengaged 16.34
unenlightened 16.45
unenlightening 26.9
unenvied 16.13
unequalize 35.12
unequipped 30.58
unerring 26.11

u

401

unestablished | unpretending

unestablished 30.59
unexamined 16.42
unexampled 16.38
unexciting 26.13
unexecuted 16.12
unexpected 16.12
unexpired 16.28
unexplained 16.41
unexploded 16.9
unexploited 16.12
unexplored 16.19
unexposed 16.50
unexpressed 31.3
unexpurgated 16.12
unfading 26.5
unfancied 16.11
unfathomed 16.39
unfazed 16.50
unfeigned 16.41
unfenced 31.30
unfermented 16.12
unfilled 16.35
unfiltered 16.29
unfinished 30.59
unfitted 16.12
unflagging 26.6
unflattering 26.11
unflavored 16.29
unflavoured 16.29
unfledged 16.34
unfleshed 30.59
unflinching 26.12
unfocused 31.25
unforced 31.18
unforgiving 26.14
unformatted 16.12
unformed 16.39
unformulated 16.12
unfortified 16.14
unfounded 16.9
unframed 16.39
unfrequented 16.12
unfriend 16.41
unfulfilled 16.35
unfulfilling 26.8
unfunded 16.9
unfurnished 30.59
ungainly 4.22
ungifted 16.12
unglazed 16.50
ungloved 16.49
unglued 16.25
ungrounded 16.9
ungrudging 26.6
unguent 30.56
unguided 16.9
ungulate 30.42
unhallowed 16.23
unhampered 16.29
unharmed 16.39
unhatched 30.46

unhealed 16.35
unheard 16.31
unheated 16.12
unhedged 16.34
unheeded 16.9
unheeding 26.5
unheralded 16.9
unhesitating 26.13
unhindered 16.28
unhonoured 16.29
unhooded 16.9
unhoped 30.58
unhyphenated 16.12
uni 4.33
Uniate 30.41
unicameral 23.36
unicorn 25.28
unicycle 23.32
unicyclist 31.8
unidentified 16.14
unidirectional 23.34
unifier 12.14
uniflow 9.17
uniform 24.9
uniformity 4.53
unify 6.7
unilateral 23.36
unilateralist 31.8
unilluminated 16.12
unillustrated 16.12
unimpaired 16.5
unimpassioned 16.45
unimpeded 16.9
unimposing 26.14
unimpressed 31.3
unimproved 16.49
unincorporated 16.12
uninflected 16.12
uninfluenced 31.30
uninformed 16.39
uninhabited 16.12
uninhibited 16.12
uninitiated 16.12
uninjured 16.28
uninspired 16.28
uninspiring 26.11
uninstructed 16.12
uninsulated 16.12
uninsured 16.28
uninterested 16.12
uninteresting 26.13
uninterrupted 16.12
uninvestigated 16.12
uninvited 16.12
uninviting 26.13
uninvolved 16.49

union 25.37
unionist 31.10
uniplanar 12.54
unipod 16.18
unique 21.8
unironed 16.45
unisex 28.38
unisexual 23.25
unison 25.48
unit 10.23
Unitarian 25.37
unitarity 4.53
unitary 4.43
unite 30.26
United Nations 35.31
United States 28.47
unitive 34.8
unitize 35.14
unity 4.53
univalve 34.15
universal 23.37
universalist 31.8
universe 28.36
university 4.53
univocal 23.32
unjustified 16.14
unlabeled 16.38
unlabelled 16.38
unlamented 16.12
unleaded 16.9
unleavened 16.45
unlettered 16.29
unliberated 16.12
unlicensed 31.30
unlighted 16.12
unlined 16.42
unlisted 16.12
unlooked 30.49
unloved 16.49
unloving 26.14
unmanaged 16.34
unmannered 16.29
unmapped 30.58
unmarred 16.2
unmatched 30.46
unmeasured 16.28
unmediated 16.12
unmelted 16.12
unmentioned 16.45
unmerited 16.12
unmetalled 16.38
unmitigated 16.12
unmixed 31.28
unmodernized 16.50
unmodified 16.14
unmodulated 16.12
unmolested 16.12
unmotivated 16.12
unmounted 16.12

unmourned 16.42
unmoved 16.49
unmoving 26.14
unmurmuring 26.11
unnamed 16.39
unneeded 16.9
unnoticed 31.14
unnumbered 16.28
Uno 9.19
unobscured 16.28
unobserved 16.49
unobstructed 16.12
unoccupied 16.14
unoffending 26.5
unoiled 16.37
unopened 16.45
unopposed 16.50
unordered 16.28
unornamented 16.12
unowned 16.43
unpadded 16.9
unpainted 16.12
unpaired 16.5
unparalleled 16.35
unpatented 16.12
unpatronizing 26.14
unpaved 16.49
unpeeled 16.35
unpersuaded 16.9
unperturbed 16.32
unpitying 26.3
unplaced 31.4
unplanned 16.40
unplanted 16.12
unplayed 16.6
unpleasing 26.14
unploughed 16.22
unplowed 16.22
unplumbed 16.39
unpointed 16.12
unpolished 30.59
unpolled 16.37
unpolluted 16.12
unpopulated 16.12
unposed 16.50
unpowered 16.28
unpracticed 31.14
unpractised 31.14
unprecedented 16.12
unpredicted 16.12
unprejudiced 31.6
unpremeditated 16.12
unprepared 16.5
unprepossessing 26.12
unpressed 31.3
unpressurized 16.50
unpretending 26.5

u

upgrader 12.26
upgrowth 32.11
upheaval 23.40
upheave 34.5
upheld 16.35
uphill 23.8
uphold 16.37
upholder 12.28
upholster 12.80
upholsterer 12.67
upholstery 4.43
upkeep 27.5
upland 16.45
uplift 30.47
uplifter 12.78
uplighter 12.79
upload 16.23
upmarket 30.21
upmost 31.20
upon 25.24
upper 12.63
upper case 28.5
upper-class 28.2
uppercut 30.40
uppermost 31.20
uppish 29.9
uppity 4.53
Uppsala 12.42
upraise 35.5
uprate 30.7
uprating 26.13
upright 30.29
uprise 35.11
uprisen 25.52
uprising 26.14
upriver 12.86
uproar 7.15
uproarious 28.23
uproot 30.37
uprooter 12.81
uprose 35.19
uprush 29.16
upscale 23.5
upset 30.4, 30.5
upsetter 12.76
upshift 30.47
upshot 30.32
upside 16.16
upside-down 25.29
upsides 35.27
upsilon 25.44
upstage 20.4
upstairs 35.4
upstanding 26.5
upstart 30.3
upstate 30.7
upstater 12.77
upstream 24.5
upstroke 21.24
upsurge 20.17
upswept 30.58

upswing 26.14
upsy-daisy 4.61
uptake 21.7
uptempo 9.20
upthrow 9.21
upthrust 31.24
uptight 30.26
up-to-date 30.7
uptown 25.29
uptowner 12.56
·upturn 25.53
upturned 16.46
upward 16.30
upwelling 26.8
upwind 16.42
Ur 13.1
uraei 6.2
uraemia 12.7
uraeus 28.22
Uralic 21.11
Urania 12.8
uranium 24.16
Uranus 28.29
urban 25.38
urbane 25.7
urbanist 31.10
urbanite 30.29
urbanity 4.53
urchin 25.13
Urdu 11.6
urea 12.3
ureter 12.77
urethra 12.65
urethral 23.36
Urey 4.43
urge 20.17
urgency 4.48
urgent 30.56
urger 12.36
urging 26.6
Uriah 12.13
Uriel 23.24
urinal 23.34
urinary 4.43
urinate 30.13
urine 25.18
urn 25.53
urogenital 23.39
urology 4.17
ursine 25.23
Ursula 12.46
Ursuline 25.22
Uruguay 6.21
Uruguayan 25.38
Uruk 21.28
us 28.21
usability 4.53
usable 23.26
usage 20.9
usance 28.45
use 28.19, 35.21

used 16.50, 31.22
useful 23.21
useless 28.27
user 12.92
user-friendly 4.22
usher 12.73
usherette 30.4
usquebaugh 7.4
Ustashe 4.50
Ustinov 17.8
usual 23.25
usurer 12.67
usurious 28.23
usurp 27.15
usurper 12.63
usury 4.43
Utah 7.18
Ute 30.37
utensil 23.9
uterine 25.23
uterus 28.31
utile 23.12
utilitarian 25.37
utility 4.53
utilizer 12.91
utmost 31.20
Utopia 12.9
Utopian 25.37
Utrecht 30.48
Utrillo 9.17
Utsire 12.67
Uttar Pradesh
    29.3
utter 12.81
utterance 28.45
utterer 12.67
uttermost 31.20
Uttley 4.26
U-turn 25.53
uvula 12.46
uvulae 4.26
uxorial 23.24
uxoricidal 23.28
uxoricide 16.16
uxorious 28.23
Uzbek 21.6
Uzbekistan 25.4
Uzi 4.62

v

Vaal 23.2
Vaasa 12.69
vac 21.1
vacancy 4.48
vacant 30.56
vacate 30.7
vacation 25.49
vacationer 12.58

vacationist 31.10
vaccinate 30.13
vaccine 25.11
vacillate 30.11
vacua 12.20
vacuity 4.53
vacuous 28.24
vacuum 24.12
vade mecum
    24.18
Vaduz 35.21
vagabond 16.42
vagabondage 20.6
vagary 4.43
vagina 12.55
vaginal 23.34
vagrancy 4.48
vagrant 30.56
vague 18.4
vaguish 29.7
vail 23.5
vain 25.7
vainglorious 28.23
vainglory 4.41
Vaishnava 12.87
Vaisya 12.89
Val 23.1
valance 28.45
valanced 31.30
Valda 12.25
Valdemar 1.13
vale 23.5
valediction 25.49
valedictorian 25.37
valedictory 4.43
valence 28.45
valency 4.48
valentine 25.23
Valentino 9.19
valerian 25.37
Valerie 4.43
valet 30.22
valetudinarian
    25.37
valetudinary 4.43
Valhalla 12.42
valiant 30.56
valid 16.10
validate 30.9
validity 4.53
valise 35.6
valium 24.16
Valkyrie 4.40
Valletta 12.76
valley 4.21
vallum 24.18
Valois 1.22
Valona 12.56
valonia 12.8
valor 12.42
valorous 28.31

u

v

valour 12.42
Valparaiso 9.29
valse 28.42
valuate 30.8
value 11.22
valuer 12.20
valve 34.15
vamoose 28.19
vamp 27.17
vampire 12.14
vampiric 21.15
vampish 29.9
vampy 4.36
van 25.1
vanadium 24.16
Vanbrugh 12.64
Van Buren 25.47
Vancouver 12.87
Vanda 12.25
vandal 23.28
Vandalic 21.11
Vanderbilt 30.51
Van Dyck 21.19
vandyke 21.19
vane 25.7
Vanessa 12.69
vang 26.1
vanguard 16.2
vanilla 12.43
vanish 29.9
vanity 4.53
vanquish 29.10
vanquisher 12.72
vantage point 30.55
vantage 20.9
Vanuatu 11.20
Vanya 12.89
vapid 16.10
vapidity 4.53
vapor 12.61
vaporetti 4.51
vaporetto 9.24
vaporish 29.9
vaporous 28.31
vapory 4.43
vapour 12.61
vapourish 29.9
vapoury 4.43
Varah 12.64
Varèse 35.3
Vargas 28.1
variance 28.45
variant 30.56
varicolored 16.29
varicoloured 16.29
varicose 28.17
varied 16.11
varietal 23.39
varietist 31.14
variety 4.53
varifocal 23.32

variform 24.9
various 28.23
varlet 30.22
varletry 4.40
varmint 30.54
varna 12.53
varnish 29.9
Varro 9.21
varsity 4.53
vary 4.39
Vasari 4.38
Vasco da Gama
   12.50
vascular 12.46
vas deferens 35.31
vase 35.2
vasectomy 4.30
vaseline 25.10
vassal 23.37
vast 31.2
vat 30.1
Vatican 25.43
Vaticanist 31.10
vaticinal 23.34
Vattern 25.53
vaudeville 23.10
vaudevillian 25.37
Vaudois 1.22
Vaughan 25.28
vault 30.51
vaulter 12.80
vaunt 30.54
vaunter 12.80
vavasory 4.43
veal 23.7
Veblen 25.44
vector 12.76
vectorial 23.24
vectorize 35.13
Veda 12.26
Vedanta 12.75
Vedantic 21.17
Vedda 12.26
vedette 30.4
Vedic 21.10
veep 27.5
veer 12.4
veg 20.3
Vega 12.31
vegan 25.41
Vegeburger 12.32
Vegemite 30.29
vegetal 23.39
vegetarian 25.37
vegetate 30.16
veggie 4.17
vehemence 28.45
vehicle 23.32
vehicular 12.46
veil 23.5
veiling 26.8

vein-like 21.19
vein 25.7
veiny 4.31
Velaazquez 35.10
velar 12.43
velcro 9.21
veld 30.51
veldskoen 25.33
veleta 12.77
vellum 24.18
Velma 12.50
velocimeter 12.78
velocipede 16.7
velocity 4.53
velodrome 24.11
velour 12.20
velouté 3.22
velum 24.18
velvet 30.25
velveteen 25.9
velvety 4.53
vena cava 12.85
venae cavae 4.58
venal 23.34
venality 4.53
vend 16.41
Venda 12.26
vendace 28.7
vendetta 12.76
vendeuse 35.25
vendible 23.26
vendor 7.5
vendue 11.1
veneer 12.4
venerate 30.15
venereal 23.24
venery 4.43
Venetia 12.72
venetian 25.49
Venezuela 12.43
Venezuelan 25.44
vengeance 35.31
venial 23.24
Venice 28.9
venison 25.48
venom 24.19
venomous 28.28
venous 28.29
vent 30.53
venti 4.51
ventiduct 30.49
ventil 23.9
ventilate 30.11
Ventolin 25.16
ventouse 28.19
ventral 23.36
ventricle 23.32
ventriloquial 23.24
ventriloquist 31.15
ventriloquize 35.15
ventriloquy 4.59

venture 12.72
venturer 12.67
venue 11.22
Venus 28.29
Venusian 25.37
Vera 12.67
veracious 28.33
veracity 4.53
Veracruz 35.21
veranda 12.25
verb 14.15
verbal 23.26
verbalist 31.8
verbalizer 12.91
verbatim 24.6
verbena 12.54
verbiage 20.6
verbose 28.17
verbosity 4.53
verboten 25.50
verdancy 4.49
verdant 30.56
Verdelho 11.22
Verdi 4.12
verdict 30.49
verdigris 4.40
Verdun 25.35
verdure 12.36
verdurous 28.31
Vere 12.4
Vereeniging 26.6
verge 20.17
verger 12.36
verglas 1.12
veridical 23.32
veriest 31.6
verifier 12.14
verify 6.7
verisimilar 12.43
verisimilitude 16.25
verism 24.21
verismo 9.18
veristic 21.17
verity 4.53
verjuice 28.19
Verlaine 25.7
Vermeer 12.4
vermeil 23.5
vermian 25.37
vermicelli 4.22
vermicular 12.46
vermilion 25.37
vermin 25.17
verminate 30.13
verminous 28.29
Vermont 30.54
vermouth 32.13
vernacular 12.46
vernacularity 4.53
vernacularize 35.13
vernal 23.34

vernalize 35.12
Verne 25.53
Verner 12.59
vernicle 23.32
vernissage 19.1
Vernon 25.46
Verny 4.34
Verona 12.56
Veronese 4.61
veronica 12.39
veronique 21.8
verruca 12.41
verrucae 4.20
Versailles 6.1
versant 30.56
versatile 23.12
versatility 4.53
verse 28.36
verselet 30.22
verset 30.24
versicle 23.32
versicolored 16.29
versicoloured 16.29
versifier 12.14
versify 6.7
version 25.49
versional 23.34
vers libre 12.65
verso 9.22
verst 31.26
versus 28.32
vert 30.45
vertebra 12.65
vertebrae 3.19
vertebrate 30.43
vertex 28.38
vertical 23.32
verticalize 35.12
vertices 35.8
vertiginous 28.29
vertigo 9.13
vervain 25.8
verve 34.14
Verwoerd 30.41
very 4.38
Vesalius 28.23
vesicle 23.32
Vespa 12.61
Vespasian 25.42
vesper 12.61
vespertine 25.23
Vespucci 4.11
vessel 23.37
vest 31.3
vesta 12.76
vestal 23.39
vestee 4.1
vestiary 4.43
vestibule 23.20
vestige 20.9
vestigial 23.24

vestiture 12.23
vestry 4.38
vestryman 25.45
vestrymen 25.45
vesture 12.23
Vesuvius 28.23
vet 30.4
vetch 15.3
vetchling 26.8
veteran 25.47
veterinarian 25.37
veterinary 4.43
veto 9.24
vetoer 12.17
vex 28.38
vexation 25.49
vexatious 28.33
vexer 12.69
vexilla 12.43
vexillum 24.18
Vi 6.1
via 12.13
viability 4.53
viable 23.26
Via Dolorosa 12.71
viaduct 30.49
Viagra 12.64
vial 23.25
viand 16.45
viatica 12.39
viaticum 24.18
vibe 14.8
vibes 35.26
vibist 31.6
vibrancy 4.48
vibrant 30.56
vibraphone 25.30
vibraphonist
  31.10
vibrate 30.7
vibrato 9.24
vibratory 4.43
Vic 21.9
vicar 12.39
vicarage 20.8
vicarial 23.24
vicariate 30.41
vicarious 28.23
vice 4.46, 28.13
vice-like 21.19
viceregal 23.30
vicereine 25.7
viceroy 10.11
viceroyal 23.25
vice versa 12.71
Vichy 4.50
vichyssoise 35.2
vicinal 23.34
vicinity 4.53
vicious 28.33
vicissitude 16.25

vicissitudinous
  28.29
Vicksburg 18.13
Vicky 4.19
Vico 9.16
vicomte 30.54
vicomtesse 28.3
victim 24.6
victimizer 12.91
victor 12.78
victoria 12.10
Victorian 25.37
Victoriana 12.53
victorious 28.23
victory 4.43
victual 23.39
victualer 12.48
victualler 12.48
vicuña 12.56
Vidal 23.2
vide 4.12
videlicet 30.5
video 9.4
videoconferencing
  26.12
videophone 25.30
video
  recorder 12.28
videorecording 26.5
videotape 27.4
vie 6.1
vielle 23.3
Vienna 12.53
Viennese 35.6
Vientiane 25.4
Vietcong 26.15
Vietminh 25.13
Vietnam 24.1
Vietnamese 35.6
vieux jeu 13.1
view 11.1
viewer 12.19
viewfinder 12.27
viewing 26.14
viewpoint 30.55
viewport 30.33
vigil 23.9
vigilance 28.45
vigilant 30.56
vigilante 4.51
vigneron 25.26
vignette 30.4
vignettist 31.14
Vignola 12.44
Vigo 9.13
vigor 12.31
vigorish 29.9
vigoro 9.21
vigorous 28.31
vigour 12.31
Viking 26.7

Vila 12.43
vile 23.11
vilifier 12.14
vilify 6.7
Villa 1.1
villa 12.43
village 20.6
villager 12.35
villagey 4.17
villain 25.44
villainous 28.29
villainy 4.34
villanelle 23.3
villein 25.16
Villon 25.24
Vilnius 28.23
vim 24.6
vin 25.1
vina 12.54
vinaigrette 30.4
Vince 28.44
Vincent 30.56
vincible 23.26
vindaloo 11.1
vindicate 30.10
vindicatory 4.43
vine 25.21
vinegar 12.31
vinegarish 29.9
vinegary 4.43
vinery 4.43
vineyard 16.30
vingt-et-un 26.19
vinho verde 4.13
viniculture 12.24
viniculturist 31.12
vining 26.9
vino 9.19
vin ordinaire 2.1
vinous 28.29
vintage 20.9
vintager 12.35
vintner 12.55
vinyl 23.9
viol 23.25
viola 12.44
Viola 12.48
violate 30.11
violence 28.45
violent 30.56
violet 30.22
violin 25.13
violinist 31.10
violist 31.8
violoncello 9.17
violone 25.30
viper 12.62
viperine 25.23
viperish 29.9
viperous 28.31
virago 9.13

v

V
W

wage 20.4
wager 12.35
Wagga
  Wagga 12.32
waggish 29.7
waggle 23.30
waggly 4.27
Wagnerian 25.37
wagon 25.41
wagoner 12.58
wagonette 30.4
wagon-lit 4.1
wagonload 16.23
wagtail 23.6
Wahhabi 4.10
wahine 4.31
wahoo 11.1
wah-wah 1.22
waif 17.4
waifish 29.7
waiflike 21.19
Waikato 9.24
Waikiki 4.1
wail 23.5
wailer 12.43
wailing 26.8
wain 25.7
wainscot 30.42
wainwright 30.29
waist 31.4
waistband 16.40
waistcoat 30.35
waistline 25.22
wait 30.7
waiter 12.77
waitress 28.10
waive 34.4
waiver 12.85
wake 21.7
Wakefield 16.35
waken 25.43
waker 12.38
wakey-wakey 4.18
Waldemar 1.13
Waldenses 35.8
Waldensian 25.37
Waldheim 24.7
Waldo 9.11
wale 23.5
Wales 35.29
walk 21.22
walkabout 30.34
walkathon 25.26
walker 12.40
walkies 35.10
walkie-talkie 4.19
walk-in 25.15
Walkman 25.45
walk-on 25.25
walkout 30.34
walkover 12.86

walk-through 11.17
walk-up 27.13
walkway 3.25
wall 23.14
wallaby 4.10
Wallace 28.8
Wallachia 12.6
wallah 12.44
wallaroo 11.1
Wallasey 4.48
wallchart 30.3
wallcovering 26.11
Wallenberg 18.13
Waller 12.44
wallet 30.22
wall eye 6.11
wall-eyed 16.14
wallflower 12.16
Walloon 25.33
wallop 27.14
walloper 12.63
wallow 9.17
wallpaper 12.61
Walls 35.29
wally 4.25
walnut 30.40
Walpole 23.18
walrus 28.31
Walsall 23.15
Walsh 29.19
Walsingham 24.19
Walter 12.80
Walton 25.50
waltz 28.42
waltzer 12.70
wampum 24.19
wan 25.24
wand 16.42
Wanda 12.28
wander 12.28
wanderer 12.67
wandering 26.11
wanderlust 31.24
wane 25.7
waney 4.31
Wanganui 4.8
wangle 23.30
wangler 12.48
wank 21.33
wanker 12.37
wanky 4.18
wanly 4.25
wanna 12.56
wannabe 4.10
wanness 28.29
want 30.54
wanter 12.79
wanton 25.50
wapentake 21.7
war 7.1
waratah 1.1

Warbeck 21.6
warble 23.26
warbler 12.44
Warburg 18.13
warby 4.10
ward 16.19
warden 25.40
warder 12.28
wardrobe 14.11
ware 2.1
warehouse 28.16
warehouseman
  25.45
warehousemen
  25.45
warfare 2.5
warfarin 25.18
Wargrave 34.4
warhead 16.3
Warhol 23.17
warhorse 28.15
Waring 26.11
warlike 21.19
warlock 21.21
warlord 16.21
warm 24.9
warm-blooded 16.9
warmer 12.52
warm-hearted 16.12
warmish 29.8
warmonger 12.32
warmth 32.18
warm-up 27.13
warn 25.28
warner 12.56
warning 26.9
warp 27.9
warpage 20.7
warpaint 30.54
warpath 32.2
warper 12.62
warplane 25.8
warrant 30.56
warrantee 4.1
warranter 12.82
warrantor 7.1
warranty 4.55
warren 25.47
warrigal 23.30
Warrington 25.50
warrior 12.10
Warsaw 7.16
warship 27.6
wart 30.33
warthog 18.8
wartime 24.7
wartorn 25.28
warty 4.54
Warwick 21.15,
  21.18
Warwickshire 12.11

wary 4.39
was 35.16
wash 29.11
washbag 18.1
washbasin 25.48
washboard 16.20
washcloth 32.8
washday 3.9
washer 12.73
washerman 25.45
washermen 25.45
washerwoman
  25.45
washerwomen
  25.17
Washington 25.50
Washingtonian
  25.37
washing-up 27.13
washland 16.40
washout 30.34
washroom 24.12
washstand 16.40
washtub 14.13
wash-up 27.13
washy 4.50
wasn't 30.56
wasp 27.18
waspie 4.36
waspish 29.9
waspy 4.36
wassail-bowl 23.17
wassail 23.6
wassailer 12.43
wastage 20.9
waste 31.4
wasteland 16.40
waster 12.77
wastrel 23.36
Wat 30.31
watch 15.7
watch chain 25.7
watchdog 18.8
watcher 12.24
watchfire 12.14
watchmaker 12.38
watchman 25.45
watchmen 25.45
watchnight 30.29
watch spring 26.11
watchtower 12.16
watchword 16.31
water 12.80
waterbed 16.3
waterbird 16.31
waterboarding 26.5
waterborne 25.28
watercolor 12.47
watercolour 12.47
watercourse 28.15
watercraft 30.47

w

watercress 28.3
waterer 12.67
waterfall 23.15
waterfowl 23.16
waterfront 30.55
watergate 30.9
waterhole 23.17
Waterhouse 28.16
watering 26.11
waterline 25.22
waterlogged 16.33
Waterloo 11.1
waterman 25.45
watermark 21.5
watermelon 25.44
watermen 25.45
watermill 23.9
water power 12.16
waterproof 17.13
waterproofer 12.30
water-
    repellent 30.56
water-
    resistant 30.56
Waters 35.24
watershed 16.4
waterside 16.16
waterspout 30.34
watertight 30.30
waterway 3.25
waterweed 16.7
waterwheel 23.7
water wings 35.32
waterworks 28.41
watery 4.43
Watford 16.28
Watkin 25.15
Watson 25.48
Watt 30.31
wattage 20.9
Watteau 9.25
wattle 23.39
Watts 28.47
Watusi 4.47
Waugh 7.1
waul 23.14
wave 34.4
waveband 16.40
wavelength 32.20
wavelet 30.22
waver 12.85
waverer 12.67
wavery 4.43
wavy 4.58
wax 28.38
waxberry 4.43
waxbill 23.8
waxcloth 32.8
waxen 25.48
waxer 12.69
waxing 26.12

waxwing 26.14
waxwork 21.31
waxy 4.45
way 3.1
waybill 23.8
wayfarer 12.65
wayfaring 26.11
waylay 3.1
waylayer 12.2
waymark 21.5
waymarker 12.37
Wayne 25.7
way-out 30.34
wayside 16.16
wayward 16.30
wazzock 21.30
we 4.1
weak 21.8
weaken 25.43
weakener 12.58
weakish 29.8
weak-kneed 16.7
weakling 26.8
weakly 4.23
weal 23.7
wealden 25.40
wealth 32.17
wealthy 4.56
wean 25.9
weaner 12.54
weapon 25.46
weaponry 4.43
wear 2.1
Wear 12.4
wearer 12.65
wearing 26.11
weary 4.43
weasel 23.41
weaselly 4.27
weather 12.84
weatherbeaten
    25.50
weatherboard 16.20
weatherbound
    16.43
weathercock 21.20
weathergirl 23.42
weather glass 28.2
weatherly 4.27
weatherman 25.2
weathermen 25.5
weatherproof 17.13
weatherstrip 27.6
weathervane 25.8
weave 34.5
weaver 12.85
weaverbird 16.31
weaving 26.14
web 14.3
Webb 14.3
Weber 12.21

webinar 1.14
webisode 16.23
weblog 18.8
webmail 23.5
website 30.30
Webster 12.76
we'd 16.7
wed 16.3
wedding 26.5
Wedekind 16.42
wedge 20.3
wedgie 4.17
Wedgwood 16.26
wedlock 21.21
Wednesday 3.9
wee 4.1
weed 16.7
weeder 12.26
weedkiller 12.43
weedy 4.12
week 21.8
weekday 3.9
weekend 16.41
weekender 12.26
weekly 4.23
Weeks 28.38
ween 25.9
weeny 4.31
weep 27.5
weeper 12.61
weepy 4.36
weever 12.85
weevil 23.10
weevily 4.24
weewee 4.59
weft 30.47
Wehrmacht 30.48
Wei 3.1
weigh 3.1
weigher 12.2
weigh-in 25.13
weight 30.7
weighting 26.13
weightlifter 12.78
weightlifting 26.13
weight-watchers
    35.24
weighty 4.52
Weil 23.11
Weimar 1.13
weir 12.4
weird 16.28
weirdo 9.11
Weismann 25.45
Weissmuller 12.46
weka 12.37
welcome 24.18
welcomer 12.52
weld 16.35
welder 12.26
welfare 2.5

welfarist 31.12
welkin 25.15
well 23.3
we'll 23.7
well-being 26.3
wellington 25.50
Wells 35.29
wellspring 26.11
well-to-do 11.1
well-wisher 12.72
welly 4.22
welsh 29.19
welsher 12.72
Welshman 25.45
Welshmen 25.45
Welshwoman 25.45
Welshwomen 25.17
welt 30.51
welter 12.76
welterweight 30.17
Weltschmerz 28.47
Wenceslas 28.27
wench 29.20
wencher 12.72
wend 16.41
Wenda 12.26
Wendell 23.28
Wendic 21.10
Wendish 29.6
Wendy 4.12
Wensleydale 23.5
went 30.53
wept 30.58
were 13.1
we're 12.4
weren't 30.57
werewolf 17.18
werewolves 35.35
Werner 12.59
Weser 12.90
Wesker 12.37
Wesley 4.22
Wesleyan 25.37
Wessex 28.39
west 31.3
westbound 16.43
West Bromwich
    20.7
westerly 4.27
western 25.50
westerner 12.58
westernizer 12.91
westernmost 31.20
westing 26.13
Westmeath 32.5
Westminster 12.78
Westmorland 16.45
Weston-super-
    Mare 2.1
Westphalia 12.6
Westphalian 25.37

westward 16.30
wet 30.4
wetback 21.2
wether 12.84
wetland 16.40
wet look 21.28
wetly 4.22
wetness 28.29
wet nurse 28.36
wetsuit 30.38
wetting 26.13
wettish 29.10
we've 34.5
Wexford 16.28
wey 3.1
Weymouth 32.13
whack 21.1
whacker 12.37
whacking 26.7
whacko 9.1
whale 23.5
whaleback 21.2
whaleboat 30.35
whalebone 25.30
whaler 12.43
wham 24.1
whammy 4.29
whang 26.1
Whangarei 3.1
whare 4.41
wharf 17.9
wharfie 4.14
wharfinger 12.35
Wharton 25.50
wharves 35.35
what 30.31
whatever 12.85
whatnot 30.32
whatsit 30.24
whatsoever 12.85
whaup 27.9
wheat 30.18
wheatear 12.12
wheaten 25.50
wheatgerm 24.22
wheatgrass 28.2
wheatmeal 23.7
Wheatstone 25.31
whee 4.1
wheedle 23.28
wheedler 12.48
wheel 23.7
wheelbarrow 9.21
wheelbase 28.5
wheelchair 2.4
wheel clamp 27.17
wheeler 12.43
wheeler-dealer
  12.43
wheeler-dealing
  26.8

wheelhouse 28.16
wheelie 4.23
wheeling 26.8
wheelsman 25.45
wheelsmen 25.45
wheelspin 25.18
wheelwright 30.29
Wheen 25.9
wheeze 35.6
wheezer 12.90
wheezy 4.61
whelk 21.32
whelp 27.16
when 25.5
whence 28.44
whenever 12.85
whensoever 12.85
where 2.1
whereabouts 28.47
whereafter 12.75
whereas 35.1
whereat 30.1
whereby 6.1
wherefore 7.6
wherefrom 24.8
wherein 25.13
whereof 34.10
whereon 25.24
wheresoever 12.85
whereto 11.1
whereupon 25.24
wherever 12.85
wherewith 33.4
wherewithal 23.14,
  23.15
wherry 4.38
whet 30.4
whether 12.84
whetstone 25.31
whetter 12.76
whew 11.1
whey 3.1
which 15.6
whichever 12.85
whichsoever 12.85
whicker 12.39
whiff 17.6
whiffle 23.29
whiffy 4.14
Whig 18.6
whiggery 4.43
whiggish 29.7
while 23.11
whilom 24.18
whilst 31.29
whim 24.6
whimbrel 23.36
whimper 12.62
whimperer 12.67
whimpering 26.11
whimsical 23.32

whimsy 4.61
whim-wham 24.1
whin 25.13
whinchat 30.1
whine 25.21
whiner 12.55
whinge 20.19
whinger 12.35
whingy 4.17
whinny 4.32
whinstone 25.31
whiny 4.32
whip 27.6
whipcord 16.21
whiplash 29.1
whipper-in 25.13
whippersnapper
  12.61
whipper 12.62
whippet 30.23
whipping 26.10
whippoorwill 23.10
whippy 4.36
whip-round 16.43
whipsaw 7.16
whirl 23.42
whirler 12.49
whirligig 18.6
whirlpool 23.20
whirlwind 16.42
whirlybird 16.31
whirr 13.1
whisht 30.59
whisk 21.35
whisker 12.39
whiskery 4.43
whisky 4.19
whisper 12.62
whisperer 12.67
whispering 26.11
whist 31.6
whistle 23.37
whistler 12.48
whistle-stop 27.8
whit 30.20
Whitby 4.10
white 30.26
whitebait 30.9
whiteboard 16.20
whitecap 27.1
white currant 30.56
white-collar 12.44
whiteface 28.5
whitefish 29.7
whitefly 6.11
Whitehall 23.15
whitehead 16.3
Whitehorse 28.15
White House 28.16
whiten 25.50
whitener 12.58

white-out 30.34
whitethroat 30.35
whitewall 23.15
whitewash 29.11
whitewasher 12.73
Whitewater 12.80
whitewood 16.26
whitey 4.54
whither 12.84
whiting 26.13
whitish 29.10
Whitlam 24.18
Whitman 25.45
Whitney 4.32
Whitsun 25.48
Whitsuntide 16.17
Whittier 12.12
Whittington 25.50
whittle 23.39
Whitworth 32.14
whiz-bang 26.1
whizz 35.10
whizz-kid 16.10
whizzo 9.29
who 11.1
whoa 9.1
who'd 16.25
whodunit 30.23
whodunnit 30.23
whoever 12.85
whole 23.17
wholefood 16.25
wholegrain 25.8
wholehearted 16.12
wholemeal 23.7
wholesale 23.6
wholesaler 12.43
wholewheat 30.19
whom 24.12
whomever 12.85
whomp 27.17
whomsoever 12.85
whoop 27.11
whoopee 4.1, 4.37
whooper 12.63
whoops 28.46
whoosh 29.15
whop 27.8
whopper 12.62
who're 12.19
whore 7.1
whoredom 24.17
whorehouse 28.16
whoremonger 12.32
Whorf 17.9
whorish 29.9
whorl 23.42
whortleberry 4.38
who's 35.21
whose 35.21
whosoever 12.85

w

whump 27.17
why 6.1
Whyalla 12.42
whydah 12.27
Whymper 12.62
Wicca 12.39
Wiccan 25.43
Wichita 7.18
wick 21.9
wicked 16.10
wicker 12.39
wickerwork 21.31
wicket 30.21
wicketkeeper 12.61
wicketkeeping 26.10
Wicklow 9.17
Wicks 28.39
widdershins 35.31
wide 16.14
wide-angle 23.30
wideawake 21.7
widen 25.40
widener 12.58
widening 26.9
widescreen 25.11
widespread 16.4
widget 30.21
widish 29.6
Widnes 28.9
widow 9.11
widower 12.17
widowhood 16.26
width 32.15
widthways 35.5
Wieland 16.45
wield 16.35
wielder 12.26
wieldy 4.12
wiener 12.54
Wiesbaden 25.40
Wiesel 23.37
Wiesenthal 23.2
wife 17.7
wifehood 16.26
wifely 4.25
wife-swapping 26.10
wig 18.6
Wigan 25.41
wigeon 25.14
wigging 26.6
wiggle 23.30
wiggler 12.48
wiggly 4.27
wight 30.26
Wigtownshire 12.11
wigwag 18.1
wigwam 24.1
Wilberforce 28.15

Wilbur 12.21
Wilcox 28.40
wild 16.36
wildcat 30.1
Wilde 16.36
wildebeest 31.5
Wilder 12.27
wildfire 12.14
wildfowl 23.16
wilding 26.5
wildish 29.6
wildlife 17.7
wildwood 16.26
wile 23.11
Wilfred 16.11
wilful 23.21
Wilhelmina 12.54
Wilhelmshaven 25.51
Wilkie 4.19
Wilkins 35.31
will 23.8
Willa 12.43
Willard 16.2
willer 12.43
willet 30.22
willful 23.21
William 24.20
Williams 35.30
Williamsburg 18.13
Williamson 25.48
willing 26.8
will-o'-the-wisp 27.18
Willoughby 4.10
willow 9.17
willowherb 14.15
willowy 4.7
willpower 12.16
Wills 35.29
willy-nilly 4.24
willy 4.24
Wilma 12.51
Wilmer 12.51
Wilmot 30.31
Wilson 25.48
wilt 30.51
Wilton 25.50
Wiltshire 12.5
wily 4.25
Wimbledon 25.40
wimp 27.17
wimpish 29.9
wimple 23.35
wimpy 4.36
win 25.13
wince 28.44
wincer 12.70
wincey 4.46
winceyette 30.4
winch 29.20

wincher 12.72
Winckelmann 25.2
wind 16.42
windage 20.6
Windaus 28.16
windbag 18.1
windbound 16.43
windblown 25.30
windborne 25.28
windbreak 21.7
Windbreaker 12.38
windcheater 12.77
wind chill 23.8
winder 12.27
Windermere 12.7
windfall 23.15
wind farm 24.2
Windhoek 21.28
windhover 12.86
windjammer 12.50
windlass 28.27
windmill 23.9
window 9.11
windowpane 25.8
window seat 30.18
window-shop 27.8
window-shopper 12.62
windowsill 23.9
windpipe 27.7
windproof 17.13
windrow 9.21
windsail 23.37
Windscale 23.5
windscreen 25.11
windshield 16.35
windsock 21.21
Windsor 12.90
windstorm 24.9
windsurf 17.17
windsurfer 12.30
windswept 30.58
wind-up 27.13
windward 16.30
windy 4.12
wine 25.21
winebibber 12.21
winebibbing 26.4
wine glass 28.2
winegrower 12.17
winemaking 26.7
winery 4.43
wineskin 25.15
wing 26.3
wingback 21.2
winging 26.5
winged 16.10, 16.47
winger 12.35, 12.60
wing half 17.2
winglet 30.22
wing-like 21.19

wingman 25.2
wingmen 25.5
wing nut 30.40
wingover 12.86
wingspan 25.3
wingspread 16.4
wingtip 27.6
Winifred 16.11
wink 21.33
winker 12.39
winkle 23.32
winkler 12.43
winless 28.8
Winnebago 9.13
winner 12.55
winning 26.9
Winnipeg 18.3
winnow 9.19
winnower 12.17
wino 9.19
Winona 12.56
winsome 24.20
Winston 25.50
winter 12.78
winterbourne 25.28
wintergreen 25.11
winterize 35.13
winterly 4.27
Winters 35.24
wintertime 24.7
Winthrop 27.8
Winton 25.50
wintry 4.40
wipe 27.7
wipeout 30.34
wiper 12.62
wire 12.13
wire-draw 7.15
wire-drawn 25.28
wireman 25.2
wiremen 25.5
wirepuller 12.46
wirepulling 26.8
wirer 12.67
wiring 26.11
Wirral 23.36
wiry 4.43
Wisconsin 25.19
Wisden 25.40
wisdom 24.17
wise 35.11
wiseacre 12.38
wisecrack 21.3
wisecracker 12.37
Wiseman 25.45
wish 29.6
wishbone 25.30
wishing well 23.4
wish-list 31.8
wish-wash 29.11
wishy-washy 4.50

wisp 27.18
wispy 4.36
wist 31.6
wisteria 12.10
wit 30.20
witan 25.50
witch 15.6
witchcraft 30.47
witchdoctor 12.79
witchery 4.43
witchetty 4.53
witch-hunt 30.55
witchlike 21.19
with 33.4
withal 23.14
withdraw 7.1
withdrawal 23.25
withdrawn 25.28
withdrew 11.1
wither 12.84
withers 35.24
withheld 16.35
withhold 16.37
withholder 12.28
within 25.13
without 30.34
withstand 16.40
withstander 12.25
withstood 16.26
withy 4.57
witless 28.8
witling 26.8
witness 28.9
Wittenberg 18.13
witter 12.78
wittering 26.11
Wittgenstein 25.23
witting 26.13
witty 4.53
Witwatersrand
　16.40
wives 35.35
wiz 35.10
wizard 16.30
wizardly 4.27
wizardry 4.43
wizened 16.45
wo 9.1
woad 16.23
wobble 23.26
wobbler 12.48
wobbly 4.27
Wodehouse 28.16
wodge 20.11
woe 9.1
woebegone 25.25
woeful 23.21
wog 18.8
woggle 23.30
wok 21.20
woke 21.24

woken 25.43
Woking 26.7
wold 16.37
Wolf 17.18
wolfberry 4.38
wolfcub 14.13
Wolfe 17.18
Wolfgang 26.1
wolfhound 16.43
wolfish 29.7
wolf-like 21.19
wolfram 24.19
wolfskin 25.15
Wolfson 25.48
Wollaston 25.50
Wollongong 26.15
Wollstonecraft
　30.47
Wolof 17.8
Wolsey 4.62
Wolverhampton
　25.50
wolverine 25.11
wolves 35.35
woman 25.45
womanhood 16.26
womanish 29.9
womanizer 12.91
womankind 16.42
womanlike 21.19
womanly 4.27
womb 24.12
wombat 30.1
women 25.17
womenfolk 21.24
womenswear 2.15
won 25.24, 25.35
wonder 12.29
wonderer 12.67
wondering 26.11
wonderland 16.40
wondrous 28.31
wonky 4.19
won't 30.55
wont 30.55
wonted 16.12
wonton 25.24
woo 11.1
wooable 23.26
wood 16.26
woodbine 25.21
woodblock 21.21
woodcarver 12.85
woodcarving 26.14
woodchip 27.6
woodchuck 21.29
woodcock 21.20
woodcraft 30.47
woodcut 30.40
woodcutter 12.81
woodcutting 26.13

wooded 16.9
wooden 25.40
wooden-head 16.3
wooden-headed
　16.9
woodland 16.45
woodlander 12.29
woodlark 21.5
woodlice 28.13
woodlouse 28.16
woodman 25.45
woodmen 25.45
woodnote 30.35
woodpecker 12.37
wood pigeon 25.14
woodpile 23.11
Woodrow 9.21
woodruff 17.15
woodrush 29.16
Woods 35.27
woodscrew 11.17
woodshed 16.4
woodsman 25.45
woodsmen 25.45
woodsmoke 21.24
Woodstock 21.21
woodsy 4.62
woodturner 12.59
woodturning 26.9
Woodward 16.30
woodwasp 27.18
woodwind 16.42
woodwork 21.31
woodworker 12.41
woodworm 24.22
woody 4.13
woodyard 16.2
wooer 12.19
woof 17.13, 17.14
woofer 12.30
wool 23.21
woolen 25.44
Woolf 17.18
woolgathering
　26.11
woollen 25.44
Woolley 4.26
wool-like 21.19
woolly 4.26
woolpack 21.3
woolsack 21.4
woolshed 16.4
Woolworth 32.13
woomera 12.67
woosh 29.15
woozy 4.62
wop 27.8
Worcester 12.81
Worcestershire
　12.11
word 16.31

wordage 20.6
wordbook 21.28
wording 26.5
word-perfect 30.49
wordplay 3.15
wordsearch 15.14
wordsmith 32.6
Wordsworth 32.13
wordy 4.13
wore 7.1
work 21.31
workaday 3.9
workaholic 21.11
workbench 29.20
workboat 30.35
workbook 21.28
workbox 28.40
workday 3.9
worker 12.41
workflow 9.17
workforce 28.15
workhorse 28.15
workhouse 28.16
working 26.7
Workington 25.50
workload 16.23
workman 25.45
workmanlike 21.19
workmate 30.12
workmen 25.45
workout 30.34
workpeople 23.35
workpiece 28.6
workplace 28.5
workroom 24.12
worksheet 30.19
workshop 27.8
work-shy 6.17
worksite 30.30
workspace 28.5
worktop 27.8
workwear 2.15
workweek 21.8
world 16.38
worldly 4.28
worldwide 16.14
worm 24.22
worm cast 31.2
wormer 12.52
wormhole 23.17
worm-like 21.19
Worms 35.30
wormwood 16.26
wormy 4.30
worn 25.28
worrier 12.10
worrit 30.24
worry 4.42
worrywart 30.33
worse 28.36
worsen 25.48

worship 27.6
worshiper 12.62
worshipper 12.62
worst 31.26
worsted 16.12
wort 30.45
worth 32.14
Worthing 26.14
worthwhile 23.11
worthy 4.57
wot 30.31
wotcha 12.24
would 16.26
would-be 4.10
wouldn't 30.56
wouldst 31.27
wound 16.43
wounding 26.5
wove 34.11
woven 25.51
wow 8.1
wowser 12.92
wrack 21.1
wraith 32.4
wraithlike 21.19
wrangle 23.30
wrangler 12.42
wrangling 26.8
wrap 27.1
wrapper 12.61
wrapping 26.10
wrasse 28.1
wrath 32.8
wrathy 4.56
wreak 21.8
wreaker 12.38
wreath 32.5
wreathe 33.3
wreck 21.6
wreckage 20.6
wrecker 12.37
wren 25.5
wrench 29.20
wrest 31.3
wrestle 23.37
wrestler 12.42
wrestling 26.8
wretch 15.3
wretched 16.8
Wrexham 24.20
wriggle 23.30
wriggler 12.48
wriggly 4.27
wright 30.26
wring 26.3
wringer 12.60
wrinkle 23.32
wrinkly 4.24
wrist 31.6
wristband 16.40
wristlet 30.22

wristwatch 15.7
wristy 4.53
writ 30.20
write 30.26
writer 12.79
writerly 4.27
writhe 33.5
writhing 26.14
writing 26.13
written 25.50
Wroclaw 34.2
wrong 26.15
wrongdoer 12.19
wrongdoing 26.3
wronger 12.60
wrong-foot 30.39
wrong-footed 16.12
wrong-headed 16.9
wrong'un 25.46
wrote 30.35
wrought 30.33
wrung 26.18
wry 6.1
wryly 4.25
wryness 28.9
Wu 11.1
Wuhan 25.1
wunderkind 16.42
Wuppertal 23.2
Wurlitzer 12.70
wurst 31.26
Wurzburg 18.13
wuss 28.20
Wyandot 30.31
Wyatt 30.41
wychelm 24.18
Wycherley 4.27
wych hazel 23.41
Wyclif 17.6
Wye 6.1
wynd 16.42
Wyndham 24.17
Wynne 25.13
Wyoming 26.9
Wystan 25.50

Xanadu 11.6
Xanthe 4.56
Xanthippe 4.36
Xavier 12.12
xenon 25.26
Xenophanes 35.7
xenophobe 14.11
xenophobia 12.5
xenophobic 21.9
Xenophon 25.25
xeric 21.15

xerographic 21.10
xerox 28.40
Xhosa 12.70
xi 6.1
Xian 25.1
Xingtai 6.1
Xining 26.3
Xinjiang 26.1
Xizang 26.1
xoanon 25.26
X-rated 16.12
X-ray 3.19
Xuzhou 9.1
xylophone 25.30
xylophonist 31.10

yabber 12.21
yabby 4.10
yacht 30.31
yachtie 4.54
yachtsman 25.45
yachtsmen 25.45
yachtswoman 25.45
yachtswomen 25.17
yah 1.1
yahoo 11.10
Yahweh 3.25
yak 21.1
yakka 12.37
Yakut 30.39
Yakutia 12.12
Yakutsk 21.35
yakuza 12.92
Yale 23.5
Yalu 11.13
yam 24.1
Yama 12.50
Yamamoto 9.25
yammer 12.50
Yamoussoukro 9.21
Yancheng 26.2
yang 26.1
Yangshao 8.1
Yangtze 4.45
yank 21.33
Yankee 4.18
Yanomami 4.29
Yantai 6.1
yantra 12.64
Yaoundé 3.9
yap 27.1
yapok 21.20
yapper 12.61
yappy 4.36
yard 16.2
yardage 20.6
yardarm 24.2

yardbird 16.31
Yardie 4.12
yardman 25.2
yardmen 25.5
yardstick 21.17
yarmulke 12.41
yarn 25.4
yarran 25.47
yarrow 9.21
yashmak 21.3
Yasmin 25.17
yatter 12.74
yaw 7.1
yawl 23.14
yawn 25.28
yawp 27.9
yaws 35.17
Yayoi 10.15
yclept 30.58
ye 4.1
yea 3.1
yeah 2.1
yean 25.9
year 12.4
yearbook 21.28
yearling 26.8
yearly 4.27
yearn 25.53
yearner 12.59
yearning 26.9
yeast 31.5
yeasty 4.52
Yeats 28.47
yegg 18.3
Yehudi 4.13
yell 23.3
yellow 9.17
yellowback 21.2
yellow-belly 4.22
yellowfin 25.14
yellowhammer
12.50
yellowish 29.6
yellowlegs 35.28
yellowy 4.7
yelp 27.16
yelper 12.61
Yeltsin 25.19
Yemen 25.45
Yemeni 4.34
yen 25.5
yeoman 25.45
yeomanly 4.27
yeomanry 4.43
yeomen 25.45
Yerevan 25.1
yes 28.3
yesterday 3.9
yesteryear 12.12
yet 30.4
yeti 4.51

w

x

y

Yevtushenko 9.16
yew 11.1
Y-fronts 28.47
yid 16.8
Yiddish 29.6
Yiddisher 12.72
yield 16.35
yielder 12.26
yielding 26.5
yikes 28.39
yin 25.13
Yinchuan 25.4
yip 27.6
yippee 4.1
ylang-ylang 26.1
Ymir 12.7
yo 9.1
yob 14.9
yobbish 29.6
yobbo 9.9
yodel 23.28
yodeler 12.48
yodeller 12.48
yoga 12.32
yogi 4.15
yogic 21.10
yogurt 30.42
yohimbe 3.7
yo-ho-ho 9.1
yoicks 28.40
yoke 21.24
yokel 23.32
Yokohama 12.50
yokozuna 12.56
yolk 21.24
Yom Kippur 12.20
yomp 27.17
yon 25.24
yonder 12.28
yonks 28.41
yoo-hoo 11.10
yore 7.1
Yorick 21.15
york 21.22
yorker 12.40
Yorkist 31.7
Yorkshire 12.11
Yoruba 12.21
you 11.1
you'd 16.25
you'll 23.20
young 26.18
Younger 12.32
youngish 29.9
youngling 26.8
youngster 12.81
your 7.1
you're 12.20
yours 35.17
yourself 17.18

yourselves 35.35
youse 35.21
youth 32.12
you've 34.12
yowl 23.16
yo-yo 9.28
Ypres 12.65
ytterbium 24.16
yttrium 24.16
yuan 25.4
Yucatán 25.4
yucca 12.41
yuck 21.29
yucky 4.20
Yugoslav 34.2
Yugoslavia 12.12
Yugoslavian 25.37
Yuit 30.20
Yukon 25.25
yule 23.20
Yuletide 16.17
yummy 4.30
yum-yum 24.14
Yunnan 25.1
Yupik 21.14
yuppie 4.37
yuppiedom 24.17
yuppify 6.7
yurt 30.45
Yves 34.5
Yvette 30.4
Yvonne 25.24

Z

zabaglione 4.33
Zachary 4.43
Zack 21.1
Zadok 21.20
zag 18.1
Zagazig 18.6
Zagreb 14.3
Zaire 12.4
Zairean 25.37
zakat 30.3
Zambezi 4.61
Zambia 12.5
Zambian 25.37
Zamboanga 12.31
zamindar 1.6
zander 12.25
Zante 4.51
Zanuck 21.30
zany 4.31
Zanzibar 1.4
Zanzibari 4.38
Zaozhuang 26.1
zap 27.1

Zapata 12.75
Zapotec 21.6
Zappa 12.61
zappy 4.36
Zara 12.64
Zarathustra 12.66
Zarathustrian 25.37
Zaria 12.10
zariba 12.21
Zarqa 12.37
zazen 25.5
zeal 23.7
Zealand 16.45
zealot 30.42
zealotry 4.43
zealous 28.27
zebra 12.64
Zechariah 12.13
Zedekiah 12.13
Zeebrugge 12.32
Zeeland 16.45
Zeffirelli 4.22
Zeiss 28.13
Zeitgeist 31.16
Zelda 12.26
Zen 25.5
Zena 12.54
zenana 12.53
Zenist 31.10
zenith 32.6
Zeno 9.19
Zenobia 12.5
Zephaniah 12.13
zephyr 12.30
zeppelin 25.16
Zermatt 30.1
zero 9.21
zest 31.3
zester 12.76
zesty 4.51
zeta 12.77
zetetic 21.17
zeugma 12.52
Zeus 28.19
Zhanjiang 26.1
Zhdanov 34.10
Zhengzhou 9.1
Zhenjiang 26.1
Zhongshan 25.1
Zhou 9.1
Zhukov 34.10
Ziegfeld 16.35
ziggurat 30.2
zigzag 18.1
zilch 15.15
zillion 25.52
zillionth 32.19
Zimbabwe 4.59
Zimbabwean 25.37

zimmer 12.51
zinc 21.33
zinfandel 23.3
zing 26.3
zinger 12.60
zingy 4.35
zinnia 12.8
Zion 25.38
Zionist 31.10
zip 27.6
zip code 16.23
ziplock 21.21
zipper 12.62
zippy 4.36
zip-up 27.13
zircon 25.25
zirconia 12.8
zirconium 24.16
zit 30.20
zither 12.84
zitherist 31.12
zizz 35.10
zloty 4.54
zodiac 21.1
zodiacal 23.32
Zoë 4.7
zoetrope 27.10
Zoffany 4.34
Zola 12.44
zombie 4.10
zonal 23.34
zonation 25.49
zone 25.30
zonk 21.34
zoo 11.1
zookeeper 12.61
zoologist 31.7
zoology 4.17
zoom 24.12
zoomorphic 21.10
zorbing 26.4
zorilla 12.43
Zoroaster 12.74
Zoroastrian 25.37
Zouave 34.2
zouk 21.27
zounds 35.27
zucchetto 9.24
zucchini 4.31
Zuider Zee 4.1
Zulu 11.13
Zurich 21.15
zwieback 21.2
Zwingli 4.24
Zworykin 25.15
zydeco 9.16
zygote 30.35
zygotic 21.17
zymotic 21.17
zymurgy 4.17

More Literature titles from OUP

The Oxford Companion to Charles Dickens
edited by Paul Schlicke

Reissued to celebrate the bicentenary of Charles Dickens's birth, this companion draws together an unparalleled diversity of information on one of Britain's greatest writers; covering his life, his works, his reputation, and his cultural context.

Reviews from previous edition:
'comes about as close to perfection as humanly possible'
Dickens Quarterly

'will prove invaluable to scholars, readers and admirers of Dickens'
Peter Ackroyd, *The Times*

The Oxford Companion to the Brontës
Christine Alexander and Margaret Smith

This Companion brings together a wealth of information about the fascinating lives and writings of the Brontë sisters.

'This book is a must ... a treasure trove of a book'
Irish Times

The Oxford Companion to Classical Literature
edited by M. C. Howatson

A broad-ranging and authoritative guide to the classical world and its literary heritage.

Reviews from previous edition:
'a volume for all seasons ... indispensable'
Times Educational Supplement

'A necessity for any seriously literary household.'
History Today

OXFORD

Oxford Paperback Reference

The Concise Oxford Dictionary of English Etymology
T. F. Hoad

A wealth of information about our language and its history, this reference source provides over 17,000 entries on word origins.

'A model of its kind'

Daily Telegraph

A Dictionary of Euphemisms
R. W. Holder

This hugely entertaining collection draws together euphemisms from all aspects of life: work, sexuality, age, money, and politics.

Review of the previous edition
'This ingenious collection is not only very funny but extremely instructive too'

Iris Murdoch

The Oxford Dictionary of Slang
John Ayto

Containing over 10,000 words and phrases, this is the ideal reference for those interested in the more quirky and unofficial words used in the English language.

'hours of happy browsing for language lovers'

Observer

Oxford Paperback Reference

The Concise Oxford Companion to English Literature
Dinah Birch and Katy Hooper

Based on the best-selling *Oxford Companion to English Literature*, this is
an indispensable guide to all aspects of English literature.

Review of the parent volume
'the foremost work of reference in its field'

view

A
S

s,

ogy

RD